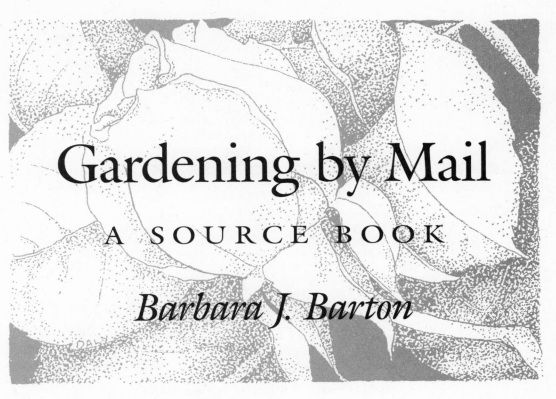

Gardening by Mail

A SOURCE BOOK

Barbara J. Barton

Everything for the Garden and Gardener

A directory of mail-order resources for gardeners in
the United States and Canada, including seed companies,
nurseries, suppliers of all garden necessaries and ornaments,
horticultural and plant societies, magazines, libraries,
and a list of useful books on plants and gardening.

A TUSKER PRESS BOOK

Houghton Mifflin Company · Boston · 1990

Dedicated to my parents, Hildor and Marguerite Barton,
and to my aunt, Margit Barton McNulty;
they thought I could do anything, made it possible,
and it worked!

Library of Congress Cataloging-in-Publication Data
Barton, Barbara J.
Gardening by mail : a source book / Barbara J. Barton. — 3rd ed.,
updated and expanded.
p.   cm.
Subtitle: A directory of mail-order resources for gardeners in the
United States and Canada, including seed companies, nurseries,
suppliers of all garden necessaries and ornaments, horticultural and
plant societies, magazines, libraries, and a list of useful books on
plants and gardening.
"A Tusker Press book."
Includes bibliographical references.
ISBN 0-395-52280-3
1. Gardening — United States — Directories.   2. Horticulture — United
States — Directories.   3. Gardening — Canada — Directories.
4. Horticulture — Canada — Directories.   5. Mail-order business —
United States — Directories.   6. Mail-order business — Canada —
Directories.   I. Title.
SB450.943.U6B37   1990   89-71641
635′.029′4 — dc20   CIP

Printed in the United States of America

BTA 10 9 8 7 6 5 4 3 2 1

Originated and composed by Tusker Press
P.O. Box 1338
Sebastopol, California 95473
(707) 829-9189

Programming by Nancy D. H. Jacobsen
BobRed Co.
Forest Knolls, California 94933

TABLE OF CONTENTS

Introduction

i Introduction

ii Important information for using this source book

iv A few words about ordering plants by mail

vi State, provincial and country abbreviations used in the listings and indexes

Listings

A Plant and seed sources

B Garden suppliers and services

C Professional societies, trade associations, conservation and umbrella groups

D Horticultural and plant societies

E Magazines and newsletters

F Libraries

G Books

Indexes

H Plant and seed sources index

J Geographical index of plant and seed sources

K Products and services index

L Society index

M Magazines and newsletters indexed by title

Practical Matters

- Catalog and information request form
- Record of catalog orders and requests
- Request for listing or update of current listing
- Reader feedback and update order form

A table of the symbols and abbreviations used in this book appears on the bookmark.

Dear Gardener:

I don't know how you fell in love with growing things, but I came home from work one day to find a Wayside Gardens catalog in the mail. It was as fatal and irresistible as Cupid's dart — soon I was carrying seed catalogs to read on the bus, rushing to secondhand book stores during my lunch hour, always trying to learn more.

As this insatiable habit was developing, one of my greatest frustrations was that there seemed to be no easy way to find out everything I wanted to know. If I saw a lovely plant, where could I get one to try to grow myself? Surely there must be wonderful gardening magazines, but there were very few on newsstands — what did *real* gardeners do? Were there plant and horticultural societies? Would they allow *me* to join? Where might I find a horticultural library to browse in? Even though I'm a reference librarian myself, it all seemed so difficult! Only *old* gardeners knew — and it took them years to find out.

When suddenly I had the time and the opportunity, I decided to "whip together" the ideal reference book for people like me — full of sources of seeds, plants and garden supplies, societies to join, libraries to haunt, magazines to curl up with, and a list of good books on plants and practical gardening, "good reads" and books with inspiring pictures to feast the imagination.

My mind began to spin with grandiose ideas. I'd index the sources in many ways to make the book even more useful. I'd describe their catalogs, whether you could visit them and when, and whether they had display gardens to visit, and I'd list them by location so I could plan trips to include horticultural high spots! I'd mention their shipping seasons, whether they sold wholesale to the trade, what their minimum order was, whether they shipped to buyers overseas, and whether they listed their plants by botanical name. Every day I thought of some new and indispensable tidbit of information that the gardeners of North America just had to be told!

Seven years later I'm much wiser; putting together the ideal reference book is nearly impossible. It's impossible to get thousands of people to send back information in a standard format, and it's only current on the day they mail it! Many people are very cooperative, some are uncooperative, and quite a few will reply long after the book goes to press, with a note saying "I just found this on my desk ..."

Readers of the two earlier editions, which I published myself as Tusker Press, know the stirring saga of the plucky librarian who forged ahead, undeterred by rejection slips, with money cascading out of her pockets and double chins set at a determined angle. The first good reviews, the stream of letters from delighted readers, the agony of schlepping boxes of books anywhere people who garden might gather, orders from all over the world — all true, and very thrilling and fun in a roller-coasterish way, but I was thinking about giving it all up for a real job. I was simply delighted when Houghton Mifflin wanted to publish it. Overnight success at last!

Those readers may want to know how it's going here at Tusker Press World Headquarters. Since the last edition I have become a great-aunt and taken the Master Gardener course at the University of California Cooperative Extension (and I recommend the program highly). I've been whacking away at my garden, which like me seems bigger and more derelict with each passing year; it still has not progressed beyond the "great potential" stage! My dog Alice and cats Kelpie and Trout are happy company and do their best to help control the moles and pocket gophers. It is surely true that with a garden comes work to fill all available time, and also great contentment; my urge to travel has nearly disappeared, since there never seems to be a good time to leave home without missing a vital fleeting moment.

This book is the result of a lot of work on my part, but I have had the assistance of many others. Over the years gardening friends and readers have made many suggestions for improvements and additions. Many thanks are due to the companies who have given me permission to use the charming drawings from their catalogs. Again Jim Robertson has been my kind mentor and adviser, and Alan Freeland has been kindness and helpfulness rolled into one. Frances Tenenbaum of Houghton Mifflin has been very encouraging and supportive of my original concept. Lois De Pue spent days helping me put information into the computer, Kathy Spalding kept all my files in order, and Heather, Danielle and Susan cheerfully sent my mailings on their way. Rick Ryall patiently kept my computers from driving me crazy. The drawing on the title page was given to me by Cathleen Daly, a dear friend and well-known artist; it's brought me lots of luck. There is no way to describe the contribution of Georgie March, who galloped to the rescue when I needed her to help me pull it all together again. Credit for everything else should go to Nancy Jacobsen — another dear friend of many years, whose programming genius made it easy to handle the huge database and print out all the information in it. I am *very* lucky in my friends!

Important Information for Using this Source Book

This is an annotated directory of sources for everything that a gardener might want or need to purchase through the mail. My purpose is to provide you with information that will help you find what you want: this is not a "buyer's guide" which rates or recommends companies. I make every effort to describe the contents of catalogs or other sales material as fairly and accurately as I can.

Remember, this book is meant to be *useful*, not permanent, so mark it up all you want!

Who's Listed — Almost every mail-order garden business I could locate and find enough information about by my cut-off date; a few companies previously listed have been dropped for a variety of reasons, some because of reader complaints. In all but the cases noted, everyone listed has been sent a questionnaire and letter asking for detailed information and their catalog. For those who didn't reply fully, the notes give you all the information I could find; I'm sorry that it isn't always complete. Alphabetizing follows library conventions: Mc and Mac interfiled, and acronyms before words, i.e. A.B.C. before Abbott.

Addresses — When I know them, I have given both the mailing address and the sales location of the business (these are sometimes the same). Please use the first address given for inquiries by mail. Where the nursery or shop has a different town address from the post office, this is given in parentheses after the street address.

Call Ahead or **By Appointment Only** — Many of the smaller businesses are run by one person who sometimes has a full-time job elsewhere or has to run the mundane errands of us ordinary folk. Please honor their requests that you contact them before coming to visit, and please don't try to visit those companies that don't welcome visitors; if they don't give a sales location or other information on how to visit, they probably sell only by mail order.

Retail & Wholesale — It is common for businesses to sell multiple items at a declining cost per item; many also sell "wholesale to the trade" (those who buy the merchandise for resale or other business uses). Unless I indicate that they will sell wholesale to anyone who will buy the minimum amount, do not ask to buy wholesale unless you qualify. It's best to send your inquiry on business letterhead.

Payment To Other Countries — I have tried to indicate where you may pay with international reply coupons, available at most post offices, or international money orders, available at larger post offices (ask for Form 6701 in the U.S.). Some overseas businesses ask for U.S. bills, as changing checks sometimes costs more than the check is worth. Others will accept U.S. personal checks, and will inform you of the amount to send. You can sometimes charge purchases to your credit card, which automatically takes care of foreign exchange. I have also indicated where I could how much Canadians should send to the U.S. to take into account the dollar difference; you should check with your post office or bank about other forms of payment. Except as noted, all prices not in U.S. or Canadian dollars are in the currency of the country where the business or organization is located. Orders from overseas should be paid by international money orders or checks in U.S. dollars.

Self-addressed Stamped Envelopes — Always send a business-size envelope (10 inches or 27 cm.) as your SASE — most of the lists will not fit into anything smaller. Also note if the business has requested more than the usual first-class postage; the list may well be too heavy for one stamp. Foreign companies that request an SASE should be sent a self-addressed long envelope and an international reply coupon.

Plant and Agricultural Regulations — You should check with local offices of the U.S. Department of Agriculture or Agriculture Canada to see whether seeds, bulbs or plants from other countries may be imported and what permits are needed. You will notice that some companies will not ship to certain states because of agricultural regulations, and many Canadian companies will not ship to the U.S. for the same reason; I have tried to indicate where companies say they cannot ship. Because of regulations, companies are justified in charging a fee for the preparation of export papers. Please do not ask companies to send catalogs if they do not ship to your area.

Endangered Plants — In most cases, endangered plants are protected by international treaty. Ethical companies indicate the sources of their rare or endangered seeds, bulbs and plants; look for companies that say they sell nursery-propagated plants and bulbs. If in doubt, ask.

Botanical and Common Names — When I have seen the catalog, I try to indicate whether botanical names are used, but I have not checked on the correctness or currency of the names. Some catalogs are maddeningly inconsistent, using botanical names for some plants and not for others, or making up their own fanciful common names. It is common for herbs, fruits and vegetables to be listed by common and cultivar names, and many popular garden plants are listed by their cultivar names, frequently without botanical names. I have used the term "collectors' list" to indicate plant lists that assume fairly knowledgeable buyers, usually list plants only by botanical/cultivar name and have brief or no plant descriptions.

Trade Names — In the Product Sources Index I have identified trade names as either registered trademarks (R) or trademarks (TM).

Notes on Catalogs — The notes are based on a study of the catalog; if I have not received one, the notes are necessarily very brief. I have used the expressions "nice," "good," "wide," "broad" or " huge selection" and so forth to indicate the breadth of selection offered, **not** as a quality judgment on what's offered. I try to get as much information as I can into limited space, including items that cannot be included among the twelve specialties indexed. You should always read the notes with a pencil in hand so that you can highlight notes or items of special interest that you want to locate again.

Listings — Being in *Gardening by Mail* costs nothing to those listed; these listing are **not** advertisements, and all the descriptions are mine, based on a study of catalogs or literature. I do ask every company that wants to be listed to fill out a detailed questionnaire every few years and return it with their catalog; the choice of listings is mine alone. Companies and organizations that would like to be listed in future editions will find a form in the Practical Matters section at the back of the book.

Ordering Catalogs/Literature — One thing businesses like to know is where their customers heard about them. To let people know that you found them in *Gardening by Mail,* and to encourage them to provide me with complete information, I have included a form for ordering/requesting catalogs and information in the Practical Matters. If you don't use the form, please tell them you read about them in *Gardening by Mail.*

Please keep in mind that catalogs and postage are expensive and request only catalogs for merchandise that is truly of interest to you. An avalanche of requests can be considered more disaster than benefit to a small business; please be patient and considerate of the effort that goes into offering something special and working without much help. One company asked not to be listed again because my readers "never" sent the SASE requested for a list; in such situations the company is justified in not replying to your request.

Reader Feedback — Hearing from readers has been the greatest pleasure of working on this book — you've given me pats on the back and complaints when deserved, and a lot of good suggestions for improving the book and new sources to list. One complaint I don't deserve is that I enticed you into requesting more catalogs or ordering more plants than you really needed to have — self-control is *your* problem! There's a Reader Feedback form in the Practical Matters section. I'd love to hear from you.

Updates — We discovered with the first edition that companies constantly move, change their names and owners, or go out of business, so in order to keep the book current we started selling regular updates. For this third edition the updates will be issued three times a year, starting in August 1990, for a total of six updates. The changes are cumulative, so you only need to order the most recent one; new sources discovered and new books received will be mentioned as space permits. We've combined the Update order form with the Reader Feedback form — see Practical Matters.

A Few Words About Ordering Plants By Mail

Why do people order plants and seeds by mail? Most of us have local sources for ordinary or even unusual plants; but some of us live where few nurseries exist, others are so besotted by rarities that only specialist nurseries have what we want, and still others grow orchids or tropical fruit in greenhouses and need to order from other climates. Some of us order for reasons of perceived economy, and some for greater selection or just to have something exotic from a faraway source. Whatever the reason, there's a time of the year when only a good seed or nursery catalog can warm the gardener's heart.

I've been working with plant and seed catalogs for seven years now and have inadvertently become something of an expert on catalogs and what they convey to their readers. I'd like to share some thoughts and warnings so that you'll be happy with your purchases and avoid unpleasant experiences as much as possible.

There is a science to reading a catalog which will almost always repay you in good results. When you receive a catalog, don't go first to the plants and their prices; search first for information on the company. I always look to see if the the catalog gives the name of the proprietor or someone to contact if need be; if there is no name and no telephone number, read on with increased caution. After all, these people are in business and should be willing to communicate with their customers.

Does the company list plants by correct botanical names and/or specific cultivar names? Does it guarantee that plants are true to name? Does it offer to replace plants that arrive in bad condition, and how long do you have to request a replacement? Does it tell you frankly what size the plants or bulbs will be? If the plants are endangered, does the company specify that their plants are nursery grown and propagated? When will it ship your plants? Beware of companies that ship live plants all year; harsh winters or hot summers can ruin even healthy plants in transit, and companies shouldn't try to blame predictable weather problems on the carrier.

When you feel some confidence in the company, then you can study the plant lists. You will quickly notice that there are catalogs aimed at all levels of plant expertise, starting with those that list plants only by common name and topping off with catalogs that list plants only by botanical name. Each is meant for a particular audience. Catalogs aimed at unsophisticated gardeners have an obligation to give good descriptions of the plants and how to grow them; they can also educate their customers when they include the correct botanical names where appropriate. Catalogs that make up fanciful common names such as "dainty little dancing alpine fairy bells" or are deliberately vague, using "Viburnum sp." for a plant they should easily be able to identify, should go to the bottom of your catalog pile.

I particularly like a catalog that gives good and honest plant descriptions. Some catalogs would have you believe that every plant they sell is perfect; the plain truth is that some varieties are much better behaved, some need special coddling, some reseed all over the garden, some smell not so sweet! The descriptions should offer the pros *and* the cons in addition to height and color of flower; they should also tell you something about growing the plant — soil, exposure, hardiness, need for water and fertilizer, division and pruning; it simply isn't true that most plants will grow happily anywhere you live or under any conditions. Catalogs meant for sophisticated plant collectors do not to go into such detail but rely on the advanced knowledge of their readers.

Finally, the price! Which do you think is cheapest, the $10 plant from a reputable nursery which will replace it for up to a year, or the $3.95 runt that arrives half dead from a company which won't answer your letters of complaint or sends a plant in the same condition to replace it? This is an extreme example, and I hope I have eliminated companies like the latter, but we all know there's no free lunch. It's expensive to grow good plants, especially those that take years to reach shipping size.

Use your own judgment about how difficult or expensive a plant is to grow. Daylilies are obviously easier to propagate than specially grafted dwarf conifers and are priced not by difficulty of propagation but by the newness and rarity of the cultivar. Plants are also priced by size, and if you are willing to take them small and grow them on yourself, you can save money.

When ordering plants, first try to pick a company you feel comfortable with, then place a small trial order. It's a good idea when ordering plants to be shipped at another season to include a self-addressed postcard, already written for the company to fill in the blanks, stating when it received the order and amount of payment and when it expects to ship the order; be sure to include the company's name and address so you won't confuse your orders.

There are fads in plants as in all things. Many people want only the newest and rarest and are willing to pay steep prices; there are usually older varieties on the same list that are just as lovely and cost a fraction of the price. If you're just starting out, or want to try a number of varieties to see what you like best, many nurseries offer collections, which are good bargains.

One reader complained because I did not describe the condition and size of plants received from each company. How could I possibly order a wide selection of plants and seeds from 1,000 catalogs, then evaluate and grow them on to see how healthy they are? To be fair I would somehow have to order without giving my name, I'd have to have enormous test gardens and greenhouses, unlimited water and expert help; and I would have to be rich beyond my wildest dreams!

Finally, if you do have reason to complain, write to the company at once and detail your complaint. Be sure to mention the date of your order, when it was received, and what was wrong; keep a copy of all correspondence for your records. If you do not receive a reply within a few weeks, telephone or photocopy your original letter and send it again with another letter. If you still receive no reply, or have ordered and paid for merchandise that did not arrive at the proper shipping season, write to the postal inspector in care of the post office where the business is located (check with the country's consulate or embassy in the case of foreign companies). I cannot straighten out consumer disputes, but I do drop companies about which I have received several complaints; please let me know of such instances. I would never knowingly list a company I even suspect of being shady; such businesses don't belong in this book.

I'd love to see a day when all catalogs are botanically correct, honest and forthcoming, informative, well illustrated and fun to read. I'd also like to see an end to pocket gophers, poison oak and wild blackberries and see the San Francisco Giants win the World Series. Until that day we must all navigate as best we can by using common sense. Read carefully, study catalogs, enjoy your garden!

State, Provincial and Country Abbreviations
Used in Tables and Indexes

U.S. and Canada

AB	Alberta, Canada
AK	Alaska
AL	Alabama
AR	Arkansas
AZ	Arizona
BC	British Columbia, Canada
CA	California
CO	Colorado
CT	Connecticut
DC	District of Columbia
DE	Delaware
FL	Florida
GA	Georgia
HI	Hawaii
IA	Iowa
ID	Idaho
IL	Illinois
IN	Indiana
KS	Kansas
KY	Kentucky
LA	Louisiana
MA	Massachusetts
MB	Manitoba, Canada
MD	Maryland
ME	Maine
MI	Michigan
MN	Minnesota
MO	Missouri
MS	Mississippi
MT	Montana
NB	New Brunswick, Canada
NC	North Carolina
ND	North Dakota
NE	Nebraska
NF	Newfoundland, Canada
NH	New Hampshire
NJ	New Jersey
NM	New Mexico
NS	Nova Scotia, Canada
NV	Nevada
NY	New York
OH	Ohio
OK	Oklahoma
ON	Ontario, Canada

U.S. and Canada (continued)

OR	Oregon
PA	Pennsylvania
PE	Prince Edward Island, Canada
PQ	Province of Quebec, Canada
PR	Puerto Rico
RI	Rhode Island
SC	South Carolina
SD	South Dakota
SK	Saskatchewan, Canada
TN	Tennessee
TX	Texas
UT	Utah
VA	Virginia
VT	Vermont
WA	Washington
WI	Wisconsin
WV	West Virginia
WY	Wyoming

Overseas

Au	Austrlia
En	England
In	India
Ja	Japan
Ne	New Zealand
No	Northern Ireland
So	South Africa
Sw	Switzerland
Wa	Wales
We	West Germany

Plant and Seed Sources

Plant and seed sources are listed alphabetically. Former company names and alternative names used in advertising are cross-referenced to the main listing. Specialties (plants, seeds, supplies, books, bulbs) are indicated on the top line of the notes on catalogs. If no shipping season information is given, the company will ship at any time during the year.

For display gardens, greenhouses, orchards and other plant displays, the months given are the best months to visit. Check to see whether you can visit at other times; if the nursery has regular hours, you can probably visit the plant display anytime it is open.

See the Index section for:

H. Plant Sources Index: an index of plant and seed sources by plant specialties. A two-letter code tells you which state/province/country the source is located in, so that you can order from the nearest source or a source in a similar climate zone if you like.

J. Geographical Index: an index of plant and seed sources by location. Sources in the U.S. and Canada are listed by state or province and then by city or post office; other sources are listed by country only. Symbols indicate which sources have nurseries or shops and plant displays; those without symbols sell by mail order only. Always check the main listing to see if you should call ahead or make an appointment to visit.

Other Sources of Seeds and Plants

In addition to using the sources listed, you can sometimes locate harder-to-find plants in the seed exchanges and plant sales of horticultural societies or botanical gardens. You can also place an advertisement in the "plants wanted" section of many society magazines. These are usually free, but the plant must be rare in commerce. See also the seed exchanges listing in the plant sources index.

Many societies provide their members with lists of specialist nurseries, and there is a list of plant-finding source books in the Books section.

Finally, many gardeners are very generous with seeds and cuttings of their plants when they are properly asked — be you likewise!

A table of the symbols and abbreviations used
in this book appears on the bookmark.

A & P Orchids
110 Peters Road
Swansea, MA 02777
(508) 675-1717
Penny & Azhar Mustafa

Plants
Small nursery offers a list of **hybrid orchids** written in "orchidese" but welcome to collectors. Among the plants unfamiliar to me are hawkinsara, brownara and cattleytonia. Plants available in several sizes and seedling flats. They also have a blooming-orchid-of-the-month plan. (1985)
❑ Catalog: Free, R&W, CAN, SS:4-10, $20m
⌂ Nursery: All year, daily, by appointment only
▼ Garden: Winter-spring, by appointment only

Abbey Gardens
4620 Carpinteria Avenue
Carpinteria, CA 90313
(805) 684-5112 or 1595 TO/CC $20m
Lem Higgs

Plants ↯ Books
Catalog offers a broad selection of **cacti and succulents** to hobbyists and collectors; some b&w photos, plants briefly described. I don't know why, but I can't look at a cactus catalog without wanting one of everything -- they are very fascinating plants! The nursery also sell books. (1968)
❑ Catalog: $2, R&W, CAN/OV, SS:3-11, $10m, bn
⌂ Nursery: All year, Tu-Su
▼ Garden: March-October, Tu-Su

Abundant Life Seed Foundation
P.O. Box 772
1029 Lawrence Street
Port Townsend, WA 98368
(206) 385-5660 or 7192 TO/CC $20m
Forest Shomer, Mgr.

Seeds ↯ Books
"A non-profit educational foundation...raising and collecting open-pollinated cultivars without chemicals." Offers a wide choice of seeds: **vegetables, Northwestern native plants, Native American grains, garden flowers** and books on many garden subjects. Bulk prices available. (1975)
❑ Catalog: $1, R&W, CAN/OV, bn/cn
⌂ Nursery: All year, M-F
▼ Garden: Growing area, M-F, call ahead

Adagent Acres
2245 Floral Way
Santa Rosa, CA 95403
(707) 575-4459
Arnold Adams, Julius Sargent

Plants
A hobby started in 1965 with one **orchid** plant (the same old story); now offering a good selection of paphiopedilum, cattleya, cymbidium and other hybrids, each briefly to very well described.
❑ Catalog: 1 FCS, SS:W, $20m

Adamgrove
Route 1, Box 246
California, MO 65018
Eric & Bob Tankesley-Clarke

Plants
Catalog offers a huge selection of bearded, beardless, Siberian, arilbred and species **irises**, all well described, with some cultural information. Also offers a somewhat smaller selection of **daylilies**, both diploid and tetraploid, and some **herbaceous peonies**, too. (1983)
❑ Catalog: $2d ($5 OV), CAN/OV, SS:7-9, $15m

Adams County Nursery, Inc.
P.O. Box 108
Aspers, PA 17304
(717) 677-8105
Phillip Baugher, Tom Callahan, Mgrs.

Plants
Offers a broad variety of **fruit** -- apples, pears, peaches and nectarines, sweet and sour cherries, plums and apricots, on a variety of rootstocks for various growing conditions, for both home gardeners and large commercial growers. Informative color catalog. (1905)
❑ Catalog: Free, R&W, CAN/OV, SS:11-12,2-5
⌂ Nursery: All year, M-F
▼ Garden: All year, M-F

Ahrens Nursery & Plant Labs
RR 1, Box 351
Huntingburg, IN 47542-9589
(812) 683-3055 TO/CC $25m
Philip & Linda Ahrens

Plants ↯ Books ↯ Supplies
Informative color catalog offers 35 varieties of **strawberries** and other **berries, grapes, dwarf fruit trees, asparagus and rhubarb**, as well as specialized supplies for the commercial strawberry grower. They also sell cook- books for fruit growers. (1929)
❑ Catalog: Free, R&W, SS:10-7, $10m
⌂ Nursery: All year, M-F
▼ Garden: March-May, M-F

Air Expose
4703 Leffingwell Street
Houston, TX 77026
George Haynes III

Plants
Offers a wide selection of **hibiscus**, both subtropical and hardy, described only by color of flowers.
❑ Catalog: Long SASE, R&W, CAN/OV, $25m
⌂ Nursery: April-October, after 4 pm weekdays

Aitken's Salmon Creek Garden
608 N.W. 119th Street
Vancouver, WA 98685
(206) 573-4472 TO $10m
Terry & Barbara Aitken

Plants
"Hybridize and sell all varieties of **bearded irises** in addition to a small selection of Japanese, Siberians, Pacific Coast Natives and a few species irises." A wide selection with plants very briefly described, some shown in color and b&w photos. (1978)
❒ Catalog: $1d, R&W, CAN, SS:7-9, $10m
⌂ Nursery: April-June, evenings & weekends, call ahead
▼ Garden: April-June, evenings & weekends, call ahead

Alberta Nurseries & Seed Company
P.O. Box 20
Bowden, AB, Canada T0M 0K0
(403) 224-3544
Ed Berggren

Plants ～ Seeds ～ Supplies
Offers a good selection of **vegetable and flower seeds** to the US and Canada and general nursery stock only in Canada; varieties are specially selected for short-season climates. Also sells general growing supplies.
❒ Catalog: Free ($2 US), R&W, US, SS:4-5
⌂ Nursery: All year, M-F

Alberts & Merkel Bros., Inc.
2210 S. Federal Highway
Boynton Beach, FL 33435-7799
(407) 732-2071
J. L. Merkel

Plants
Specializes in **orchids, bromeliads and other tropical foliage plants.** Issues three catalogs at $1 each; request catalog of orchids, bromeliads or other tropical plants. (1890)
❒ Catalog: See notes, CAN/OV
⌂ Nursery: All year, M-Sa
▼ Garden: All year, greenhouse

Albiflora, Inc.
P.O. Box 24, Gyotoku
Ichikawa, Chiba, Japan 272-01
0473-58-7627
Mah Yanagisawa

Seeds ～ Books
Offer a broad range of seed of **Japanese native plants**, including many primulas (will ship named varieties of Primula sieboldii 'Sakurasoh' and wild species plants to the fanatic). Also carry books on alpine plants, Japanese gardening and flora of Japan and China with Latin and English plant names. (1984)
❒ Catalog: 2 IRC, OV, bn

Alfrey -- Peter Pepper Seeds
P.O. Box 415
Knoxville, TN 37901
H. W. Alfrey

Seeds
List of **unusual hot and sweet peppers**, also okra, luffa, castor beans (as a deterrent to moles) and some **novelty tomatoes**; plants briefly described, some photographs. Offers a **pepper tomato** that looks like a bell pepper, but is hollow for stuffing.
❒ Catalog: Long SASE, CAN

Alice's Violet Room
Route 6, Box 233
Waynesville, MO 65583
(314) 336-4763 TO
Alice & Leon Pittman

Plants
List features **African violets** from many well-known hybridizers, both recent and older favorites, including trailers, miniatures and semi-miniatures; a broad selection, plants briefly described. Also sells leaves. (1980)
❒ Catalog: Long SASE, R&W, CAN/OV, SS:5-10
⌂ Nursery: All year, daily, call ahead

Allen Company
P.O. Box 1577
Salisbury, MD 21801
(301) 742-7122 TO/CC
Richard & Nancy Allen

Plants
Color catalog of **strawberries, asparagus, raspberries, blueberries** and a **thornless blackberry**; plants are well described with growing suggestions. Check with your local agricultural authorities about ordering these plants from out of state -- some states have strict regulations. (1885)
❒ Catalog: Free, R&W, SS:11-6, $15m
⌂ Nursery: January-May, M-F, by appointment only

Allen, Sterling & Lothrop
191 US Route 1
Falmouth, ME 04105
(207) 781-4142 TO/CC
Shirley Brannigan

Seeds ～ Supplies
Catalog offers a good selection of **short-season vegetable seeds**, annual and perennial flowers, all well described with cultural suggestions. They also sell growing and greenhouse supplies, fertilizers and supplies for basket-making! Basket-making classes are offered in Falmouth. (1911)
❒ Catalog: $1d, R&W
⌂ Nursery: All year, M-Sa

Allgrove Farm, Inc.
P.O. Box 459
Wilmington, MA 01887
(508) 658-4869
Bruce Allgrove

Plants ～ Supplies
Selection of **carnivorous and "woodsy" terrarium plants** and collections of plants for "partridge berry bowls" -- sound charming, don't they? Also several booklets by the proprietor on terrarium growing, grapevine and moss baskets, and wreaths to be decorated by the buyer. (1932)
❒ Catalog: $.50, SS:10-4, $15m, cn/bn
⌂ Nursery: May-September, Sa, call ahead

Allwood Bros.
Mill Nursery
Hassocks, W. Sussex, England BN6 9NB
Hassocks 4229
W. Rickaby

Seeds
This firm is famous for its hybrid **dianthus and carnations**. Catalog lists the seed of over 30 species and hybrids. Also offers a special plant support for taller growing carnations and Rickaby's "Allwood's Guide to Perpetual Flowering Carnations," a 22-page pamphlet (£1.65 ppd. OV). (1911)
❏ Catalog: Free, R&W, OV, cn/bn
⌂ Nursery: All year, M-F, call ahead

Alpen Gardens
173 Lawrence Lane
Kalispell, MT 59901
(406) 257-2540 TO/CC
Bill & Lois McClaren

Plants
"Specializing in early varieties, new introductions and cream-of-the-crop **dahlias**." A collectors' list that gives brief descriptions of each plant and stars their top choices; plants listed by size and type of flower. (1979)
❏ Catalog: Free, CAN/OV
⌂ Nursery: All year, daily, call ahead
▼ Garden: August-September, growing area, call ahead

Alpenflora Gardens
17985 - 40th Avenue
Surrey, BC, Canada V3S 4N8
(604) 576-2464
C. & H. Fischer

Plants
A broad selection of **rock garden and alpine plants**, perennials and miniature shrubs, shipped to the US in eighteen-packs of the buyer's choice. Plants not described, listed only by botanical name.
❏ Catalog: $2, R&W, US, SS:W, $75m, bn
⌂ Nursery: All year, daily

Alpine Gardens & Calico Shop
12446 County F
Stitzer, WI 53825
(608) 822-6382 TO $15m
Charlotte Nelson

Plants
A broad selection of sedums, sempervivums and jovibarbas and other **alpine plants**, listed only by botanical name with no plant descriptions. All are grown outside all year in Wisconsin, so they're very hardy. (1976)
❏ Catalog: $1, R&W, SS:4-10, $20m
⌂ Nursery: March-October, daily, call ahead
▼ Garden: May-June, daily, call ahead

Alpine Valley Gardens
2627 Calistoga Road
Santa Rosa, CA 95404
(707) 539-1749
Wilbur & Dorothy Sloat

Plants ⦿ Seeds
A small family nursery offers over 500 named **daylilies** in limited quantities for the gardener wanting named and newer hybrids; new varieties are added every year. Also sells **alstroemeria** seeds from a "grandparents" patch of Ligtu hybrids (mixed colors). Plants very briefly described. (1979)
❏ Catalog: Long SASE, CAN, $10m
⌂ Nursery: All year, daily, call ahead
▼ Garden: June-July, daily, call ahead

Alston Seed Growers
Littleton, NC 27850
Clifton C. Alston

Seeds
"Rare old-time **non-hybrid corn**," several varieties, and an "everlasting old garden tomato which has volunteered for over 100 years in a few old Southern gardens." Also **moon and stars watermelon** and "bushel" gourds. (1975)
❏ Catalog: $1, R&W, CAN, SS:11-4

Alta Seeds
P.O. Box 253
Potrero, CA 92063
Peter Ewaniuk

Seeds
Small seed company engaged in a breeding program to develop "**vegetable** varieties for home-garden use with emphasis on better flavor and nutritional value." They are expanding their list to a full line of vegetables and flowers, with special varieties for the Southwest and short seasons.
❏ Catalog: $2d, CAN/OV, SS:3-6,10, $2m

Jacques Amand, Ltd.
The Nurseries, Clamp Hill
Stanmore, Middlesex, England HA7 3JS
01-981-8138 FAX 6784

Bulbs
A well-known British supplier of **spring- and summer-blooming bulbs** offers a broad selection of alliums, colchicums, corcus, cyclamen, fritillaria, hybrid and species lilies, daffodils, tulips and others. Each plant is briefly described, some shown in color. You may need an import permit to order.
❏ Catalog: $2(US bills), bn/cn

Amaryllis, Inc.
P.O. Box 318
1452 Glenmore Avenue
Baton Rouge, LA 70821
(504) 924-5560 or 4521 TO/CC
Ed Beckham

Plants ⦿ Bulbs
Offers a broad variety of named hybrid and species **amaryllis**, as well as a few other bulbs -- **Lycoris radiata, habranthus, agapanthus and daylily** seedlings; very brief descriptions. (1942)
❏ Catalog: $1, R&W, CAN/OV, SS:9-5, $15m
⌂ Nursery: All year, call ahead

Ambergate Gardens
8015 Krey Avenue
Waconia, MN 55387
(612) 443-2248
Michael & Jean Heger

Plants
Small nursery specializing in **Martagon lilies** and other hardy **perennials**, **native plants and ornamental grasses**, some of them unusual, as well as a good selection of **hostas**; all plants are well described. They also supply durable custom-engraved plastic plant labels. (1985)
❏ Catalog: $1, R&W, CAN, SS:4-5,8-9, $20m, bn/cn
⌂ Nursery: March-November, Tu-Su, call ahead
▼ Garden: May-September, Tu-Su, call ahead

Amenity Plant Products
RD 5, Box 265
Mt. Pleasant, PA 15666
Guy W. Metzler

Plants & Seeds
Offers **wildflower** seeds both by individual species and in mixtures, and **shrubs and trees** for wildlife enhancement and land reclamation; each plant is well described with hints on use and culture. A number of the wildflowers are also available as plants, with good descriptions. (1987)
❒ Catalog: $1d, R&W, CAN/OV, SS:9-6, cn/bn

Ameri-Hort Research
P.O. Box 1529
Medina, OH 44258
(216) 723-4966
Dr. Karen T. Murray

Plants
Offers the **lilac** introductions of Fr. John Fiala of Falconskeape Gardens. The plants are very well described, and a number of them are shown in his book "Lilacs: the Genus Syringa" (Timber Press, 1988). Eight cultivars are offered in quantity as cultured cuttings, liners or single potted plants.
❒ Catalog: $2

American Bamboo Company
345 W. Second Street
Dayton, OH 45402
Todd Mumma

Plants
Sells rhizomes of **bamboo** hardy in Northern climes -- Phyllostachys bissettii and other varieties. Availability list issued in January. (1956)
❒ Catalog: Free, SS:4, bn

American Daylily & Perennials
P.O. Box 210
Grain Valley, MO 64029
(816) 224-2852 TO/CC
Jack & Jo Roberson

Plants
Color catalog of **daylilies, cannas** and a few award-winning **irises**, most illustrated and all well described. They also offer some **hostas, chrysanthemums and herbaceous peonies.** (1976)
❒ Catalog: $3d (7 IRC), R&W, CAN/OV, SS:3-6,9-10, $20m

American Forest Foods Corp.
Route 5, Box 84E
Henderson, NC 27536
(919) 438-2674
Marlene Smith

Seeds & Supplies
Formerly called Carolina Agro-Tech, this company sells kits for growing **shiitake and oyster mushrooms** and supplies and tools for growers; they have also written a booklet, "Forest Mushroom Farming and Gardening," on how to grow shiitake. They also buy mushrooms from growers under contract and market dried mushrooms nationwide. (1982)
❒ Catalog: $1d, R&W, CAN/OV, SS:9-5, $18m
⌂ Nursery: All year, M-Sa, call ahead

Ames' Orchard and Nursery
6 E. Elm Street
Fayetteville, AR 72703
(501) 443-0282
Guy & Carolyn Ames

Plants & Supplies
Small nursery specializes in disease- and insect-resistant **fruit stock:** antique apples, hardy blueberries, thornless blackberries, strawberries and raspberries, grapes and peaches, each well described in an informative catalog. Also offers books and supplies and encourages low-spray growing. Apple trees also sold in combinations. (1983)
❒ Catalog: 2 FCS, R&W, SS:11-4

Anderson Iris Gardens
22179 Keather Avenue North
Forest Lake, MN 55025
(612) 433-5268 TO
Sharol Longaker

Plants
Offers a broad selection of **tall bearded iris and herbaceous peonies;** all plants are briefly described. Some iris are their own introductions, many are recent award winners. (1978)
❒ Catalog: $.50, SS:7-10
⌂ Nursery: June-October, daily
❦ Garden: June, daily

The Angraecum House
P.O. Box 976
Grass Valley, CA 95945
(916) 273-9426 TO
Fred Hillerman

Plants & Books
Specialist in **species and hybrid Angraecum orchids** from Africa and Madagascar. Offers a cultural manual for $4 as well as his own book, "Introduction to Cultivated Angraecoid Orchids of Madagascar," for $32.95 autographed and postpaid.
❒ Catalog: Free, CAN/OV, SS:4-11, $20m, bn
⌂ Nursery: March-November, M-F, by appointment only

Annabelle's Fuchsia Garden
32531 Rhonda Lane
Fort Bragg, CA 95437
Bruce & Regine Plows

Plants
Offer a very large selection of hybrid **fuchsias,** from the old tried and true to the most recent, and some species fuchsias, each briefly described and rooted to order. They also offer **orchids,** particularly cymbidiums, paphiopedilums, and other hybrids; are issuing an orchid list.
❒ Catalog: $1d, CAN, SS:12-6
⌂ Nursery: March-October, W-Su; other months call ahead
❦ Garden: July-October, W-Su

Antique Rose Emporium
Route 5, Box 143
Brenham, TX 77833
(409) 836-9051 TO/CC
Mike Shoup

Plants & Books
Color/b&w catalog offers a broad selection of **old garden roses,** each well described, with a good deal of historical and cultural information. Roses grown on their own roots, selected for fragrance and long bloom in Zones 6 and above. They also offer books for rosarians. (1983)
❒ Catalog: $2, R&W, CAN, SS:1-5, $10m
⌂ Nursery: All year, Tu-Su
❦ Garden: Spring & fall, Tu-Su

Antonelli Brothers, Inc.
2545 Capitola Road
Santa Cruz, CA 95062
(408) 475-5222 TO/CC $25m
Edward Antonelli

Bulbs
Well known for their **tuberous begonias**, their lath houses are a glorious sight in the summer. They offer a good selection, including hanging-basket begonias and a number of collections. In addition, they offer **tigridia, tuberoses, gladiolus, gloxinias, dahlias, ranunculus and anemones**. (1935)
❏ Catalog: $1d, R&W, CAN/OV, SS:2-6, $2m
⌂ Nursery: All Year, daily
▼ Garden: June-October, daily

Apacha Cactus
3441 Road B
Redwood Valley, CA 95470
(707) 485-7088 or 485-5188
Aldean Keefer

Plants
Offer a nice selection of **cactus**, grown outdoors in northern California: chamaecereus, echinocereus, ferrocactus, lobivia, mammillaria, notocactus, opuntia and others, many suitable for dish gardens. They also sell **aloes, euphorbias, mesembs** and **yuccas**. Very brief plant descriptions. (1983)
❏ Catalog: $.50, R&W, SS:3-11, bn
⌂ Nursery: March-December, W-Su, call ahead
▼ Garden: March-November, W-Su, call ahead

Appalachian Gardens
P.O. Box 82
Waynesboro, PA 17268
(717) 762-4312 TO/CC $25m
Tom McCloud & Ezra Grubb

Plants
Good list of **hardy ornamental trees** and **shrubs**: azaleas, holly, conifers, dogwoods, box, berberis, viburnums, kalmias, rhododendrons; all plants very well described, some hard to find, such as Franklinia alatamaha. (1986)
❏ Catalog: Free, R&W, $5m, bn/cn
⌂ Nursery: All year, M-F
▼ Garden: All year, M-F

Appalachian Wildflower Nursery
Route 1, Box 275A
Honey Creek Road
Reedsville, PA 17084
(717) 667-6998
Don Hackenberry

Plants
Small nursery specializes in **rock garden plants and garden perennials**, with emphasis on local native plants descended from known wild colonies or from Soviet Central Asia, China and Japan. Lists species iris, gentians, phlox, primula, gaultheria, hellebores, dianthus and others.
❏ Catalog: $1.25, R&W, SS:4-5,9-10, bn
⌂ Nursery: All year, M-Sa (Th-Sa in shipping season)

Applesource
Route 1
Chapin, IL 62628
(217) 245-7589
Tom Vorbeck

Applesource is not a source of plants, but a service that will send you unusual **varieties of antique apples** during harvest season so that you can taste before you decide which cultivars to plant. A really nifty idea -- even if you don't have room for a tree! Good holiday gift for yourself or a friend. Catalog is mailed in September. (1983)
❏ Catalog: Free, SS:10-1, $16m

Arbor & Espalier
201 Buena Vista Avenue East
San Francisco, CA 94117
(415) 626-8880
John C. Hooper & Harry Hull

Plants
Offers old-fashioned and unusual **apples** and **pears** already trained in several styles of espalier. (1986)
❏ Catalog: Free, R&W
⌂ Nursery: By appointment only

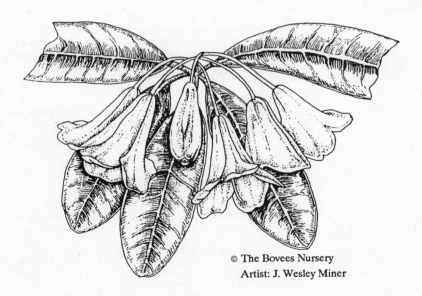

© The Bovees Nursery
Artist: J. Wesley Miner

Archias' Seed Store
106 E. Main Street
Sedalia, MO 65301
(816) 826-1330
Gary Eck & Kevin Daniel

Seeds ～ Supplies
Wide selection of **vegetable seeds and some asparagus and vegetable plants**, all well described. They also sell flower seeds, plants and bulbs and **berry plants**, as well as a good selection of growing supplies, birdhouses and feeders, fertilizers, insecticides and beekeeping aids. (1884)
❑ Catalog: Free, R&W, CAN/OV, SS:3-6, $5m

Artistic Plants
P.O. Box 1165
608 Holly Drive
Burleson, TX 76028
(817) 295-0802 TO/CC
Estella Flather

Plants ～ Books ～ Supplies ～ Tools
A **bonsai** nursery, offering plants for bonsai, accent plants and some succulents and tropical plants for display with bonsai, all briefly described. Also sells bonsai tools, pots and books; finished bonsai, some "in training" for many years, are available at the nursery. (1985)
❑ Catalog: $1, R&W, $20m, bn
⌂ Nursery: Th-Su, call ahead
▼ Garden: Th-Su, call ahead

Ashwood Nurseries
Greenforge
Kingswinford, W.Mid., England DY6 0AE
(0384) 401996

Seeds
Seeds of **lewisia** species and hybrids; they have hybridized a number of colors not found in the species. Their catalog shows the plants in color and gives good cultural information. Seed list available in September.
❑ Catalog: $1(US Bills), US/CAN, bn

Avid Gardener

See Springvale Farm Nursery.

Avon Bulbs
Upper Westwood
Bradford-on-Avon, England BA15 2AT
(02216) 3723
Chris Ireland Jones

Bulbs
Source for many **spring- and summer-blooming bulbs**: alliums, calanthe, crocosmia, galanthus, pleione, lilies, hardy cyclamen, arums, colchicum, crocus, fritillaries, erythronium, species gladiolus, irises, tulips, narcissus and trilliums. Plants briefly described; import permit needed for some, CITES certificate needed for others.
❑ Catalog: $3(US bills), OV, SS:2-3,9-11, bn

Avonbank Iris Gardens
Box 5691, Radford University
Radford, VA 24142
(703) 639-1333
Lloyd Zurbrigg

Plants
A selection of **reblooming iris**, bred for the Mid-Atlantic states. Most are quite hardy and succeed in other climate zones as well. Each plant is well described; many are their own introductions.
❑ Catalog: 2 FCS, $18m
▼ Garden: By appointment only

Aztekakti/Desertland Nursery
P.O. Box 26126
11306 Gateway East
El Paso, TX 79927
(915) 858-1130 TO/CC
David & Lupina Guerra

Plants ～ Seeds
Specializes in rare and hard-to-find **Mexican and South American cactus** and some **succulents and desert and subtropical trees** -- plants and seeds, some habitat-collected. It's a collectors' list, just names, but seems to be a broad selection, available in large and small quantities. Also sells pottery and Indian crafts at the nursery. (1976)
❑ Catalog: 3 FCS, R&W, bn
⌂ Nursery: All year, daily, call ahead
▼ Garden: Spring-summer, daily, call ahead

B & B Laboratories
1600 D Dunbar Road
Mt. Vernon, WA 98273
(206) 424-5647
Bonnie N. Brown

Plants
Propagates **ornamental trees and shrubs, perennials and species lilies** by tissue culture. Plants are seedling size and are delivered in sterile rooting medium; they will also do custom propagation. Plants and bulbs sold only in quantities of twenty-five or more.
❑ Catalog: Long SASE, CAN/OV, $50m

B & D Lilies
330 P Street
Port Townsend, WA 98368
(206) 385-1738 TO/CC $20m
Bob & Dianna Gibson

Bulbs
Offers a broad selection of **hybrid and species lilies** and several special collections of lilies; each is well described, many are shown in color. A second catalog lists their "heirloom" collection, tried and true hybrids which perform well in home gardens. Also sells alstroemerias. (1978)
❑ Catalog: $1d, R&W, CAN/OV, SS:10-12, bn
⌂ Nursery: July-August, daily, call ahead
▼ Garden: July-August, daily, call ahead

B & T Associates
Whitnell House, Fiddington
Bridgwater,Somerset, England TA5 1JE
David Sleigh

Seeds
Seed for thousands of species of **tropical and subtropical plants**: fruit, cactus, palms, proteas, bromeliads, carnivorous plants, flowering trees and shrubs. They publish seed lists in 37 categories; for two International Reply Coupons they'll send a list of seed lists. Their alphabetical species list with 25,000 entries will sell for about $20. Many seeds are collected to order and sent when viable; tell them what you're looking for. (1985)
❑ Catalog: 2 IRC, R&W, $5m, bn

BDK Nursery
P.O. Box 628
2091 Haas Road
Apopka, FL 32712
(305) 889-3053
Bill & Dee Downham

Plants
Offers a good selection of **miniature roses**, many of them prize winners; all
are well described. They also will custom propagate from their huge personal collection and have a limited selection of perpetual old garden roses.
❑ Catalog: Free, R&W, $5m

Fred Bach Epiphyllums
414 South Street
Elmhurst, IL 60126
Frederick O. Bach

Plants ❧ Seeds
Sells only unrooted cuttings of **epiphyllums** ("orchid cactus"). They
specialize in their own hybrids, with a limited number of other varieties
available. At present concentrating on **aporophyllum** (aporocactus X
epiphyllum) interspecies crosses, with seed and cuttings available. Plants
very briefly described, with some cultural information. (1987)
❑ Catalog: Long SASE, SS:4-10

Bailey's
P.O. Box 654
Edmonds, WA 98020
(206) 774-7528
Larry A. Bailey

Plants
Small nursery specializes in **exhibition auriculas and Juliana hybrid primulas**; plants very briefly described. You can also make special requests
for other hybrid and species primulas.
❑ Catalog: Free, SS:4-5,9-10, bn

Baker & Chantry Orchids
P.O. Box 554
18611-132nd Street N.E.
Woodinville, WA 98072
(206) 483-0345 TO/CC $20m
Gary Baker & Will Chantry

Plants
Offers many types of **hybrid orchids** -- masdevallia, paphiopedilum,
miltonia, cattleya, brassia, dracula, pleurothallid -- and also **species
orchids**. Send your "want list" for items not listed. (1978)
❑ Catalog: Long SASE(2FCS), SS:4-11
⌂ Nursery: Daily
▼ Garden: Greenhouse, daily

Bakker of Holland
US Reservation Center
Louisiana, MO 63353-0050
(314) 454-4525 TO/CC
Clay Logan, Mgr.

Bulbs
A Dutch bulb company affiliated with Stark Bros. offers a good selection of
tulips, daffodils, crocus, lilies, iris and other **spring- and summer-blooming bulbs** in a color catalog; somewhat florid plant descriptions, some cultural information.
❑ Catalog: Free, SS:fall,spring, cn/bn

A Bamboo Shoot
1462 Darby Road
Sebastopol, CA 95472
(707) 823-0131
Richard Waters

Plants
Good selection of **bamboo**, both clumping and running, from timber to pigmy,
hardy and tropical, listed by botanical and common name. (1985)
❑ Catalog: $1($1.50 IMO), R&W, CAN/OV, SS:11-5, bn
⌂ Nursery: All year, daily, by appointment only
▼ Garden: All year, daily, by appointment only

Bamboo Sourcery
666 Wagnon Road
Sebastopol, CA 95472
(707) 823-5866
Gerald Bol

Plants
Collectors' list of **bamboos** -- 97 forms, listed by botanical and cultivar
name with good descriptions and cultural information -- available in 4-inch
pots or one-gallon or five-gallon containers. Some are rare or newly
imported varieties; some are non-invasive and make handsome garden
ornamentals; some are very hardy (to -20F). (1985)
❑ Catalog: $1, R&W, CAN/OV, $20m, bn
⌂ Nursery: By appointment only
▼ Garden: By appointment only

The Banana Tree
715 Northampton Street
Easton, PA 18042
(215) 253-9589
Fred Saleet

Seeds
Seeds of a wide selection of **tropical plants** for collectors and "astute
growers of tropicals"; offers many types of bananas and other tropical
fruits, ferns and bromeliads, palms, gingers, proteas, phormiums, cashews
carambola and much more; all plants are well described. Also rhizomes of
heliconia and the "tuber-like bulbs" of **bananas**. Sells plants at the
nursery. (1960)
❑ Catalog: $1, CAN/OV, $5m, bn
⌂ Nursery: All year, daily, call ahead

Barber Nursery
23561 Vaughn Road
Veneta, OR 97487
(503) 935-7701
William Barber

Plants
Nice selection of **seedling trees and shrubs** -- conifers, maples, oaks,
crabapples, dogwoods, species roses and more ornamental species -- listed by
botanical and common name only. Small plants at reasonable prices. Garden
described as "pretty acreage and nice collection of woody plants"; it's on my
travel list! Formerly Mountain Mist Nursery. (1983)
❑ Catalog: Free, R&W, CAN/OV, SS:11-4, $25m, bn
⌂ Nursery: All year, daily, call ahead
▼ Garden: All year, daily, call ahead

Barnee's Garden
Route 10, Box 2010
Nacogdoches, TX 75961
(409) 564-2920
Jean Barnhart

Plants
Offers a broad selection of **daylilies**; grows 2,500 registered cultivars, not all listed in the catalog. She has bought the Bob Dove Daylily Gardens and has added his hybrids to her list.
❑ Catalog: 1 FCS, R&W, SS:9-10, 3-4
⌂ Nursery: All year, M-T,Th-Sa; Su, call ahead
▼ Garden: May-June, M-T,Th-Sa; Su, call ahead

Vernon Barnes & Son Nursery
P.O. Box 250
McMinnville, TN 37110
(615) 668-8576 or 2165 TO/CC

Plants
A very broad selection of **fruit and nut trees, berries** of all kinds and **ornamental trees and shrubs**; many available in small sizes in quantities for hedges or windbreaks. Some plants can't be shipped to CA or AZ. (1950)
❑ Catalog: Free, R&W, SS:10-5, $50m, cn

Bay View Gardens
1201 Bay Street
Santa Cruz, CA 95060
(408) 423-3656
Joseph Ghio

Plants ⚬ Seeds
A broad selection of **irises**: tall bearded, Louisiana, spuria and Pacific Coast natives. Their famous hybrid 'Pacificas' have good northern California place names (they offer seeds of these, too); plants are well described. Also sell collections and even "surprise packages" at season's end. (1965)
❑ Catalog: $1.50, CAN/OV, SS:7-10, $10m

The Beall Orchid Company
3400 Academy Drive S.E.
Auburn, WA 98002
(206) 735-1140
Daniel S. Harvey

Plants
Nice selection of **orchids** -- cattleyas, miltonias, phalaenopsis and odonto-glossum-odontioda complex, Colombian miltonias and other species and hybrid orchids; all plants well described. Offers "experienced" cattleyas which have bloomed, stress service to hobbyists and serious collectors. (1906)
❑ Catalog: Free, R&W, CAN/OV
⌂ Nursery: All year, Su-F
▼ Garden: November-March, Su-F

Bear Creek Nursery
P.O. Box 411
Bear Creek Road
Northport, WA 99157-0411
Donna & Hunter Carleton

Plants ⚬ Tools
"Hardy fruits, nuts, shrubs and rootstocks for the home gardener and orchardist." Large selection of antique apples, berries and hardy nut trees; good plant descriptions and cultural information. Specializes in cold-hardy and drought-resistant stocks -- trees and shrubs for windbreaks, wildlife and hardwood; also sells pruning tools. (1979)
❑ Catalog: 2 FCS, R&W, SS:3-5,11, cn/bn
⌂ Nursery: By appointment only

Beaver Creek Nursery
7526 Pelleaux Road
Knoxville, TN 37938
(615) 922-3961
Mike Stansberry

Plants
Specializes in collectors' **trees and shrubs**: species maples, stewartias, viburnums, magnolias, kalmias, hollies, mildew-resistant crape myrtles and other ornamental plants, most of them Southern natives. A good selection; each plant well described. Some of the plants are quite recent introductions.
❑ Catalog: $1d, SS:W, $20m, bn/cn
⌂ Nursery: All year, by appointment only

Becker's Seed Potatoes
RR 1
Trout Creek, ON, Canada P0H 2L0
J. Murray Becker

Plants
Offers 36 varieties of **seed potatoes**, listed by maturity date and well described by flavor and use. Also offers "garden packs" -- ten eyes each of four varieties that will mature over a long period. (1983)
❑ Catalog: Free, US, SS:4-5, $6m

Bedford Dahlias
65 Leyton Road
Bedford, OH 44146
(216) 232-2852
Eugene A. Woznicki

Plants
Offers a good selection of **dahlias**, many of them newer introductions and show varieties, some imported from England and Japan. Most varieties are well described; they are shipped at the planting time specified by you.
❑ Catalog: FCS

Beersheba Wildflower Garden
P.O. Box 551
Stone Door Road
Beersheba Springs, TN 37305
(615) 692-3575
Lloyd Tate

Plants
Color catalog offers a nice selection of **Southeastern wildflowers**, many shown in photographs and described only by botanical and common name. Included are **species orchids and lilies, trilliums, ferns** and more.
❑ Catalog: Free
⌂ Nursery: All year, M-F

Bernardo Beach Native Plant Farm
1 Sanchez Road
Veguita, NM 87062
Judith & Roland Phillips

Plants ⚬ Seeds ⚬ Books
Small nursery specializes in **Southwestern native plants** that are tolerant of drought, wind and cold -- trees, shrubs, perennials, wildflowers, vines, grasses and cactus, each well described. Plants are shipped only to areas with appropriate hot/dry climates. Also offers seeds of native plants and a book, "Southwestern Landscaping with Native Plants." (1980)
❑ Catalog: $1, R&W, SS:10-3, $20m, cn/bn
⌂ Nursery: April-Oct, Tu,Th,Sa, 520 Montano NW, Albuquerque
▼ Garden: Growing area, Veguita, by appointment only

Betsy's Brierpatch
1610 Ellis Hollow Road
Ithaca, NY 14850
(607) 273-6266

Plants
Offers a variety of **houseplants**, both foliage and cacti and succulents;
each plant is well described, with some cultural information.
❏ Catalog: Long SASE, SS:4-10, bn/cn

Bio-Quest International
P.O. Box 5752
Santa Barbara, CA 93150-5752
(805) 969-4072 TO
Dr. Richard Doutt

Seeds ⌁ Bulbs
Specializes in **South African bulbs** -- collectors' list offers a good selection of bulbs, mostly from Cape Province. Small but choice selections --
babiana, lachenalia, ixia, moraea, gladiolus, watsonia and many more. Seed
is collected on special order; archival collection is listed. (1980)
❏ Catalog: $2, CAN, SS:1,6-9, $10m, bn
⌂ Nursery: All year, daily, by appointment only

Birch Farm Nursery
Gravetye
East Grinstead, England R19 4LE
(0342) 810236
W. E. Th. Ingwersen, Ltd.

Seeds
One of the best-known nurseries in England, specializing in **alpine and
rock garden** plants. They publish a seed list, on which you would be sure
to find desirable plants -- they no longer ship plants outside Great Britain.
The seed list is 2 IRC to the US, 1 IRC to Europe.
❏ Catalog: 2 IRC, US/CAN, bn

Bird Rock Tropicals
6523 El Camino Real
Carlsbad, CA 92009-4843
(619) 483-9393 FAX 438-1316 TO
Pamela Koide

Plants
A collectors' list of **tillandsias**. A very broad selection, adding more all
the time; no plant descriptions. Plants available individually or mounted
in a variety of ways. (1981)
❏ Catalog: Long SASE, R&W, CAN/OV, $25m, bn
⌂ Nursery: All year, M-Sa, call ahead
▼ Garden: April-August, M-Sa, call ahead

Bisnaga Cactus Nursery

See New Mexico Cactus Research.

Black Copper Kits
111 Ringwood Avenue
Pompton Lakes, NJ 07442
(201) 831-6484
Harold Welsh

Plants ⌁ Supplies
Offers a small selection of **carnivorous plants**, terrariums, leaflets and
growing supplies; plants not described. (1972)
❏ Catalog: $.25, SS:2-11, $5m, cn/bn

Blackmore & Langdon
Pensford
Bristol, England BS18 4JL
(0272) 33-2300
J. S. Langdon

Seeds
Offers seed of their well-known **tuberous begonias and delphiniums**, plus
polyanthus primroses, gloxinias and aquilegias. Catalogs and seed orders
must be paid in US bills or money orders for pounds, due to cost of changing foreign checks. Delphiniums and begonias are world famous. (1900)
❏ Catalog: $3(US bills), R&W, OV, $5m
⌂ Nursery: All year, M-F

Bloomingfields Farm

See Lee Bristol Nursery.

Blue Dahlia Gardens
P.O. Box 316
San Jose, IL 62682
(309) 247-3210
G. Kenneth Furrer

Plants
Dahlia collectors' list: names of cultivars, types and flower color given;
only new introductions are described briefly -- fanatics will know them!
Offers about 600 cultivars.
❏ Catalog: Free, CAN/OV, SS:12-6

Blue Star Lab
P.O. Box 173
Route 3
Williamstown, NY 13493
(315) 964-2295 TO
David & Joan De Graff

Plants
Specializes in **hardy blueberries, raspberries and asparagus crowns**. These
are grown by special methods to reduce transplant shock and lengthen trans-
plant season.   Seven varieties of blueberry, four varieties of raspberry,
Jersey Giant asparagus transplants. (1981)
❏ Catalog: Free, CAN/OV, SS 4-11
⌂ Nursery: All year, M-F, call ahead
▼ Garden: All year, growing fields, call ahead

Blueberry Hill
RR 1
Maynooth, ON, Canada K0L 2S0
Roger & Valerie Kelly

Plants
Sells **native lowbush blueberry** plants for home gardeners; also to commercial growers under the name Kelly's Farm. Lowbush blueberries are about a
foot high and spread by rhizomes; they are very hardy and need cold winters.
❏ Catalog: Free, US, SS:4-5, $10m

Kurt Bluemel, Inc.
2740 Greene Lane
Baldwin, MD 21013-9523
(301) 557-7229
Kurt Bluemel

Plants
A very extensive list of **ornamental grasses, sedges and rushes**, as well as
perennials, bamboos, ferns and aquatic plants, all very briefly described,
with uses and hardiness zones. There are also useful tables listing grasses
by desirable traits and for specific purposes. (1964)
❏ Catalog: $2, R&W, CAN/OV, SS:3-5, $25m, bn/cn
⌂ Nursery: All year, by appointment only
▼ Garden: All year, by appointment only

Bluestone Perennials
7211 Middle Ridge Road
Madison, OH 44057
(800) 852-5243 TO/CC
R. N. Boonstra

Plants
A broad selection of **hardy perennials**. They seem to specialize in chrysan-
themums, sedums and ground covers, but offer a choice of many, many other
plants for a perennial border; good plant descriptions with cultural informa-
tion and many color photos. Small plants at moderate prices. (1972)
❐ Catalog: Free, R&W, SS:3-6,8-11, bn/cn
⌂ Nursery: February-June, August-November, M-Sa, call ahead
▼ Garden: April-June, M-Sa, call ahead

Boehlke's Woodland Gardens
W 140 N 10829 Country Aire Road
Germantown, WI 53022
Daniel Boehlke

Plants
"**Native plants and hardy perennials** for Northern gardens." Offers plants
that naturalize in woodlands, some marsh plants, prairie plants and native
Midwestern wildflowers and ferns. Nice selection; plants well described with
cultural suggestions.
❐ Catalog: $.50d, R&W, SS:5-6,9-10, cn/bn

Bonnie Brae Gardens
1105 S.E. Christensen Road
Corbett, OR 97019
(503) 695-5190
Jeanie Driver

Bulbs
A nice selection of show quality **novelty daffodils**; varieties described by
name, class and hybridizer with very brief personal comments and descriptions
of growth habit and season of bloom. Many of the varieties are good
naturalizers. Seller pays postage in the US. (1984)
❐ Catalog: Free, R&W, CAN/OV, SS:9, $5m
⌂ Nursery: Call ahead.
▼ Garden: March-May, call ahead.

Bonsai Farm
P.O. Box 130
Lavernia, TX 78121
(512) 649-2109 TO/CC
Edith Sorge

Plants ⬧ Books ⬧ Supplies ⬧ Tools
List offers a number of plants to use for **bonsai**, both indoor and outdoor,
as well as a large selection of bonsai supplies -- pots, tools, planting supplies, soil amendments, bonsai display stands and books. Plants very well
described. (1971)
❐ Catalog: $1, R&W, $10m, cn/bn

Bonsai of Georgia
4096 Clairmont Road
Atlanta, GA 30341
(404) 451-5356 TO/CC
David E. Cook

Plants ⬧ Supplies
Publishes no catalog at present; you'll have to send a "want list" to see if
they have the **bonsai plants or supplies** you are looking for. Also sells
waterlilies, lotus and bamboo. Ships overnight anywhere in the US. For
locals they offer bonsai classes, maintenance and boarding of bonsai. (1975)
❐ Catalog: See notes
⌂ Nursery: All year, T-Sa
▼ Garden: All year, T-Sa

The Bonsai Shop
43 William Street
Smithtown, NY 11787
(516) 724-3055
Rhys & Kathy O'Brien

Plants
Specialize in finished **bonsai**; several examples are shown in color, though
not all plants will look just like the pictures. They sell many more kinds
at the nursery, along with books, tools and growing supplies. (1986)
❐ Catalog: Free, R&W, CAN, SS:W, cn
⌂ Nursery: By appointment only

Boordy Nursery
P.O. Box 38
Riderwood, MD 21139
(301) 823-4624
J. & P. Wagner

Plants ⬧ Books ⬧ Supplies
Proof that "Wine Country" is rapidly spreading all over the country -- here's
a nursery in Maryland offering **hardy wine grapes** for colder areas, a good
selection for both red and white wines and a few table grapes, all well
described in an informative catalog. Sells two books on winemaking by Philip
M. Wagner and carries winemaking equipment not listed in the catalog. (1942)
❐ Catalog: Free, SS:3-5, $16m

Borbeleta Gardens
15980 Canby Avenue
Faribault, MN 55021
(507) 334-2807
Julius Wadekamper

Plants ⬧ Bulbs
"Introduce **daylilies, Siberian and bearded iris and lilies** developed by
amateur gardeners who in the past have had no commercial outlet. We also
develop and introduce our own originations." Catalog has many color illus-
trations; plants are briefly described. (1972)
❐ Catalog: $3(4 IRC), R&W, CAN/OV, SS:4-10
⌂ Nursery: All year, M-F, call ahead
▼ Garden: April-September, growing area, call ahead

Boston Mountain Nurseries
Route 2, Box 405-A
Mountainburg, AR 72946
(501) 369-2007
Pense Family

Plants
A good selection of **cane berries (brambles), strawberries, blueberries** and
table grapes in quantities for home gardeners and for large commercial
growers; all plants well described and hardy to Zones 4 or 5.
❐ Catalog: 1 FCS, R&W, SS:fall,spring

Botanic Garden Company
9 Wyckoff Street
Brooklyn, NY 11201
(718) 624-8839
Jon Peterson & Elan Zamora

Seeds ⊗ Supplies ⊗ Tools
Wildflower seeds from all regions of the US, sold by individual packets or
in six-packs or in mixes. They also sell some tools, supplies and gifts for
gardeners, greeting cards, handsome posters and tee-shirts. Not a large
selection, but lovely presentation packs for gifts. (1984)
❐ Catalog: $1d, R&W, CAN/OV, $15m

Botanicals
219 Concord Road
Wayland, MA 01778
(508) 358-4846 TO/CC $25

Plants
Small nursery specializes in **plants for difficult situations** in USDA Zones
5 to 7; they've tested many plants and list about 100 species of perennials,
shrubs and trees which are hardy, soil- and drought-tolerant for "water- and
soil-sensible landscapes."
❐ Catalog: $1, SS:4-9

Bountiful Gardens
19550 Walker Road
Willits, CA 95490
(707) 459-3390 TO/CC $5m
Bill & Betsy Bruneau, Mgrs.

Seeds ⊗ Books ⊗ Supplies ⊗ Tools
Catalog offers a broad selection of **open-pollinated vegetable seeds** from
Chase Seeds in England, as well as seeds of herbs, flowers, green manure
crops and grains; all well described in informative catalog. Also sells a
wide selection of gardening books, tools and organic supplies. (1983)
❐ Catalog: Free(4 IRC), R&W, CAN/OV, cn/bn
⌂ Nursery: Common Ground Garden Supply, Palo Alto, CA
▼ Garden: Tours, write for information

The Bovees Nursery
1737 S.W. Coronado
Portland, OR 97219
(503) 244-9341 TO/CC
Lucille Sorensen, Mgr.

Plants ⊗ Supplies
A collector's catalog of **species and hybrid rhododendrons**, as well as Jap-
anese maples, camellias, lilacs, clematis, dwarf conifers, alpine and rock
garden plants, dwarf shrubs, ground covers and woodland plants -- all well
described. They have a separate list offering Vireya rhododendrons. (1953)
❐ Catalog: $2d, CAN/OV, SS:9-11,2-4, $20m, bn/cn
⌂ Nursery: September-December, Feb-July, W-Su
▼ Garden: February-June, W-Su

S & N Brackley
117 Winslow Road, Wingrave
Aylesbury, Bucks., England HP22 4QB
(0296) 681384
S. & N. Brackley

Seeds
Specializes in **sweet peas**: offers many cultivars, including many old-fash-
ioned sweet-smelling varieties. Sold by individual cultivar, each briefly
described, or in several special mixes. (1890)
❐ Catalog: 2 IRC, R&W, OV
⌂ Nursery: All year, daily
▼ Garden: June-August, daily

Brand Peony Farm
P.O. Box 842
St. Cloud, MN 56302
Gerald Lund

Plants
A good selection of herbaceous **peonies**, many developed by Ben Gilbertson.
All plants well described, including Tenuifolia flora plena, the fern leaf
peony. Also sells some **tall bearded iris**. (1868)
❐ Catalog: $1d, SS:9-10

Breck's
US Reservation Center
6523 North Galena Road
Peoria, IL 61656
Spring Hill Nurseries Co., Inc.

Plants ⊗ Bulbs
Color catalog offers a large selection of **spring-blooming bulbs** -- tulips,
daffodils, alliums, iris and more; each plant glowingly described, some given
rather fanciful names. Also have a catalog of **summer-blooming bulbs** --
lilies, daylilies, gladiolus, dahlias and tuberous begonias. (1818)
❐ Catalog: Free, SS:4-5,8-11, cn

Breckinridge Orchids
6201 Summit Avenue
Brown Summit, NC 27214-9744
(919) 656-7991 TO/CC
Mark Rose

Plants ⊗ Supplies
Because of rapid turnover they issue only a price list, not a catalog. Offer
a good selection of **blooming orchids** all year; specialize in phalaenopsis,
vanda, cattleya, dendrobium, oncidium, paphiopedilum and species orchids.
Prices by size of pot and number of bloom spikes. Some supplies. (1957)
❐ Catalog: Long SASE, R&W, CAN/OV, SS:3-11, $35m
⌂ Nursery: All year, M-Sa
▼ Garden: March-July, M-Sa

Briarwood Gardens
RFD 1
14 Gully Lane
East Sandwich, MA 02537
(617) 888-2146 TO
Jonathan Leonard

Plants
Nursery specializing in choice selections of **Dexter hybrid rhododendrons**
which were originally bred in Sandwich, a few miles away. They also have
other hybrids, as well as pieris, kalmia and holly at the nursery. Plants
are very well described. (1984)
❐ Catalog: $1, R&W, SS:5-6
⌂ Nursery: May-September, Tu-Su
▼ Garden: May, Tu-Su

Lee Bristol Nursery
Bloomingfields Farm
Route 55
Gaylordsville, CT 06755-0005
(203) 354-6951 TO/CC $15m
Lee Bristol

Plants
Daylilies listed by color with an index of cultivar names; plants are very well described, with season of bloom and cultural hints given. Offers a broad selection, quantity discounts and several collections for long seasons of bloom. (1969)
❒ Catalog: Free, R&W, CAN/OV, SS:4-11
⌂ Nursery: June-August, W-Su
▼ Garden: July-August, W-Su

Brittingham Plant Farms
P.O. Box 2538
Salisbury, MD 21801
(301) 749-5153 TO/CC
Wayne Robertson & James Brittingham

Plants
Specializes in virus-free **strawberry** plants, as well as **asparagus roots, raspberries, blackberries, blueberries and grapes**; all very well described, with cultural and hardiness information. (1945)
❒ Catalog: Free, R&W, CAN/OV
⌂ Nursery: All year, M-F

Broadleigh Gardens
Bar House, Bishops Hull
Taunton, Somerset, England TA4 1AE
(0823) 286231
Christine Skelmersdale

Bulbs
A well-known English specialist in **"small bulbs"** -- crocus, hyacinths, fritillarias, species iris, daffodils, scillas, species tulips and many others, some quite unusual. As with all foreign bulb imports, you may need an import permit; payment possible by credit card.
❒ Catalog: $1(US bills), bn

Broken Arrow Nursery
13 Broken Arrow Road
Hamden, CT 06518
Richard & Sally Jaynes

Plants
Specializes in **kalmias, species and hybrid rhododendrons** and a number of other choice **woodland trees and shrubs** -- fothergilla, pieris, Japanese lilac, enkianthus, dawn redwood and others. Mr. Jaynes is the author of "Kalmia: The Laurel Book" ($32 ppd.); many of the kalmia are his own selections. Cannot ship to CA or AZ. (1984)
❒ Catalog: Free, SS:3-4,10-11, $20m, bn/cn
⌂ Nursery: By appointment only
▼ Garden: June, by appointment only

Brookfield Nursery & Tree Plantation
P.O. Box 2490
Christiansburg, VA 24068
(703) 382-9099 or (800) 443-TREE TO/CC
David G. Larsen

Plants
Sells **living or fresh-cut Christmas trees**, delivered direct by UPS, plus tree stands and wreaths; can't ship to HI or AK. (1969)
❒ Catalog: Free, R&W, SS:11-12

Brooksfield Farm
426 Byrd Street
Centralia, WA 98531
(206) 736-8209
Ric and Cathy Cavness

Bulbs
A small family nursery growing and selling **daffodils and tulips** -- a nice selection in an informative catalog, with a table of blooming sequence.
❒ Catalog: Free, SS:9-10

Brookside Wildflowers
Route 3, Box 740
Boone, NC 28607
(704) 963-5548
Jo Boggs

Plants ⌖ Books
Offer nursery-propagated **wildflowers**; a good selection, all very well described with good cultural information. Plants are one-year-olds and shipped in pots; cannot ship to CA. Also offer books on growing and identifying wildflowers and a line of birdhouses. (1987)
❒ Catalog: See notes, SS:3-5,9-11, $10m, bn/cn
⌂ Nursery: May-October, Th-Tu
▼ Garden: May-August, Th-Tu

Joseph Brown, Native Seeds
Star Route, Box 226
Gloucester Point, VA 23062
(804) 642-4602 TO
Joseph Brown

Seeds
A wide selection of seeds of **native plants**, some of them habitat-collected. Selection includes asclepias, asters, echinaceas, eupatorium, liatris, rudbeckias, species iris and a number of native orchids. Included are seeds of **trees and shrubs of the Southeast**. No plant descriptions. (1984)
❒ Catalog: $1, R&W, CAN/OV, $12m, bn

Brown's Omaha Plant Farms, Inc.
P.O. Box 787
Omaha, TX 75571
Brown Family

Plants
Offers **onion plants** in bunches of about 75 -- several varieties including 'Texas Sweeties' in quantities from 2 bunches to 60. They have added other **vegetable plants**: cabbages, cauliflower, brussels sprouts and broccoli. Also known as W. G. Farrier Plant Co. or Jim Brown Plants. (1935)
❒ Catalog: Free, R&W

Brown's Kalmia & Azalea Nursery
8527 Semiahmoo Drive
Blaine, WA 98230
(206) 371-2489 TO/CC
Ed & Barbara Brown

Plants
Specialize in **kalmias**, offering a nice selection of hybrids from liners to blooming sizes with good plant descriptions. They will be adding azaleas, clematis, dwarf conifers and hybrid lilies -- ask for that list. (1983)
❒ Catalog: Long SASE, R&W, CAN/OV, SS:3-6,9-11
⌂ Nursery: March-December, daily, call ahead
▼ Garden: May-June, call ahead

John Brudy Exotics
3411 Westfield Drive
Brandon, FL 33511
(813) 684-4302
John Brudy

Seeds ∾ Books ∾ Bulbs
Offers a selection of seeds for **tropical trees, shrubs and fruits**; each plant well described, and germination instructions given for each. Many are suitable for greenhouses or as houseplants. Also sells some bulbs and corms and his own book on growing, "How to Do It in a Tub." (1965)
❑ Catalog: $2, CAN/OV, cn/bn

Brussel's Bonsai Nursery
8365 Center Hill Road
Olive Branch, MS 38654
(601) 895-7457 TO/CC
Brussel & Maury Martin, Susan Straus

Plants ∾ Books ∾ Supplies ∾ Tools
Grower and importer offers specimen finished **bonsai** and plants for bonsai, as well as plastic and clay bonsai pots, pruners and a soft spray nozzle for bonsai culture. Plants briefly described, some specimen plants illustrated. Cannot ship to AK or HI. Ask for book list. (1975)
❑ Catalog: $1d, R&W, SS:9-5, $20m, cn/bn
⌂ Nursery: All year, M-F, by appointment only
▼ Garden: By appointment only

Elizabeth Buck African Violets
9255 Lake Pleasant Road
Clifford, MI 48727
(517) 761-7382
Elizabeth Buck

Plants
Does not publish a catalog; sells only **African violet leaves** of newest varieties by well-known hybridizers. The leaves come labeled, but the choice is hers. Come in quantities of 12, 25, 50 and 100; a good way to start a collection. Write for further information. (1968)
❑ Catalog: See notes, SS:5-10, $5m
⌂ Nursery: All year, M-F

Buckley Nursery
646 N. River Road
Buckley, WA 98321
(206) 829-1811
Don & Penny Marlow

Plants
A broad selection of **fruit for the Pacific Northwest**: apples, apricots, cherries, peaches, plums and prunes, Asian pears, nuts and many berries, as well as table and wine grapes. They have added French hybrid lilacs and other **flowering deciduous shrubs**; all plants briefly but well described.
❑ Catalog: Free, R&W, SS:1-4
⌂ Nursery: All year, daily
▼ Garden: All year, daily

Buell's Greenhouse, Inc.
P.O. Box 218
Weeks Road
Eastford, CT 06242
(203) 974-0623
Albert & Diantha Buell

Plants ∾ Seeds ∾ Books ∾ Supplies
A collectors' list of **African violets and exotic gesneriads** -- plants, tubers, rhizomes and seeds plus some supplies and books; plants briefly described in concise tables of information. Noted for their 'Buell's Hybrid Gloxinias.' Catalog $.25 plus long SASE with 2 FCS for postage. (1940)
❑ Catalog: See notes, SS:2-6,9-10, $10m, bn
⌂ Nursery: All year, M-Sa
▼ Garden: All year, greenhouse, M-Sa

The Bulb Crate
2560 Deerfield Road
Riverwoods, IL 60015
Alice Hosford

Plants ∾ Bulbs
Small company sells **hybrid lilies, peonies, tall and dwarf bearded iris**, some **daffodils and species tulips**; some plants shown in color, all are briefly described. (1987)
❑ Catalog: Free, R&W, CAN/OV, $10m

Bull Valley Rhododendron Nursery
214 Bull Valley Road
Aspers, PA 17304
(717) 677-6313
Faye & Ray Carter, Kim Altice

Plants
Specializes in Dexter and Wister-Swarthmore **hybrid rhododendrons**, "plants for the serious collector," described only by color of bloom. Have added Gable, Pride, Consolini and Leach hybrids and unnamed hybrids of Jack Cowles. They also offer several varieties of holly. (1979)
❑ Catalog: $2, SS:5-6,9
⌂ Nursery: All year, by appointment only
▼ Garden: May, Rhododendrons, by appointment only

Bundles of Bulbs
112 Green Springs Valley Road
Owings Mills, MD 21117
(301) 363-1371
Kitty Washburne

Bulbs
A broad selection of **spring-blooming bulbs**: tulips, daffodils, crocus, lilies and various small bulbs; all are well described and illustrated with nice block prints. Also offer "span" collections for long seasons of bloom. Recent additions are hybrid lilies and herbaceous peonies and some flower arranging and growing supplies. (1984)
❑ Catalog: $2d, SS:10-11, $10m
⌂ Nursery: By appointment only
▼ Garden: March-June, Th, Sa-Su

Burford Brothers
Monroe, VA 24574
(804) 929-4950
Tom & Russell Burford

Plants ∾ Supplies
Offer a wide variety of **antique and modern apples**; their brochure, which sells for $1, describes 60 varieties by taste, appearance and time of ripening. They also offer a hefty catalog for $8, deductible from your first order, which gives much fuller descriptions and history of the apples and includes more varieties. They also sell orchard supplies. (1983)
❑ Catalog: See notes, SS:11-12,3-5, $10m
⌂ Nursery: March-December, daily, by appointment only
▼ Garden: September-October, daily, by appointment only

Burk's Nursery
P.O. Box 1207
Benton, AR 72015-1207
(501) 794-3266
Bob & Lois Burks

Plants
Former owners of California Epi Center have a new nursery specializing in **haworthias and gasterias**; a very broad selection with good brief plant descriptions; all plants seed-grown or nursery-propagated. Nursery is in Alexander, AR; write or call for directions. (1988)
☐ Catalog: Free, CAN/OV, SS:4-11, $10m, bn
⌂ Nursery: By appointment only
▼ Garden: April-October, by appointment only

Burnt Ridge Nursery
432 Burnt Ridge
Onalaska, WA 98570
(206) 985-2873
George Michael Dolan

Plants
Small nursery specializes in **perennial crops** -- hardy and regular kiwis, as well as beeches, Asian pears, dawn redwood, bald cypress, fig trees, hybrid chestnuts, walnuts and filberts and other **fruiting trees**; all plants well described. (1980)
☐ Catalog: Long SASE, R&W, $20m, cn/bn
⌂ Nursery: All year, call ahead

W. Atlee Burpee Company
300 Park Avenue
Warminster, PA 18974
(215) 674-4900 TO/CC $25m
Jon Burpee, Cust. Svs.

Plants ⟳ Seeds ⟳ Books ⟳ Supplies ⟳ Tools ⟳ Bulbs
A **gardening fixture** for many years, they offer flowers, vegetables, perennial plants, berries and fruit trees in a fat color catalog; each plant well described. Offer spring bulbs in a separate summer catalog. Also carry many tools, supplies, canning equipment and beekeeping supplies. (1876)
☐ Catalog: Free, cn/bn
⌂ Nursery: All year, daily
▼ Garden: Summer, daily, by appointment only

D. V. Burrell Seed Growers Co.
P.O. Box 150
Rocky Ford, CO 81067-0150
(719) 254-3318
William E. Burrell

Seeds ⟳ Books ⟳ Supplies ⟳ Tools
A good selection of **vegetable seed**, especially watermelons, canteloupes, hot peppers, corn and popcorn, tomatoes and onions, as well as **annual flowers**. Also offers growing supplies and a good deal of growing information. (1899)
☐ Catalog: Free, R&W, CAN/OV

Bushland Flora (Australian Seed Specialists)
P.O. Box 189
Hillarys, Australia 6025
(09) 401-0187
Brian Hargett

Seeds ⟳ Books
Collectors' list with seeds of hundreds of **Australian plants**, each briefly described; also offers some color-illustrated books on these plants. Many acacias, banksias, eucalyptus, melaleucas, callistemons, helicrysums and helipterums (everlastings) and others; planting guides with orders. Send your "want list" for species not listed; they're sometimes available. (1972)
☐ Catalog: 3 IRC, OV, bn/cn
⌂ Nursery: By appointment only

Busse Gardens
Route 2, Box 238
Cokato, MN 55321
(612) 286-2654 TO/CC
Ainie H. Busse

Plants
A very extensive catalog of **hardy perennials** of all types; offers an especially large selection of hostas, Siberian iris, peonies, daylilies, ferns, astilbe, heuchera, phlox, hardy geraniums, herbaceous peonies and wildflowers for rock gardens and woodland, well to briefly described. (1973)
☐ Catalog: $2d, R&W, SS:4-10, $20m, bn/cn
⌂ Nursery: April-October, M-Sa
▼ Garden: July, call ahead

The Butchart Gardens
Box 4010, Sta. A
Victoria, BC, Canada V8X 3X4
(604) 652-4422
R. I. Ross

Seeds
Butchart Gardens in Victoria sells seed of many of the **annual and perennial flowers** grown in their famous gardens; plants are well described, and prices are very reasonable. They also sell a number of collections: cottage garden, window box, rock garden, children's and hanging baskets. (1904)
☐ Catalog: $1d, US/OV, $2m
▼ Garden: All year, daily, admission charge

Butterbrooke Farm
78 Barry Road
Oxford, CT 06483-1598
(203) 888-2000
Tom & Judy Butterworth

Seeds
Offers seed of **open-pollinated, short-season vegetables** for Northern climates, not treated chemically. Regular packets $.45 each; also available at four times regular size. Sells booklets and a video cassette on organic vegetable growing; customers may join their seed co-op. (1979)
☐ Catalog: Long SASE(1 IRC), CAN/OV
⌂ Nursery: Daily, call ahead
▼ Garden: May-September, call ahead

CRM Ecosystems

See Prairie Ridge Nursery.

Cactus by Dodie
934 E. Mettler Road
Lodi, CA 95242
(209) 368-3692 TO/CC $25m
Dick & Dodie Suess

Plants ∾ Books ∾ Supplies
A broad selection of **cacti and succulents** in a collectors' list: mammillaria, lobivia, gymnocalcium, echinocereus, coryphantha, notocactus, parodia, rebutia, aloes, agaves, crassulas, euphorbias and haworthias; no plant descriptions, a few illustrated in b&w photos. Also offers pots, labels, supplies and a few books on cacti. (1981)
❒ Catalog: $1d($2 OV), CAN/OV, SS:W, $15m, bn
⌂ Nursery: All year, Th-Sa, call ahead
▼ Garden: All year, sales area, Th-Sa

Cactus by Mueller
10411 Rosedale Highway
Bakersfield, CA 93312
(805) 589-2674
Gus & Maria Piazza

Plants
A collectors' list of **cacti and succulents**: cereus, echinocereus, echinopsis, gymnocalycium, lobivia, mammillaria, notocactus, opuntia, rebutia, aloe, caralluma, crassula, echeveria, haworthia, huernia, senecio and many more. Also some **mesembs**. No plant descriptions, but many shown in color. (1966)
❒ Catalog: $1d, R&W, bn
⌂ Nursery: All year, Th-Tu
▼ Garden: Spring-fall, Th-Tu

Cactus Gem Nursery
5485 White Drive
Batesville, AR 72501
Jim & Betty Daniel

Plants ∾ Books ∾ Supplies
Specializes in **cactus and succulents**: echeverias, lithops and epiphyllums. Catalog is a quarterly newsletter offering plants, books and growing supplies. "A wide variety of all succulent plants." (1966)
❒ Catalog: Free, SS:3-11, $15m
⌂ Nursery: By appointment only

The Cactus Patch
RR 2, Box 159
Radium, KS 67550-9111
(316) 982-4670
John Cipra, Jr.

Plants ∾ Books
Small nursery offers **winter-hardy cactus**: opuntias, echinocereus, coryphanthas, as well as yuccas -- a very broad selection of opuntias. All plants well described. Also recommends and sells "Cacti of the Southwest, Revised with Color," by W. Hubert Earle. (1975)
❒ Catalog: $.25 or FCS, SS:4-10, $5m, bn
⌂ Nursery: Call ahead
▼ Garden: May-June, call ahead

Caladium World
P.O. Drawer 629
Sebring, FL 33871
(813) 385-7661 TO/CC
L. E. & Daniel Selph

Bulbs
Specialize in **caladium bulbs**, those brilliantly colored fancy leaved plants that survive so well through the Southern summers. Several are illustrated in their color leaflet. (1979)
❒ Catalog: Free, R&W, CAN, SS:1-5, $10m
⌂ Nursery: January-August, M-F, call ahead
▼ Garden: July-September, growing area, call ahead

California Epi Center

See Rainbow Gardens Nursery & Bookshop.

© Good Seed Co.
Artist: Will Ross

California Nursery Co.
P.O. Box 2278
Fremont, CA 94536
(415) 797-3311
George Roeding, Jr.

Plants
List offers a broad selection of **fruit and nut trees** for home gardeners and commercial orchardists, including kiwis, persimmons, pistachios, grapes, citrus, avocados, nut trees, bamboo; no plant descriptions. (1865)
❑ Catalog: Free, CAN/OV, $30m

Callahan Seeds
6045 Foley Lane
Central Point, OR 97502
(503) 855-1164
Frank T. Callahan II

Seeds
An extensive list of seeds of **native Northwestern trees and shrubs** as well as some from most other continents, listed by botanical and common names only. They will also custom-collect seeds from "want lists" -- seeds available in small packets and in bulk. Small supplier, good list. (1977)
❑ Catalog: Long SASE, R&W, CAN/OV, bn/cn
⌂ Nursery: All year, daily, by appointment only

Camellia Forest Nursery
P.O. Box 291
125 Carolina Forest
Chapel Hill, NC 27516
(919) 967-5529
Kai-Mei Parks

Plants
Camellias selected for hardiness and disease resistance, both species and unusual hybrids just being introduced; also species maples and rhododendrons, unusual **ornamental trees and shrubs**, dwarf conifers, holly and evergreen azaleas. Wide selection of collectors' plants; some are recent collections from China and Japan. Plants are briefly described. (1978)
❑ Catalog: 2FCS, CAN/OV, SS:11-5, $15m
⌂ Nursery: All year, by appointment only
▼ Garden: Spring, fall, by appointment only

Camelot North
RR 2, Box 398
Pequot Lakes, MN 56472
(218) 568-8922 or 8789
Jerry & Ruth Peltier

Plants ⬙ Books
List offers a good selection of **perennials and perennial herbs** hardy to Zone 3; very brief plant descriptions. Also listed are a few books on growing annuals, perennials and herbs and a list of plants suitable for drying. (1981)
❑ Catalog: $1d, SS:6-8, $10m, bn
⌂ Nursery: May-June, daily; July-August, M-Sa
▼ Garden: Growing area, M-Sa

Canyon Creek Nursery
3527 Dry Creek Road
Oroville, CA 95965
(916) 533-2166
John & Susan Whittlesey

Plants
A good selection of **perennials**, including many violas and violets, species geraniums, the "chocolate" cosmos, euphorbias, salvias, campanulas and many more; all very well described with cultural suggestions. Surely the chief attraction of the Oroville area! (1985)
❑ Catalog: $1, SS:2-5,9-11, bn
⌂ Nursery: All year, M-Sa

Cape Cod Violetry
28 Minot Street
Falmouth, MA 02540
(508) 548-2798
John & Barbara Cook

Plants ⬙ Supplies
A collectors' list of **African violets**, many from well-known hybridizers, and **episcias, sinningias and miniature streptocarpus**; all very briefly described and available as plants or by leaves and stolons. Also sells growing supplies and African violet gift items.
❑ Catalog: $1d ($2 OV), R&W, CAN/OV, SS:5-10
⌂ Nursery: By appointment only

Cape Seed & Bulb
P.O. Box 4063, Idasvalley
Stellenbosch, Cape, South Africa 7609
(02231) 78418
J. L. Holmes

Seeds
Color catalog shows a number of the plants offered: a very broad selection of seeds of **South African bulbous and other plants**. Descriptions include only height and color, but these plants are worth looking up elsewhere for more complete descriptions. They are introducing a smashing clear yellow **Clivia miniata var. citrina** -- a bit less expensive than diamonds. (1981)
❑ Catalog: $2d (US bills), R&W, OV, SS:12-3, $40m, bn

Caprice Farm
15425 S.W. Pleasant Hill Road
Sherwood, OR 97140
(503) 625-7241 TO/CC
Allan, Dorothy & Richard Rogers, Robin Blue

Plants
A good selection of **hostas, Japanese and Siberian irises, daylilies** and **peonies**, both herbaceous and tree cultivars, some quite rare. All plants are very well described, and some are illustrated in color; much here to gladden the heart. (1978)
❑ Catalog: $1d, R&W, CAN/OV, $10m
⌂ Nursery: All year, daily, call ahead
▼ Garden: May-September, call ahead

Cardinal Nursery
Route 1, Box 316
State Road, NC 28676
(919) 874-2027 TO/CC
Bill & Barbara Storms

Plants
Two catalogs, "Rhododendrons for Eastern Gardens" and "Rhododendrons for Collectors and Hobbyists," each listing over 200 **rhododendron hybrids**, with several sizes available for most plants; all well described with notes on hardiness and bloom time. List is arranged by cultivar name; names of hybridizers read like a Who's Who of Rhodoland! Cannot ship to CA, OR, WA.
❑ Catalog: Free
⌂ Nursery: All year, Sa or by appointment

Carino Nurseries
P.O. Box 538
Indiana, PA 15701
(412) 463-3350 or 7480, (800) 223-7075

Plants
Specializes in **seedling trees** for windbreaks, wildlife food and Christmas trees and ornamental trees for general garden use. Plants are available as seedlings and as larger transplants, source of plant introductions given for many plants.
❒ Catalog: Free

Carlson's Gardens
P.O. Box 305
South Salem, NY 10590
(914) 763-5958
Bob Carlson

Plants
A broad selection of **azaleas and rhododendrons** for collectors: native and hybrid azaleas such as Knaphill-Exbury, Robin Hill, Gable, North Tisbury, Glenn Dale and their own 'Face 'em Down' evergreens. Also large and small leafed hybrid rhododendrons (Dexter, Leach, Gable) and **kalmias**. (1970)
❒ Catalog: $2d, SS:4-6,9-11, bn/cn
⌂ Nursery: Daily, by appointment only

Carncairn Daffodils, Ltd.
Carncairn Lodge
Broughshane
Ballymena, Co.Antrim, No. Ireland BT43 7HF
(0266) 861216
Kate Reade

Bulbs
Collectors' list of **daffodils**: a broad selection of types with division and color class given for each, along with a good description; many are their own introductions. Bulbs are shipped airmail.
❒ Catalog: $2(US bills), US/CAN, SS:8

Carolina Exotic Gardens
Route 5, Box 283-A
Greenville, NC 27834
(919) 758-2600
D. R. Minton

Plants ❧ Seeds
Sells **carnivorous plants** and seeds, particularly Venus's-flytrap, drosera, sarracenia, nepenthes and other bog plants; each well described with growing suggestions. (1973)
❒ Catalog: $1, R&W, CAN/OV, $10m

Carroll Gardens
P.O. Box 310
444 E. Main Street
Westminster, MD 21157
(301) 848-5422 or (800) 638-6334
Alan L. Summers

Plants ❧ Books ❧ Tools
Informative catalog lists a huge selection of **perennials, herbs, roses, vines, conifers, trees, shrubs and summer bulbs**, all very well described with cultural information. Many hollies, lilies, yews, viburnums, box, clematis, species geraniums, dianthus, campanulas and much more; many fine woody plants suitable for small gardens.
❒ Catalog: $2d, CAN, SS:W, bn/cn
⌂ Nursery: All year, daily

Carter & Holmes, Inc.
P.O. Box 668
1 Old Mendenhall Road
Newberry, SC 29108
(803) 276-0579 TO
Owen Holmes & Gene Crocker

Plants ❧ Supplies
A broad selection of **orchids**; they are especially well known for their cattleya and phalaenopsis hybrids, many of which are shown in color and are irresistible. Plants are listed by color, with good descriptions. Also sell orchid and greenhouse growing supplies. (1948)
❒ Catalog: $1.50d, R&W, CAN/OV, SS:W, $15m
⌂ Nursery: All year, M-F, Sa am
▼ Garden: March-April, October-November, M-F, Sa am

Carter Seeds
475 Mar Vista Drive
Vista, CA 92083
(619) 724-5931 FAX 8832, (800) 872-7711
Mrs. M. K. Frick

Seeds ❧ Books ❧ Supplies
Essentially a wholesale seed company, their smallest quantity is one ounce of seed, but they offer a broad selection of seeds of **ornamental trees** and **shrubs**, including palms, eucalyptus, acacias, conifers, as well as ornamental and lawn **grasses, perennials, annuals and wildflowers**. They have also added books on plants and some propagation and growing supplies.
❒ Catalog: Free, R&W, CAN/OV, $15m ($25m flowers), cn/bn
⌂ Nursery: All year, M-F, call ahead

Casa Yerba Gardens
3459 Days Creek Road
Days Creek, OR 97429
(503) 825-3534
Jim & Carol Hilderbrand

Plants ❧ Seeds
Price list, send long SASE; catalog $1d. Offers a nice selection of **herb** seeds and some shallots, Egyptian onions, goldenseal roots and elephant garlic; no plant descriptions.
❒ Catalog: See notes, CAN/OV, SS:4-6,9-10, cn/bn

Cascade Forestry Nursery
Route 1
Cascade, IA 52033
(319) 852-3042

Plants
Offers **hardy nut trees, conifers and other trees and shrubs** primarily for reforestation, woodlots and windbreaks; plants not described, informative leaflet free of charge. Plants offered from seedling size to several feet tall, depending on variety.
❒ Catalog: Free, R&W, CAN/OV, $20m, SS:4-5, cn/bn

Cascade Daffodils
1790 Richard Circle
West St. Paul, MN 55118-3821
(612) 455-6177
David & Linda Karnstedt

Bulbs
A very broad selection of **show daffodils**, both standard and miniature categories. Each plant is described by name of hybridizer, class and brief comments; collectors will know and want them -- they sound delicious. (1986)
❒ Catalog: Free, SS:8-9, $15m
⌂ Nursery: By appointment only
▼ Garden: April-May, by appointment only

Catalpa Nursery
P.O. Box 1599
Catalpa Point, Oxford Road
Easton, MD 21601
(301) 822-0242

Plants
Offer three cultivars of **Leyland cypress:** 'Leighton Green,' 'Castlewellen Gold' and 'Naylor's Blue.' These trees are hardy to Zone 5, are very fast-growing and are much used for hedges and screens.
❒ Catalog: Free, R&W
⌂ Nursery: All year, M-Sa

Catnip Acres Herb Nursery
67 Christian Street
Oxford, CT 06483-1224
(203) 888-5649
Dean & Gene Pailler

Seeds
Seeds of over 350 varieties of **herbs and everlastings;** each very well described with good germination and cultural information. Also sell books on herbs, herb gifts and supplies and over 400 varieties of herb plants and 100 varieties of **scented leaf geranium** plants at the nursery. (1978)
❒ Catalog: $2, CAN/OV, cn/bn
⌂ Nursery: April-December, Tu-Su
▼ Garden: June-August, Tu-Su

Richard G. M. Cawthorne
Lower Daltons Nursery
Swanley Village
Swanley, Kent, England BR8 7NU
Richard G. M. Cawthorne

Seeds
Seeds from the world's largest collection of **violas, violettas and viola species,** with 450 named varieties. Plants are for sale at the nursery only, but he will send mixed viola seed overseas (packet is $5 in US bills). Plants are well described, selection is mouth-watering. (1951)
❒ Catalog: See notes, OV

Cedar Ridge Nurseries
Cedar Ridge Road
Allison Park, PA 15101
(412) 443-6060
Walter L. Greenwood

Plants ❧ **Supplies**
Here is a one-plant nursery, but what a choice! They offer **nepenthes,** the Asian pitcher plants, both species and hybrids, easily grown in greenhouse, under lights or in terraria; dozens of varieties, well described. Also sell many color slides. Catalog gives good cultural information.
❒ Catalog: Free, R&W, CAN, SS:5-10, bn

Chadwell Himalayan Seed
81 Parlaunt Road
Slough, Berks., England SL3 8BE
(0753) 42823
Christopher Chadwell

Seeds
"Free-lance plant hunter/botanist, specializing in the **flora of the northwest Himalaya and the Orient,** seed available from expeditions and local collectors." List has section of easy seeds for beginners, good plant descriptions and lovely line drawings of many of the plants. Collectors will crow! New lists of trees and shrubs, Japanese plants and tropical/greenhouse plants are forthcoming. (1984)
❒ Catalog: 4 IRC(or $3 US bills), OV, bn

John Chambers
15 Westleigh Road, Barton Seagrave
Kettering, Northants, England NN15 5AJ
(0933) 681 632
John Chambers

Seeds
Seeds of **British wildflowers, herbs, grasses and wildflower bulbs,** mostly by their British common names -- you'll have to use British reference books. Also offers plants to attract butterflies, bees and birds -- should work just as well this side of the ocean. Also herbs and grasses. (1979)
❒ Catalog: Free, R&W, OV, cn/bn
⌂ Nursery: All year, daily

Chambers Nursery
26874 Ferguson Road
Junction City, OR 97448
(503) 998-2467 TO/CC
Vic Chambers

Plants
A collectors' list of **rhododendrons and azaleas;** all plants well described with information on hardiness, season of bloom, size and rating. A very broad selection.
❒ Catalog: Free, $30m

Champlain Isle Agro Associates
East Shore
Isle La Motte, VT 05463
(802) 928-3425
Randy & Amy McCoy

Plants
Propagators of virus-tested "Vermont Premium" **small fruit nursery stock.** Sixteen cultivars of raspberries, including red, yellow, black and thornless, and French tarragon; they are adding hardy table grapes and **daylilies.** "Vermont Premium" stock meets stringent standards of certification for virus testing, are shipped direct from the greenhouse in a soilless medium. (1985)
❒ Catalog: Free, R&W, OV, $20m

Charles Island Gardens
P.O. Box 91471
West Vancouver, BC, Canada V7V 3P2
(604) 921-7383
Wally Thomas

Plants
Small nursery specializes in **odontoglossum and miniature cymbidium orchids**; each plant described by parentage and color or expected bloom appearance. The cymbidiums are meristems from the McBeans collection, all have 'Cooksbridge' names. (1977)
❏ Catalog: Free, R&W, US/OV, SS:4-10
⌂ Nursery: By appointment only

Chehalem Gardens
P.O. Box 693
Newberg, OR 97132
(503) 538-8920
Tom & Ellen Abrego

Plants
A list for lovers of **Siberian and spuria irises**. They have "regular" and tetraploid Siberian irises; the latter are sturdier and richer in color with larger blooms. Each plant briefly but well described. A small nursery; stock may be limited on some plants. Can't ship to FL or HI. (1982)
❏ Catalog: Free, SS:8-9
♥ Garden: May, weekends, by appointment only

Chehalis Rare Plant Nursery
2568 Jackson Highway
Chehalis, WA 98532
(206) 748-7627
Herbert Dickson

Seeds
Small specialty nursery offers only **primula** seed by mail: single, double, show and alpine auricula, florindae, some petite hybrids and mixed candelabra. Ask for seed list. At the nursery they sell miniature and unusual alpine and rock garden plants, dwarf conifers and trees and shrubs. (1968)
❏ Catalog: Long SASE, CAN/OV, $5m
⌂ Nursery: All year, call ahead

Chestnut Hill Nursery, Inc.
Route 1, Box 341
Alachua, FL 32615
(904) 462-2820
R. D. Wallace & Deborah Gaw

Plants ☙ Books
Specialize in blight-resistant hybrid **chestnuts** -- Dunstan hybrids and the 'Revival,' 'Carolina' and 'Heritage' chestnuts -- all well described and illustrated in a color pamphlet. They also offer 34 varieties of **Oriental persimmons**, most described in their order form, and a book on chestnut orcharding in America. (1980)
❏ Catalog: Free, R&W, CAN/OV, SS:1-4
⌂ Nursery: All year, M-F, call ahead
♥ Garden: November-March, orchard, call ahead

Chiltern Seeds
Bortree Stile
Ulverston, Cumbria, England LA12 7PB
G. D. and B. S. Bowden

Seeds
Catalog is a sure delight; offers a very extensive selection of plants for every purpose, each very well described. The catalog is a useful reference book containing **ornamental plants** from all over the world. Also sells seed of Oriental, unusual and common vegetables and herbs and British wildflowers.
❏ Catalog: $2d(US bills), OV, bn/cn

Choice Edibles
584 Riverside Park Road
Carlotta, CA 95528
(707) 768-3135
Dan Harkins

Seeds
A small company specializing in cultures and spawn of morel, shiitake, oyster and stropharia **mushrooms**; they will also do custom tissue culturing of customers' mushrooms. Will provide detailed indoor and outdoor growing instructions. Cannot ship to South Africa. (1985)
❏ Catalog: Long SASE(2FCS), R&W, CAN/OV, $10m

David Chopin Nursery
17005 Black Mountain Road
Livingston, LA 70754

Plants
Hybridizer of a number of named cultivars of **miniature weeping crape myrtles**; plants are described by color of flower, type of leaf and size of plant. They are perfect for planters and hanging baskets. (1977)
❏ Catalog: Long SASE

Christa's Cactus
529 W. Pima
Coolidge, AZ 85228
(602) 723-4185
Christa Roberts

Seeds
Offers a collectors' list of **cacti and succulents, desert trees and shrubs**; some quite rare, very briefly described in tiny print. A broad selection, including some caudiciforms and succulents used for bonsai; geographical sources of habitat-collected seed mentioned where known. (1979)
❏ Catalog: 1 FCS(3 IRC), R&W, CAN/OV, bn
⌂ Nursery: All year, M-F, call ahead
♥ Garden: March-June, M-F, call ahead

Paul Christian -- Rare Plants
P.O. Box 468
Wrexham, Clwyd, Wales LL11 3DP
(0978) 366399

Bulbs
Source of rare **bulbs, corms and tubers**: alliums, anemones, arums, colchicum, corydalis, crocus, erythroniums, fritillaria, galanthus, species irises, trillium and species tulips, among others. Plants briefly described. Accepts credit card orders; £11 fee for health certificate and postage.
❏ Catalog: $3(US bills), US/CAN, bn

City Gardens
11850 Van Dyke Avenue
Detroit, MI 48234-4191
(313) 921-5033
Bob Barnhart & Mike Stevenson

Plants ∾ Supplies
Occupying greenhouses established seventy-five years ago, they list a good selection of "**horticultural exotica**" -- flowering houseplants, bromeliads, ferns, tropical foliage plants of all kinds and orchids. They also offer bonsai, using tropical shrubs and trees for indoor culture. Plants are briefly described in tables; there's some cultural information.
❑ Catalog: $1.50d, R&W, SS:3-10, $15m
⌂ Nursery: All Year, daily
▼ Garden: October-June, daily

Clargreen Gardens, Ltd.
814 Southdown Road
Mississauga, ON, Canada L5J 2Y4
(416) 822-0992 TO/CC
Mike Dytnerski, Mgr.

Plants ∾ Books ∾ Supplies ∾ Tools
Offers **orchids**: phalaenopsis, cattleyas and miniature cattleyas, vandas, paphiopedilums and other species, each very briefly described. Another catalog lists **tropical plants, roses, perennials, bonsai, general nursery stock** and books, tools, supplies and pots. (1918)
❑ Catalog: Free, R&W, US/OV, SS:5-11, $45m, bn/cn
⌂ Nursery: All year, daily
▼ Garden: All year, greenhouses, daily

Clifford's Perennial & Vine
Route 2, Box 320
East Troy, WI 53120
(414) 968-4040 April-Sept, 642-7156 Oct-March
Ken & Connie Clifford

Plants
"Suppliers of the Cottage Garden," offer a good selection of **perennials** -- iris, peonies, Oriental poppies, rhododendrons, azaleas, daylilies and clematis and other flowering vines; each plant very well described with cultural notes. (1982)
❑ Catalog: $1d, CAN, SS:4-5,9-10, $15m, bn/cn

Cloud Forest Orchids
P.O. Box 370
Honokaa, HI 96727
(808) 775-9850
Erik & Hillery Gunther

Plants
Small nursery specializes in **species and hybrid orchids** for the collector, offered in flasks or as seedlings and mericlones in individual pots; all well described, some shown in color photos. Ship around the world.
❑ Catalog: Free, R&W, CAN/OV, bn
⌂ Nursery: By appointment only
▼ Garden: By appointment only

Cloud Mountain Nursery
6906 Goodwin Road
Everson, WA 98247
(206) 966-5859
Tom & Cheryl Thornton

Plants
Offers a nice selection of **fruit trees and berries**: apples, European and Asian pears, plums, cherries, kiwis, peaches, table grapes and currants, blueberries, raspberries and strawberries. They also offer filberts, walnuts and chestnuts. Informative catalog, fruit growing classes at the nursery. They also sell special fruit assortments for Thanksgiving and Christmas.
❑ Catalog: Free, SS:2-5, $15m
⌂ Nursery: All year, F-Sa

Coastal Gardens & Nursery
4611 Socastee Boulevard
Myrtle Beach, SC 29575
(803) 293-2000 TO/CC $35m
Rudy & Ursula Herz

Plants
A large selection of **hostas**, as well as Japanese and Siberian irises, daylilies, ground covers, perennials, woodland, bog and aquatic plants. I saw only the hosta list; cultivar names only, no plant descriptions. (1974)
❑ Catalog: $2d, R&W, CAN/OV, SS:3-11, $35m, bn
⌂ Nursery: All year, daily, call ahead
▼ Garden: April-July, daily, call ahead

Coburg Planting Fields
573 East 600 North
Valparaiso, IN 46383
(219) 462-4288 TO/CC $50m
Philipp Brockington & Howard H. Reeve, Jr.

Plants
Small nursery offering **daylilies** -- a nice selection of both old and new varieties, grown in the rich farm soil of Indiana; all are shipped with double fans. Some varieties may be limited, so they suggest calling to check on availability; each plant is briefly described by color, season of bloom and name of hybridizer. (1984)
❑ Catalog: Free, CAN, SS:5-10
⌂ Nursery: May-October, daily, call ahead
▼ Garden: July, call ahead

Coenosium Gardens
6642 S. Lone Elder Road
Aurora, OR 97002
(503) 266-5471
Robert & Dianne Fincham

Plants ∾ Books
A collector of conifers who offers a very broad selection of **conifers, dwarf conifers, Japanese maples, many beeches, kalmias** and other plants for bonsai. Each plant well described; some rarer items propagated to order.
❑ Catalog: $3d, CAN/OV, SS:4-6, 9-11, bn
⌂ Nursery: All year, M-F, call ahead
▼ Garden: May-September, M-F, call ahead

Cold Stream Farm
2030 Free Soil Road
Free Soil, MI 49411-9752
(616) 464-5809 TO
Mike & Kay Hradel

Plants
Specializes in hybrid poplars for woodlots, wildlife habitat and erosion
control. Offers other **trees and shrubs** useful for woodland planting in
seedling size and collections for wildlife cover plantings; no descriptions.
Nice selection of native trees and shrubs, including American chestnut.
❐ Catalog: Free, R&W, SS:10-7, $5m, cn
⌂ Nursery: October-July, daily, call ahead

Color Farm Growers
2710 Thornhill Road
Auburndale, FL 33823
(813) 967-9895
Vern Ogren

Plants
Specializes in **old-fashioned heirloom types of coleus**, which they consider
superior garden plants -- some are sun-tolerant. They have also hybridized
from these plants and offer a large selection; each plant well described in
all its glowing colors. New introductions yearly. (1985)
❐ Catalog: $.50, SS:W, $7m

Colorado Alpines, Inc.
P.O. Box 2708
Avon, CO 81620
(303) 949-6464 or 6672
Marty & Sandy Jones

Plants ⚘ Seeds
Specializes in **alpine and rock garden plants** grown at 7,500 feet in the
Rocky Mountains. Offers a good selection, plants well but fairly briefly
described: androsaces, dianthus, erysimums, gentians, lewisias, penstemons,
phlox, primulas, saxifragias and sempervivums. Seed list not seen.
❐ Catalog: $2, CAN/OV, SS:4-6,9-10, $10m, bn
⌂ Nursery: All year, daily

Colvos Creek Nursery & Landscaping
1931 - 2nd Avenue #215
Seattle, WA 98101
(206) 441-1509
Mike Lee & Hector Gaxiola

Plants
A broad selection of unusual **trees and shrubs**: acacias, species maples,
eucalyptus, conifers, flowering shrubs, oaks, palms and yuccas, among others.
They are adding plants all the time and send out catalog supplements as new
items are ready for sale; newest list has hardy bamboos.
❐ Catalog: $2d, R&W, SS:W, $15m, bn
⌂ Nursery: By appointment only

Comanche Acres Iris Gardens
Route 1, Box 258
Gower, MO 64454
(816) 424-6436 TO
Jim, Vivian & Tanya Hedgecock

Plants ⚘ Bulbs
Specializes in **tall bearded irises** and offers a selection that includes a
number of award winners, all well described in a color catalog. Also offers
a few dwarf bearded and border bearded irises, "horned" and Louisiana irises
and **daylilies and mixed daffodils**. (1981)
❐ Catalog: $2d, R&W, CAN/OV, SS:7-10, $10m
⌂ Nursery: April-October, daily
▼ Garden: April-May, daily

Companion Plants
7247 N. Coolville Ridge Road
Athens, OH 45701
(614) 592-4643 TO/CC $20
Peter & Susan Borchard

Plants ⚘ Seeds ⚘ Books
Over 400 **herb** plants for sale and about 120 varieties of seed -- all very
well described in an informative catalog. Selection includes **scented
geraniums, everlastings, woodland plants** and a few books on herbs
and herb growing. Will ship only seeds to Canada and overseas. (1982)
❐ Catalog: $2, R&W, SS:W, $15m, cn/bn
⌂ Nursery: March-November, Th-Su
▼ Garden: April-June, Th-Su (closed August 1-15)

Comstock, Ferre & Co.
P.O. Box 125
263 Main Street
Wethersfield, CT 06109
Richard G. Willard, Jr.

Seeds
Offering older varieties of **vegetables** and new varieties proven to be
more disease-resistant and productive; plants are well described with some
cultural information for each. Also offer seeds of annuals and perennials,
a good selection including everlastings. (1820)
❐ Catalog: Free, R&W, CAN/OV, $10m, cn/bn
⌂ Nursery: All year, daily
▼ Garden: August, call ahead

Conley's Garden Center
Boothbay Harbor, ME 04538
(207) 633-5020
Conley Family

Plants ⚘ Seeds
Plants well described in catalog -- a larger selection is offered in the
price list, including **native bulbs and orchids, ferns, wildflowers, vines**
and **ground covers**. Also offers some wildflower seed and seed mixtures.
❐ Catalog: $1.50, SS:3-6,9-11, $25m, bn/cn
⌂ Nursery: January-March, M-Sa
▼ Garden: Spring-fall, "idea" garden, M-Sa

Connell's Dahlias
10216 - 40th Avenue East
Tacoma, WA 98446
(206) 531-0292 TO/CC $20m
Les Connell

Plants
Offers a broad selection of **dahlias**, grouped by type; each briefly but well
described, some illustrated in color. Several collections are available for
those who want to start with only a few! Also offers **gladiolus** and the
wonderful annual publication "Dahlias of Today." (1973)
❐ Catalog: $1d, R&W, CAN/OV, SS:1-5, $10m
⌂ Nursery: All year, daily, call ahead
▼ Garden: August-September, daily

The Cook's Garden
P.O. Box 65
Moffits Bridge
Londonderry, VT 05148
(802) 824-3400 TO/CC $20m
Shepherd & Ellen Ogden

Seeds ✍ Books ✍ Supplies
Specializes in **vegetables and salad greens, edible flowers and ornamental vegetables** for home gardeners/cooks and specialty market gardeners. A very broad selection with good plant descriptions and growing hints; also some seed starting supplies and their book, "The Cook's Garden." (1977)
❒ Catalog: $1, R&W, CAN/OV
▼ Garden: June-August, call ahead

Cook's Geranium Nursery
712 N. Grand
Highway 14 North
Lyons, KS 67554
(316) 257-5033
Waldo L. Cook

Plants
Sells a huge selection of **geraniums and pelargoniums**: dwarf, fancy leaved (zonal), stellar, scented, ivy leaf, Regal -- 850 varieties by their count. There are no species geraniums but some species pelargoniums; all plants are well described. They also offer a number of collections. (1944)
❒ Catalog: $1d, CAN/OV, $15m
⌂ Nursery: All year, M-Sa; Su, call ahead

Cooley's Gardens
P.O. Box 126
11553 Silverton Road N.E.
Silverton, OR 97381
(503) 873-5463 TO/CC
Richard C. Ernst & Georgie Johnson

Plants
Color catalog offers large selection of **tall bearded irises**; many are shown in photographs, all are well described. They also offer a number of irises which can be selected as a your-choice collection at a good savings. (1928)
❒ Catalog: $2d, R&W, CAN/OV, SS:7-9, $10m
⌂ Nursery: All year, daily, call ahead
▼ Garden: May, daily, call ahead

Cooley's Strawberry Nursery
P.O. Box 472
Augusta, AR 72006
(501) 347-2026

Plants
Offers 23 types of everbearing and June-bearing strawberries; each variety is well described with some cultural information. Minimum order is 100 plants, so you'll have to share an order or set up a pick-your-own operation.
❒ Catalog: Free

Cooper's Garden
212 W. County Road C
Roseville, MN 55113
(612) 484-7878
Joan Cooper

Plants ✍ Bulbs
Small nursery specializes in species, Siberian and Louisiana **irises, daylilies, perennials and wildflowers** and, in a separate list, **daffodils** and sometimes **lilies**. A nice selection, particularly species irises; plants briefly described. Send long SASE for daffodil list. (1975)
❒ Catalog: 1 FCS(2 IRC), CAN, SS:8-9, bn
⌂ Nursery: May-September, call ahead
▼ Garden: May-September, call ahead

Copacabana Gardens
P.O. Box 323
234 Hall Drive
Moraga, CA 94556
(415) 254-2302 TO
Lee Anderson & James Larsen

Plants
Small nursery specializing in unusual **tropical and subtropical plants** for collectors and landscapers; a broad selection, each plant is very briefly described with notes on minimum temperature. Among the offerings are eucalyptus, palms, tropical fruit, proteas, bamboos, and a number of **subtropical flowering trees**. The catalog is not dated, but updated from time to time. Formerly called L & L Landscape & Rare Plant Nursery. (1980)
❒ Catalog: $2, R&W, CAN, SS:W, $25m, bn/cn
⌂ Nursery: By appointment only
▼ Garden: By appointment only

Cordon Bleu Farms
P.O. Box 2033
418 Buena Creek Road
San Marcos, CA 92069
Bob Brooks, Ray Chesnik & Steve Bingham

Plants
Offers a very broad selection of **daylilies** of all types -- tetraploids, diploids, miniatures and doubles -- plus **spuria and Louisiana irises**; plants well described, many illustrated in color. (1970)
❒ Catalog: $1, CAN/OV, SS:2-5,7-11, $12m
⌂ Nursery: All year, daily
▼ Garden: April-July, daily

Corns
Route 1, Box 32
Turpin, OK 73950
(405) 778-3615
Carl & Karen Barnes

Seeds
Corns is a membership organization, devoted to growing and preserving **open-pollinated varieties of corn** of all kinds: dent, flour, flint, popcorns and pod corns. They have available several hundred varieties, with about 1,000 varieties being maintained in living seed banks. Write for information.
❒ Catalog: $1d, R&W, CAN, $3m
⌂ Nursery: All year, daily, call ahead

Cottage Gardens
11314 Randolph Road
Wilton, CA 95693
(916) 687-6134
James McWhirter & Larry Lauer

Plants
A small nursery with a broad selection of recent and new **tall bearded** irises. Quite a few are their own introductions; new introductions are well described, all others are given brief descriptions. (1974)
❒ Catalog: $.50, R&W, CAN/OV, SS:7-8, $10m
⌂ Nursery: April-May, call ahead
▼ Garden: April-May, call ahead

The Cottage Herb Farm Shop
311 State Street
Albany, NY 12210
(518) 465-1130 TO/CC $10m
Betty Jane King

Seeds
Sells only seeds of **herbs**: plants for cooking, fragrance and medicinal purposes.
❒ Catalog: $.50, CAN, $5m
⌂ Nursery: All year, M-Sa

Country Bloomers Nursery
20091 E. Chapman Avenue
Orange, CA 92669
(714) 633-7222
Mike Morton

Plants
A good selection of **old garden roses and miniature roses**, listed by name, color, year of introduction and hybridizer (and old roses by type of rose). The old garden roses are available as liners or as year-old bare-root plants and should be reserved in advance of bare-root season. (1982)
❒ Catalog: Free, R&W, CAN/OV, bn
⌂ Nursery: All year, Tu-Su
▼ Garden: April-May, October-November, Tu-Su

Country Cottage
Route 2, Box 130
Sedgwick, KS 67135
Micki Crozier

Plants
"Catering to the enthusiastic gardener," collectors' list of **sempervivums, sedums and jovibarbas**, well to briefly described, with some cultural notes. It makes you think that you must have room for a few of these plants, with their "flushes" of various colors -- they sound irresistible. (1983)
❒ Catalog: 1 FCS(1 IRC), SS:4-9, bn
⌂ Nursery: April-October, by appointment only
▼ Garden: By appointment only

The Country Garden
Route 2, Box 455A
Crivitz, WI 54114-9645
(715) 757-2045 TO/CC $20m
Joseph Seals

Plants ✑ Seeds
Specializes in seeds of **flowers for cutting gardens** -- a broad selection; many of the annuals and perennials are available in separate colors for creating special effects. Also offers some plants of perennials and ornamental grasses. Includes many old-fashioned varieties and new introductions from abroad -- delightful! Catalog available in August.
❒ Catalog: $1, R&W, SS:9-10, bn/cn
⌂ Nursery: May-June, Tu-Su; July-Oct, call ahead
▼ Garden: June-September, call ahead

Country View Gardens
13253 McKeighan Road
Chesaning, MI 48616
(517) 845-7556
Barb Gibson

Plants
Small nursery growing different types of **bearded irises**; specializes in miniature dwarf, standard dwarf and miniature and standard tall bearded and some Siberians and spurias. Also offers some **daylilies**. The list is extensive, with brief plant descriptions. (1985)
❒ Catalog: Long SASE w/2 FCS, SS:7-9, $10m
⌂ Nursery: May-September, daily, call ahead
▼ Garden: May-June, call ahead

Country Wetlands Nursery
P.O. Box 126
Muskego, WI 53150
(414) 679-1268 TO/CC $50m
JoAnn Gillespie

Plants ✑ Seeds ✑ Books ✑ Supplies
This nursery specializes in wetland plants and will help you create wildlife ponds and natural wetland habitats. They sell both plants and seeds (some habitat-collected) and a few books on wetland plants. They also sell a special pot-within-a-pot for growing sedge and other plants. Plants given only a general description, listed by botanical and common names. (1986)
❒ Catalog: $1, SS:4-6,9-10, bn/cn
⌂ Nursery: April-November, M-Sa
▼ Garden: May-September, by appointment only

Creole Orchids
P.O. Box 24458
New Orleans, LA 70184-4458
(504) 282-5191 or (800) 634-4860 TO/CC
Harry A. Freiberg, Jr.

Plants
Hybrid orchids of all kinds: cattleya alliance, oncidium alliance, paphiopedilum alliance, dendrobium alliance and cymbidium alliance, both divisions and seedlings. Good selection, brief plant descriptions. (1981)
❒ Catalog: Free, R&W, CAN/OV, $30m
⌂ Nursery: All year, by appointment only
▼ Garden: All year, by appointment only

Cricket Hill Herb Farm, Ltd.
Glen Street
Rowley, MA 01969
(508) 948-2818 TO/CC
Judy Kehs

Plants ✑ Seeds ✑ Books
Offers a nice selection of **herbs**, both plants and seeds, and **scented geraniums**; no plant descriptions. Also sells herb blends for cooking and books on herbs and offers lectures, classes and tours of the gardens. (1976)
❒ Catalog: $1, R&W, SS:5-6,9, $15m, cn/bn
⌂ Nursery: April-December, M-Sa, Su pm; January-March, Th,Sa
▼ Garden: Summer, call ahead

Cricklewood Nursery
11907 Nevers Road
Snohomish, WA 98290
(206) 568-2829
Evie Douglas

Plants ⬿ Tools
Small nursery specializes in old-fashioned "**English border perennials**" and rock garden plants -- a very nice selection listed only by botanical name. Offers species geraniums, hebes, species primulas, species bulbs and many others. Also offers a selection of quality tools. (1982)
❑ Catalog: $2d, R&W, SS:3-4,9-10, $20m, bn
⌂ Nursery: April-June, September, F-Sa
▼ Garden: May-June, F-Sa

C. Criscola Iris Garden
Route 2, Box 183
Walla Walla, WA 99362
(509) 525-4841
Carrie Criscola

Plants
Offers a good selection of tall bearded, dwarf and intermediate **irises**, listed only by name.
❑ Catalog: 1 FCS

Crosman Seed Corp.
P.O. Box 110
507 W. Commercial Street
East Rochester, NY 14445
(716) 586-1928
William & Justine Mapstone, Mgrs.

Seeds
Calling themselves "America's oldest packet seed house," they offer a good selection of **vegetable, herb and annual flower** seeds on a combined seed list/order form; no descriptions of plants, prices very reasonable. (1838)
❑ Catalog: Free, R&W, CAN/OV, $3m
⌂ Nursery: All year, M-F

Cross Seed Company
HC-69, Box 2
Bunker Hill, KS 67626-9701
(913) 483-6163 or 6240
Dale K. Cross

Seeds
A small supplier of **grain, bean, sprouting and sunflower seeds**, most available organically grown. Offered are: lentils, adzuki, popcorn, mung beans, barley, rye, oats, wheat, buckwheat, millet, triticale, black and striped sunflower seeds and various seeds for sprouting. (1943)
❑ Catalog: Free(1 IRC), R&W, CAN/OV
⌂ Nursery: All year, M-F, Sa am
▼ Garden: Summer, M-F, Sa am

Crownsville Nursery
P.O. Box 797
Crownsville, MD 21032
(301) 923-2212
Charles Wasitis

Plants
Catalog offers a large selection of **perennials, ornamental grasses, herbs, wildflowers and ferns and some azaleas** -- each very well described with cultural information. Many aquilegias, dianthus, campanulas, species geraniums, geums and hostas.
❑ Catalog: $2d, SS:3-5,9-11, $25m, bn/cn

Cruickshank's, Inc.
1015 Mount Pleasant Road
Toronto, ON, Canada M4P 2M1
(416) 488-8292 TO/CC
Laura Rapp & Linda Ledgett

Plants ⬿ Books ⬿ Supplies ⬿ Tools ⬿ Bulbs
Spring catalog offers a large selection of **summer-blooming bulbs**: begonias, gladiolus, dahlias, amaryllis, cannas, caladiums and lilies. Also offers **perennials** such as peonies, daylilies, clematis and many irises. Another catalog offers a broad selection of **spring bulbs**, major and minor. (1927)
❑ Catalog: $3, R&W, US/OV, SS:W, $20m, bn/cn
⌂ Nursery: Summer, daily; all year, M-F

Cumberland Valley Nurseries, Inc.
P.O. Box 471
McMinnville, TN 37110-0471
(615) 668-4153 or (800) 492-0022
W. W. Bragg, Pres.

Plants
Specializes in **peaches, plums and nectarines** for larger plantings. Also offers apples (hardy and low-chill), cherries, pears, apricots and pecans. Informative leaflet -- a very large selection of peaches listed by ripening sequence. Can't ship to CA, OR or WA. (1902)
❑ Catalog: Free, R&W, SS:12-3, $25m

The Cummins Garden
22 Robertsville Road
Marlboro, NJ 07746
(201) 536-2591 TO/CC
Elizabeth K. Cummins

Plants
Specialize in **rhododendrons, azaleas and dwarf conifers** for the rock garden and bonsai, also kalmias, heathers, pieris, box and other acid-loving plants; all well described. They are adding new varieties all the time and have an annual plant propagation workshop -- call for details. (1972)
❑ Catalog: $2d(2 IRC), R&W, CAN/OV, SS:3-5,9-11, $15m, bn/cn
⌂ Nursery: All year, daily, call ahead
▼ Garden: April-October, call ahead

Cycad Gardens
4524 Toland Way
Los Angeles, CA 90041
(213) 255-6651
Loran M. Whitelock

Plants
Specializes in **cycad seedlings** -- bowenia, ceratozamia, cycas, dioon, encephalartos, lepidozamia, macrozamia, stangeria and zamia -- with notes on origins. Some plants also available in gallon sizes; you can send a "want list" for other rare items that may be available from time to time.
❑ Catalog: Long SASE, R&W, $25m, bn
⌂ Nursery: By appointment only

Dabney Herbs
P.O. Box 22061
Louisville, KY 40222
(502) 893-5198 TO/CC $20m
Davy Dabney

Plants ✿ Books ✿ Supplies
Offers a good selection of **herbs, scented geraniums, ginseng, perennials** and **wildflowers**, all well described, as well as books, gardening supplies and natural pest controls for pets in an informative catalog. (1986)
❑ Catalog: $2, R&W, SS:9-6, cn/bn

Dacha Barinka
25232 Strathcona Road
Chilliwack, BC, Canada V2P 3T2
(604) 792-0957
David Schmierbach

Seeds
Offers seeds for **everlasting flowers, vegetables, herbs** and Chinese vegetables, as well as seeds and starts of onions, garlic and chives. Also some table and wine grapes, nuts and miscellaneous ornamental plants.
❑ Catalog: Long SASE, US/OV, SS:3-5

The Daffodil Mart
Route 3, Box 794
Gloucester, VA 23061
(804) 693-3966 TO/CC $20m
Brent & Becky Heath

Books ✿ Tools ✿ Bulbs
A very extensive catalog of novelty **daffodils** -- hundreds of varieties, as well as miniature and species daffodils. Plants are arranged by divisions; all are well described. Request the wholesale catalog if you want to order spring-blooming bulbs in quantities of 100+. Offer growing supplies, tools and books; they do consultation and will give illustrated lectures. (1935)
❑ Catalog: $1d, R&W, CAN/OV, SS:9-11, $15m, bn
⌂ Nursery: March-April, Sept.-October, by appointment only
▼ Garden: March-April, by appointment only

Dahlias by Phil Traff
10717 Orting Highway East
Puyallup, WA 98373
(206) 863-0542
C. Phillip Traff

Plants
A collectors' list of **dahlias** -- many are medal winners; all varieties briefly but well described. Also sells the annual "Dahlias of Today," a publication of the Puget Sound Dahlia Association, very informative and full of the latest dahlia news. (1978)
❑ Catalog: Free, SS:1-5
⌂ Nursery: August-Sept, call ahead
▼ Garden: August-September, call ahead

The Nursery at the Dallas Nature Center
7575 Wheatland Road
Dallas, TX 75249
(214) 296-1955
John H. Weller, Mgr.

Plants ✿ Seeds
A source of plants and seeds of **native plants of Texas**; a nice selection listed only by common and botanical name. At the nursery they also sell nature books, birdhouses, feeders and other gifts for nature lovers.
❑ Catalog: Free, R&W, CAN/OV, $10m, cn/bn
⌂ Nursery: All year, Th-Su, call ahead
▼ Garden: Spring-fall, daily

William Dam Seeds
P.O. Box 8400
279 Highway 8 (West Flamboro)
Dundas, ON, Canada L9H 6M1
(416) 628-6641
Rene Dam

Seeds ✿ Books ✿ Supplies
Color catalog of short-season **vegetables, herbs, annuals and perennials**: varieties of European and Oriental vegetables and seeds for **houseplants**. Plants are well described; all seeds are untreated. Some organic growing supplies, propagation supplies and gardening books. (1949)
❑ Catalog: $1, US/OV, SS:W
⌂ Nursery: Winter-spring, M-Sa, call ahead
▼ Garden: Summer, M-F

© Vermont Bean Seed Co.
Artist: F. Allyn Massey

Dan's Garden Shop
5821 Woodwinds Circle
Frederick, MD 21701
(301) 695-5966 TO/CC $10m
Dan Youngberg

Seeds ⚘ Supplies
Seeds for **annuals, perennials and vegetables**, all very well described.
Also carries a good selection of growing and propagation supplies and gives
general seed-starting instructions. Woodwinds Circle sounds the perfect
place to do business -- Mozart, Haydn, Schumann! (1975)
☐ Catalog: Free

Dane Company
4626 Lamont Street
Corpus Christi, TX 78411
(512) 852-3806
Rosa Meilleur

Plants
A collectors' list of **bromeliads** -- aechmea, billbergia, cryptanthus, many
neoregelias (including their own "neo" hybrids), tillandsia species and
hybrids; no plant descriptions. Plants shipped bare-root by Priority Mail.
☐ Catalog: Long SASE, SS:W, $20m, bn
⌂ Nursery: All year, daily, call ahead

Davidson-Wilson Greenhouses
RR 2, Box 168
Ladoga Road
Crawfordsville, IN 47933-9423
(317) 364-0556
Barbara Wilson, Marilyn Davidson

Plants ⚘ Supplies
Specializes in **geraniums, begonias, African violets and other gesneriads,
ferns, cactus, ivy, hoyas, herbs, succulents, hibiscus** and much more; b&w
catalog illustrates many plants, each briefly to well described. Also sells
indoor growing supplies. (1980)
☐ Catalog: $1, R&W, SS:W
⌂ Nursery: All year, M-Sa; April-June, Su pm
▼ Garden: May-September

Corwin Davis Nursery
20865 Junction Road
Bellevue, MI 49021
(616) 781-7402
Corwin Davis

Plants ⚘ Seeds
Sells plants and seeds of **pawpaw**; plants are either seedlings or grafts.
He calls pawpaw the "forgotten fruit: edible and beautiful trees for land-
scaping, nothing bothers them, insects or pests or diseases." Sound ter-
rific! Send SASE for price list; $3.70 ppd. for informational bulletin.
☐ Catalog: See notes, SS:4
⌂ Nursery: All year, call ahead

Daylily World
P.O. Box 1612
254 N. Old Monroe Road
Sanford, FL 32772-1612
(407) 322-4034
David Kirchhoff

Plants
A very broad selection of **daylilies** in a catalog with color and b&w photos;
new introductions well described, older varieties briefly described. They
have many diploids and tetraploids, and many blooms seem to be double.
Their new hybrids were created by David Kirchhoff, a Silver Medal winner for
hybridizing.
☐ Catalog: $2(2 IRC), CAN/OV, $25m
⌂ Nursery: Daily, call ahead
▼ Garden: May-June, call ahead

Daylily Discounters
Route 2, Box 24
Alachua, FL 32615
(904) 462-1539
Ara Das

Plants
A new **daylily** nursery which offers varieties with a proven track record
nationally; all are very well described, and many are illustrated in color
photographs. They will be adding **liriope**. At present they cannot ship
to CA. (1988)
☐ Catalog: $2d, R&W, CAN/OV, $25m
⌂ Nursery: Daily, call ahead
▼ Garden: April-May, call ahead

Daystar
Route 2, Box 250
Litchfield-Hallowell Road (West Gardiner)
Litchfield, ME 04350
(207) 724-3369
Marjorie & George Walsh

Plants
An extensive list of **alpine, rock garden and dwarf plants**; many are choice,
including dwarf conifers and shrubs, daphnes, hardy ferns, ornamental
grasses, heathers, dianthus, phlox, holly, azaleas, rhododendrons; plants
are very briefly described. (1969)
☐ Catalog: $1d, R&W, CAN, SS:4-6, 9-11, $15m, bn
⌂ Nursery: March-November, call ahead
▼ Garden: By appointment only

Peter De Jager Bulb Co.
P.O. Box 2010
188 Asbury Street
South Hamilton, MA 01982
(508) 468-4707 TO/CC
Peter De Jager

Bulbs
A very broad selection of **Dutch bulbs** -- tulips, daffodils, crocuses,
alliums, amaryllis, hybrid lilies, hyacinths and other spring and fall bulbs.
Well illustrated and described briefly in a color catalog. (1954)
☐ Catalog: Free, R&W, SS:9-12, $10m
⌂ Nursery: M-Sa, call ahead

T. DeBaggio Herbs by Mail
923 N. Ivy Street
Arlington, VA 22201
(703) 243-2498
Thomas DeBaggio

Plants
Specializes in **rosemary and lavender** and has originated new varieties.
He also sells special rosemary plants for Christmas gifts and decorations.
Be sure to specify the mail order catalog when you write. (1976)
☐ Catalog: $1, SS:3-4,11-12, cn/bn
⌂ Nursery: April-June, daily
▼ Garden: April-June, daily

DeGiorgi Seed Company
1529 N. Saddle Creek Road
Omaha, NE 68104
(402) 544-1520
Betty Gray

Seeds
A good old-fashioned catalog, offering a broad selection of garden **annuals, perennials and vegetables** for home and commercial growers. All varieties are well described, with cultural suggestions; packets of many sizes. (1905)
❑ Catalog: $1, CAN/OV, bn/cn
⌂ Nursery: All year, by appointment only

DeGrandchamp's Blueberry Farm
15037 - 77th Street
South Haven, MI 49090
(616) 637-3915 FAX (616) 637-2351
Mike DeGrandchamp

Plants
Specializes in **blueberries** -- 19 kinds by their count -- as well as some small and large leafed **rhododendrons, Northern Lights azaleas, pieris kalmias, Meserve hollies and heathers**. Also offer tissue cultured hostas, daylilies and Gerbera daisies; no plant descriptions.
❑ Catalog: Free, R&W, CAN/OV, $25m
⌂ Nursery: March-December, M-F

Del's Japanese Maples
4691 River Road
Eugene, OR 97404
(503) 688-5587 or 688-2174 (evenings)
Del & Pat Loucks

Plants
Small nursery sells grafted **Japanese maples** as liners -- offers a broad selection with Japanese cultivar names, no descriptions. Collectors and bonsai folks will be delighted; they grow more than 200 varieties. (1979)
❑ Catalog: $1, R&W, CAN/OV, SS:10-4, $50m
⌂ Nursery: All year, M-Sa, call ahead
▼ Garden: Spring-fall, call ahead

Delegeane Garlic Farms
P.O. Box 2561
Yountville, CA 94599
(707) 944-8019
James & Nyda Delegeane

Plants
Sells elephant, white and red garlic cloves for planting, with growing and harvesting instructions. Also sells various seasonings, wildflower honey and garlic and shallots for cooking. (1979)
❑ Catalog: Free, CAN, $3m

Desert Nursery
1301 S. Copper
Deming, NM 88030
(505) 546-6264
Shirley J. Nyerges

Plants
Small nursery offers a good selection of **cacti and succulents** for the collector, some very hardy; descriptions are sketchy but geographical origins are given. Plants include: echinocereus, opuntias, mammillarias, parodias, rebutias, euphorbias and haworthias. Hours vary; call ahead. (1977)
❑ Catalog: 1 FCS, SS:3-12, $12m, bn
⌂ Nursery: March-September, M-Sa, call ahead
▼ Garden: March-September, greenhouse, call ahead

Desert Theatre
17 Behler Road
Watsonville, CA 95076
(408) 728-5513
Kate & Jay Jackson

Plants
A broad selection of **cactus and succulents** including aloes, lithops, noto-cactus, haworthias, echeverias, euphorbias, gymnocalyciums, mammillarias, rebutias and sulcorebutias, listed by botanical name; catalog gives brief descriptions, has some b&w photos. (1980)
❑ Catalog: $2, R&W, CAN/OV, $10m, bn
⌂ Nursery: All year, by appointment only
▼ Garden: All year, by appointment only

Howard W. Dill
RR 1
400 College Road
Windsor, NS, Canada B0N 2T0
(902) 798-2728
Howard N. Dill

Seeds
Sells only seed of 'Dill's Atlantic Giant' **pumpkin**, which has obtained a world class weight of over 600 pounds -- up 200 pounds just since I did the first edition of this book!
❑ Catalog: 2 FCS, R&W, US/OV

Dionysos' Barn

See The Herb Barn.

Dominion Seed House
115 Guelph Street
Guelph Street & Maple Avenue
Georgetown, ON, Canada L7G 4A2
(416) 877-7802 FAX 873-4648 TO/CC

Seeds ❧ Books ❧ Supplies ❧ Tools
A Canadian garden emporium selling seeds of **annuals, perennials and vegetables**, as well as summer-blooming bulbs, berries and seed potatoes; many illustrated in color and all well described. In addition, they sell tools, gardening supplies, canning equipment and books. (1927)
❑ Catalog: Free, SS:W, cn/bn
⌂ Nursery: All year, M-Sa

Don's Daylily Garden
10211 N.E. 38th Street
Kansas City, MO 64161
(816) 454-9163
Donald L. Long

Plants
A very extensive list of **daylilies**, including a long list of diploids and triploids, all briefly described. A large selection sure to appeal to collectors; cannot ship to CA. (1952)
❑ Catalog: $.50, R&W, SS:4-5,8-9, $20m
⌂ Nursery: April-September, M, W-Sa, by appointment only
▼ Garden: June-July, M, W-Sa, by appointment only

Donaroma's Nursery
P.O. Box 2189
Upper Main Street
Edgartown, MA 02539
(508) 627-8366 or 3036 TO/CC
Michael Donaroma

Plants
Nursery on Martha's Vineyard that specializes in **perennials** and
wildflowers; a very good selection, well described in their "listing of
choice perennials." They send out availability lists in spring and fall.
Broad choice of aquilegia, astible, campanula, delphinium, dianthus,
inula, lupine, meconopsis, papaver, silene and veronica and many others.
They encourage the use of wildflowers. (1977)
☐ Catalog: Free, R&W, CAN/OV, SS:3-5,9-10, bn/cn
⌂ Nursery: All year, M-Sa; July-August, daily
▼ Garden: Summer, M-Sa

Donnelly's Nursery
Route 7, Box 420
Fairview, NC 28730
(704) 298-0851
Russell Donnelly

Plants
A nice selection of **hosta**, all briefly but well described, and about 60
cultivars of **ivy**, very briefly described. (1975)
☐ Catalog: $1d, SS:4-10, $15m
⌂ Nursery: April-October, M-Sa, call ahead
▼ Garden: April-June, M-Sa, call ahead

Dooley Gardens
Route 1
Hutchinson, MN 55350
(612) 587-3050
Dooley Family

Plants
Offers a broad selection of **chrysanthemums**, sold as rooted cuttings; each
plant well described. Brochures give some cultural information. (1968)
☐ Catalog: Free, R&W, SS:3-6, $10m
⌂ Nursery: Call ahead

Dunford Farms
P.O. Box 238
Sumner, WA 98390
Donald Duncan & Warren Gifford

Plants
Sells only **Agapanthus** 'Headbourne Hybrids' and **Alstroemeria** aurantiaca or
Alstroemeria 'Ligtu Hybrids' -- request price list.
☐ Catalog: Free, SS:9-10

Dutch Gardens, Inc.
P.O. Box 200
Adelphia, NJ 07710
(201) 780-2713

Plants & **Bulbs**
Color catalog of spring-flowering **Dutch bulbs** offers all of the most
popular hybrids, with some cultural information. They have bulk order plans
for groups and a catalog of **summer-blooming bulbs** -- lilies, gladiolus,
dahlias, cannas and amaryllis. A wide selection in both catalogs. (1960)
☐ Catalog: Free, SS:9-10,3-4, $20m, cn/bn

Dutch Mill Herb Farm
Route 2, Box 190
Forest Grove, OR 97116
(503) 357-0924
Barbara J. Remington

Plants
Sells a very broad selection of **herbs** of all kinds: artemisias, lavenders,
mints, monardas, oreganos, rosemary, sages, santolinas, thymes, violas,
yarrows and scented geraniums. A long list, with no plant descriptions;
botanical and common names mixed together. (1973)
☐ Catalog: Long SASE, R&W, SS:3-5, cn/bn
⌂ Nursery: March-November, M-Sa, call ahead
▼ Garden: June-July, September, call ahead

Dyke Bros. Nursery
Route 1, Box 251-S
Vincent, OH 45785
(614) 678-2192
David Dyke

Plants
Offer four varieties of highbush **blueberries** -- 'Blueray,' 'Berkeley,'
'Colville' and 'Jersey' -- and the 'Cheyenne' blackberry. Minimum order
for blueberries is eighteen plants; varieties can be mixed. Blackberries
available as single plants.
☐ Catalog: Long SASE, SS:2-6,9-11
⌂ Nursery: All year, call ahead
▼ Garden: Pick your own berries, call ahead

E & H Products
78260 Darby Road
Bermuda Dunes, CA 92201
(619) 345-0147
Ruben M. Villegas

Seeds
Offers a good selection of **wildflower** seeds, both by individual species
and in mixes for all regions of the US. Each plant is well described; seed
available from 1/4 oz. to 1/4 lb. Also sells some **herb** seeds and
potpourris for various uses. (1985)
☐ Catalog: Free, R&W, CAN, cn/bn

Early's Farm & Garden Centre, Inc.
P.O. Box 3024
2615 Lorne Avenue South
Saskatoon, SK, Canada S7K 3S9
(306) 931-1982 TO/CC
J. C. Bloski, Mgr.

Seeds & **Supplies** & **Tools** & **Bulbs**
This old firm re-entered the mail order business in 1985 with a color catalog offering **garden flower and vegetable seeds, gladiolus bulbs** and a huge
selection of supplies and tools -- everything for Northern gardening. I love
the name Saskatoon, Saskatchewan -- say it slowly, with feeling. (1907)
☐ Catalog: $2d, R&W, US, $25m
⌂ Nursery: All year, M-Sa

Earthstar Herb Gardens
P.O. Box 1022
Chino Valley, AZ 86323
(602) 636-4910
Robert A. Leckliter

Plants & Seeds
Small nursery offers a good selection of **herb plants**, including several
types of garlic, basil, artemisia, echinacea, rosemary and scented geraniums,
as well as some herb seeds; all plants are organically grown at 5,000 feet
and are very hardy. Common and botanical names only; no plant descriptions.
❏ Catalog: $1d, SS:4-9, cn/bn
⌂ Nursery: April-September, M-Sa, call ahead
▼ Garden: May-June, August-September, M-Sa

Earthworks Herb Garden Nursery

See T. DeBaggio Herbs by Mail.

Eastern Plant Specialties
P.O. Box 226
Georgetown, ME 04548
(207) 371-2888 TO/CC $25m
Mark Stavish

Plants & Supplies
A broad selection of hardy **rhododendrons and azaleas**, unusual and dwarf
conifers, kalmias, pieris, holly, ornamental trees, dwarf shrubs and ground
cover plants; all well described, some illustrated. Catalog full of rare and
hardy collectors' plants; lists of plants for special uses. (1982)
❏ Catalog: $2, R&W, CAN, SS:4-11, $15m, bn
⌂ Nursery: By appointment only
▼ Garden: May-October, by appointment only

Eco-Gardens
P.O. Box 1227
1346 S. Indian Creek Drive (Stone Mountain)
Decatur, GA 30031
(404) 294-6468
Don L. Jacobs, Ph.D.

Plants & Books
Eco-Gardens is a collection of **native and exotic plants** hardy in the Pied-
mont region; they sell surplus plants, some of their own breeding, to raise
operating funds. Nice selection of **perennials, bog plants, ferns** and
shrubs; brief descriptions. Also offers plant books at a discount. (1976)
❏ Catalog: $1, R&W, CAN/OV, SS:3-6,9-1, bn
⌂ Nursery: All year, by appointment only
▼ Garden: All year, by appointment only

Edible Landscaping
P.O. Box 77
Afton, VA 22920
(804) 361-9134 TO
Michael McConkey

Plants
A selection of **fruit for Mid-Atlantic gardens**, including Actinidia arguta
(hardy kiwi), black currants, several gooseberries, Oriental persimmons,
mulberries, jujube, pawpaw and grapes; most plants are well described
in a charmingly hand-lettered and illustrated catalog. (1980)
❏ Catalog: $2, R&W, CAN/OV, $7m
⌂ Nursery: All year, M-F, call ahead

Emlong Nurseries
P.O. Box 236
2671 W. Marquette Woods Road
Stevensville, MI 49127
(616) 429-3431 TO/CC $10m
C. R. Emlong, Pres.

Plants
Offers a broad selection of **fruit trees, roses and general nursery stock**;
catalog shows many plants in color or b&w photographs. All plants are well
described. Among those offered are many berries, grapes, flowering shrubs
and other shrubs for hedging and conifers.
❏ Catalog: Free, R&W, SS:4-6,10-11, $5m
⌂ Nursery: All year, daily, call ahead (closed Su in July)
▼ Garden: April-May, daily

Enchanted Garden
1524 Pike Place
Pike Place Market
Seattle, WA 98101
(206) 625-1205
Doreen Kost

Plants
This small plant shop in the Pike Place Market offers **tillandsias** by mail
order -- a good selection of species plants, briefly described. Varieties
that grow well for beginners are indicated. (1979)
❏ Catalog: Long SASE, R&W, CAN, SS:4-10, $25m, bn
⌂ Nursery: All year, daily

Endangered Species
P.O. Box 1830
Tustin, CA 92681-1830
(714) 544-9505 TO/CC
Roger & Hermine Stover

Plants & Books
Large selection of **tropical plants**, including many large and small bamboo
varieties, palms, cycads, ferns, grasses, tropical foliage plants, sansevierias and phormiums. A collectors' list; plants are well described. They
also sell Hermine's "The Sansevieria Book." Catalog is $6 for three years;
price list is free. (1978)
❏ Catalog: See notes, R&W, CAN/OV, $100m, bn

Englerth Gardens
2461 - 22nd Street
Hopkins, MI 49328
(616) 793-7196
Mary Englerth Herrema

Plants
Specializes in **perennials** -- daylilies, hosta, Japanese and Siberian
iris -- and offers a good selection, especially of daylilies, as well as
collections of iris and daylilies for naturalizing. Each plant is briefly
described. (1931)
❏ Catalog: $.50, R&W, SS:4-6,8-10, $10m
⌂ Nursery: April-June, August-October, F-Sa
▼ Garden: July, F-Sa

Enoch's Berry Farm
Route 2, Box 227
Fouke, AR 71837
(501) 653-2806
A. B. Enoch

Plants
Offer three **blackberries** released by the Arkansas Experimental Station: 'Navaho' (thornless), 'Choctaw' and 'Shawnee.' They claim that the fruit is very high quality. (1980)
☐ Catalog: Free, R&W, SS:12-3, $8m
⌂ Nursery: All year, M-F, call ahead

Ensata Gardens
9823 E. Michigan Avenue
Galesburg, MI 49053
(616) 665-7500 TO
Bob Bauer & John Coble

Plants
Small nursery specializing in **Japanese and Siberian iris** only. They have a broad selection of Japanese iris, smaller selection of Siberian iris; all plants are well described, and some shown in color. Also have a Japanese garden display area, for those lucky enough to be close. (1985)
☐ Catalog: $2, R&W, CAN/OV, SS:5-10, $15m
⌂ Nursery: May-September, daily, call ahead
▼ Garden: June-July, daily, call ahead

Ernst Crownvetch Farms
RD 5, Box 806
Meadville, PA 16335
(814) 425-7276 or 7897
Calvin & Ted Ernst

Plants ⟋ Seeds
Mail order farm seed house can supply many **grains**; also sells several fast-growing **trees, crownvetch and grasses** for erosion control, reclamation and groundcover.
☐ Catalog: Free, CAN/OV, SS:4-12, $2m
⌂ Nursery: March-November, M-F

Murray Evans Daffodils

See Oregon Trail Daffodils.

Evergreen Acres Dahlia Gardens
682 Pulaski Road
Greenlawn, NY 11740
(516) 261-1024 TO $50m
Joe & Nedra Marsh

Plants
Offers a good selection of **dahlias**, with new introductions from the US, Canada, Japan, England and New Zealand, as well as established cultivars. Plants are described by form and color in table form, no plant descriptions.
☐ Catalog: $.50, R&W, CAN/OV, SS:5-6
⌂ Nursery: May-September, daily, by appointment only
▼ Garden: August-September, daily, by appointment only

Evergreen Y. H. Enterprises
P.O. Box 17538
Anaheim, CA 92817-7538
W. S. Hwang

Seeds ⟋ Books ⟋ Supplies
Offers a good selection of **Oriental vegetables**, listed in English and Chinese and well described. Also offers Oriental cookbooks and unspecified "cooking items"; ask for list, as they don't appear in seed catalog. (1978)
☐ Catalog: $1d, R&W, CAN/OV, $5m

John Ewing Orchids, Inc.
P.O. Box 1318
487 White Road (Watsonville)
Soquel, CA 95076
(408) 684-1111
John & Loraine Ewing

Plants
Collectors' list of seedling phalaenopsis **orchids**, available in several sizes; in pink, white, yellow, tan and red stripes or spots on colored backgrounds; available in flasks, as stem propagations or seedlings. Informative catalog. Also cymbidiums, miltonias and cattleyas in season.
☐ Catalog: Free, R&W, CAN/OV, SS:3-11
⌂ Nursery: All year, M-Sa, call ahead
▼ Garden: March-June, greenhouse

Exeter Wild Flower Gardens

See Oakridge Nurseries.

Exotic Seeds, Lothar Seik
Postfach 13 48
Tubingen 1, West Germany D 7400
Lothar Seik

Seeds
Seeds from all continents except Europe; the catalog I received is in German, but a new catalog in English is on the way. Luckily, the use of botanical names lets me tell you that he lists **palms, cycads, proteas, passifloras, cassias, eucalyptus, ferns, cactus** and more. (1980)
☐ Catalog: $3(US bills), US, SS:4-10, bn

Exotica Rare Fruit Nursery
P.O. Box 160
2508-B E. Vista Way
Vista, CA 92083
(619) 724-9093
Steve Spangler & Jessica Leaf

Plants
Offers **tropical fruits and flowering trees and nuts**, Hawaiian ornamentals, palms and Mexican and South American vegetables and fruit -- all for southern climates. Among the plants: bananas, figs, sapotes, annonas, low-chill apples and palms. They also do consultation on edible landscaping. (1975)
☐ Catalog: Long SASE, R&W, CAN/OV, cn/bn
⌂ Nursery: All year, daily
▼ Garden: All year, daily

Exotics Hawaii, Ltd.
P.O. Box 10416
1344 Hoakoa Place
Honolulu, HI 96816
(808) 732-2105 FAX 373-3868
Kalfred K. Yee

Plants
A grower of mericloned **orchids**, but also offers a nice variety of other **tropical foliage plants**, such as dracaenas, polyscias, aroids, ficus, anthuriums and bromeliads. Specify which plants you're interested in. (1958)
☐ Catalog: Long SASE, R&W, $20m
⌂ Nursery: All year, daily, Royal Hawaiian Shopping Center

F W H Seed Exchange
P.O. Box 651
Pauma Valley, CA 92061

Seeds ⁊ Bulbs
Not a seed company, but dedicated gardeners who collect seed of garden flowers and heirloom vegetables and exchange among themselves. Their newsletter has a bit of the flavor of Elizabeth Lawrence's "Gardening for Love," lists what people have and what they want; you must be willing to contribute, too.
❐ Catalog: $2 and Long SASE w/2 FCS

Fackler Nursery

See Rocky Meadow Orchard & Nursery.

Fairway Enterprises
114 The Fairway
Albert Lea, MN 56007
(507) 373-5290
Eldren & Nancy Minks

Plants
A nice selection of **hostas**, listed by color or leaf type with brief descriptions. Many are their own introductions; they also offer three daylilies which they hybridized. (1986)
❐ Catalog: Free, SS:8-9, $30m
⌂ Nursery: August-September, by appointment only

Fairyland Begonia & Lily Garden
1100 Griffith Road
McKinleyville, CA 95521
(707) 839-3034
Winkey & Leslie Woodriff

Plants ⁊ Seeds ⁊ Bulbs
Hybridizes **lilies and begonias**, also sells streptocarpus, hybrid calla lilies and lily seed. Offers a nice selection, including mixed collections of lilies and "yearling" lilies which will bloom in two years; all plants very well described.
❐ Catalog: $.50(10 IRC), R&W, CAN/OV, SS:W, $10m
⌂ Nursery: All year, daily

Fancy Fronds
1911 - 4th Avenue West
Seattle, WA 98119
(206) 284-5332
Judith I. Jones

Plants
A good selection of **hardy ferns**, including ferns from England, China, Japan and New Zealand and other temperate areas, all very well described and some illustrated with line drawings -- special requests invited. (1976)
❐ Catalog: $1d, R&W, CAN, SS:3-6,9-10, $10m, bn/cn
⌂ Nursery: All year, by appointment only
▼ Garden: May-October, by appointment only

Far North Gardens
16785 Harrison Street
Livonia, MI 48154
(313) 422-0747
Karen J. Ness

Seeds
An extensive list of seeds, offered in a confusing jumble of categories rather than alphabetically, but intriguing to the collector. Specialties include seed of Barnhaven primroses. They are adding more **perennials** and **rock garden** plants; brief to no plant descriptions. (1962)
❐ Catalog: $2d, CAN/OV, bn/cn

Farmer Seed & Nursery
P.O. Box 129
818 N.W. 4th Street
Faribault, MN 55021
(507) 334-1623 TO/CC $20m
Plantron, Inc.

Plants ⁊ Seeds ⁊ Supplies ⁊ Tools
A **garden emporium** in your mailbox: vegetable seeds, trees and shrubs, fruit and berries, roses, summer-blooming bulbs, tools, supplies, canning equipment. Color catalog offers broad selection of Northern-grown hardy stock, giant and midget vegetables and the gooseneck hoe that I still love! (1888)
❐ Catalog: Free, R&W, SS:3-5
⌂ Nursery: All year

Farnsworth Orchids
606 N. Lanikai Place
Haiku, Maui, HI 96708
(808) 572-7528 TO
Larry & Kathy Farnsworth

Plants
"Our **orchids** are bred and grown for the home environment, for ease of culture and frequent blooming...bright, colorful, and fragrant." Good selection, especially mini-cattleyas, also cattleyas, phalaenopsis, vandaceous and others; plants briefly to well described. (1978)
❐ Catalog: Free, CAN/OV, $25m
⌂ Nursery: All year, by appointment only
▼ Garden: All year, greenhouse, by appointment only

Fedco Seeds
52 Mayflower Hill Drive
Waterville, ME 04901
C. R. Lawn & Gene Frey, Mgrs.

Plants ⁊ Seeds ⁊ Books ⁊ Supplies
Seeds of **short-season vegetables, herbs, annual and perennial flowers**, the only list that I've seen with "Yuppie Vegetables" as a special category! A very extensive list with every variety well described; they try to keep costs down by encouraging group orders. Also sell **hardy fruit and nut trees, berries and fruiting shrubs** -- $50 minimum order, ask for "Fedco Trees" list -- and some supplies and books on gardening. (1978)
❐ Catalog: Free, SS:4-9, $25m (see notes)

Fedco Trees

See Fedco Seeds.

Fennell's Orchid Jungle
26715 S.W. 157th Avenue
Homestead, FL 33031
(305) 247-4824 or (800) 327-2832 TO/CC
The Fennell Family

Plants ⁊ Books ⁊ Supplies
Catalog offers a huge selection of **hybrid orchids** -- dendrobiums, epidendrums, miltonias, miltassias, oncidiums, phalaenopsis, vandas, cattleyas; plants well described. Sells other tropical plants as well. Also sells orchid supplies and books and offers orchid tours and tissue culture. (1888)
❐ Catalog: Free, R&W, CAN/OV, SS:W
⌂ Nursery: All year, daily
▼ Garden: All year, daily

Fern Hill Farm
P.O. Box 185
Clarksboro, NJ 08020
John F. Gyer

Seeds
Sells only **'Dr. Martin' Pole Lima Bean** seed; there's no description of this particular variety, but it must be something special. Pre-germinated seed is available in April.
❑ Catalog: Long SASE, CAN/OV, $5m

Fernald's Hickory Hill Nursery
RR 2
Monmouth, IL 61462
(309) 734-6994
Gary Fernald

Plants
Informative leaflet offers lots of growing advice and a good selection of hardy nuts: pecans, hicans, shagback and shellbark hickory, butternuts, black walnuts and hazelnuts. He will do custom-grafting to preserve a favorite old nut tree for you. (1980)
❑ Catalog: 1 FCS, CAN
⌂ Nursery: All year, daily, call ahead
▼ Garden: Orchard, call ahead

Fiddyment Farms
5000 Fiddyment Road
Roseville, CA 95678
(916) 771-0800 TO
David Fiddyment

Plants ◡ Seeds
Small nursery specializes in **pistachios**, both seeds and seedling and budded trees, as well as nuts for eating. (1978)
❑ Catalog: Free, R&W, CAN/OV, SS:12-1, $4m
⌂ Nursery: All year, M-F, call ahead
▼ Garden: All year, M-F, call ahead

Field and Forest Products, Inc.
N3296 Kuzuzek Road
Peshtigo, WI 54157
(715) 582-4997 TO/CC $10m
Joseph H. Krawczyk & Mary Ellen Kozak

Seeds ◡ Books ◡ Supplies ◡ Tools
Small company selling **shiitake mushroom spawn** (eleven strains for growing under various temperatures and conditions), **oyster mushroom spawn** and complete growing supplies, books and tools. Shiitake strains well described for commercial and home growers. They also sell their how-to book, "Growing Shiitake Mushrooms in a Continental Climate." (1983)
❑ Catalog: $2, CAN/OV, SS:5-11, $5m
⌂ Nursery: All year, by appointment only
▼ Garden: Summer, by appointment only

Henry Field Seed & Nursery Co.
407 Sycamore Street
Shenandoah, IA 51602
(712) 246-2011 or (605) 665-9391 TO/CC $10m
Don Kruml, Mgr.

Plants ◡ Seeds ◡ Supplies ◡ Tools
A true **garden emporium**: vegetable and flower seeds, fruit and nut trees, grapes, berries, roses, ornamental flowering trees, shrubs and vines and growing supplies and tools. Color catalog shows most of the plants offered and gives good plant descriptions and some growing hints. (1892)
❑ Catalog: Free, R&W, SS:2-6,10-11

Fieldstone Gardens, Inc.
620 Quaker Lane
Vassalboro, ME 04989-9713
(207) 923-3836
Steven D. Jones

Plants
Extensive list of **perennials and rock garden plants**: Japanese and Siberian irises, astilbe, campanulas, clematis, delphiniums, epimediums, species geraniums, herbaceous and tree peonies, phlox and much more. Plants are well described, with cultural suggestions. (1981)
❑ Catalog: $2, CAN/OV, SS:4-6,9-11, $15m, bn/cn
⌂ Nursery: February-December, Tu-Su
▼ Garden: June-July, Tu-Su

The Fig Tree Nursery
P.O. Box 124
Gulf Hammock, FL 32639
(904) 486-2930
Gertrude Watson

Plants ◡ Books
Offers a variety of **fig trees**, as well as **pears, muscadine grapes, mulberries and pomegranates**, each well but briefly described. Also sells her own book on "Growing Fruit Trees and Vines," $3.45 ppd. Can't ship plants to CA or AZ.
❑ Catalog: $1, CAN, SS:10-3
⌂ Nursery: M-Sa, call ahead

Finch Blueberry Nursery
P.O. Box 699
Bailey, NC 27807
(919) 235-4662 or 4664

Plants
Offers a nice selection of **rabbiteye blueberries**, each variety well described. Flier gives good information on blueberry culture; they also sell mixed selections for cross-pollination and long bearing season.
❑ Catalog: Free, SS:10-5

Fischer Greenhouses
Blackman Road & Poplar Avenue
Bargaintown, NJ 08221
(609) 927-3399
Charles W. Fischer, Jr.

Plants ◡ Supplies
Color catalog offers a wide selection of **African violets** and other gesneriads; most plants shown in photographs, all briefly described. (1888)
❑ Catalog: $.35, CAN/OV, SS:4-11, $15m
⌂ Nursery: All year, daily
▼ Garden: All year, daily

Flad's Glads

See Skolaski's Glads & Field Flowers.

Flickingers' Nursery
P.O. Box 245
Sagamore, PA 16250
(412) 783-6528 or 397-4953 TO/CC
Richard Flickinger

Plants
A wholesaler of **seedling trees** -- the same price to everyone, but a minimum of fifty trees of one variety. A nice selection of spruces, pines and firs and Canadian and Carolina hemlocks, as well as Vinca minor and birch, mountain ash and dogwood. Cannot ship to CA. (1947)
❏ Catalog: Free, SS:4-10, $30m
⌂ Nursery: All year, M-Sa, call ahead

Floating Mountain Seeds
P.O. Box 1275
Port Angeles, WA 98362
(206) 457-1888
Roger Lemstrom

Seeds
A source of **antique and heirloom vegetable seeds** from the Pacific Northwest and elsewhere, some very intriguing such as broomcorn, Einkhorn wheat found in a Neolithic grave site (that's antique!), Cuban cigar tobacco and the "mortgage-lifter" tomato; all well described. Adding herbs and flowers.
❏ Catalog: $1.50
⌂ Nursery: By appointment only

Flora Favours
Route 4, Box 370
Elkhorn, WI 53121
(414) 742-3342
Thomas Olechowski

Plants
A very good selection of **hardy perennials** suitable for the hard winters of the Midwest; very brief plant descriptions. Among plants offered are anemones, aquilegias, asters, astilbes, campanulas, coreopsis, dianthus, species geraniums, monardas, phlox, sedums and veronicas. (1981)
❏ Catalog: $1, SS:3-5,9, $20m, bn
⌂ Nursery: April-October, Tu-Su, call ahead
▼ Garden: April-June, Tu-Su, call ahead

Flora Lan Nursery
Route 1, Box 357
Forest Grove, OR 97116
(503) 357-3500
Larry Landauer

Plants
An extensive list of **rhododendron and azalea hybrids** and magnolias, camellias, Japanese maples, pieris japonica, daphnes, heathers, brooms and other **ornamental plants**; no plant descriptions. They're just starting to mail order, have been wholesaling since 1945.
❏ Catalog: Free, R&W, CAN, SS:10-4, bn/cn
⌂ Nursery: April-June, daily
▼ Garden: April-May, daily

Florida Colors Nursery
23740 S.W. 147th Avenue
Homestead, FL 33032
(305) 258-1086
Luc & Carol Vannoorbeeck

Plants
Offers a good selection of grafted hybrid **hibiscus**; plants are listed by cultivar name with only information on size and color of flower. For more complete information they sell a "Hibiscus Catalogue" for $7.50 ppd.; it has 144 color photos.
❏ Catalog: Free, R&W, CAN/OV, $30m
⌂ Nursery: All year, M-Sa
▼ Garden: April-December, M-Sa

Florida Keys Native Nursery, Inc.
102 Mowhawk Street
Tavernier, FL 33070
(305) 852-2636 or 5515
Dona Sprunt

Plants
Native trees and shrubs of south Florida.
❏ Catalog: Free

Floridel Gardens
P.O. Box 514
330 George Street
Port Stanley, ON, Canada N0L 2A0
(519) 782-4015 TO
Tom & Rosita Morgan

Plants ✍ Supplies
Offers **phalaenopsis orchids**, as well as others, and orchid growing supplies; they send growing instructions with every purchase and will give personalized instructions and repotting demonstrations at the nursery.
❏ Catalog: $2d, CAN, SS:5-9, $20m
⌂ Nursery: All year, M-Sa, call ahead

The Flower & Herb Exchange
604 North Street
Decorah, IA 52101
(319) 382-5990
Diane Whealy

Seeds
A **seed exchange** for old-fashioned flowers and herbs not commercially available; as with all seed exchanges you must be willing to share your treasures. You may also advertise for plants you are trying to find.
❏ Catalog: $3, CAN/OV

Flowerland
P.O. Box 26
Wynot, NE 68792
Hans Anderson

Plants
A good selection of field-grown garden **perennials** at reasonable prices; plants are briefly described. Also offers a number of **hardy ferns** and **wildflowers** and mixed "get-acquainted" collections. (1977)
❏ Catalog: Long SASE, SS:4-6,9-10

Flowerplace Plant Farm
P.O. Box 4865
Meridian, MS 39304
(601) 482-5686
Gail Barton & Richard Lowery

Plants
"We sell only perennials which prove tough in [the South]. We like old-fashioned flowers and select those which tolerate drought and heavy clay soils and have few (if any) pests." Their nursery is new, and selection is fairly limited; plants are very well described. (1988)
☐ Catalog: $1, R&W, SS:10-3, $10m, cn/bn
⌂ Nursery: By appointment only

Floyd Cove Nursery
11 Shipyard Lane
Setauket, NY 11733-3038
(516) 751-1806
Patrick M. Stamile

Plants
A very broad selection of **daylilies**, many of them new cultivars, many diploids and tetraploids, as well as recent introductions and classics. Plants very briefly described.
☐ Catalog: $1d, SS:4-11
⌂ Nursery: July-August, daily, call ahead
▼ Garden: July, daily, call ahead

Foliage Gardens
2003 - 128th Avenue S.E.
Bellevue, WA 98005
(206) 747-2998
Sue Olsen

Plants ~ Books
A very good selection of **ferns, both hardy and for greenhouses**, listed by botanical name with good plant descriptions. All plants grown from spore; new varieties being added all the time. They have also produced a video-cassette, "Short Course on Ferns," and offer some books. (1976)
☐ Catalog: $1, SS:4-6,9-10, $15m, bn
⌂ Nursery: All year, by appointment only
▼ Garden: Spring-summer, by appointment only

Fordyce Orchids
1330 Isabel Avenue
Livermore, CA 94550
(415) 447-7171 or 828-3211 TO/CC $25m
Frank & Madge Fordyce

Plants
Specialists in **miniature cattleya orchid hybrids**, splashed-petal cattleyas and yellow and red cattleyas -- rooted seedlings in flasks or pots. Offer a broad selection; all plants briefly described.
☐ Catalog: Free, R&W, CAN/OV, SS:3-11, $10m
⌂ Nursery: All year, M-Sa, by appointment only
▼ Garden: All year, greenhouse, by appointment only

Forestfarm
990 Tetherow Road
Williams, OR 97544
(503) 846-6963 (9-4 PST)
Ray & Peg Prag

Plants
A collectors' list of many interesting **Western natives, garden perennials and trees and shrubs**. Offers small plants at reasonable prices, some quite unusual; each plant well described. Also sells hardy eucalyptus, bee plants, conifers, woodland plants and much more -- a curl-up-with list, now bound into a booklet! Starting to offer larger plants by popular request. (1973)
☐ Catalog: $3, CAN, SS:W, $30m, bn/cn
⌂ Nursery: All year, daily, call ahead
▼ Garden: All year, growing area, call ahead

Forevergreen Farm
70 New Gloucester Road
North Yarmouth, ME 04021
(207) 829-5830
Suzy Verrier

Plants ~ Tools
Offers a good selection of old-fashioned, hardy and uncommon **roses**: old garden varieties and species roses, and more modern shrubs roses such as those hybridized in Canada and the Midwest and some of the David Austin roses. Emphasis is on the hardy growers. (1983)
☐ Catalog: Free, SS:11,4-5
⌂ Nursery: March-October, daily
▼ Garden: June-July, daily

Fort Caroline Orchids
13142 Fort Caroline Road
Jacksonville, FL 32225
(904) 641-9788 TO/CC
W. C. Guthrie

Plants
Have started publishing catalogs; specify **bromeliads, epiphyllums, ferns or orchids**. The orchid list offers a huge selection of hybrid and species orchids of many kinds; information on crosses but no plant descriptions.
☐ Catalog: See notes, R&W, OV, $20m
⌂ Nursery: All year, M-Sa
▼ Garden: All year, greenhouses, M-Sa

Foster Nurseries
P.O. Box 150
Fredonia, NY 14063
(716) 672-6234
Andrew W. Dorn, Jr.

Plants
A wholesale nursery which offers a broad selection of **table and wine** grapes; they are categorized as American Grape varieties, French hybrid varieties, Florida bunch varieties, American premium seeded and seedless varieties, grafted Vinifera varieties and rootstocks; no descriptions. Minimum order is fifty vines or $50.
☐ Catalog: Free, $50m

Four Winds Growers
P.O. Box 3538
42186 Palm Avenue
Fremont, CA 94539
(415) 656-2591
Donald F. Dillon

Plants
Specializes in **dwarf citrus**: oranges, tangerines, mandarin oranges, limes, grapefruit, lemons, tangelos and kumquats -- 30 varieties in all. These are true dwarf trees, growing to eight feet; informative leaflet tells how to grow them. Cannot ship to FL, TX or AZ. (1954)
☐ Catalog: Long SASE, R&W, SS:4-11, $17m
⌂ Nursery: All year, M-F

Fowler Nurseries, Inc.
525 Fowler Road
Newcastle, CA 95658
(916) 645-8191 TO/CC
Robert & Richard Fowler, Nancy F. Johnson

Plants
Offers a broad selection of **fruit for the home garden**, including red and Asian "crunch" pears (first planted in California in the 1850's), European, Chinese and hybrid chestnuts, berries, table and wine grapes, pecans and walnuts. Price list is free; informative, descriptive catalog is $2. (1912)
❐ Catalog: See notes, R&W, SS:1-2, $20m
⌂ Nursery: All year, daily
❦ Garden: All year, daily

Fox Hill Farm
P.O. Box 9
443 W. Michigan Avenue
Parma, MI 49269-0009
(517) 531-3179 TO
M. J. Hampstead

Plants ❧ Books ❧ Supplies
Broad selection of **herbs and scented geraniums, bee and dye plants** -- some 350 varieties by their count -- listed only by common name. They also offer herbal products, books and videotapes about herbs and a computer program for making plant lists and printing plant labels. (1972)
❐ Catalog: $1, plant/price list free
⌂ Nursery: March-December, W-Su
❦ Garden: April-October, W-Su

Fox Hollow Herbs
P.O. Box 148
McGrann, PA 16236
(412) 763-8247
Carol & Tom Porter

Plants ❧ Seeds ❧ Books
Small seed company offers open-pollinated varieties of **herbs and vegetables** and **garlic, shallot and Egyptian onion** sets, as well as old-fashioned annuals. All plants are well described, with suggestions for use and some recipes. They also sell some books, English watering cans and wrought-iron planters. (1987)
❐ Catalog: Free, CAN, cn/bn

Fox Orchids, Inc.
6615 W. Markham Street
Little Rock, AR 72205
(501) 663-4246
John M. Fox

Plants ❧ Books ❧ Supplies
A very extensive list of cattleya hybrids and many other **hybrid orchids, bromeliads, ferns and other tropical plants**; all plants briefly described. Also sell orchid books and growing supplies which they ship at any time of the year. (1945)
❐ Catalog: Free, CAN, SS:3-11, bn
⌂ Nursery: All year, M-F, call ahead
❦ Garden: All year, greenhouse, call ahead

Foxborough Nursery, Inc.
3611 Miller Road
Street, MD 21154
(301) 836-7023
David Thompson

Plants
A collectors' list of **dwarf and unusual conifers, shrubs and trees**. The selection is broad -- plants for bonsai, heathers, kalmias, holly, pieris, rhododendrons, hamamelis, Camperdown elm and other treasures. The plants are not described; many are very special. (1976)
❐ Catalog: $1d, R&W, CAN/OV, $25m, bn/cn
⌂ Nursery: Sa, by appointment only
❦ Garden: May-November, Sa, by appointment only

The Fragrant Path
P.O. Box 328
Ft. Calhoun, NE 68023
E. R. Rasmussen

Seeds
Catalog is devoted to seeds of **fragrant, rare and old-fashioned plants** of all kinds, with irresistible descriptions, literary quotations and charming sketches. A wide selection; can you live without trying "Kiss-me-over-the-garden-gate"? Cottage gardeners beware! (1982)
❐ Catalog: $1, CAN, $5m, bn/cn

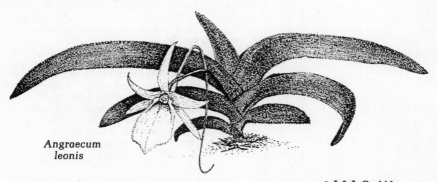

*Angraecum
leonis*

© J & L Orchids
Artist: Richard Gates

Fred's Plant Farm
P.O. Box 707
Route 1, Dresden Road
Dresden, TN 38225
(901) 364-3754 or (800) 243-9377
Fred C. Stoker

Plants ∾ Seeds
Sells only **sweet potato plants**, but fifteen kinds, all described by color of "meat." Also sells tobacco seed, pipes and tobacco humidifiers, a machine for making filtered cigarettes, and "country-made sorghum molasses." Fred's hats are back again this year, in three styles. (1947)
❏ Catalog: Free, R&W, SS:4-6
⌂ Nursery: April-June, daily, call ahead

Lorine Friedrich
9130 Glenbury Street
Houston, TX 77037
(713) 448-8976
Lorine H. Friedrich

Plants
Offers a nice selection of **sinningias, episcias, columneas and African violets** from leading growers in many sizes; plants briefly described.
❏ Catalog: $.50

Frosty Hollow Nursery
P.O. Box 53
Langley, WA 98260
(206) 221-2332
Marianne Edain & Steve Erickson

Seeds
Small company does habitat collection of pre-ordered seeds; they offer a wide variety of Northwestern native plants for which they collect seed -- **wildflowers, ornamental trees and shrubs and conifers**. Will collect to order; also consult on landscape restoration and permaculture design. (1982)
❏ Catalog: Long SASE, R&W, CAN/OV, $10m, bn/cn

Fruit Spirit Botanical Gardens
Dorroughby, Australia 2480
(066) 89-5192
Paul Recher

Seeds
Here's something different: seeds of **exotic fruits and nuts**, more than 160 species, some collected fresh at a botanical garden which specializes in tropical plants. Also Australian native plants, palms and ornamentals. Seeds available in "home packs" and larger quantities; will also trade seed.
❏ Catalog: $1(US bills), OV, A$15m, bn

Fungi Perfecti
P.O. Box 7634
Olympia, WA 98507
(206) 426-9292 TO/CC
Paul & Cruz Stamets

Seeds ∾ Books ∾ Supplies
Catalog offers **mushroom spawn**, growing kits, supplies and books for the amateur and commercial grower. Varieties include shiitake, oyster, button, enoki, Coprinus comatus and Stropharia rugoso-annulata. Paul is co-author of "The Mushroom Cultivator," which they sell. (1980)
❏ Catalog: $3, R&W, CAN/OV, SS:9-6, $10m, bn/cn

G & B Orchid Lab & Nursery
2426 Cherimoya Drive
Vista, CA 92084
(619) 727-2611 TO/CC
Barry L. Cohen

Plants ∾ Supplies
Specializes in phaleneopsis, cymbidium, cattleya and dendrobium **orchids** in great variety, each briefly described. Also sells several types of flasking media, laboratory glassware and a variety of fertilizers and chemicals for orchid hobbyists and hybridizers. (1970)
❏ Catalog: Free, R&W, CAN/OV, SS:4-12, $20m
⌂ Nursery: All year, M-F
▼ Garden: All year, glasshouse, M-F

G & G Gardens and Growers
6711 Tustin Road
Salinas, CA 93907
(408) 663-6252 TO/CC
Sharon Gayman

Plants
A collectors' list of **fuchsias**, over 150 cultivars and a few species -- each very well described -- as well as collections of their choice. They also offer **tuberous begonias** of many types and forms. (1980)
❏ Catalog: $1d, SS:W, bn/cn

Garden City Seeds
P.O. Box 297
Victor, MT 59875
(406) 961-4837
Down Home Project

Seeds
A cooperative that offers heirloom and open-pollinated seeds for short growing seasons: vegetables, flowers, herbs, potatoes, garlic and strawberries, as well as books, organic pest controls and fertilizers. The catalog is informative, with good information on growing and seed saving.
❏ Catalog: $2, CAN/OV

Garden Grains

See The Grain Exchange.

Garden of Delights
2018 Mayo Street
Hollywood, FL 33020
(305) 923-2087 TO
Murray & Debby Corman

Plants ∾ Seeds
Here's a list of **tropical fruits and nuts** so unusual that I've never heard of many of them -- collectors will swoon! A source of seeds and plants of cherimoyas, cashews, maya breadnut, jelly palm, star apple, governor's plum, lovi-lovi, ice cream bean and yam bean. Intrigued? Super stuff! Sells both seeds and small plants, some fruits by the dozen. (1975)
❏ Catalog: $2d, R&W, CAN/OV, $50m, bn/cn
⌂ Nursery: All year, daily, call ahead
▼ Garden: All year, daily, call ahead

Garden of the Enchanted Rainbow
Route 4, Box 439-B
Killen, AL 35645
(205) 757-1518
Jordan & Bernice Miller

Plants
Specializes in **tall bearded, median and reblooming irises**, "the best of the old, and the best of the new"; some are their own introductions. Offers a wide selection; plants very briefly described. (1977)
☐ Catalog: $1d, CAN/OV, SS:7-9, $30m
⌂ Nursery: July-September, call ahead

Garden Perennials
Route 1
Wayne, NE 68787
(402) 375-3615
Gail Korn

Plants
Sells a broad selection of **perennials**, including many daylilies; all plants are very well described with cultural symbols and information, some illustrated in line drawings. Plants are field-grown clumps. (1982)
☐ Catalog: $1d, SS:4-10, bn
⌂ Nursery: April-October, daily
▼ Garden: June-July, September, daily

Garden Place
P.O. Box 388
6780 Heisley Road
Mentor, OH 44061-0388
(216) 255-3705 TO
Jack, John, Jim & Dave Schultz

Plants
A very large selection of **perennials**, each well but briefly described. Catalog gives growing tips and has informative tables of plants by color, height, use, exposure, etc. Plants sold singly or in groups of 3 or 12 and shipped bare-root. Selection too broad to describe! (1972)
☐ Catalog: $1, CAN, SS:9-5, $10m, bn/cn

The Garden Source, Ltd.

See Bonsai of Georgia.

Garden Valley Dahlias
406 Lower Garden Valley Road
Roseburg, OR 97470
(503) 673-8521
Leon V. Olson

Plants
A collectors' list of **dahlias**, only briefly described as to color and form.
☐ Catalog: 1 FCS, SS:3-5
⌂ Nursery: August-October, daily

Garden World
2503 Garfield Street
Laredo, TX 78043
(512) 724-3951
Tony Ramirez

Plants ⬳ Supplies
Bananas -- over 40 varieties -- and citrus, bougainvilleas, bromeliads, cactus, bamboo, papayas and other **tropicals**, briefly to well described. Also offer some growing supplies, including their own "Bio-Force" bio-catalyst, humic acids and seed inoculant. (1976)
☐ Catalog: $1, R&W, CAN/OV, SS:W, $2m, cn/bn
⌂ Nursery: All year, daily, call ahead
▼ Garden: All year, daily, call ahead

Gardenimport, Inc.
P.O. Box 760
Unit 5, 2 Essex Avenue
Thornhill, ON, Canada L3T 4A5
(416) 731-1950 TO/CC $20m
Dugald Cameron

Seeds ⬳ Supplies ⬳ Tools ⬳ Bulbs
Distributor of Sutton's Seeds in Canada. Color catalog offers a broad selection of **garden annuals, perennials, summer-flowering bulbs** and **vegetables** and imported garden tools. A separate catalog offers **spring bulbs**. All plants are well described, many illustrated. Bought the business of A. J. Woodward & Sons. (1982)
☐ Catalog: $3(2 years), R&W, US/OV, SS:W, $15m, bn/cn
⌂ Nursery: All year, M-F, call ahead

Gardens of the Blue Ridge
P.O. Box 10
US 221 North
Pineola, NC 28662
(704) 733-2417
Edward P. Robbins

Plants
Catalog lists a good selection of **wildflowers, ferns, native orchids** and **native trees and shrubs**, all well described and some illustrated in color photos. Many are hard-to-find Southeastern native plants at reasonable prices. (1892)
☐ Catalog: $2, R&W, CAN/OV, SS:3-4,9-11, $10m, bn/cn
⌂ Nursery: March-December, M-Sa, call ahead
▼ Garden: April-September, M-Sa, call ahead

Gaze Seed Company, Inc.
P.O. Box 640
St. John's, NF, Canada A1C 5K8

Seeds
Open-pollinated **vegetable seeds**.
☐ Catalog: Free to NF & LB, $1 other

Georgetown Greenhouse & Nursery
RD 1, Box 108-B
Georgetown, PA 15043
Joseph Iannetti

Plants ⬳ Books ⬳ Supplies
This nursery specializes in **episcias** (called "Flame Violets"), greenhouse tools and supplies and Ortho gardening books. The plant selection is small, some not always available. They sell several computer programs, too. (1982)
☐ Catalog: Free, R&W, SS:4-10, $5m

Louis Gerardi Nursery
1700 E. Highway 50
O'Fallon, IL 62269
(618) 632-4456
Vernon R. Reinacher & David E. Frost

Plants
Scionwood of nuts for grafting: American persimmons, mulberries, pecans and hicans, hickory, black walnuts, Carpathian walnuts, heartnuts, butternuts and Chinese chestnuts. A good selection, listed by size of nut, flavor, cracking quality, bearing habit and years to bearing.
☐ Catalog: Long SASE, CAN/OV, 11-4, $10m
⌂ Nursery: Daily, call ahead

Gilson Gardens
P.O. Box 277
US Route 20
Perry, OH 44081
The Gilson Family

Plants
Specializes in plants for **ground cover** and offers a broad selection: 100
varieties of ivy, pachysandra, sedums, plumbago, primroses, vincas, lamiums
and others. Each plant is well described, with good general cultural
information. (1947)
☐ Catalog: Free, SS:W, $10m, bn/cn
⌂ Nursery: Call ahead

Girard Nurseries
P.O. Box 428
6839 North Ridge East, Route 20
Geneva, OH 44041
(216) 466-2881 or 969-1636 TO/CC
Peter Girard, Jr.

Plants ⌇ Seeds
Color catalog offers a broad selection of **rhododendrons and azaleas**: their
own Girard Evergreen azaleas; Gable, Exbury, Knaphill, Ilam, Mollis and Ghent
azaleas; rhododendrons chosen for hardiness. Also sells a good selection of
conifers, flowering trees and shrubs, holly, specimens, mixed collections
of seedling trees and shrubs and seeds of trees, shrubs and conifers. Cannot
ship to CA, HI, AK or CAN; no seeds to SD. (1946)
☐ Catalog: Free, SS:4-6,10-11, $20m
⌂ Nursery: All year, M-Sa; Su spring only
▼ Garden: April-May, daily

Gladside Gardens
61 Main Street
Northfield, MA 01360
(413) 498-2657 TO $20m
Mr. & Mrs. Corys M. Heselton

Plants ⌇ Bulbs
Specializes in **summer-blooming and tender bulbs**, particularly gladiolus,
cannas, crinums, oxalis, dahlias, Siberian and Japanese irises and many
others, each well described. Also offers some perennials and greenhouse
plants. (1940)
☐ Catalog: $1d (4 IRC), R&W, CAN/OV, SS:3-7, $15m, cn/bn
⌂ Nursery: March-October, daily, call ahead
▼ Garden: July-October, call ahead

Glasshouse Works
P.O. Box 97
10 Church Street
Stewart, OH 45778-0097
(614) 622-2142 TO/CC $20m
Tom Winn & Ken Frieling

Plants
A very extensive list of **exotic and tropical plants** -- a list to thrill the
collector with a greenhouse or tropical climate. Among the many: ferns,
gingers, bromeliads, succulents, aroids, acanthus, cactus, euphorbias,
all briefly described. Specialty is variegated plants of all kinds and
plants for tropical indoor bonsai. (1973)
☐ Catalog: $1.50d, R&W, CAN/OV, $15m, bn/cn
⌂ Nursery: All year, Th-Su
▼ Garden: All year, Th-Su

Glendale Enterprises
Route 3, Box 77 P
DeFuniak Springs, FL 32433
(904) 859-2141 or 2341
John Alex Wilkerson

Seeds
Sells seeds of **chufa (Cyperus esculentus)** to feed wild turkeys and other
wildlife (cannot be shipped to Canada); offers advice on how to manage wild
turkey habitat and seed of other wildlife food plants -- velvet bean,
partridge pea, beggarweed and cowpeas. (1979)
☐ Catalog: Long SASE, R&W, cn/bn
⌂ Nursery: All year, daily, call ahead

Global Seed Exchange
P.O. Box 2631
Longview, WA 98632
Dale C. Sullivan

Seeds
A **seed exchange** with a quarterly newsletter to members; emphasis is on
ornamentals and exotics, with some edibles as well. The newsletter gives
information on various types of plants; members list their wants and what
they have to trade. Charge is for four newsletters and membership. (1988)
☐ Catalog: $6(US$10 OV)

Gloria Dei
36 East Road
High Falls Park
High Falls, NY 12440
(914) 687-9981
Marty & Norma Kelly

Plants
Specializes in new and recently introduced **miniature roses** from well-known
hybridizers, plus some old favorites; a nice selection, each well described.
☐ Catalog: Free, R&W, SS:W, $14m
⌂ Nursery: By appointment only

Golden Bough Tree Farm
Marlbank, ON, Canada K0K 2L0
Josef Reeve

Plants
A good selection of **hardy fruit trees and grapes** for Northern climates, as
well as **ornamental trees and conifers**, English oak, larch, birch and maples
and plants for bonsai; all well described with cultural suggestions. (1973)
☐ Catalog: $1, R&W, US/OV, SS:W, $25m, bn/cn

Golden Lake Greenhouses
10782 Citrus Drive
Moorpark, CA 93021
Paula Lake

Plants ⌇ Books
Specializes in **bromeliads**, offering a wide selection of tillandsias,
aechmeas, billbergias, cryptanthus, dykias, guzmanias, neoregelias and
vreiseas; most with very brief descriptions. Also sells hoyas, ceropegias,
rhipsalis and epiphyllums, as well as a few books on bromeliads. (1968)
☐ Catalog: $1(2 IRC), CAN/OV, bn

Good Hollow Greenhouse & Herbarium
Route 1, Box 116
Taft, TN 38488
(615) 433-7640
Frank & Triss Peterson

Plants & Supplies
A nice selection of **herbs, perennials, scented geraniums and wildflowers**; each well described. They also offer a large selection of dried herbs and spices, teas, essential oils and potpourris. (1986)
☐ Catalog: $1, SS:4-11, $10m, cn/bn
⌂ Nursery: All year, Tu-Sa, call ahead
▼ Garden: April-October, Tu-Sa, call ahead

Good Seed Co.
Star Route, Box 73 A
Oroville, WA 98844
Harris Dunkelberger, T. Peyton, M. Baka

Seeds & Books & Supplies
Good Seed has changed hands -- in good hands, we hope; they offer the same broad selection of open-pollinated, untreated **heirloom vegetable seeds** in packets of three sizes. All varieties are well described, with good cultural and seed-saving information. They also offer some flower and herb seeds, cover crop seed, Oriental vegetables and books on gardening. (1980)
☐ Catalog: $1, R&W, CAN, $10m, bn/cn

Goodwin Creek Gardens
P.O. Box 83
Williams, OR 97544
(503) 846-7357 or 488-3308
Jim & Dotti Becker

Plants & Seeds & Books
Sells plants and seeds of **everlasting annual and perennial flowers, herbs and wildflowers**. A good selection; plants are well but briefly described. They also sell their book, "A Concise Guide to Growing Everlastings," with illustrations and instructions on growing and drying many plants. They have opened a shop on Oak Street in Ashland for Shakespeare fans. (1978)
☐ Catalog: $1, SS:4-6,9-11, cn/bn
⌂ Nursery: All year, by appointment only
▼ Garden: By appointment only

John H. Gordon, Jr., Grower
1385 Campbell Boulevard
North Tonawanda, NY 14120-9715
(716) 691-9371 (early or evenings)
John H. Gordon, Jr.

Plants & Seeds
Small nursery sells **hardy nut trees and seeds, persimmons and pawpaws**; a nice selection, each very briefly described. Also sells sample nuts by variety to taste before buying. Offers almonds, filberts, hazels, hickory, sweet chestnuts, pecans and walnuts. Can't ship to West Coast; will ship seed only to Canada and overseas. (1980)
☐ Catalog: Free, SS:3-4,10, $3m
⌂ Nursery: Spring to fall, call ahead
▼ Garden: September-October, call ahead

Gossler Farms Nursery
1200 Weaver Road
Springfield, OR 97478-9663
(503) 746-3922 or 747-0749
Marjory & Roger Gossler

Plants
A very large selection of **magnolias**, each well described. Also a number of **daphnes, stewartias, franklinia, hamamelis, kalmias, beeches, viburnums** and many other unusual trees and shrubs, well described with cultural suggestions. Collectors of very special trees and shrubs will be delighted! (1968)
☐ Catalog: $1, R&W, SS:10-12,2-3, bn/cn
⌂ Nursery: All year, by appointment only
▼ Garden: March-June, by appointment only

Grace's Gardens

See Ripley's Believe It or Not Seed Catalog.

Russell Graham, Purveyor of Plants
4030 Eagle Crest Road N.W.
Salem, OR 97304
(503) 362-1135
Russell & Yvonne Graham

Plants & Bulbs
A collectors' catalog, full of unusual plants such as **species bulbs** and lilies, iris, fritillaria, hardy cyclamen, novelty daffodils, **hardy ferns**, trillium and **ornamental grasses**; all plants well described and sure to tempt plant fanatics. Small nursery with a large selection. (1980)
☐ Catalog: $2d, R&W, SS:9-12, $20m, bn/cn
⌂ Nursery: Sa, by appointment only
▼ Garden: Sa, by appointment only

The Grain Exchange
2440 E. Water Well Road
Salina, KS 67401
Thom Leonard

Seeds
A non-profit seed exchange specializing in **grains**: wheat, rice, oats, rye, barley, sorghum, amaranth, buckwheat and grain corn (flint, flour, dent and popcorn). Varieties are well described; they also sell a few books on bread making. (1986)
☐ Catalog: $1

Grandview Iris Gardens
HC 86, Box 91
Bayard, NE 69334
(308) 586-1471
Viola Schreiner

Plants
A broad selection of **tall bearded iris** for the collector, listed by cultivar name; very brief plant descriptions.
☐ Catalog: 1 FCS, SS:7-9, $10m
▼ Garden: June, growing area

The Green Escape
P.O. Box 1417
Palm Harbor, FL 34682
(813) 784-1132
Joan & Marshall Weintraub

Plants
Offers close to 300 species of rare and uncommon **palms**: indoor and cold hardy species, many that do well in low light and others very hardy. List arecas, arenga, calamus, chamaedorea, gaussia, howea, licuala, pinanga, johannesteijsmannia, livistona, sabal, thrinax and veitchia; all well described. Each plant comes with specific cultural information. (1988)
☐ Catalog: $6d, CAN/OV, $20m, bn/cn

Green Horizons
218 Quinlan, #571
145 Scenic Hill Road
Kerrville, TX 78028
(512) 257-5141 TO/CC
Sherry Miller

Seeds ⬥ Books
Devoted to preserving and protecting **Texas wildflowers**, company offers a number of them in small packets to bulk supplies. Also offers scarified bluebonnet seeds for better germination and books on wildflowers and gardening in Texas and the South.
☐ Catalog: Long SASE, CAN/OV, cn/bn
⌂ Nursery: January-November, M-Sa

Green Plant Research
P.O. Box 735
Kaaawa, HI 96730
(808) 237-8672
Ted Green

Plants
A broad selection of **hoyas, dischidias and other asclepiads**, each very well described. These plants come from private collections and collecting trips in Samoa, Australia, New Guinea, the Solomon Islands, New Hebrides, Java, Singapore, Malaysia and the Philippines; a few are hybrids.
☐ Catalog: $1, CAN/OV, $25m, bn/cn
⌂ Nursery: By appointment only
♥ Garden: By appointment only

Green Valley Orchids
77200 Green Valley Road
Folsom, LA 70437
(504) 796-5785
Don Saucier

Plants
Specialize in phalaenopsis and cattleya alliance **orchids**, most of their own hybridizing; they also sell ascocendas, vandas and dendrobiums. List is written in that secret code known to orchidists which always sounds like gossip, but has to do with pedigree. (1979)
☐ Catalog: $1d, R&W, CAN/OV, SS:3-11
⌂ Nursery: All year, Sa-Su, call ahead
♥ Garden: March-June, Sa-Su, call ahead

The Greenery
14450 N.E. 16th Place
Bellevue, WA 98007
(206) 641-1458
Lynn & Marilyn Watts

Plants
A broad selection of **species rhododendrons and azaleas**, as well as a selection of hybrids -- collectors will crow! Each plant is briefly to well described. Also sells dwarf hybrid rhododendrons and **trilliums** not listed in in the catalog; ask if you are looking for a particular species.
☐ Catalog: $2, R&W, OV, SS:3-6,9-10, bn
⌂ Nursery: March-November, by appointment only

Greenleaf Orchids
158 S. Winterset Avenue
Crystal River, FL 32629
(904) 795-3785
Ralph & Rochelle Flowers

Plants
A broad selection of **orchids** -- cattleyas, angraecum, phalaenopsis, vandas and various miniatures and dwarfs -- each briefly described, listed by color.
☐ Catalog: Free, R&W, CAN/OV, SS:W, $25m
⌂ Nursery: All year, M-Sa

Greenlee Nursery
301 E. Franklin Avenue
Pomona, CA 91766
(714) 629-9045
John Greenlee

Plants
Broad selection of **ornamental grasses**; very informative catalog gives good descriptions of each plant and its performance in the **West**, with cultural suggestions and tables of plant by use and best planting location. (1986)
☐ Catalog: $2.50, R&W, CAN, SS:3-5, $25m
⌂ Nursery: Call ahead

Greenlife Gardens Greenhouses
101 County Line Road
Griffin, GA 30223
(404) 228-3669 (evenings) TO/CC
Ira & Linda Slade

Plants
Flowering epiphytic cacti, dwarf crape myrtles, succulents and cacti; most plants are briefly described. The catalog is in color; you'll have a hard time choosing only a few, especially when you're winter-housebound. (1967)
☐ Catalog: $2, $15m, cn/bn

Greenmantle Nursery
3010 Ettersburg Road
Garberville, CA 95440
(707) 986-7504
Ram & Marissa Fishman

Plants
Catalog packed with cultural information, offers **antique apples**, many collected from old homesteads in Humboldt County. Also about 200 **old garden roses**, many rare varieties and species imported from England. Still more: pears, cherries, plums, quinces and disease-resistant chestnuts. (1983)
☐ Catalog: $3, (rose list, long SASE), SS:1-4, cn
⌂ Nursery: All year, by appointment only
♥ Garden: May-June, by appointment only

Greenwood Daylily Gardens
4905 Pioneer Boulevard, #10
Whittier, CA 90601
(213) 699-8144 TO $50m
John Schoustra & Mike McKain

Plants
A huge selection of **daylilies**, each well described in a color catalog.
They have recently bought the Greenwood Nursery in Goleta and moved it
to Whittier; some varieties not listed are available at the nursery. (1989)
❒ Catalog: $3, CAN/OV, $25m
⌂ Nursery: 1st & 3rd Sa of each month
▼ Garden: April-June, 1st & 3rd Sa

Greer Gardens
1280 Goodpasture Island Road
Eugene, OR 97401-1794
(503) 686-8266 TO/CC
Harold E. Greer

Plants ↝ Books ↝ Supplies ↝ Tools
Color catalog offers a very large selection of **rhododendrons and azaleas**,
vireyas, **ornamental trees**, maples (many palmatum cultivars), dwarf
conifers, acid-loving **shrubs and vines and bonsai materials**; all well
described in a very informative catalog (famous for its enthusiasm!). Also
many books on trees and plants. (1955)
❒ Catalog: $3(5 IRC), R&W, CAN/OV, bn
⌂ Nursery: All year, daily
▼ Garden: All year, March-June, daily

Grianan Gardens
P.O. Box 14492
San Francisco, CA 94114
Colleen O'Meara Thomas

Seeds
Small company offering a nice selection of seeds for garden **annuals** and
perennials; all plants well described. Packets available in sample and
regular sizes; many of the seeds are imported from Europe and Canada.
Since I can't bear to thin seedlings overmuch, I like small packets! (1985)
❒ Catalog: $1d(2 IRC), R&W, CAN/OV, $3m

Griffey's Nursery

See Wildflower Nursery.

Grigsby Cactus Gardens
2354 Bella Vista Drive
Vista, CA 92084
(619) 727-1323 FAX 727-1578 TO/CC
David B. Grigsby

Plants
Catalog profusely illustrated with b&w photos -- a real collectors' list of
unusual **cacti & succulents**, all well described. They specialize in euphorbias, sansevierias, aloes, haworthias, mammillarias and other specimen plants
and rare succulents. Also send "wish letters" to regular customers, offering
new and unusual plants. (1965)
❒ Catalog: $2d, R&W, CAN/OV, SS:W, $20m, bn
⌂ Nursery: All year, Tu-Sa
▼ Garden: April-June, Tu-Sa

Grimo Nut Nursery
RR 3, Lakeshore Road
Niagara on the Lake, ON, Canada L0S 1J0
(416) 935-9773 TO
Ernest & Marion Grimo

Plants
A selection of **hardy nuts** for Northern climates, seedlings and grafted
trees: persian walnuts, black walnuts, heartnuts, butternuts, Chinese chest-
nuts, apricots (sweet kernels), filberts, hickory and more -- well described
in an informative list. Sells seed nuts, does custom grafts. (1974)
❒ Catalog: $1d, R&W, US/OV, SS:4, $10m
⌂ Nursery: All year, Sa-Su, by appointment only
▼ Garden: July-August, Sa-Su, by appointment only

Grootendorst Nurseries
15310 Red Arrow Highway
Lakeside, MI 49116
(616) 469-2865 TO
Theo Grootendorst

Plants
Offers **rootstocks** in small quantities for home gardeners, as well as in
quantity: 'East Malling' and 'Malling-Merton' varieties for apples, also
rootstocks for plums, peaches and cherries. Will do custom-grafting.
Propagates old fruit varieties for Southmeadow Fruit Gardens. (1957)
❒ Catalog: Free, R&W, OV, SS:10-5, $20m
⌂ Nursery: All year, M-F, call ahead
▼ Garden: All year, M-F, call ahead

Gulf Coast Plantsmen
15680 Perkins Road
Baton Rouge, LA 70810
(504) 291-0395
Ralph Helms

Plants
"Supplies plants adapted to the rather adverse conditions of the lower
South": **evergreen azaleas, bamboo, crape myrtles, gingers, ornamental
grasses, hardy hibiscus, aroids, crinums** and others. All are briefly
described. (1982)
❒ Catalog: Long SASE w/2 FCS, SS:2-4, $15m
⌂ Nursery: February-July, October-November, Tu-Su, call ahead

---

Gurney Seed & Nursery Co.
2nd & Capital
Yankton, SD 57078
(605) 665-4451 or 1930 TO/CC $10m
Don Kruml, Pres.

Plants ↝ Seeds ↝ Supplies
Color tabloid catalog offers a very **broad selection of plants and seeds** for
the home gardener -- fruit trees, roses, flowering trees and shrubs, nuts,
berries, grapes and vegetable and flower seeds, all well described. Also
gardening and canning supplies and advice in an informative catalog. (1866)
❒ Catalog: Free, SS:1-5,9-10, cn
⌂ Nursery: All year, M-Sa

Hahn's Rainbow Iris Garden
200 N. School Street
Desloge, MO 63601
(314) 431-3342
Clyde & Anna Hahn

Plants
A real collectors' list, tightly packed, offers a broad selection of
irises, but gives only name, hybridizer, year and price -- hundreds of
cultivars. List includes tall bearded, intermediate and dwarf bearded
irises and a nice selection of **daylilies**. (1981)
❐ Catalog: $1d, CAN/OV, SS:4-7,8-9
⌂ Nursery: May-September, call ahead
▼ Garden: May-July, call ahead

Halcyon Gardens
P.O. Box 75
Wexford, PA 15090
(412) 935-2233 TO/CC $15m
Elizabeth Bair

Seeds
Offers a nice selection of **herb** seeds; each plant very well described with
germination and cultural information. They also sell a number of seed collections for various uses and a kit for growing culinary herbs at home.
❐ Catalog: $1d, R&W, CAN, cn/bn

Haley Nursery Company, Inc.
Route 5
Smithville, TN 37116
(615) 597-7333 FAX 1838; (800) 251-1878

Plants
Offers a very broad selection of **peaches**, including a number of low-chill
varieties for Florida and the far South. They also sell **nectarines, plums,
apricots, cherries, apples and Asian pears**. There are no plant
descriptions, but number of chilling hours is given for peaches and
nectarines.
❐ Catalog: Free

Dr. Joseph C. Halinar
2334 Crooked Finger Road
Scotts Mills, OR 97375
Dr. Joseph C. Halinar

Plants ✑ Seeds
Small grower specializing in seed of **species and hybrid lilies, daylilies,
Siberian irises and alliums** for hybridizers and collectors; brief plant
notes include information on hybridizing qualities. Supplies limited; you'll
have to choose substitutes, but they all sound desirable. Some plants
available; list distributed in November. (1980)
❐ Catalog: Long SASE(1 IRC), R&W, CAN/OV, SS:10-4
⌂ Nursery: By appointment only
▼ Garden: July, by appointment only

Hall Rhododendrons
P.O. Box 62
6924 Highway 38
Drain, OR 97435
(503) 836-2290 TO/CC
Jan D. Kelley

Plants ✑ Supplies
Collectors' list -- a huge selection of **species and hybrid rhododendrons**.
The nursery has recently been sold to the Kelley brothers of Drain, OR, and
they will be adding **azaleas, pieris and kalmias** to the 1,450 rhododendrons
they offer now. All varieties are well described, and there is good general
cultural information. (1978)
❐ Catalog: $1, R&W, CAN/OV, bn
⌂ Nursery: March-June, call ahead

Robert B. Hamm
10065 River Mist Way
Rancho Cordova, CA 95670
(916) 366-7835
Robert B. Hamm

Plants
Specializing in **begonias, peperomias, cacti and succulents, scented
geraniums, stapeliads and achimenes** and increasing variety all the time:
"odd and rare items for indoors and out." Plants are briefly described;
price of catalog includes 4 newsletters a year. Formerly called Plants
Etcetera. (1981)
❐ Catalog: $3, R&W, CAN/OV, SS:W, $25m
⌂ Nursery: By appointment only

Hammond's Acres of Rhodys
25911 - 70th Avenue N.E.
Arlington, WA 98223
(206) 435-9206 or 9232
David & Joan Hammond

Plants
Offer a broad selection of **rhododendrons and azaleas**, both hybrids and
species, listed only by name, hardiness, season and color of bloom. They
grow 3,000 hybrids and species, so if you don't find what you want in the 600
or more listed in the catalog, send them your "want list." They offer other
ornamentals at the nursery, will try to fill special requests if plants are
available from other local nurseries. (1976)
❐ Catalog: Free, R&W, SS:3-6,8-10
⌂ Nursery: All Year, daily
▼ Garden: April-May, daily

Marilyn Hampstead

See Fox Hill Farm.

Hardscrabble Enterprises
Route 6, Box 42
Cherry Grove, WV 26804
(304) 567-2727
Paul & Nan Goland

Seeds ✑ Books ✑ Supplies
Sell spawn of **shiitake mushrooms** and all of the equipment necessary to grow
them in your own woodlot. Price of the catalog includes growing instructions
and their newsletter; they also buy dried shiitake mushrooms from organic
growers. Also sell a professional dehydrator expandable to 35 trays. (1985)
❐ Catalog: $3, R&W

James Harris Hybrid Azaleas
538 Swanson Drive
Lawrenceville, GA 30245
(404) 963-7463

Plants
I received only the plant list, which offers **hybrid evergreen azaleas** and cutting-grown **native azaleas** (species). The hybrids are well described, with information on crosses, color, size of bloom and size of plant at maturity -- a nice selection. Ten species azaleas are offered. (1965)
☐ Catalog: Long SASE

Harris Seeds
961 Lyell Avenue
Rochester, NY 14606
(716) 458-2882
Garden Trends, Inc.

Seeds ⬿ Supplies ⬿ Tools
Color catalog offers a broad selection of **flower and vegetable seeds**, many developed by their own research staff and all well described. They list "special merit" vegetables which they feel perform best -- and have those cute "baby" pumpkins. They also sell some tools and growing supplies. (1879)
☐ Catalog: Free, R&W

Hartman's Herb Farm
Old Dana Road
Barre, MA 01005
(617) 355-2015 TO/CC
Lynn & Peter Hartman

Plants ⬿ Supplies
Offers a selection of **herb and scented geranium plants**, as well as essential oils, herb teas, potpourris, dried flower arrangements and wreaths, note papers and an herbal calendar. (1980)
☐ Catalog: $1, $10m
⌂ Nursery: Feb-December, daily
▼ Garden: May-November, daily

Hartmann's Plantation, Inc.
P.O. Box E
310 - 60th Street
Grand Junction, MI 49056
(616) 253-4281 TO/CC $10m
Patrick & Daniel Hartmann

Plants ⬿ Supplies
Selection of **Northern and Southern blueberries**, as well as "Arctic" kiwis, pineapple guava, pawpaw, wintergreen, lemongrass and a new "Baba" berry, a red raspberry for the South. They also carry supplies for fruit growers, including bird repellent devices, and the book "Blueberry Culture" by Dr. Paul Eck. Another address is Box 524, Earleton, FL 32631. (1942)
☐ Catalog: $2.25d, R&W, CAN/OV
⌂ Nursery: All year, M-F, Sa am, call ahead

Hass Nursery
24105 Ervin Road
Philomath, OR 97370
(503) 929-3739
Henrietta Hass

Plants
A collectors' list of **rhododendrons and azaleas** and several cultivars of Pieris japonica, all well described. The many azalea hybrids include those of Back Acres, Gable, Glenn Dale, Harris, Greenwood, Linwood, North Tisbury and others. Also offers a large selection of Satsuki azaleas.
☐ Catalog: $2, SS:9-6, $15m
⌂ Nursery: By appointment only

Hastings
P.O. Box 115535
Atlanta, GA 30310-8535
(404) 755-6580, (800) 334-1771 TO/CC

Plants ⬿ Seeds ⬿ Supplies
A **regional garden emporium**: fruit and nut trees, berries, grapes, kiwis and seed for vegetables and garden annuals. Color catalog has good plant descriptions, also offers tools and supplies. They sell a broad selection of plants suitable for Southern gardens. (1889)
☐ Catalog: Free, CAN, SS:1-4

Hatfield Gardens
22799 Ringgold Southern Road
Stoutsville, OH 43154
(614) 474-5719 TO/CC $25m
Handy Hatfield

Plants
Broad selection of **daffodils, hostas, daylilies, bearded irises, ornamental grasses** and some **perennials and herbaceous peonies**; no room for more than brief plant descriptions and a few b&w photos. Garden looks lovely.
☐ Catalog: $2, SS:4-10, $15m
⌂ Nursery: April-September, daily, call ahead
▼ Garden: April-September, daily, call ahead

Hauser's Superior View Farm
Route 1, Box 199
County Highway J
Bayfield, WI 54814
(715) 779-5404 TO
Jim Hauser

Plants
Offers a good selection of hardy field-grown **perennials** -- sold only by the dozen or hundred; only name and flower color given. A good choice of chrysanthemums, lupines, sedums, delphiniums and others; also asparagus and rhubarb. Also offers homemade jams, jellies and apple butter. (1908)
☐ Catalog: Free, R&W, CAN, SS:4-7,9-11, $10m
⌂ Nursery: April-November, M-Sa, call ahead
▼ Garden: May-June, September-October, M-Sa, call ahead

Havasu Hills Herbs
3717 Stoney Oak Road
Coulterville, CA 95311
(209) 878-3102
Kathy Seaton & Dodie Heiny

Plants ⬿ Books ⬿ Supplies
Offer a broad selection of organically grown **herbs and scented geraniums**; all plants are well described. They also sell herb and cookbooks and potpourri supplies and offer classes at their farm. (1984)
☐ Catalog: $1d, R&W, SS:9-6, $10m, cn/bn
⌂ Nursery: Daily, by appointment only
▼ Garden: April-June, by appointment only

Heard Gardens, Ltd.
5355 Merle Hay Road
Johnston, IA 50131
(515) 276-4533 TO/CC
W. R. Heard

Plants
Specialize in **lilacs** propagated on their own roots; some 60 varieties, each briefly described. They have the lovely variety, 'Primrose,' which is a soft pale yellow and hard to find. Have added **flowering crabapples** -- about 20 varieties -- and viburnums, not given in the lilac list -- ask! (1959)
❒ Catalog: $2d ($5 US bills), SS:3-5,10-11, $15m
⌂ Nursery: All year, M-Sa
▼ Garden: All year, M-Sa (special tours call ahead)

Heaths and Heathers
P.O. Box 850
62 Elma-Monte Road
Elma, WA 98541
(206) 482-3258 TO/CC
Bob, Alice & Cindy Knight

Plants
A collectors' list of many species and cultivars of **erica, calluna** and **daboecia**, each described by color, season of bloom, size and color of foliage. Offers about 280 varieties; if you don't see what you want, write and ask if they have it. (1982)
❒ Catalog: Long SASE, CAN, SS:2-6,9-11, $10m
⌂ Nursery: All year, M-F, call ahead
▼ Garden: June-October, call ahead

Heirloom Garden Project
    Dept. of Vegetable Crops
Plant Science Building
Cornell University
Ithaca, NY 14853-0327

Seeds
Seed kits of typical **vegetables grown a century ago**.
❒ Catalog: $1 and SASE

Heirloom Garden Seeds
P.O. Box 138
Guerneville, CA 95446

Seeds
Offer 200 varieties of **culinary herbs and heirloom flowers**.
❒ Catalog: $2

Heirloom Seeds
P.O. Box 245
West Elizabeth, PA 15088-0245
Tom Hauch

Seeds ⬿ Supplies
New company specializing in seeds of open-pollinated **heirloom vegetables** "that taste good." Catalog has good descriptions of each variety and lots of cultural information. They also offer a few "old-fashioned" annual flowers and will be adding more. (1988)
❒ Catalog: $1d

Heliconia Haus
12691 S.W. 104th Street
Miami, FL 33186
Charles D. Ullman

Plants
Small nursery specializing in **heliconias and gingers**, with a few musaceae and species cannas. Offers a collectors' list with only brief descriptions of these hard-to-find plants, a few of which have been habitat-collected in Central America. (1984)
❒ Catalog: Free, R&W, CAN/OV, bn
⌂ Nursery: February-November, daily, by appointment only
▼ Garden: February-November, daily, by appointment only

Henrietta's Nursery
1345 N. Brawley Avenue
Fresno, CA 93722-5899
(209) 275-2166 TO/CC
Jerry & Sylvia Hardaway

Plants ⬿ Seeds
A very large selection of **cactus and succulents**: euphorbias, cereus, caudiciforms, notocactus, mammillaria, crassula, sedum, rhipsalis, parodia and far too many more to list! Each plant is very well described, and some are shown in b&w photos; they also offer a number of inexpensive collections to get you started, as well as mixed seeds. (1958)
❒ Catalog: 1FCS, R&W, CAN/OV, $20m
⌂ Nursery: All year, M-Sa
▼ Garden: Growing area, M-Sa

The Herb Barn
P.O. Box 31
Bodines, PA 17722
(717) 995-9327
Sandy Nelson

Plants
A nice selection of **herb plants**, especially artemisia, mint, thyme and scented leaved geraniums; each plant very briefly described. (1977)
❒ Catalog: $.50, R&W, SS:W, $5m, cn/bn
⌂ Nursery: Sa-Su, call ahead

Herb Gathering, Inc.
5742 Kenwood Avenue
Kansas City, MO 64110-2732
(816) 523-2653 TO/CC $20m
Paula Winchester

Seeds ⬿ Books
A fresh-herbs business which also imports European **gourmet vegetable and herb seeds**; offers many seeds wanted by cooks. Also sells herb and cookbooks and will ship fresh herbs by Express Mail. Plants and seed germination well described. (1978)
❒ Catalog: $2, R&W, CAN/OV

The Herbfarm
32804 Issaquah-Fall City Road
Fall City, WA 98024
(206) 784-2222
The Zimmerman Family

Plants ⬿ Books ⬿ Supplies
Free regular catalog lists many **herb plants** and a large selection of herb products, gifts and courses offered. They also print a plant list of 425 **herbs, sedums and sempervivums** which they sell ($1.75, ask for #0100). Catalog also lists books and herbal flea collars for cats and dogs. (1974)
❒ Catalog: See notes, CAN/OV, cn/bn
⌂ Nursery: All year, hours vary, call ahead
▼ Garden: April-September

Herbs-Liscious
1702 S. Sixth Street
Marshalltown, IA 50158
(515) 752-4976
Carol Lacko-Beem

Plants
Offers a good selection of **herb plants** with no plant descriptions; plants come at the end of a catalog packed with dried herbs for flavorings, herb baths, essential oils, porcelain garden markers, etc. They will search for and fill requests for more unusual herbs if asked. (1987)
☐ Catalog: $1d, R&W, $10m
⌂ Nursery: All year, M-Sa, by appointment only
▼ Garden: May-September, M-Sa, by appointment only

Heritage Gardens
1 Meadow Ridge Road
Shenandoah, IA 51602
(605) 665-1080 or 5188
Donald Leighton, Pres.

Plants ⚭ Bulbs
A new upscale subsidiary of Henry Field Seed & Nursery Company, offering a wide selection of **perennials, flowering trees and shrubs, roses, grapes and berries and summer-blooming bulbs**; color catalog shows many of the plants, gives good plant descriptions with some growing information. (1989)
☐ Catalog: Free, cn/bn

Heritage Rosarium
211 Haviland Mill Road
Brookville, MD 20833
(301) 774-2806
Nicholas & Rosanne Weber

Plants
Offers a large selection of **old garden, modern shrub and species roses**, available on a custom-root basis. About 400 varieties are listed only by cultivar or species name, with symbols for type, color and date of introduction; get out your "old rose" books. Regularly stock 50 to 75 varieties.
☐ Catalog: $1d, SS:11, $20m
⌂ Nursery: April-October, Sa-Su, by appointment only

Heritage Rose Gardens
16831 Mitchell Creek Drive
Ft. Bragg, CA 95437
(707) 984-6959 or 964-3748
Virginia Hopper & Joyce Demits

Plants
A broad selection of **species and old garden roses**, including unidentified roses found at old North Coast homesteads and named for the location found. Specializes in teas/Chinas, ramblers/climbers and many more and will do custom-rooting of additional rare varieties. Garden visits in June and July, by appointment only. (1981)
☐ Catalog: $1d, CAN/OV, SS:1-2, bn
▼ Garden: 40350 Wilderness Road, Branscomb, see notes

Heronswood Nursery
7530 - 288th Street N.E.
Kingston, WA 98346
(206) 297-4172
Daniel J. Hinkley & Robert L. Jones

Plants
Small nursery offers a good list of **ornamental woody plants**: maples, berberis, box, callicarpa, cercidiphyllum, cotoneaster, daphne, eucryphia, hydrangea, holly, mahonia, pernettya, pieris, rubus, willows, sarcococca, many conifers and viburnums. Plants are small; no plant descriptions.
☐ Catalog: Long SASE, SS:10-3, $20m
⌂ Nursery: Sa-Su, by appointment only
▼ Garden: Sa-Su, by appointment only

Heymaqua Seed Service
2286 South Face Road
Garberville, CA 95440
Stan Heymann & Lily Aquarian

Seeds
Organically grown and open-pollinated **vegetables, herbs and flowers** for mild winter climates like coastal northern California; salad greens a specialty. Varieties chosen to be vigorous and easily grown, with "nutritional content, flavor and beauty given important consideration."
☐ Catalog: $1d, CAN/OV, $3m

© Holly Hills, Inc.
Artist: Tom Horner

Hickory Hill Gardens
RD 1, Box 11
Loretto, PA 15940
(814) 886-2823
Clayton Burkey

Plants
A very broad selection of **daylilies**, also Siberian irises, hosta, bearded
irises, herbaceous peonies and other perennials. Each plant briefly but
well described. Also advertises as Burkey Gardens. (1981)
▢ Catalog: $1, CAN, SS:5-6,8-10, $10m
⌂ Nursery: June-October, by appointment only
▼ Garden: July-August, by appointment only

Hidden Garden Nursery, Inc.
13515 S.E. Briggs
Milwaukie, OR 97222
(503) 653-8189
Wayne & Kathy Lauman

Plants
A small family nursery which offers a nice selection of **miniature roses**,
each variety very well described. Plants are available "pre-finished" and
"finished," but there's no further explanation of what that means. They also
sell WaterWorks hydrogels to reduce watering. (1986)
▢ Catalog: Free, R&W, CAN
⌂ Nursery: All year, M-Sa
▼ Garden: April-September, M-Sa

Hidden Springs Herb and Fuchsia Farm
Route 14, Box 159-1A
Cookeville, TN 38501
(615) 268-9354
Jomo & Turtle MacDermott

Plants
Fuchsias, hardy and for warm climates, including varieties which bloom
well in hot weather, with cultural hints and good plant descriptions.
Another list offers **herbs, scented geraniums and sedums**. (1968)
▢ Catalog: $1d, R&W, SS:9-6
⌂ Nursery: All year, daily, call ahead
▼ Garden: Spring, daily, call ahead

Hidden Springs Nursery -- Edible Landscaping
Route 14, Box 159
Cookeville, TN 38501
(615) 268-9889
Hector Black

Plants
Offers plants for **edible landscaping and low maintenance fruits for**
sustainable agriculture. Antique apples, apricots, figs, grapes, mayhaws,
hardy kiwis, medlars and quinces, pears, plums, jujube, goumi and several
nitrogen-fixing shrubs for reclamation. (1978)
▢ Catalog: $.50, CAN/OV, SS:10-4, $15m
⌂ Nursery: March-December, by appointment only
▼ Garden: March-December, by appointment only

High Altitude Gardens
P.O. Box 4619
620 Sun Valley Road
Ketchum, ID 83340
(208) 726-3221 TO/CC
Bill McDorman

Seeds ✎ Books ✎ Supplies ✎ Tools
Seed of open-pollinated **gourmet and heirloom vegetables, herbs, wild-**
flowers and **native grasses**, adapted to the cold, short-season, high-
altitude climate of the mountain West. Informative catalog with cultural
suggestions; also sells tools, growing supplies and books. (1984)
▢ Catalog: $2, R&W, CAN/OV, SS:5-8, cn/bn
⌂ Nursery: All year, M-F, call ahead
▼ Garden: July-September, by appointment only

High Country Rosarium
1717 Downing Street
Denver, CO 80209
(303) 832-4026
William Campbell; John Ray, Mgr.

Plants ✎ Books
Very hardy **old garden roses** grown in the Rockies -- a nice selection of
species, old garden varieties and shrub roses, all well described. Also
offers several collections -- for hedges, bird lovers and dry climates -- and
rose books and rose growing supplies. (1971)
▢ Catalog: $1, SS:11-3, bn/cn
⌂ Nursery: First 2 weekends in June
▼ Garden: May-June, by appointment only

Highland Succulents
Eureka Star Route, Box 133
Gallipolis, OH 45631
(614) 256-1428 TO/CC
William Ballard

Plants
"We specialize in hard-to-find **succulents** -- no common varieties." A col-
lectors' list, with periodic specialty lists of new and unusual items; a very
large selection. Plants briefly described, many shown in b&w photographs.
▢ Catalog: $2, R&W, CAN/OV, $15m, bn
⌂ Nursery: W-F, by appointment only

Highlander Nursery
P.O. Box 177
Pettigrew, AR 72752
(501) 677-2300
Lee & Louise McCoy

Plants
Specializes in hardy and low-chill **blueberries**, a dozen varieties which
bear from early to late in the season. Also offers one dwarf variety,
'Tophat,' which grows less than twenty-four inches high and makes a nice
container or border plant. (1986)
▢ Catalog: Free, R&W, CAN/OV, SS:W
⌂ Nursery: All year, daily, call ahead
▼ Garden: May-June, October, daily, call ahead

Hildenbrandt's Iris Gardens
HC 84, Box 4
Lexington, NE 68850-9304
(308) 324-4334
Les & Tony Hildenbrandt

Plants ✎ Bulbs
Very extensive list of **tall bearded and dwarf irises**, each briefly described. Also offers a good selection of **herbaceous peonies, Oriental**
poppies, hostas and a few hybrid **lilies**. The color selection of Oriental poppies seems wonderful: apricot, black raspberry, purple and
yellow-orange! (1956)
▢ Catalog: 2 FCS(2 IRC), R&W, CAN/OV, SS:7-9, $10m
⌂ Nursery: All year, call ahead
▼ Garden: May-Sept, call ahead

Hill 'n dale
6427 N. Fruit Avenue
Fresno, CA 93711
(209) 439-8249
Dale Kloppenburg

Plants
A very extensive list of **hoyas**, both species and named cultivars, with a number of **dischidias** (cousins of the hoya) and some **aeschynanthus**. Have added to their collection during trips to Australia, Guadalcanal, the Solomon Islands and the Philippines, so there are more to come. Cuttings only.
☐ Catalog: Long SASE w/2 FCS, R&W, $25m, bn
⌂ Nursery: All year, by appointment only
▼ Garden: June-August, by appointment only

Hillhouse Nursery
90 Kresson-Gibbsboro Road
Voorhees, NJ 08043
(609) 784-6203 TO/CC $10m
Theodore S. Stecki

Plants
Specializes in the **Linwood hardy azaleas**, hybridized by the late G. Albert Reid -- all either double, semi-double or hose-in-hose varieties, which come in a range of habits from prostrate and compact to tall -- all very hardy. Very brief descriptions; plants grown in 3" pots. (1968)
☐ Catalog: Free, R&W, SS:4-6,9-11
⌂ Nursery: Sept-June, evenings & weekends, call ahead
▼ Garden: April-June, Sept-October, call ahead

Hilltop Herb Farm
P.O. Box 325
Chain-O-Lakes Resort near Cleveland
Romayor, TX 77368
(713) 592-5859

Plants ⟿ Seeds ⟿ Books
Hilltop Herb Farm is well known in Texas for its restaurant; the founder and her daughter are the authors of "Southern Herb Growing." They also sell **herb plants, scented geraniums and seeds**, a nice selection with no plant descriptions, and gift baskets of preserves.
☐ Catalog: Free, SS:W, $20m
⌂ Nursery: By appointment only

Historical Roses
1657 W. Jackson Street
Painesville, OH 44077
(216) 357-7270
Ernest J. Vash

Plants
Small nursery offers a wide selection of **old garden roses** of all kinds, a number of fragrant hybrid teas and the very hardy shrub roses of Griffith Buck. All plants very briefly described; over 100 in all. Ships only to the lower forty-eight states. (1982)
☐ Catalog: Long SASE, SS:3-4,10-1, $7m
⌂ Nursery: All year, M-Sa, call ahead

Holbrook Farm & Nursery
Route 2, Box 223 B
Fletcher, NC 28732
(704) 891-7790 TO/CC $25m
Allen W. Bush

Plants
Offers a broad selection of **garden perennials, native wildflowers, hardy geraniums, hostas and trees and shrubs, including heaths and heathers**; all are very well described, with cultural information. The catalog has a homey touch which enhances the grand selection of fine perennials. (1980)
☐ Catalog: $2d, SS:3-5,9-11, $15m, bn/cn
⌂ Nursery: April-October, M-Sa
▼ Garden: May-August, M-Sa

Holladay Jungle
P.O. Box 5727
1602 E. Fountain Way
Fresno, CA 93755
(209) 229-9858
Barbara Holladay

Plants
A broad selection of **tillandsias** available bare-root; there are no plant descriptions, but you should be able to find them in a good book. They "grow on trees and rocks without soil and all flower." They also have a **bromeliad** list which I did not see. (1984)
☐ Catalog: Free, R&W, CAN/OV, $15m, bn
⌂ Nursery: All year, by appointment only
▼ Garden: All year, by appointment only

Holland Wildflower Farm
290 O'Neal Lane
Elkins, AR 72727
(501) 643-2622 TO/CC
Bob & Julie Holland

Plants ⟿ Seeds
Small nursery sells plants and seeds of **prairie wildflowers** ideal for harsh winters and hot summers; each plant is very well described, with cultural suggestions and a nice sketch. They also sell dried flowers and grasses, wildflower notecards with seeds and other gifts. (1985)
☐ Catalog: $1.50, R&W, CAN, $10m, bn/cn
⌂ Nursery: March-December, by appointment only
▼ Garden: March-October, by appointment only

Holly Hills, Inc.
1216 Hillsdale Road
Evansville, IN 47711
(812) 867-3367
Stephen, David & Helen Schroeder

Plants
Offer their own very hardy H. R. Schroeder **evergreen azaleas**, thirty-eight named cultivars bred for Midwestern winters; plants well described. They also sell species azaleas, hybrid rhododendrons, American holly and dwarf conifers -- tell them which plants you are interested in. (1974)
☐ Catalog: Free, CAN/OV, SS:3-6,9-11, $25m, bn/cn
⌂ Nursery: March-November, M-Sa, call ahead
▼ Garden: April-May, M-Sa, call ahead

Hollydale Nursery
Pelham, TN 37366
(615) 467-3600 or (800) 222-3026
Dale M. Bryan

Plants
Offers a very broad selection of **peaches, nectarines and plums** and a few table grapes. Obviously they sell mostly to orchardists, but will sell in small quantities as well. Trees grown on 'Nemaguard' and 'Lovell' rootstock in fumigated soil. List includes a number of low-chill peach varieties.
☐ Catalog: Free, R&W

Hollyvale Farm
P.O. Box 69
Humptulips, WA 98552
(206) 987-2218
Bonnie L. Heintz & Alice M. Reid

Plants
Offer over 50 varieties of **holly**, including many Wieman hybrids: 'Wieman's Variegated,' 'Gold Edge,' 'Night Glow,' 'Moon Bright,' 'Screw Leaf' and others. Mr. Wieman and his wife, both in their 90's, have registered more holly varieties than anyone else in the US.
☐ Catalog: Long SASE, R&W, SS:4-9

Homestead Division of Sunnybrook Farms
9448 Mayfield Road
Chesterland, OH 44026
(216) 729-9838
Peter & Jean Ruh

Plants ∾ Seeds ∾ Tools
A retirement business of the founders of Sunnybrook Farms -- huge selection of **hostas** (and hosta seeds), also a number of **ivies, epimediums, daylilies and two Japanese ferns** -- some retirement! Plants briefly to well described. They also offer a few of their favorite hand tools and plant labels. (1980)
☐ Catalog: $1, CAN/OV, SS:4-10, $25m
⌂ Nursery: February-September, Sa-Su, by appointment only
▼ Garden: June-September, Sa-Su, by appointment only

Honeywood Lilies
P.O. Box 63
Parkside, SK, Canada S0J 2A0
(306) 747-3296 or 3776
Dr. A. J. Porter & Allan B. Daku

Plants ∾ Bulbs
Specializes in **lilies**, offering a nice variety of all types and some collections. Also offers herbaceous peonies and some iris, alliums, species tulips, hardy daylilies and a few "minor bulbs," all well described.
☐ Catalog: $1d, R&W, US/OV, SS:4-5,9-11, cn/bn
⌂ Nursery: April-October, M-Sa, Su by appointment only
▼ Garden: July-September, M-Sa

Hookland's Dahlias
1096 Horn Lane
Eugene, OR 97404
(503) 688-7792
Robert B. Hookland & Dwayne Dickson

Plants
Offer a good selection of **dahlias**, listed by type with very brief descriptions. Grow more varieties than they list, so you can send a "want list" to ask for desired cultivars. (1968)
☐ Catalog: Free, R&W, CAN/OV, SS:12-5
⌂ Nursery: Hours vary, call ahead

Horizon Seeds

See Miller Grass Seed Company.

Jerry Horne -- Rare Plants
10195 S.W. 70th Street
Miami, FL 33173
(305) 270-1235
Jerry Horne

Plants
A collectors' list of rare and exotic **tropical plants**. A good selection of of bromeliads, platyceriums, ferns, palms, cycads, aroids and others, all briefly described with cultural suggestions. (1975)
☐ Catalog: Long SASE, CAN/OV, $10m, bn
⌂ Nursery: All year, M-Sa, call ahead
▼ Garden: All year, M-Sa, call ahead

Hortense's African Violets
12406 Alexandria Street
San Antonio, TX 78233
(512) 656-0128
Hortense Pittman

Plants
Offer a selection of standard, compact standard, miniature and semi-miniature **African violets**, including their own hybrids, "Hortense's Honeys" -- both plants and leaves and several collections; all plants briefly described.
☐ Catalog: $.25, SS:W, $10m

Hortico, Inc.
RR 1
723 Robson Road
Waterdown, ON, Canada L0R 2H0
(416) 689-6984
William Vanderkruk

Plants
A very broad selection of garden **perennials**, hardy ornamental trees and shrubs, roses, lilacs, ferns, wildflowers and conifers, briefly described. Essentially a wholesale nursery, but will sell in small quantities to home gardeners at retail prices. Ask for rose or perennial list, $2 each.
☐ Catalog: See notes, R&W, US/OV, bn

Horticultural Enterprises
P.O. Box 810082
Dallas, TX 75381-0082

Seeds
"Chilies are our business." **Chilies and sweet peppers** from around the world -- each briefly described and illustrated as to size and shape. Also some **Mexican herbs and vegetables**. Included is a bibliography of cookbooks with publishers' addresses -- uses galore for your harvest! (1973)
☐ Catalog: Free, CAN

Spencer M. Howard Orchid Imports
11802 Huston Street
North Hollywood, CA 91607
(818) 762-8275
Spencer & Marjorie Howard

Plants
Only **species orchids**, collected from all over the world. A collectors'
list offers dendrobium, epidendrum, angraceum, oncidium, laelia,
rhyncostylis, paphiopedilum, phalaenopsis, cirrhopetalum, pleurothallis
and many others; very brief descriptions -- get out your reference books
and dream. (1957)
❑ Catalog: Long SASE w/2 FCS, R&W, CAN/OV, $25m, SS:W, bn
⌂ Nursery: All year, by appointment only
▼ Garden: Spring, by appointment only

Huan Bui Orchids, Inc.

See Limrick, Inc.

J. L. Hudson, Seedsman
P.O. Box 1058
Redwood City, CA 94064
J. L. Hudson

Seeds ❧ Books
"Specialize in **rare seeds** from all over the world -- except Antarctica."
Now called the "Ethnobotanical Catalog of Seeds," it's informative, with a
broad selection, historic, cultural and literary references and current
scientific information, illustrated with old prints. More than a catalog,
it's an education. Also offers some books. (1911)
❑ Catalog: $1(9 IRC), R&W, CAN/OV, bn/cn

Huff's Garden Mums
P.O. Box 187
618 Juniatta
Burlington, KS 66839-0187
(316) 364-2933
Charles A. Huff

Plants
A huge selection of **chrysanthemums** -- a collectors' list -- each very
briefly described and organized by type. Also offers a number of collections
by type or use for those who are bewildered by the choice. Still carries
some old favorites. (1955)
❑ Catalog: Free, R&W, OV, SS:3-6, $5m
⌂ Nursery: September-June, M-F
▼ Garden: September-October, M-F

Huggins Farm Irises
Route 1, Box 348
Hico, TX 76457
(817) 796-4041
Pete & Mary Huggins

Plants
Broad selection of **bearded irises**: tall bearded, reblooming, intermediate,
border, dwarf, horned, "space age" and "antique" (before 1950 -- by which
measure, I'm an antique, too). The "antiques" are used for landscaping re-
stored older homes.
❑ Catalog: $1d, CAN/OV, SS:7-10, $10m
⌂ Nursery: Weekends & eves, call ahead
▼ Garden: March-May, Sept-Nov., weekends & eves, call ahead

Hughes Nursery
1305 Wynooche West
Montesano, WA 98563
Howard Hughes

Plants
A collectors' list of **Japanese maples**, mostly listed by their Japanese
cultivar names, and a few other species maples; all are well described with
cultural suggestions. A broad selection of hard-to-find trees, listed by
shape and leaf color/character. Have added rare **beech** cultivars. (1964)
❑ Catalog: $1.50d, CAN, SS:10-3
⌂ Nursery: All year, by appointment only
▼ Garden: All year, by appointment only

Ed Hume Seeds, Inc.
P.O. Box 1450
Kent, WA 98035
Jeff Hume

Seeds ❧ Books ❧ Supplies ❧ Tools ❧ Bulbs
Sells a wide variety of untreated **vegetable** seeds for short-season and cool
climates, both new and old varieties; also **perennials, annuals, dahlias** and
gladiolus. Also sells some tools and supplies, a greenhouse, some books on
gardening by Ed Hume and others and Ed's video cassettes. (1978)
❑ Catalog: Free, R&W, CAN

Hummingbird Gardens
P.O. Box 225
461 Scenic Drive
La Honda, CA 94020
(415) 747-0679
Karen Sullivan

Seeds
Specializing in **plants that attract hummingbirds**, including many California
native plants. At present offer only a seed list; plants are available only
at the nursery. An extensive list of hummingbird plants with brief descrip-
tions and growing information is available for $12.50 ppd. (1988)
❑ Catalog: Long SASE, R&W, CAN/OV
⌂ Nursery: All year, by appointment only
▼ Garden: May-October, by appointment only

Huronview Nurseries & Garden Centre
1811 Brigden Side Road
Bright's Grove, ON, Canada N0N 1C0
(519) 869-4689 or 2837 TO $25m
Dick & Mary Kock

Plants ❧ Supplies
Wide selection of **orchids**: cattleyas, oncidiums, vandas, cymbidiums, paph-
iopedilums, phalaenopsis and some species orchids, each briefly described.
Two other catalogs offer either a wide selection of nursery stock, roses,
ornamental and fruit trees or perennials, wildflowers and ferns. (1950)
❑ Catalog: $1d, R&W, US/OV, SS:4-10, $20m
⌂ Nursery: All year, M-Sa
▼ Garden: All year, M-Sa

Hurov's Tropical Seeds
P.O. Box 1596
Chula Vista, CA 92012
(619) 426-0091 TO $10m
H. Ron Hurov

Seeds
Offers a huge selection of seeds for "**useful plants**" from all over the
world; he says he offers 6,000 species of mostly wild harvested seeds.
Seed lists are organized by edible fruits, fragrant plants, houseplants,
dye plants, landscape plants and so forth; each is briefly described. (1969)
❑ Catalog: $1, R&W, CAN/OV, $5m, bn/cn
⌂ Nursery: M-Sa, by appointment only

Brenda Hyatt
1 Toddington Crescent, Bluebell Hill
Chatham, Kent, England ME5 9QT
(0634) 63251
Brenda Hyatt

Seeds
Specializes in **Auricula primroses**, both Alpine and show varieties; sells
seeds of both types in packets of mixed colors. She now keeps the National
Collection of P. auricula, including the collection of Gordon Douglas; seeds
available of cowslips, candelabras, double Jack-in-the-Green and double and
single gold-laced. She has recently written a book on these plants.
❑ Catalog: 1 IRC (20p), OV, $5m
⌂ Nursery: By appointment only

Illinois Foundation Seeds, Inc.
P.O. Box 722
Route 45
Champaign, IL 61820
(217) 495-6260
Dale E. Cochran, Gen. Mgr.

Seeds
Sells only new hybrid "**sweet corn**": 'Ivory 'n Gold,' 'Illini Gold,' 'Illini
Xtra-Sweet,' 'Xtra-Sweet 82,' 'Northern Xtra-Sweet' and 'Florida Staysweet.'
All are well described, some shown in color in their leaflet.
❑ Catalog: Free, R&W, CAN/OV
⌂ Nursery: All year, M-F

Indigo Knoll Perennials
16236 Compromise Court
Mt. Airy, MD 21771
(301) 489-5131
Steve Harsy

Plants
Offers a good selection of **perennials**: alliums, asters, chrysanthemums,
dianthus, echinaceas and heleniums, monardas, sedums, verbascums and
veronicas. All of the plants are very well described, with a list of plants
for beginners and busy people. Plants chosen on the basis of ease of
culture, quality of display and lack of general availability in the trade.
❑ Catalog: $1d, SS:4-5,9-10

W. E. Th. Ingwersen, Ltd.

See Birch Farm Nursery.

Inland African Violets
1216 - 24th Avenue
Coaldale, AB, Canada T0K 0L0
(403) 345-4662
Mary Thompson & John Insley

Plants ∽ Supplies
Offer 500 cultivars of **African violets** from leading American and Canadian
hybridizers and specialize in micro-miniatures. Not all 500 are listed in
their catalog, but they offer a nice selection; each plant well described.
Also offer African violet growing supplies. Sell other gesneriads at the
nursery. (1978)
❑ Catalog: $1, SS:5-9
⌂ Nursery: Daily, by appointment only

Intermountain Cactus
2344 S. Redwood Road
Salt Lake City, UT 84119
(801) 972-5149
Robert A. Johnson

Plants
Offers a selection of **very hardy cactus** (some to -20 to -50F), most of
which are profuse bloomers, including opuntia, pediocactus, corypantha and
neobesseya. Each plant well described; opuntias sold by pad or by clump.
❑ Catalog: Long SASE, SS:4-11, $15m, bn/cn
⌂ Nursery: Spring-fall, M-Sa, by appointment only
▼ Garden: May-September, M-Sa, by appointment only

Intermountain Seeds
P.O. Box 40
Rexburg, ID 83440
(208) 356-9805
Allen Wilson

Seeds
A nice selection of **flowers, herbs and vegetables** for the intermountain
climate of the northern Rockies or any short growing season. Most of the
seeds are hybrids; each is very well described. Also sell black plastic
mulch and row covers to help you get a jump on the season.
❑ Catalog: 1 FCS

International Seed Supplies
P.O. Box 538
Nowra, NSW, Australia 2541
(044) 48 7563
Neville & Pamela Burnett

Seeds
A very broad selection of seeds, including **Australian native plants**, regular garden flowers, shrubs and trees from all over; each plant is briefly
described, and there are color photographs of many. They sell seed six-packs
of Australian native plants -- a dozen assortments. (1983)
❑ Catalog: A$3(IMO), OV, $30m, bn/cn

Inter-State Nurseries
P.O. Box 208
Hamburg, IA 51640-0208
(314) 754-4525 or (800) 325-4180 TO/CC
Stark Bros.

Plants ∽ Bulbs
Color catalog offers a good selection of **hybrid roses and perennials**; each
plant well described, most shown in photographs. Common names only.
❑ Catalog: Free, SS:9-11,2-5, cn

Iris Acres
RR 4, Box 189
Winamac, IN 46996
(219) 946-4197
Thurlow & Jean Sanders

Plants
A very extensive list of **bearded irises in all sizes**, including reblooming and "space age" types; all plants briefly described. List offers general information on planting and care of irises. (1959)
❏ Catalog: $.50, CAN, SS:7-8
⌂ Nursery: May-September, call ahead
▼ Garden: May-June, call ahead

Iris Gardens
109 Sourdough Ridge Road
Bozeman, MT 59715
Maureen K. Blackwell

Plants
Offers older, often hard-to-find varieties of **tall bearded, intermediate and dwarf irises**; list not seen.
❏ Catalog: Long SASE, SS:7-8, $6m
⌂ Nursery: June-September, by appointment only
▼ Garden: June, by appointment only

The Iris Pond
7311 Churchill Road
McLean, VA 22101
(703) 893-8526
Clarence Mahan

Plants
Offers tall bearded, Japanese, Siberian, reblooming and species **irises** and a large selection of miniature tall bearded irises; good selection, plants very briefly described. (1985)
❏ Catalog: $1, CAN/OV, SS:7-9, $12m
▼ Garden: May-June, by appointment only

Iris Test Gardens
1010 Highland Park Drive
College Place, WA 99324
(509) 525-8804
Austin & Ione Morgan

Plants
Very extensive list of tall bearded **irises** and some dwarfs; brief descriptions. Many offerings are their own hybrids, including 'Morgan's Double Rimmers.' Shipments to Canada and overseas must be over $400 and include permit costs. (1977)
❏ Catalog: $.50, R&W, CAN/OV, SS:7-9, $5m
⌂ Nursery: July-September, call ahead
▼ Garden: May, daylight hours

Island Seed Mail Order
P.O. Box 4278, Station A
Victoria, BC, Canada V8X 3X8
(604) 384-0345

Seeds
A good selection of seeds of **annual flowers, vegetables and herbs**. List is combined with the order form; there are no plant descriptions. (1960)
❏ Catalog: Free, US/OV

Ison's Nursery
Route 1, Box 191
Brooks, GA 30205
(404) 599-6970
William G. Ison

Plants
Specialize in **muscadine-scuppernong grapes**; offer many varieties and have a seedless muscadine on the way. They also sell many other fruits -- blackberries, blueberries, raspberries, apricots, low-chill apples, figs, plums, pomegranates, nut trees; well described, with cultural hints. (1936)
❏ Catalog: Free, R&W, CAN/OV, SS:11-4
⌂ Nursery: September-June, M-F
▼ Garden: Orchard, M-F

Ivies of the World
P.O. Box 408
Highway 42 (2 miles East)
Weirsdale, FL 32195
(904) 821-2201 or 2322 TO/CC
Tim & Judy Rankin

Plants
Offers more than 200 cultivars of **ivy**, mainly rooted cuttings; plants are grouped by type and well described. This nursery was formerly Tropexotic Growers, and before that The Alestake of Elkwood, VA (for those of you who haven't been keeping track). Adding new varieties all the time. (1986)
❏ Catalog: $1.50, CAN/OV, $20m
⌂ Nursery: All year, M-F, call ahead

J & L Orchids
20 Sherwood Road
Easton, CT 06612
(203) 261-3772 TO/CC
C. Head, M. Webb & L. Winn

Plants
A broad selection of **species orchids** from all over the world, as well as hybrids; all well described with lovely illustrations. Specializes in rare and unusual species and miniatures which can be grown in the home under lights or on the windowsill; also offers "beginners' specials." (1960)
❏ Catalog: $1, CAN/OV, bn
⌂ Nursery: All year, M-Sa
▼ Garden: All year, greenhouse, M-Sa

J. E. M. Orchids
6595 Morikami Park Road
Delray Beach, FL 33446
(407) 498-4308
Gene Monnier

Plants
Offers **hybrid orchids**: oncidium intergenerics, minicattleyas, phalaenopsis, dendrobiums, catasetum and others, each very briefly described with information on crosses. Also sells tropical fruit trees and tropical fruit in season at the nursery. (1974)
❏ Catalog: $1d, R&W, CAN/OV, SS:4-11
⌂ Nursery: September-June, M-Sa
▼ Garden: September-June, M-Sa

Jackson & Perkins Co.
P.O. Box 1028
Medford, OR 97501
Shacklee Corp.

Plants ❧ Bulbs
Color catalogs (which sometimes come smelling of roses in mid-winter) offer a wide selection of modern **hybrid tea, floribunda, grandiflora and climbing roses**, as well as rhubarb, asparagus, dwarf fruit trees, flowering trees and summer-blooming bulbs. Descriptions are effusive. (1872)
☐ Catalog: Free, R&W, CAN
▼ Garden: May-August, roses

Jasperson's Hersey Nursery
2915 - 74th Street
Wilson, WI 54027
(414) 772-4749 TO
Lu M. Jasperson

Plants
Small nursery specializes in **tall bearded irises**, listed only by cultivar name. Fresh cut flowers and fresh vegetables are available at the nursery, where you can choose and dig other perennials on the spot. (1987)
☐ Catalog: Long SASE, R&W, SS:4-9, $10m
⌂ Nursery: April-October, Tu-Sa
▼ Garden: April-October, Tu-Sa

Jeannette's Jesneriads
2173 Leslie Street
Terrytown/Gretna, LA 70056
(504) 393-6977
Jeannette Domiano

Plants ❧ Supplies
Offers her own hybrid **African violets**, standard to large-sized, a number of which have been prize winners. She also offers **aeschynanthus, columnea, nemantanthus** and a few other gesneriad cuttings; plants are well to briefly described. Sells growing supplies for pick-up at the nursery. (1982)
☐ Catalog: $1, SS:4-10, $19m
⌂ Nursery: All year, daily, call ahead
▼ Garden: All year, daily, call ahead

The Thomas Jefferson Center
for Historic Plants
Monticello
P.O. Box 316
Charlottesville, VA 22902
(804) 979-5283 or 295-2657 TO/CC $10m
John Fitzpatrick & Catherine Claffin, Mgrs.

Seeds
Seeds from the **historic flowers and vegetables** grown at Monticello and at Tufton Farm. The center is a force in the preservation of garden plants grown in the 18th century. They also offer books on historic or old-fashioned flowers, including reprints of early books, and books by and about Jefferson as a gardener. Many historic plants are sold at Monticello. (1987)
☐ Catalog: Long SASE, R&W, SS:1-10, $5m, bn/cn
⌂ Nursery: April-October, daily
▼ Garden: April-June, October, daily

Klaus R. Jelitto
P.O. Box 560127
D 2000 Hamburg 56, West Germany
(0 41 03) 89752 FAX 15258

Seeds
A very broad selection of **rock garden and alpine plants, perennials and ornamental grasses** listed by botanical name. Catalog is in German, with cultural instructions for germinating seeds in English and French, symbols for use and some color photographs. (1957)
☐ Catalog: Free, R&W, OV, $20m, bn
⌂ Nursery: September-July, M-F

Jernigan Gardens
Route 6, Box 593
Dunn, NC 28334
(919) 567-2135 (8-9 pm)
Bettie Jernigan

Plants
Long collectors' list of **daylilies**, very briefly described, with concise tables of information. Also offers a good selection of **hostas** and some **irises** by mail; other perennials are available only at the nursery.
☐ Catalog: Long SASE, R&W, SS:4-11, $15m
⌂ Nursery: April-July, daily (closed 12 to 3), call ahead
▼ Garden: April-July, daylilies (closed 12 to 3)

Johnny's Selected Seeds
310 Foss Hill Road
Albion, ME 04910
(207) 437-9294 or 4301 TO/CC $15m
Robert L. Johnston, Jr.

Seeds ❧ Books ❧ Supplies
Catalog lists a broad selection of **vegetables, herbs and garden annuals**, as well as specialty grains and seed for commercial crops; also a good selection of growing supplies and books. All plants are very well described, with cultural suggestions and germination guides; particularly suited to Northern growing. (1973)
☐ Catalog: Free, CAN/OV
⌂ Nursery: April-June, M-Sa
▼ Garden: July-August, call ahead

Johnson Nursery
Route 5
Ellijay, GA 30540
(404) 276-3187 TO $20m
Johnson Family

Plants ❧ Supplies ❧ Tools
Catalog offers a good selection of **fruit trees** -- apples, old peach varieties, pears, plums, cherries, nuts, many kinds of berries and some grapes -- all well described, with b&w photos. Also sells supplies and tools.
☐ Catalog: Free, R&W, SS:12-4, $13m
⌂ Nursery: All year, M-Sa
▼ Garden: May-December, M-F, by appointment only

Johnson Seed Company
P.O. Box 543
Woodacre, CA 94973
Cathy Johnson

Seeds
A small company specializing in **seed of California native grasses**: twelve
varieties, mostly habitat-collected. She will try to collect wanted seed if
she can locate habitat; send "want list." Latest catalog has added wildflowers, herbs and wilflower seed mixes.
❏ Catalog: $.50, R&W, CAN/OV, bn/cn

Jones & Scully
18955 S.W. 168th Street
Miami, FL 33187-1112
(305) 238-7000 or (800) 672-4437
Wm. Peters, Lou Lodyga & Julie Gregory, Mgrs.

Plants
Color catalog offers a broad selection of **orchids**, especially cattleyas,
phalaenopsis, vanda and many species. They will assist customers over the
phone with cultural challenges; most plants are shipped Federal Express.
Plants are well described, photos mouthwatering! (1945)
❏ Catalog: $5d, R&W, CAN/OV, $25m, bn
⌂ Nursery: All year, daily
▼ Garden: All year, greenhouses

Jordan Seeds
6400 Upper Afton Road
Woodbury, MN 55125
(612) 738-3422
Dan, Jake & Nancy Jordan

Seeds ⬦ Supplies
Offer a broad variety of **vegetable seeds**, each very briefly described by
days to maturity, size and appearance. Seeds are sold in bulk, with one
ounce being the smallest size. Also sell some growing and marketing supplies
and mechanical planters for big operations.
❏ Catalog: Free

JoS Violets
402 Dundee Street
Victoria, TX 77904
(512) 575-1344 TO
Joanne Schrimsher

Plants ⬦ Supplies
List of standard, miniature, semi-miniature and trailing **African violets**
for sale as plants or leaves; each briefly described. Also sells growing
supplies and ceramic, Swift Moist-rite and Oyama Texas-style pots. (1983)
❏ Catalog: Long SASE, R&W, SS:4-11, $5m
⌂ Nursery: All year, evenings & weekends, by appointment only
▼ Garden: All year, by appointment only

Joyce's Garden
64640 Old Bend Redmond Highway
Bend, OR 97701
(503) 388-4680
Joyce Macdonald Glimm

Plants
Offers "ultra-hardy" **perennials, ground covers and herbs**; Bend even gets
freezes in July and August! Good selection, including achillea, asters,
campanulas, dianthus, helianthemums, phlox, veronicas, sages and more;
plants are briefly described. (1987)
❏ Catalog: $2, R&W, SS:4-6,9-10, bn/cn
⌂ Nursery: February-November, M-Sa, call ahead
▼ Garden: July-September, M-Sa, call ahead

J. W. Jung Seed Co.
335 S. High Street
Randolph, WI 53957-0001
(414) 326-4100 TO/CC
The Jung Family

Plants ⬦ Seeds ⬦ Supplies ⬦ Bulbs
Color catalog offers a broad selection of seeds for the flower and vegetable
garden, as well as nursery stock -- **fruit trees, roses, perennials,
ornamental trees, shrubs and vines**. Also issues a bulb catalog in the
summer. Carries tools and supplies, too. (1907)
❏ Catalog: Free, R&W, SS:4-11
⌂ Nursery: All year, M-Sa

Jungle Gems, Inc.
300 Edgewood Road
Edgewood, MD 21040
(301) 676-0672 TO/CC
Charles Williamson

Plants
Sells **phalaenopsis orchids** from blooming size to seedlings, as well as
miltonopsis, cattleyas, tillandsias and mericlones in mini-flasks. All
plants are very briefly described. Their clones include hybrids of the
special Phalaenopsis violacea 'Harfords Orange' in orange and red. (1975)
❏ Catalog: Free, R&W, CAN/OV,
⌂ Nursery: All year, M-Sa
▼ Garden: All year, glasshouse, M-Sa

Justice Gardens
107 Hight Drive
Watkinsville, GA 30677
(404) 769-8379
Louis Justice

Plants
Sells a wide selection of **hybrid azaleas and some rhododendrons** (and some
rhododendron species) from a number of well-known hybridizers; plants listed
only by species or cultivar name and name of hybridizer. Also sells dwarf
crape myrtles, dwarf nandina and Franklinia in 4-inch pots.
❏ Catalog: Long SASE, R&W, SS:3-6,9-12

Justice Miniature Roses
5947 S.W. Kahle Road
Wilsonville, OR 97070
(503) 682-2370
Jerry, June & Tara Justice

Plants
A broad selection of **miniature roses**, all very well described, with some
growing advice. In 1987 they started introducing varieties hybridized in
Ireland by Sean McCann.
❏ Catalog: Free, R&W,
⌂ Nursery: All year, daily

K & L Cactus Nursery
12712 Stockton Boulevard
Galt, CA 95632
(209) 745-4756 TO/CC
Keith & Lorraine Thomas

Plants ⟋ Seeds ⟋ Books ⟋ Supplies
Color and b&w catalog offers extensive list of **flowering desert and jungle cacti, succulents** and some seed; each well but briefly described. Also sells some cactus books and a few supplies, including handsome pots. (1971)
❑ Catalog: $2d, CAN/OV, SS:W, $20m, bn
⌂ Nursery: All year, F-Su

KSA Jojoba
19025 Parthenia Street
Northridge, CA 91324
(818) 701-1534 FAX 993-0194
Kathie Aamodt

Plants ⟋ Seeds ⟋ Supplies
Sells only **jojoba** -- seeds, seedlings, rooted cuttings and a variety of jojoba products such as soap, shampoos, lotions and automotive products. Cuttings, seedlings may be purchased in bulk; no plant descriptions. (1979)
❑ Catalog: Long SASE w/2 FCS, R&W, CAN/OV
⌂ Nursery: All year, M-F, call ahead

Kalmia Farm
P.O. Box 3881
Charlottesville, VA 22903
Ken Klotz

Plants
Sell only varieties of **garlic, shallots and onions** -- but some interesting onions: potato onions, bird's nest onions, Egyptian top onions; all well described. The potato onions are an old variety which they say is perennial.
❑ Catalog: Free, SS:9-11

Karleens Achimenes
1407 W. Magnolia
Valdosta, GA 31601-4235
(912) 242-1368
Karleen Lane

Plants
A small hobby business, but offers a wide selection of achimenes and other **gesneriads** -- sinningias, gloxinias, smithiantha, eucodonias and kohlerias. Also offers variegated plants; most briefly but well described. Get out your glasses; one of those tightly packed lists for the collector! (1978)
❑ Catalog: $1.50, CAN/OV, SS:1-6, $12m, bn
⌂ Nursery: By appointment only
▼ Garden: April-September, by appointment only

Kartuz Greenhouses
1408 Sunset Drive
Vista, CA 92083
(619) 941-3613 TO/CC
Michael Kartuz

Plants
The catalog, a collectors' dream, offers flowering plants for the home, greenhouse and outside in warm areas -- **begonias, gesneriads and African violets** and many other rare flowering plants and vines -- all very well described. (1960)
❑ Catalog: $2, R&W, CAN/OV, SS:W, $15m, bn
⌂ Nursery: All year, W-Sa
▼ Garden: All year, W-Sa, greenhouses

Kawamoto Orchid Nursery
2630 Waiomao Road
Honolulu, HI 96816
(808) 732-5808 TO/CC $25m
Leslie Kawamoto

Plants
Color catalog of **hybrid and species orchids** -- cattleyas, oncidiums, vandas, dendrobiums -- many illustrated, all briefly described. A number of mericlones are listed. They also have three orchid-of-the-month clubs with various offerings. A wide selection, available in various sizes. (1947)
❑ Catalog: $2d, R&W, CAN, $25m, bn
⌂ Nursery: All year, M-Sa, call ahead
▼ Garden: All year, M-Sa, call ahead

Kay's Greenhouses
207 W. Southcross
San Antonio, TX 78221
(512) 922-6711
Kay Tucker

Plants
A good selection of **rhizomatous and cane begonias**, both cuttings and plants. Each plant is briefly described by color of leaves and bloom; cuttings are rooted to order and may take some time. (1987)
❑ Catalog: $1, R&W, CAN, SS:W, $10m
⌂ Nursery: Weekends, by appointment only
▼ Garden: January-May, by appointment only

Kelly Nurseries
P.O. Box 800
Dansville, NY 14437
(716) 335-2211 or (800) 828-6977 TO/CC $10m
Thomas Kelly, Gen. Mgr.

Plants
Formerly Kelly Bros., they offer a broad selection of **general nursery stock**: hardy fruit trees, ornamental trees and shrubs, berries, grapes, ground covers and conifers. Many plants illustrated in color catalog, each well described. Cannot ship to CA, OR or WA. (1986)
❑ Catalog: Free, R&W, SS:3-6,9-11, $2m, cn/bn
⌂ Nursery: February-June, daily
▼ Garden: May-June, M-Sa

Kelly's Plant World
10266 E. Princeton
Sanger, CA 93657
(209) 294-7676
Herbert Kelly, Jr.

Bulbs
Summer-blooming bulbs: crinums, amarcrinums, amaryllids, cannas, irises, daylilies, hymenocallis and more. His canna list has 115 varieties. Also has a broad selection of crinums.
❑ Catalog: $1

Kensington Orchids
3301 Plyers Mill Road
Kensington, MD 20895
(301) 933-0036
Merritt W. Huntington

Plants ✍ Books ✍ Supplies
List offers phalaenopsis, doritaenopsis and oncidium hybrids, cattleyas, "Cambria types," miltonias and paphiopedilum **orchids** in seedling and flowering sizes, very briefly described. Also sells books and orchid-growing supplies.
☐ Catalog: Free, R&W, CAN/OV, SS:W, $25m
⌂ Nursery: All year, daily
▼ Garden: All year, greenhouses, daily

Kent's Flowers
320 W. Eagle Street
Arlington, NE 68002-0398
(402) 478-4011 TO/CC
Kent & Joyce Stork

Plants
New and recent **African violets** from various leading hybridizers such as Grodon Boone -- including their own prize winners; plants well described. Sells both plants and leaves. (1977)
☐ Catalog: $.50, CAN/OV, SS:9-10, $15m, bn
⌂ Nursery: All year, M-Sa, call ahead
▼ Garden: All year, M-Sa, call ahead

Keith Keppel
P.O. Box 8173
451 N. Lillian
Stockton, CA 95208
(209) 463-0227
Keith Keppel

Plants
An extensive list of **tall bearded irises**, many his own introductions; plants very well described, with good information on parentage. A small nursery -- a hobby gone mad! Stock is sometimes limited. What's really amazing is that there are any names left for iris cultivars! (1955)
☐ Catalog: $1, CAN/OV, SS:7-8, $10m
⌂ Nursery: April-May, by appointment only
▼ Garden: April-May, by appointment only

Kester's Wild Game Food Nurseries
P.O. Box 516
4582 Highway 116 East
Omro, WI 54963
(414) 685-2929 TO/CC
David & Patricia Kester

Plants ✍ Seeds
A wide selection of **plants to feed wildlife**: plants for ponds, various grains and wild rice (including an edible variety). The catalog offers a lot of cultural and wildlife food management information, lists seed and plants, including **aquatic plants**, and seed for feeding pet birds. (1899)
☐ Catalog: $2, CAN, SS:2-10
⌂ Nursery: All year, M-Sa, call ahead

Kilgore Seed Company
1400 W. First Street
Sanford, FL 32771
(407) 323-6630
J. H. Hunziker

Seeds ✍ Supplies ✍ Tools
A regional seed company, offering **vegetables and flowers** for the Gulf Coast area of the US, but suited to any subtropical or tropical climate. A wide selection, each very well described, with cultural suggestions; they also sell gardening supplies and tools. (1918)
☐ Catalog: $1d, CAN/OV
⌂ Nursery: All year, M-Sa

Kilworth Flowers
RR 3
County Road 14
Komoka, ON, Canada N0L 1R0
(519) 471-9787
Jim & Jo-Anne Eadie

Plants ✍ Books ✍ Supplies
Seedling to blooming size **orchids**: cattleya, phalaenopsis, dendrobium, ascocendas, cymbidium and paphiopedilum hybrids and sophronitis and paphiopedilium species; all briefly described. Also orchid books and grow-ing supplies. (1983)
☐ Catalog: Free, R&W, SS:3-10
⌂ Nursery: All year, Tu-Su, call ahead
▼ Garden: May-June, Tu-Su, call ahead

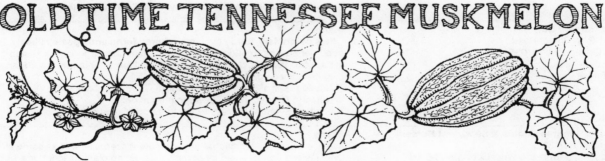

OLD TIME TENNESSEE MUSKMELON

© Southern Exposure Seed Exchange
Artist: Lucia Stanton

Kimberly Garden on Oregon Hill
RR 1, Box 44 G
Lisle, NY 13797
(607) 849-6554 TO/CC $10m
David & Kimberly Armstrong

Plants
Catalog offers a wide selection of **perennials and some unusual annuals**, all very well described, with good cultural information; many are illustrated with handsome line drawings. Price of each plant includes shipping. (1986)
❑ Catalog: $2d, R&W, CAN, SS:4-5,9-11, bn/cn

Kinder Canna Farm
P.O. Box 7706
Lawton, OK 73506
(405) 353-5118 TO/CC $10m
Johnny & Connie Kinder

Plants
Small nursery specializing in **cannas**; color pamphlet illustrates plants and describes them briefly. Selection is limited, prices very reasonable.
❑ Catalog: Free, R&W, CAN/OV, SS:12-6

King's Mums
P.O. Box 368
20303 E. Liberty Road
Clements, CA 95227
(209) 759-3571
Ted & Lanna King

Plants
Color catalog offers wide choice of **chrysanthemums** -- a real collectors' list; all plants well described, with cultural information. Also sells collections and the handbooks of the National Chrysanthemum Society. (1964)
❑ Catalog: $2d, CAN, SS:2-6, $10m
⌂ Nursery: All year, daily
♥ Garden: October-November, daily

Kings Herb Seeds
P.O. Box 14
Glenbrook, NSW, Australia 2773
Mike & Tricia Healy

Seeds
Offers 400 varieties of herbs, annual and perennial flowers, everlastings, oriental and gourmet vegetables; all well described and many shown in color. Australian seed houses seem to have unusual everlastings -- there's an almost black Nigella which is outstanding.
❑ Catalog: A$4.50

Kirkland Iris Garden
725 - 20th Avenue West
Kirkland, WA 98033
(206) 828-4907
Carol & George Lankow

Plants
Specializes in **dwarf and median bearded irises**, but offers a good selection of all types; all plants are well described, and some cultural information is included in the catalog. (1981)
❑ Catalog: Free, SS:7-8, $10m
⌂ Nursery: Call ahead
♥ Garden: April-May, call ahead

Kitazawa Seed Co.
1748 Laine Street
Santa Clara, CA 95051-3012
Ernest Kitazawa

Seeds
A good selection of seeds for **Oriental vegetables**; plants are briefly described. Nine varieties of daikon, the Japanese radish, and seven kinds of mustard. Cannot ship to Mexico. (1917)
❑ Catalog: Free, R&W, CAN/OV

Arnold J. Klehm Grower, Inc.
44 W 637, Route 72
Hampshire, IL 60193
(312) 683-4761 TO/CC
Arnold J. Klehm

Plants
A nice selection of **orchids**, mostly hybrid seedlings of phalaenopsis, but also vandaceous, cattleya alliance, paphiopedilums, ascocenda and species; some are their own "Meriklehms" (an orchid witticism, theirs). All briefly described, some illustrated in color. Special offers, too. (1980)
❑ Catalog: $1d, R&W, CAN/OV, SS:W, bn
⌂ Nursery: All year, M-F, call ahead

Klehm Nursery
Route 5, Box 197
Penny Road
South Barrington, IL 60010-9555
(800) 553-3715 TO/CC
Art Landen, Jr., Mgr.

Plants ✿ Books
Color catalog offers many cultivars of **hosta, daylilies, irises and herbaceous and tree peonies, ferns, ornamental grasses and perennials**; all plants well described and many illustrated, with good cultural information. They also offer a few books on plants which are their specialty. (1852)
❑ Catalog: $4d, R&W, CAN/OV, SS:W, bn
♥ Garden: Two open-house days a year; call for information.

Kline Nursery Co.
17401 S.W. Bryant Road
Lake Oswego, OR 97035
(503) 636-3923
Phil Parker

Plants
Offers **perennials, hardy cyclamen, hardy ferns and species lilies**; good general information and very brief plant descriptions. Also listed are species irises, rock garden narcissus, trilliums. This was the Edgar L. Kline Nursery for many years. (1987)
❑ Catalog: $2d, R&W, CAN/OV, $15m
⌂ Nursery: All year, Tu-Sa, by appointment only
♥ Garden: September-May, Tu-Sa, by appointment only

Gerhard Koehres Cactus & Succulent Nursery
Wingertstrasse 33
Erzhausen/Darmstadt, West Germany D-6106
(0 61 50) 72 41
Gerhard Koehres

Seeds
A very extensive list of **cactus and succulent** seeds, as well as some tillandsias and palms, listed by botanical name; no plant descriptions, but sure to please collectors. Offered are aylostera, copiapoa, frailea, gymnocalciums, parodia, agaves, aloes, euphorbias, mesembs and much more!
❑ Catalog: 1 IRC, R&W, OV, bn

P. Kohli & Co.
Park Road, near Neelam Theater
Srinagar, Kashmir, India 190009
73061
Mrs. Urvashi Suri

Seeds ❧ Bulbs
Seeds of a broad selection of **Himalayan plants** -- trees, shrubs, vines, perennials, alpines and bulbs from Kashmir and the western Himalayas. Can also arrange the purchase of subtropical seeds and bulbs of India -- write for information. Plants listed by botanical name only; some briefly described on gossamer paper lists. (1928)
❑ Catalog: 5 IRC, R&W, OV, $25m, bn

Kordonowy's Dahlias
P.O. Box 568
401 Quick Road (Castle Rock)
Kalama, WA 98625
(206) 673-2426
Sam & Katherine Kordonowy

Plants
A collectors' catalog of **dahlias** of all kinds, in a very broad selection: about 300 varieties, each very briefly described as to color and type, with general information. Offers a few collections. (1953)
❑ Catalog: Free, R&W, CAN, SS:3-5
⌂ Nursery: March-September, call ahead
▼ Garden: July-September, call ahead

V. Kraus Nurseries, Ltd.
Centre Road
Carlisle, ON, Canada L0R 1H0
(416) 689-4022 or 5704
Victor & Eva Kraus

Plants
A broad selection of **flowering and ornamental trees and shrubs,** including many hybrid tea roses, grandifloras, floribundas, climbers, modern shrub and miniature roses. Also sells fruit trees, grapes, berries, rhubarb and asparagus, including many apples and plums. No descriptions. (1951)
❑ Catalog: Free, R&W, US/OV, SS:10-11,4-5, $6m, bn/cn
⌂ Nursery: All year, M-Sa
▼ Garden: June-August, M-Sa

L. Kreeger
91 Newton Wood Road (SF)
Ashtead, Surrey, England KT21 1NN
L. Kreeger

Seeds
A good selection of seeds of **alpine and rock garden** plants; all plants well described, with country and site of origin of wild-collected seed and type of growing conditions which suit them best. Be sure to send US$ bills only for list, no checks. (1985)
❑ Catalog: $2(US bills), OV, bn

Krider Nurseries
P.O. Box 29
Middlebury, IN 46540
(219) 825-5714 TO/CC
Tim Barwick

Plants
Offers a nice selection of **roses,** mostly hybrid teas, many illustrated in color and all well described. I may have the wrong impression of Indiana; they offer a hardy rose called 'Hoosier Hysteria,' pretty enough to warm the blood anywhere. A reader tells me that "Hoosier Hysteria" refers to winter basketball madness! (1896)
❑ Catalog: Free, R&W, SS:2-6,9-11
⌂ Nursery: All year, M-Sa
▼ Garden: April-November, M-F

Michael & Janet Kristick
155 Mockingbird Road
Wellsville, PA 17365
(717) 292-2962
Michael & Janet Kristick

Plants
The sort of catalog that makes a collector's heart sing! Hundreds of culti-vars: **conifers, including many dwarfs, and Japanese and species maples.** No descriptions, just pages and pages of names. Japanese maples listed by Japanese cultivar names. (1970)
❑ Catalog: Free, CAN/OV, SS:4-12, bn
⌂ Nursery: All year, daily, by appointment only
▼ Garden: May-October, daily, by appointment only

Krohne Plant Farms
Route 6, Box 586
Dowagiac, MI 49047
(616) 424-3450 or 5423
William & Shiela Krohne

Plants
Fifteen varieties of **strawberries** which will produce in Northern climates; informative leaflet. Will sell in quantities as low as 25 per customer; quantity discounts for commercial growers. Also offers two kinds of asparagus crowns and horseradish. (1974)
❑ Catalog: Free, R&W, SS:3-6, $6m
⌂ Nursery: All year, daily, call ahead
▼ Garden: Spring-summer, daily, call ahead

Kusa Research Foundation
P.O. Box 761
Ojai, CA 93023
Non-Profit Foundation

Seeds
Group devoted to **seedcrops of folk origin, especially cereal grains.** Sells seed of crops which can be grown by home gardeners and small-scale farm-ers: special strains of millet, hull-less barley, Swiss gourmet baking wheat, lentils, sesame, oats and others; all well described. Also offers literature and publishes a newsletter called "Cerealist." (1980)
❑ Catalog: Long SASE, CAN/OV

LBG Nursery
Route 5, Box 130
Princeton, MN 55371
(612) 389-4920
Frank Foltz

Plants
Small family nursery offers a nice selection of organically grown **fruit trees**: apples, plums, pears, cherries, crabapples, mulberries, as well as wine grapes, raspberries, filberts and miscellaneous fruiting trees and shrubs for **edible landscaping**, each well described for habit and flavor of fruit. They'll provide advice on organic pest controls. (1983)
❑ Catalog: 2FCS, R&W, SS:4-5, $10m, cn/bn
⌂ Nursery: April-May, by appointment only
▼ Garden: June-September, by appointment only

LaFayette Home Nursery, Inc.
RR 1, Box 1A
Lafayette, IL 61449
(309) 995-3311
Corliss Jock Ingels

Seeds
Broad selection of **prairie grasses, forbs, trees, shrubs and wildflowers** for prairie restoration and development; all plants listed by botanical and common name. They also offer a number of grass and wildflower mixes for various conditions and do consulting and installation. (1887)
❑ Catalog: Free, R&W, bn/cn

Lagomarsino Seeds
5675-A Power Inn Road
Sacramento, CA 95824
(916) 381-1024 TO/CC $20m
Thomas & Janna Reimers

Plants ～ Seeds
A broad selection of **vegetable and herb** seeds; no plant descriptions. They ship onion plants from February to May; then in May start shipping sweet potato and yam plants. Seeds available in sizes from garden packets to one pound. Also sell grass seed for lawns, erosion control, field and pasture and wildflower mixes.
❑ Catalog: Free, $1m
⌂ Nursery: All year, M-Sa

Lake Odessa Greenhouse
1123 Jordan Lake Street
Lake Odessa, MI 48849
(616) 374-8848
Mark Potter

Plants
They offer a large selection of **geraniums** -- scented, brocade, rosebud, zonal, "tulip" and ivy types -- as well as a variety of houseplants such as ivies, wandering jews, peperomias and more. All plants well but briefly described.
❑ Catalog: Free, R&W, SS:5-10
⌂ Nursery: All year, M-Sa
▼ Garden: All year, greenhouse, M-Sa

Lakeshore Tree Farms, Ltd.
RR #3
Saskatoon, SK, Canada S7K 3J6
(306) 382-2077
Rob Krahn, Mgr.

Plants
Hardy fruit trees, berries and a nice selection of **ornamental trees, shrubs and perennials**. Catalog gives good plant descriptions, lists plants by common names. Fruit, including saskatoons, are hardy to 50 below zero. They have a landscaping service for local customers. (1936)
❑ Catalog: $1, R&W, US/OV, SS:4-5,9, $30m, cn
⌂ Nursery: April-November, M-Sa; May-September, daily
▼ Garden: June-July, daily

Lamb Nurseries
E. 101 Sharp Avenue
Spokane, WA 99202
(509) 328-7956
Nicola Luttropp

Plants
Catalog packed with **rock garden and perennial plants, vines, ground covers, succulents, clematis, violets and flowering shrubs**; a wide selection of collectors' plants, each very well described with cultural notes. They supply many botanical gardens, as well as people like us. (1938)
❑ Catalog: Free, R&W, CAN/OV, SS:W, bn/cn
⌂ Nursery: February-October, F-Sa

Lamtree Farm
Route 1, Box 162
Warrensville, NC 28693
(919) 385-6144
Lee A. Morrison

Plants
My heart leaps at the word "Franklinia," and here it is! Small nursery sells a limited but choice selection of **trees and shrubs**: franklinia, leucothoe, native rhododendrons and azaleas, kalmia, seedling maples and conifers and 'Lu shan' (Rhododendron fortunei); no plant descriptions. Also sells Christmas wreaths and garlands, lovely gifts for city folk! (1979)
❑ Catalog: Long SASE w/2FCS, R&W, SS:9-4, $25m, bn
⌂ Nursery: All year, daily, by appointment only
▼ Garden: All year, daily, by appointment only

D. Landreth Seed Company
P.O. Box 6426
180 W. Ostend Street
Baltimore, MD 21230
(301) 727-3922 or 3923

Seeds
"America's oldest seed house" -- they had George Washington and Thomas Jefferson as early customers! Offers a broad selection of **new and old varieties of vegetables**, all well described with cultural information, as well as a smaller selection of **herbs and garden annuals**. (1784)
❑ Catalog: $2d, R&W, CAN/OV, $15m
⌂ Nursery: All year, M-F

Landscape Alternatives, Inc.
1465 Pascal Street
691 W. Carpenter Avenue (Roseville)
St. Paul, MN 55108
(612) 647-9571
Karl Ruser, Gen. Mgr.

Plants
Specializes in nursery-propagated native Minnesota **wildflowers** and prairie and other ornamental **grasses** for distinctive low-maintenance landscapes. A good selection, with very brief plant descriptions. They also offer a few cultivated perennials. (1986)
❒ Catalog: $1d, R&W, CAN, SS:W, $25m, cn/bn
⌂ Nursery: April-September, M-Sa, by appointment only
▼ Garden: May-September, M-Sa, by appointment only

Larner Seeds
P.O. Box 407
Bolinas, CA 94924-0407
(415) 868-9407
Judith Larner Lowry

Seeds ⬿ Books
Seed for the Western landscape -- a good selection of **native wildflowers**, annual and perennial, and **trees, shrubs, vines and grasses**. Catalog emphasizes use in natural landscaping and offers several mixes for various habitats. Also offers books on natural landscaping and their own series of pamphlets on growing native plants. (1978)
❒ Catalog: $1.50, R&W, CAN/OV, bn/cn
⌂ Nursery: All year, by appointment only
▼ Garden: April-August, by appointment only

Las Pilitas Nursery
Star Route, Box 23 X
Las Pilitas Road
Santa Margarita, CA 93453
(805) 438-5992
Bert & Celeste Wilson

Plants ⬿ Seeds ⬿ Bulbs
A very extensive list of **California native plants** of all kinds, including a few wildflower seeds. Price list gives the number of plants available -- a good indication of what's rare or hard to propagate; list gives botanical and common name only. Excellent for landscaping and revegetation projects. The catalog is a series of lists by plant use; very informative. (1975)
❒ Catalog: $4 (price list free), R&W, $2m, bn/cn
⌂ Nursery: All year, Sa or by appointment only
▼ Garden: All year, Sa or by appointment only

Lauray of Salisbury
Undermountain Road (Route 41)
Salisbury, CT 06068
(203) 435-2263
Laura & Judy Becker

Plants
A very extensive collectors' list of **begonias, gesneriads, cacti, succulents, epiphyllums and hybrid and species orchids**, all briefly described, with some cultural notes by genera.
❒ Catalog: $2(3 IRC), SS:4-10, $10m, bn
⌂ Nursery: All year, daily, call ahead
▼ Garden: All year, glasshouse, call ahead

Laurie's Garden
41886 McKenzie Highway
Springfield, OR 97478
(503) 896-3756
Lorena M. Reid

Plants
Specializes in **beardless irises** -- Western natives, Japanese, Siberian, Evansia, water irises and other species and crosses between Pacific Coast and Siberian irises; broad selection, all briefly described. Also lists a few other hardy perennials. (1964)
❒ Catalog: Long SASE(3 IRC), SS:8-11, bn/cn
⌂ Nursery: March-November, call ahead
▼ Garden: May-July, call ahead

Lawson's Nursery
Route 1, Box 472
Yellow Creek Road
Ball Ground, GA 30107
(404) 893-2141 TO/CC $25m
Jim & Bernice Lawson

Plants ⬿ Books
A good selection of **antique apple and pear trees**; all well described with historical background -- even a 14th century apple called "Rambo"! They have added **blueberries, grapes, plums, peaches, apricots and nuts**. Also the Potter Walnut Cracker and books on fruit growing and cookbooks. (1968)
❒ Catalog: Free, R&W, CAN/OV, SS:11-3
⌂ Nursery: All year, M-Sa
▼ Garden: September, M-Sa

Lawyer Nursery, Inc.
950 Highway 200 West
Plains, MT 59859
(406) 826-3881 TO/CC
John N. Lawyer

Plants ⬿ Seeds
Supplies many types of **ornamental trees, fruit and nut trees, rootstock** in larger quantities for commercial growers, landscaping and reclamation uses. Also seeds of trees and woody plants, including subtropical trees and shrubs. Minimum $50 on seed orders, $150 on plants. (1959)
❒ Catalog: Free, R&W, CAN/OV, SS:10, $50m, bn/cn

Lazarus Enterprises
P.O. Box 69325
34114 Smith Road
Portland, OR 97201
(503) 695-2575
Mariel Lazarus

Plants
Sell **gladiolus** corms "by the bag"; you can buy bags of 2, 4, 6 and 8 ounces of mixed large and small corms by color and by size of flower. They also offer seed. List is the order form; no plant descriptions. (1981)
❒ Catalog: Free, CAN/OV
⌂ Nursery: Call ahead

Le Champion Heritage Seeds
P.O. Box 1602
Freedom, CA 95019-1602
(408) 724-5870
Fred Deghuee

Seeds
Specializes in old-fashioned **open-pollinated vegetable** varieties, including some heirloom types. A good selection, including some Oriental vegetables, popcorn and edible flowers; each very well described, with some suggestions for growing and using. (1985)
❑ Catalog: $1d, CAN/OV

Le Marche Seeds International

Mail order retail and bulk seed sales acquired by Shepherd's Garden Seeds.

Orol Ledden & Sons
P.O. Box 7
Center & Atlantic Avenues
Sewell, NJ 08080-0007
(609) 468-1000 TO/CC
Don & Dale Ledden

Seeds ～ Supplies ～ Tools ～ Bulbs
Catalog offers over 600 varieties of **flowers, vegetables, grasses and cover crops and some summer-blooming bulbs**, all well described; varieties are both hybrid and open-pollinated, and most seed is available untreated if desired. Also sells a full line of growing supplies and tools, organic pest controls and fertilizers. (1904)
❑ Catalog: Free, R&W, CAN/OV, SS: 2-5,9-10, $10m
⌂ Nursery: All year, daily
▼ Garden: April-September, daily

Ledgecrest Greenhouses
1029 Storrs Road
Storrs, CT 06268
(203) 487-1661

Plants
Offers a good selection of **hardy perennials** in three-inch pots, each briefly described. Plants in larger sizes are available at the nursery, as are general growing supplies.
❑ Catalog: 2 FCS, SS:4-9, bn/cn
⌂ Nursery: All year

Lee's Botanical Gardens
12731 S.W. 14th Street
Miami, FL 33184
(305) 223-0496 TO
Bruce Lee Bednar

Plants
Collectors' list of **carnivorous plants** -- sarracenia, nepenthes, dionaea, drosera, pinquicula, utricularia, catopsis; plants are listed in a jumble of botanical names, but collectors will know them. Some are rare and limited to one per customer. (1980)
❑ Catalog: Free(1 IRC), R&W, CAN/OV, $10m, bn
⌂ Nursery: March-October, weekends, by appointment only
▼ Garden: By appointment only

Lee's Gardens
P.O. Box 5
Tremont, IL 61568

Plants
Hostas, iris, daylilies, wildflowers and other sun- and shade-loving perennials, both common and rare.
❑ Catalog: $1d

Lenette Greenhouses
4345 Rogers Lake Road
Kannapolis, NC 28081
(704) 938-2042
K. G. Griffith

Plants
Catalog offers cattleya and phalaenopsis **hybrid orchids**, in community pots, flasks and blooming sizes, even "stud plants"; plants very briefly described. Also offers miniature cymbidium crosses and a few oncidiums, vandas and paphiopedilums. Most are their own hybrids. (1961)
❑ Catalog: Free, R&W, CAN/OV, SS:W, $20m
⌂ Nursery: All year, M-Sa
▼ Garden: All year, greenhouses, M-Sa

Les Violettes Natalia
124 Ch. Grapes
Sawyerville, PQ, Canada J0B 3A0
(819) 889-3235
Roch & Natalie Pineault

Plants ～ Supplies
A huge selection of **African violets** from many prominent hybridizers -- standards, miniatures and semi-miniatures and trailers, all well described, with a "!" for nearly every one! They also offer a broad selection of other **gesneriads** -- sinningeas, columneas, kohlerias, streptocarpus, gloxinias, achimenes, episcias and aeschynanthus -- and indoor growing supplies. (1987)
❑ Catalog: $2, US/OV, SS:5-10, $15m, bn/cn

W. O. Lessard Nursery
19201 S.W. 248th Street
Homestead, FL 33031
(305) 247-0397 or 248-2666
William O. Lessard

Plants
Catalog lists 31 varieties of **bananas** -- even more sold at the nursery. Some available as corms or plants, some up to large specimens; each plant is very well described. Formerly "Tropical Spices, Etc." (1978)
❑ Catalog: $1, R&W, CAN/OV, SS:3-11
⌂ Nursery: By appointment only

Henry Leuthardt Nurseries, Inc.
P.O. Box 666
Montauk Highway
East Moriches, NY 11940
(516) 878-1387
Henry P. Leuthardt

Plants
A selection of **fruit trees, berries and grapes**, including some old varieties; all briefly to well described. This nursery is also a source of espaliered apple and pear trees in several styles. Their "handbook" is $1, gives more information than the free catalog.
❑ Catalog: Free, R&W, SS:10-12,3-5
⌂ Nursery: All year, daily, call ahead

Lewis Strawberry Nursery
P.O. Box 24
Rocky Point, NC 28457
(919) 675-2394 or 9409 TO
C. E. Lewis

Plants
Fifty varieties of **strawberries**, sold in quantities of 100 and up; no descriptions. Most of the plants are June-bearers; they also carry six everbearing kinds. (1954)
☐ Catalog: Free, R&W, CAN/OV, $12m
⌂ Nursery: All year, M-Sa

Liberty Seed Company
P.O. Box 806
128 - 1st Drive S.E.
New Philadelphia, OH 44663
(216) 364-1611 TO/CC $10m
William & Connie Watson

Seeds ⁊ Supplies
Color and b&w catalog offers a broad selection of garden **annuals** and **perennials**, **vegetables** (including heirloom and open-pollinated varieties), giant pumpkins and super sweet corn; all well described and adapted to the Midwest. Also offers a broad selection of propagation and growing supplies. (1981)
☐ Catalog: Free, R&W, SS:2-5
⌂ Nursery: All year, M-F; March-June, Sa

Life-Form Replicators
P.O. Box 857
Fowlerville, MI 48836
(517) 223-8750
Bob & Layne Stewart

Plants ⁊ Seeds
It may not sound like a nursery, but this small firm specializes in **perennials** grown from selected imported seed from plant breeders in Britain and some Soviet bloc countries. A nice selection which shows their bias for heirloom varieties; all plants are very well described. (1982)
☐ Catalog: $2d, R&W, SS:3-5,9-11, bn
⌂ Nursery: All year, by appointment only
▼ Garden: May-September, by appointment only

Lilypons Water Gardens
P.O. Box 10
6800 Lilypons Road
Lilypons, MD 21717-0010
(301) 874-5133 TO/CC
Charles B. Thomas

Plants ⁊ Books ⁊ Supplies
Color catalog offers a broad selection of **water lilies, lotus, bog plants**, garden ponds, statues, fountains, fish and water gardening supplies. They also have a nursery in Texas, at 839 FM 1489 (P.O. Box 188), Brookshire, TX 77423, (713) 934-8525, with a display garden, too. The photographs are irresistible! (1917)
☐ Catalog: $5(8 IRC), R&W, CAN/OV, SS:3-11, cn/bn
⌂ Nursery: March-October, daily; November-February, M-F
▼ Garden: All year, sales area, M-F

Limerock Ornamental Grasses
RD 1, Box 111C
Port Matilda, PA 16870
(814) 692-2272
Norman Hooven III

Plants
Offers 60 varieties of **ornamental grasses**, each well described, with a list of grasses for various growing conditions and uses. There is a nice introduction to grasses with comments on form, color, texture and motion. (1981)
☐ Catalog: $1, R&W, CAN/OV, SS:3-11, bn/cn
⌂ Nursery: March-November, call ahead
▼ Garden: September-October, call ahead

Limrick, Inc.
6900 S.W. 102nd Avenue
Miami, FL 33173
(305) 595-7919 FAX 595-3520 TO/CC
Kerry Richards

Plants
Offers a broad selection of **hybrid orchids** and a few **species orchids**: broughtonia, many cattleyas, paphiopedilums, phalaenopsis and others; some color photographs and the kind of telegraphic plant descriptions which require some orchid fever to decipher.
☐ Catalog: $2, R&W, CAN/OV, $25m
⌂ Nursery: All year, daily
▼ Garden: Greenhouses, daily

Lindel Lilies
5510 - 239th Street
Langley, BC, Canada V3A 7N6
(604) 534-4729
Linda & Del Knowlton

Bulbs
Offers a broad selection of **hybrid lilies**: trumpets (including sunburst forms), Oriental hybrids, Asiatic hybrids (including Columbia-Platte Asiatics) and some species lilies; all are well described. (1986)
☐ Catalog: Free, R&W, US, SS:fall
⌂ Nursery: June-October, Su-F, call ahead
▼ Garden: June-August, Su-F, call ahead

Linn Farm Perennials
Route 3, Box 281
Charlottesville, VA 22901
Mary Linn Wolf

Plants
Small nursery specializing in **perennial plants**; a nice selection, with each plant very well described and suggestions for use in the garden, many plants illustrated with line drawings. Future catalogs will offer an expanding selection of **gray and silver leaved plants** and other ornamental foliage plants. (1986)
☐ Catalog: $1.50, SS:4-9, bn/cn

Little Valley Farm
RR 3, Box 544
Spring Green, WI 53588
(608) 935-3324
Barbara Glass

Plants ⌘ Seeds ⌘ Books
Small nursery specializes in native plants of the Midwest -- **wildflowers, trees, shrubs and vines** for woods, wetlands and prairie; a nice selection, all plants well described. Also offers some seeds, books on prairie and woodland plants and local workshops on prairie planting. (1978)
❏ Catalog: $.25, R&W, SS:4-5,9-10, cn/bn
⌂ Nursery: May-October, call ahead
▼ Garden: May-October, call ahead

Living Tree Centre
P.O. Box 797
Bolinas, CA 94924
(415) 868-2224
Dr. Jesse Schwartz, John Kozak

Plants
Historic **apples** from England, France, Russia and California's pioneering days, including some "highly aromatic" apples -- over 80 kinds, all well described, with cultural information on apple growing. Also offers apple scion wood, apricots, quince and pears. (1979)
❏ Catalog: $7d, R&W, CAN, SS:1-4
⌂ Nursery: By appointment only

Lloyd's African Violets
2568 E. Main Street
Cato, NY 13033
(315) 626-2314
JoAnn Lloyd

Plants
Sells **African violets**, new introductions of well-known hybridizers: Fredette, Tremblay, Boone, 'Rainbow' (Wasmund), Lyons Greenhouse, Rob's Mini-o-lets, Croteau and others, each well but briefly described. Sells only leaves by mail, plants and growing supplies at the shop. (1975)
❏ Catalog: 1 FCS, CAN/OV, SS:5-11
⌂ Nursery: All year, daily, call ahead
▼ Garden: All year, daily, call ahead

Lockhart Seeds
P.O. Box 1361
3 N. Wilson Way
Stockton, CA 95201
(209) 466-4401 TO/CC
Lockhart Family

Seeds ⌘ Supplies
Color catalog with a broad selection of **vegetables** (both hybrid and open-pollinated) and **Oriental vegetables**, with comparative tables on size, season and disease resistance. Specializes in crops for central California; also offers some growing supplies. (1948)
❏ Catalog: Free, R&W, CAN, $10m, cn/bn
⌂ Nursery: All year, M-F

Lofts Seed, Inc.
P.O. Box 146
Bound Brook, NJ 08805
(800) 526-3890 or (800) 624-1474 (NJ)
Marie Pompei, Mgr.

Seeds
A large dealer in turfgrass seed, Lofts also distributes "Pinto" wildflower seed mixes for Northern, Southern and tropical growing conditions, as well as mixes of perennial or annual wildflowers or wildflowers for semi-shade. Seed is sold in half-pound minimum quantity and in bulk. (1923)
❏ Catalog: Free, R&W, CAN/OV

Logee's Greenhouses
141 North Street
Danielson, CT 06239
(203) 774-8038
Joy Logee Martin

Plants ⌘ Books
A very extensive list of **begonias and other greenhouse and exotic plants** -- many are outdoor plants in warmer climates; all well described with some cultural suggestions, many illustrated in color. It's impossible to convey the variety -- a collector's dream, a houseplant lover's candy store. Catalog published every other year, price refundable with purchase. (1892)
❏ Catalog: $3, CAN/OV, SS:W, $15m, bn/cn
⌂ Nursery: All year, daily
▼ Garden: All year, daily

Lon's Oregon Grapes
P.O. Box 7632
Salem, OR 97303
Lon Rombough

Plants
New company trying to list **table and wine grapes** for as many climates as possible; offers plants and cuttings of over 50 varieties, with more to come. If he doesn't have it, he'll try to find a source. All plants very well described, with notes on hardiness.
❏ Catalog: Long SASE, R&W, CAN/OV, SS:12-4
⌂ Nursery: By appointment only

Long Hungry Creek Nursery
Red Boiling Springs, TN 37150
(615) 699-2784
Jeff Poppen

Plants
Specializing in antique **apples**, as well as newer, hardy, disease-resistant varieties with great taste -- about 50 varieties, including 'Liberty,' 'Arkansas Black,' 'Griffith,' 'Grimes Golden,' 'Spigold,' 'Jonagrimes,' 'Mollies Delicious' -- very brief descriptions. Choice of two rootstocks; some espaliered trees. (1976)
❏ Catalog: Long SASE, R&W, CAN/OV, SS:11-4, $20m
⌂ Nursery: All year, call ahead
▼ Garden: All year, call ahead

Long's Gardens
P.O. Box 19
3240 Broadway
Boulder, CO 80306
(303) 442-2353
Catherine Long Gates

Plants
List offers broad selection of **tall bearded irises**, with several collec-
tions and progressive savings on larger purchases. During blooming time
you can visit the nursery, select your favorites and dig them up on the spot.
Sells a few border, intermediate and dwarf bearded irises as well; brief
descriptions. (1905)
❑ Catalog: Free, SS:7-8
⌂ Nursery: Late May-early June, daily, call ahead
▼ Garden: May-June, tall bearded irises, call ahead

Lost Prairie Herb Farm
805 Kienas Road
Kalispell, MT 59901
(406) 755-3742 TO/CC $12m
Diane Downs

Plants ⌇ **Supplies**
Hardy herbs, ground covers and perennials for Northern climates, briefly to
well described; a broad selection of very hardy plants for extreme winters.
Also offers organic pest controls and flea controls for pets. (1977)
❑ Catalog: $2, SS:4-10, $6m, cn/bn
⌂ Nursery: April-October, daily, call ahead
▼ Garden: June-August, daily, call ahead

Loucks Nursery
P.O. Box 102
14200 Campground Road
Cloverdale, OR 97112
(503) 392-3166 TO
Mert & Marjorie Loucks

Plants
Specializes in **Japanese maples** for bonsai and container growing. Offers
a broad selection of cultivars by their Japanese cultivar names; each plant
well described. Small nursery offers over 100 cultivars. (1955)
❑ Catalog: $1, R&W, CAN
⌂ Nursery: All year, daily, call ahead
▼ Garden: All year, daily, call ahead

Louisiana Nursery
Route 7, Box 43
Highway 182
Opelousas, LA 70570
(318) 948-3696 or 942-6404
Ken, Albert & Dalton Durio

Plants
Magnolias -- 350 cultivars -- and many other unusual trees, shrubs, vines
and other collectors' plants in catalog (M); catalog (D) has a huge selection
of daylilies, Louisiana, spuria and Pseudacorus irises, cannas, ginger,
liriope and related plants. Catalog (C) lists **crinums**. Endless lovely
choices; plants are briefly but well described. (1950)
❑ Catalog: $5(M),$3(D),$2(C), R&W, CAN/OV, bn/cn
⌂ Nursery: All year, daily

Paul P. Lowe
5741 Dewberry Way
West Palm Beach, FL 33415
Paul P. Lowe

Plants
A collectors' list of **bromeliads, species orchids and begonias**; plants very
briefly described. Bromeliads sold as unrooted offsets ("pups"), begonias in
quantities of 50 or 100 unrooted cuttings. Wide selection; you might send a
"want list" for special items. Cannot ship to Hawaii. (1957)
❑ Catalog: $1, SS:4-11, $10m

Lowe's own-root Roses
6 Sheffield Road
Nashua, NH 03062
(603) 888-2214
Malcolm (Mike) Lowe

Plants
A catalog of **old roses**, grown on their own roots; a wide selection of many
types, including species roses and some of the modern shrub roses of contemporary hybridizers in Europe and the US. For $5 they also sell a collectors'
list of hundreds of rare roses which they will custom-bud or propagate to
order; these might take up to eighteen months to deliver. (1979)
❑ Catalog: $2($3 OV), CAN/OV, SS:10, $8m, bn/cn
▼ Garden: June, by appointment only

The Lowrey Nursery
2323 Sleepy Hollow Road
Conroe, TX 77385
(713) 367-4076
Katie Ferguson

Plants
Offers **Southwestern native plants** for use in the landscape; many are
selections or hybrids of their own propagation. Plants are well adapted to
home or commercial environments. (1970)
❑ Catalog: Free, R&W, SS:11-2, $25m
⌂ Nursery: All year, M-Sa
▼ Garden: March-June, M-Sa

Lyndon Lyon Greenhouses, Inc.
14 Mutchler Street
Dolgeville, NY 13329-0249
(315) 429-8291
Paul & Sidney Sorano

Plants
This firm is the originator of many favorite **African violets** and also sells
streptocarpus, episcias, columneas and other houseplants; many are illus-
trated in color photographs, with good brief plant descriptions. (1954)
❑ Catalog: $1, R&W, CAN/OV, SS:5-10, $14m
⌂ Nursery: All year, daily
▼ Garden: All year, daily

McClure & Zimmerman
P.O. Box 368
108 W. Winnebago
Friesland, WI 53935
(414) 326-4220 TO/CC $20m
J. W. Jung Seed Co.

Books ⌇ **Bulbs**
A very large selection of **bulbs**, both the common spring Dutch bulbs and a
wide selection of species bulbs not so easy to find -- species tulips, bulbous irises, hardy cyclamen, summer-blooming bulbs; all very well described,
many charmingly illustrated. Books on bulbs, too. (1980)
❑ Catalog: Free, SS:8-11, bn

McConnell Nurseries, Inc.
RR 1
Port Burwell, ON, Canada N0J 1T0
(519) 874-4405 or 4800 TO/CC
James G. Collins, Pres.

Plants ◈ Bulbs
Color catalog offers a large selection of **general nursery stock** -- roses, berries of all kinds, ornamental trees and shrubs, spring bulbs and garden perennials; all plants well described. They also advertise under other names. (1912)
❏ Catalog: Free, R&W, SS:3-11, cn/bn
⌂ Nursery: All year, M-S

McCrory's Sunny Hill Herb Farm
35152 LaPlace Court
Eustis, FL 32726
(904) 357-9876
Ward & Dolores McCrory

Plants
A nice selection of **herbs and scented geraniums**, each very briefly described, with notes on use. They also sell **bromeliads** at the nursery.
❏ Catalog: $.50d, R&W, $8m, cn/bn
⌂ Nursery: All year, daily, call ahead

Boris McCubbin
508 Cappy Drive
Knoxville, TN 37920
(615) 579-1218

Seeds
"Seeds for nearly every kind of **gourd** imaginable, from the charming and colorful to the giant dippers and kettles." Seed list not received. (1982)
❏ Catalog: $.50, CAN/OV

McDaniel's Miniature Roses
7523 Zemco Street
Lemon Grove, CA 92045
(619) 469-4669
Earl & Agnes McDaniel

Plants
List offers about a hundred **miniature roses**, listed by color; all briefly described, petal count frequently given. Many are their own hybrids. (1973)
❏ Catalog: Free, CAN/OV
⌂ Nursery: All year, M-Sa, call ahead
▼ Garden: April-May, call ahead

McFayden Seeds
P.O. Box 1800
Brandon, MB, Canada R7A 6A6
(204) 727-0766

Plants ◈ Seeds ◈ Books ◈ Supplies ◈ Tools ◈ Bulbs
Offers a broad selection of **general nursery stock**, flower and vegetable seeds, spring-blooming bulbs and perennials; color catalog also offers tools and supplies as well as kitchen and canning items.
❏ Catalog: $2, SS:4-5,9

McKinney's Glasshouse
89 Mission Road
Wichita, KS 67207
(316) 686-9438 or 684-5333
James McKinney & Charles Pickard

Plants ◈ Supplies
"We are **gesneriad specialists**, with a large supply of African violets, episcias and diminutive terrarium plants." Also lists growing supplies and terrariums in many styles. (1946)
❏ Catalog: $1.50, CAN/OV, bn/cn
⌂ Nursery: By appointment only

Rod McLellan Co.
1450 El Camino Real
South San Francisco, CA 94080
(415) 871-5655 TO/CC $20m
David Balster, Mgr.

Plants ◈ Books ◈ Supplies
Color catalog offers many types of **orchids**. Nursery specializes in hybridizing cattleyas and cymbidiums, but also offers miltonias, oncidiums, brassias, odontoglossums, phalaenopsis and more. Also sells books on orchids, orchid food and potting mixture. (1895)
❏ Catalog: $2(3 IRC), R&W, CAN/OV, SS:4-10, $10m
⌂ Nursery: All year, daily
▼ Garden: All year, greenhouses, tours

McMillen's Iris Garden
RR 1
Norwich, ON, Canada N0J 1P0
(519) 468-6508
John & Gloria McMillen

Plants
Offers a very large selection of **daylilies and irises**; they grow over 100 daylilies and 1,000 irises in their gardens. Irises are tall, border and dwarf bearded, "novelty" and Siberian; good plant descriptions. (1973)
❏ Catalog: $1, US, SS:8-9, $30m
⌂ Nursery: All year, call ahead
▼ Garden: June-July, daily

Ma-Dot-Cha Hobby Nursery
300 Montezuma Avenue
Dothan, AL 36303
(205) 792-6970
Mark S. Cannon

Plants
Sells only **camellia scions** from his personal collection. Write and ask if he has the cultivars you're looking for; send long SASE for reply.
❏ Catalog: See notes, $10m
⌂ Nursery: All year, call ahead

Mad River Imports
P.O. Box 1685
North Fayston Road
Moretown, VT 05660
(802) 496-3004
Jeffrey M. Rice

Books ◈ Bulbs
Offers a wide selection of **spring-flowering bulbs** -- tulips, daffodils, crocus and the "minor bulbs" -- all briefly described; bulbs are sold by five, ten and twenty-five. They also sell hybrid Asiatic lilies and some books on growing special bulbs.
❏ Catalog: Free, SS:10, cn/bn

Magnolia Nursery & Display Garden
12615 Roberts Road
Chunchula, AL 36521
(205) 675-4696 or 8471 (evenings)
David Ellis

Plants
Offers a good selection of **Southeastern native plants**: species azaleas, Louisiana irises, native magnolias such as the "bigleaf," as well as Gresham hybrid magnolias, camellias, evergreen azaleas, holly, Japanese irises and other desirable landscape plants. (1985)
❏ Catalog: $1d, R&W, CAN/OV, SS:11-3, $50m, bn
⌂ Nursery: All year, M-F; by appointment only on weekends
▼ Garden: All year, M-F; by appointment only on weekends

Makielski Berry Farm & Nursery
7130 Platt Road
Ypsilanti, MI 48197
(313) 434-3673 or 572-0060 TO/CC
Edward & Diane Makielski

Plants
Specializes in **bramble berries**: raspberries, blackberries, currants, gooseberries, all state-inspected. Also sells strawberries, rhubarb, blueberries, asparagus, grapes and fruit trees. All plants well described, with good information on bearing season, flavor and use. (1954)
❏ Catalog: Free, R&W, CAN/OV, SS:11-5
⌂ Nursery: November-June, daily

Ann Mann's Orchids
9045 Ron-Den Lane
Windemere, FL 34786
(407) 876-2625
Ann Mann

Plants ⌇ Books ⌇ Supplies
Very large selection of orchids, bromeliads, hoyas, anthuriums, alocasias and other **exotic plants**, all briefly described with cultural notes. Also sells water purifiers, cork, charcoal and other growing supplies, including their own potting fiber, "Husky-Fiber," and New Zealand sphagnum moss.
❏ Catalog: $1, SS:W, $20m, bn
⌂ Nursery: By appointment only

Maple Leaf Nursery
4236 Greenstone Road
Placerville, CA 95667
(916) 622-2265
Bob Barnard

Plants
A small new nursery which offers **plants for bonsai** and other unusual plants for the garden: deciduous and evergreen azaleas, both species and hybrids, ornamental trees and shrubs, cistus, halimiocistus, helianthemum, unusual lavenders and rosemary; every plant very well described. (1987)
❏ Catalog: $1.50, SS:2-5,9-11, bn/cn
⌂ Nursery: February-November, M-W, by appointment only

Maple Tree Gardens
P.O. Box 547
208 First Street
Ponca, NE 68770
(402) 755-2615
Larry L. Harder

Plants
Bearded irises: standard tall, miniature and standard dwarf, intermediate, miniature tall and border, as well as arilbred and Siberian irises. Also **daylilies**, a real collectors' list; broad selection with brief plant descriptions. (1961)
❏ Catalog: Free, CAN/OV, SS:7-10, $10m
▼ Garden: May, July, by appointment only

Maplewood Seed Company
311 Maplewood Lane
Lake Oswego, OR 97470-9236
(503) 672-1023
J. D. Vertrees

Seeds
Offers seed of many cultivars of **Acer palmatum and other species maples**; all seed is freshly harvested. Maples for specialists, collectors and bonsai; no plant descriptions. Japanese maples listed by Japanese cultivar names. Mr. Vertrees is the author of **the** book on maples. Seed list sent in autumn. (1980)
❏ Catalog: Long SASE(2 IRC), CAN/OV, SS:11-5, $2m, bn
⌂ Nursery: By appointment only
▼ Garden: May-June, October, by appointment only

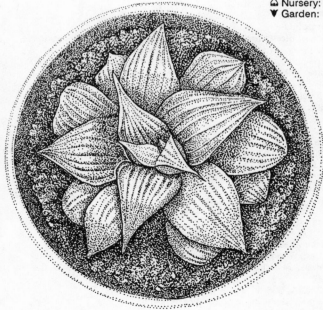

© Succulent Plants
Artist: Lisa Moran

Marilynn's Garden
13421 Sussex Place
8184 Katella Ave (Stanton)
Santa Ana, CA 92705
(714) 995-4133
Marilynn Cohen

Plants
Offers a nice selection of **drought-tolerant plants** and **bromeliads** on two separate lists; no plant descriptions. The drought-tolerant list offers aloes, agaves, crassulas, euphorbias, kalanchoe, opuntias, epiphyllums, hoyas and rhipsalis. Also offers plumerias and Mexican species orchids. (1972)
⬜ Catalog: $2, R&W, CAN/OV, $50m, bn
⌂ Nursery: By appointment only

Maroushek Gardens
120 E. 11th Street
Hastings, MN 55033
(612) 437-9754
Lillian Maroushek

Plants
An extensive selection of **hostas** -- about 100 varieties -- with no plant descriptions. They also have a nice selection of hybrid **clematis**, some not listed often, and some rock garden plants and shade perennials for sale only at the nursery. (1976)
⬜ Catalog: $.50d, SS:5,8-9, bn/cn
⌂ Nursery: May-October, call ahead
▼ Garden: May-August, rock garden, call ahead

Marrs Tree Farm
9802 - 62nd Avenue, Ct. E.
Payallup, WA 98373
(206) 848-4833
Gevan R. Marrs

Plants
Small nursery specializing in **plants for bonsai**, both conifers and broadleaved. Most seem to be seedlings of up to seven years; all are well described -- a nice selection. (1986)
⬜ Catalog: $1d, R&W, SS:10-4, $25m, cn/bn

Marston Exotics
Brampton Lane
Madley, Hereford, England HR1 9LX
(0981) 251140
Paul F. Gardner

Plants ⚭ **Books** ⚭ **Supplies**
Very wide selection of **carnivorous plants**; each plant lovingly described and many illustrated in charming drawings. Export orders require a permit; plants are shipped bare-root; minimum overseas orders £100.
⬜ Catalog: $1(US bills), R&W, CAN/OV, UK100m, bn/cn
⌂ Nursery: All year, M-F, by appointment only
▼ Garden: All year, M-F, by appointment only

Marvelous Minis
30840 Wentworth Street
Livonia, MI 48154
(313) 261-6767
Ron Brenton

Plants
Specializes in **miniature African violets**, with a few standards from well-known hybridizers. Also other **miniature plants** for terraria and dish gardens -- begonias, gesneriads, ferns and other very small plants; all plants briefly described.
⬜ Catalog: $1d, R&W, SS:5-10, $15m, bn
⌂ Nursery: By appointment only

Mary's Plant Farm
2410 Lanes Mill Road
Hamilton, OH 45013
(513) 892-2055 or 894-0022
Mary & Sherri Harrison

Plants
Offer a wide selection of **perennials**, including species geraniums, irises, ornamental grasses, herbs and hostas. Also sell a number of **trees and shrubs**, many good for smaller gardens: berberis, hydrangeas, spireas, lilacs, viburnums, amelancheir, dogwood and crabapples, as well as some wildflowers and ferns. Plants very briefly described; they send a newsletter to their customers. (1977)
⬜ Catalog: $1d, SS:3-11, bn/cn
⌂ Nursery: March-October, Tu-Sa
▼ Garden: March-October, Tu-Sa

Maryland Aquatic Nurseries
3427 N. Furnace Road
Jarrettsville, MD 21084
(301) 557-7615
Richard J. Schuck

Plants ⚭ **Supplies**
Good selection of **plants for ponds, pools and bogs**: water lilies, Japanese and Louisiana irises, ornamental grasses. All plants are well but briefly described. They also sell a unique "clear-water" treatment system to keep water algae-free. (1986)
⬜ Catalog: $2, R&W, CAN, $25, bn
⌂ Nursery: All year, daily, call ahead
▼ Garden: All year, daily, call ahead

Maryott's Gardens
1073 Bird Avenue
San Jose, CA 95125
(408) 971-0444 TO/CC
Marilyn Harlow, Mgr.

Plants
A good choice of **tall and standard dwarf bearded irises** for collectors; new introductions are well described, others fairly briefly. They also offer a number of collections of special irises. (1978)
⬜ Catalog: $1d, R&W, OV, SS:7-8, $15m
⌂ Nursery: April-May, W-Su
▼ Garden: April, W-Su

Matsu-Momiji Nursery
P.O. Box 11414
410 Borbeck St.
Philadelphia, PA 19111
(215) 722-6286 (after 4 pm)
Steve Pilacik

Plants ⚭ **Supplies** ⚭ **Tools**
A collectors' list of many cultivars of Japanese black pine (Pinus thunbergii), spruces, Japanese maples and other **plants for bonsai**, each fairly briefly described. The pines cannot be shipped to several Western states -- inquire for details. Also finished bonsai, pots, supplies and courses at the nursery. (1980)
⬜ Catalog: $2, CAN, $35m
⌂ Nursery: All year, daily, by appointment only
▼ Garden: April-September, daily, by appointment only

Mauna Kea Orchids
206 Ainako Avenue
Hilo, HI 96720
(808) 935-4081 or 961-7316
Wendell J. Cabanas

Plants
"Concentrates on offering promising **cattleya and phalaenopsis** clones
for the home grower." (1980)
❑ Catalog: Free, CAN/OV, SS:3-11, $25m

Maver Rare Perennials

See The Seed Source.

Maxim's Greenwood Gardens
2157 Sonoma Street
Redding, CA 96001
(916) 241-0764
Georgia Maxim

Plants ⚭ Bulbs
A huge selection of **irises**: bearded in various sizes, Japanese and Siberian
irises, Pacific Coast Hybrids, arilbreds, spuria and Louisiana irises. Also
some tetraploid and diploid daylilies and a broad selection of novelty daffo-
dils (offered every three years). All briefly described. (1955)
❑ Catalog: $1, CAN, SS:7-11
⌂ Nursery: All year, call ahead
▼ Garden: March-June, call ahead

Earl May Seed & Nursery Co.
208 N. Elm Street
Shenandoah, IA 51603
(712) 246-1020 or (800) 831-4193 TO/CC
Rankin Family

Plants ⚭ Seeds ⚭ Supplies ⚭ Tools ⚭ Bulbs
Seasonal color catalogs offer general nursery stock, seeds, bulbs, peren-
nials and garden supplies -- a traditional **garden emporium**; all plants well
described, with cultural suggestions. (1919)
❑ Catalog: Free, R&W, SS:2-5, cn/bn
⌂ Nursery: 58 garden centers in the Midwest
▼ Garden: Test garden open to the public

Meadowlake Gardens
Route 4, Box 709
Walterboro, SC 29488
(803) 844-2359 or 2545 TO/CC $50m
John Allgood

Plants
Offer a wide selection of **daylilies**, including a number of new introductions from various hybridizers. They also sell **Japanese irises** and
hostas which will be listed again in the next catalog. Plant descriptions
vary from very detailed to good but brief. (1960)
❑ Catalog: $3d, R&W, CAN/OV, SS:3-5,8-11, $20m
▼ Garden: Garden open May 22-June 22

Mellinger's, Inc.
2310 W. South Range Road
North Lima, OH 44452
(216) 549-9861 or (800) 321-7444 TO/CC
Philip & Jean Steiner

Plants ⚭ Seeds ⚭ Books ⚭ Supplies ⚭ Tools ⚭ Bulbs
Catalog is a large general store of home and commercial gardening supplies,
books, seeds and plants of all kinds -- impossible to fit into any category.
It's hard to believe that they can carry so many items -- 4,000 by their
count! It's a jumble of delights with plants in no logical order, and great
fun to peruse. (1927)
❑ Catalog: Free, R&W, CAN/OV, $10m, cn/bn
⌂ Nursery: All year, M-Sa
▼ Garden: All year, M-Sa

Merry Gardens
P.O. Box 595
Mechanic Street
Camden, ME 04843
(207) 236-9064
Mary Ellen Ross

Plants
Catalog lists **herbs, scented and miniature geraniums, many ivy culti-
vars** and **fuchsias**, as well as flowering vines, ferns, succulents and
other foliage plants for home and conservatory. Collectors' list; plants
very briefly described. (1947)
❑ Catalog: $1, CAN, SS:3-12, $10m, bn/cn
⌂ Nursery: All year, M-Sa
▼ Garden: May-October, M-Sa

Mesa Garden
P.O. Box 72
Belen, NM 87002
(505) 864-3131
Steven & Linda Brack

Plants ⚭ Seeds
A very extensive collectors' list of **cacti and succulents**, both seed and
seed-grown plants, with very brief descriptions including habitat data.
German and British customers may send orders in local currency to agents
in those countries. Seed list in January, plant list in spring; guaranteed
to thrill collectors! (1976)
❑ Catalog: 2 FCS(2 IRC), R&W, CAN/OV, SS:W, bn
⌂ Nursery: By appointment only
▼ Garden: By appointment only

Messelaar Bulb Co.
P.O. Box 269
County Road, Route 1-A
Ipswich, MA 01938
(508) 356-3737
Pieter Messelaar

Bulbs
Importer of **spring- and summer-flowering Dutch bulbs** sells in quantities
from five to hundreds; plants are briefly described, and many are illustrated
in color. (1946)
❑ Catalog: Free, R&W, SS:9-12,2-5, $10m
⌂ Nursery: September-December, M-Sa, Su pm

Meta Horticultural Labs
Meta, KY 41501
(606) 432-1516 TO/CC
James W. Lawson

Seeds
Sells seeds of 95 kinds of Northeastern **deciduous fruit and nut trees** --
black mulberry, pawpaws, persimmons, black walnuts and some species
maples -- some of these seeds are habitat-collected. They also sell 15 "true
strains" of **gourd** seeds.
❒ Catalog: $1d, CAN/OV
⌂ Nursery: All year, call ahead

Roger & Shirley Meyer
16531 Mount Shelly Circle
Fountain Valley, CA 92708
(714) 839-0796 (evenings)
Roger & Shirley Meyer

Plants ❧ Seeds
Small nursery offers scionwood of thirty varieties of **kiwi and hardy kiwi,**
ten varieties of **jujube** (bare-root jujube trees available from January to
March) and other **unusual fruits** such as Surinam cherry, lychee, Mexican
yellow guava and dwarf banana. Also offers seeds of jujube, cherimoya,
yellow tamarillo and horned melon. No plant descriptions. (1975)
❒ Catalog: Long SASE, CAN/OV, SS:1-3, cn
⌂ Nursery: By appointment only
▼ Garden: By appointment only

Meyer Seed Co.
600 S. Caroline Street
Baltimore, MD 21231
(301) 342-4224

Seeds ❧ Supplies ❧ Tools ❧ Bulbs
Specializes in **vegetable and flower seeds** which do well in the Baltimore-
Washington, DC, area. Catalog is informative to the home or commercial grow-
er and also offers supplies, equipment and summer-blooming bulbs. (1910)
❒ Catalog: Free, R&W

Miami Orchids
22150 S.W. 147th Avenue
Miami, FL 33170
(305) 258-2664 TO/CC
Milton Millon

Plants
List offers dendrobium, phalaenopsis, oncidium, cattleya and minicattleya
orchids in various-sized pots, and some **species orchids** mounted on
driftwood or in cedar baskets; descriptions are very brief. Also sells
orchid growing supplies. (1987)
❒ Catalog: $1, R&W, CAN/OV, $20m
⌂ Nursery: All year, M-Sa
▼ Garden: All year, M-Sa

MicroCulture, Inc.
P.O. Box 3004-222
Corvallis, OR 97339
(503) 754-7771 TO/CC
Shel Perrigan & Mike O'Hare

Plants
Sells mini-tubers of several varieties of **potatoes:** 'All Blue,' 'Desiree,'
'Yellow Finn,' 'Russett Burbank' and 'Red Pontiac.' New varieties being
added; list available in September. (1984)
❒ Catalog: Free, R&W, CAN/OV, SS:12-5

Mid-America Iris Gardens
3409 N. Geraldine Avenue
Oklahoma City, OK 73112
(405) 946-5743
Paul W. Black

Plants
Color catalog offers a very broad selection of **bearded and reblooming
irises** in several sizes; each plant very briefly described, but new
introductions and his twenty favorites get lots of ink. (1978)
❒ Catalog: $1($4 OV), CAN/OV, SS:7-8, $10m
⌂ Nursery: March-September, daily
▼ Garden: March-September, daily

Midwest Cactus
P.O. Box 163
New Melle, MO 63365
(314) 828-5389
Chris M. Smith

Plants
Specializes in hardy **opuntia cacti** for year-round outdoor gardens; plants
are shown in b&w photographs, briefly described with good growing information, grouped by best cultural conditions. (1984)
❒ Catalog: $.50, CAN, SS:4-9, $5m, bn

Mighty Minis
7318 Sahara Court
Sacramento, CA 95828
(916) 421-7284
Jean Stokes

Plants ❧ Supplies
A small nursery selling **miniature African violets** (plants and leaves) and
mini-begonias and other gesneriads. A broad selection; each brief
description has lots of !!! They also sell plastic "egg" terrariums for use
with tiny plants. (1982)
❒ Catalog: $1d, CAN/OV, SS:5-10, $15m
⌂ Nursery: All year, by appointment only
▼ Garden: All year, by appointment only

Milaeger's Gardens
4838 Douglas Avenue
Racine, WI 53402-2498
(414) 639-2371 or 2040 TO/CC
Kevin D. Milaeger

Plants
A broad selection of **perennials,** including a good selection of mostly
modern roses, clematis, shade plants, prairie wildflowers and ornamental
grasses; all very well described, many illustrated in color photographs.
The catalog is accurately called "The Perennial Wishbook." (1960)
❒ Catalog: $1d, R&W, SS:3-6, $25m, bn/cn
⌂ Nursery: All year, daily
▼ Garden: Spring-summer, daily

Miller Grass Seed Company
P.O. Box 886
Hereford, TX 79045
(806) 258-7288
Joe & Tom Miller

Seeds
Offers seeds of **native grasses, wheatgrasses, legumes and pasture grasses**
as well as seeds of **Southwestern wildflowers and native plants,** such as
"rubber rabbitbrush." Many seeds are habitat-collected; there are no plant
descriptions. (1939)
❐ Catalog: Free, R&W, cn/bn

J. E. Miller Nurseries, Inc.
5060 W. Lake Road
Canandaigua, NY 14424
(716) 396-2647 or (800) 828-9630 TO/CC $10m
John & David Miller

Plants ∾ Supplies
Color catalog offers a broad selection of **fruit and nut trees,** berries of
all kinds, grapes, ornamental trees and supplies; each plant well described,
many illustrated. (1936)
❐ Catalog: Free, R&W, SS:2-6, 10-11, $5m, cn
⌂ Nursery: All year, M-Sa
▼ Garden: April-May, growing area, M-Sa

Miller's Manor Gardens
3167 E. US 224
Ossian, IN 46777
(219) 597-7403
Roger & Lynda Miller

Plants
Offers **bearded irises** of all types: an extensive list featuring newer
median and dwarf irises, each very briefly described. Also offers a number
of **Siberian iris** cultivars, as well as a nice selection of **daylilies.**
Small nursery; some plants may be in short supply. (1976)
❐ Catalog: $.50, R&W, CAN/OV, SS:7-9, $10m
⌂ Nursery: April-October, M-Tu, Th-Sa
▼ Garden: May, M-Tu, Th-Sa

Miller-Bowie County Farmers Assn.
P.O. Box 1110
1007 W. 3rd Street
Texarkana, TX 75502
(214) 794-3631
Harlon Robinson, Seed Dept.

Seeds
Formerly Bunch's Seeds, and more recently Aurora Gardens. They offer, among
other regional crops, cowhorn okra, rattlesnake beans, willow leaf pole lima
beans and many varieties of Southern peas: **vegetables for Southern gardens.**
❐ Catalog: Free, R&W, CAN/OV, $5m
⌂ Nursery: All year, M-F, Sa am

Miniature Plant Kingdom
4125 Harrison Grade Road
Sebastopol, CA 95472
(707) 874-2233
Don Herzog

Plants
Offers a good selection of **miniature roses,** including their own hybrids, as
well as **Japanese maples, conifers and plants for bonsai.** The bonsai list
has grown to take over most of the catalog; desirable plants, many of which
have fruit and/or flowers. (1965)
❐ Catalog: $2.50, R&W, SS:W, $7m
⌂ Nursery: All year, Th-Su
▼ Garden: Spring-summer, Th-Su

Grant Mitsch Novelty Daffodils
P.O. Box 218
Hubbard, OR 97032
(503) 651-2742 (evenings)
Dick & Elise Havens

Bulbs
Specialize in rarer hybrids of **daffodils,** including those of Grant E.
Mitsch, as well as many others; each plant is very well described, and many
are illustrated in color in an informative catalog. Grant Mitsch was
introducing new cultivars until the time of his death at 81; the Havenses
carry on the family tradition. (1927)
❐ Catalog: $3d, CAN/OV, SS:9-10
▼ Garden: Spring, daffodils, call ahead

Mohns, Inc.
P.O. Box 2301
Atascadero, CA 93423
(805) 466-4362
Jim DeWelt, Mgr.

Plants
Offer their own 'Minicaps' strain of perennial **Oriental poppies,** bred
especially for the warm winter climate of central and southern California.
They come in a choice of several shades of red, pink and orange and in
dwarf, standard and tall heights. (1983)
❐ Catalog: 2 FCS, SS:3-5

Monashee Gardens
Site 6, Box 9, RR 7
Vernon, BC, Canada V1T 7Z3
(604) 542-2592
John & Margaret Montgomery

Plants
A new nursery offering a nice selection of **daylilies, dwarf bearded irises,
Siberian irises, alliums and hybrid lilies;** plants are briefly described.
Customers will receive their "Monashee Bulletin Board" three times a year;
it's full of planting and cultural information. (1988)
❐ Catalog: Long SASE, US, SS:7-10

Montrose Nursery
P.O. Box 957
Hillsborough, NC 27278
(919) 732-7787
Nancy Goodwin

Plants
Small nursery specializes in seed-grown hardy **species cyclamen** (large
selection) and **primulas,** but also offers other perennials and rock garden
plants -- asters, aquilegias, irises, phlox, salvias, helibores and more; all
very well described. Many are Southeastern native plants, tested at the
nursery for heat and cold tolerance. Collectors' delight! (1984)
❐ Catalog: $1.50, SS:2-5,9-12, bn
⌂ Nursery: All year, M-Sa, by appointment only
▼ Garden: All year, by appointment only

Moon Mountain Wildflowers
P.O. Box 34
864 Napa Avenue
Morro Bay, CA 93442-0034
(805) 772-2473 TO/CC $15m
Donna Vaiano

Seeds ⬥ Books
Informative catalog lists **annual and perennial wildflowers** of many areas, including mixes suitable for many habitats or uses, sold in packets and in bulk. Plants well described with cultural suggestions. Also sells wild-flower posters of Calif. Native Plant Society and wildflower books. (1981)
▢ Catalog: $1(5 IRC), R&W, CAN/OV, bn/cn
⌂ Nursery: All year, M-Sa
▼ Garden: Spring-summer, call ahead

Moonshine Gardens
P.O. Box 367
Potter Valley, CA 95469
(707) 998-3055 or 743-1570
Monty Byers

Plants
A very large selection of **bearded irises** of all types: tall bearded, dwarf, border, median, intermediate, horned, many reblooming; all plants very well described. Growing area is at 12570-A Powerhouse Road, Potter Valley. (1985)
▢ Catalog: Free, OV, SS:7-9
⌂ Nursery: April-May, Oct, daily (take orders at garden)
▼ Garden: April-May, October, daily (see notes)

Moore Water Gardens
P.O. Box 340
Highway 4
Port Stanley, ON, Canada N0L 2A0
(519) 782-4052
Sue See

Plants ⬥ Books ⬥ Supplies
A good selection of **water lilies, lotus, aquatic plants,** supplies and ponds for water gardens, all well described in an informative catalog, some illustrated in color. Also a number of books on water gardening. (1930)
▢ Catalog: Free, R&W, SS:4-9, $5m, bn/cn
⌂ Nursery: All year, call ahead
▼ Garden: May-August, call ahead

Moosebell Flower, Fruit & Tree Co.
Route 1, Box 240
St. Francis, ME 04774
Paul Sprung

Plants
Small nursery offering **very hardy fruit trees** for cold climates: apples, crabapples, cherry plums, Siberian pears, gooseberries and currants. All plants are very well described as to taste, habit and culture.
▢ Catalog: Free, SS:4-5

Morden Nurseries, Ltd.
P.O. Box 1270
Morden, MB, Canada R0G 1J0
(204) 822-3311
Herman Temmerman

Plants
A good selection of **hardy fruit trees, ornamental trees and shrubs, roses,** and **perennials.** Color catalog, some plants illustrated. Offers fruiting and ornamental crabapples, apples, plums, apricots and berries -- all very hardy; plants briefly described. (1964)
▢ Catalog: Free
⌂ Nursery: All year, M-F; hours vary, call ahead

Mt. Leo Nursery
P.O. Box 135
603 Beersheba Street
McMinnville, TN 37110
(615) 473-7833
Virginia Pearsall

Plants
List offers a nice selection of **evergreens, flowering trees and shrubs, ground covers and fruit and nut trees;** sizes listed but no descriptions. List includes thorn-free blackberries, apples, apricots, pears, peaches, plums, berries and grapes, flowering and shade trees and shrubs. (1982)
▢ Catalog: Free, R&W, CAN/OV, SS:10-4, cn
⌂ Nursery: All year, daily

Mt. Tahoma Nursery
28111 - 112th Avenue East
Graham, WA 98338
(206) 847-9827 TO/CC
Rick Lupp

Plants
Small nursery offers a very nice selection of **alpine plants** for collectors, as well as a number of **small shrubs and dwarf conifers** ideal for gardeners with limited space. All plants very well described, with brief indications as to culture. Troughs for trough gardens available at the nursery. (1985)
▢ Catalog: $1, R&W, CAN, bn
⌂ Nursery: Weekends, by appointment only
▼ Garden: Weekends, April-May, by appointment only

Mountain Mist Nursery

See Barber Nursery.

Mountain Seed & Nursery

See Northplan/Mountain Seed.

Mountain Valley Seeds & Nursery
1798 North 1200 East
Logan, UT 84321
(801) 752-0247 TO/CC $5m
D. Agathangelides

Seeds ⬥ Supplies
A selection of **vegetable seed,** many open-pollinated and suitable for short-season regions, and **annual garden flowers;** all plants well described with planting suggestions. Also sells Treesaver trunk protectors and Solarcap plant protectors for starting vegetables in cold climates. (1974)
▢ Catalog: Free, R&W, CAN/OV
⌂ Nursery: All year, M-Sa

Mowbray Gardens
3318 Mowbray Lane
Cincinnati, OH 45226
(513) 321-0694 TO
Christopher Trautmann

Plants
Sells very hardy **species and hybrid rhododendrons** for cold climates, including hybrids of Leach, Pride and Delp; nursery is in Zone 6. Also offers a rhododendron seed list of hand-pollinated crosses (seed list $1). (1976)
▢ Catalog: Free, $25m

Mums by Paschke
12286 E. Main Road
North East, PA 16428
(814) 725-9860
Jack Paschke

Plants
A good selection of hybrid **chrysanthemums** available to home gardeners from
a large wholesaler. Pamphlet gives good plant descriptions, offers 78
varieties to choose from, listed by color. (1933)
☐ Catalog: Free, R&W, SS:3-6, $10m
⌂ Nursery: April-November, daily

Mushroompeople
P.O. Box 159
Inverness, CA 94937
(415) 663-8504
Jennifer Snyder & Bob Harris

Seeds ᘒ Books ᘒ Supplies ᘒ Tools
Specializes in spawn of **shiitake mushrooms**, both cold and warm weather
strains, and advises farmers and home growers on setting up shiitake growing
operations. Also offers complete growing supplies, books on mushroom
growing, hunting and cooking and a video cassette on shiitake growing in
Japan. (1976)
☐ Catalog: Free, R&W, CAN/OV, $3m, cn/bn
▼ Garden: M-F, by appointment only

Musser Forests Inc.
P.O. Box 340
Route 119 North
Indiana, PA 15701
(412) 465-5686 TO/CC
Fred A. Musser

Plants
Supplies a broad selection of ornamental trees and shrubs in transplant
sizes: **conifers, flowering trees and shrubs, hedging plants and ground
covers** for the gardener and commercial grower. Good descriptions, some
color photographs. (1928)
☐ Catalog: Free, R&W, CAN/OV, SS:3-5,9-12, $10m, cn/bn
⌂ Nursery: March-November, daily
▼ Garden: April-May, trees & shrubs, daily

National Heirloom Flower Seed Exchange
136 Irving Street
Cambridge, MA 02138
Robert Bourne

Seeds
New **seed exchange** formed by an estate gardener looking for heirloom and
rare flowers to use in reproductions of period gardens or plants historically
used as medicines or insecticides. He will act as the clearinghouse for
information; write and tell him what you want and what you have to offer.
☐ Catalog: Long SASE, CAN/OV

Native Gardens
Route 1, Box 464
Greenback, TN 37742
(615) 856-3350
Edward & Meredith Clebsch

Plants ᘒ Seeds
Nursery-propagated **native plants** (and seeds) for meadow and natural land-
scaping. Very informative tables in the catalog give information on growing
conditions, season and color of flower, habitat and soil, with very concise
comments. (1983)
☐ Catalog: $1, R&W, $10m, cn/bn
⌂ Nursery: By appointment only
▼ Garden: By appointment only

Native Seed Foundation
Star Route
Moyie Springs, ID 83845
(208) 267-7938 TO/CC
David & Simon Ronniger

Seeds
Seeds of **interior Pacific Northwest native conifers and shrubs** and several
hardy nut species, all providing wildlife food and shelter; most are
habitat-collected and sold by the pound. There are no plant descriptions,
but list notes location of collection. (1977)
☐ Catalog: 1FCS, R&W, CAN/OV, $20m, bn

Native Seeds, Inc.
14590 Triadelphia Mill Road
Dayton, MD 21036
(301) 596-9818 TO
Dr. James A. Saunders

Seeds
Color brochure offers seed of individual **wildflowers**, chosen to flourish in
many regions of the country. Also offers seed mixes with a broad variety of
wildflowers and seeds in bulk. Some plants illustrated, all well described.
☐ Catalog: Free, R&W, CAN/OV, bn/cn

Native Seeds/SEARCH
2509 N. Campbell Avenue, #325
Tucson, AZ 85719
(602) 327-9123
Mahina Drees, Dir.

Seeds ᘒ Books ᘒ Supplies
Non-profit group offers traditional **Southwestern native crops**, many by
Spanish names, as well as **wild food plants**; all plants briefly described,
with cultural suggestions. Offers a few related publications, occasional
workshops and Indian seed-drying baskets. A wide selection of open-
pollinated corn, beans, amaranth, gourds, squash and hot peppers. (1983)
☐ Catalog: $1, CAN/OV, $2m
⌂ Nursery: September-July, Tu-Th, call ahead
▼ Garden: January-October, daily, call ahead

Natural Gardens
113 Jasper Lane
Oak Ridge, TN 37830
Maureen & Jim Cunningham

Plants ᘒ Books
A good selection of **Southeastern native plants and wildflowers** for wetland,
woodland, perennial gardens and wildlife food, all very well described, with
a guide to naturalization and information on butterfly gardens. Also sells
books on growing wildflowers and perennials. (1984)
☐ Catalog: $1d, SS:3-11, $8m, bn/cn

Nature's Garden Nursery
Route 1, Box 488
Beaverton, OR 97007
Frederick W. Held

Plants ✥ Seeds
A good selection of plants for the woodland, shady or sunny garden, including some **sedum and sempervivums, hardy ferns, gentians and helebores, species primulas, violas** and other choice rock garden plants, each very briefly described. Also sells seed of a number of garden perennials in a separate winter seed list. (1974)
❑ Catalog: $1.25d, R&W, CAN, SS:2-5,9-11, $15m, bn/cn

E. B. Nauman, Nurseryman
688 Saint Davids Lane
Schenectady, NY 12309
E. B. Nauman

Plants
"I specialize in **broadleaf evergreens** which are hardy in the Northeast and and Midwest: **rhododendrons, azaleas and mountain laurels**, featuring young plants of quality, named varieties." A brief list, but each plant is well described, with detailed cultural notes. (1973)
❑ Catalog: Free, SS:4-6,9-11, $10m

Neon Palm Nursery
1560 Sebastopol Road
Santa Rosa, CA 95407
(707) 578-7467
Dale Motiska

Plants
A good selection of **hardy subtropical plants**: many palms, cycads, winter-hardy cactus, yuccas, agaves, ferns, bamboos and others. There are no plant descriptions, but there are notes as to hardiness. (1983)
❑ Catalog: $1, SS:4-10, $50m, bn
⌂ Nursery: February-December, Tu-Su

New Mexico Cactus Research
P.O. Box 787
1132 E. River Road
Belen, NM 87002
(505) 864-4027
Horst Kuenzler

Seeds
A very extensive collectors' list of **cacti and succulent** seeds and mixtures of seeds by genus, listed by botanical name only, with very brief notes on origin. Many of the seeds are habitat-collected; no plant descriptions for most, brief notes on some. Also sells winter-hardy cactus under the name Bisnaga Cactus Nursery. (1955)
❑ Catalog: $1, R&W, CAN/OV, $5m, bn
⌂ Nursery: By appointment only
♥ Garden: By appointment only

The New Peony Farm
P.O. Box 18105
St. Paul, MN 55118
(612) 457-8994
Kent Crossley

Plants
Catalog lists only a few of the 350 varieties of herbaceous **peonies** which they grow; each plant well described. They are particularly interested in offering fine older cultivars in danger of being lost in commerce; they also offer single and double fernleaf peonies, mixed assortments by color. (1980)
❑ Catalog: Free, R&W, CAN, SS:9-10
♥ Garden: June, by appointment only

New York State Fruit Testing Coop. Assn.
P.O. Box 462
Geneva, NY 14456
(315) 787-2205
David A. Gripe, Gen. Mgr.

Plants
For a $5 membership fee, fruit testers may buy a large selection of new and older varieties of **hardy fruit**. They must agree not to distribute the new varieties, as well as to report on how their choices perform. All plants well described; prices seem about average. (1918)
❑ Catalog: Free

Niche Gardens
1111 Dawson Road
Chapel Hill, NC 27516
(919) 967-0078
Kim & Bruce Hawks

Plants
Small nursery specializing in **Southeastern wildflowers and native plants, perennials, ornamental grasses and herbs** for rock gardens, bogs and dry areas. Plants are well described, with notes on use and placement, and come in four-inch pots, quart or gallon sizes; all are nursery-propagated. (1984)
❑ Catalog: $3, CAN/OV, SS:3-11, $15, bn/cn
⌂ Nursery: March-November, Tu-Sa
♥ Garden: April-October, Tu-Sa

Nicholls Gardens
4724 Angus Drive
Gainesville, VA 22065
(703) 754-9623 TO
Diana & Mike Nicholls

Plants
Small nursery sells a good selection of **irises** -- Siberian, Japanese, Louisiana, species and bearded, dwarf to tall -- as well as **daylilies** and **dahlias**. All plants are briefly described -- and would provide something in bloom from early spring to late fall. They are the official display garden for the Society for Japanese Iris. (1984)
❑ Catalog: $1d, CAN/OV, SS:4-5,7-9, $10m
⌂ Nursery: April-September, daily, call ahead
♥ Garden: April-September, daily, call ahead

Nichols Garden Nursery, Inc.
1190 N. Pacific Highway
Albany, OR 97321
(503) 928-9280 TO/CC $10m
E. R. Nichols, Keane & Rose Marie McGee

Plants ✥ Seeds ✥ Books ✥ Supplies
An extensive selection of **herbs, vegetables and flowers**; many vegetables selected for the coastal conditions of the Northwest. All plants very well described with cultural hints -- also garden, herbal and winemaking supplies and books on rural subjects. They've introduced a lovely lavender, 'Sharon Roberts,' reblooming, very hardy and a deep lavender-blue. They also specialize in elephant garlic. (1950)
❑ Catalog: Free, R&W, CAN, SS:4-5,9-10
⌂ Nursery: All year, M-Sa
♥ Garden: Spring, summer, M-Sa

Nindethana Seed Service
RMB 939, Washpool Road
Woogenilup, Australia 6324
(098) 541066 FAX 541011
Peter C. Luscombe

Seeds
A collectors' list of **Australian native plants**, listed only by botanical name with no descriptions; a very broad selection of trees, shrubs and wildflowers, including eucalyptus, acacias, banksias, stylidiums, hakeas, callistemons, cassias, dryandras, leptospermums and grevilleas. (1956)
❐ Catalog: 2 IRC, R&W, OV, $10m, bn
⌂ Nursery: By appointment only

Nolin River Nut Tree Nursery
797 Port Wooden Road
Upton, KY 42784
(502) 369-8551
John & Lisa Brittain

Plants
Formerly the Leslie Wilmoth Nursery, specializing in grafted **nut trees** -- pecans, hicans, hickories, heartnuts, butternuts, black and Persian walnuts, chestnuts -- over 100 varieties; also grafted **persimmons**. Listed by variety name, with very brief plant descriptions. (1985)
❐ Catalog: Free, R&W, SS:3-4, cn/bn
⌂ Nursery: All year, M-Sa, by appointment only
▼ Garden: June-September, by appointment only

Nooitgedag Disa Nursery
7 Sunnybrae Road
Rondebosch, Cape, South Africa 7700
(021) 689-1919
Dr. L. Vogelpoel

Seeds
A hobbyist specializing in seed of **Disa orchids**: uniflora, tripetaloides and cardinalis and hybrids -- Veitchii, Diores, Kewensis, Watsonii, Kirstenbosch Pride and Langleyensis. Plants well described; grow to flowering size in three years. Growing information included with seeds. (1980)
❐ Catalog: Free, OV, SS:2-6, $20m

Nor'East Miniature Roses
58 Hammond Street
Rowley, MA 01969
(617) 948-7964
Harmon & John Saville

Plants
Color catalog of **miniature roses**, including "mini" tree roses and climbers, both single plants and collections. Another branch at P.O. Box 473, Ontario, CA 91762, (714) 988-7222. Nice selection, plants well described. (1972)
❐ Catalog: Free, R&W, $6m
⌂ Nursery: May-September, daily, call ahead
▼ Garden: June-September, AARS Garden, call ahead

North Coast Rhododendron Nursery
P.O. Box 308
Bodega, CA 94922
Parker Smith & Becky Duckles

Plants
Rhododendron nursery specializes in plants for mild climates, even some hot ones, and for greenhouses in cold climates. They offer both hybrids and Maddenii and other species; all plants are very well described.
❐ Catalog: $1, CAN/OV, SS:fall-winter

North Pine Iris Gardens
P.O. Box 595
308 N. Pine
Norfolk, NE 68701
Chuck & Mary Ferguson

Plants
Specializes in **bearded irises of all sizes**, a broad selection with brief plant descriptions. Also sells some **hosta**, as well as windsocks, wind chimes and hand-carved iris letter openers in wood.
❐ Catalog: $1, CAN/OV, SS:4-9, $10m
⌂ Nursery: By appointment only

North Star Gardens
19060 Manning Trail North
Marine, MN 55047-9723
(612) 433-5850 or 5851
Paul M. Otten, Gen. Mgr.

Plants ～ Supplies
"We are the **raspberry** specialists," and they offer over 30 cultivars: red, purple, black and yellow, each variety compared by qualities and very well described. They also offer the new European "Jostaberry," a cross between a currant and gooseberry -- vigorous, tasty and a thousand other qualities.
❐ Catalog: 2 FCS, R&W, CAN/OV, SS:3-10, $25m
⌂ Nursery: All year, M-Sa
▼ Garden: July, September, call ahead

Northern Kiwi Nursery
RR 3
Niven Road
Niagara-on-the-Lake, ON, Canada L0S 1J0
(416) 468-7573 TO
Paul, Peter & David Klassen

Plants
A Canadian source for several varieties of very **hardy kiwis**; list gives good information on each variety and on culture generally. (1985)
❐ Catalog: Free, R&W, US/OV, $20m
⌂ Nursery: All year, M-Sa, call ahead
▼ Garden: May-September, M-Sa, call ahead

Northplan/Mountain Seed
P.O. Box 9107
Moscow, ID 83843-1607
(208) 882-8040 TO/CC
Loring M. Jones

Seeds
Seeds of **native trees and shrubs** for disturbed land restoration, erosion control and highway landscaping; **wildflower** mixes for various habitats and **range and reclamation grasses**. Garden seed catalog lists **short-season vegetables and annuals**. Garden seed catalog $1d; send long SASE for native plant list. (1975)
❐ Catalog: See notes, R&W, CAN/OV
⌂ Nursery: By appointment only
▼ Garden: By appointment only; call (208) 286-7004

Northwest Biological Enterprises
23351 S.W. Bosky Dell Lane
West Linn, OR 97068
(503) 638-6029
Stanley G. Jewett, Jr.

Plants
Specializes in **Northwestern native plants**, including ferns and azaleas (R. occidentale), conifers, ornamental trees and shrubs and perennials and rock garden plants. Plants briefly but well described. (1971)
▢ Catalog: $2d, R&W, CAN, SS:10-4, $10m, bn/cn
⌂ Nursery: February-Nov, M-F, call ahead
▼ Garden: March-May, M-F, call ahead

Northwest Mycological Consultants
702 N.W. 4th Street
Corvallis, OR 97330
(503) 753-8198

Seeds
Offer a good selection of **mushroom spawn**: shiitake, enoki, reiski, morel and black morel, several types of oyster and several others such as "hen of the woods" and "shaggy mane." They also sell books and mushroom growing supplies and consult with growers.
▢ Catalog: $2

Northwoods Nursery
28696 S. Cramer Road
Molalla, OR 97038
(503) 651-3737 TO/CC
Jim Gilbert & Kathy Fives

Plants ∾ Books ∾ Supplies ∾ Tools
Offers **hybrid chestnuts, berries, apples, figs, hardy kiwis, pawpaws** and **oriental pears**, grown by organic methods "as much as possible." A good variety of kiwis, other fruits and nuts and many ornamental shrubs and trees which do well in the Northwest and which are, in many cases, suited to the urban-sized lot. (1979)
▢ Catalog: Free, R&W, SS:1-5, $10m
⌂ Nursery: January-May, Tu-Su
▼ Garden: January-May, Tu-Su

Nourse Farms, Inc.
RFD, Box 485
River Road (Whately)
South Deerfield, MA 01373
(413) 665-2658
Tim Nourse

Plants
Growers of tissue-cultured **strawberries** as a means of producing "virus-free" plants -- 31 varieties. They also sell **blackberries, raspberries, rhubarb, horseradish** and the Rutgers University "all-male" **asparagus** hybrids 'Jersey Centennial', 'Jersey Giant' and 'Greenwich' -- more vigorous and do not set seed. Informative catalog with cultural suggestions. (1969)
▢ Catalog: Free, R&W, CAN/OV, SS:3-6
⌂ Nursery: April-May, M-Sa
▼ Garden: June-September, growing area, call ahead

Novelty Nurseries
P.O. Box 382
Novelty, OH 44072
(216) 338-4425
Patty & Michael Artino

Plants
Offers **hardy ferns** suitable to harsh Midwestern winters (Zone 5); each plant well described, grown from spore.
▢ Catalog: Long SASE, R&W, CAN, $10m, bn

Nuccio's Nurseries
P.O. Box 6160
3555 Chaney Trail
Altadena, CA 91003
(818) 794-3383

Plants
A very large selection of **camellias and azaleas**; all plants well to briefly described. Camellias include japonica, sasanqua, reticulata, rusticana and higo hybrids and a number of species; some camellia scions are also available. Azalea hybrids of many types, including many of their own and a huge selection of Japanese satsukis. Also sell a few gardenias. (1935)
▢ Catalog: Free, R&W, SS:1-11
⌂ Nursery: All year, F-Tu; June-December, closed Su

Oak Hill Farm
204 Pressly Street
Clover, SC 29710
(803) 222-4245 TO
Betsy & E. Y. Johnson

Plants
Small nursery offers **species azaleas** -- atlanticum, austrinum, bakerii, prunifolium, slippenbachi, roseshell, canescens, vaseyi; hardy to -10F, container-grown from seed, six-year plants, but no plant descriptions. (1977)
▢ Catalog: Long SASE, R&W, CAN, SS:11-3, $50m, bn
⌂ Nursery: All year, call ahead, 6-8 am
▼ Garden: April, call ahead

Oak Hill Gardens
P.O. Box 25
37W 550 Binnie Road
Dundee, IL 60118-0025
(708) 428-8500 TO/CC
Hermann & Dorothy Pigors

Plants ∾ Books ∾ Supplies
Informative catalog offers a broad selection of **species and hybrid orchids**, as well as **bromeliads** and other flowering and foliage indoor plants; each plant briefly described in table format. Also offers growing supplies and books on orchids and houseplants. (1973)
▢ Catalog: Free, R&W, CAN/OV, SS:W, bn
⌂ Nursery: All year, M-Sa
▼ Garden: All year, M-Sa

Oakes Daylilies
8204 Monday Road
Corryton, TN 37721
(615) 689-3036 or 687-1268
Stewart Oakes

Plants
Just **daylilies**, a collectors' list of hundreds of varieties from many noted hybridizers and AHS award winners. Grows over 1,500 varieties, with concentration on award winners; plants are described in concise but informative tables -- a mind-boggling choice. (1979)
▢ Catalog: Free, R&W, CAN/OV
⌂ Nursery: March-October, daily, call ahead
▼ Garden: June-July, AHS Display Garden, daily

Oakridge Nurseries
P.O. Box 182
East Kingston, NH 03872
(603) 642-8227
Richard Marcella & Glen Taylor

Plants
Small nursery offers nice selection of **ferns and wildflower plants**, mature and ready for planting. Plants are well but briefly described, a few shown in color photographs. Formerly called Exeter Wild Flower Gardens. (1971)
❏ Catalog: $1, R&W, CAN/OV, SS:3-5,9-10, cn/bn

Oikos Tree Crops
721 N. Fletcher
Kalamazoo, MI 49007-3077
(616) 342-6504 TO
Ken Asmus

Plants
Small nursery offers seedling **nut trees**, **pines** with edible nuts, **oaks** with edible acorns and hybrid **chestnuts**; no plant descriptions. Also **berrying shrubs**: bayberry, dwarf cherries, serviceberry, rugosa roses, persimmons and pawpaws. Will be adding more oaks and other ornamental trees. Can't ship to CA; some restrictions to OR, FL, WA and AR. (1980)
❏ Catalog: Free, R&W, CAN/OV, SS:3-5,10-12, $30m, cn/bn
⌂ Nursery: March-December, daily, by appointment only
▼ Garden: Growing area, by appointment only

Old Farm Nursery
5550 Indiana Street
Golden, CO 80403
(303) 278-0754 or 0755 TO/CC $20m
Larry Schlichenmayer

Plants
Offers a good selection of **hardy perennials**, some of which are hard to find; all plants are well described. Among the offerings are aquilegias, penstemons, helichrysums, salvias, veronicas, species geraniums, dianthus and some small shrubs and ornamental grasses, as well. (1984)
❏ Catalog: Free, R&W, CAN, SS:3-6,9-10, bn
⌂ Nursery: March-October, M-Sa; May-August, Su
▼ Garden: May-September, daily

Old Thyme Flowers & Herbal Seed Exchange

See The Flower & Herb Exchange.

Ontario Seed Company, Ltd.
P.O. Box 144
16 King Street South
Waterloo, ON, Canada N2J 3Z9
(519) 886-0557 or 2990 TO/CC $10m
Scott Uffelman

Seeds
Offer a wide selection of **vegetables, annuals and perennials** for Canadian gardens; each variety well described with some seed starting suggestions. They also offer general gardening supplies, seeders, row covers, some books and bird feeders. (1899)
❏ Catalog: $2, R&W, $5m, cn

Orchibec
200 Jean Gauvin
Ste. Foy, PQ, Canada G2E 3L9
(418) 871-2155
Laurier Nappert

Plants
A nice selection of **orchids**: laeliinae, phalaenopsis, paphiopedilum, cattleyas, doritaenopsis and species; plants are very briefly described. Catalogs are available in French and English; specify which you want. (1983)
❏ Catalog: $2, SS:5-9
⌂ Nursery: Daily, by appointment only
▼ Garden: Daily, summer, by appointment only

Orchid Gardens
2232 - 139th Avenue N.W.
Andover, MN 55304
(612) 755-0205
Carl Phillips

Plants
Collectors' list of **wildflowers and hardy ferns**; a good selection with good descriptions and concise cultural notes in an informative catalog. Most plants are native to northern Minnesota, including native orchids, violets, ferns, vines, club mosses and a few trees and shrubs. (1945)
❏ Catalog: $.50, SS:4-5,8-10, cn/bn
⌂ Nursery: By appointment only
▼ Garden: By appointment only

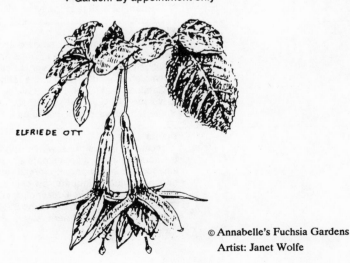

ELFRIEDE OTT

© Annabelle's Fuchsia Gardens
Artist: Janet Wolfe

Orchid Haven
900 Rossland Road East
Whitby, ON, Canada L1N 5R5
(416) 668-8534 TO/CC
Joy & Mal Bain

Plants
A good selection of **orchids**, both hybrids and species in seedling and
blooming sizes; each briefly but well described. Sells phalaenopsis,
paphiopedilums, cattleyas, dendrobiums and epidendrums and others. (1982)
⬚ Catalog: Free, R&W, US/OV, SS:4-10, $35m, bn
⌂ Nursery: Daily, call ahead
♥ Garden: Daily, call ahead

The Orchid House
1699 Sage Avenue
Los Osos, CA 93402
(805) 528-1417 or (800) 235-4139 TO
N. H. Powell

Plants
Specialist in **hybrid and species orchids** -- paphiopedilums, odontoglossums,
phalaenopsis, cymbidiums, cattleyas and oncidiums; request list of variety
you're interested in. Plants available as seedlings or in flowering size;
orchid lovers and collectors can decipher the "orchid-speak." (1943)
⬚ Catalog: See notes, R&W, CAN/OV, SS:W
⌂ Nursery: All year, call ahead
♥ Garden: All year, call ahead

Orchid Species Specialties
42314 Road #415
Raymond Road
Coarsegold, CA 93614
(209) 683-3239 TO
Walter J. Rybaczyk

Plants
Extensive collectors' lists of **species orchids**, collected by the proprie-
tors or other well-known jungle collectors; no descriptions. Award-winning
species cattleya and laelia clones a specialty, much wanted by hybridizers.
Three lists: general botanical, laelia and species cattleya, $1 each. They
also sell some growing supplies. (1972)
⬚ Catalog: See notes, R&W, CAN/OV, SS:W, $50m, bn
⌂ Nursery: All year, daily, call ahead
♥ Garden: All year, call ahead

Orchid Thoroughbreds
731 W. Siddonsburg Road
Dillsburg, PA 17019
(717) 432-8100
Diane Vickery

Plants
Offers a good selection of **hybrid orchids** of all kinds: cattleyas,
ascocendas, paphiopedilums, phalaenopsis, vandas, angraecums, miltonias,
dendrobiums and some **species orchids**, as well. Most plants are briefly
described.
⬚ Catalog: Free, R&W, CAN/OV
⌂ Nursery: By appointment only
♥ Garden: By appointment only

Orchids by Hausermann, Inc.
2N 134 Addison Road
Villa Park, IL 60181
(708) 543-6855 FAX 9842 TO/CC
Eugene Hausermann

Plants ⚭ Books ⚭ Supplies
Color catalog gives brief descriptions of hundreds of species and hybrid
orchids, all described in informational tables. Also offers cultural
suggestions, orchid growing supplies and books about orchids. (1920)
⬚ Catalog: $1.25, R&W, CAN/OV, SS:3-12, $10m, bn
⌂ Nursery: All year, M-Sa
♥ Garden: January-May, M-Sa, greenhouses

Orchids for Everyone
P.O. Box 72
Glenburnie, ON, Canada K0H 1S0
(613) 548-4647 TO/CC
Sylvia Moreau

Plants
Nice selection of **hybrid orchids** -- cattleyas, phalaenopsis -- and a number
of **species orchids**. All plants briefly described in "orchid-talk." They
also sell African violets, cactus and garden shrubs at the nursery. (1987)
⬚ Catalog: Free, US, SS:4-11, bn
⌂ Nursery: All year, daily
♥ Garden: Greenhouse, daily

Orchids Royale
P.O. Box 1289
5902 Via Real
Carpinteria, CA 93013
(805) 684-8066
James Burkey

Plants
A very large selection of standard and miniature **orchids** -- cymbidiums,
miltonias, odontoglossum alliance and paphiopedilum divisons -- some
obviously very rare. Plants very briefly described, some in a sort of
"orchid shorthand" known to the fanatic. (1978)
⬚ Catalog: Free, CAN/OV, SS:W
⌂ Nursery: All year, M-F, call ahead
♥ Garden: All year, M-F, call ahead

Oregon Exotica Nursery
1065 Messinger Road
Grants Pass, OR 97527
Jerry Black

Plants
"Specializes in rare fruits, with emphasis on **hardy subtropical fruits** and
their culture in Northern climates." Offers hardy citrus (citranges),
ichandarins, hardy grapefruit relatives, dwarf citrus, feijoas, hicans,
bananas, jujubes, loquats, low-chill apples, hardy kiwis and many varieties
of figs. All are very well described. (1985)
⬚ Catalog: Free, R&W, CAN/OV, SS:11-4, $5m
⌂ Nursery: By appointment only

Oregon Miniature Roses
8285 S.W. 185th Avenue
Beaverton, OR 97007
(503) 649-4482 TO/CC $20m
Ray Spooner

Plants
Color catalog offers a good selection of **miniature roses**, each well described and many illustrated. Sells a few of their own hybrids, miniature tree roses and roses for hanging baskets. (1978)
❑ Catalog: Free, R&W, CAN, $10m
⌂ Nursery: All year, daily, call ahead

Oregon Trail Daffodils
3207 S.E. Mannthey Road
Corbett, OR 97019
(503) 695-5513
Bill & Diane Tribe

Bulbs
Specializing in the **novelty daffodils** of the late Murray Evans and new cultivars of Bill Pannill, a broad selection of specialty daffodils. Each variety is well described by class, breeding and seedling number; the owners are the fourth generation of the Evans family in the daffodil trade. (1989)
❑ Catalog: Free, R&W, CAN/OV, SS:9-10, $5m
▼ Garden: April, call ahead

Orgel's Orchids
18950 S.W. 136th Street, Box K-6
Miami, FL 33187
(305) 233-7168
Orgel C. Bramblett

Plants
Collectors' list of **carnivorous plants** -- an especially large selection of nepenthes, droseras, sarracenias and pinguiculas -- and **species orchids** -- dendrobiums, vandas, aerides, cymbidiums, ascocentrums, phalaenopsis and more. Will export plants covered by CITES convention. (1972)
❑ Catalog: Free, R&W, CAN/OV, bn
⌂ Nursery: All year, by appointment only
▼ Garden: All year, growing area, by appointment only

D. Orriell -- Seed Exporters
45 Frape Avenue
Mt. Yokine, WA, Australia 6060
(09) 344-2290 FAX 344-8980
Patricia B. Orriell

Seeds
Very extensive list of **Australian native plants** for collectors or botanical gardens; each plant briefly described. Includes hardy eucalyptus, wildflowers, ferns, palms, proteas, banksias and cycads, acacias and many tropical/greenhouse plants. Also has list of native plants for bonsai. (1979)
❑ Catalog: $4(US bills), R&W, OV, $25m, bn/cn
⌂ Nursery: Daily, by appointment only

Owen Farms
Route 3, Box 158-A
Curve-Nankipoo Road
Ripley, TN 38063
(901) 635-1588 (6-9 pm CST)
Edric & Lillian Owen

Plants
Offers a nice selection of collectors' **trees, shrubs and perennials**: birch, dogwood, hydrangea, crape myrtle (including mildew-resistant cultivars), Satsuki azaleas and garden perennials. All plants are well described. Finished bonsai are available at the nursery. (1985)
❑ Catalog: $2(2 IRC), R&W, CAN/OV, SS:W, bn/cn
⌂ Nursery: All year, M-Sa, call ahead
▼ Garden: April-November, M-Sa, call ahead

Owen's Vineyard & Nursery
Georgia Highway 85
Gay, GA 30218
(404) 538-6983 or 6810
Robert L. Owen

Plants
Family nursery specializing in **muscadine grapes and rabbiteye blueberries**; the catalog gives very detailed information on growing muscadines; each of the twenty-eight varieties is well described. They also sell **hostas**, not included in the catalog I received.
❑ Catalog: Free
⌂ Nursery: All year, M-Sa

Owens Orchids
P.O. Box 365
18 Orchidheights Drive
Pisgah Forest, NC 28768-0365
(704) 877-3313 TO/CC
William & Joyce Owens

Plants
Good selection of **orchids** -- phalaenopsis and cattleya hybrids, many meristems and some seedlings, briefly described. Also offers an orchid-a-month plan and starter collections for beginners. Several lists a year.
❑ Catalog: Free, SS:W
⌂ Nursery: All year, M-Sa
▼ Garden: All year, greenhouse, M-Sa

Ozark National Seed Order
P.O. Box 932
Woodstock, NY 12498
(914) 246-1488
Stuart Leiderman

Seeds
Offers **open-pollinated, untreated garden seeds**: vegetables, herbs and flowers. Price of list includes a sample packet; all packets are $.25.
❑ Catalog: $.50, R&W, CAN/OV

Pacific Berry Works
963 Thomas Road
Bow, WA 98232
(206) 757-4385 TO/CC
Mintz & Sakuma

Plants ⬿ Books
A small nursery specializes in "**day neutral**" strawberries, which bear three months after planting, and **cane berries** -- raspberries, boysenberries, loganberries and tayberries from Scotland. Plants well described. Also sells a couple of berry cookbooks. (1985)
❑ Catalog: Free, R&W, CAN, SS:2-5
⌂ Nursery: Call ahead
▼ Garden: Growing area, call ahead

Pacific Coast Hybridizers
P.O. Box 972
1170 Steinway Avenue
Campbell, CA 95009-0972
(408) 370-2955
Bryce Williamson

Plants
Hobbyist hybridizers turned nurserymen; the color catalog is informative and offers a wide selection of **tall bearded and reblooming irises**. Plants very well described, many shown in photos. (1970)
❒ Catalog: $1d, R&W, CAN/OV, SS:7-9
⌂ Nursery: April 15-May 15, daily, call ahead
❦ Garden: April 15-May 15, daily, call ahead

Pacific Tree Farms
4301 Lynwood Drive
Chula Vista, CA 92010
(619) 422-2400 TO/CC
William L. Nelson

Plants ∾ **Books** ∾ **Supplies** ∾ **Tools**
A broad selection of **fruit, nut and ornamental trees** (including 90 varieties of pine), California native trees and shrubs and tender warm-climate fruits like banana, cherimoya, lychee, date palm, pistachio and more; good selection, no plant descriptions. Adding new trees all the time. Also books, grafting supplies and fertilizers. (1970)
❒ Catalog: $1.50(US$3 OV), R&W, CAN/OV, bn/cn
⌂ Nursery: All year, W-M
❦ Garden: All year, W-M

Carl Pallek & Son Nursery
P.O. Box 137
Highway 55
Virgil, ON, Canada L0S 1T0
(416) 468-7262
Otto Pallek

Plants
An extensive list of hybrid tea **roses**, as well as floribundas, grandifloras, climbers and a selection of old garden roses, each very briefly described. Sells in Canada only, but Americans may pick up orders at the nursery; order early to allow preparation of inspection papers. (1959)
❒ Catalog: Free, SS:11-12,3-4
⌂ Nursery: All year, M-Sa
❦ Garden: July-September, M-Sa

Palms for Tropical Landscaping
6600 S.W. 45th Street
Miami, FL 33155
(305) 666-1457
Carol Graff

Plants ∾ **Seeds**
Small nursery offers a wide selection of **palms**; over 130 individual species and varieties listed only by botanical name. They can be shipped in three-inch, one-gallon or three-gallon pots. Seeds are available for some species; supplies might be limited. Plants not listed might be obtainable. (1983)
❒ Catalog: Long SASE($2 OV), CAN/OV, SS:3-11, $50m, bn
⌂ Nursery: Daily, by appointment only
❦ Garden: Daily, by appointment only

The PanTree
1150 Beverly Drive
Vista, CA 92084
John Rubesha

Plants
Specializing in euphorbias, aloes, crassulas, aeoniums, echeverias, haworthias, gasterias, kalanchoes, monadeniums and other **succulents**. Collectors' list with no plant descriptions; over one hundred euphorbias. Stocks sometimes limited. (1978)
❒ Catalog: $.50, SS:2-11, $10m, bn

Paradise Water Gardens
62 May Street
Whitman, MA 02382
(716) 447-4711 TO/CC

Plants ∾ **Books** ∾ **Supplies**
Specializes in plants and supplies for **water gardens** -- water lilies, aquatic plants, books on water gardening, supplies for pools and ponds.
❒ Catalog: $3

Park Seed Company, Inc.
P.O. Box 46
Highway 254 North
Greenwood, SC 29648-0046
(803) 223-7333 TO/CC $20m
Park Family

Plants ∾ **Seeds** ∾ **Books** ∾ **Supplies** ∾ **Tools** ∾ **Bulbs**
Park offers a huge selection of seeds for the home gardener, many illustrated in color. In addition to the usual **flowers and vegetables**, they also have some harder-to-find seeds, plants and bulbs. The catalog seems to arrive on December 26th to fight the post-Christmas blues (it works!). (1868)
❒ Catalog: Free, R&W, CAN, cn/bn
⌂ Nursery: All year, M-F
❦ Garden: May-July, M-F

Parsley's Cape Seeds
1 Woodlands Road
Somerset West, Cape, South Africa 7130
(024) 512630
Alan and Renate Parsley

Seeds
Specializes in **Proteaceae**. Collectors' list of South African plants: leucodendrons, proteas, leucospermums, ericas, species pelargoniums, Australian banksias, carnivorous plants, as well as shrubs and trees. (1953)
❒ Catalog: $1d, R&W, OV, bn

Paul's Premium Seeds
P.O. Box 370147
San Diego, CA 92137-0147
Paul E. Barbano

Seeds
New seed company specializes in seed of **heirloom vegetables**, including the 'Jenny Lind' melon and my father's favorite 'Country Gentleman' corn; a small but enticing selection, all well described. (1988)
❒ Catalog: Free, CAN/OV

Theodore Payne Foundation
10459 Tuxford Street
Sun Valley, CA 91352
(818) 768-1802
Non-Profit Foundation

Seeds ⟳ Books
This non-profit foundation honors the work of Theodore Payne, who made **California wildflowers and native plants** admired the world over. They sell seeds by mail and plants at their headquarters; no plant descriptions. They also sell many books on native flora -- including Payne's original 1956 catalog with good plant descriptions ($3.50 ppd). From March to May call their southern California wildflower viewing hotline, (818) 768-3533. (1963)
❐ Catalog: $2, R&W, CAN/OV, $3m, bn/cn
⌂ Nursery: All year, Tu-Sa
♥ Garden: October-June, Tu-Sa

Peace Seeds
2385 S.E. Thompson Street
Corvallis, OR 97333
Dr. Alan Kapuler

Seeds
"A planetary gene pool and research service." They offer a wide variety of seeds for **vegetables, native plants, herbs, heirloom potatoes and tomatoes** and **medicinal plants**. Seed list is $1; their catalog and research journal is $5 and presents "an integrated view of the Plant Kingdom." (1979)
❐ Catalog: See notes, R&W, CAN/OV, cn/bn
⌂ Nursery: By appointment only
♥ Garden: April-October, by appointment only

Peaceful Valley Farm Supply
P.O. Box 2209
110 Springhill Boulevard
Grass Valley, CA 95945
(916) 265-4769 TO/CC (M-Sa)
Mark & Kathleen Fenton

Plants ⟳ Seeds ⟳ Books ⟳ Supplies ⟳ Tools ⟳ Bulbs
Thick catalogs which offer **everything for the organic grower**: pest controls, fertilizers, beneficial insects, green manure crops and pasture grasses, soil testing, books and tools and growing supplies. Their fall catalog offers seed potatoes, garlic, onions, strawberries and flower bulbs. Full of information; real "take-to-bed" catalogs. (1975)
❐ Catalog: $2d, R&W, CAN/OV, SS:1-4, $20m
⌂ Nursery: All year, Tu,Th,Sa, call ahead

Peekskill Nurseries
Shrub Oak, NY 10588
(914) 245-5595

Plants
Specializes in **ground covers**: pachysandra, vinca minor, euonymus, Baltic ivy and Bar Harbor juniper. Plants well described and sold in quantities from ten to thousands.
❐ Catalog: Free

Penn Valley Orchids
239 Old Gulph Road
Wynnewood, PA 19096
(215) 642-9822
William W. Wilson

Plants
A very broad selection of **hybrid orchids**, some one of a kind, with some **species orchids** as well; most well but briefly described. Offers a huge list of paphiopedilums, also cattleya alliance and others. Sells antique orchid prints; ask for special list of prints and old journals. (1946)
❐ Catalog: $1, R&W, CAN/OV, SS:W, bn
⌂ Nursery: All year, by appointment only

Pense Nursery
Route 2, Box 330-A
Mountainburg, AR 72946
Phillip D. Pense

Plants
Specializes in **berries and table grapes** -- boysenberries, youngberries, raspberries, blackberries, gooseberries and seedless Concord, Mars, Venus and Reliance table grapes. Berry plants available in quantities of 25, 50 and 100; single grapevines available with orders of berry plants. (1981)
❐ Catalog: Free, R&W, SS:10-4, $25m

The Pepper Gal
10536 - 119th Avenue North
Largo, FL 34643
Dorothy L. Van Vleck

Seeds
An extensive list of **ornamental, hot and sweet peppers**, 200 varieties by her count; no plant descriptions, but she does list her favorites.
❐ Catalog: Free, CAN

Perry's Water Gardens
191 Leatherman Gap Road
Franklin, NC 28734
(704) 524-3264 or 369-5648
Ben R. Gibson

Plants ⟳ Books ⟳ Supplies
Complete **aquatic nursery**, offering water lilies, lotus and other aquatic plants, as well as books, fish and water garden supplies. A nice selection of plants, all well described; some are shown in color photographs. (1979)
❐ Catalog: $2, R&W, CAN/OV, SS:3-9, cn/bn
⌂ Nursery: March-September, daily
♥ Garden: March-September, daily

Peter Pauls Nurseries
RD #2
Canandaigua, NY 14424
(716) 394-7397 TO/CC $15m
James & Patricia Pietropaolo

Plants ⟳ Seeds ⟳ Books
A good selection of **carnivorous plants**, and seeds thereof, as well as growing supplies, terrarium kits, plant collections and their book, "The Carnivorous Plants of the World," on how to identify and grow carnivorous plants from seed to maturity. Featured are Venus's-flytrap, sarracenias, droseras, darlingtonia and pinguiculas. (1957)
❐ Catalog: Free(4 IRC), R&W, CAN/OV, SS:4-11, $5m, bn

Piccadilly Farm
1971 Whippoorwill Road
Bishop, GA 30621
(404) 769-6516 TO $20m
Sam & Carleen Jones

Plants
A nice selection of **hardy perennials for Southern gardens** -- hostas, Helleborus orientalis, phlox, ajuga, coreopsis and ornamental grasses can be shipped; hardy ferns and other perennials available only at the nursery. Brief plant descriptions. (1979)
□ Catalog: $1,50, R&W, SS:4-10, $20m
⌂ Nursery: April-September, F-Sa, by appointment only
▼ Garden: May-September, F-Sa, by appointment only

Pick's Ginseng
Crawford Street
Tomkinsville, KY 42167
(502) 487-6441
Morris Pickerel, Sr.

Plants ⚘ Seeds ⚘ Books
Offers **ginseng** roots and seeds, goldenseal and comfrey roots and books on their uses. Also buys ginseng roots.
□ Catalog: Free, R&W, CAN, SS:9-12, $18m
⌂ Nursery: All year, daily, call ahead
▼ Garden: Spring, daily, call ahead

Pickering Nurseries, Inc.
670 Kingston Road (Highway 2)
Pickering, ON, Canada L1V 1A6
(416) 839-2111
Joseph G. Schraven

Plants
An extensive list of **roses** -- hybrid tea, floribunda and many old garden roses, with tables of information for size, ARA rating, fragrance and color and a section on how to winterize roses in very cold climates. Many roses shown in color photographs. (1956)
□ Catalog: $2, R&W, US/OV, SS:10-4, $12m
⌂ Nursery: All year, call ahead

Piedmont Gardens
533-577 Piedmont Street
Waterbury, CT 06706
(203) 754-8534 or 3535 TO/CC
Henry & Philip Payne

Plants
A good selection of **hostas**, grouped by leaf size and briefly but well described. They also have a nice selection of hardy ferns and a few other native woodland plants. (1970)
□ Catalog: $.50, R&W, CAN, SS:4-9, bn/cn
⌂ Nursery: April-September, M-F, call ahead
▼ Garden: April-September, M-F, call ahead

Piedmont Plant Company
P.O. Box 424
807 N. Washington Street
Albany, GA 31703
(912) 435-0766 or 883-7029 TO/CC $10m
DuVernet, Jones & Parker

Plants
Offers over 60 varieties of **vegetable plants** -- onions, cabbage, lettuce, broccoli, cauliflower, tomatoes, peppers and eggplant, some illustrated in color, all well described. Also sells collections and complete vegetable gardens; can't ship to Western and Gulf states, AK or HI. (1906)
□ Catalog: Free, R&W, SS:4-6

Pine Heights Nursery
Pepper Street
Everton Hills, Australia 4053
(07) 353-2761
Donald & Marina Rix

Bulbs
An Australian source of **spring- and summer-blooming bulbs**: alliums, crinums, gingers, haemanthus, hymenocallis, kaempferia, moraea, sprekelia, velthemia, watsonia and many more. Also specialize in species and hybrid **hippeastrum** (amaryllis), both bulbs and seeds. Brief plant descriptions.
□ Catalog: $1(US bills), OV, bn/cn

Pinecliffe Daylily Gardens
6604 Scottsville Road
Floyds Knob, IN 47119
(812) 923-8113 or 8132
Donald & Kathy Smith

Plants
Huge selection of **daylily** cultivars; plants are very briefly described in informative tables, many are recent or brand new introductions. They have ten thousand seedlings in their trial beds. (1982)
□ Catalog: $1d, R&W, CAN/OV, SS:4-11, $25m
⌂ Nursery: April-November, daily, call ahead
▼ Garden: June-August, daily, call ahead

Pinetree Garden Seeds
Route 100
New Gloucester, ME 04260
(207) 926-3400
Dick Meiners

Seeds ⚘ Books ⚘ Supplies ⚘ Tools ⚘ Bulbs
Catalog offers a very broad selection of **flower and vegetable** seed in smaller, less expensive packets; specializes in space-saving vegetable cultivars; all well described in an informative catalog. Also sells spring-blooming bulbs, tools and supplies and 250 books on gardening and self-sufficiency. (1979)
□ Catalog: Free, CAN/OV, bn
⌂ Nursery: All year, M-F

Pixie Treasures Miniature Rose Nursery
4121 Prospect Avenue
Yorba Linda, CA 92686
(714) 993-6780 TO/CC
Dorothy Cralle & Laurie Chaffin

Plants
A huge selection of **miniature roses** -- over 125 varieties, including their own hybrids. Many are illustrated in the color catalog; all are well described. They also offer several special collections. (1972)
□ Catalog: $1d, $15m
⌂ Nursery: All year, M-Sa
▼ Garden: April-November, M-Sa

Plant City Bonsai
609E Shallowford Road
Gainesville, GA 30501
(404) 535-2991
Steve & Chery Cratty

Plants ☙ Supplies ☙ Tools
Offers a nice selection of **plants for bonsai** and **finished bonsai,** as well
as bonsai growing supplies, pots and tools. (1986)
❏ Catalog: 2 FCS
⌂ Nursery: All year, Th-Sa, Su pm
▼ Garden: All year, Th-Sa, Su pm

Plant Factory
2414 Saint Charles Place
Cinnaminson, NJ 08077
(609) 829-5311
Roger Bower, Jr.

Plants ☙ Supplies
Small nursery specializes in **African violets and rex begonias;** the catalog
offers a nice selection, with good plant descriptions and all the necessary
supplies for growing them. (1985)
❏ Catalog: Long SASE, R&W, SS:5-10, $10m
⌂ Nursery: By appointment only
▼ Garden: By appointment only

The Plant Shop's Botanical Gardens
18007 Topham Street
Reseda, CA 91335
(818) 881-4831
Bob Cole & Bill Cook

Plants
Good luck! This catalog offers plants so unusual that I hardly know where to
start; there are those among you who will swoon! They offer **begonias,
species orchids, bromeliads, cacti and succulents, aroids, platyceriums,
carnivorous plants, plumerias, tender bulbs:** over 2,000 of their plants are
registered by the CITES Convention. First, get a greenhouse... (1967)
❏ Catalog: $3.50d, OV, bn, $25m
⌂ Nursery: All year, F-Su

Plant Villa
16 Fullerton
Belleville, IL 62221
(618) 235-6694
Wayne Guttersohn

Plants
A long list of **African violets** offered as starter plants or fresh cut
leaves, well described. Also offers other gesneriads such as columneas,
aeschynanthus, episcias and compact gloxinias.
❏ Catalog: $.35, R&W, SS:4-10
⌂ Nursery: All year, by appointment only
▼ Garden: All year, by appointment only

Plant World
Route 12, Box 18
McMinnville, TN 37110
J. Dale Bennett

Plants
A nice selection of **ornamental trees, shrubs and ground covers;** many
are desirable plants but are not listed by botanical name -- I'm sure they'll
correct this in their next catalog. The plants are well described, and new
plants are being added all the time; they encourage "want lists" from their
customers. (1987)
❏ Catalog: $1d, SS:10-6, cn

Plants of the Southwest
930 Baca Street
Santa Fe, NM 87501
(505) 983-1548 TO/CC $20m
Gail Haggard

Seeds ☙ Books
Catalog full of landscaping and cultural information, with the object of sug-
gesting water-saving gardens. Offers seeds of **native trees and shrubs,
wildflowers, grasses, cacti and succulents -- also native vegetable seeds**
and recipes for New Mexican foods. Very useful in the Southwest! (1977)
❏ Catalog: $1.50, R&W, CAN/OV, bn/cn
⌂ Nursery: All year, daily
▼ Garden: May-September, daily

Plants of the Wild
P.O. Box 866
Willard Field
Tekoa, WA 99033
Kathy Hutton, Mgr.

Plants
Broad selection of seedling **Western native trees and shrubs,** all well de-
scribed with notes on uses. Minimum order is ten plants of each species;
plants are useful for natural landscaping, wildlife cover, erosion control
and reclamation.
❏ Catalog: Long SASE, R&W, SS:spring,fall, $10m, bn/cn
⌂ Nursery: All year, M-F, by appointment only
▼ Garden: Spring, M-F, by appointment only

Pleasant Hill African Violets
Route 1, Box 73
Brenham, TX 77833
(409) 836-9736 TO/CC
Ruth Goeke

Plants ☙ Supplies
"**African violet leaves and plants,** episcia stolons and other gesneriads --
aeschynanthus, nemantanthus and columnea cuttings -- at the moment we
have about 200 varieties of episcias." Large selection, brief plant descriptions. Also offer growing supplies. (1980)
❏ Catalog: $1, R&W, SS:4-10

Pleasant Valley Glads
P.O. Box 494
Agawam, MA 01001
(413) 786-9146 or 789-0307
Gary Adams

Bulbs
Offers a wide selection of **gladiolus;** many are recent introductions and
prize winners. Each plant is well described. In addition, a number of
dahlias are offered, listed by size of bloom and very briefly described.
❏ Catalog: Free, R&W, CAN/OV, SS:3-6, $20m
⌂ Nursery: All year, M-Sa, call for appointment & directions

Pleasure Iris Gardens
425 East Luna
Chaparral, NM 88021
(505) 824-4299 after 6 pm
Henry & Luella Danielson

Plants
A very extensive list of **irises** for collectors, including a number of their own hybrids -- bearded of all types, Japanese and Siberians, aril and arilbred, Louisiana, Sino-Siberian and spuria, oncocylus and regelia species and hybrids -- all briefly described with cultural notes. (1938)
❐ Catalog: $1d, CAN/OV, SS:7-9
▼ Garden: April, call ahead

The Plumeria People
P.O. Box 820014
Houston, TX 77282-0014
(713) 496-2352
Mary Helen Eggenberger

Plants ❧ Books ❧ Supplies ❧ Bulbs
Tropical plant specialists: **plumerias, bougainvillea, gingers, hibiscus, tender bulbs, flowering vines and shrubs and heliconias**; a good selection, all very well described. Also several books on growing tropical plants, including their own very comprehensive "Handbook on Plumeria Culture," and some growing supplies. (1981)
❐ Catalog: $2, R&W, CAN/OV, SS:3-10, $15m, cn/bn
⌂ Nursery: By appointment only
▼ Garden: By appointment only

Plumtree Nursery
387 Springtown Road
New Paltz, NY 12561
(914) 255-0417
Christine Marmo & Lee Reich

Plants
Small nursery offers unusual fruit and vegetable plants: **musk strawberries, 'Consort' European and clove currants, chuffa and skinless garlic**, each well described. They also offer soil testing kits and organic pest controls by mail. (1984)
❐ Catalog: Long SASE, SS:4,10-11

Pollen Bank
2065 Walnut Boulevard
Walnut Creek, CA 94596
(415) 939-7744
Jack S. Romine

Plants
A former President of the California Horticultural Society, Jack is noted as a hybridizer of **daylilies**; he sells unusual tetraploid conversions and seedlings for hybridizers. Pretty special stuff -- but hybridizing daylilies seems to be a national mania. Detailed family trees given.
❐ Catalog: Long SASE, SS:W, $20m
⌂ Nursery: All year, M-Sa, by appointment only

Pony Creek Nursery
Tilleda, WI 54978
(715) 787-3889 TO/CC
Jenny Schultz

Plants ❧ Seeds ❧ Books ❧ Supplies
Tabloid catalog lists a wide selection of **fruit and nut trees**, ornamental shrubs, berries, flower and vegetable seeds, books, growing supplies and beneficial insects; all well described. Plants best suited to the Midwest; cannot ship to CA. (1950)
❐ Catalog: Free, SS:5-10, cn/bn
⌂ Nursery: April-October, daily
▼ Garden: Growing area, daily

Portable Acres
2087 Curtis Drive
Penngrove, CA 94951
Colin Rigby

Plants
A small nursery specializing in **Pacific Coast native irises and beardless species irises**; a good selection, each plant very briefly described with some cultural information. (1984)
❐ Catalog: Long SASE w/2FCS, SS:11-4

Porter & Son
P.O. Box 104
1510 E. Washington Street
Stephenville, TX 76401-0104
Gene R. Porter

Seeds ❧ Books ❧ Supplies
A long-time family business offering a good selection of **vegetable and flower** seeds for the South, especially melons, tomatoes and hot peppers; each variety very well described. Also a good selection of gardening supplies, including drip irrigation, and gardening books. (1912)
❐ Catalog: Free, SS:1-4, $3m
⌂ Nursery: All year, M-F
▼ Garden: Spring-summer, M-F

Possum Trot Tropical Fruit Nursery
14955 S.W. 214th Street
Miami, FL 33187
(305) 251-5040
Robert Barnum, Mgr.

Plants
Tropical fruit for climates that never freeze; a good selection on a price list with no descriptions. Due to problems with shipping, they will not ship in the US, except for large shipments for which the buyer is willing to pay air freight. Cannot ship to CA.
❐ Catalog: Long SASE, R&W, CAN/OV, SS:W, $20m
⌂ Nursery: All year, daily
▼ Garden: All year, daily

Potterton & Martin
The Cottage Nursery
Moortown Road, Nettleton
Caistor, Lincs., England LN7 6HX
0472 851792

Bulbs
A British bulb specialist offering **dwarf bulbs**, which we would call the "minor bulbs" -- a good selection of alliums, anemones, corydalis, crocus, cyclamen, erythronium, fritillaria, species iris, narcissus, oxalis and pleione, among others. Good plant descriptions.
❐ Catalog: $3(US bills), US/CAN, SS:9, bn

Powell's Gardens
Route 3, Box 21
Highway 70
Princeton, NC 27569
(919) 936-4421
S. E. Powell

Plants
A huge selection of **irises, many daylilies and hosta**, and a broad selection of **perennials, dwarf conifers and some ornamental trees and shrubs**; the pages are tightly packed, with only the briefest of descriptions -- a true collectors' list. (1953)
❒ Catalog: $2.50, R&W, CAN/OV, bn/cn
⌂ Nursery: All year, M-Sa
▼ Garden: All year, M-Sa

Prairie Moon Nursery
Route 3, Box 163
Wiscoy Community Farm
Winona, MN 55987
(507) 452-5231 or 1362
Alan Wade

Plants ～ Seeds ～ Books
A good selection of **grasses and wildflowers** for prairie restoration and wild gardens, both plants and seeds, listed by botanical and common name and habitat only, with coded information on germination. Also sells books on prairie gardening. (1983)
❒ Catalog: $1, R&W, CAN, SS:4-5,10-11, bn/cn
⌂ Nursery: All year, call ahead
▼ Garden: April-November, restored prairie, call ahead

Prairie Nursery
P.O. Box 306
Westfield, WI 53964
(608) 296-3679 TO/CC
Brian Bader & Neil Diboll

Plants ～ Seeds
A small nursery specializing in **prairie plants and seed, grasses and forbs** (flowering herbaceous plants other than grasses); all plants well described, some color pictures and some line drawings. Also a list of plants to feed birds and butterflies. Sells only seeds overseas. (1974)
❒ Catalog: $2, R&W, CAN/OV, SS:4-6,9-11, $15m, cn/bn
▼ Garden: June-August, M-F, by appointment only

Prairie Orchid Company
515 Elmhurst Road
Winnipeg, MB, Canada R3R 0V2
(204) 889-0269
Ed Maza

Plants ～ Books ～ Supplies
A good selection of **hybrid and species orchids**: cattleyas, dendrobiums, encyclias, laelias, oncidiums, lycastes, odontoglossums, sophronitis, miltonias and paphiopedilums; no plant descriptions except for hybrids. Also offers growing supplies, plant lights and books. (1984)
❒ Catalog: $1, R&W, SS:5-9, bn
⌂ Nursery: All year, daily, by appointment only
▼ Garden: By appointment only

Prairie Ridge Nursery/CRM Ecosystems, Inc.
9738 Overland Road
Mt. Horeb, WI 53572
(608) 437-5245
Joyce Powers

Plants ～ Seeds
Specializing in **prairie wildflowers, grasses and forbs**, both plants and seeds; plant information given in concise tables. They also sell plant and seed collections for various growing conditions and do consulting on the establishment of low-maintenance erosion-control plantings. (1974)
❒ Catalog: Free, R&W, CAN, SS:5-6,9-10, bn/cn

Prairie Seed Source
P.O. Box 83
North Lake, WI 53064
Robert Ohrenhoerster

Seeds
Another company striving to recreate the prairie ecosystems and to encourage people to create their own. Offers seed of many **prairie plants**, with very brief information in table form and outlines showing size and form of each plant. They also rent slide sets on prairie plants and restoration.
❒ Catalog: $1, CAN/OV, bn/cn

Prairie State Commodities
P.O. Box 6
Main Street
Trilla, IL 62469
(217) 235-4322 FAX 3246 or (800) 777-7458
Charles L. Stodden

Seeds
Seeds for agriculture, including **open-pollinated corn, alfalfa, clovers, soybeans, buckwheat, sorghum, lawn grasses and cover crops**; also sell seed cleaners, can supply "organically grown" on some items. All items sold in fairly large quantities. (1975)
❒ Catalog: $1, R&W, $5m
⌂ Nursery: All year, M-Sa, call ahead

Prentiss Court Ground Covers
P.O. Box 8662
Greenville, SC 29604
(803) 277-4037 TO/CC
Lesesne & Gene Dickson

Plants
A small family enterprise offers **ground cover plants**: ajuga, cotoneaster, euonymous, ivy, hypericum, liriope, jasmine, daylilies, vincas, sedums and more. Plants offered bare-root or in pots, in quantities of fifty or more; no plant descriptions. (1978)
❒ Catalog: $.25, R&W, SS:4-10, $15m, bn

The Primrose Path
RD 2, Box 110
Scottdale, PA 15683
(412) 887-6756
Charles & Martha Oliver

Plants
A broad selection of **perennials**, including rock garden and woodland plants, all well described and with lists of plants for special uses. They have an active hybridization and selection program in phlox, heuchera, tiarella; good selection of primulas, aquilegias, phlox and hardy ferns. (1985)
❒ Catalog: $1.50d, R&W, SS:W, bn/cn
⌂ Nursery: All year, M-Sa, call ahead
▼ Garden: April-October, M-Sa, call ahead

Protea Seed & Nursery Suppliers
P.O. Box 98229
Sloanpark, South Africa 2152
011-7825215
Mrs. I. M. Bruens

Seeds ∾ Books
Offers seeds of proteas, leucodendrons, banksias, ericas and other **South African native plants**, all briefly described. They will also try to supply seeds that are not on their list. Also list several books on growing these plants. (1979)
☐ Catalog: $1(US bills), US/CAN/OV, $20m, bn

Putney Nursery, Inc.
Route 5
Putney, VT 05346
(802) 387-5671
C. J. & Ruth Gorius

Seeds
Offers seeds of **wildflowers, herbs, perennials and alpines**; the wildflowers are sold in seed mixes for various growing conditions, as well as seeds of individual plants. Color catalog, each plant well described. Also sells Christmas greens by mail; request that brochure separately. (1928)
☐ Catalog: $1d, $6m, bn/cn
⌂ Nursery: February-December, daily
♥ Garden: April-September, M-Sa

Qualitree Nursery
11110 Harlan Road
Eddyville, OR 97343
(503) 875-4192 TO
Donna Frank

Plants
"We grow **conifers and deciduous seedlings** for Christmas tree growers, reforesters and small woodlot owners. We will grow almost any species on contract." Sells only in quantity. (1981)
☐ Catalog: Free, R&W, CAN/OV, SS:11-2, $50m
⌂ Nursery: All year, by appointment only
♥ Garden: All year, by appointment only

Quality Dutch Bulbs
P.O. Box 225
50 Lake Drive
Hillsdale, NJ 07642
(201) 391-6586 TO/CC $25m
Peter Langeveld

Bulbs
Dutch bulbs imported and distributed by the grower -- a broad selection of hybrid tulips, daffodils, crocus, hyacinths and amaryllis in a color catalog offering collections and pre-season specials. (1982)
☐ Catalog: Free, R&W, SS:8-11, $5m, cn

Rainbow Gardens Nursery & Bookshop
1444 E. Taylor Street
Vista, CA 92084
(619) 758-4290 TO/CC
C. H. Everson

Plants ∾ Books
Specializes in **epiphyllums and other rainforest cacti, hoyas, haworthia** and **"holiday" cacti**; a large selection. Plants well described, many shown in color photos. Bookshop has a separate catalog offering a huge selection of books on cacti, succulents, bromeliads, ferns and greenhouse/propagation. Bought out California Epi Center, the greatest nursery name ever! (1977)
☐ Catalog: $2(6 IRC), CAN/OV, SS:4-11, $14m, bn/cn
⌂ Nursery: All year, Tu-Sa, by appointment only
♥ Garden: All year, Tu-Sa, by appointment only

Rainforest Flora, Inc.
1927 W. Rosecrans Avenue
Gardena, CA 90249
(213) 515-5200 TO
Jerrold Robinson

Plants
Offers bromeliads, tillandsias, platyceriums, cycads, neoregelia and other **tropical plants**. (1976)
☐ Catalog: Long SASE, R&W, CAN/OV, $30m
⌂ Nursery: All year, daily
♥ Garden: All year, daily

Rainforest Plantes et Fleurs, Inc.
1550 Roycroft Street
Honolulu, HI 96814
(808) 942-1550
Michael Miyashiro

Plants ∾ Seeds
Growers and shippers of **hoyas and other tropical plants**; hoya list has good plant descriptions of rare varieties -- they can also provide seeds. Also ship plumeria and bougainvillea and will air-ship tropical cut flowers and other flower-arranging material. (1985)
☐ Catalog: $1d(2 IRC), R&W, CAN/OV, $30m, bn
⌂ Nursery: All year, M-Sa
♥ Garden: By appointment only

Raintree Nursery
391 Butts Road
Morton, WA 98356
(206) 496-5410 TO/CC
Sam Benowitz & Maida Richman

Plants ∾ Books ∾ Supplies
Offer **edible plants, many fruit and nut varieties** in a very informative catalog full of orchard lore, edible landscaping and cultural suggestions. They also offer some ornamental trees and shrubs, grafting and pruning supplies and books on fruit growing and edible landscaping. (1976)
☐ Catalog: Free, R&W, SS:1-5, $10m, cn/bn
⌂ Nursery: February-April, Sa-Su
♥ Garden: Growing area, Sa-Su

Ramona Gardens
2178 El Paso Street
Ramona, CA 92065
(619) 789-6099
Linda Moore

Plants
Offers **bearded irises, daylilies and daffodils**; a good selection of the first two, each well but briefly described. Daffodil list not seen. (1985)
☐ Catalog: $1d, CAN/OV, SS:3-11, $12m
⌂ Nursery: All year, by appointment only
♥ Garden: April-June, by appointment only

Rancho Nuez Nursery
1378 Willow Glen Road
Fallbrook, CA 92028
(619) 728-6407
Tom & Cindy Cooper

Plants ～ Seeds
Specialize in **macadamia nuts**; plants, seeds and scionwood are available.
They also publish "The Macadamia Nut Grower Quarterly," consult with those
who wish to grow macadamias (the only edible protea!) and sell grafting
supplies. Ask for ordering information; they don't publish a catalog. (1970)
🗀 Catalog: See notes, R&W, CAN/OV, $5m
⌂ Nursery: September-July, daily
▼ Garden: September-July, daily

Randy's Iris Garden
186 West 800 North
Sunset, UT 84015
Randy & Shelly Brown

Plants
A real collectors' list of **tall bearded and standard dwarf bearded irises**:
huge selection, tiny print, brief descriptions. Many seem to be fairly
recent introductions, others obviously old favorites; they also will put
together special collections of their choice. (1984)
🗀 Catalog: 1 FCS, SS:7-8, $10m
▼ Garden: By appointment only

Rare Seed Locator Network
2140 Shattuck Avenue
Berkeley, CA 94704
Abdal Singh

Seeds
Oh agony! I found this **seed exchange** the night before this book went
to press, so was unable to contact them. According to Hortideas, it is
an "organization [of private collectors] with over 300 participants in ten
countries," formed because most botanical gardens do not exchange
seeds with individuals.
🗀 Catalog: Long SASE

Rasland Farm
NC 82 at US 13
Godwin, NC 28344
(919) 567-2705
Sylvia Tippett

Plants ～ Supplies
A good selection of **herb plants and scented geraniums**; good but brief plant
descriptions. Also a broad selection of herbal products: teas, potpourris
and supplies, cooking herbs, wreaths and more. No shipments to HI. (1981)
🗀 Catalog: $2.50, R&W, SS:3-10, $10m, cn/bn
⌂ Nursery: All year, M-Sa
▼ Garden: May-September, M-Sa

Ravenswood Seeds
6525 W. Bluemound Road
Wauwatosa, WI 53213-4094
Sue Fisher

Seeds
New seed company offering **flower and herb seeds** imported from Europe;
has a nice selection of annuals and perennials, especially sweet peas, and
also many culinary herbs. Also offers seed collections. Catalog price will
bring the next three catalogs and a sample packet of seed.
🗀 Catalog: $1.50, bn

Rawlinson Garden Seed
269 College Road
Truro, NS, Canada B2N 2P6
Bill Rawlinson

Seeds
Catalog offers seeds for a broad selection of **vegetables, some herbs** and
flowers, all very well described, with cultural information. Included is a
heritage baking bean called 'Jacob's Cattle'; it's got to be good! Catalog
free in eastern Canada, $1 elsewhere in Canada, US$1 or £1 overseas. (1979)
🗀 Catalog: See notes, US/OV
⌂ Nursery: February-June, M-Sa

© Edible Landscaping
Artist: Sher Bell

Steve Ray's Bamboo Gardens
909 - 79th Place South
Birmingham, AL 35206
(205) 833-3052
Steve Ray

Plants
Specializes in **hardy bamboos**; 17 varieties listed in the catalog, all very well described, with many culms shown in b&w photographs. They have other varieties planted on 50 acres, and new varieties will become available as the supply builds up. (1976)
☐ Catalog: $1, SS:9-2, $20m, bn/cn
⌂ Nursery: All year, by appointment only
▼ Garden: All year, by appointment only

Rayner Bros.
P.O. Box 1617
Mt. Herman Road
Salisbury, MD 21801
(301) 742-1594 TO/CC
P. Curtis Massey

Plants
Offers a wide selection of **strawberries** for many climates; all well described with cultural information. Also offers **dwarf fruit trees, blackberries, raspberries, blueberries, asparagus roots and table grapes** in a color catalog.
☐ Catalog: Free, SS:2-5

Reasoner's, Inc.
P.O. Box 1881
2501 - 53rd Avenue East
Oneco, FL 34264-1881
(813) 756-1881
Bud Reasoner

Plants ✍ Books
Here's a source for **hibiscus**; not the hardy variety but the lovely, tender kind that grows in Florida and Hawaii. They have a very large selection, described only by letter codes; scionwood also available. Also sell an American Hisbiscus Society book on growing hibiscus. (1881)
☐ Catalog: $1, CAN/OV, SS:W, $5m
⌂ Nursery: All year, daily

Reath's Nursery
P.O. Box 521
100 Central Boulevard
Vulcan, MI 49892
(906) 563-9321
David Reath

Plants ✍ Bulbs
Offers **herbaceous and tree peonies**, including hybrids of Daphnis, Saunders and his own. Japanese tree peonies listed by Japanese cultivar name -- a true collectors' list; catalog has color photographs and good plant descriptions. Has started selling **hostas**, too.
☐ Catalog: $1, SS:9-10

Recor Tree Seed
9164 Huron Street
Denver, CO 80221
Anvanette Recor

Seeds
Offer seeds of **conifers and maples** (not Japanese) by common name; plants briefly described. Seeds offered in packets and in bulk. They will try to locate seeds of trees not listed and help customers with information if needed. (1981)
☐ Catalog: Long SASE, R&W, CAN, $5m, cn

Red's Rhodies
15920 S.W. Oberst Lane
Sherwood, OR 97140
(503) 625-6331 TO
Dick & Karen Cavender

Plants
In a slight change of direction, "Red" now specializes in **vireya rhododendrons** by mail order; he has a good selection of species and hybrids, each well described. He still offers selected clones of Rhododendron occidentale and other rhododendron hybrids at the nursery. (1977)
☐ Catalog: Long SASE, CAN, SS:4-10, bn/cn
⌂ Nursery: All year, daily, call ahead
▼ Garden: April-June, call ahead

Redlo Cacti
2315 N.W. Circle Boulevard
Corvallis, OR 97330
(503) 752-2910 TO/CC
Lorne & Lola Hanna

Plants
Good selection of **cacti, succulents and lithops**; each given a good, brief description, many available in more than one size. There are several pages of detailed cultural information. (1984)
☐ Catalog: $2d, bn
⌂ Nursery: All year, daily, by appointment only

Redwood City Seed Co.
P.O. Box 361
Redwood City, CA 94064
(415) 325-SEED
Craig & Sue Dremann

Seeds ✍ Books
Old-fashioned open-pollinated **vegetables and herbs**, mostly developed before 1906; unusual varieties, including Oriental types and Native American beans, corn, hot peppers and squash. These and other "useful" plants are very well described, with growing hints. Books on plants and organic gardening, too.
☐ Catalog: $1(5 IRC), R&W, CAN/OV, cn/bn

Rex Bulb Farms
P.O. Box 774
4310-B Highway 20
Port Townsend, WA 98368
(206) 385-4280 TO/CC
Nethalie Shaver

Plants ✍ Bulbs
Color catalog offers a good selection of American-grown **lilies**, both species and hybrids, for garden, greenhouse or patio; plants briefly to well described, some illustrated. They have also added some **dahlias**. (1946)
☐ Catalog: $1d, CAN/OV, SS:10-12,3-5, $20m
⌂ Nursery: All year, M-F, call ahead

Rhapis Gardens
101 Rhapis Road, Box 287
Gregory, TX 78359
(512) 643-2061 or 5814 TO/CC $20m
Lynn McKamey

Plants ✍ Books ✍ Supplies
Sells **Rhapis excelsa**, grown in the US by division, and offers a number of varieties; these subtropical palms have been collectors' plants in Japan for centuries. Also offers cycads, Cissus rhombifolia and 'Ming' aralias; all plants well described. Also designer pottery and a book on Rhapis palms called "Secret of the Orient," by Lynn McKamey. (1976)
☐ Catalog: $1, R&W, CAN/OV, SS:2-11, $18m
⌂ Nursery: All year, M-F, call ahead
▼ Garden: All year, growing area, call ahead

Rhapis Palm Growers
P.O. Box 84
31350 Alta Vista Drive
Redlands, CA 92373
(714) 794-3823 TO
Leland & Anna Hollenberg

Plants
"We offer more than 40 named varieties of **Rhapis excelsa and R. humilis**
palms, imported from Japan -- including variegated and all-green varieties."
Color catalog is in Japanese, with anglicized Japanese species names given
on price list. (1976)
❑ Catalog: $2, R&W, CAN/OV, $25m
⌂ Nursery: All year, by appointment only
▼ Garden: All year, by appointment only

Rice Creek Gardens
1315 - 66th Avenue N.E.
Minneapolis, MN 55432
(612) 574-1197 or 755-8484 TO/CC
Betty Ann Mech

Plants ∾ Books ∾ Tools
A collectors' list of **alpine and rock garden plants**: dwarf conifers, ground
covers, dwarf flowering shrubs, dwarf ferns and waterside plants. Broad
selection of very hardy plants, well but briefly described. Also offers some
books on rock gardening and prairie plants. Has another shop at 11506
Highway 65, Blaine, MN. (1972)
❑ Catalog: $2, R&W, OV, SS:5-9, $35m, bn
⌂ Nursery: May-October, M-Sa
▼ Garden: May-October, M-Sa

Richardson's Seaside Banana Garden
6823 Santa Barbara Avenue
La Conchita, CA 93001
(805) 643-4061
Doug Richardson

Plants
Offers both bare-root and containered **banana** plants, each very well
described for habit of growth and flavor of fruit, with good cultural
information. They also sell bananas to eat, so you can taste several
varieties before investing in a tree. (1985)
❑ Catalog: $2, R&W, $20m
⌂ Nursery: All year, daily, call ahead
▼ Garden: April-December, daily, call ahead

Richters
P.O. Box 26
Highway 47
Goodwood, ON, Canada L0C 1A0
(416) 640-6677 TO/CC
Otto Richter

Plants ∾ Seeds ∾ Books ∾ Supplies ∾ Tools
Catalog offers seed and plants of many **herbs, wildflowers and everlasting
flowers,** as well as dried herbs and spices, herbal gifts and books and
posters on herbs; will ship plants in Canada and by UPS to the United States.
All plants are well described, with information on culture and traditional
uses. (1971)
❑ Catalog: $2.50(6 IRC), R&W, US/OV, cn/bn
⌂ Nursery: All year, M-Sa; spring & fall, daily
▼ Garden: Summer, M-Sa

Rider Nurseries
Route 2, Box 90A
Farmington, IA 52626
(319) 878-4148 TO/CC
Geri & William Rider

Plants
Specializes in **strawberries**. Also offers asparagus, horseradish, rhubarb,
grapes, raspberries, blackberries and hardy blueberries, some roses, fruit
trees, dwarf fruit trees and ornamental shrubs. Very brief plant descriptions. Offers several "collections" of fruit, berries and roses. (1930)
❑ Catalog: Free, R&W, SS:3-5
⌂ Nursery: March-May, M-Sa, call ahead

Ripley's Believe It or Not Seed Catalog
10 Bay Street
Westport, CT 06880-4800
(203) 454-1919
Jess F. Clarke, III

Seeds
Formerly listed as Grace's Garden, this small company specializes in "amazing
vegetables" -- largest, smallest, tallest, strangest, and so forth, all well
described. Children might have fun growing things such as birdhouse gourds,
large and small pumpkins and broom corn to make their own brooms.
❑ Catalog: $1, $15m

Riverbend Orchids
14220 Lorraine Road
Biloxi, MS 39532
(601) 392-2699 TO/CC
Morton Engelberg & James Phillips

Plants ∾ Supplies
List offers a number of cattleyas, including mini-cattleyas, phalaenopsis and
paphiopedilum **hybrids and some species orchids** and miscellaneous hybrids,
all briefly described. Sold in flasks, community pots and individually.
❑ Catalog: Free, R&W, $15m
⌂ Nursery: All year, daily, call ahead
▼ Garden: All year, greenhouse, call ahead

Clyde Robin Seed Co.
P.O. Box 2366
Castro Valley, CA 94546
(415) 581-3468
Clyde Robin

Seeds ∾ Books
Color catalog offers a broad selection of **wildflowers**; plants briefly
described. Also available are a number of native seed mixes suitable for
any climate. They also offer books on wildflowers, note paper and herb
seed collections.
❑ Catalog: $2, R&W, CAN/OV, bn/cn
⌂ Nursery: All year, M-F (3670 Enterprise Ave., Hayward, CA)

Robinett Bulb Farm
P.O. Box 1306
Sebastopol, CA 95473-1306
James Robinett

Seeds ✍ Bulbs
Seeds and bulbs of **West Coast native bulbs**: alliums, brodiaea, calochortus, species lilies, fritillaries, erythroniums and others; also alstroemerias. Bulbs are nursery-grown and, because the business is small, may be in short supply. New list every August. Minimum overseas order is $20. (1983)
❏ Catalog: Long SASE, SS:9-11, $10m, bn/cn

Robyn's Nest Nursery
7802 N.E. 63rd Street
Vancouver, WA 98662
(206) 256-7399
Robyn Duback

Plants
A small nursery offering a nice selection of **perennials and rock garden plants**, particularly dianthus, ornamental grasses, and many hostas; each plant well described, some of them hard to find. (1983)
❏ Catalog: $1d, SS:spring,fall, bn/cn
⌂ Nursery: Call ahead

Rock Spray Nursery
P.O. Box 693
Depot Road
Truro, MA 02666
(508) 349-6769
Betsy Erickson & Kate Herrick

Plants
Suppliers of heaths and heathers; they offer a number of species and varieties of **erica** and **calluna**, briefly described by size, color and season of bloom, habit and color of foliage. They sell other seaside plants at the nursery. (1981)
❏ Catalog: Free, R&W, $25m, bn
⌂ Nursery: Summer, daily; October-March, by appointment only

Rocknoll Nursery
9210 US 50 East
Hillsboro, OH 45133-8546
(513) 393-1278 TO/CC $25m
Eleanor Saur

Plants ✍ Seeds
Catalog offers a broad selection of **rock garden plants**, shade and native plants, some dwarf evergreens and flowering shrubs and perennials; very brief plant descriptions. Features hostas, dianthus, phlox, penstemons, irises, daylilies, epimediums. Separate seed list available. (1928)
❏ Catalog: 2 FCS, SS:3-11, $20m, bn/cn
⌂ Nursery: March-November, M-Sa, call ahead

Rocky Meadow Orchard & Nursery
Route 2, Box 2104
New Salisbury, IN 47161-9716
(812) 347-2213
Ed & Pat Fackler

Plants ✍ Supplies
Specializes in **apples, pears and Oriental pears, cherries and plums** and rootstocks for these fruit trees; some trees available as espaliers. Also does custom propagation, sells grafting supplies and does consultation on fruit culture. All fruit varieties are chosen with flavor as first priority. Informative catalog. (1975)
❏ Catalog: $.50, R&W, SS:11-5
⌂ Nursery: All year, Tu-Sa, by appointment only
▼ Garden: September-October, by appointment only

Grace Rollerson
5512 Clinton Street
Burnaby, BC, Canada V5J 2L8
(604) 435-0560
Grace E. Rollerson

Plants
Known by collectors of **cactus and succulents** as editor of the now defunct "Cactus & Succulent Information Exchange" newsletter, Mrs. Rollerson sells surplus plants from her own collection: many species of cactus, mesembs, lithops, adromischus, cotyledon, crassula, echeveria, euphorbia, haworthia, sedum and others. Canada only; some in short supply. Write for information on back issues of the newsletter.
❏ Catalog: Long SASE, SS:4-10, bn
⌂ Nursery: By appointment only
▼ Garden: April-October, by appointment only

Ronniger's Seed Potatoes
Star Route
Moyie Springs, ID 83845
(208) 267-7938
David Ronninger

Plants
Offer a broad selection of **seed potatoes**: 23 early-maturing varieties, 25 that mature in mid-season, 16 late-maturing varieties and 5 varieties of fingerlings, with more choices to come. Each variety is well described by color, flavor, disease resistance and keeping qualities.
❏ Catalog: 2FCS, R&W, SS:3-5,9-10, $7m
⌂ Nursery: All year, M-Sa, call ahead

Roris Gardens
7851 Carmencita Avenue
Sacramento, CA 95829
(916) 689-7460
Joseph B. Grant II, Mgr.

Plants
Offer a good selection of tall bearded **irises**, all shown in lovely color photographs, with good plant descriptions.
❏ Catalog: $2d, CAN/OV, SS:6-9, $10m
⌂ Nursery: All year, M-F
▼ Garden: Late March-early May, daily

Rose Acres
6641 Crystal Boulevard
Diamond Springs, CA 95619
(916) 626-1722
Muriel Humenick

Plants
Collectors' list offers a selection of hybrid tea, shrub and old garden **roses** and a few species roses; descriptions in letter code. Many plants are "own root"; they specialize in singles and shrub hybrid musks and can propagate special requests. They also offer Daphne odora. (1979)
❏ Catalog: Long SASE, R&W, SS:10-2, $10m, bn
⌂ Nursery: All year, call ahead
▼ Garden: April-June, call ahead

The Rose Garden & Mini Rose Nursery
P.O. Box 203
SC Highway 560 (Austin Street)
Cross Hill, SC 29332-0203
(803) 998-4331 TO/CC $20m
Michael & Betty Williams

Plants
List offers a selection of award-winning **miniature roses** chosen for best performance; each briefly but well described, a few illustrated in color, including their own introductions -- 'Sox' will knock yours off! (1983)
☐ Catalog: Free, R&W
⌂ Nursery: All year, daily, call ahead
▼ Garden: May-October, daily, call ahead

Rose Hill Herbs and Perennials
Route 4, Box 377
Amherst, VA 24521
Joan Rothemich

Plants
A good selection of **herbs, perennials, scented geraniums and everlastings**; plants briefly to well described. They also offer several collections of plants for salad lovers, vinegar makers, everlastings and scented geraniums. Good selections of rosemary, mints, basils, sages and thymes. (1976)
☐ Catalog: $2d, SS:4-6,9-10, $10m

Rosehill Farm
Gregg Neck Road
Galena, MD 21635
(301) 648-5538 TO/CC $20m
Patricia Berlen

Plants
Color catalog offers a good selection of **miniature roses** and several collections; each plant well described. (1977)
☐ Catalog: Free, R&W, CAN/OV
⌂ Nursery: All year, M-Sa
▼ Garden: May, September, M-Sa

The Rosemary House
120 S. Market Street
Mechanicsburg, PA 17055
(717) 697-5111 or 766-6581
Bertha Reppert

Plants ⬥ Seeds ⬥ Books ⬥ Supplies
Offers a good selection of **herb seeds, some herb plants, scented geraniums** and herbal gifts, supplies, teas, books, cards and kitchenware. Also cookbooks, herb garden plans, bus trips to herb gardens, tea parties and makings for potpourri. Can't ship plants to CA, mints to MT. (1968)
☐ Catalog: $2, R&W, CAN/OV, SS:4-6,9-11, cn
⌂ Nursery: All year, Tu-Sa
▼ Garden: May-October, Tu-Sa

Roses by Fred Edmunds
6235 S.W. Kahle Road
Wilsonville, OR 97070
(503) 682-1476 FAX 682-1275
Fred Edmunds

Plants ⬥ Supplies
An informative color catalog offers a broad selection of modern hybrid tea, floribunda, grandiflora and climbing **roses**, all well described with cultural suggestions. The "gambler's special" is a new European rose on trial. They also offer goatskin gloves, leaky pipe and Felco pruning shears. (1950)
☐ Catalog: Free, CAN/OV, SS:11-5
⌂ Nursery: November-May, M-F
▼ Garden: September, M-F, call ahead

Roses of Yesterday & Today
802 Brown's Valley Road
Watsonville, CA 95076-0398
(408) 724-3537 or 2755 TO/CC $20m
Patricia S. Wiley, Kathryn Wiley Minier

Plants
Informative catalog lists a broad selection of "old garden" and many other types of **roses** -- modern shrubs, climbers and ramblers, hybrid teas and **species roses**; plants very well described, some illustrated in b&w photos. Included are rare, highly perfumed and some very hardy roses. (1948)
☐ Catalog: $3, CAN/OV, SS:1-5
⌂ Nursery: All year, M-F
▼ Garden: May-June, M-F

Roslyn Nursery
211 Burrs Lane
Dix Hills, NY 11746
(516) 643-9347 TO/CC
Philip & Harriet Waldman

Plants
Collectors' list of hybrid and species rhododendrons, evergreen and deciduous azaleas, dwarf conifers, hollies, pieris, kalmias, other **ornamental shrubs and trees and perennials**; each plant briefly described, with some color photographs. A large selection of choice landscape plants. (1980)
☐ Catalog: $2, CAN/OV, SS:4-6,9-12, $25m, bn
⌂ Nursery: All year, Tu-Sa; April-June, Tu-Su
▼ Garden: April-June, growing area, Tu-Su

Roswell Seed Co.
P.O. Box 725
115-117 S. Main
Roswell, NM 88202-0725
(505) 622-7701 TO/CC
Jim, Ivan & W. L. Gill

Seeds ⬥ Supplies
Regional seed company sells **vegetables, grains and grasses** for New Mexico, Arizona, Oklahoma and Utah. Hybrid and open-pollinated crops well described; offers a good variety of grains, cover crops, native grasses, some annual flowers and growing supplies. Can't ship to CA. (1900)
☐ Catalog: Free, R&W, $5m
⌂ Nursery: All year, M-Sa

Rupp Seeds, Inc.
5-17919 County Road 13
Wauseon, OH 43567
(419) 337-1841 TO/CC $5m
Roger L. Rupp

Seeds
A big supplier to commercial farms, they will sell **sweet corn** seeds to home gardeners. They run extensive trials on sweet corn and sell seed from many sources; ask for the corn list for home growers. (1946)
☐ Catalog: Free, R&W

Jim & Irene Russ Quality Plants
P.O. Box 6450
Buell Road
Igo, CA 96047
(916) 396-2329
Jim & Irene Russ

Plants
Very broad selection of **sedums, sempervivums, jovibarba and heuffeliis**, well described in a tightly packed collectors' list, with good cultural information (they are happy to help with specific cultural questions). Most of the plants are hardy to Zone 1 and come in many colors, leaf textures, even cobweb types. No shipping to Eastern Bloc countries. (1956)
❑ Catalog: $.50(2 IRC), R&W, CAN/OV, SS:3-11, $10m, bn
⌂ Nursery: April-October, W-M, call ahead
▼ Garden: March-May, W-M, call ahead

Rust-En-Vrede Nursery
P.O. Box 231
Constantia, South Africa 7848
(021) 74-2574
Hendrik van Zijl

Seeds
Specializes in the seeds of **South African bulbous plants and disa orchids**; plants listed by botanical name with no descriptions, but collectors will know them. List includes lachenalia, cyrtanthus, moraea, romulea, babiana, species iris and gladiolus, geissorhiza, brunsvigia and many more. (1978)
❑ Catalog: Free, OV, SS:12-5, $15m, bn

S & H Organic Acres
P.O. Box 1531
Watsonville, CA 95077
(408) 893-1226 TO/CC $10m
Marlene Courselle

Plants ⌖ Books
A brief list, but offers "breathtaking" **elephant garlic**, other garlics, shallots, Egyptian and potato onions, garlic braids and garlic books -- powerful stuff! (1971)
❑ Catalog: $1d, R&W, SS:8-10
⌂ Nursery: August-February, daily, call ahead

SLO Gardens
4816 Bridgecreek Road
San Luis Obispo, CA 93401
(805) 544-3122 TO
Rudy Bachmann

Plants
A very extensive list of **hoyas**, many species and cultivars, offered as cuttings or rooted plants; all briefly described, some cultural information is included.
❑ Catalog: 1 FCS($1 OV), CAN/OV, SS:2-11, $20m
⌂ Nursery: All year, Sa-Su, call ahead
▼ Garden: All year, Sa-Su, call ahead

SPB Sales
P.O. Box 278
Nash, TX 75569
(214) 838-5616
Mark Peyton

Seeds ⌖ Supplies ⌖ Tools
Regional seed company specializing in **vegetables for Southern gardens**, particularly tomatoes, melons, onions and onion plants, corn, **peas and gourds**, all briefly described. Also a good selection of growing supplies. (1984)
❑ Catalog: Free, R&W, SS:2-4

Saginaw Valley Nut Nursery
8285 Dixie Highway, Route 5
Birch Run, MI 48415
Richard D. Goldner

Plants ⌖ Seeds
A selection of **hardy nut trees** (to -30F) -- black and Persian walnuts, butternuts, buartnuts (butternut X heartnut), hickory, Chinese and Korean chestnuts, mulberries and pawpaws -- all very briefly described. Cultivars also listed by state of origin. Inquire about seed nuts and scions. (1980)
❑ Catalog: Long SASE, SS:10-12,4-5

St. Lawrence Nurseries
RD 2
Route 345, Potsdam-Madrid Road
Potsdam, NY 13676
(315) 265-6739
Diana & Bill MacKentley

Plants ⌖ Books
A broad selection of organically grown **cold-hardy fruit and nut trees**, other edible fruits, berries and scionwood; plants very well described, with comparative tables on hardiness, fruit color and harvest season in an informative catalog. Books on fruit culture available.
❑ Catalog: Free, CAN, SS:4-5, cn/bn
⌂ Nursery: M-Sa, call ahead
▼ Garden: June-March, call ahead

Salter Tree Farm
Route 2, Box 1332
Madison, FL 32340
(904) 973-6312
Charles E. Salter

Plants ⌖ Bulbs
A good selection of **Southern native trees and shrubs**, with some lilies, ground covers and non-natives; there are no plant descriptions, but they are well worth looking up elsewhere.
❑ Catalog: Long SASE, R&W, SS:11-3, bn/cn
⌂ Nursery: M-Sa, call ahead
▼ Garden: M-Sa, growing area, call ahead

Saltspring Primroses
2426 W. 47th Avenue
Vancouver, BC, Canada V6M 2N2
John Kerridge

Seeds
Offers seed of prize-winning **primroses**, all hand-pollinated: gold-laced polyanthus, blue cowichan, mixed cowichan and gold-laced polyanthus X polyanthus. All seed packets are $2 -- Canadian dollars for Canada, US dollars for the US and overseas. (1985)
❑ Catalog: Free, US/OV, $2m

Sanctuary Seeds/Folklore Herb Co., Ltd.
2388 W. 4th Avenue
Vancouver, BC, Canada V6K 1P1
(604) 733-4724
Maha Sarsthi

Seeds ✍ Books
Catalog offers a broad selection of **open-pollinated and untreated vegetable and herb seeds**, with detailed growing instructions; they do not print instructions on their seed packets. They also sell dried herbs, teas, natural foods and herb and garden books. (1970)
☐ Catalog: $1, R&W, US, cn/bn
⌂ Nursery: All year, M-Sa

Sandy Mush Herb Nursery
Route 2, Surrett Cove Road
Leicester, NC 28748
(704) 683-2014 TO $25m
Fairman & Kate Jayne

Plants ✍ Seeds ✍ Books
A very broad selection of **herbs**, both seeds and plants, all very well described in a lovely italic hand. Also offers scented geraniums, irises, ornamental grasses, primulas, heathers, other perennials, herbal gifts and books. Also salvia, lavender, rosemary, thyme, mints and more. (1978)
☐ Catalog: $4d, R&W, CAN, $10m
⌂ Nursery: All year, Th-Sa, call ahead
▼ Garden: May-October, Th-Sa, call ahead

Santa Barbara Orchid Estate
1250 Orchid Drive
Santa Barbara, CA 93111
(800) 553-3387 FAX (805) 683-3405 TO/CC
Anne P. Gripp

Plants ✍ Supplies
Offers many **cymbidium orchids** which do well outdoors in coastal California, as well as a huge selection of **species and other orchids** -- far too many to list! Each is briefly described; get out your orchid reference books. They also offer growing supplies and plants in flasks. (1957)
☐ Catalog: Free, R&W, CAN/OV, SS:W
⌂ Nursery: All year, daily
▼ Garden: All year, daily

Santa Barbara Water Gardens
P.O. Box 4353
160 E. Mountain Drive
Santa Barbara, CA 93140
(805) 969-5129
Stephne Sheatsley & Virginia Hayes

Plants ✍ Books ✍ Supplies
A nice selection of **water lilies, lotus, aquatic and bog plants**, each very briefly described. Also sells books and supplies for water gardening and does local water garden design, construction and maintenance. (1980)
☐ Catalog: $1.50d, SS:W, cn/bn
⌂ Nursery: All year, W,Sa
▼ Garden: June-August, W,Sa

Savage Farms Nursery
P.O. Box 125 K
Highway 56 South
McMinnville, TN 37110
(615) 668-8902

Plants
Color catalog offers **fruit trees, nuts, grapes, berries** and a selection of ornamental trees, shrubs and conifers, each briefly described. Some of the plants cannot be shipped to CA, OR and WA. (1942)
☐ Catalog: Free, SS:10-4, cn
⌂ Nursery: October-May, daily
▼ Garden: October-May, daily

Savory's Gardens, Inc.
5300 Whiting Avenue
Edina, MN 55435
(612) 941-8755 TO/CC $35m
Arlene, Robert & Dennis Savory

Plants
Around 200 varieties of **hosta** are listed. Plants are briefly but well described, some illustrated in color; many are their own introductions. They grow over 800 varieties of hosta at the nursery, also sell daylilies, ground covers and other perennials there. (1946)
☐ Catalog: $2, R&W, CAN, SS:4-5,9-10, $25m, bn
⌂ Nursery: April-October, M-F; May, daily
▼ Garden: June-August, M-F, call ahead

Saxton Gardens
1 First Street
Saratoga Springs, NY 12866
Stanley Saxton

Plants ✍ Bulbs
A broad selection of **daylilies, lilies and hostas** -- their own "Adirondack" daylily introductions, which are extra-hardy, as well as others. Plants well described, some illustrated in color. Ask for the lily or hosta lists; they aren't in the daylily catalog. (1945)
☐ Catalog: $.50, R&W, CAN, SS:4-5,9-10, $10m
⌂ Nursery: May-October, daily, by appointment only
▼ Garden: July-August, by appointment only

John Scheepers, Inc.
RD 6, Phillipsburg Road
Middletown, NY 10940
(914) 342-1135
Steven Van Eeden, Mgr.

Plants ✍ Bulbs
Issues seasonal catalogs offering **spring- and summer-blooming bulbs**, many illustrated in color, all well described. Spring catalog also offers perennials, as well as dahlias, begonias, lilies, gladiolus and daylilies.
☐ Catalog: Free

S. Scherer & Sons
104 Waterside Road
Northport, NY 11768
(516) 261-7432
Robert W. Scherer

Plants ✍ Supplies
Offers everything necessary for a garden pool or pond: **waterlilies** and other **aquatic plants**, fiberglass pools, pool liners, fountain heads, pumps and low-voltage garden lights. Everything briefly but well described. (1907)
☐ Catalog: Free, SS:4-12, cn/bn
⌂ Nursery: All year, daily
▼ Garden: April-October, daily

Schlichenmayer's

See Old Farm Nursery.

Schreiner's Gardens
3625 Quinaby Road N.E.
Salem, OR 97303
(503) 393-3232
David Schreiner

Plants
Color catalog describes tall bearded **irises**, "lilliputs" and intermediates and offers a number of collections; a very large selection. All plants very well described, with cultural advice; many are illustrated. (1925)
❑ Catalog: $2d, R&W, CAN/OV, SS:7-9, $10m

Schulz Cactus Gardens
1095 Easy Street
Morgan Hill, CA 95037
(408) 683-4489
Ernst Schulz

Plants
A broad selection of **cactus** -- coryphanthus, echinocereus, escobaria, ferocactus, matucana, neochilenia, neoporteria, parodia and others, as well as a very large number of mammillaria; listed by botanical name only. (1979)
❑ Catalog: Free, R&W, bn
⌂ Nursery: All year, daily, call ahead
▼ Garden: All year, daily, call ahead

F. W. Schumacher Co.
36 Spring Hill Road
Sandwich, MA 02563-1023
(508) 888-0659
Donald H. Allen

Seeds ⌦ Books
A very broad selection of seeds of **trees, shrubs, conifers, rhododendrons** and **azaleas** listed by botanical and common name, and with geographical source where important. Offers species maples, birches, dogwoods, cotoneasters, crabapples, hollies, species roses, viburnums and much more; they will also buy seed of rare plants. Some books on propagation, too. (1926)
❑ Catalog: $1, R&W, bn
⌂ Nursery: All year, M-F

Scotty's Desert Plants
11588 S. Academy
Selma, CA 93662
(209) 891-1026 TO/CC
Mel & Mike Scott

Plants ⌦ Books ⌦ Supplies
Their "Catalog of Unusual Succulents" is just that -- offers a good selection of **cacti and succulents**, as well as bonsai pots and books on cacti and succulents. Plants briefly described, many illustrated in b&w photographs. Formerly Altman's Specialty Plants. (1974)
❑ Catalog: $1, R&W, SS:3-12, $15m, bn

Sea-Tac Gardens
20020 Des Moines Memorial Drive
Seattle, WA 98198
(206) 824-3846
Louis & Patti Eckhoff

Plants
Collectors' list of **dahlias**, with information given in a compact table; a broad selection. Their own introductions begin with 'Sea' -- as in 'Sea-Miss' -- a real winner. (1978)
❑ Catalog: Long SASE, R&W, CAN/OV, SS:4, $10m
⌂ Nursery: February-October, daily
▼ Garden: August-October, daily

Seagulls Landing Orchids
P.O. Box 388
Glen Head, NY 11545
(516) 367-6336 TO/CC
Shell Kanzer

Plants
Original hybridizers of **"Mini Cats"** and **"Compact Cats"** -- cattleya hybrids which will bloom two to four times a year. They also sell standard **cattleyas and miltonias** and other hybrids. Plants well described.
❑ Catalog: Free, R&W, CAN/OV, SS:4-11
⌂ Nursery: All year, Tu-Su, 1702 Route 25A (Laurel Hollow)
▼ Garden: All year, Tu-Su

Seaside Banana Garden

See Richardson's Seaside Banana Garden.

Seawright Gardens
134 Indian Hill
Carlisle, MA 01741
(508) 369-2172 TO/CC
Robert D. Seawright

Plants
A collectors' list of **daylilies** -- both diploids and tetraploids -- a wide selection; each very well described, with good general cultural advice. Includes eyed and blotched tetraploids bred by Don Stevens. (1976)
❑ Catalog: $1d(4 IRC) R&W, CAN/OV, SS:5-9, $15m
⌂ Nursery: May-October, daily (sales at 201 Bedford Road)
▼ Garden: June-August, daily

Sedona Gardens
P.O. Box 318
Osoyoos, BC, Canada V0H 1V0
(604) 446-2428
Carol A. Spooner

Plants
Offers many **houseplants** to gladden a Northern heart: African violets, hibiscus, bougainvillea, begonias, geraniums, hoyas, jasmines and epiphyllums. Firm has just changed hands; catalogs will be issued in January.
❑ Catalog: $1, SS:5-9

Seed Centre, Ltd.
Box 3867, Station D
14510 - 127th Street
Edmonton, AB, Canada T5L 4K1
(403) 456-1052 or 1054
Wigglesworth, Moore & Van Brederode

Seeds ⌦ Supplies ⌦ Tools
Color catalog offers **flower and short-season vegetable seeds**, as well as general nursery stock, conifers and ornamental trees and shrubs. They also carry a full line of growing supplies, fertilizers, pest controls and tools.
❑ Catalog: Free(1 IRC), R&W, US/OV, SS:3-5, $5m
⌂ Nursery: Spring, daily; all year, M-Sa

Seed Saving Project
Dept. LAWR, 139 Hoagland Hall
University of California
Davis, CA 95616
(916) 752-7645

Seeds
A seed savers' exchange for the preservation of **rare and endangered vegetable varieties**. Sponsored by the University of California's Sustainable Agriculture Program, it is open to dedicated gardeners who are committed to genetic preservation; membership is $3. Varieties listed are particularly adapted to the interior valleys of California.
❏ Catalog: $3

The Seed Shop
Tongue River Stage, HC-32
Mile City, MT 59301-9804
(406) 784-2213
Jim & Barbara Linaburg

Seeds
Small company offering seeds of **cactus** of many kinds and a few **succulents** -- a nice selection. Also lists seeds of some endangered or threatened species, habitat-collected from privately owned land and in compliance with all federal and state laws. Plants well described. (1988)
❏ Catalog: $2, bn/cn

The Seed Source
Route 68, Box 301
Tuckasegee, NC 28783
Majella Larochelle & Vee Sharp

Plants ⬥ Seeds
A new location for The Seed Source and Sharp Plants, formerly Maver Rare Perennials. They offer a broad selection of seeds -- the following lists are available for $1 each: Alpines, Bulbous Plants, Ornamental Grasses, Herbs, Wildflowers, Rock Garden Plants, Perennials and Trees & Shrubs. They also sell perennial plants by mail. The lists I've seen have brief to no plant descriptions.
❏ Catalog: See notes, R&W, $50m

Seedalp
P.O. Box 282
Meyrin, Geneve, Switzerland CH 1217
(022) 82 48 78
Idem Kroner

Seeds
Broad selection of **alpine and rock garden plants**, listed by botanical name; color descriptions and brief information in French, key to symbols in French, German and English. Anemones, aquilegias, campanulas, dianthus, digitalis, gentians, hellebores, irises, poppies, primulas, pulsatillas. (1981)
❏ Catalog: Free, R&W, OV, $5m, bn
⌂ Nursery: All year, M-F, call ahead

Seeds Blum
Idaho City Stage
Boise, ID 83706
(208) 343-2202
Jan Blum

Seeds ⬥ Books
Pronounced "Seeds Bloom" -- their catalog is informative, fun and helpful. They offer a number of **vegetables, annuals and perennials** for various conditions, advice on saving seed and opportunities for gardeners to test new "old" seeds and do research. They also sell books -- "fireside friends."
❏ Catalog: $2, CAN/OV, cn/bn

Seedway, Inc.
P.O. Box 250
Hall, NY 14463-0250
(315) 526-6391 TO/CC $10m

Seeds
Color catalog of **vegetable and flower seeds**; each well described and available in quantities suitable for home gardens as well as large commercial operations. They distribute "Bejo" vegetable seeds in the US and parts of Canada and have their own varieties of sweet corn.
❏ Catalog: Free, R&W, CAN/OV
⌂ Nursery: All year, M-F

Lothar Seik, Exotic Seeds

See Exotic Seeds, Lothar Seik.

Select Seeds
81 Stickney Hill Road
Union, CT 06076
Marilyn Barlow

Seeds
This seed business grew out of an old-garden restoration project; they specialize in **old-fashioned and heirloom perennials** found in cottage and period gardens, chosen for fragrance and flower cutting. Plants are well described -- there's not a "cultivar" on the list -- and listed by botanical name, with "old" common names given. (1986)
❏ Catalog: $2, R&W, CAN/OV, $2m, bn/cn
⌂ Nursery: By appointment only
▼ Garden: May-July, by appointment only

Sequoia Nursery -- Moore Miniature Roses
2519 E. Noble Avenue
Visalia, CA 93277
(209) 732-0190 or 0309 TO/CC $20m
Ralph S. Moore

Plants
Specializes in the hybrids of Ralph Moore, a pioneer in **miniature roses**, patenter of over 150 cultivars and the first to introduce striped flowers to minis. Color leaflets introduce new varieties twice a year and offer popular varieties for sale, including a few new hybrids which are bigger than minis. (1937)
❏ Catalog: Free, R&W
⌂ Nursery: All year, daily
▼ Garden: March-June, September, daily

Sevenoaks Nursery
3530 N.W. Roosevelt Drive
Corvallis, OR 97330
Barbara & Ron Cameron

Plants
Small nursery offers a nice selection of **hardy native plants**: species maples, creeping Oregon grape, kalmia (including several hybrid cultivars), quaking aspen, several willows and a dwarf mountain ash. Plants well described, offered in containers or bare-root. (1979)
❑ Catalog: $1.50d, R&W, $15m, bn

Shackleton's Dahlias
30535 Division Drive
Troutdale, OR 97060
(503) 663-7057
Steve & Linda Shackleton

Plants
"Heavy emphasis is placed on quality exhibition **dahlia** varieties -- we carry newer show varieties." A real collectors' list; information given in concise tables, with only color descriptions. (1981)
❑ Catalog: 1 FCS, CAN/OV, SS:12-5
⌂ Nursery: August-October 10, daily, call ahead
▼ Garden: September, call ahead

Shady Hill Gardens
821 Walnut Street
Batavia, IL 60510-2999
Chuck & Mary Ellen Heidgen

Plants ⟨⟩ Seeds
Sells over 1,100 **geraniums and pelargoniums**, some of their own hybridizing. The selection is huge -- plants of all sizes, indoor and out, scented, varie- gated, stellar, ivy, dwarf and a nice selection of species geraniums. All plants briefly but well described; also sells geranium seed. Nursery is also open on Sundays during April-June and Thanksgiving-Christmas. (1974)
❑ Catalog: $2d, R&W, CAN, SS:3-5,10-11, $5m, cn
⌂ Nursery: All year, M-Sa; see notes
▼ Garden: All year, glasshouses, M-Sa

Shady Oaks Nursery
700 - 19th Avenue N.E.
Waseca, MN 56093
(507) 835-5033
Clayton R. Oslund

Plants ⟨⟩ Books
This nursery specializes in **plants which grow well in shade** and offers a good selection of perennials, ferns, wildflowers, ground covers, hostas and a number of shrubs which tolerate shade; each plant well described. Also offers several books on shade gardening and woodland plants. (1979)
❑ Catalog: $1d, SS:4-5,9-10, bn/cn

Shannon Gardens of Oak Brook Farm
P.O. Box 175
Northfield, MN 55057-0175
(612) 644-0598 (evenings)
David E. Shannon

Plants
A hobby operation that has grown and grown -- a good selection of **tall bearded irises** for the collector; no plant descriptions. Be sure to call well in advance before trying to visit -- gardens are not at mailing address.
❑ Catalog: SS:8, $10m
▼ Garden: By appointment only; call (612) 257-1153

Shanti Bithi Nursery
3047 High Ridge Road
Stamford, CT 06903
(203) 329-0768 FAX (203) 329-8872

Plants ⟨⟩ Books ⟨⟩ Supplies ⟨⟩ Tools
Importers of finished **bonsai**, some quite mature; various plants are shown in color photos. Also sell bonsai tools, pots, supplies and books and two styles of stone lantern. (1970)
❑ Catalog: Free, OV, bn
⌂ Nursery: By appointment only

Sharp Plants

See The Seed Source.

Sheffield's Seed Co.
273 Route 34
Locke, NY 13092
(315) 497-1058 FAX 497-1059
Richard R. Sheffield

Seeds
Their main emphasis is on **tree and shrub seeds** for ornamental, forestry and Christmas tree production; seeds are sold by the ounce to the pound. There are many fine ornamental conifers and broadleaved trees and shrubs on the list: maples, birches, hickories, cotoneasters, walnuts, magnolias, pines, cherries, oaks, viburnums, dogwoods and much more. (1978)
❑ Catalog: Free, R&W, CAN/OV, bn/cn
⌂ Nursery: All year, M-Sa, call ahead

Shein's Cactus
3360 Drew Street
Marina, CA 93933
(408) 384-7765
Rubin & Annemarie Shein

Plants
A collectors' list of **cactus and succulents** by botanical name; no descrip- tions, but a large selection of rare and unusual plants. Offered are copi- apoa, coryphanthas, echinocereus, lobivia, gymnocalycium, parodia, rebu- tia, sulcorebutia, wiengartia, haworthias and many mammillarias; all plants seed-grown or nursery-propagated. (1977)
❑ Catalog: $1, SS:2-10, $15m, bn
⌂ Nursery: December-October, Sa-Su, by appointment only
▼ Garden: April-September, Sa-Su, by appointment only

Shelldance Nursery
2000 Cabrillo Highway (Highway 1)
Pacifica, CA 94044
(415) 355-4845 TO/CC
Michael Rothenberg

Plants
Offer a broad selection of **bromeliads, primarily tillandsias**, in a collec- tors' list; no plant descriptions. They suggest sending a "want list," as sizes and varieties available change so rapidly. Sell aechmea, billbergia, guzmania, neoregelia, nidularium, vriesea and many other tillandsias.
❑ Catalog: $1, R&W, CAN/OV, $25m, bn
⌂ Nursery: All year, M-F, call ahead

Shepard Iris Garden
3342 W. Orangewood Avenue
Phoenix, AZ 85051
(602) 841-1231 TO/CC
Don & Bobbie Shepard

Plants
A collectors' list offers a very large selection of tall bearded, aril and arilbred, Louisiana, spuria and median **irises**; each plant briefly described with useful cultural notes. (1970)
❒ Catalog: $1, SS:8-10
⌂ Nursery: April; by appointment only at other times
▼ Garden: April, Th, Su

Shepherd's Garden Seeds
6116 Highway 9
Felton, CA 95018
(408) 335-5311 or (203) 482-3638 TO/CC $15m
Renee Shepherd

Seeds
European **vegetables, salad and herb varieties** for the cooking gardener and collections of seeds for various tastes -- Italian, French, Oriental and Mexican. Each vegetable is carefully described, with cultural information and recipes. Also sells **everlasting, annual and edible flowers** and a super "fresh-from-the-garden" cookbook. (1983)
❒ Catalog: $1, R&W, CAN, cn/bn
⌂ Nursery: All year, M-F, call ahead
▼ Garden: June-October, M-F, call ahead

Sherwood's Greenhouses
P.O. Box 6
Sibley, LA 71073
(318) 377-3653
Sherwood Akin

Plants
Small nursery sells a selection of **unusual fruits**: mayhaws (hawthorne), jujubes, pawpaw, keriberry, citrange and other citrus, chinknut and goumi. Among the more common fruits are hardy kiwis, pears, grapes and blackberries; all plants very briefly described on single-page list. (1975)
❒ Catalog: Long SASE, R&W, SS:1-2
⌂ Nursery: All year, M-Sa, call ahead

Shissler Seed Company
RR #3
Elmwood, IL 61529
(309) 742-2211 TO
Jeff Campbell

Seeds
A big commercial seed supplier; sells seed of three varieties of sweet corn and one variety of popcorn to home gardeners. The sweet corns are 'Great Sweetness,' 'Great Feast' and 'Super Duper' -- all their own hybrids. (1934)
❒ Catalog: Long SASE, R&W, CAN/OV, SS:12-5, $5m
⌂ Nursery: By appointment only

R. H. Shumway Seedsman
P.O. Box 1
Route 1, Whaley Pond Road
Graniteville, SC 29829
(803) 663-9771 or 6276 TO/CC $15m
J. Wayne Hilton

Seeds
An old seed house operating in both South Carolina and Illinois (Box 777, Rockford, IL 61105). Catalog offers a good variety of open-pollinated **vegetables, annual and perennial flowers, green manure crops, fruit trees and berries**, illustrated with old-style line art. (1870)
❒ Catalog: $1d(4 IRC), R&W, CAN/OV, SS:1-5,9-11
⌂ Nursery: All year, M-Sa

Siegers Seed Co.
8265 Felch Street
Zeeland, MI 49464
(800) 962-4999
Richard L. Siegers

Seeds
Offers a wide selection of **vegetable** seed, both hybrid and open-pollinated, and some annual flowers as well. All seeds sold in bulk; minimum seems to be based on size of seed. Also offers growing supplies and seeders. (1957)
❒ Catalog: Free, R&W, CAN
⌂ Nursery: All year, M-F

Purple Coneflower

Wild Geranium

Joe Pye Weed

© Prairie Nursery
Artist: Helen Mortensen

Silvaseed Company, Inc.
P.O. Box 118
317 James Street
Roy, WA 98580
(206) 843-2246
David & Mike Gerdes

Seeds
Sell seed of **Pacific Northwest conifer species**; minimum order is one pound of seed. List includes abies, chamaecyparis, pinus, pseudotsuga, picea, sequoia, thuja and tsuga species; no plant descriptions. They will do custom seed collecting and seed stratification; also sell seedling plants. (1968)
❒ Catalog: $1d, R&W, CAN/OV, bn/cn
⌂ Nursery: All year, M-F, call ahead

Silver Springs Nursery
HCR 62, Box 86
Moyie Springs, ID 83845
(208) 267-5753
James Kramer

Plants
Offers a number of **native plants as ground covers**: Arctostaphylos uva-ursi, Ceanothus prostratus, Cornus canadensis, Gaultheria ovatifolia, Linnaea borealis and Mahonia repens; each plant is well described. Also offers several ornamental grasses, some pines and other conifers. (1987)
❒ Catalog: Free, R&W, SS:3-11, bn/cn

Singers' Growing Things
17806 Plummer Street
Northridge, CA 91325
(818) 993-1903 TO/CC
Joseph & Bertha Singer

Plants ✍ Books ✍ Supplies
"Specialize in **caudiciform plants**, plants suitable for **bonsai** and unusual **succulents**: sansevierias, monadeniums, pachypodiums, euphorbias and low-light plants, as well as other unusual members of the plant kingdom, such as the baobab tree." Also sell a number of books, some supplies. (1968)
❒ Catalog: $2(5 IRC), R&W, CAN/OV, $15m, bn
⌂ Nursery: All year, F-Sa
▼ Garden: All year, greenhouse, F-Sa

Siskiyou Rare Plant Nursery
2825 Cummings Road
Medford, OR 97501
(503) 772-6846
Baldassare Mineo

Plants ✍ Books
A collectors' catalog of **alpine and rock garden plants** offers about 1,500 plants, with rarer items available in small quantities; all very well described with cultural information. Fall supplement with plants for fall planting. Also sells books on alpine and rock garden plants. (1964)
❒ Catalog: $2d, CAN, SS:2-5,9-10, bn
⌂ Nursery: All year, M-F, by appointment only
▼ Garden: April-May, rock garden, by appointment only

Anthony J. Skittone
1415 Eucalyptus
San Francisco, CA 94132
(415) 753-3332
Anthony Skittone

Plants ✍ Seeds ✍ Books ✍ Bulbs
Huge selection of **spring and summer bulbs**, many rare species from around the world, including South Africa; also some perennials, irises, lilies and seed of Australian and South African plants. Many shown in color; all well described. Also some books on Australian and South African plants. (1980)
❒ Catalog: Free, R&W, CAN/OV, SS:8-4, bn
⌂ Nursery: August-May, M-F, by appointment only

Skolaski's Glads & Field Flowers
4821 County Trunk Highway Q
Waunakee, WI 53597
(608) 836-4822
Stan & Nancy Skolaski

Bulbs
Formerly Flad's Glads, they offer **gladiolus, pixiolas, hybrid lilies** and other summer-blooming bulbs, mostly plants suitable for cut flowers. Each variety is very well described. They also offer collections of bulbs.
❒ Catalog: Free, R&W, CAN/OV, SS:3-6, $15m
⌂ Nursery: All Year, M-Sa, call ahead
▼ Garden: August, M-Sa, call ahead

Skyline Nursery
264-B Heath Road
Sequim, WA 98382
Herb Senft

Plants
Small nursery offers a good selection of **perennials, alpines and rock garden plants**: anemones, aquilegias, astilbes, campanulas, dianthus, gentians, hellebores, heucheras, penstemons, saxifrages, sisyrinchiums, violets and grasses. No plant descriptions. Willing to trade plants; write. (1982)
❒ Catalog: $1, SS:2-6,9-11, $15m
⌂ Nursery: All year, Tu-Sa
▼ Garden: April-June, Tu-Sa

Sleepy Hollow Herb Farm
P.O. Box 1411
Danville, KY 40422
(606) 269-7601
Steve & Julie Marks

Plants ✍ Seeds
Offers a wide selection of organically grown **herb plants** and perennials, each very well described; good choices of lavenders, scented geraniums, mints, rosemary, salvias and thymes, among others. Also some seeds of culinary herbs and everlastings and herb teas and other herbal items.
❒ Catalog: Free, CAN/OV, SS:4-1, $14m, cn/bn

Slocum Water Gardens
1101 Cypress Gardens Boulevard
Winter Haven, FL 33880-6099
(813) 293-7151
Peter D. Slocum

Plants ✍ Books ✍ Supplies
Color catalog offers a wide selection of **water lilies and lotus**, aquatic and bog plants and aquarium plants, all well described. Also offers growing supplies and books for water gardening.
❒ Catalog: $2, R&W, CAN/OV, SS:4-10
⌂ Nursery: All year, M-F, Sa pm
▼ Garden: June-November, M-Sa

Smirnow's Son
11 Oakwood Drive West, Route 1
Huntington, NY 11743

Plants
This is a famous **tree peony** nursery; they have never replied to any
of my inquiries, but so many people have asked why I don't list them that
I've decided to give you their address. I hope you'll have better luck!
❐ Catalog: $2

Smith Nursery Co.
P.O. Box 515
Charles City, IA 50616
(515) 228-3239
Bill Smith

Plants ∾ Seeds
A good selection of **ornamental shrubs and trees** in small sizes. The list I
received had a jumble of common and botanical names -- dogwoods, linden,
elderberries, lilacs, euonymus, sumacs, birch, locust, species maples,
poplars and willows, among others; no plant descriptions. Seed, too. (1962)
❐ Catalog: Free, R&W, CAN/OV
⌂ Nursery: All year, M-Sa, call ahead

Solar Green, Ltd.
Route 1, Box 115 A
Moore, ID 83255
(208) 554-2821
Patty Slayton

Seeds
Offers seed of **alpine, rock garden plants and wildflowers** from southeast
Idaho, including rare seed collected from the Lost Rivers Range, Snake River
Plains into the Wood River areas around Sun Valley, and the Saw Tooth
Mountains. List will be different each year.
❐ Catalog: Free, bn

Solomon Daylilies
105 Country Club Road
Newport News, VA 23606
(804) 595-3850
Sandra Solomon

Plants
Tetraploids, miniature and small-flowered, doubles, spiders, **daylilies** for
both North and South -- all daylilies from tiny to huge, "from oldies-but-
goodies to the very newest." Plant descriptions given in concise but in-
formative tables. A very large selection. (1981)
❐ Catalog: Long SASE(2FCS), SS:4-5,9-11
⌂ Nursery: March-November, call ahead
▼ Garden: May-June, call ahead

Somers' Greenhaven Farm Nursery
3426 Greenlund Road, Route 1
Perrinton, MI 48871
Wendell A. Somers

Seeds
A source of seed nuts of very hardy **Carpathian walnuts**; they claim that
these are the equal of the "English" walnuts grown in warmer climates. The
source of the original seeds was Poland. (1939)
❐ Catalog: Free

Sonoma Antique Apple Nursery
4395 Westside Road
Healdsburg, CA 95448
(707) 433-6420 TO/CC $20m
Carolyn & Terry Harrison

Plants ∾ Books
Offer old English and American cider **apples**, other varieties for cooking or
eating and books on fruit growing and cider making. Will select trees suitable for espalier or train them for you. Sell apples to taste, too. They
have added other fruits: antique and Oriental pears, figs, peaches, plums.
❐ Catalog: $1d, R&W, CAN, SS:1-4, $10m
⌂ Nursery: January-April, Tu-W,F-Sa; all year, W

Sonoma Grapevines
1919 Dennis Lane
Santa Rosa, CA 95403
(707) 542-5510 FAX 4801
Rich Kunde

Plants
A source of **varietal wine and table grapevines, grafting scions** and
rootstocks; you have to want to start your vineyard on a scale of at least
100 plants or have like-minded neighbors. Chardonnay, semillon, cabernet
sauvignon, merlot, pinot noir and chenin blanc from excellent sources.
❐ Catalog: Long SASE, R&W, SS:2-3

Sorum's Nursery
Route 4, Box 308J
Sherwood, OR 97140
(503) 628-2354

Plants
Offer large leaf, dwarf and small leaf **rhododendrons** and **pieris**; the list
groups plants by type and color, with no descriptions. They offer about 100
cultivars, most in several sizes; in addition they will do custom propagating
of evergreen azaleas, Daphne odora and several varieties of **figs** from the
old Willamette Fig Gardens.
❐ Catalog: Long SASE

South Florida Seed Supply
16361 Norris Road
Loxahatchee, FL 33470
(407) 790-1422
Carl Bates

Seeds
Seeds of **tropical and subtropical trees and shrubs**, available only in large
quantites, usually 1,000. Source of many palms, also poinciana, bauhinia,
jacaranda, frangipani, Florida native plants, beach, bog and aquatic plants
and more. Seedlings available at their nursery, formerly called "Plants for
Tomorrow." (1975)
❐ Catalog: Free, CAN/OV, $25m, bn/cn
⌂ Nursery: All year, M-F, call ahead

South Seas Nursery
P.O. Box 4974
1419 Lirio Avenue
Ventura, CA 93004
(805) 647-6990
Rob Brokaw

Plants
Sells a wide selection of **tropical fruits**: sapote, carambola, cherimoya, atemoya, feijoa, guava, lychee, loquat, macadamia, papaya, pitanga and others, including a dozen varieties of avocado. Plants are greenhouse-grown, need a tropical or subtropical climate or greenhouse. (1985)
☐ Catalog: Long SASE, R&W, CAN/OV, cn/bn
⌂ Nursery: All year, M-F, Sa am

Southern Exposure
35 Minor Street
Beaumont, TX 77702
(409) 835-0644
Bob Whitman

Plants
Offers a huge selection of **cryptanthus**: 300 hybrids from Europe, Australia, the Orient and the US, as well as Brazilian species. Also sells aroids, bromeliads and philodendrons.
☐ Catalog: 3 FCS, R&W, CAN/OV, SS:W
⌂ Nursery: All year, daily, by appointment only

Southern Exposure Seed Exchange
P.O. Box 158
North Garden, VA 22959
Jeff McCormack

Seeds ⚘ Books ⚘ Supplies
Thick catalog offers a broad selection of **heirloom vegetables**: corn, tomatoes, onions and garlic, beans, squash, grains, herbs, peas and much more; each variety well described. They also offer supplies for seed savers and books on seed saving and on food growing. (1982)
☐ Catalog: $3, R&W, CAN/OV

Southern Seeds
The Vicarage, Sheffield
Canterbury, New Zealand 8173
(0516) 38 814
The Vestry, Malvern Parish

Seeds
Specializes in **alpine and rock garden plants of New Zealand**, collected from the scree and tussock-grassland of the Waimakariri Catchment. Plants listed by botanical name only; list of reference books on New Zealand plants is included. Hebes, celmisias, coprosmas, schizeilemas, more. (1982)
☐ Catalog: $2(US bills), OV, NZ$10m, bn
⌂ Nursery: By appointment only
▼ Garden: By appointment only

Southern Seeds
P.O. Box 2091
Melbourne, FL 32902
(407) 727-3662 TO
Wae & Kathy Nelson

Seeds
A source of **open-pollinated vegetables** for really hot climates; they offer grain, amaranth, beans, Cuban squash, carrots, Hawaiian sweet corn, gourds, eggplant, lettuce, okra, onions, peas, tomatoes and peppers. But that's not all -- also bananas, boniato, chayote, coffee, jicama, papaya, peanuts and roselle. All very well described in an informative catalog. (1987)
☐ Catalog: $1, CAN/OV, $3m

Southmeadow Fruit Gardens
15310 Red Arrow Highway
Lakeside, MI 49116
(616) 469-2865
Theo Grootendorst

Plants ⚘ Books
Offers a huge selection of **fruit trees**, many of them antique varieties -- apples, pears, peaches, plums, cherries, grapes, gooseberries, even medlars; no descriptions. Sells a detailed reference guide to antique fruit varieties for $8; offers "conservation fruits" for wildlife. (1961)
☐ Catalog: Free, SS:10-5, $14m
⌂ Nursery: All year, M-F, call ahead

Southwest Seeds
200 Spring Road, Kempston
Bedford, England MK42 8ND
(0234) 58970
Doug & Vivi Rowland

Seeds ⚘ Books
The ultimate collectors' list -- thousands of **cactus, succulents** and other **desert plants**, densely typed in tiny print; no descriptions, enough to make make your heart sing! They specialize in desert plant seed of all kinds, including seed of **carnivorous plants and South African bulb seed**, and also sell books on desert and carnivorous plants. (1971)
☐ Catalog: Free, OV, bn
⌂ Nursery: All year, call ahead
▼ Garden: All year, call ahead

Southwestern Native Seeds
P.O. Box 50503
Tucson, AZ 85703
Tim & Sally Walker

Seeds
Collectors' list of about 385 species of **Western, Southwestern and Mexican natives** "for gardens, nurseries, rock gardens, landscaping, botanical gardens and for many other uses." Information on type, outstanding qualities, size, hardiness and rarity are given in concise tables; many seeds are habitat-collected, listed by state of origin. (1975)
☐ Catalog: $1, CAN/OV, bn

Specialty Seeds
24 Jolimont Terrace
Jolimont, Victoria, Australia 3002
(03) 65 03448
Sarah Guest

Seeds
The distributor of Suttons Seeds in Australia, they also offer seeds from other sources: **annuals, perennials, everlastings, herbs and vegetables**. Each variety is well described.
☐ Catalog: A$4
⌂ Nursery: By appointment only

Spring Hill Nurseries Co.
P.O. Box 1758
Peoria, IL 61656
Spring Hill Nurseries Co., Inc.

Plants & Bulbs
Color catalog offers a broad selection of **perennials, flowering shrubs, ground covers and some roses, summer-blooming bulbs and houseplants,** all well described. Another address: 110 W. Elm Street, Tipp City, OH 45371.
☐ Catalog: Free, SS:2-5,9-11, cn/bn

Springvale Farm Nursery
Mozier Hollow Road
Hamburg, IL 62045
(618) 232-1108
Will & Jeanne Gould

Plants & Supplies & Tools
This nursery, which also advertises as "Avid Gardener," offers a nice selection of **rock garden plants, dwarf conifers and shrubs** for bonsai and small gardens, as well as **ground covers and perennials.** All plants container-grown and well described; they also sell bonsai supplies and tools and birdhouses and feeders. (1980)
☐ Catalog: $2d, R&W, SS:3-11, $20m, bn/cn

Spruce Gardens
RR 2, Box 101
Wisner, NE 68791
Calvin Reuter

Plants
Offers a broad selection of **tall bearded irises,** about 600 cultivars, with a few smaller bearded irises as well, all very briefly described. (1987)
☐ Catalog: $1d, CAN, SS:7-8, $10m
⌂ Nursery: May-June, daily
▼ Garden: May-June, daily

Squaw Mountain Gardens
36212 S.E. Squaw Mountain Road
Estacada, OR 97023
(503) 630-5458 TO $25m
Joyce Hoekstra, Janis & Arthur Noyes

Plants
A broad selection of **sedums, sempervivums** and some **arachnoideums, calcareums, ciliosums, jovibarbas, mamoreums and tectorums**; all briefly described with general cultural instructions. They have added some perennials, ground covers, hardy ferns, dwarf evergreens, azaleas and hardy ivy. (1983)
☐ Catalog: Free, R&W, SS:3-9, $10m, bn
⌂ Nursery: All year, daily, call ahead
▼ Garden: All year, daily, call ahead

Stallings Exotic Nursery
910 Encinitas Boulevard
Encinitas, CA 92024
(619) 753-3079
Dale Kolaczkowski, Mail Order Mgr.

Plants & Bulbs
Hold your breath -- hibiscus, jasmines, gingers, ornamental grasses and bamboos, lilies, heliconias, bananas, palms, abutilons, bougainvilleas, cannas. They grow about 1,000 **tropical and subtropical plants**; all well described with growing suggestions. A collector's feast! (1945)
☐ Catalog: $3d, CAN/OV, SS:4-11, $25m, bn
⌂ Nursery: All year, daily
▼ Garden: All year, daily

Stanek's Garden Center
2929 - 27th Avenue East
Spokane, WA 99223
(509) 535-2939

Plants
Offers a wide selection of **hybrid roses,** including floribundas, grandifloras, climbers and standard tree roses, all briefly described. They also offer table grapes, raspberries, hardy kiwis, semi-dwarf fruit trees, nut trees, gladiolus and tuberous begonias. (1913)
☐ Catalog: Free, SS:4-5
⌂ Nursery: All year; also at 16023 Sprague Avenue East

Stark Bro's Nurseries & Orchards Co.
Highway 54 West
Louisiana, MO 63353-0010
(314) 754-5511 or (800) 325-4180 TO/CC
Family Corporation

Plants & Supplies
This firm -- made famous by the 'Delicious' apples they developed many years ago -- offers **fruit trees, grapes, ornamental trees and shrubs and roses** in a color catalog, including good plant descriptions and some cultural hints. Lots of mouth-watering pictures of pies! (1816)
☐ Catalog: Free, R&W, SS:2-5,10-12, cn
⌂ Nursery: February-December, M-Sa

Steele Plant Company
P.O. Box 191
212 Collins Street
Gleason, TN 38229
(901) 648-5476
Ken Sanders

Plants
They offer eight varieties of **sweet potato** plants, yam plants and other **vegetable plants** such as onions, cabbage, brussels sprouts, broccoli and cauliflower. Plants are available in quantities from a dozen to hundreds. Can't ship to CA.
☐ Catalog: $.50, SS:5-6
⌂ Nursery: January-June, September-October, M-Sa

Arthur H. Steffen, Inc.
P.O. Box 184
1259 Fairport Road
Fairport, NY 14450
(716) 377-1665
Arthur Steffen, Jr.

Plants
A large wholesale grower of **clematis,** sells well-rooted plants of over 200 varieties by mail order if you order several plants. Catalog gives very good cultural and pruning information and shows many species and cultivars in color; be sure to ask for the mail order price list with the catalog. Also offers **silver lace vine and Dutchman's pipe.** (1949)
☐ Catalog: $2, R&W, CAN/OV, SS:10-5, $30m, bn

Stewart Orchids, Inc.
P.O. Box 550
3376 Foothill Road
Carpinteria, CA 93013
(805) 684-5448 TO/CC $10m
Leo Holguin

Plants ∾ Books ∾ Supplies
Color catalog of **hybrid orchids**, also special lists of paphiopedilums, cattleyas and phalaenopsis; a broad selection, all plants well described. They also offer several orchid "plant-of-the-month" plans, orchid growing supplies and orchid books. (1926)
▢ Catalog: $2, R&W, CAN/OV
⌂ Nursery: All year, daily
▼ Garden: Sales areas, daily

Stock Seed Farms, Inc.
Route 1, Box 112
Murdock, NE 68407
(402) 867-3771
Stock Family

Seeds
Offers seed of **prairie wildflowers and grasses native to the Midwest**; all plants are well described in a pamphlet which contains good information on how to get started. They also sell wildflower mixes and literature. (1958)
▢ Catalog: Free, R&W, cn/bn

Stocking Rose Nursery
785 N. Capitol Avenue
San Jose, CA 95133
(408) 258-3606 TO/CC
George S. Haight

Plants ∾ Supplies ∾ Tools
Broad selection of hybrid tea roses, floribundas, climbers and tree **roses**, all well described and some illustrated in color, with good cultural instructions. Also offers some miniature tree roses, supplies and gifts.
▢ Catalog: Free, SS:12-4
⌂ Nursery: All year, F-W
▼ Garden: April-November, F-W

Stoecklein's Nursery
135 Critchlow Road
Renfrew, PA 16053
(412) 586-7882
Marc & Carol Stoecklein

Plants
Specializing in **ground covers**, this nursery offers a very good selection of plants for use in shade and woodlands, too: **daylilies, hostas, ornamental grasses, ivy, irises and other perennials**. Each plant is briefly described, with information on culture and use in the landscape. (1977)
▢ Catalog: $1d, R&W, SS:4-9, bn/cn
⌂ Nursery: March-November, M-Sa, call ahead
▼ Garden: May-September, call ahead

Stokes Seed Company
P.O. Box 548
Buffalo, NY 14240
(416) 688-4300 FAX (416) 684-8411 TO/CC
John F. Gale

Seeds ∾ Supplies
Publish a very informative catalog aimed at commercial farmers and growers, but also sell in smaller packets to home gardeners; each plant is well described, with a lot of cultural information. They offer a huge selection of **vegetable and flower** seeds, some available precision-sized or pelleted, and some supplies. Have added a lot of color photos to their catalog. (1881)
▢ Catalog: Free, R&W, bn/cn
▼ Garden: July-August, M-F, trial gardens, call ahead

Stokes Seed Company
39 James Street
St. Catharines, ON, Canada L2R 6R6
(416) 688-4300 FAX (416) 684-8411
John F. Gale

Seeds ∾ Supplies
Stokes is really a Canadian company, doing a lot of business in the US as well: see catalog notes for the US branch in Buffalo, NY, above.
▢ Catalog: Free, R&W, bn/cn

Stubbs Shrubs
23225 S.W. Bosky Dell Lane
West Linn, OR 97068
(503) 638-5048
Arthur & Eleanor Stubbs

Plants
Small nursery specializes in newer hybrid **evergreen azaleas** -- Kurume, Satsuki, Gable, Glenn Dale, Beltsville Dwarfs, Back Acres, Robin Hill, Linwood Hardy, Harris, North Tisbury and Greenwood; plants well described in an informative catalog. Offers about 600 varieties. (1978)
▢ Catalog: $2d, R&W, SS:3-10
⌂ Nursery: All year, call ahead
▼ Garden: Spring, daily, call ahead

Succulent Plants
3123 Pierce Street N.E.
Minneapolis, MN 55418
(612) 781-1293
Dennis Hoidal

Plants
A small nursery with a fine selection of **succulent plants**: haworthias, euphorbias, sansevierias, agaves and caudiciforms of many families -- some illustrated with lovely line drawings. Several collections are also offered. There are no plant descriptions, so you will either want to have reference books handy or already know what you're looking for. (1985)
▢ Catalog: $1d, CAN, SS:4-11, $10m, bn
⌂ Nursery: Daily, by appointment only

Succulenta
P.O. Box 480325
Los Angeles, CA 90048
(213) 933-8676
Deborah Milne & Lykke Coleman

Plants
Collectors' lists of **cactus and succulents**, including rare haworthias and euphorbias; plants briefly described in their periodic lists of new and special items. No longer publish a catalog, but send lists of new plants; you can always send a "want list." Plants are nursery-propagated. (1978)
▢ Catalog: $1, SS:4-10, bn

Alex Summerville
RD 1, Box 449
Glassboro, NJ 08028
(609) 881-0704
Alex Summerville

Plants
Offers a broad selection of **gladiolus**; new varieties from well-known hybridizers and many favorites both new and old, including some miniatures. Each plant very well described, some available as bulbs or bulblets.
❑ Catalog: Free, R&W, SS:2-5

Sunlight Gardens
Route 1, Box 600-A
Andersonville, TN 37705
(615) 494-8237
Andrea Sessions & Marty Zenni

Plants & Books
Specializes in **wildflowers of southeastern and northeastern North America**; a nice selection, very well described, and with the easy ones pointed out. Also offers collections for special conditions and books on growing wildflowers and perennials. (1984)
❑ Catalog: $2, R&W, CAN, SS:9-5, $15m, bn
⌂ Nursery: All year, by appointment only

Sunnybrook Farms Nursery
P.O. Box 6
9448 Mayfield Road
Chesterland, OH 44026
(216) 729-7232 TO/CC $20m
Timothy Ruh & Martha Sickinger

Plants & Books & Supplies
Specializing in **herbs, perennials, scented geraniums, hostas, ivies**, and **houseplants**; a very good selection in each category, each well described. They also offer herb books, dried herbs and essential oils and hold herb workshops and a Herb & Garden Fair (September) at the nursery. (1928)
❑ Catalog: $1d, SS:3-6,9-10, $10m, cn/bn
⌂ Nursery: All year, daily
▼ Garden: July-September, daily

Sunnyslope Gardens
8638 Huntington Drive
San Gabriel, CA 91775
(818) 287-4071

Plants
Color catalog offers a large selection of **chrysanthemums** of many types, including spiders, cascades, brush, spoon, anemones, cushion types and even mums for bonsai culture. Also sells a selection of giant everblooming **carnations**; brief descriptions with some cultural suggestions.
❑ Catalog: Free, SS:mums 3-6; carnations 2-9, $5m

Sunnyvale Cactus Nursery
679 Pearl Street
Reading, MA 01867
(617) 944-5959
Art Scarpa

Plants
Specializes in outdoor **cactus** hardy in New England, needing only protection from moisture during the winter -- most are opuntias -- briefly but well described. Sells mail order only. (1982)
❑ Catalog: Long SASE, R&W, SS:5-9, $15m, bn

Sunrise Oriental Seed Co.
P.O. Box 10058
Elmwood, CT 06110-0058
Lucia Fu

Plants & Seeds & Books
Catalog, in both Chinese and English, offers over a hundred varieties of **Oriental vegetables**; also some flowers, sprouting seeds and gardening and cookbooks in Chinese and English. This year they have added a few hard-to-germinate plants, including several jasmines. They send information sheets with their seeds and will answer questions from customers on growing and serving Oriental vegetables. (1976)
❑ Catalog: $1d, R&W, CAN, SS:4-10, $5m, cn/bn

Sunshine Caladium Farms
P.O. Box 969
Sebring, FL 33871-0969
(813) 385-0663 or 655-3530 TO/CC
Eldridge D. Pollard

Bulbs
Color brochure offers about thirty varieties of **caladiums**; no plant descriptions, all illustrated. Favorite plants for color in hot summer areas.
❑ Catalog: Free, R&W, CAN, SS:1-5

Sunshine State Tropicals
P.O. Box 1033
7845 Grand Boulevard
Port Richey, FL 34673-1033
(813) 845-5340 or 841-9618 TO/CC $15m
Gregory R. Sytch

Plants
Sells **houseplants and tropical plants**: gesneriads, begonias, peperomias, cannas, gingers, episcias, aeschynanthus, columneas, bougainvilleas. Plants are potted, clumps, bulbs or rooted cuttings. Catalog not seen. (1988)
❑ Catalog: Free, R&W, CAN, SS:W, $10m
⌂ Nursery: All year, M-Sa
▼ Garden: October-April, M-Sa

Sunshine Violets & Gesneriads
Fruitland Road
Barre, MA 01005
(508) 355-2089
Elojzia Bardossy

Plants & Books
A division of Sunshine Orchids International that sells a broad selection of **African violets**, both hybrids and species, as well as **other gesneriads**: episcias, achimenes, aeschynanthus, codonanthes and columneas. Also offered are **orchid hybrids, ferns, fuchsias, begonias, succulents** and other houseplants and books about them. (1978)
❑ Catalog: $1d, R&W, CAN/OV, SS:W
⌂ Nursery: All year, W-Su, call ahead

Sunswept Laboratories
P.O. Box 1913
Studio City, CA 91604
(818) 506-7271 TO/CC
Robert C. Hull

Plants
Good selection of **hybrid and species orchids**; flask list includes brough-
tonias, catasetums, cattleyas, epidendrums, laelias, miltonias, oncidiums,
paphiopedilums, phalaenopsis, stanhopeas and other rare and endangered
orchids from seed or tissue culture, each briefly described. Also do custom
seed-sowing and micropropagation. (1980)
❑ Catalog: $2, CAN/OV, bn
⌂ Nursery: By appointment only
▼ Garden: By appointment only

Surry Gardens
P.O. Box 145
Surry, ME 04684
(207) 667-4493 or 4493 TO
James M. Dickinson

Plants
Offers a good selection of **perennials and rock garden plants**, listed in
compact tables with zone, bloom season, exposure, height and soil needs
and very brief description given; gentians, campanulas, primulas, asters,
dianthus, platycodon, thyme, veronica and more. (1978)
❑ Catalog: Free, R&W, SS:5-6,9-11, $15m, bn
⌂ Nursery: All year, daily
▼ Garden: May-September, daily

Suttons Seeds (England)

See Gardenimport, Inc. (Canada) and Specialty Seeds (Australia).

Swan Island Dahlias
P.O. Box 700
Canby, OR 97013
(503) 266-7711 TO/CC
Nicholas, Ted & Margaret Gitts

Plants
Color catalog offers a broad selection of **dahlias**, many shown in photos
and all well described. They offer several collections and, for the dahlia
fanatic, a powdered drink made from dahlia tubers (caffeine-free). Good
cultural and historical information on dahlias. (1930)
❑ Catalog: $2d, CAN, SS:3-6, $10m
⌂ Nursery: All year, M-F
▼ Garden: August-September, daylight hours

T & T Seeds, Ltd.
P.O. Box 1710
Winnepeg, MB, Canada R3C 3P6
(204) 943-8483 or 956-2777 TO/CC
P. J. & Kevin Twomey

Plants ∾ Seeds ∾ Supplies ∾ Bulbs
Color catalog offers good selection of **vegetables, annuals and perennials**,
summer-blooming bulbs, trees, shrubs, vines, fruit trees and berries, all
well described. They also carry a broad selection of growing supplies. Ship
only seeds to the US. (1946)
❑ Catalog: $1, US, SS:W
⌂ Nursery: All year, M-Sa

A. P. & E. V. Tabraham
Saint Mary's
Isles of Scilly, England TR21 0JY
(0720) 22759
A. P. Tabraham

Seeds
The Tabrahams sell seed of their hybrid **fuchsias**, which they claim to be
winter-hardy in Britain -- specify the seed list. A good selection, well de-
scribed. They have added "rock garden" fuchsias, 4-6 inches high. (1972)
❑ Catalog: 3 IRC (free in UK), OV, $10m
⌂ Nursery: By appointment only
▼ Garden: May-June, by appointment only

Talavaya Seeds
Route 2, Box 2
36A Tesuque Drive
Espanola, NM 87532
(505) 753-5801 or 5802 TO/CC $20m
Carol Underhill, Dir.

Seeds
A non-profit organization devoted to seed preservation and research in
sustainable agriculture. To raise funds, they sell organic, open-pollinated
native seed: **corn, beans, melons, squash, amaranth, peppers and quinoa**.
Varieties well described with information on dry land culture. (1984)
❑ Catalog: $1, R&W, CAN/OV, $3m, cn/bn
⌂ Nursery: All year, M-F, call ahead
▼ Garden: Call ahead

Dave Talbott Nursery
4038 Highway 17 South
Green Cove Springs, FL 32043
(904) 284-9874
David L. Talbott

Plants
Specialize in **daylilies**, including hybrids of their own. New introductions
shown in color; all plants well described, some in glowing prose! A wide
selection of recent introductions and some older favorites. At the nursery
they offer flowering shrubs and perennials for northern Florida. (1974)
❑ Catalog: $1d, CAN, $25m
⌂ Nursery: All year, M-Sa; May-June, daily
▼ Garden: May-June, M-Sa, call ahead

Taylor's Herb Gardens
1535 Lone Oak Road
Vista, CA 92084
(619) 727-3485
Kent Taylor

Plants ∾ Seeds
A wide selection of **herb plants and seeds**, each well described in an in-
formative catalog with recipes; some plants illustrated in color. (1947)
❑ Catalog: $1, R&W, $18m, cn/bn
⌂ Nursery: All year, M-F

Ter-El Nursery
P.O. Box 112
Orefield, PA 18069
Cathy Bennett

Plants ❧ Supplies
Small nursery offers a nice selection of **ground covers, perennials** and **chrysanthemums**; all plants very well described. They also grow plants not listed and invite "want lists" for special requests. Offer a few propagating and growing supplies. (1976)
☐ Catalog: $1d, R&W, SS:4-10, bn

Territorial Seed Company
P.O. Box 27
80030 Territorial Road
Lorane, OR 97451
(503) 942-9547 TO/CC $20
Tom & Julie Johns

Seeds ❧ Books ❧ Tools ❧ Bulbs
Informative catalog specializes in **vegetables** for the maritime climate areas of Oregon, Washington, British Columbia and northern California. Also offers sprinklers, tools, books and a list of local organic fertilizer suppliers. Also seeds of annuals, herbs and green manure crops and, in a separate catalog, spring- and summer-blooming bulbs and irises. (1979)
☐ Catalog: Free, R&W
⌂ Nursery: March-August, M-F
▼ Garden: July-September, M-F, Su

Terrorchids
Am Atzumer Weg 18
Wolfenbuttel, West Germany 3340
05331/62999
Heinz Pinkepank

Plants
Specializes in "nearly" **hardy orchids**: cypripediums, orchis, ophrys, himantoglossum, calanthe, platanthera and pleione. I received only the pleione list, which has no plant descriptions, but lists both species (16) and hybrids (21). Write for information on import permits, etc.
☐ Catalog: $1(US bills), OV

Thomasville Nurseries
P.O. Box 7
1842 Smith Avenue
Thomasville, GA 31799-0007
(912) 226-5568
A. Paul Hjort

Plants
All sorts of modern **roses, native deciduous and evergreen azaleas, daylilies, liriope and ophiopogon**; each well described and illustrated in color or b&w. Also has a large AARS test garden next to the nursery. (1898)
☐ Catalog: Free, R&W, SS:W
⌂ Nursery: All year, M-Sa am; December-May, Sa & Su pm
▼ Garden: April-November, roses, daylight hours

Thompson & Morgan
P.O. Box 1308
Farraday & Gramme Avenues
Jackson, NJ 08527
(201) 363-2225 or (800) 367-7333 TO/CC
Bruce J. Sangster

Seeds
Color catalog with a huge selection of **plants of all types**. Good descriptions of plants and good germination and cultural information; the catalog creates yearnings on a grand scale. They have recently started a new magazine, "Growing from Seed"; see magazine section. (1855)
☐ Catalog: Free, CAN/OV, bn/cn
⌂ Nursery: All year, M-F

Tiki Nursery
P.O. Box 187
Fairview, NC 28730
(704) 628-2212
Jack & Claire Pardo

Plants
Offers a wide selection of **African violets**, sinningias, achimenes, streptocarpus and **other gesneriads** as well as begonias, fuchsias and a few other exotic houseplants. Each plant very briefly described.
☐ Catalog: $2, CAN, SS:4-10, $15m, bn
⌂ Nursery: By appointment only
▼ Garden: By appointment only

Tile Barn Nursery
Standen Street, Iden Green
Benenden, Kent, England TN17 4LB
(0580) 240221
Liz & Peter Moore

Plants
Specialists in **hardy cyclamen**, offering many varieties, each very well described; their focus is on the rarer types. There is a mandatory CITES and Health Certificate Fee added to the price of the tubers, as well as the cost of postage.
☐ Catalog: $1(US bills), US/CAN, SS:6-7, bn

Tilley's Nursery/The WaterWorks
111 E. Fairmount Street
Coopersburg, PA 18036
(215) 282-4784 TO/CC
Tom Tilley

Plants ❧ Books ❧ Supplies
Good selection of **water lilies, bog and aquatic plants**, all well described. They also sell pools, pond liners, fish and snails, water gardening supplies and books on how to go about it. (1975)
☐ Catalog: $1, R&W, SS:3-10, cn/bn
⌂ Nursery: Spring & summer, daily, call ahead
▼ Garden: June-October, daily, call ahead

Tinari Greenhouses
P.O. Box 190
2325 Valley Road
Huntingdon Valley, PA 19006
(215) 947-0144
Frank & Anne Tinari

Plants ❧ Seeds ❧ Books ❧ Supplies
A good selection of **African violets** -- many are their own hybrids; all briefly described, many illustrated in color. To my delight, they carry a green African violet called 'Kermit'! Also sell seeds, books and growing supplies, including plant stands and carts, and Anne Tinari's book on the development of African violets, "Our African Violet Heritage." (1945)
☐ Catalog: $.50, SS:5-10
⌂ Nursery: All year, M-Sa; October-May, Su pm
▼ Garden: All year, M-Sa; October-May, Su pm

Tinmouth Channel Farm
RR 1, Box 428B
Tinmouth, VT 05773
(802) 446-2812 TO/CC $20m
Carolyn Fuhrer & Kathleen Duhnoski

Plants ⬯ Seeds
Small nursery offers more than 80 varieties of annual and perennial **herbs** and hardy plants, all organically grown; each plant well described. Cultural hints are offered, including the formula of their own insecticide -- secret ingredients are red pepper and garlic -- don't see how it could fail! (1987)
🔲 Catalog: $1, SS:5-10, $18m, cn/bn
⌂ Nursery: All year, F-Sa, call ahead

Tiny Petals Nursery
489 Minot Avenue
Chula Vista, CA 92010
(619) 422-0385 TO
Patrick & Susan O'Brien

Plants
A broad selection of **miniature roses**, featuring the hybrids of Dee Bennett: minis, micro-minis, trailers and climbers, all well described; they offer 300 cultivars, not all listed in the catalog. Can't ship to AZ and FL, but will refer you to nurseries under contract. (1973)
🔲 Catalog: Free, SS:1-11, $5m
⌂ Nursery: All year, W-M
▼ Garden: Spring-summer, W-M

Tischler Peony Garden
1021 E. Division Street
Faribault, MN 55021
(507) 334-7242
R. W. Tischler

Plants
Offers a nice selection of **herbaceous peonies** from a number of hybridizers, including many of their own; each plant is very well described. He also grows varieties not listed, so you can send a "want list." (1976)
🔲 Catalog: Free, SS:8-9

Tolowa Nursery
P.O. Box 509
8653 Wagner Creek Road
Talent, OR 97540
(503) 535-5557 TO $10m
Jeanne Bieg & Greg Carey

Plants
A broad variety of **fruit and nut trees**: antique apples, pears and Asian pears, figs and cherries, plums and prunes, apricots, persimmons, kiwis, various berries and grapes. Also offers walnuts, filberts, Chinese chestnuts, almonds, pecans, ornamental trees and rootstock for fruit trees. Brief plant notes. (1981)
🔲 Catalog: Free, R&W, CAN/OV, SS:1-4, $5m
⌂ Nursery: January-April, daily, call ahead

Tomato Growers Supply Company
P.O. Box 2237
Fort Myers, FL 33902
(813) 768-1119 TO/CC $20m
Linda & Vincent Sapp

Seeds ⬯ Books ⬯ Supplies
Over 150 varieties of **tomato** seed, growing supplies and books; all plants well described, with good general cultural instructions and days to maturity for each variety -- oh, the agony of choices, but they all sound so good it must be hard to go wrong! They've added hot and sweet peppers, too. (1984)
🔲 Catalog: Free, $2m

The Tomato Seed Company, Inc.
P.O. Box 323
Metuchen, NJ 08840
Martin Sloan

Seeds
The ultimate in a world of specialization: **tomato** seed only. Varieties are listed by type and shape and are well described in a hand-lettered catalog; over 100 varieties -- hybrid, heirloom, red, yellow, large and small, round and plum -- I'm suddenly starving! Also offers a few tomato relatives in the solanum, physalis and cyphomandra familiies. (1983)
🔲 Catalog: Free, R&W, CAN/OV

Torbay's Plant World
St. Marychurch Road
Newton Abbot, Devon, England
(08047) 2939
Ray & Lin Brown

Seeds
Offers seed of **perennials, alpine and rock garden plants**: aquilegia, digitalis, gentians, lewisias, meconopsis, primulas (including double auriculas), saxifragias, silenes and violas. Visitors to the garden will find a giant planted map of the world.
🔲 Catalog: Free

Tradewinds Nursery
P.O. Box 70
Calpella, CA 95418
(707) 485-0835 TO
Gib & Diane Cooper

Plants
Offers a selection of **bamboos** -- Phyllostachys pubescens (Moso or Giant Timber Bamboo) and eight other genera -- arundinaria, chimonobambusa, sasa, bambusa, pseudosasa and other phyllostachys. Also sells bamboo timber, 1/2 inch to 6 inches in diameter, for special projects. (1986)
🔲 Catalog: Long SASE, CAN/OV, $40m, bn
⌂ Nursery: All year, by appointment only
▼ Garden: All year, by appointment only

Tranquil Lake Nursery
45 River Street
Rehoboth, MA 02769-1395
(508) 336-6491 or 252-4310
Warren P. Leach & Philip A. Boucher

Plants ⬯ Books
Catalog offers a good selection of **daylilies, Japanese and Siberian irises** and two good border **sedums**; plants well described. Many more are available at the nursery; they grow many older varieties, so send a "want list." Sell other perennials at the nursery; also sell a few books. (1958)
🔲 Catalog: FCS, CAN/OV, SS:4-6,8-10, $10m
⌂ Nursery: March-November, Th-Su, call ahead
▼ Garden: May-September, Th-Su, call ahead

Trans Pacific Nursery
16065 Oldsville Road
McMinnville, OR 97128
(503) 472-6215
Jackson Muldoon

Plants
A wide selection of **trees, shrubs, vines and perennials** from all over the world, many not easy to find; each plant well described. Among the plants are chianochloa, clianthus, cotula, dryandra, hardenbergia, kennedia, moraea, pleione, parahebe, rhodohypoxis, violas, South African bulbs and Japanese maples. (1982)
☐ Catalog: $1d, CAN/OV, SS:W, $10m, bn
⌂ Nursery: All year, daily, by appointment only
▼ Garden: May-August, October-February, by appointment only

Transplant Nursery
Parkertown Road
Lavonia, GA 30553
(404) 356-8947
Mary, Jeff & Lisa Beasley

Plants
Collectors' list of Dexter **rhododendrons**, rare **native deciduous azaleas** and **hybrid azaleas** of James Harris, Robin Hill, Ralph Pennington, North Tisbury and several others; brief descriptions and some color photographs. Many are suitable for bonsai. Also offer kalmia, leucothoe and pieris. Catalogs come out in September each year. (1975)
☐ Catalog: Free, R&W, CAN/OV, SS:10-4, $25m, bn
⌂ Nursery: April-May, daily, call ahead
▼ Garden: April-May, daily, call ahead

Travis' Violets
P.O. Box 42
Ochlochnee, GA 31773-0042
(912) 574-5167 or 5236 TO/CC $25m
Travis Davis

Plants ⬥ Supplies
African violets, including their own hybrids and many others: Hortense's Honeys, Lyon's, Betty Bryant's and Fredettes included. Sell both leaves and plants; all are well described. They also sell pots, fertilizer and a violet potting mix. (1980)
☐ Catalog: $1d, R&W, CAN/OV, SS:W, $15m
⌂ Nursery: All year, daily, call ahead

Tregunno Seeds
126 Catharine Street North
Hamilton, ON, Canada L8R 1J4
(416) 528-5983
H. Tregunno

Seeds ⬥ Supplies ⬥ Bulbs
A very broad selection of **vegetable and flower seeds** for home garden and commercial grower; brief plant descriptions, available in various quantities. Also sells gladiolus, tuberous begonias and lawn grass seed. Offers many garden supplies and fertilizers; Canadian orders only.
☐ Catalog: Free, R&W, $10m
⌂ Nursery: All year, M-Sa

William Tricker, Inc.
P.O. Box 31267
7125 Tanglewood Drrive
Independence, OH 44131
(216) 524-3491
Richard Lee

Plants ⬥ Books ⬥ Supplies
Color catalog of **water lilies and other aquatic and bog plants**, even a Victoria trickeri with leaves up to 6 feet across. In addition to a broad selection of plants, they sell books on water gardening, fancy fish, pool supplies and remedies in an informative catalog. (1895)
☐ Catalog: $2d, R&W, CAN/OV, cn/bn
⌂ Nursery: All year, daily
▼ Garden: May-August, daily

© Oregon Trail Daffodils
Artist: Estella Evans

Trillium Lane Nursery
18855 Trillium Lane
Ft. Bragg, CA 95437
(707) 964-3282
Bruce & Eleanor Philp

Plants
Rhododendrons; they claim to offer 1,000 cultivars and varieties -- species, dwarf and standard hybrids. They issue no catalog, but you can send a "want list".
❑ Catalog: See notes

Triple Oaks Nursery
Route 47
Franklinville, NJ 08322
(609) 694-4272 TO/CC $15m
Ted & Lorraine Kiefer

Plants ∾ Supplies
A list of **herb plants and scented geraniums**; no descriptions. Also offers lectures and classes on herbs and herb crafts at the nursery and a selection of herb products and essential oils for making potpourri.
❑ Catalog: Long SASE, SS:4-10
⌂ Nursery: All year, daily
▼ Garden: May-October, daily

Tripple Brook Farm
37 Middle Road
Southampton, MA 01073
(413) 527-4626 (evenings)
Stephen Breyer

Plants
Small nursery with a good selection of **Northeastern native plants**, hardy bamboos, fruiting mulberries and hardy kiwi, irises, flowering shrubs and more -- catalog full of good cultural information, as well as drawings of many plants and the nursery cat and dog -- a delight!
❑ Catalog: Free, R&W, CAN/OV, SS:4-11, bn
⌂ Nursery: By appointment only
▼ Garden: Growing area, by appointment only

Tropicals Unlimited
P.O. Box 1261
595 Uluhaku Street
Kailua, HI 96734
(808) 262-6040
Eileen J. Laughlin

Plants ∾ Seeds ∾ Books
Offers **tropical and greenhouse plants**, some orchids and seeds of tropical fruit. Also offers a few books on Hawaiian plants and gardens and greeting cards with seeds of tropical plants. (1980)
❑ Catalog: $1, R&W, SS:W, cn/bn

Tsang & Ma
P.O. Box 5644
Redwood City, CA 94063
(415) 595-2270 TO/CC $10m
Paul Shleffar

Seeds ∾ Books ∾ Supplies ∾ Tools
Offers a selection of **Oriental vegetables**, seasonings, flavored oils and stir-fry sauces, kitchen equipment, utensils and dinnerware -- grow it, cook it, serve it, enjoy it! (1974)
❑ Catalog: Free, R&W, CAN/OV

Tsolum River Fruit Trees
P.O. Box 68
Merville, BC, Canada V0R 2M0
(604) 337-8004
Renee Poisson

Plants
A very broad selection of organically grown **heirloom fruit trees** -- apples, pears, plums, crabapples, medlars and quinces, each very well described in an informative catalog. Ship only within Canada. (1983)
❑ Catalog: $3.50, SS:12-4
⌂ Nursery: December-April, Su, call ahead
▼ Garden: April, Su, call ahead

Turner Seed Company
Route 1, Box 292
Breckenridge, TX 76024
(817) 559-2065
Bob Turner

Seeds
Offers a good selection of seed for **native grasses, wildlife food** and **forbs** for reclamation, grazing and pastureland. List is by common name, with no descriptions.
❑ Catalog: Long SASE, R&W, cn

Turnipseed Nursery Farms
P.O. Box 792
685 S. Glynn Street
Fayetteville, GA 30214
(404) 461-1654
Steven Stinchcomb

Plants
A nice selection of **ground covers** -- ajuga, euonymus, ivy, liriope, mondo grass, vinca minor and daylilies -- each plant well described.
❑ Catalog: SS:W, $25m

21st Century Gardens
885 Ohio Street
Prescott, AZ 86303
Patrick K. Spence

Plants
Broad selection of **bearded irises** in all sizes, including the "Space-Age" irises of Lloyd Austin and newer hybrids of this type, which are horned, spooned or flounced. Plants well described, many shown in color. (1979)
❑ Catalog: $2d, R&W, CAN/OV, SS:7-8, $5m
▼ Garden: By appointment only

Otis Twilley Seed Co.
P.O. Box 65
Trevose, PA 19047
(800) 622-7333 or 232-7333 (PA) TO/CC $25m
Philip Lewandowski, Gen. Mgr.

Seeds ∾ Supplies
Color catalog offers a large selection of **vegetables and garden flowers** -- all very well described and with growing suggestions -- available in packets or in bulk. Also offers growing supplies and the new seed company status symbols, tee-shirts and caps. (1920)
❑ Catalog: Free, R&W, CAN/OV

Twin Peaks Seeds
1814 Dean Street
Eureka, CA 95501
(707) 442-6142
Mark & Susanne Moore

Seeds
"Hardy, easy to grow, adaptable, **annual and perennial California native wildflowers**"; small company, brief list, plants very well described. (1982)
☐ Catalog: Long SASE, R&W, CAN/OV, cn/bn

Twombly Nursery
163 Barn Hill Road
Monroe, CT 06468
(203) 261-2133
Kenneth & Priscilla Twombly

Plants
Offers a broad selection of **ornamental plants** of all kinds: dwarf conifers, ornamental grasses, flowering trees and shrubs, perennials, alpine and rock garden plants. Each plant is concisely described; some plants are available in quite large sizes for pickup at the nursery. (1964)
☐ Catalog: $2, R&W, SS:3-5,9-10, $25m, bn/cn
⌂ Nursery: Spring & fall, daily; summer, M-Sa
▼ Garden: April-October, same hours as nursery

TyTy Plantation
P.O. Box 159
TyTy, GA 31795
(912) 382-0404

Plants ᔥ Bulbs
Color catalog offers many **tender summer-blooming bulbs** -- cannas, crinums, lilies, daylilies, hymenocallis, gingers, caladiums, agapanthus -- as well as pansies, ferns and other perennials and shrubs; each plant well described. There are many hardy plants as well as tender Southerners. (1833)
☐ Catalog: Free, R&W, CAN/OV, $5m
⌂ Nursery: All year, M-Sa
▼ Garden: July-Nov, M-Sa

TyTy South Orchards
P.O. Box 159
TyTy, GA 31795
(912) 382-0404 or 386-1919 TO/CC
Larry Butler

Plants
This is the **fruit orchard** of TyTy Plantation; from January to April they ship peaches, plums, pears, apples, pomegranates, Japanese persimmons, nuts, berries, nectarines and mulberries. They specialize in plants adapted to the South (Zones 7 to 10).
☐ Catalog: Free, R&W, CAN/OV, $15m
⌂ Nursery: All year, M-Sa

Upper Bank Nurseries
P.O. Box 486
670 S. Ridley Creek Road
Media, PA 19063
(215) 566-0679 TO $10m
Wirt L. Thompson, Jr.

Plants
A nursery selling a nice selection of ornamental trees and shrubs, but they ship only **bamboo**: eleven varieties of phyllostachys, arundinaria, semi-arundinaria, pseudosasa, shibataea and sasa. No plant descriptions. (1925)
☐ Catalog: Long SASE, R&W, SS:fall,spring, bn/cn
⌂ Nursery: All year, M-F
▼ Garden: Spring, M-F

Valente Gardens
RFD 2, Box 234
Dillingham Road
East Lebanon, ME 04027
(207) 457-2076
Ron & Cindy Valente

Plants
Small family-run nursery, shipping only **daylilies** at present; broad selection of newer hybrids and miniatures, briefly described. Visitors to the nursery can buy and dig other perennials, including Siberian and Japanese irises and hostas. Daylilies shipped when it's nice weather in Maine. (1983)
☐ Catalog: 2FCS, SS:W
⌂ Nursery: April-September, Sa-Su
▼ Garden: July-August, Sa-Su

Valley Nursery
P.O. Box 4845
2801 N. Montana Avenue
Helena, MT 59601
(406) 442-8460
Clayton Berg

Plants
"Best of the old plus newer, hardier plants for cold climates." Ornamental and berrying trees, conifers and shrubs are listed by size or use, then by common or botanical name. Prices not shown on list but will be quoted on available plants as requested. (1961)
☐ Catalog: Free, R&W, CAN/OV, SS:3-11, $15m, cn/bn
⌂ Nursery: All year, daily
▼ Garden: June-October, daily

Valley Vista Kiwi

See Meyer, Roger & Shirley.

Van Bourgondien Bros., Inc.
P.O. Box A
245 Farmingdale Road
Babylon, NY 11702
(516) 669-3523 or (800) 645-5830 TO/CC
John & Debbie Van Bourgondien

Plants ᔥ Bulbs
Color catalogs offer **spring- and summer-blooming bulbs and perennials**; each plant briefly described, with cultural information given in symbols. Large selection, especially of bulbs, all shown in color; catalogs sent in fall and spring. (1919)
☐ Catalog: Free, R&W, SS:2-6,9-12, cn/bn
⌂ Nursery: August-May, M-Sa, call ahead

Van Engelen, Inc.
313 Maple Street
Litchfield, CT 06759
(203) 567-5662 or 8734 TO/CC
J. S. Ohms

Bulbs
Sells **Dutch bulbs** in quantities of 50 and 100 per variety, but anyone who orders a minimum of $50 may take advantage of their bulk prices. Offers a broad selection; brief plant descriptions, cultural suggestions. (1946)
☐ Catalog: Free, R&W, SS:9-12, $50m, cn/bn

Van Ness Water Gardens
2460 N. Euclid
Upland, CA 91786-1199
(714) 982-2425 TO/CC
William C. Uber

Plants ∾ Books ∾ Supplies
Color catalog offers **everything for water gardens** -- water lilies and other aquatic plants, fish, ponds and supplies and books on water gardening, as well as a lot of information on how to do it. They also consult worldwide on fresh-water ecosystems and water gardens. (1932)
☐ Catalog: $2($5 OV), OV, SS:W, $15m, cn/bn
⌂ Nursery: All year, Tu-Sa
▼ Garden: June-August, Tu-Sa

Mary Mattison van Schaik
RR 1, Box 181
Cavendish, VT 05142-9725
(802) 226-7338

Bulbs
Importer of **spring-blooming Dutch bulbs** -- hybrid and species tulips, daffodils, hyacinths, crocus and other "little" bulbs. Very brief plant descriptions.
☐ Catalog: Free, SS:10, $10m

Vandenberg
3 Black Meadow Road
Chester, NY 10918
(914) 469-2633 TO/CC $15m
John & Connie Vandenberg

Plants ∾ Bulbs
A color catalog of **Dutch and other spring and summer bulbs** -- irises, lilies, daylilies, woodland wildflowers and ferns and other perennials, many illustrated and all briefly described. (1860)
☐ Catalog: $2d, R&W, SS:8-10,3-5
⌂ Nursery: August-May, M-F, call ahead

VanWell Nursery, Inc.
P.O. Box 1339
1000 N. Miller Street
Wenatchee, WA 98801
(509) 663-8189
Peter VanWell

Plants
A broad selection of **fruit trees**: apples, cherries, pears, peaches, plums and prunes, apricots, berries, nuts, grapes -- all well described in an informative catalog. Some apple trees are available on standard-to-dwarf rootstocks, other dwarf fruit trees are available.
☐ Catalog: Free, R&W, CAN, SS:11-6, $15m
⌂ Nursery: All year, M-Sa, call ahead
▼ Garden: July-September, M-Sa, call ahead

Varga's Nursery
2631 Pickertown Road
Warrington, PA 18976
(215) 343-0646
Barbara L. Varga

Plants
Very wide selection of **hardy and greenhouse ferns**, listed only by botanical and common name, with brief notes on size or use. A list of source books is given to help you work your way through the jungle. They have added a tissue-culture lab and are propagating more difficult ferns. (1975)
☐ Catalog: $1, R&W, CAN/OV, SS:W, $25m, bn
⌂ Nursery: All year, daily, by appointment only
▼ Garden: Spring & fall, greenhouse, by appointment only

Veldheer Tulip Gardens
12755 Quincy Street
Holland, MI 49424
(616) 399-1900 FAX 399-1900 TO/CC
Vernin Veldheer

Bulbs
Specializes in **spring- and summer-blooming Dutch bulbs** -- tulips, daffodils, crocus, hyacinths, lilies, alliums and others -- all briefly described in a color catalog. (1950)
☐ Catalog: Free, R&W, SS:4-10
⌂ Nursery: All year, M-Sa, call ahead
▼ Garden: April-September, daily, call ahead

Vermont Bean Seed Co.
Garden Lane
Fair Haven, VT 05743
(802) 265-4212 TO/CC
Jack Burke

Seeds ∾ Supplies ∾ Tools
Specializes in **bean and vegetable seeds**; informative catalog with good descriptions, growing instructions, even a number to call when customers need help! Also a selection of growing supplies, some annual, herb and perennial seeds; some color photos and many beautiful drawings. (1975)
☐ Catalog: Free, R&W, CAN/OV
⌂ Nursery: All year, M-Sa
▼ Garden: Trial garden, July-September, M-Sa

Vermont Wildflower Farm
Route 7
Charlotte, VT 05445
(802) 425-3500 or 3931 TO/CC
Chy & Ray Allen

Seeds
The garden is a tourist attraction in Vermont; they have seeded "thousands" of wildflower species in their six-acre test garden. Offer **wildflower seeds and seed mixes** for sun or shade, regionalized for the entire US. Color catalog gives basic how-to information on getting started. (1982)
☐ Catalog: Free, R&W, CAN/OV, $7m, cn/bn
⌂ Nursery: May-October, daily
▼ Garden: July-August, wildflowers, daily

Vesey's Seeds, Ltd.
P.O. Box 9000
Charlottetown, PE, Canada C0A 1P0
(902) 892-1048 TO/CC $15m
B. E. & S. F. Simpson

Seeds ∾ Books ∾ Supplies
A broad selection of **vegetables and flowers**, all well described with cultural information. Specializes in short-season varieties for Canada and New England (order catalog from Box 6000, Houlton, ME 04730-0814). Also offers growing supplies, gardening books and hand-made black-ash baskets. (1939)
❑ Catalog: Free, R&W, US
⌂ Nursery: All year, M-Sa
▼ Garden: July-September, M-Sa

Andre Viette Farm & Nursery
Route 1, Box 16
State Route 608
Fisherville, VA 22939
(703) 943-2315 TO/CC
Andre Viette

Plants
A very broad selection of **garden perennials**; very brief plant descriptions. Plants are grouped by use or cultural conditions, shade or sun, or by type. Many daylilies, irises, hostas, peonies, ornamental grasses, epimediums, astilbes, liriopes, Oriental poppies and more. Cannot ship to CA.
❑ Catalog: $2, R&W, SS:3-6,9-11, $25m
⌂ Nursery: April-October, M-Sa
▼ Garden: May-July, M-Sa

Village Arbors
1804 Saugahatchee Road
Auburn, AL 36830
(205) 826-3490
Jeannette Frandsen & Betty Breyer

Plants
Specializing in **plants that do well in the Gulf South**: herbs, perennials and scented geraniums; each plant very sell described. They have nice selections of lavender, rosemary, basil and mint.
❑ Catalog: $1, R&W, $25m
⌂ Nursery: All year, M-Sa
▼ Garden: May, M-Sa

The Violet Showcase
3147 S. Broadway
Englewood, CO 80110
(303) 761-1770
Douglas Crispin

Plants ∾ Seeds ∾ Books ∾ Supplies
A broad selection of **African violets**, each well described. Also some other **gesneriads**. Their supplies catalog offers a wide selection of growing supplies, lights, plant carts, books, pots, fertilizers (supplies sold in bulk to hobbyists gone mad). Some seed available, too. (1969)
❑ Catalog: $1, CAN, SS:5-10
⌂ Nursery: All year, M,W-Sa

Violets Collectible
1571 Wise Road
Lincoln, CA 95648
(916) 645-3487
Jeani Hatfield

Plants
Fanatic's list of **African violets**; a very large selection -- regular, miniature, semi-miniature and trailers -- with good brief plant descriptions. The list is tightly packed; settle down with your reading glasses. Big display at the greenhouse; available as either plants or leaves. (1981)
❑ Catalog: $1, R&W, CAN/OV, SS:4-10, $10m
⌂ Nursery: All year, daily, call ahead
▼ Garden: Growing area, call ahead

Vireya Specialties Nursery
2701 Malcolm Avenue
Los Angeles, CA 90064
(213) 475-2679
Bette & Bill Moynier

Plants
A selection of **hybrid and species Vireya rhododendrons**, suitable for garden and greenhouse/houseplant culture -- they are garden plants in climates warmer than those of other rhododendrons (Zone 10) and will bloom any time during the year, some even year-round. Some color pictures; very good plant descriptions of about 50 varieties. (1980)
❑ Catalog: Long SASE, CAN/OV, bn

Volkmann Bros. Greenhouses
2714 Minert Street
Dallas, TX 75219
(214) 526-3484
Walter & Henry Volkmann

Plants ∾ Supplies
A nice selection of **African violets**, many of their own hybridizing, each briefly described and some shown in color. Also offer growing supplies, equipment and plant stands. (1949)
❑ Catalog: Free, R&W, SS:3-11, $5m
⌂ Nursery: All year, M-F, Sa am
▼ Garden: January-June, M-F, Sa am

Volkmann Gardens
3714 Old Settlers Road
Flower Mound, TX 75028
(214) 539-7714
Henry Volkmann

Plants ∾ Seeds ∾ Supplies
A new "spare time" venture of Henry Volkmann, this nursery offers **African violets**, both plants and seeds, and growing supplies. He will be adding other gesneriads, orchids and houseplants in his next catalog. (1988)
❑ Catalog: Free, R&W, SS:3-11, $5m
⌂ Nursery: All Year, daily
▼ Garden: January-June, daily

Walden -- West
5744 Crooked Finger Road N.E.
Scotts Mills, OR 97375
(503) 873-6875
Charles Purtymun & Jay Hyslop

Plants
Offer a broad selection of **hostas**, some of which are their own introductions. Plants are briefly described.
❑ Catalog: Long SASE, SS:5-9, $15m
⌂ Nursery: May-September, daily, call ahead
▼ Garden: May-August, daily, call ahead

Mary Walker Bulb Company
P.O. Box 256
Omega, GA 31775
(912) 386-1919

Bulbs
A good selection of **summer-blooming bulbs** -- cannas, crinums, gingers, caladiums, gladiolus, agapanthus, callas, lycoris and others -- mostly listed by common name and color, many shown in color photographs. Also offers a few perennials. Shares a phone number with TyTy South Orchards.
☐ Catalog: Free

Wapumne Native Plant Nursery
3807 Mt. Pleasant Road
Lincoln, CA 95648
(916) 383-5154
Everett D. Butts

Plants
Specializes in **California native plants**. No catalog; write for information.
☐ Catalog: See notes, R&W

Wyrttun Ward
18 Beach Street
Middleboro, MA 02346
(617) 866-4087
Gilbert A. Bliss

Plants
Specializes in perennial **herbs, Northeastern wildflowers, woodland plants** and **dye plants**. (1976)
☐ Catalog: $1, CAN/OV, SS:4-6,9-11
⌂ Nursery: April-November, daily, call ahead

Washington Evergreen Nursery
P.O. Box 388
Brooks Branch Road
Leicester, NC 28748
(704) 683-4518 (April-Oct); or (803) 747-1641
Jordan Jack

Plants
A collectors' catalog of **dwarf conifers and other dwarf shrubs** such as kalmias and rhododendrons; all very well described, with cultural information and estimated size after ten years. (1978)
☐ Catalog: $2d, SS:4-6,9-10, $15m, bn
⌂ Nursery: April-October, by appointment only
♥ Garden: May-October, by appointment only

Water Ways Nursery
Route 2, Box 247
Lovettsville, VA 22080
(703) 822-9052 TO
Sarah R. Kurtz

Plants
Small nursery on a historic Virginia farm offers **waterlilies, lotus** and **aquatic plants**. Plants are sold bare-root or potted; brief plant descriptions. (1985)
☐ Catalog: Long SASE, R&W, SS:3-9, $25m, cn/bn
⌂ Nursery: March-October, by appointment only
♥ Garden: June-August, by appointment only

Waterford Gardens
74 E. Allendale Road
Saddle River, NJ 07458
(201) 327-0721 or 0337 TO/CC $10m
James A. Lawrie, Mgr.

Plants ⌾ Books ⌾ Supplies
Complete selection of **water lilies, lotus and other aquatic and bog plants**, as well as pools, supplies, fish, pumps, filters, remedies and books on water gardening. Many color photographs and good descriptions. I have one water lily, which every visitor is rushed to see when it's blooming! (1985)
☐ Catalog: $4, R&W, CAN, SS:4-8, cn/bn
⌂ Nursery: All year, M-Sa
♥ Garden: May-September, M-Sa

The WaterWorks

See Tilley's Nursery.

The Waushara Gardens
Route 2, Box 570
Plainfield, WI 54966
(715) 335-4462 or 4281
George & Robert Melk

Plants ⌾ Books ⌾ Bulbs
Color brochure offers a wide selection of gladiolus and "Pixiolas," lilies, cannas, dahlias, callas and other **summer-blooming bulbs**, well described. Sold in quantities suitable for the cut flower trade as well as for the home gardener. Also a few books on glads and lilies. (1924)
☐ Catalog: $1, R&W, CAN/OV, $12m, SS:1-6
⌂ Nursery: January-September, M-Sa, call ahead
♥ Garden: August-September, M-Sa, call ahead

Wavecrest Nursery & Landscaping Co.
2509 Lakeshore Drive
Fennville, MI 49408
(616) 543-4175
Carol T. Hop

Plants ⌾ Supplies
Offers a nice selection of **ornamental trees and shrubs** -- Japanese maples, berberis, hollies, larch and other conifers -- with brief plant descriptions. They also have a shop called The Barn Owl which sells a broad selection of birdhouses and feeders and books about birds. (1955)
☐ Catalog: Free, R&W, CAN/OV, SS:W, bn
⌂ Nursery: All year, daily, by appointment only

Wayside Gardens
P.O. Box 1
Hodges, SC 29695-0001
(800) 845-1124 TO/CC $25m
William J. Park

Plants ⌾ Supplies
Color catalog of **ornamental trees and shrubs, perennials and roses**, all well described and illustrated, with good cultural information and a cultural card with each plant purchased. A Wayside catalog that chanced my way started my passion for ornamental garden plants and was my first tutor. Wide selection; they introduce many new cultivars from Europe and England.
☐ Catalog: $1d, SS:1-5,9-11, bn/cn

We-Du Nurseries
Route 5, Box 724
Marion, NC 28752
(704) 738-8300
Richard Weaver & Rene Duval

Plants
A collectors' catalog of **rock garden and woodland plants**, Southern natives, American, Japanese, Korean and Chinese wildflowers; some are very unusual. Each plant lovingly described; it's almost impossible to convey the pleasure of reading such a catalog and looking up the new plants. (1981)
☐ Catalog: $1d, CAN/OV, SS:2-5,8-11, $20m, bn
⌂ Nursery: All year, M-Sa, call ahead
▼ Garden: April-May, M-Sa, call ahead

Wedge Nursery
Route 2, Box 114
Albert Lea, MN 56000
Donald & Bradford Wedge

Plants
Specializing in own-root **lilacs**, both "French lilacs" and other hybrids such as 'Josiflexa' (S. josikaea X S. reflexa), 'Hyacinthiflora' (S. vulgaris X S. oblata) and 'Prestoniae' (S. reflexa X S. villosa), as well as some species and miscellaneous hybrids. Each plant very well described. (1878)
☐ Catalog: Free, R&W, CAN/OV, SS:3-5, $10m

Wee Gems Minature Roses
2197 Stewart Avenue
St. Paul, MN 55116
(612) 699-2694
Ted Le Boutillier

Plants
"Newest and best miniature roses"; over 200 varieties.
☐ Catalog: Free

Chris Weeks Peppers
P.O. Box 3207
Kill Devil Hills, NC 27948
Chris Weeks

Seeds
New small supplier of **hot pepper** seeds, he lists 60 varieties, some of which he claims are quite rare. Calculating his profits at a dime an hour, he does it for the desire to distribute peppers to the other folks who appreciate the beauty, taste and pizzazz that hot peppers add to life. (1983)
☐ Catalog: Long SASE, CAN/OV

Weiss Brothers Nursery
11690 Colfax Highway
Grass Valley, CA 95945
(916) 272-7657
Weiss-Baldoni Nurseries, Inc.

Plants ⚭ Supplies
Offer a good selection of **perennials**, each briefly but well described; in a separate color catalog they offer **spring-blooming bulbs**. They also offer a broad selection of drip irrigation supplies and systems, fertilizers and fertilizer injectors and the Blackhole Gopher Trap.
☐ Catalog: $1d, CAN, SS:2-6, bn/cn
⌂ Nursery: Daily

Well-Sweep Herb Farm
317 Mt. Bethel Road
Port Murray, NJ 07865
(201) 852-5390
Louise & Cyrus Hyde

Plants ⚭ Seeds ⚭ Books ⚭ Supplies
A very broad selection of **herb plants, perennials and scented geraniums**; no plant descriptions. Also offers some herb seeds, dried flowers and other herb gifts, supplies and books. Lectures and open houses in the spring and fall. (1971)
☐ Catalog: $1, SS:4-10, $5m, cn/bn
⌂ Nursery: April-December, Tu-Sa
▼ Garden: June-July, Tu-Sa

West Coast Violets
2692 E. 45th Avenue
Vancouver, BC, Canada V5R 3C1
(604) 435-6382
Sylvia Sutton

Plants ⚭ Supplies
A good selection of **African violets**: minis, semi-minis, standards, trailers and chimeras from a number of prominent hybridizers. Each plant is well described. Also offers indoor growing supplies. (1986)
☐ Catalog: $1, US, SS:5-9
⌂ Nursery: By appointment only
▼ Garden: By appointment only

Ken West Orchids
P.O. Box 1332
Pahoa, HI 96778
(808) 965-9895 TO/CC
Ken & Jean West

Plants
Offer a number of **cattleya hybrids**, listed by color, either in small pots or in community pots; each thoroughly described. Some of their hybrids have won awards from the American Orchid Society. They also offer a few other hybrids. (1979)
☐ Catalog: Free, R&W, CAN/OV, SS:W
⌂ Nursery: All year, daily, call ahead
▼ Garden: All year, daily, call ahead

Western Biologicals, Ltd.
P.O. Box 283
Aldergrove, BC, Canada V0X 1A0
(604) 856-3339
William Chalmers

Seeds ⚭ Books ⚭ Supplies
Offer live cultures and granular spawn for a broad selection of **mushrooms**, with pages of cultural instructions. They also offer complete growing supplies and books for commercial or home growers. They will also do tissue culture and hold workshops in tissue culture and mushroom growing. (1983)
☐ Catalog: C$2, R&W, US/OV, $10m, bn
⌂ Nursery: Call ahead

Westgate Garden Nursery
751 Westgate Drive
Eureka, CA 95501
(707) 442-1239 TO $100m
Catherine Weeks

Plants
Catalog offers a large selection of **species and hybrid rhododendrons and azaleas**, with good plant descriptions, and some unusual ornamental shrubs and trees as companion plants -- crinodendron, eucryphia, halesia, kalmia, stewartia, styrax -- a real collectors' list. (1965)
❐ Catalog: $4d, SS:10-4
⌂ Nursery: All year, daily
♥ Garden: March-June, daily

Westside Exotics Palm Nursery
P.O. Box 156
6030 River Road
Westley, CA 95387
(209) 894-3492 or 575-2168 TO
Daniel and Susan Lara

Plants ✎ Seeds
A very good selection of **palms**, available as seedlings or small plants; no plant descriptions. A small nursery with a fast turnover of plants; not all palms available at all times; palm and flowering tree seed available in season only. Also a few tropical palms, some hardy to 28F. (1983)
❐ Catalog: Long SASE, SS:2-11, $20m, bn
⌂ Nursery: All year, by appointment only
♥ Garden: May-October, growing area, by appointment only

Westwind Seeds
2509 N. Campbell, #139
Tucson, AZ 85719
Regina Smith

Seeds
Specialize in **open-pollinated vegetables and herbs** for short seasons and heat- and drought-resistant. A good selection, with each variety very well described; also offer a few hot-season annual flowers. (1980)
❐ Catalog: $1d, R&W

Whayes End Nursery
P.O. Box 310
South Highway 653
Burgess, VA 22432
(804) 453-3807
Dorothy S. Webb

Plants
Small nursery offers a nice selection of **hardy perennials**, both old garden favorites and new varieties; plants available in quart and half-gallon sizes, well described, with tables of information on growing and use. (1986)
❐ Catalog: Free, R&W, SS:3-5,9-11, $35m, bn/cn
⌂ Nursery: March-November, Th-Su, call ahead
♥ Garden: April-October, Th-Su, call ahead

Frank B. White, Jr.
6419 Princess Garden Parkway
Lanham, MD 20706

Plants
Huge list of **azaleas**. I received no reply, but a friend from Bethesda tells me that he has a wonderful selection and that I must list him.
❐ Catalog: $1

White Flower Farm
Route 63
Litchfield, CT 06759-0050
(203) 567-0801 or 496-9600 TO/CC
Eliot Wadsworth II

Plants ✎ Books ✎ Supplies ✎ Tools ✎ Bulbs
Color catalog offers a broad selection of **shrubs and perennials**; very good plant descriptions and detailed cultural suggestions. They offer many **spring- and summer-flowering bulbs** in their fall catalog. Also offer books, supplies and tools and have a staff horticulturist who will consult with customers over the phone. Cost of catalog includes three issues. (1950)
❐ Catalog: $5d, SS:3-5,8-12, bn/cn
⌂ Nursery: April-October, daily
♥ Garden: June-August, garden & trial garden, daily

Whitman Farms
1420 Beaumont Street
Salem, OR 97304
(503) 363-5020 or 364-3076
Lucile Whitman

Plants
Seedling trees and rooted cuttings, including **species maples, beeches, dogwood, franklinia, oaks, zelkova, stewartia**, and other desirable landscape trees and shrubs. Also offers rooted cuttings of **currants, table grapes, gooseberries and raspberries**. Ask for plant list and a price list.
❐ Catalog: Long SASE, CAN, SS:W, $10m, bn

Whitney Gardens
P.O. Box F
31600 Highway 101
Brinnon, WA 98320
(206) 796-4411
Anne Sather

Plants
Offers a large selection of **hybrid and species rhododendrons and azaleas** and **kalmias**: some plants illustrated in color, all very well described, with cultural information. They have a seven-acre display garden; sounds lovely in spring and fall. (1955)
❐ Catalog: $2.50($3 OV), CAN/OV, SS:W
⌂ Nursery: All year, daily
♥ Garden: April-May, daily

Wicklein's Aquatic Farm & Nursery, Inc.
1820 Cromwell Bridge Road
Baltimore, MD 21234
(301) 823-1335 TO/CC
Mr. & Mrs. Walter Wicklein

Plants ✎ Supplies
Offers a good selection of **water lilies, lotus and other aquatic and bog plants**, all well to briefly described. Also sells fiberglass ponds, PVC pond liners, pumps and other supplies and fancy goldfish and koi.
❐ Catalog: $1, R&W, CAN, $25m
⌂ Nursery: April-August, daily; other months, call for hours

Gilbert H. Wild & Son, Inc.
P.O. Box 338
1112 Joplin Street
Sarcoxie, MO 64862-0338
Jim Wild, Pres.

Plants
Color catalog offers a large selection of **daylilies and herbaceous peonies**; all plants very well described, many illustrated. Offers a number of collections and several your-choice collections at considerable savings. Many of the plants are their own hybrids. (1885)
☐ Catalog: $2d(12 IRC), R&W, CAN/OV, SS:4-11, $10m
⌂ Nursery: January 15-December 15, M-F, call ahead
▼ Garden: May-August, M-Sa, call ahead

Wild Seeds
Brannas
Llandderfel, Gwynedd, Wales LL23 7RF
Mike Thorne

Seeds ⮂ Bulbs
Seed of **British wildflowers** for climates which can grow them; plants are listed by their common names, with no plant descriptions. There are also collections for woodlands (which include bluebells and wild daffodils), meadows, riverside and coastal sites, cottage gardens and bogs. He also sells bulbs, for which you may need an import permit.
☐ Catalog: $1(US bills), cn

Wildflower Nursery
1680 Highway 25-70
Marshall, NC 28753
(704) 656-2681
Maggie Griffey

Plants ⮂ Bulbs
Specializing in **Southeastern native plants**, a nice selection of hardy native orchids and ferns, violas, trilliums, bog plants, lilies and other bulbous plants, perennials and some desirable native trees and shrubs; each plant briefly described. Formerly "Griffey's Nursery." (1968)
☐ Catalog: Free, R&W, CAN/OV, bn
⌂ Nursery: All year, daily
▼ Garden: April-May, daily

Wildflower Seed Company
P.O. Box 406
St. Helena, CA 94574
(707) 963-3407
Michael Landis

Seeds ⮂ Books
Specialize in **wildflower** seed for the home landscape; collections for a cottage garden, cutting garden, dried flowers, patio gardens and for dry places, as well as mixtures for every region of the country. They also offer a few books on wildflowers and gardening. (1988)
☐ Catalog: $1d, R&W, CAN/OV, $17m

The Wildflower Source
P.O. Box 312
Fox Lake, IL 60020
Elaine & Phill King

Plants
Offer hardy **native orchids, asarums and trilliums, native woodland plants and hardy ferns**; all plants very well described, with cultural suggestions. They offer nine trilliums and other charmers for shady acid soil. (1984)
☐ Catalog: $1d, R&W, SS:4-5,8-11, bn

Wildginger Woodlands
P.O. Box 1091
Webster, NY 14580
Phyllis Farkas

Plants ⮂ Seeds ⮂ Books
A collectors' list of **rock garden and woodland plants**, including Northeastern native plants, shrubs, trees and ferns, offered as plants or seeds; no descriptions of plants, but many choice items such as trillium and violas. Also sells a few recommended books on growing ferns and wildflowers. (1983)
☐ Catalog: $1d, SS:4,10, $10m, bn/cn

Wildlife Nurseries
P.O. Box 2724
Oshkosh, WI 54903-2724
(414) 231-3780
John J. Lemberger

Plants ⮂ Seeds ⮂ Supplies
Offers **native grasses, perennials and annuals for wildlife food**; brief plant descriptions. Also aquatic plants, pond creatures, wood duck houses, pond supplies and even wild ducks and pheasants for release.
☐ Catalog: Free

Wildseed, Inc.
P.O. Box 308
Eagle Lake, TX 77434
(409) 234-7353 or (800) 848-0078 TO/CC $5m
John Thomas & Tom Kramer

Seeds ⮂ Books
Wildflower seed for every region; many plants are illustrated in a color catalog, but without plant descriptions. They do, however, list all of the plants in each regional seed mix and percent of each by weight. They also sell a "Wildflower Grower's Guide," with detailed growing instructions for many of the plants and pictures of the seedlings. (1983)
☐ Catalog: Free, R&W, CAN/OV, cn/bn
⌂ Nursery: All year, M-F, call ahead
▼ Garden: April, daily tours

The Wildwood Flower
Route 3, Box 165
Pittsboro, NC 27312
(919) 542-4344
Thurman Maness

Plants
Nursery-propagated **wildflowers**, including crosses between Lobelia cardinalis and L. siphilitica which have created several new color forms, as well L. cardinalis in white and pink forms. Also **hardy ferns, hydrangeas,** and other ornamental shrubs; all plants well described. (1975)
☐ Catalog: Long SASE, R&W, SS:3-6, bn
⌂ Nursery: All year, daily, by appointment only

Wildwood Gardens
14488 Rock Creek
Chardon, OH 44024
(216) 286-3714 TO
Mrs. Anthony J. Mihalic

Plants
A collectors' list of **dwarf conifers and other dwarf shrubs**, primarily for bonsai, as well as some ferns, ground covers and rock garden plants; each plant is very briefly described. They also import bonsai specimens from Japan and the Far East.
☐ Catalog: $.50, CAN/OV, SS:4-5,9-11, $25m, bn
⌂ Nursery: All year, daily
▼ Garden: All year, daily

Wildwood Nursery
P.O. Box 1334
Claremont, CA 91711
(714) 593-4093 or 621-2112 TO
Ray Walsh

Plants ✍ Seeds
Offers plants and seeds of **California natives and other Mediterranean climate plants**, for habitat restoration of rare and endangered species and drought-tolerant landscaping. Good selection of trees, shrubs and ground covers, herbaceous perennials, grasses and herbs; no plant descriptions.
☐ Catalog: $1, R&W, $15m, bn/cn
⌂ Nursery: All year, M-Sa, 3975 Emerald Avenue, La Verne
▼ Garden: Spring, M-Sa, 3975 Emerald Avenue, La Verne

Wiley's Nut Grove
2002 Lexington Avenue
Mansfield, OH 44907-3024
(419) 756-0697
Dr. Robert F. Wiley

Plants
Specializes in **hardy Northern nut trees**: chestnuts and Chinese chestnuts, filberts, walnuts, butternuts, hickory nuts, pecans, hicans, as well as persimmons and pawpaws. Varieties listed but not described; scionwood is also available. (1955)
☐ Catalog: Long SASE, R&W, CAN/OV, SS:10-5, $5m
⌂ Nursery: March-November, M-Sa, by appointment only
▼ Garden: August-October, M-Sa, by appointment only

Wilk Orchid Specialties
P.O. Box 1177
45-212 Nohonani Place
Kaneohe, HI 96744
(808) 247-6733
Alice & Chet Wilk

Plants
Offer hybrids of many types of **orchid**: cattleyas, dendrobiums, ascocendas, phalaenopsis, vanda, oncidiums and others; each very briefly described. Also offer a number of mericlones. They will try to locate any orchid, not just those listed. (1978)
☐ Catalog: Free, R&W, CAN/OV, bn
⌂ Nursery: All year, by appointment only
▼ Garden: April-November, by appointment only

Willhite Seed Co.
P.O. Box 23
Poolville, TX 76076
(817) 599-8656 TO/CC $25m
Don Dobles

Seeds
Color catalog features **watermelons, melons, pumpkins huge and small**, and a broad line of **garden vegetables** -- all very well described. Big selections of corn, tomatoes, cowpeas, peppers, cucumbers, gourds and squash, including many favorite old varieties. (1920)
☐ Catalog: Free, R&W, CAN/OV

Nancy Wilson Species & Miniature Narcissus
571 Woodmont Avenue
Berkeley, CA 94708
Nancy Wilson

Bulbs
A very small nursery specializing in **species and miniature narcissus**. Each well described, but stock is limited; these are real collectors' items. She is looking for collectors willing to trade unusual items and wants to create a gene bank and recover old varieties. These are delightful plants. (1980)
☐ Catalog: Free, R&W, SS:8-11, $10m, bn

Wilson's Violet Haven
3900 Carter Creek Parkway
Bryan, TX 77802
(409) 846-8970 TO/CC $25m
Dottie & Bud Wilson

Plants ✍ Supplies
Offer **African violets** by a number of prominent hybridizers, both plants and leaves; a wide selection listed by hybridizer and each briefly described.
Other gesneriads include aescananthus, columneas and episcias. Also offer growing supplies, including their own Violet Haven Soil. (1982)
☐ Catalog: $1.50, R&W, CAN/OV SS:W, $16m
⌂ Nursery: All year, call ahead
▼ Garden: Spring-fall, call ahead

Wilton's Organic Seed Potatoes
P.O. Box 28
Aspen, CO 81612
(303) 925-3433
Wilton Jaffee

Plants
Sells only 'Norlands' (red) and 'Norgolds' (russet) **seed potatoes**, the "only organic, high altitude certified seed potato in the US" -- grown at 8,000 feet. Planting instructions sent with the potatoes; he says they're crisper, firmer, more prolific and flavorful than those grown at lower elevations. (1980)
☐ Catalog: Free, R&W, CAN, SS:12-6, $10m

Wimberlyway Gardens
7024 N.W. 18th Avenue
Gainesville, FL 32605-3237
(904) 331-4922
R. W. Munson, Jr.

Plants
A very broad selection of **daylilies**; most plants very well described, many shown in b&w photos. Many are their introductions and those of Betty Hudson; many of her introductions are lower growing and have dark "eyes."
☐ Catalog: $3, CAN/OV
⌂ Nursery: May-September, M,Th,Sa

Windy Ridge Nursery
P.O. Box 301
Hythe, AB, Canada T0H 2C0
(403) 356-2167 FAX (403) 356-3694
John & Carol Jones

Plants
Hardy and native fruit and a few ornamental trees, all briefly to well described. Offer apples, saskatoons, raspberries and strawberries, Nanking cherries, currants and gooseberries. Will ship only their saskatoons to the US. Also sell some growing supplies and offer seminars in the winter on Northern fruit growing.
❑ Catalog: $2d, R&W, SS:4-5,9-10, $10m
⌂ Nursery: April-October, daily
▼ Garden: July-August, daily

Winter Greenhouse
Route 2, Box 24
Winter, WI 54896
(715) 266-4963
Mikael Wilsdahl

Plants
A broad selection of **hardy perennials** -- aquilegia, asters, chrysanthemums, delphiniums, dianthus, Oriental poppies, phlox, primulas and violas -- very briefly described in informative tables. (1984)
❑ Catalog: $1, CAN, SS:5, $10m, bn/cn
⌂ Nursery: All year, daily
▼ Garden: May-September, daily

Womack's Nursery Co.
Route 1, Box 80
Highway 6 between De Leon and Gorman
De Leon, TX 76444-9660
(817) 893-6497
Larry J. Womack

Plants ⬥ **Supplies**
Specialist in **fruits and nuts for the Southwest**: pecans, peaches, pears, apricots, apples, wine and table grapes, as well as shade trees, flowering trees and shrubs and roses; all plants are well described. They also sell pruning and propagation tools and supplies, and sprayers. (1937)
❑ Catalog: Free, R&W, SS:12-3, $15m
⌂ Nursery: Mid-December-March, M-Sa

Tom Wood, Nurseryman
P.O. Box 100
Archer, FL 32618
(904) 495-9168
Tom Wood

Plants
Offers a very good selection of **gingers**: alpinias, costus, curcumas, globbas, kaempgerias, hedychiums, zinzibers and others. Plants are listed by common names with very brief but informative descriptions. Plants can only be sent bare root to CA and HI. He has a collection of 150 species and hybrids and will trade for new kinds.
❑ Catalog: Free, R&W, SS:W, $20m

Woodlanders, Inc.
1128 Colleton Avenue
Aiken, SC 29801
(803) 648-7522 TO
R. Mackintosh, R. McCartney & G. Mitchell

Plants ⬥ **Books**
A collectors' list of **Southeastern native trees, vines, shrubs, ferns, ground covers and perennials** and new or hard-to-find exotics; briefly described, with sources of further information. Looking up the plants is well worth the trouble; list contains many treasures. Also sells books on plants and field guides. (1980)
❑ Catalog: Long SASE w/2 FCS, CAN/OV, SS:10-3, $15m, bn
⌂ Nursery: All year, by appointment only
▼ Garden: March-April, call ahead

A. J. Woodward & Sons

See Gardenimport.

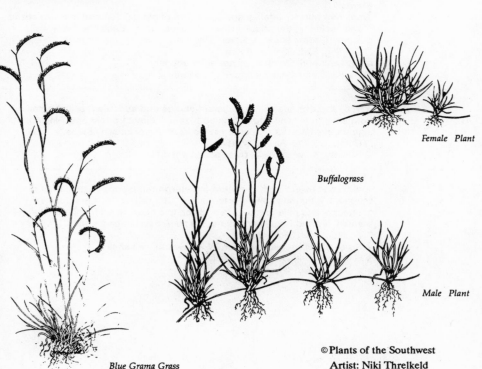

Blue Grama Grass

Buffalograss

Female Plant

Male Plant

© Plants of the Southwest
Artist: Niki Threlkeld

Galleta

Woody's Liriope Farm
Route 3, Box 356
Royston, GA 30662
(404) 245-6880

Plants
A wholesale source of **liriope**; nine varieties (and Mondo grass) available in quantites of 100 or 1,000. Some varieties are well described for use and appearance.
☐ Catalog: Long SASE

Worel's Iris Gardens
10930 Holly Lane
Osseo, MN 55369
(612) 420-4876
Jack J. Worel

Plants
Offers a broad selection of **bearded irises**: tall, border and dwarf bearded, as well as Siberians, some species and arilbreds, also daylilies and hosta; each plant briefly described.
☐ Catalog: Free

Wrenwood of Berkeley Springs
Route 4, Box 361
Berkeley Springs, WV 25411
(304) 258-3071
Flora & John Hackimer

Plants
Large selection of **herbs, perennials, scented geraniums, sedums and rock garden plants**, listed in an informative catalog. Many thymes, dianthus, salvias, oreganos, mints, basils and other temptations -- so many herbs also make wonderful garden perennials. (1981)
☐ Catalog: $1.50, R&W, SS:4-10, $30m, bn/cn
⌂ Nursery: All year, W-Su
▼ Garden: May-September, W-Su

Wright Iris Nursery
6583 Pacheco Pass Highway
Gilroy, CA 95020
(408) 848-5991 TO/CC $20m
Ean St. Claire

Plants
Offers two lists: tall bearded, standard dwarf bearded and Siberian **irises** and another list of forty varieties of **canna**; each plant described briefly. Lists are free in California, $3d each outside California. (1984)
☐ Catalog: See notes, R&W, SS:7-8, $15m
⌂ Nursery: All year, Tu-Su, call ahead
▼ Garden: May-June, Tu-Su, call ahead

Guy Wrinkle Exotic Plants
11610 Addison Street
North Hollywood, CA 91601
(818) 766-4820
Guy Wrinkle

Plants ⬥ Bulbs
Specializes in **collectors' plants** -- haworthia, species pelargoniums, species bulbs from South Africa, euphorbias, species orchids and a large selection of cycads and rare succulents from trips to Africa and Mexico. Some are rare and in short supply; no plant descriptions. (1980)
☐ Catalog: $1d, R&W, CAN/OV, SS:3-12, $15m, bn
⌂ Nursery: All year, by appointment only
▼ Garden: All year, by appointment only

Wyatt-Quarles Seed Co.
P.O. Box 739
331 S. Wilmington Street (Raleigh)
Garner, NC 27529
(919) 832-0551 TO/CC $10m
Corporation

Seeds ⬥ Supplies ⬥ Bulbs
Color catalog offers seeds of **flowers and vegetables** especially adapted to the Southern states; each briefly described. Also offers some growing supplies and a spring bulb catalog. (1881)
☐ Catalog: Free, R&W, CAN, $5m
⌂ Nursery: All year, M-F, Sa am

Yesterday's Rose
572 Las Colindas Road
San Rafael, CA 94903
(415) 472-2119 TO $25m
Georgia A. Shields

Plants
Small new nursery offers a good selection of **old garden and modern shrub roses**, including the popular roses of David Austin. Each plant very well described, some shown in color. Planning a display garden soon. (1989)
☐ Catalog: $2d, SS:12-3, $18m
⌂ Nursery: April-October, by appointment only
▼ Garden: May-June, by appointment only

Roy Young, Seedsman
23, Westland Chase, West Winch
King's Lynn, Norfolk, England PE33 0QH
(0553) 840 867
Roy Young

Seeds
"List of approximately 2,000 different **cactus and succulent** seeds obtained from either my own hand-pollinated plants or direct from habitat. Includes a guaranteed accurately named selection of every known lithops."
☐ Catalog: 3 IRC, R&W, OV, $6m
⌂ Nursery: All year, M-Sa, by appointment only

Young's Mesa Nursery
2755 Fowler Lane
Arroyo Grande, CA 93420
(805) 489-0548
Kay & Bill Young

Plants
A very large selection of **geraniums (pelargoniums)** of all types; brief descriptions with good cultural information. They also offer a few species geraniums and pelargoniums in addition to a huge selection of miniature, scented, ivy and Regal geraniums. Be sure to call ahead. (1977)
☐ Catalog: $2d, SS:W, $15m
⌂ Nursery: February-November, W-Sa, Su pm, call ahead
▼ Garden: April-November, call ahead

Yucca Do Nursery
P.O. Box 655
Waller, TX 77484
John Fairey & Carl Schoenfeld

Plants
A nice selection of unusual **trees, shrubs and perennials** for Zones 8 and 9: azaleas, cryptomeria, magnolias, maples, itea, cliftonia, cephalotaxus and styrax, listed only by botanical name. Also listed are garden perennials that grow well in that tough summer climate: mostly native Texas plants and their Mexican, Asian and southeastern US counterparts. (1986)
☐ Catalog: $2(2IRC), SS10-12,1-4, $15m, bn
▼ Garden: April-June, by appointment only

Zaca Vista Nursery
1190 Alamo Pintado Road
Solvang, CA 93463
(805) 688-2585
Steve & Addie Stephens

Plants ❧ **Seeds** ❧ **Books** ❧ **Supplies**
Offers a very broad selection of **African violets**, many from well-known hybridizers -- plants, leaves and some seed -- and some other Saintpaulia species. Standards, miniatures, semi-miniatures, trailers; all very briefly described. Also African violet supplies and books. (1980)
☐ Catalog: $1d, R&W, CAN/OV, SS:W
⌂ Nursery: All year, W-Su
▼ Garden: All year, W-Su

Zuma Canyon Orchids
5949 S. Bonsall Drive
Malibu, CA 90265
(213) 457-9771
Amado Vazquez

Plants
Specialize in **phalaenopsis orchids**. The color catalog shows a number of their very beautiful hybrids, many of which have been award winners. Most of the plants for sale are seedlings or in community pots.
☐ Catalog: $3, R&W, CAN/OV, SS:W, $15m
⌂ Nursery: All year, daily

©LBG Nursery
Artist: Sharla Foltz

hemerocallis

B

Garden Suppliers and Services

Sources of garden supplies are listed alphabetically. Their specialties (furniture, ornaments, supplies, tools, books, and services) are indicated at the top of the notes on catalogs.

See the Index section for:

K. Product Sources Index: an index of suppliers and services listed by specialties. This index also includes nurseries and seed companies that offer products or services. Within categories, sources are listed by location, and a symbol indicates whether they have a sales location or shop to visit.

Other Sources of Garden Supplies and Services

For tools and garden ornaments, keep your eye on garage sales, salvage yards and dumps — and always be alert for old houses and gardens being demolished for "progress." These are good sources of old bricks and paving stones, gates, fences, trellises, benches and more. Sometimes you can strike a deal with the wreckers and haul it away yourself, as I did with a thousand bricks on the hottest day of the year!

For books, see the many sources of new and used books listed in this section. Also, it's wise to check used bookstores and the remainder tables of new bookstores routinely. Many of the societies listed in Section D sell books, some of which are highly specialized books hard to find elsewhere, to their members.

For garden tours, also check the tour programs of horticultural and plant societies; many have excellent offerings. You might consider joining a tour of an overseas society to make new gardening friends. Several horticultural magazines, such as *Pacific Horticulture* and *Horticulture*, offer tours to their readers, and so do several specialist nurseries.

A table of the symbols and abbreviations used
in this book appears on the bookmark.

AMH Furniture
P.O. Box 610
Benton Hollow Road
Woodbourne, NY 12788-0610
(914) 434-0546 or (800) 228-2824 TO/CC
Alan Panich

Furniture
American-made **garden furniture** manufactured from kiln-dried New York white oak: benches, tables, chairs, planters and dining sets in simple, solid styles. (1988)
❏ Catalog: Free, R&W, CAN/OV, $50m
⌂ Shop: All year, M-F

ATTRA
(800) 346-9140

Services
ATTRA stands for "Appropriate Technology Transfer for Rural Areas"; it is a free **information service for low-input, sustainable agriculture** funded by the US Department of Agriculture. It can supply information to help you reduce pesticide use in your garden, farm or orchard.

Abbey Garden Sundials
P.O. Box 102
Indian Hill Road
Pakenham, ON, Canada K0A 2X0
(613) 256-3973 TO/CC
Gail Bent

Ornaments
Handsome sand-cast **sundials**, designed in Wales and made in Canada using the Welsh patterns. Available in a number of designs, some with birds as pointers. They offer several sundials which are also statues. (1987)
❏ Catalog: $2d (US bills), US/OV

Abracadata, Ltd.
P.O. Box 2440
Eugene, OR 97402
(503) 342-3030 or (800) 451-4871 TO/CC
Mark Brown, Gen. Mgr.

Services
"Design your own home landscape." **Computer program** draws landscape plans, positions plants and hard features, allows you to view plans from different angles and plants at various sizes. It comes with regional plant image libraries. They have other programs for interiors and building design and one which lets you be a train engineer, among others.
❏ Catalog: Free, R&W, CAN/OV

Acorn Services Corporation
346 Still River Road
Bolton, MA 01740
(508) 779-5515
Warren & Alice Smith

Supplies ❧ Furniture
Sell **potting benches, plant stands, patio carts and trellises**, all made of redwood for strength and durability. Potting benches come with wooden or plastic pans and with coated or stainless steel hardware for high humidity. They also sell long-lasting redwood flats for starting seeds; all products have a lifetime money-back guarantee. (1982)
❏ Catalog: $2, R&W, CAN/OV

Adirondack Designs
350 Cypress Street
Fort Bragg, CA 95437
(800) 222-0343
George Griffith

Furniture
Sell the **Adirondack garden chair**, a garden classic, as well as a similar loveseat, sunlounge and swing and side and coffee tables -- all made of California redwood for durability. They will ship to parts of Canada served by UPS. (1981)
❏ Catalog: Free, R&W, CAN

---

agAccess
P.O. Box 2008
Davis, CA 95616
(916) 756-7177 FAX 7188 TO/CC
David & Karen Katz

Books
A source for **new books in all areas of agriculture and horticulture**, from water and irrigation to specialty crops. While leaning toward agriculture, they also carry books on forestry, natural history and gardening; all are reviewed in some detail. Also carry computer software for applications in horticulture. (1979)
❏ Catalog: Free, R&W, CAN/OV
⌂ Shop: All year, M-F, 603 - 4th Street

Age-Old Garden Supply
P.O. Box 1556
Boulder, CO 80306
(303) 499-0201
Christopher Burke & Christopher Munley

Supplies
New firm offers **organic fertilizers**, including bat guano, greensand, kelp meal and soluble seaweed and fish powders for foliar feeding. Products and their uses well described in an informative list.
❏ Catalog: Free, R&W

Agrilite
P.O. Box 12
93829 River Road
Junction City; OR 97448
(503) 998-3218 TO
Veronica Bekker

Supplies
Sells **growing lights**: halide, sodium and full-spectrum high-intensity discharge lights, fertilizers and indoor growing supplies. (1979)
❏ Catalog: $2d, R&W, CAN, $20m
⌂ Shop: Daily

Alpine Millworks Company
70 S. Allison Street
Lakewood, CO 80226
(303) 238-4894
Kent Struble

Furniture
Sells **garden furniture**, manufactured in Colorado. Two styles are offered: classic British and Adirondack chairs, benches, coffee and end tables; both styles offered in either teak or mahogany. (1989)
❐ Catalog: Free, R&W, CAN/OV
⌂ Shop: By appointment only

Alsto's Handy Helpers
P.O. Box 1267
Route 150 East
Galesburg, IL 61401
(309) 343-6181 or (800) 447-0048 TO/CC
A Dick Blick Company

Supplies ✎ Tools ✎ Furniture ✎ Ornaments
Offers a broad selection of **gadgets for garden and home**: garden carts, tools, supplies, watering equipment, birdhouses, animal traps, lawn furniture, items for home and kitchen.
❐ Catalog: Free

Alternative Garden Supply, Inc.
297 N. Barrintgon Road
Streamwood, IL 60107
(800) 444-2837 or (708) 885-8282 TO/CC
David Ittel

Supplies ✎ Tools
The company has changed its focus to **hydroponic systems**; offers a good selection of plant lights, growing supplies, fertilizers and insect controls for the indoor grower. The shop is called Chicago Indoor Garden Supply.
❐ Catalog: Free, R&W, CAN
⌂ Shop: All year, M-Sa

Amaranth Stoneware
P.O. Box 243
Sydenham, ON, Canada K0H 2T0
(613) 541-0799
Paul & Marilyn King

Supplies ✎ Ornaments
Stoneware and terra cotta **garden markers** for herb and vegetable gardens; available for a number of popular plants, as well as for "weeds," "cat crossing" and "thank you for not smoking," among other choices. (1986)
❐ Catalog: Free, R&W, US/OV

Amdega Conservatories
Boston Design Center, Suite 624
Boston, MA 02210
(617) 951-2755 FAX 2717
Jim Gimbell, Sales Mgr.

Ornaments
Offers English **garden rooms and conservatories** which can be built to fit a number of situations -- even large enough to use as a pool pavilion. An elegant way to sit outside in cool or windy weather.
❐ Catalog: $3

American Arborist Supplies
882 S. Matlack Street
West Chester, PA 19382
(800) 441-8381 or (800) 352-3458 (PA) TO/CC

Supplies ✎ Tools ✎ Books
A very broad selection of **tools and supplies for tree surgeons**: chain saws, pruning tools, sprayers, climbing and safety equipment, shovels, rakes, picks and mattocks and much more. They also sell books on tree pruning and care.
❐ Catalog: Free

The American Botanist
1103 W. Truitt Avenue
Chillicothe, IL 61523
(309) 274-5254 TO/CC $25m
D. Keith Crotz

Books ✎ Services
Specialize in **rare, used and out-of-print books** in all areas of gardening, landscaping and botany. Also offer collection development, book search service and appraisals and will buy book collections in their field. (1983)
❐ Catalog: $1, CAN/OV
⌂ Shop: All year, by appointment only

American Standard Co.
P.O. Box 325
Plantsville, CT 06479
(203) 628-9643 TO/CC
Florian Family

Tools
Florian Rachet-Cut **pruning tools** with ratchet action which have increased leverage and need less hand-power; they offer hand pruners, loppers and pole pruners.
❐ Catalog: Free, R&W, CAN/OV, $17m
⌂ Shop: All year, M-F, 157 Water Street, Southington

American Sundials, Inc.
P.O. Box 677
300 Main Street
Pt. Arena, CA 95468
(707) 884-3082 TO/CC
Wendy Moss

Ornaments
A nice selection of solid **bronze sundials**, with a variety of styles and mottos, some of which are also **birdbaths**.
❐ Catalog: Long SASE, $35m

American Weather Enterprises
P.O. Box 1383
Media, PA 19063
(215) 565-1232 TO/CC $25m
R. Sanders

Supplies
A nice selection of **weather instruments**: hygrometers, thermometers, barometers, anemometers, recording equipment, remote weather stations and sundials and weathervanes. They also offer books on the weather and software for forecasting and hurricane tracking.
❐ Catalog: Free, CAN/OV
⌂ Shop: All year, M-Sa, call ahead

America's Pet Door Store

See Patio Pacific.

Anchor & Dolphin Books
P.O. Box 823
30 Franklin Street
Newport, RI 02840
(401) 846-6890
James Hinck

Books
Specialize in **rare, old and out-of-print books** on horticulture, garden-ing, plant hunting, landscape architecture and garden history. (1977)
☐ Catalog: $1d, CAN/OV
⌂ Shop: Call ahead

Anderson Horticultural Design Service
P.O. Box 5264
Minnetonka, MN 55343
(612) 545-5500

Services
Individual garden plans for outdoor rooms, borders and shade, concept and waterside gardens. Each set has various layouts and planting suggestions suitable for various climates and conditions.
☐ Catalog: $1d

Applied Hydroponics
3135 Kerner Boulevard
San Rafael, CA 94901
(800) 634-9999 TO/CC
Peter Wardenburg

Supplies
Offering Hydrofarm **hydroponic systems**, as well as supplies and other equipment, and metal halide and high-pressure sodium **light systems**. Also carbon dioxide enrichment systems for home gardeners. They now have retail stores in many locations in addition to mail order; call for information.
☐ Catalog: Free, R&W, CAN/OV
⌂ Shop: All year, M-Sa

Applied Hydroponics of Canada
2215 Walkley
Montreal, PQ, Canada H4B 2J9
(514) 489-3803 FAX 3805 TO/CC
Don Stewart

Supplies
Offer a broad selection of Hydroponix **equipment and supplies**, including complete hydroponic starter kits. They also sell plant stands, halide lights and other supplies for indoor gardeners. Catalog in English and French.
☐ Catalog: Free, R&W, US/OV, $25m
⌂ Shop: All year, M-F, call ahead

Aquacide Company
P.O. Box 10748
1627 - 9th Street
White Bear Lake, MN 55110
(800) 328-9350 or (612) 429-6742 (MN)

Supplies
Offer a variety of **products to control algae and underwater weeds** in lakes and ponds; supposed to be harmless to fish. Another product, Mosquito Beater, is a safe dry powder which keeps mosquitoes away for days. They also sell some special tools for cutting and gathering weeds from ponds.
☐ Catalog: Free

Aquamonitor
P.O. Box 327
Huntington, NY 11743
(516) 427-5664
Robert & Velma Whitener

Supplies
Complete **mist irrigation systems** and/or automatic controls to monitor soil moisture for propagation in greenhouses; useful for any greenhouse plants, seedlings or cuttings which need constant moisture. Because the system monitors the soil, it waters when needed, not on an automatic timer.
☐ Catalog: Free, CAN/OV

Arborist Supply House, Inc.
P.O. Box 23607
215 S.W. 32nd Street
Fort Lauderdale, FL 33307
(305) 561-9527
Way & Geraldine Hoyt

Tools ⌇ Books
Offers specialized **equipment for arborists**, some of which is also useful to less specialized folk: pruning tools, safety equipment, deep-root barriers and a nice little tree guard to protect from weed-whackers. Also sells books for tree workers. (1984)
☐ Catalog: Free, R&W
⌂ Shop: All year, M-F

Arctic Glass & Window Outlet
Route 1, Box 254
I-94 at Hammond Exit
Hammond, WI 54015
(715) 796-2292 or 796-2295 TO/CC
Joseph Bacon

Supplies
Ships **insulated (double) glass** nationwide at 25% to 60% below retail; used for greenhouses, sunrooms and windows, doors and roof windows. Panels are unframed; informative leaflet tells you how to install them. (1979)
☐ Catalog: $2d, R&W, CAN/OV, $100m
⌂ Shop: All year, daily

Ardisam, Inc.
Route 4, Box 666
Cumberland, WI 54829
Richard, Ronald & Mark Ruppel

Supplies
Manufacture and sell Earthquake **rototillers**; they make both front and rear tine models, depending on your need. They have cast iron housing, worm-gear drive, self-cleaning bolo tines and solid steel driveshafts -- all this tech talk is making me swoon! Send for the literature and study it yourself.
☐ Catalog: Free, R&W, CAN/OV

Arroyo Craftsman Lighting, Inc.
2080 Central Avenue, Building B
Duarte, CA 91010
(818) 359-3298 TO/CC
M. C. Barker

Ornaments
Beautiful **lighting fixtures** in the turn-of-the-century Arts and Crafts style; they remind me of old houses in Pasadena, California. They are obviously upscale in price and not suitable for every architectural style, but very lovely; would make a very special gift.
☐ Catalog: $2, R&W, CAN, $100m

Autumn Forge
1104 N. Buena Vista Avenue
Orlando, FL 32818
(407) 293-3302 TO/CC
Charter P. Murray

Ornaments
A blacksmith who makes several styles of **plant hangers in forged iron**, as well as other handsome hardware -- he also does custom work and will make almost anything else. Offers fire tools, garden dinner bells, racks and sconces, mouse-tail coat hooks and other nice touches. (1975)
❐ Catalog: $1d, R&W, $15m

Autumn Innovations

See Garden Magic.

Avant Horticultural Products
P.O. Box 15233
420 S. Military Trail
West Palm Beach, FL 33416-5233
(800) 334-7979
C. Wyclif Head III

Supplies
Manufacturers of **reacted liquid plant foods**, which they claim are more immediately available to plants. There are several formulas -- for roses, blooming plants and agricultural plants, and a spray formula compatible with fungicides and insecticides. Avant Therm-Chem offers winter protection to plants and helps them retain moisture during dry periods.
❐ Catalog: Free

BCP/Custom Software Applications
P.O. Box 3005
Arlington, WA 98223
(206) 659-1454
Alan Buck

Services
IBM **software for choosing perennials and ground covers**. The perennial program includes information on the plant's family, genus and species and allows choice by height, spacing, color of flowers and flowering season, as well as soil and light requirements, and includes 1,238 plants. Ground cover program includes 734 plants and searches on the same characteristics. (1987)
❐ Catalog: Write for information, CAN/OV, $45m

BCS Mosa, Inc.
P.O. Box 1739
13601 Providence Road
Matthews, NC 28106
(704) 846-1040 TO/CC
BCS S.p.A., Milan, Italy

Supplies
A very broad selection of **tillers, chipper/shredders, garden carts, sickle-bar mowers, sprayers and power lawn mowers**. They will sell direct if you are not near one of their dealers. (1982)
❐ Catalog: Free, R&W, CAN/OV, $15m

Bark Service Company
P.O. Box 637
Troutman, NC 28166
(800) 999-2275 TO/CC
R. K. Ferrar

Books
Offer a good selection of current and recent **garden books** at a discount; they also sell books on woodworking, home construction and needlecraft.
❐ Catalog: Free, CAN/OV, $20m

The Barn Owl

See Wavecrest Nursery & Landscaping Co. in Section A.

Carol Barnett -- Books
4408 S.E. Knapp
Portland, OR 97206
(503) 777-2933
Carol Barnett

Books ✎ Services
Specializes in **used, rare and out-of-print books** on gardens, horticulture and botany, with brief descriptions of contents as well as notes on condition. She will also do book searches if you send her a "want list." (1983)
❐ Catalog: Free, CAN/OV

Beatrice Farms
Dawson, GA 31742

Supplies
Offers **earthworms and worm castings**.
❐ Catalog: Free

Leona Bee Tours & Travel
18305 Biscayne Boulevard, #211
Miami, FL 33160-2172
(305) 935-3101

Services
Travel agency specializing in **horticultural tours**, including special tours for orchid-lovers to various habitats of species orchids.
❐ Catalog: Free

Bell's Book Store
536 Emerson Street
Palo Alto, CA 94301
(415) 323-7822 TO/CC $15m
Mr. & Mrs. Herbert Bell

Books
Offer a good selection of **new, used and out-of-print books** on gardening, as well as prints, botanic postcards and greeting cards. They have a good annotated book list on "Old Garden Roses" ($2.50), but no catalog. Send a "want list" to see if they have what you want. (1935)
❐ Catalog: See notes, CAN/OV
⌂ Shop: All year, M-Sa

Bench Craft

See Brandywine Garden Furniture.

Beneficial Insectary
14751 Oak Run Road
Oak Run, CA 96069
(916) 472-3715
Sinthya Penn

Supplies
A family-operated "bug" business offering lacewings, ladybugs, fly parasites, trichogramma wasps, predatory mites, praying mantis egg cases and other **beneficial insects and organic pest controls**. They also offer a "Garden Variety Pack" of beneficial insects to attack on every front. (1978)
❐ Catalog: Free, R&W, CAN/OV

Berry-Hill, Limited
75 Burwell Road
St. Thomas, ON, Canada N5P 3R5
(519) 631-0480 TO/CC $5m
R. C. Foster & D. L. Roberts

Supplies ⌘ Tools ⌘ Books
Here's a wonderful old-time **farm equipment and country kitchen catalog:**
full of canning supplies, equipment for dairy and poultry yards, garden
bells, weather vanes, a cider press and tools and equipment for the garden.
They also sell many practical "how-to" books. (1948)
☐ Catalog: Free (2 IRC), R&W, US/OV, $5m
⌂ Shop: All year, M-F

Better Yield Insects & Garden Houses
P.O. Box 3451
Tecumseh Station
Windsor, ON, Canada N8N 3C4
(519) 727-6108 FAX 727-5989
Mrs. Patricia Coristine

Supplies
Supplier of **beneficial insects:** whitefly parasites, spider mite predators,
aphid predators, thrip predators and nematodes. They also sell sticky
traps, strips and insect barriers. (1977)
☐ Catalog: Free, US/OV, SS:W
⌂ Shop: All year, daily, call ahead

Beth L. Bibby Books
1225 Sardine Creek Road
Gold Hill, OR 97525
(503) 855-1621
George A. Bibby & Nikki A. Wright

Books
Offers **used and out-of-print books** on plants, gardening and flower
arranging.
☐ Catalog: $2, CAN/OV

Dorothy Biddle Service
US Route 6
Greeley, PA 18425-9799
(717) 226-3239
Lynne Dodson

Supplies ⌘ Tools ⌘ Books
A broad selection of **supplies for flower arrangers** which would be useful
to all who cut and bring flowers indoors. Books on arranging and drying
flowers, tools and some houseplant supplies. (1936)
☐ Catalog: $.25, R&W, CAN/OV
⌂ Shop: All year, M-F

Bio-Control Co.
P.O. Box 337
57A Zink Road
Berry Creek, CA 95916
(916) 589-5227
Dorothy M. Neva

Supplies
Ladybugs, green lacewings, trichogramma, praying mantis egg cases, fly par-
asites and Bio-Control Honeydew to attract **beneficial insects.** An informa-
tive leaflet explains the use of these biological insect controls. (1959)
☐ Catalog: Free, R&W, CAN
⌂ Shop: All year, M,W,F, call ahead

Bio-Gard Agronomics
P.O. Box 4477
Falls Church, VA 22044
(703) 536-4076
Dr. Andrew J. Welebir

Supplies
Offer their Calcium-25, an **organic foliar fertilizer,** which they say will
increase yield 20% to 50% and can be used on any ornamental plant as
well as on food crops. (1987)
☐ Catalog: Free, R&W, CAN/OV, $13m

Bio-Resources
P.O. Box 902
1210 Birch Street
Santa Paula, CA 93060
(805) 525-0526
Jeri Brandt Mead

Supplies
Predatory mites, green lacewings, ladybugs, fly parasites, trichogramma
wasps, mealybug predators and whitefly parasites; the uses of **beneficial
insects** well described in an informative leaflet.
☐ Catalog: Free, R&W, CAN/OV

© Robinson Iron
Artist: W. Wayne Fuller

BioLogic
P.O. Box 177
Springtown Road
Willow Hill, PA 17271
(717) 349-2789
Dr. Albert Pye

Supplies
Sells Scanmask -- a strain of **beneficial, insect-eating nematodes** to control a variety of soil and boring pest insects, such as black vine weevils, white grubs, cutworms, caterpillars and fly maggots. (1985)
❏ Catalog: Long SASE, R&W, CAN/OV, $10m
⌂ Shop: By appointment only

Bird 'n Hand
40 Pearl Street
Framingham, MA 01701
(508) 879-1552
Bethany Smith

Supplies
An informative catalog for serious bird feeders -- offering several mixes of **bird food, feeders and other bird-oriented items**. They also offer an automatic resupply service so that you won't run out of bird food.
❏ Catalog: Free

Birdsong
Route 3, Box 140B
Waynesboro, GA 30830
(404) 554-9814
Patricia & Hilton Gillis

Supplies
Custom-made **birdhouses** for cavity-nesting birds (i.e., bluebirds and others), available in red cedar or a variety of other woods, carefully made to be long-lasting and trouble-free. Bird feeders are also available. (1989)
❏ Catalog: Long SASE, R&W

Geo. C. Birlant & Co.

See Charleston Battery Bench, Inc.

Mary Bland
Augop, Evenjobb
Nr. Presteign, Wales, UK
Whitton 218 or (054-76) 218

Books
Rare, used and out-of-print books for gardeners.
❏ Catalog: Free

Bloomsaver, Ltd.
2049 Paseo Dorado
La Jolla, CA 92037
(619) 456-5086
Jolene Telles & Diane Ryason

Supplies
Offers a three-partition **container for cutting and placing flowers into water** in the garden and carrying them in from the garden, as well as an additive to keep cut flowers fresh longer. (1988)
❏ Catalog: Free, R&W, CAN/OV, $23m

Blue Creek Valley Ventures
P.O. Box 1514
Route 4, Highway 255
Cleveland, GA 30528
(404) 865-4048 TO/CC
Janice Lymburner & Priscilla Wilson

Supplies
Offer **tee-shirts, sweatshirts, totes and towels** with nice Appalachian wildflower designs. Designs vary from year to year and include wildflowers, unpopular plants (kudzu, poison ivy) and "budding botanist" designs for children. They also sell gourd crafts at their shop. (1976)
❏ Catalog: Free, R&W, $13m
⌂ Shop: January-April, weekends; May-December, daily

Bonide Chemical Co., Inc.
2 Wurz Avenue
Yorkville, NY 13495
(315) 736-8231
Jim Wurz

Supplies
Offers a complete line of **home, garden and lawn pesticides**, including the organic products Rotenone, Dipel, Bacillus thuringiensis, dormant oil, oil and lime sulfur spray and many more. (1926)
❏ Catalog: Long SASE, R&W, CAN/OV
⌂ Shop: All year, M-F, call ahead

Bonsai Associates, Inc.
3000 Chestnut Avenue
Baltimore, MD 21217
(301) 235-5336 TO/CC
Barbara Bogash & Arschel Morell

Supplies ⬿ Tools ⬿ Books ⬿ Services
A wide selection of **books, tools and supplies for bonsai**; they also sell some starter plants for bonsai, each plant well described. They will repot, refine and board bonsai for local enthusiasts. (1979)
❏ Catalog: $2d, R&W, CAN/OV
⌂ Shop: All year, W-Sa, call ahead

Bonsai Creations
P.O. Box 7511
Ft. Lauderdale, FL 33338
(305) 463-8783 TO/CC
Jonathan Chavkin

Supplies ⬿ Tools ⬿ Books
Sell **bonsai tools, pots, books and supplies** -- a very broad selection shown in b&w photographs. They also sell finished and pre-bonsai trees, which cannot be shipped to CA, LA, NV or TX. (1982)
❏ Catalog: $2.50, CAN/OV

The Book Tree
12 Pine Hill Road
Englishtown, NJ 07726
(201) 446-3853 TO/CC
Anne & John Haines

Books ⬿ Services
Offer **new and recent books** on landscape architecture, horticulture, plants and gardening; they will try to locate current books for you.
❏ Catalog: Free, R&W, CAN/OV
⌂ Shop: By appointment only

Bookfinders General, Inc.
Box 837, Madison Square Station
New York, NY 10159-0837
(212) 689-0772

Books ⬿ Services
A free **book-finding** service: send your "want list," and they will search for any book and send you a price quote when they find it.
❏ Catalog: Free

Bow House, Inc.
P.O. Box 228
92 Randall Road
Bolton, MA 01740
(508) 779-6464 FAX 2272
John J. Rogers

Ornaments
Offer **gazebos and other garden structures** of classic design; the Belvedeary
can be finished in several styles, even cut in half for a bay window. Also
sell a domed temple, arbors, a pergola, changing structures, a Japanese tea
house, bridges up to 40 feet, even a dog house. All very elegant. (1971)
❏ Catalog: $3, R&W, CAN/OV
⌂ Shop: All year, daily, call ahead

Bramen Company, Inc.
P.O. Box 70
Salem, MA 01970-0070
(508) 745-7765 TO/CC
Robert Strom

Supplies ⸜ Tools
Automatic Thermafor **ventilation controllers** open and close hinged windows
as heavy as 30 pounds -- adjustable for temperatures from 55F to 105F -- and
they work without electricity. Also offer Rolcut pruners and other **hand
tools**, tool hooks, seaweed extract, seed-starting cubes and mulch mats.
❏ Catalog: Free, R&W, CAN

Brandywine Garden Furniture
24 Phoenixville Pike
Malvern, PA 19355
(215) 640-1212 or (800) 722-5434
Bruce Bassett-Powell & Christopher Gutteridge

Furniture ⸜ Ornaments
Offer several lines of **garden furniture**: Brandywine and Bench Craft teak
and white-painted hardwood benches, chairs and tables and planters; and
Trafalgar Designs traditional English garden furniture in cast aluminum.
Each line is available in a number of styles, from simple to high Victorian.
❏ Catalog: Free, R&W, CAN/OV, $100m

Bricker's Organic Farm
842 Sandbar Ferry Road
Augusta, GA 30901
(404) 722-0661
Bill Bricker & Ed Hensley

Supplies
Supplier of **organic fertilizers, soil amendments and potting soils**, as well
as other organic gardening supplies, including their Kricket Krap fertilizer
(how do they collect it?). They also sell cat bells, real fly paper, live
animal traps and automatic dog feeders and waterers. (1978)
❏ Catalog: $1d, R&W, CAN/OV, $7m
⌂ Shop: All year, M-Sa

Brighton By-Products Co., Inc.
P.O. Box 23
New Brighton, PA 15066
(800) 245-3502 or (800) 642-2668 TO/CC $30m
Nathan Ortinberg, Pres.

Supplies
A very broad selection of **growing and landscaping supplies**, sold to anyone
by mail; especially good on greenhouse and propagation supplies, irrigation
and horticultural chemicals -- including DuPont Landscape Fabric, a non-
chemical mulch/weed barrier.
❏ Catalog: $5, CAN/OV, $30m

Andy Brinkley Studios
Route 2, Box 577
Connelly Springs, NC 28612
(704) 397-3197
Andy Brinkley

Ornaments
Offers a variety of **garden sculptures and fountains** with plant, animal and
flower themes; most are made of brass, copper or bronze, some with verdigris
finish. The animals are fanciful, and the flower and tree sculptures are
very handsome; some can be made as light fixtures. (1982)
❏ Catalog: Free, R&W, CAN
⌂ Shop: All year, call ahead

Broadview Station
Route 2, Box 50A
Luverne, ND 58056
(701) 769-2273 TO/CC
Russell & Colleen Ford-Dunker

Supplies
Offer a traditional **wooden wheelbarrow** with removable sides and either a
steel or pneumatic wheel; it's made with cedar and ash woods. They also
make planters and potting benches. (1989)
❏ Catalog: Free, R&W, CAN/OV

Warren F. Broderick -- Books
P.O. Box 124
695 - 4th Avenue
Lansingburgh, NY 12182
(518) 235-4041
Warren F. Broderick

Books
A select stock of **out-of-print books** on garden design, garden art and
architecture and botanical illustration. (1977)
❏ Catalog: $1.50, R&W, CAN/OV
⌂ Shop: All year, by appointment only

Bronwood Worm Gardens
P.O. Box 28
Bronwood, GA 31726-0028
(912) 995-5994
J. F. Seymour

Supplies
Specialize in **bed-run redworms** in mixed sizes for composting and garden-
ing; they also have Gray Nightcrawlers (Georgia wigglers). All shipments are
Air Mail or UPS. Includes instructions for doing your own worm farming.
❏ Catalog: Free, R&W, $11m

Brooks Books
P.O. Box 21473
Concord, CA 94521-0473
(415) 672-4566
Philip & Martha Nesty

Books ⸜ Services
Sells **horticultural and botanical books; new, used and out-of-print** and
rare. Specializes in cacti, succulents, ornamental horticulture, floras
and botanicals, plant monographs, California native plants, Australian and
South African plants and trees and shrubs. Offers a search service; buys
book collections. (1986)
❏ Catalog: $1(2 IRC), CAN/OV
⌂ Shop: By appointment only

Brushking
4173 Domestic Avenue
Naples, FL 33941-0130
(813) 643-6368

Supplies & Tools
A manufacturer and importer of **garden and landscape maintenance tools**: pruning and grafting tools, rotary weed and brush cutters, sprayers and fertilizer injectors. Anyone may buy from their catalog.
❏ Catalog: Free

Brushy Mountain Bee Farm, Inc.
Route 1, Box 135
Moravian Falls, NC 28654
(800) BEESWAX FAX (919) 921-2681 TO/CC
Steve & Sandy Forrest

Supplies & Tools & Books
Everything for the beekeeper: books, bees, hives, supplies and equipment, including supplies for selling honey -- an informative catalog. Recent additions are video cassettes and slide shows on bees and beekeeping.
❏ Catalog: Free, R&W, CAN/OV
⌂ Shop: April-August, M-Sa; September-March, M-F

Bug-Off, The Natural Alternative
Route 3, Box 27A
Lexington, VA 24450
(703) 463-1760
Mirabai McLeod

Supplies
Offer a natural **alternative to chemical insect repellents**: no alcohol, perfumes or dyes, made from essential herbal oils. They claim it can also be used for insect control on pets.
❏ Catalog: Long SASE, R&S, CAN/OV

Builders Booksource
1817 Fourth Street
Berkeley, CA 94710
(415) 845-6874 or (800) 843-2028 TO/CC
George & Sally Kiskaddon

Books
A very broad selection of **books on architecture and design, construction, interior design, landscaping and gardening** -- everything from start to finish; the store is a delight! They produce a spring catalog and send bimonthly newsletters on what's new.
❏ Catalog: Free, CAN/OV
⌂ Shop: All year, daily

C & C Products
Route 3, Box 438
Hereford, TX 79045
(806) 276-5338 TO/CC
John & Nadine Chance

Supplies
Offers Big Drop, a **sprinkler that deep waters** up to one inch an hour in a 40-foot circle or one-half inch an hour over a 60-foot circle. The base is stable, and the head can be raised to 4 feet for broad coverage. Good for deep soaking and watering where wind usually blows spray out of the garden.
❏ Catalog: Free, R&W
⌂ Shop: All year, M-F, call ahead

C 'n' C Protea
330 N. Lantana Street
Camarillo, CA 93010
(805) 482-8905
Clifford Severn

Books
Formerly a protea nursery, they now specialize in **books on proteaceae** and will do consulting and lecturing on those South African plants.
❏ Catalog: Free, CAN/OV
⌂ Shop: All year, M-Sa, call ahead

Calendula
P.O. Box 930
Picton, ON, Canada K0K 2T0
(613) 476-3521
Heiko Frick

Books
Offers **rare and out-of-print books** and periodicals on flowers and gardens, landscape architecture, flower arranging, pomology, floriculture and wildflowers. Ask for their horticultural catalog.
❏ Catalog: Free, US/OV

Capability's Books
P.O. Box 144
Highway 46
Deer Park, WI 54007
(800) 247-8154 or (715) 269-5346 TO/CC
Pauline Rickard & Kris Gilbertson

Books
A very broad selection of **horticultural and gardening books**, new or recently published in the US or Britain. They have nearly 1,000 books in 84 categories -- something for any special interest. They have added computer programs and some video cassettes, too. (1978)
❏ Catalog: Free, R&W, CAN/OV
⌂ Shop: All year, M-F

Cape Cod Worm Farm
30 Center Avenue
Buzzards Bay, MA 02532
(508) 759-5664

Supplies
Sells **earthworms and worm castings**.
❏ Catalog: Free

Carruth Studio
760 Warehouse Road, Suite E
Toledo, OH 43615
(419) 382-7790 or 382-7898
George & Deborah Carruth

Ornaments
Offer cast concrete and terra cotta **wall plaques, birdfeeders, birdbaths, statues, planters and garden accessories**. They say, "Plant a smile in your garden"; all have a charming, whimsical feeling, some are slyly medieval! Great gifts. (1975)
❏ Catalog: $1d, R&W, CAN/OV
⌂ Shop: All year, M-F

Carter Fishworm Farm
Plains, GA 31780

Supplies
Offers **earthworms and worm castings**.
❏ Catalog: Free

Carts Warehouse

See Peter Reimuller's Cart Warehouse.

Cedar Hill Books
Route 8, Box 883
Tulsa, OK 74127
(918) 425-2590
Carol Bergman

Books
Offers **books on gardening, flower crafts, canning and preserving**, as well as nature books for children; a nice selection. (1986)
❏ Catalog: Free, CAN/OV

Charleston Battery Bench, Inc.
191 King Street
Charleston, SC 29401
(803) 722-3842 TO/CC
Andrew B. Slotin, Mr. & Mrs. Phil H. Slotin

Furniture
Sells only the **Charleston Battery Bench**, made using the mold patterns of the original maker; the bench has been in use in Charleston since the 1880s. It has cast iron sides painted in traditional green and cypress wood slats.
❏ Catalog: Free, R&W, CAN
⌂ Shop: All year, M-Sa

Charley's Greenhouse Supply
1569 Memorial Highway
Mt. Vernon, WA 98273
(206) 428-2626 TO/CC
Charles & Carol Yaw

Supplies ∾ Tools ∾ Books
A broad selection of **growing supplies, tools, plant lights, drip and misting systems, books** and many other items. They also sell greenhouses and greenhouse materials and accessories. (1975)
❏ Catalog: $2, CAN/OV
⌂ Shop: All year, M-F

Chicago Indoor Garden Supply

See Alternative Garden Supply, Inc.

Chippendale Home & Garden Furnishings

See Southern Statuary and Stone.

The Clapper Co.
1121 Washington Street
West Newton, MA 02165
(617) 244-7900 TO/CC
Bob & Anette Scaguetti

Tools ∾ Books ∾ Furniture ∾ Ornaments
Good selection of **tools, garden furniture and ornaments, garden supplies and books**. They sell Barlow Tyrie teak benches and furniture from England as well as classic, American-made hardwood garden furniture, swings and planters.
❏ Catalog: Free

Clarel Laboratories, Inc.
513 Grove Street
Deerfield, IL 60015
(312) 945-4013
Al Toral

Supplies
Sells Cactus Juice, Granny's Bloomers and other greenhouse and houseplant **fertilizers** especially formulated for African violets, orchids, foliage plants, cacti, ferns and tomatoes. Also sells Moonshine biodegradable leaf shine and Keep 'em Bloomin' **cut flower extender**.
❏ Catalog: Free, R&W, CAN/OV, $3m

Clothcrafters, Inc.
P.O. Box 176
90 Rhine Street
Elkhart Lake, WI 53020
(414) 876-2112 TO/CC
John & Karen Wilson

Supplies
Sell **clothing for gardeners**: boots, gloves, kneepads and aprons. In addition, they sell Poly Ban row covers, mosquito netting, cloth wares for the home and kitchen items. (1936)
❏ Catalog: Free, CAN
⌂ Shop: All year

J Collard
P.O. Box 7000A
Redondo Beach, CA 90277
(213) 543-9660 or (800) 541-4550 TO/CC
Charles E. Tressler & Jane F. Collard

Tools ∾ Furniture ∾ Ornaments
A new company offering **tools, garden ornaments, birdhouses**, even a snow shovel with a crook in its handle which will save your back. Catalog also offers many gifts for gardeners, household items with garden motifs and botanical prints. (1987)
❏ Catalog: Free

Robert Compton, Ltd.
RR 3, Box 3600
Bristol, VT 05443
(802) 453-3778 TO/CC
Christine Homer & Robert Compton

Ornaments
Sells **stoneware fountains** in a variety of configurations and will make custom orders. Fountains come with submersible pump, ready to plug in and fill; they are completely self-contained and can be used indoors or out.
❏ Catalog: $2d, R&W, CAN/OV
⌂ Shop: All year, by appointment only

CompuGarden, Inc.
1006 Highland Drive
Silver Spring, MD 20910
(301) 587-7995
Daniel Klein & Rosanne Skirble

Services
Offers **computer software** for the IBM PC -- a planning system for vegetable gardens -- and a service for an individually prepared garden plan for those without a computer which is Zip Code-specific in all regions of the US, Canada and Mexico.
❏ Catalog: Free, R&W, CAN/OV
⌂ Shop: All year, by appointment only

Computer Junction

See Infopoint Software.

Computer/Management Services
1426 Medinah Court
Arnold, MD 21012
Charles W. Barbour

Services
Custom **computer programs** for orchid lovers and for the nursery trade; both run on IBM or compatible computers. "Orchidata" is software for keeping track of an inventory of orchids; "Collector" makes an inventory of any type of collectible, including plants. Your chance to organize books or photos!
❏ Catalog: Free, CAN/OV, $40m

Coopersmith's England
6441 Valley View Road
Oakland, CA 94611
(415) 339-2499
Paul Coopersmith

Services
Offers **garden tours** to England, Scotland and France; groups are small, pace is relaxed, with several nights at each country inn or stately home. Most tours seem to include a few historical sites and private gardens; one tour includes gardens, antique shopping and London theater.
❏ Catalog: Free

Cottage Garden Collection
1269 Broadway, Suite 238
El Cajon, CA 92021
(619) 447-1554 TO/CC $30m
Marion & John Brodie

Supplies
Imported VHS **video cassettes** of British gardens of the National Trust; two cassettes offer spring and autumn gardens or summer and winter gardens. Also offer a cassette of the garden of the Royal National Rose Society.
❏ Catalog: Free, R&W, CAN/OV

Country Casual
17317 Germantown Road
Germantown, MD 20874-2999
(301) 540-0040 FAX 7364 TO/CC
Mrs. Bobbie Goldstein

Furniture
Offer Lister and Verey British **teak benches and tables** in a variety of styles and sizes, as well as their own Chippendale II designs; also several styles of garden swing, wooden planting tubs and deck chairs. Suppliers have Friends of the Earth (UK) approval. They pay the freight on purchases.
❏ Catalog: $2, R&W, CAN/OV
⌂ Shop: All year, call ahead

Country Home Products, Inc.
P.O. Box 89
Cedar Beach Road
Charlotte, VT 05445
(802) 425-2196 TO/CC
Mary Clark

Supplies
Offers the Dick Raymond **trimmer/mower** and **field and brush cutter**-- two well-thought-out pieces of equipment. The trimmer/mower is a string-type weed cutter on big wheels, which makes it possible to cut high weeds and grass easily; the field and brush mower will cut saplings up to an inch thick and has a steel cutting blade and powered wheels. (1985)
❏ Catalog: Free, CAN/OV
⌂ Shop: All year, M-F, call ahead

Country House Floral Supply
P.O. Box 4086, Bvl. Station
Andover, MA 01810
(508) 475-8463 TO/CC $20m
Helga J. Frazzette

Supplies ❧ Tools ❧ Books ❧ Ornaments
Offers **flower arranging supplies**, a very broad selection, including many styles of vases, bonsai stands, pruning tools and books on flower arranging.
❏ Catalog: $1, CAN/OV

Cox & Kings Travel
21 Dorset Square
London, England NW1 6Q9
(01) 724-6624
Anne Crawshay-Williams

Services
Offers a number of **horticultural and botanical tours** in Europe and world-wide; flower-painting and birdwatching tours, too, all led by experts. (1758)
❏ Catalog: Free

Creative Playgrounds, Ltd.
P.O. Box 10
McFarland, WI 53558
(608) 838-3326 or (800) 338-0522 TO/CC
Jim Lee, V.P., Sales

Furniture
Sells TimberGym **play structures**, which can be put together in several configurations of various complexity, depending on space and size of family. Even comes with a tented clubhouse for secret meetings. (1974)
❏ Catalog: Free, R&W, CAN/OV

Critter Creek Laboratory & Orchids
400 Critter Creek Road
Lincoln, CA 95648
(916) 645-8520
Arthur & Beverly Allison

Services
Offer **orchid testing** for cymbidium mosaic virus and tobacco mosaic virus, using the accurate ELISA technique, and the capability of testing other plants for viruses. They also offer a self-testing kit and virus testing anti-serums.
❏ Catalog: Free, R&W
⌂ Shop: By appointment only, Allison Ranch

Cropking, Inc.
P.O. Box 310
4930 Chippewa Road
Medina, OH 44258
(216) 725-5656 TO $25m
Dan J. Brentlinger

Supplies
Specialize in **greenhouses and supplies** and equipment for the larger-scale hydroponic grower; they offer a hydroponic growers' newsletter and an annual growers' seminar in March. Much of their equipment is suitable for any greenhouse. They sell rockwool, the last word in growing media. (1981)
❏ Catalog: $2d, R&W, CAN/OV
⌂ Shop: All year, M-F, call ahead

Cross T Products, Inc.
P.O. Box 10012
Knoxville, TN 37939
(615) 588-1948

Supplies
Manufactures and sells the Mighty Mover, a **garden cart** with a polyethelene body that will carry up to 400 pounds and cannot be harmed by weather.
❐ Catalog: Free

Cross VINYLattice
3174 Marjan Drive
Atlanta, GA 30340
(404) 451-4531
Susan M. Boyd

Ornaments
Here's a great idea! Lattice made of vinyl in nine colors; they say it never needs painting, it's impact resistant, it won't rot, it has no staples to rust and termites won't eat it. They will only sell by mail if you're not near one of their dealers; call or write for information. (1981)
❐ Catalog: Free

Cumberland Woodcraft
P.O. Drawer 609
Carlisle, PA 17013
(717) 243-0063
John Lopp, Mgr.

Ornaments
Offers a broad line of Victorian gingerbread for remodeling, but also two charming **gazebos**, garden benches and other historical reproductions.
❐ Catalog: $4.50, R&W, CAN/OV, $75m
⌂ Shop: All year, M-F

D.I.G. Corporation
7916 Ajay Street
Sun Valley, CA 91352
(818) 504-1188 or (800) 322-9146 TO/CC
David Levy

Supplies
Drip and mist irrigation supplies for the do-it-yourselfer -- including micro-sprinklers for indoors and out. Informative brochure gives basics on how to get started and what you'll need. Also offer Liquick sprayers and fertilizer injectors. (1982)
❐ Catalog: Free, R&W, CAN/OV, $50m
⌂ Shop: All year, M-F, call ahead

Daffodrill, Inc.
P.O. Box 248
Salt Point, NY 12578
(800) 635-5137 TO/CC
Carroll Reisner, V.P. & Gen. Mgr.

Tools
Sells an **earth auger** for planting bulbs, fertilizing trees and shrubs and planting seedings and ground covers. It fits a standard quarter-inch drill and is made of durable steel. (1988)
❐ Catalog: Free, R&W, CAN/OV, $43m

Dalton Pavilions, Inc.
7260-68 Oakley Street
Philadelphia, PA 19111
(215) 342-9804
James, Gerald & Glenn Dalton

Ornaments
Offers Western red cedar gazebos in various sizes and several charming styles -- Victorian, classic, Colonial or Victorian pagoda -- all available with screening. Also sells benches and tables to fit each size.
❐ Catalog: $3, CAN/OV

Dataplant
25, Malgraves Place
Basildon, Essex, England SS13 3PY
(0) 268 556683
Barry Hennessey

Services
For those who are looking for the very unusual, here's a **plant-finding service** in England with a database of 45,000 plants available from British nurseries, quite a few of which will export plants or seeds. They also encourage nurseries in the US and Canada who export to Britain to send their catalogs to be entered into the database. (1986)
❐ Catalog: 1 IRC, OV

Dave's Aquariums & Greenhouse
RR 1, Box 97
Kelley, IA 50134
(515) 769-2446
Dave Lowman

Supplies ∾ Tools ∾ Books
The name will fool you -- they sell **bonsai pots, books and tools**; a good selection of their own pots and imported pots as well. They also sell Artstone slabs and planting stones for bonsai and can make them to order from your sketch. (1981)
❐ Catalog: 3 FCS, CAN/OV, $10m
⌂ Shop: All year, daily, by appointment only

Day-Dex Co.
4725 N.W. 36th Avenue
Miami, FL 33142
(305) 635-5241 or 5259
Ernie & Kim Motsinger

Supplies
Offer **galvanized steel tiered benches** in several styles and sizes for orchids and other indoor and patio plants; also sell shade canopies with 55% to 80% shade. In addition, they manufacture and sell Kinsman carts, dollies and flat barrows for moving heavy nursery loads.
❐ Catalog: Free, R&W, CAN/OV
⌂ Shop: All year, M-F, call ahead

Deer Meadow
P.O. Box 175
Manset, ME 04656
(207) 244-7214
Peter Dolliver

Supplies
Seed-starting flats made of Eastern white cedar, sized for thirty-two 2-1/2-inch square peat pots; other sizes can be made to order.
❐ Catalog: Free

John Deere Catalog
1400 Third Avenue
Moline, IL 61265
(800) 544-2122
John Deere Company

Supplies ∾ Tools ∾ Books ∾ Ornaments
A new venture of an old company -- a home and garden catalog offering **tools and supplies, garden ornaments and games, fireplace equipment** and more -- even John Deere maple syrup! Color catalog; nice selection. (1838)
❐ Catalog: Free, CAN/OV

Denman & Co.
2913 Saturn Street, Suite H
Brea, CA 92621
(714) 524-0668
Bob & Rita Denman

Supplies
Manufacture and sell **gardening pants** with pockets for knee pads, called Greenknees (TM). Their line has expanded to garden chaps, picking aprons, holsters for trowels and shears; the **tools** they offer are a dispenser for vinyl garden tape, Hole Hog (a stainless steel bulb planter) and other unusual American-made tools. (1987)
❏ Catalog: Free, R&W, CAN/OV
⌂ Shop: All year, M-F, call ahead

Digger's Product Development Co.
P.O. Box 1551
Soquel, CA 95073
(408) 462-6095
Wayne Morgan

Supplies
Ever notice that every letter to the editor about pocket gophers comes from Sebastopol, CA? They are an obsession here with both gardeners and cats, but this might be the answer -- prefabricated wire gopher baskets, which are shipped flat but pop open easily for planting. They come in three sizes, and Sebastipudlians can buy them by the case. Minimum order is twelve.
❏ Catalog: Free, R&W, CAN, $20m

Direct Book Service
P.O. Box 230
Rose Bay, NSW, Australia 2029

Books
A source of all **new and current books published in Australia**; send your "want list." Payment is by bank draft in Australian currency.
❏ Catalog: See notes

Dirt Cheap Organics
5645 Paradise Drive
Corte Madera, CA 94925
(415) 924-0369
Donna & Keith Wolfe

Supplies
A source of **earthworms, bat guano, fish emulsion, beneficial insects** and a "special potion for slugs and snails." They also offer a variety of soil amendments and organic fertilizers.
❏ Catalog: Free
⌂ Shop: All year, call ahead

DoDe's Gardens, Inc.
2085 Leeward Lane
Merritt Island, FL 32953
(305) 452-5670 TO/CC
Dorothy & James Whitaker

Supplies ⚘ Books
Growing supplies and equipment for African violets and other indoor plants, including some books and the Floracart for indoor light gardening.
❏ Catalog: 2 FCS, R&W, CAN/OV, $7.50m
⌂ Shop: By appointment only

The Dramm Company
P.O. Box 1960
Manitowoc, WI 54221
(414) 684-0227 TO/CC
Kurt Dramm

Supplies ⚘ Tools
Known for the Dramm Water Breaker nozzles which break water flow into a gentle shower, offers a whole line of **watering equipment**, including watering cans and sprayers. Also sells hand-forged plant hangers, dinner bells, birdhouses, feeders and grafting and budding knives. (1945)
❏ Catalog: Free, R&W, CAN/OV, $10m

Dressler & Co.
P.O. Box 67
Silver City, NV 89428
(702) 847-0519
Chad Dressler

Ornaments
Offers a Victorian-style **cast-iron boot scraper.**
❏ Catalog: Free, R&W, CAN/OV, $20m
⌂ Shop: Spring-fall, daily, Chollar Mine, Virginia City

Drip Irrigation Garden

See D.I.G. Corporation.

Duncraft, Inc.
Penacook, NH 03303-9020
(603) 224-0200 TO/CC $15m
Mike Dunn

Supplies ⚘ Books
Broad selection of **birdfeeders, bird houses and other bird-related items**, including birdbaths and books on bird watching and identification. Also specialized bird seed mixes, depending on the birds you want to attract. (1952)
❏ Catalog: Free, R&W

Earlee, Inc.
2002 Highway 62
Jeffersonville, IN 47130-3556
(812) 282-9134 TO/CC $5m
Earl, Mary & Brent Stewart

Supplies
A broad selection of **organic products** for farmer and gardener; they manufacture Nature's Way growing supplies and sell many soil amendments, fertilizers, live animal traps, pest controls and bird repellents.
❏ Catalog: Free, R&W, CAN/OV, $3m

Earthly Goods Farm & Garden Supply
Route 3, Box 761
Mounds, OK 74047
(918) 827-3238
Debbie S. Pleu

Supplies ⚘ Tools ⚘ Books ⚘ Services
Supplies for the organic farmer and gardener: soil amendments, fertilizers, pest controls, hand tools, sprayers, animal care products and a number of books; all in an informative catalog. They also do soil testing by mail.
❏ Catalog: Free
⌂ Shop: 14 W. Brady, Tulsa

East Coast Hydroponics
432 Castleton Avenue
Staten Island, NY 10301
(718) 727-9300 or (800) 255-0121
Bill Ross

Supplies & Books
Offer a complete selection of **hydroponic growing supplies**: irrigation kits, rockwool, growing media, fans, timers, growing lights, pH testers, meters and fertilizers. They also sell beneficial insects, propagation supplies and books on organic and hydroponic gardening.
❒ Catalog: Free

east/west Gardens
1259 El Camino Real, Suite 196
Menlo Park, CA 94025
(415) 326-3151 or 321-2571 TO/CC $50m
Lisa Williams

Ornaments
Suppliers of ceramic, bronze, marble and terra cotta garden ornaments from the Orient, in classic styles. There are Chinese garden seats, statues, fishbowls, Tang style horses; my favorites are the simple terra cotta animals, especially the "laughing dog," which belongs on my verandah.
❒ Catalog: $1d, R&W, CAN/OV, $25m

Economy Label Sales Co., Inc.
P.O. Box 350
Daytona Beach, FL 32115
(904) 253-4741 or (800) 874-4465 TO/CC
Barbara Powell-Cameron

Supplies
Various styles of **plastic, paper and metal plant and garden labels**, label printers and custom labels to customer design, computer labels and software. Minimum order for most items is 1,000 blank or 500 printed of any one style, but you can get your friends or club to share an order.
❒ Catalog: Free, R&W, CAN/OV

Editions
Boiceville, NY 12412
(914) 657-7000 TO/CC $25m
Joan & Norman Levine

Books
A dealer in **used and out-of-print books** in many fields; each catalog has a nice selection of books on gardening and horticulture. (1948)
❒ Catalog: $2, CAN/OV

The Empire Gnome Manufacturing Co.
Box 453
Gormley, ON, Canada L0G 1H0

Ornaments
At last! A source of **gnomes**! They are made in limited editions of 500 copies of each little character, hand-painted and numbered. It appears that new characters are offered each year; one imagines a line of little men marching out of Gormley, singing, "Heigh ho! Heigh ho!"
❒ Catalog: Free, US/OV

The English Garden from Machin
652 Glenbrook Road
Stamford, CT 06907
(203) 348-3048 TO/CC
David Kettlewell

Furniture & Ornaments
Offers period design English **summerhouses, gazebos and covered seats**, as well as planters and trellises. Styles are charming, and they are used both in gardens and in commercial installations. (1983)
❒ Catalog: $6, CAN
⌂ Shop: All year, M-F

EnP Inc.
2001 Main Street, Box 218
603 14th Street
Mendota, IL 61342
(815) 539-7471 or (800) 255-4906 TO/CC $20m
Tom Smith

Supplies
Offer various **seed treatments, soil amendments, wetting agents, seaweed concentrate and humic acid products**. Informative leaflet explains purpose and use of each product. They offer Enliven and Fertile Grower products; demonstrate the effectiveness of the products in their own greenhouses.
❒ Catalog: Free
⌂ Shop: All year, M-Sa

Environmental Concepts
710 N.W. 57th Street
Ft. Lauderdale, FL 33309
(305) 491-4490 TO/CC $20m
Joe Lindell

Supplies
Meters to measure pH, soil salts, temperature, moisture, light intensity or soil fertility. Each comes with a comprehensive book on use. Recently introduced is a light meter which measures all types of light: sun, fluorescent, grow lights and high-intensity discharge lights. (1975)
❒ Catalog: Free, CAN/OV, $20m
⌂ Shop: All year, M-Sa

Eon Industries
315 Dodge Street
Swanton, OH 43558
John H. Noe

Supplies
Offer all-metal **plant and flower markers** -- zinc name plates will last for many years; galvanized wire standards are rust-resistant. Can be written on with pencils and markers which they also sell. Plates are sold separately, as the standards are reusable. Originally the Everlasting Label Co.
❒ Catalog: Free, R&W, CAN/OV

Erkins Studios, Inc.
662 Thames Street
Newport, RI 02840
(401) 849-2660 or 2665 TO/CC
John La Pointe

Furniture & Ornaments
Importers of **statues, fountains and other garden ornaments** in lead, iron and terra cotta; also stone, wood and metal garden benches. Styles are classic; they have some very handsome terra cotta jars and planters, as nice on city decks as in estate gardens. (1910)
❒ Catalog: $4, R&W, CAN/OV
⌂ Shop: March-December, M-F, call ahead

Evans BioControl, Inc.
895 Interlocken Parkway
Broomfield, CO 80020
(303) 460-1780 or (800) 289-6656 TO/CC

Supplies
They sell Nolo Bait, a **biological control for grasshoppers**, and De-Bug, a selective insecticide bait for grasshoppers, crickets and cutworms. They say Nolo Bait works on 58 species of grasshoppers and some crickets.
❏ Catalog: Free, R&W

Evergreen Garden Plant Labels
P.O. Box 922
Cloverdale, CA 95425
(707) 894-3225
Gary Patterson

Supplies
Sell **metal plant label holders with metal name plates** for all types of plants, available 13 inches, 20 inches and 26 inches high. They also sell 30-inch Bloomstalk Supports for taller flowers and rose-pegging hooks.
❏ Catalog: 1 FCS, CAN, $10m

Everlite Greenhouses, Inc.
9515 Gerwig Lane, Suite 115
Columbia, MD 21046
(301) 381-3881 TO/CC
William Bender

Supplies
Offer Everlite **greenhouses and solariums** in many configurations for home and commercial uses, both single and double-glazed. They have added a line of conservatories and garden rooms. (1951)
❏ Catalog: $5d, R&W, CAN/OV, $25m
⌂ Shop: All year, M-F

Exotic Blossoms
1533 Cherry Street
Philadelphia, PA 19102
(215) 963-9250
Lee-John Sobering

Furniture ∾ Ornaments
Importers of Haddonstone **garden ornaments from England**; these are made of "reconstructed" limestone and are available as planters, urns, fountains, benches, pedestals and animal figures, balustrading, even temples and pavilions. For larger gardens and deeper pockets, but very handsome indeed!
❏ Catalog: $10, R&W

FXG Corporation
3 Sullivan Street
Woburn, MA 01801
(617) 933-8428 or 935-1544
Frank Graney

Supplies
Offers two sizes of **garden cart**: the Log 'n' Lawn cart converts to carry wood or beehives in a rack; the Log 'n' Lawn Jr. will haul wood in a rack or barrels or trash containers. Also sells mechanical log-splitters.
❏ Catalog: Free, R&W, CAN/OV, $25m
⌂ Shop: All year, M-F, call ahead

Fairfax Biological Lab, Inc.
P.O. Box 300
Clinton Corners, NY 12514
(914) 266-3705
David A. Chittick, V.P. Sales

Supplies
Sell two **organic pest controls** -- Doom milky disease spore powder and Japidemic milky disease spore powder for use against Japanese beetles. They also offer Safer grub killer spore power, as well as Doom Larvo BT for use against chewing worms and caterpillars. (1945)
❏ Catalog: Free, R&W, $12m

Flora & Fauna Books
121 First Avenue South
Seattle, WA 98104
(206) 623-4727
David Hutchinson

Books
Formerly Jane Sutley Horticultural Books, they now offer a good selection of new **books** in horticulture and botany. They also offer rare, used and out-of-print books and welcome your "want lists"; will also purchase used books and collections.
❏ Catalog: Free, CAN/OV
⌂ Shop: All year, M-Sa

Floracolour
21 Oakleigh Road, Hillingdon
Uxbridge, Middlesex, England UB10 9EL
(0895) 51831
H. C. W. Shaw

Services
Here's the answer to my perennial problem of loading the film incorrectly: Mr. Shaw offers sets of slides of famous gardens, the Chelsea Flower Shows, interesting plants and flowers in England and abroad, "stately" homes and even the Pasadena Rose Parade -- and he can wait for the sun!
❏ Catalog: Free, R&W, CAN/OV
⌂ Shop: All year, daily

Floral Accents
Route 1, Box 69
Rustburg, VA 24588
Elizabeth Blanks

Supplies
Sells **flower arranging supplies** in bulk for garden clubs and classes; all supplies seem to be sold by the case. (1984)
❏ Catalog: Long SASE

The Floral Mailbox
P.O. Box 235
Lombard, IL 60148-0235
Gail Pabst

Supplies
Supplier of **professional floral supplies**: cut flower preservative, flower drying compound and arranging supplies, bouquet holders, baskets, tools and indoor plant care products such as leaf gloss and sheet moss. (1987)
❏ Catalog: $1d, CAN

Floralight Gardens Canada, Inc.
P.O. Box 247, Sta. A
Willowdale, ON, Canada M2N 5S9
(416) 920-4769 or 665-4000 TO/CC
Alan Patte

Supplies
Manufactures and sells Floralight **plant stands** -- multitiered systems for propagation or for indoor growing of African violets, orchids and other houseplants; can even be used for hydroponics.
❏ Catalog: Free, R&W, US

Florapersonnel
P.O. Box 1732
Deland, FL 32721
(904) 738-5151
Robert F. Zahra, Mgr.

Services
A **horticultural employment agency** which lists many types of jobs: managers of commercial operations, florists, landscape architects, estate managers, nursery supply and management, import and export -- you name it! A good way to find a job or a qualified worker. (1982)
❑ Catalog: Free

Florentine Craftsmen, Inc.
46-24 - 28th Street
Long Island City, NY 11101
(212) 532-3926 FAX 3928
Graham Brown

Furniture ⌘ Ornaments
A wide selection of fine **lead statuary, fountains, cast aluminum and cast iron furniture** in classic styles. Also sundials, birdbaths, weathervanes, planters and cherubs and many animals of the most appealing sort. (1928)
❑ Catalog: $4d, R&W, CAN/OV
⌂ Shop: All year, M-F

Floribunda Books
P.O. Box 203
Hamilton, NY 13346

Books
Offers a good selection of **new and recent books** on gardening, garden history and design. Seems to carry some books which "new" bookstores don't keep around long enough, but are well worth searching out.
❑ Catalog: Free

Florilegium
P.O. Box 157
Snedens Landing
Palisades, NY 10964
(914) 359-2926
Oriel Eaton Kriz

Ornaments
Offers a broad selection of **antique botanical prints**, bird prints and landscape and architectural prints for very special interiors. (1980)
❑ Catalog: $3, CAN/OV
⌂ Shop: By appointment only

Florist Products, Inc.
2242 North Palmer Drive
Schaumburg, IL 60173
(312) 885-2242
Paul Lange

Supplies ⌘ Tools
A broad selection of **gardening supplies, tools and equipment, pots, fertilizers and mist systems**; also sell the Wonder Garden, a lighted plant stand for indoor light gardening. They have another catalog for commercial growers with a complete line of supplies; send a request on your letterhead.
❑ Catalog: Free, R&W, CAN
⌂ Shop: All year, M-F (closed first two weeks of July)

Foothill Agricultural Research, Inc.
510-1/2 W. Chase Drive
Corona, CA 91720
(714) 371-0120 TO
Joe Barcinas or Viki Banks

Supplies
Offers a wide selection of **beneficial insects**: parasitic wasps, fly parasites, ladybugs, predatory mites, green lacewings, preying mantids and decollate snails. Also Chilocorus nigritus, a voracious predatory beetle which attacks scale insects, including red scale. (1978)
❑ Catalog: Free, CAN/OV, $50m
⌂ Shop: All year, daily, call ahead

Fountain Sierra Bug Company
P.O. Box 114
Rough & Ready, CA 95975
(916) 273-0513
H. H. Fountain

Supplies
Sells **ladybugs**, those little charmers who really earn their keep; offered from one-half pint to one gallon, sent by Air Mail.
❑ Catalog: Free, SS:1-9

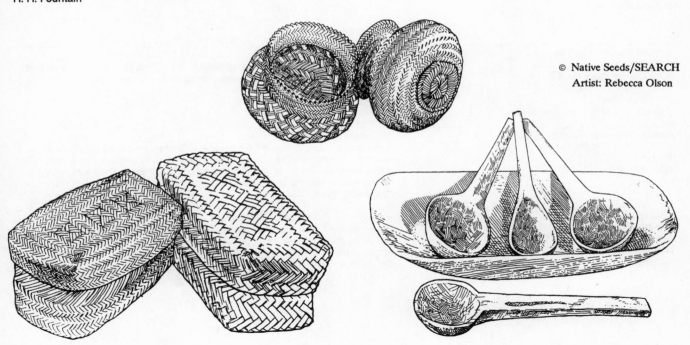

© Native Seeds/SEARCH
Artist: Rebecca Olson

Four Seasons Greenhouses
5005 Veterans Memorial Highway
Holbrook, NY 11741-4516
(516) 694-4400 or (800) 645-9527

Supplies
Sells **greenhouses and lean-to solariums**.
❒ Catalog: Free

Freedom Soil Lab
P.O. Box 1144
42 Hangar Way (Watsonville)
Freedom, CA 95019-1144
(408) 724-4427 FAX 3188
Frank Shields

Services
Offers **soil testing** by mail; issues a report showing your results in primary and secondary nutrients, toxic salts, pH value and organic matter, and compares them to typical fertile soil. Quantity discounts to clubs and garden shops. (1987)
❒ Catalog: Free, CAN/OV, $10m
⌂ Shop: All year, M-F

Full Circle Garden Products
P.O. Box 6
77 Avenue of the Giants (Phillipsville)
Redway, CA 95560
(800) 426-5511 TO/CC
Michael & Rhona Martin

Supplies ❧ Books
Offers a broad selection of **growing supplies**: fertilizers, irrigation supplies, sprayers, tools, pruning tools, plant lights and pest controls. Also sells rockwool for hydroponic growing; it's becoming "the thing" for orchids, too. Sells bat guano in 10-3-1 and 2-8-.05 formulas. (1983)
❒ Catalog: $2d, R&W, CAN/OV, $10m
⌂ Shop: All year, M-F

Full Moon Farm Products
P.O. Box 4865
217 S.W. 2nd Street
Corvallis, OR 97339
(503) 757-2532 or (800) 888-5765 TO/CC
Tom Alexander

Supplies ❧ Books
A broad selection of organic and chemical fertilizers, organic pest controls, soil amendments, irrigation supplies, plant lights, propagation supplies, drip irrigation and hydroponic systems; supplies for "high tech" gardening both indoors and out. (1980)
❒ Catalog: Free, CAN/OV
⌂ Shop: All year, M-Sa

The Garden Book Club
250 W. 57th Street
New York, NY 10107
(212) 582-6912 TO/CC
New York Review of Books

Books
Just like that big **book club**, monthly selections and other new garden books offered at a discount. Has had a series of terrific introductory offers in the past and has had the ineffable good taste to offer this book to its members since it first came out.
❒ Catalog: Write for information

The Garden Concepts Collection
P.O. Box 241233
Memphis, TN 38124-1233
(901) 756-1649
John B. Painter

Furniture ❧ Ornaments
A broad selection of **ornaments and furnishings** for the garden -- pavilions, arbors, pergolas, bridges, gates, lighting systems, planters, plant stands, garden furniture -- in a variety of historical styles. Customers may submit designs for pricing and construction. (1985)
❒ Catalog: $5d, R&W, CAN
⌂ Shop: All year, M-F

Garden Magic
2001-1/2 Fairview Road
Raleigh, NC 27608
(919) 833-7315 TO/CC $50
Darlene Welcker

Furniture ❧ Ornaments
Offer a nice selection of **garden ornaments**: light fixtures, trellises, furniture, topiary frames, Sussex trugs and thatched birdhouses. At their shop they have one-of-a-kind and antique garden ornaments in terra cotta, cast iron and copper. (1983)
❒ Catalog: Free, R&W, CAN, $25m
⌂ Shop: All year, M-Sa

Garden Variety, Limited
P.O. Box 40721
5230 Sherier Place Northwest
Washington, DC 20016
(202) 686-1229
Elaine T. Lozier & Letha Dreyfus

Books ❧ Services
New source of **general gardening books**; will do searches for specific books or by specific topic. They make every attempt to link customers with a book that will fit the expressed need."
❒ Catalog: Free

Garden Way Manufacturing Co.
102nd Street and 9th Avenue
Troy, NY 12180
(800) 828-5500 TO/CC

Supplies
They manufacture and sell Troy-Bilt tillers, Garden Way carts and Tomahawk chipper/shredders. The **tillers** come in several sizes to suit various uses and power requirements, as do the **chipper/shredders**. They also have a **sickle-bar mower** for rough stuff.
❒ Catalog: Free, CAN/OV

Gardener's Eden
Box 7307
San Francisco, CA 94120-7307
(415) 428-9292 or 421-4242 TO/CC
Williams-Sonoma

Supplies ❧ Furniture ❧ Ornaments
Offers a broad selection of **tools, equipment and gadgets** for gardening, including garden ornaments, planters, furniture and many unusual and appropriate gifts for gardeners.
❒ Catalog: Free

Gardener's Kitchen
P.O. Box 412
Farmington, CT 06034
Betty J. Rafferty

Supplies
Offer canning lids, rings and press-on labels; they still sell the #63 small canning lid which they say is still sought by many people. (1976)
❑ Catalog: Free, CAN

Gardener's Supply Company
128 Intervale Road
Burlington, VT 05401
(802) 863-1700 or 4535 TO/CC
Will Raap

Supplies ⌇ Tools ⌇ Ornaments
A broad selection of **tools and equipment, organic fertilizers and pesticides, tillers and food preservation supplies**, most illustrated in a color catalog. They also sell greenhouses, composters, irrigation equipment, shredder/chippers, carts, sprayers, knee pads, a wind-driven mole-repeller.
❑ Catalog: Free, R&W
⌂ Shop: All year, M-Sa

Gardens Alive!

See Natural Gardening Research Center.

V. L. T. Gardner
30026 Avenida Celestial
Rancho Palos Verdes, CA 90274
(213) 541-1372 TO/CC
Virginia Gardner

Books ⌇ Services
Offers **new and used books** on horticulture, gardening, botany, landscape architecture and plants and gardens appropriate to southern California and other dry areas; and will search for out-of-print books on those subjects. No catalog at present; call or send a "want list." (1982)
❑ Catalog: See notes, R&W, CAN/OV
⌂ Shop: By appointment only

E. C. Geiger, Inc.
P.O. Box 285, Route 63
Harleysville, PA 19438
(215) 256-6511 TO/CC
Ronald M. Soldo

Supplies ⌇ Tools
"**Everything for the grower.**" A thick catalog offering a huge selection of growing supplies, pruning tools, fertilizers, greenhouses and equipment, pots and flats and irrigation equipment. Also an inexpensive soil testing meter, small and accurate. (1928)
❑ Catalog: Free, R&W, CAN/OV, $50m
⌂ Shop: All year, M-F

General Hydroponics
50 Belevedere Street, Suite C
San Rafael, CA 49401-4817
(415) 457-1041
Lawrence Brooke

Supplies
Offer the Rainforest Modular Aero-Hydroponic and the Aquafarm **hydroponic systems**; the first-named system was developed in Israel. They also sell Advanced Nutrient System fertilizers and pH solutions and testing supplies.
❑ Catalog: Free

Genie House
P.O. Box 2478
56 Red Lion Road
Vincentown, NJ 08088
(609) 654-8303 or 654-8303 TO/CC
Lloyd E. Williams, Sr.

Supplies
Hand-crafted brass, copper and tin reproduction **light fixtures** in classic styles for gardens and house exteriors; they will also do custom work. (1967)
❑ Catalog: Free, R&W, CAN/OV
⌂ Shop: All year, daily

Geostar Travel
6050 Commerce Boulevard
Rohnert Park, CA 94928
(707) 584-9552 or (800) 624-6633 (CA)
Barbara Hopper

Services
A travel agency which specializes in **horticultural, botanical and natural history tours** to England, Europe, Central and South America, Hawaii and Australia. The tours are led by experts; some are organized for various societies or special interest groups.
❑ Catalog: Free
⌂ Shop: All year, M-Sa

Gladstone & Campbell
Old Stable Yard
Hawarden Castle
Hawarden, Clwyd, Wales, UK CH5 3NY
011-44-(244) 520369
Francis Gladstone

Ornaments
A source of antique and reproduction **botanical prints**, especially of gesneriads, orchids and native flowers of various continents; they do not issue a catalog, but you can write and ask if they have prints of particular plant types or styles of print. (1986)
❑ Catalog: See notes, R&W, OV
⌂ Shop: Call ahead

Glashaus/Weck Home Canning
415 W. Golf Road, Suite 13
Arlington Heights, IL 60005
Norbert Kunz, Pres.

Supplies
A source of **home canning supplies** -- jars for preserves and juices and an electric water-bath canner. (1983)
❑ Catalog: Free, R&W, CAN/OV, $10m

Gothic Arch Greenhouses
P.O. Box 1564
1059 Sutton Avenue
Mobile, AL 36633-1564
(205) 432-7529 TO/CC
W. H. Sierke, Jr.

Supplies
Redwood or red cedar **greenhouses** with fiberglass glazing in a pointed-arch style, either attached or free-standing. Also sells heating/cooling systems, shade cloth, benches and supplies. (1945)
❑ Catalog: Free
⌂ Shop: All year, M-F, call ahead

Great Lakes IPM
10220 Church Road N.E.
Vestaburg, MI 48891
(517) 268-5693
James Hansel

Supplies
A good selection of **supplies and equipment for integrated pest management**; they offer insect traps of all kinds, as well as controlled-release pheromone dispensers, all described in an informative catalog.
❑ Catalog: Free, R&W, CAN/OV
⌂ Shop: All year, M-F

Green Earth Organics
9422 - 144th Street East
Puyallup, WA 98373
(206) 845-2321
Joel & MariLou Holland

Supplies ✎ Tools
Offer a number of **organic products** for soil improvement, fertilizing and insect control; they manufacture their own Multi-Crop Liquid Seaweed. They also sell seeds for green manure crops, watering equipment and general growing supplies.
❑ Catalog: Free, R&W, CAN/OV
⌂ Shop: February-May, M-Sa; June-Jan., by appointment only

Green Thumb Hygro-Gardens
P.O. Box 1314
Sheboygan, WI 53081-1314
(414) 459-8989
Robert Van Derslice

Supplies
"We offer several **hydroponic systems** for the home hydroponic enthusiast: can be used inside or outside and can be expanded."
❑ Catalog: $1, R&W, CAN/OV
⌂ Shop: By appointment only

The Greener Thumb
P.O. Box 704
Littlefield, TX 79339
Richard A. Ferrill

Supplies ✎ Tools
New company offers Spear & Jackson and True Friends tools, organic pest controls, composting equipment, cold controls, Gloria sprayers, the Earth-tumbler compost-maker and the Nature's Raindrops sprinkler, which puts out large drops, so there's less drift in the wind. (1987)
❑ Catalog: Free

Greenhouse Builders Supply

See Progressive Building Products.

Greenleaf Industries
1200 S.W. Spruce Street
Grants Pass, OR 97526
(503) 474-0571
David James, Director

Ornaments
A sheltered workshop which has a year-round horticultural training program. For Christmas they make and sell 22-inch Christmas wreaths, which they will ship anywhere in the US; orders must be placed by December 5.
❑ Catalog: Free, SS:11-12

Grosoke, Inc.
7415 Whitehall Street #119
Ft. Worth, TX 76118
(817) 284-0696 or (800) 522-0696 TO/CC

Supplies
Sell Agrosoke hydrogels for reducing water needs of plants and Agrodip root-protecting gel to keep cuttings and bare-root stock from drying out. They also sell Aquarius, a potting soil with hydrogels already mixed in.
❑ Catalog: Free, R&W, CAN/OV, $10m

Grower's Supply Co.
P.O. Box 1123
33 N. Staebler Road
Ann Arbor, MI 48103
(313) 662-6058
Donna Draper, Mgr.

Supplies
Offer Sunlighter and Evergreen **plant stands**, with or without plant lights. They also sell Perma-Nest **plant trays** to hold potted plants or start seeds and an indoor greenhouse with automatic wick watering and an optional plant light. (1954)
❑ Catalog: Free, R&W, CAN/OV
⌂ Shop: All year, by appointment only

Growing Naturally
P.O. Box 54
Pineville, PA 18946
(215) 598-7025 FAX 598-3865
Susanne & Denis Hewitt

Supplies ✎ Tools
Sells a good selection of **organic growing supplies**, sprayers, tools, row covers, fertilizers and soil amendments, beneficial insects and insect traps, irrigation supplies and tee-shirts, of course. (1985)
❑ Catalog: Free, R&W
⌂ Shop: Call ahead

The Guano Company
3562 E. 80th Street
Cleveland, OH 44105
(216) 641-1200
Larry Pozarelli

Supplies
A source of seabird **guano** in several formulations for various uses, as well as bat guano and worm castings; literature gives good information on the benefits and use of each.
❑ Catalog: Free

H. P. Supplies, Inc.
P.O. Box 2053
Livonia, MI 48150
(313) 668-7963 TO/CC
Susan Schaaf

Supplies
Sells **lighted plant carts and stands** in several sizes, plant lights and accessories for indoor growing and seed starting. (1970)
❑ Catalog: Free, R&W, CAN/OV

Hall Enterprises
1280 Quince Drive
Junction City, OR 97448
(503) 998-2060
Stan Hall

Supplies
Stan Hall has sold his rhododendron nursery, but still offers **aluminum plant labels** in two styles; names written in pencil "weather in" and last. He will send you a sample for a SASE. He also sells sturdy polyethylene "pots" (bags) for growing on plants; they come in 1.8 and 3-gallon sizes.
❐ Catalog: Long SASE, R&W

Hangouts
P.O. Box 148
1328 Pearl Street
Boulder, CO 80302
(800) HANGOUT or (303) 442-2533
Beto Goldberg

Furniture
Offers handwoven **hammocks** in a variety of styles, materials and colors; all call out to you in insistent voices, saying, "Why not have a little lie-down now and finish that later when it's cooler?"
❐ Catalog: Free, R&W, CAN/OV
⌂ Shop: All year, daily

Happy Valley Ranch
Route 2, Box 83
Paola, KS 66071
(913) 849-3103 TO/CC
Ray & Wanda Stagg

Supplies
Offer **cider and wine presses** for the home orchardist or winemaker: single and double presses and presses in kit form, as well as separate apple grinders and picking bags, loppers, pole saws and pruners. They also have a cider cookbook.
❐ Catalog: $1, CAN/OV
⌂ Shop: All year, M-F, call ahead

Harlane Company, Inc.
266 Orangeburgh Road
Old Tappan, NJ 07675
Frank & June Benardella

Supplies ∾ Tools
Sell **garden markers** with removable name plates, marking pens, Felco **pruning shears**, a rose pruning saw, goatskin gloves and pH testing meters. They will custom-print rose nameplates.
❐ Catalog: Free

Harmony Farm Supply
P.O. Box 451
3320 Gravenstein Highway North (Sebastopol)
Graton, CA 95444
(707) 823-9125 FAX 823-1734
Kate Burroughs & David Henry

Supplies ∾ Tools ∾ Books
Only a mile or so from Tusker Press World Headquarters; I know it well! It's a real **emporium**, serving organic farmers/gardeners with a huge selection of drip and regular irrigation supplies, tools, organic pest controls, books, traps, fertilizers and soil amendments, beneficial insects and canning supplies. They are adding drought-tolerant and edible landscape plants; all described in a very informative catalog. (1980)
❐ Catalog: $2d, R&W, CAN
⌂ Shop: All year, daily

Harper Horticultural Slide Library
219 Robanna Shores
Seaford, VA 23696
(804) 898-6453 (after 3 pm)
Pamela Harper

Services
Huge selection of **photographic slides of plants, gardens, landscaping and natural scenery**, available for purchase or rent (some sets with lecture notes); catalog well arranged by subject. Ms. Harper is a well-known photographer and garden writer. (1973)
❐ Catalog: $2, CAN/OV

Hatchard's
187 Piccadilly
London, England W1V 9DA
(01) 439-9921 FAX 494-1313

Books
Long-established bookseller issues a periodic catalog offering a broad selection of **gardening and horticultural books** -- and will accept credit card orders from overseas. The Royal Horticultural Society was founded in the back room.
❐ Catalog: Free, OV
⌂ Shop: All year, M-Sa

Philip Hawk & Company
159 E. College Avenue
Pleasant Gap, PA 16823
(814) 355-7177
Philip Hawk

Ornaments
Hand-carved **stone lanterns** for outdoor lighting, in traditional Japanese and original designs; they are naturally not cheap, but beautiful, and would make a lovely commemorative gift. (1978)
❐ Catalog: $3, R&W, CAN/OV
⌂ Shop: By appointment only

Hen-Feathers & Company
10 Balligomingo Road
Gulph Mills, PA 19428
(215) 828-1721 FAX 8617
Beth & Tad Featherman

Ornaments
Offers a number of charming **statues, sundials, planters** and other garden ornaments, most in classic styles with an antique lead finish.
❐ Catalog: Free, R&W

Heritage Arts
16651 S.E. 235th Street
Kent, WA 98042
(206) 631-1318
Sharon Muth

Supplies ∾ Tools ∾ Books ∾ Services
A broad selection of **bonsai pots, tools, supplies** and some books; they offer Kaneshin bonsai tools and Tokoname bonsai pots. They also offer classes on bonsai and repotting and styling services at the shop.
❐ Catalog: $2, R&W, CAN
⌂ Shop: All year, Th-Sa

Heritage Center for the Preservation
**   of Antique Fruit, Nut & Vegetable Varieties**
RR 2, Box 201
Jamestown, IN 46147
(317) 676-5872 or 5289
John E. Perkins

Supplies ⁊ Books ⁊ Services
A new organization dedicated to preserving old fruit and nut varieties; sells new books and reprints of old **books for the heirloom gardener**, publishes a list of varieties and variety descriptions, sells supplies for seed savers, will do **plant searches** for old varieties and rent old and rare books on agriculture.
❒ Catalog: Free

Heritage Lanterns
70A Main Street
Yarmouth, ME 04096
(207) 846-3911 or (800) 544-6070 TO/CC
H. William Geoffrion

Ornaments
Beautiful hand-crafted **lanterns and light fixtures in copper, pewter and brass**, available in a variety of classic styles for outdoors and indoors. They will also do custom work.
❒ Catalog: $3, R&W, CAN/OV
⌂ Shop: All year, M-F

Hermitage Gardens
P.O. Box 361
Canastota, NY 13032
(315) 697-9093 TO/CC
Russell Rielle

Ornaments
Sell a number of fiberglass **fountains, pools, waterfalls**, redwood water-wheels and equipment for water gardening such as pumps and lights; many of their illustrations show indoor installations. They also sell ornamental **bridges** in several styles. (1946)
❒ Catalog: $1, R&W, CAN/OV
⌂ Shop: All year, daily, call ahead

Historic Hardware, Ltd.
P.O. Box 1327
1000 Washington Road (Rye)
North Hampton, NH 03862
(603) 964-2280
John De Waal

Ornaments
Hand-forged period hooks for plant hangers, plant stands, hooks to hang drying herbs, other indoor and outdoor hardware and exterior lanterns and post lights in very handsome Colonial styles. (1987)
❒ Catalog: $3, R&W, CAN
⌂ Shop: All year, Tu-Sa

Holland's Organic Garden
8515 Stearns
Overland Park, KS 66214
(913) 888-6817
Matt Holland

Supplies ⁊ Tools ⁊ Books
A "full-service exclusively **organic lawn and landscape service**". Offers Double Duty Feed Meals, Erth-Rite, Maxicrop and other fertilizers, pest controls such Scanmask and diatomaceous earth, tools, irrigation systems, garden carts, books, birdhouses and Protect-O-Mat pot mats.
❒ Catalog: Free

Hollister's Hydroponics
P.O. Box 16601
Irvine, CA 92713
(714) 551-3822 TO/CC
Steve & Jorgeen Hollister

Supplies
Offer **hydroponic kits and supplies** in an informative catalog which explains how to go about it; they sell books on hydroponics for those who want to plunge in. They also offer a water purifier. (1975)
❒ Catalog: $1, CAN/OV

Hollowbrook Pottery and Tile
P.O. Box 413
Hollowbrook Road
Lake Peekskill, NY 10537
(914) 526-3786
Roger L. Baumann

Ornaments
Stoneware planters for indoors and outdoors (frostproof to withstand harsh winters); available in handsome colors -- green, "shino," white, oxblood, celadon, stoney and woodfire; also tiles for floors, walls and patios. (1976)
❒ Catalog: Free, R&W, CAN/OV
⌂ Shop: By appointment only

Holz-Ems, Inc.
1704 N. Tustin Avenue, Suite 242
Orange, CA 92665
A. Grewall

Supplies
Offers **wire pot hangers, plant supports and label stakes** for orchid growers -- though many gardeners might like the pot hangers, which come in either fixed or swivel models to fit 4-inch to 7-inch plastic or clay pots.
❒ Catalog: Free

Homestead Carts
6098 Topaz Street N.E.
Salem, OR 97305
(503) 390-5586
Marvin Botts

Supplies
Offer a 26-inch **garden cart** with a 400-pound carrying capacity -- also available as a kit -- and a 20-inch cart for smaller gardens. They will sell wheels and axles separately.
❒ Catalog: Free

Honingklip Nurseries & Book Sales
13 Lady Anne Avenue
Newlands, Cape Town, South Africa 7700
(021) 644410 FAX 0027-21-643460
Mrs. E. R. Middelmann

Books ⁊ Services
Offer a broad selection of **books on South African plants and gardens**; they also will search for used and out-of-print books. Prices given in US$.
❒ Catalog: Free, R&W, OV
⌂ Shop: All year, M-F

Hortopaper Growing Systems
4111 N. Motel Drive, Suite 101
Fresno, CA 93722
(209) 275-3600
Gerald Nordstrom

Supplies
Offer eight-inch **plant food discs** made of Hortopaper which fertilize as you water and suppress weeds around your vegetables and ornamentals; the discs have an analysis of 5-5-5. Also sell Hortopaper as a ground cover/paper mulch made of peat moss and cellulose fibers.
❒ Catalog: Free, R&W, CAN, $3m
⌂ Shop: All year, M-F

Hortulus
139 Marlborough Place
Toronto, ON, Canada M5R 3J5
(416) 920-5057 TO/CC
Bruce & Linda Marshall

Books
Sell a broad selection of **used, out-of-print and rare books** on gardening, landscape architecture, herbs, garden history and specific plants; prices are in US dollars. They are adding books on flower painting. (1976)
❏ Catalog: $2d, R&W, US/OV

Hosta Resources
7180 N. 82nd Plaza
Omaha, NE 68122
Anne Thomsen

Services
A **plant-finding service** which searches only for cultivars of hostas; she will prepare a list of catalogs offering the plant you're searching for. Charge is $6 per plant; the original check is refunded if she fails. (1986)
❏ Catalog: See notes

Hubbard Folding Box Co.
15980 Rush Creek Road
Osseo, MN 55369
(612) 420-2875
Floyd Nelson

Supplies
Folding wooden fruit harvesting boxes; can have names or logos printed on the side; can be used over and over again. They come in several sizes and styles. Great for moving all sorts of belongings; nice gift. (1898)
❏ Catalog: Free, R&W, CAN/OV

H. D. Hudson Mfg. Co.
500 N. Michigan Avenue
Chicago, IL 60611
(312) 644-2830
R. C. Hudson, Jr.

Supplies
Offer many styles of **garden sprayers**, from hand-pumping sprayers and dusters to backpacks and a power sprayer on wheels; offer economy to top-of-the-line models.
❏ Catalog: Free, R&W, CAN/OV

Hurley Books
RR 1, Box 160
Westmoreland, NH 03467
(603) 399-4342
Henry & Janet Hurley

Books
Historical or textual books on agriculture, horticulture, animal husbandry, cottage industry and rural miscellany. They also have older seed catalogs, 19th century horticultural periodicals; more than 2,000 titles. (1966)
❏ Catalog: $1, CAN, $10m
⌂ Shop: All year, call ahead

Hyde Bird Feeder Co.
P.O. Box 168
Waltham, MA 02254
(617) 893-6780
Donald B. Hyde, Jr., & Jim Flewelling

Supplies ∾ Ornaments
Sells **birdhouses, feeders, bird seed and gifts for the bird-lover.** Canadian customers can contact Yule-Hyde Associates, 329 Rayette, Unit 7 & 8, Concord, ON L4K 2G1. (1942)
❏ Catalog: Free, R&W

Hydro-Gardens, Inc.
P.O. Box 9707
Colorado Springs, CO 80932
(303) 495-2266 or (800) 634-6362 TO/CC
Mike Morton or Stan Benson

Supplies
Greenhouse and hydroponic growing supplies of all kinds for the home grower or commercial operator, including their Chem-Gro Nutrient. A very broad selection; ask for either the home or the commercial catalog. (1972)
❏ Catalog: Free, R&W, CAN/OV, $10m
⌂ Shop: All year, M-F

I. F. M.
333 Ohme Garden Road
Wenatchee, WA 98801
(509) 662-3179 or (800) 332-3179 TO/CC
Phillip Unterschuetz

Supplies ∾ Services
Organic garden products and pest controls: a good selection, with products and their uses well described. They are specialists in organic fruit production and toxic residue testing. They offer soil amendments, natural pest controls, beneficial insects, traps and baits, soaps and green manure seed.
❏ Catalog: Free, R&W, CAN/OV
⌂ Shop: All year, M-Sa

IPM Computer System
IPM Implementation Group
University of California
Davis, CA 95616

Services
On-line database with up-to-date information on controlling home and garden pests: available anytime EXCEPT 8 to 5 on weekdays. Specific recommendations for controlling most pests, text from Extension bulletins, data from weather stations in California and a bulletin board. Fee $13 for manual & password.
❏ Catalog: Write for information

Idaho Wood Industries, Inc.
P.O. Box 488
3425 Meadow Creek Drive
Sandpoint, ID 83864-0488
(800) 635-1100 or (208) 263-9521 TO/CC
Leon Lewis & Linda Mitchell

Ornaments
Natural wood garden lights, mostly lights on standards for paths and gardens; they have a number of handsome styles made of either cedar or oak. Also sell handsome indoor and outdoor wall and ceiling fixtures in natural wood and wooden bathroom accessories. (1975)
❏ Catalog: Free, R&W, CAN/OV
⌂ Shop: All year, M-F, call ahead

Indoor Gardening Supplies
P.O. Box 40567
Detroit, MI 48240
(313) 668-8384 TO/CC
Nancy Allen

Supplies
Offers a good selection of **growing supplies** for indoor and light gardening and plant propagation: lighted plant stands, plant lights, capillary matting, meters, timers, trays and more. (1973)
❏ Catalog: Free, CAN/OV

Infopoint Software
P.O. Box 83
Arcola, MO 65603
(417) 424-3424 or 3327
Dorothy Nichols

Services
Offers several MS DOS **computer programs** for hobbyists and commercial green-houses and nurseries: three programs help you find the right flower, bulb or shrub for various uses and give germination and growing information. A cost analysis program helps growers keep track of costs for pricing. (1988)
❐ Catalog: Free, CAN/OV, $50m

Innis Violets
8 Maddison Lane
Lynnfield, MA 01979
(617) 334-6679
Reuben & Kathy Innis

Supplies
Offers **African violet growing supplies**: plant lights, insecticides and fungicides, fertilizers, pots, leaf support rings and high-dome terrariums.
❐ Catalog: $.50d
⌂ Shop: All year, by appointment only

Innovative Geotextiles Corp
P.O. Box 34221
Charlotte, NC 28234
(704) 553-1125

Supplies
Manufacturers and sells Geoscape Landscape Fabric for **weed control**. It comes in standard and commercial grades and lasts longer than black plastic film; it can also be used to prevent the silting up of drain trenches.
❐ Catalog: Free

Integrated Fertility Management

See I.F.M.

International Irrigation Systems
P.O. Box 1133
St. Catharines, ON, Canada L2R 7A3
(416) 688-4090
Robert L. Neff

Supplies
Irrigro **drip irrigation systems** based on microporous tubing, for continuous watering from a gravity flow tank or house faucet. They also offer the Fertil-Matic system for continuous **fertilizing**. US buyers may request a catalog from Irrigro, LPO 160, Niagara Falls, NY 14304.
❐ Catalog: Free, R&W, US/OV
⌂ Shop: All year, M-F, by appointment only

International Reforestation Suppliers
P.O. Box 5547
2100 West Broadway
Eugene, OR 97405
(503) 345-0597 or (800) 321-1037

Supplies ✎ Tools
Tools and equipment for gardeners, foresters, Christmas tree growers and surveyors: weather instruments, safety equipment, pruning tools, supplies for wreath makers, sprayers, animal traps and tree planting supplies.
❐ Catalog: Free
⌂ Shop: All year, M-F

InterNet, Inc.
2730 Nevada Avenue North
Minneapolis, MN 55427
(800) 328-8456 or (612) 541-9690
William B. Richardson

Supplies
Offers two weights of black polypropylene **bird netting** with an ultraviolet inhibitor, used by home gardeners and to keep birds from nesting on build-ings, etc. Also sells clips to attach the panels to buildings or cables.
❐ Catalog: Free, R&W, CAN/OV
⌂ Shop: All year, M-F, by appointment only

Irrigro

See International Irrigation Systems.

Irving & Jones
Village Center
Colebrook, CT 06021
(203) 379-9219
Irving Slavid

Furniture
Offers **wrought iron furniture** in reproductions of several Regency designs: chairs, benches and a Gothic rose arch. They are available in white, black or woodlands green or in custom colors of your choice.
❐ Catalog: $2, US/CAN

Ivelet Books
18 Fairlawn Drive
Redhill, Surrey, England RH1 6JP
(0737) 64520 or (+44) 737-64520 TO/CC $10m
S. A. Ahern

Books
Used, out-of-print and rare books on horticulture, gardening, garden design and history, plant collecting and related subjects.
❐ Catalog: Free, R&W, OV
⌂ Shop: By appointment only

Ivywood Gazebo
P.O. Box 9
Fairview Village, PA 19409
(215) 584-9699 or 631-9104
John L. Huganir

Ornaments
Manufacture **gazebos** of red cedar or pressure-treated Southern pine in four sizes from nine feet to fifteen feet across; another model is available with screening. They also make birdfeeders and a rose arbor.
❐ Catalog: $3, R&W, CAN/OV

JC's Garden Center
9915 S.E. Foster Road
Portland, OR 97266
(503) 771-6804 or (800) 233-5729 TO/CC
George F. Van Patten

Supplies ✎ Books
Offers a full line of **hydroponic growing supplies**: growing lights, timers, vent fans, carbon dioxide generators, meters, rockwool, pumps, fertilizers and transplanting hormones and books on indoor food production. (1983)
❐ Catalog: Free, R&W, $10m
⌂ Shop: All year, daily

JRM Chemical, Inc.
13900 Broadway
Cleveland, OH 44125
(216) 475-8488 or (800) 962-4010 TO
Dave Czehut, V.P.

Supplies
Offer Soil Moist granules made of **water-retaining polymers**. Also sell granules and houseplant spikes called Soil Moist Plus, which contain a balanced fertilizer (5-5-5) slowly released with regular watering. Their FAX number is (216) 475-6517. (1988)
❐ Catalog: Free, R&W, CAN/OV, $20m
⌂ Shop: All year, M-F

Janco Greenhouses
9390 Davis Avenue
Laurel, MD 20707-1993
(800) 323-6933 or (301) 498-5700 (MD)
J. A. Nearing Co., Inc.

Supplies
Offers **greenhouses and greenhouse additions** in a variety of configurations for home and commercial uses. Also sells accessories, controls and ventilators for greenhouses. FAX number is (301) 497-9751.
❐ Catalog: $2, R&W

Janziker
P.O. Box 957
Davis, CA 95617
(916) 753-7046 or (213) 202-1839
Kathy Huntziker & Janet Ferrari

Supplies
Distributors of SuperSorb-C -- coarse **water-absorbing polymer particles** that slowly release water to plants, will reduce watering need by 30% to 50%, can be used for garden or potted plants. (1988)
❐ Catalog: Free, CAN/OV, $5m

Johima Books
P.O. Box C255
51 Grasmere Lane
Cremorne, NSW, Australia 2090
(02) 953 8554 or 6310
Chris Adams

Books
They specialize in books on **Australian plants**, horticulture and agriculture. (1983)
❐ Catalog: $2d (US bills), US/CAN, $10m

David Kay Garden & Gift Catalogue, Inc.
4509 Taylor Lane
Cleveland, OH 44128
(216) 464-5125 or (800) 872-5588 TO/CC
David A. Kay

Supplies ❧ Tools ❧ Furniture ❧ Ornaments
A good selection of **tools, supplies and gifts for gardeners** and nature lovers, garden ornaments and furniture, decorations for the lunch table -- all shown in a color catalog. They also offer wildflower seeds and plants and some exotic plants for indoors. (1982)
❐ Catalog: Free, CAN/OV
⌂ Shop: All year, M-F, call ahead

Walter T. Kelley Co.
Clarkson, KY 42726
(502) 242-2012 or (800) 553-2012 FAX 242-4801
Doris J. Pharris

Supplies
Huge selection of **supplies for beekeepers**, from a "beginner's outfit" with your first swarm of bees to professional honey-producing equipment. They also offer books and will take subscriptions to beekeeping periodicals.
❐ Catalog: Free

Kemp Company
160 Koser Road
Lititz, PA 17543
(717) 627-7979 TO/CC

Supplies
Offer **shredder/chippers** in various models, depending on the volume of material to be handled. Also sell a **compost-tumbler**, which they claim makes compost in two weeks, and **gloves** for gardeners.
❐ Catalog: Free, CAN/OV, $10m
⌂ Shop: All year, M-F

The Ken-L-Questor
32255 N. Highway 99 West
Newburg, OR 97132
(503) 538-2051
Kenneth M. Lewis

Books
Specializes in **used, rare and out-of-print books** on cacti and succulents, ferns, lilies, mushrooms and fungi. Each is on a separate list; please specify which list you want ($1 each). Lots of dog books, too! (1935)
❐ Catalog: $1, R&W, CAN/OV
⌂ Shop: All year, daily, call ahead

The Keth Company
P.O. Box 645
Corona del Mar, CA 92625
Mary Keth

Supplies
A good selection of **supplies for flower arrangers**, including the Keth Candlestick Cup for putting flowers on candle holders and sets of tiny lights which run off small batteries and would make flower arrangements really sparkle. Also sell the Original Stem Stripper to remove thorns from rose stems and books on flower arranging. (1981)
❐ Catalog: $1d, CAN/OV

Myron Kimnach
550B N. Astell Avenue
Azusa, CA 91702
(818) 334-7349
Myron Kimnach

Books
Specializes in new, used and out-of-print **books on ferns, bromeliads** and **cacti and succulents** -- quite a large selection. (1984)
❐ Catalog: Free, CAN/OV

Kinco Manufacturing
170 N. Pascal Street
St. Paul, MN 55104
(612) 644-4666 TO/CC
John Kinkead & Tom Fiske

Supplies
Manufacture and sell a gas-powered heavy-duty **sickle-bar mower** for cutting heavy weeds and brush, even saplings; can be used over rough terrain. (1972)
❑ Catalog: Free, R&W, CAN/OV
⌂ Shop: All year, M-F

Kingsley-Bate, Ltd.
P.O. Box 6797
3826 S. 4 Mile Run
Arlington, VA 22206
(703) 931-9200 FAX 9201 TO/CC
Clay Kingsley

Furniture ～ Ornaments
Elegant teak and mahogany garden **furniture, planters and window boxes**; some are decorated with hand carving, all are solid and handsome.
❑ Catalog: $1, R&W, CAN/OV

Kinsman Company, Inc.
River Road
902 Cross Keys Drive (Doylestown)
Point Pleasant, PA 18950
(215) 297-5613 TO/CC
Graham & Michele Kinsman

Supplies ～ Tools
Importers of English **garden tools and equipment**, electric and hand-powered shredders, compost bins, sieves, strawberry tubs and modular arbors. It's always fun to see what they've added; their new catalog has capillary matting, cold frames, rain gutter guards, great weathervanes and more.
❑ Catalog: Free, R&W
⌂ Shop: All year, M-F, call ahead (215) 348-0840

Kunafin
Route 1, Box 39
Quemado, TX 78877
(512) 757-1181 or (800) 832-1113
Frank & Adele Junfin

Supplies
Specialists in biocontrol of insects and suppliers of **beneficial insects**: trichogramma wasps, fly parasites, Pymotes tritici and lacewings. They consult with farmers and livestock operations (up to 10,000 head). (1959)
❑ Catalog: Free, R&W, CAN
⌂ Shop: All year, daily

La Jolla Sales
6910 Dennison Street
San Diego, CA 92122
(619) 452-2044 TO/CC
Robert C. Oster

Furniture ～ Ornaments
Cast aluminum **garden furniture and plant stands** in very ornate designs for period gardens and courtyards; all are painted white.
❑ Catalog: $2, CAN/OV

Ladd Research Industries
P.O. Box 1005
Burlington, VT 05401
(802) 658-4961 TO $20m
William Ladd

Supplies
A source of **insect traps** for apple maggots, coddling moths, oblique-banded leafrollers and plum curculio; they are available as kits, and the components are available separately so you can reuse them. They come with information sheets which contain color pictures of the insects and damage.
❑ Catalog: Free, R&W, CAN/OV

Ladybug Sales

See West Coast Lady Bug Sales.

Landscape Books
P.O. Box 483
Exeter, NH 03833
(603) 964-9333
Jane W. Robie

Books
A very broad selection of **books on garden history, landscape architecture and city planning**: books are new, used and out-of-print and rare; all are well described as to contents and condition. (1972)
❑ Catalog: $3, CAN/OV

Landscapes & Accents
3045 S.W. 66th Court
Portland, OR 97225
(503) 292-2363
Myrna Dowsett

Ornaments
Designs garden **banners and flags** for festive occasions, as well as plant hangers and a triangle bell for calling gardeners to the house for lunch. The banners swivel to act as weathervanes; they're made of durable cloth in several seasonal designs. (1980)
❑ Catalog: $1d, R&W, $25m

Langenbach Fine Tool Co.
P.O. Box 453
Blairstown, NJ 07825
(201) 362-5886 TO/CC
Paul Langenbach

Tools
Offers imported **garden tools** from many countries: spades and forks, hoes, pruning and weeding tools, watering cans, sprinklers, axes and machetes, sprayers and a hand-reel mower. (1986)
❑ Catalog: Free, R&W, CAN/OV

LaRamie Soils Service
P.O. Box 255
Laramie, WY 82070
(307) 742-4185
Michael McFaul

Services
Soil testing by mail for organic and nonorganic gardeners, with suggestions for amendments, crop suitability and rotation -- designed to build organically rich soils as quickly as possible. They do not send a catalog, but mail you collection instructions.
❑ Catalog: See notes, CAN/OV, $16m

Laurelbrook Book Services
5468 Dundas Street West, Suite 600
Toronto, ON, Canada M9B 6E3
(416) 234-6811
Douglas Paton

Books
Offers a good selection of new **horticultural and gardening books**. (1988)
❏ Catalog: Free, US

Lazy Hill Farm Designs
Lazy Hill Road
Colerain, NC 27924
(919) 356-2828
Betty Baker

Ornaments
Hand-crafted **birdhouses, feeders** and a figure of St. Francis which also
serves as a small feeder. All are charmingly designed with little shingled
roofs; not cheap, but perfect for period or cottage gardens.
❏ Catalog: Free

A. M. Leonard, Inc.
P.O. Box 816
6665 Spiker Road
Piqua, OH 45356-0816
(800) 543-8955, (513) 773-2694 FAX 8640 TO/CC
Howard Kyle

Supplies & Tools
A very broad selection of **tools, supplies and equipment** for home and
commercial gardeners -- almost everything for gardening and growing. They
specialize in supplies for commercial operators, so some of the supplies come
in large quantities. Most orders shipped UPS within 24 hours. (1885)
❏ Catalog: Free, R&W, CAN/OV, $20m
⌂ Shop: All year, M-F

Limewalk Tours
102 Lake Street
Burlington, VT 05401
(802) 863-5790
Cecelia M. Lindberg

Services
Offers **garden tours** to Britain, Ireland and Europe -- different tours each
year; gardens always visited with the owner and/or head gardener, and
tours include significant historical and cultural sites.
❏ Catalog: Free

Liteform Designs
P.O. Box 3316
Portland, OR 97208
(800) 458-2505 TO/CC
Don King

Ornaments
Manufacture and sell redwood, metal and ceramic **outdoor light fixtures** in
contemporary and postmodern styles and many sizes and configurations: the
catalog I received had no price list, so be sure to ask for one. (1985)
❏ Catalog: $1, OV, $25m

Living Green, Inc.
977 McFarlane Road
Sebastopol, CA 95472
(707) 928-9556 TO/CC $20m
Frank Bramante

Supplies
Sells a self-contained **hydroponic planter/garden** for the home; it takes up
about 3 square feet and can provide tomatoes all winter, herbs or whatever
you want. (1985)
❏ Catalog: Free, R&W, CAN/OV

Living Wall Gardening Co.
2044 Chili Avenue
Tobey Street (Naples)
Rochester, NY 14624
(716) 247-0080 or 374-2340 TO/CC

Supplies
Sells polyethylene modules which fit together and form **vertical planters**
with many planting pockets -- good for small spaces such as decks or patios,
can be joined together to make a screen or hedge for privacy and beauty --
planted with vegetables or ornamentals. Great for the handicapped.
❏ Catalog: Free, R&W, CAN/OV
⌂ Shop: All year, M-Sa

© Shepherd's Garden Seeds
Artist: Mimi Osborne

Lloyds' of Kew
9, Mortlake Terrace
Kew, Surrey, England TW9 3DT
(01) 940-2512 TO/CC
Daniel Lloyd

Books & Services
A very broad selection of **used and out-of-print books** on gardening and horticulture, with many new and recent books; they will search for wanted items not on their list. Shop is very near to Kew Gardens and fun to include on a visit there -- or to the Maids of Honour tea shop down the road.
❐ Catalog: $1d (2 IRC), OV
⌂ Shop: All year, M-Tu, Th-Sa

Lord & Burnham
P.O. Box 1074, Falls Station
Niagara Falls, NY 14303
Burnham Corp.

Supplies
Offers Evenspan **greenhouses and lean-to additions**.
❐ Catalog: $2

Kenneth Lynch & Sons, Inc.
84 Danbury Road
Wilton, CT 06897
(203) 762-8363
The Lynch Family

Furniture & Ornaments
Offers a huge selection of **garden ornaments**: furniture, statues, planters and urns, gates, topiary frames, weathervanes, fountains and pools. Over 10,000 different items. Heaven must look like the Lynch catalog!
❐ Catalog: $8, CAN/OV

Mrs. McGregor's Garden Shop
4801 - 1st Street North
Arlington, VA 22203
(703) 528-8773 TO/CC
Nancy Schuhmann

Tools & Books & Ornaments
Offers several styles of **natural wood planters**; some carved with rabbits and cabbages, others in simple classic styles. Also sells other garden ornaments, hand tools, window boxes, a carved bench -- and gifts for your gardening friends.
❐ Catalog: Free, R&W, CAN/OV
⌂ Shop: All year, daily

MacKenzie Nursery Supply
P.O. Box 322
Perry, OH 44081

Supplies & Tools
Offers Felco, Coronoa and True Friends **pruning tools, watering cans** and **nozzles, sprayers**, rain gear and boots; Spear & Jackson garden tools, Safer products and BG Ultra-Gro fertilizer.
❐ Catalog: Free

McQuerry Orchid Books
5700 W. Salerno Road
Jacksonville, FL 32244
(904) 387-5044 (8-8 EST) TO/CC
Mary & Jack McQuerry

Books
Specialize in **new, used, out-of-print and rare books on orchids** and also offer back issues of orchid magazines, old plant catalogs (orchids only) and antique orchid prints. They also publish and sell the "You Can Grow Orchids" series by Mary Noble.
❐ Catalog: Free, CAN/OV
⌂ Shop: By appointment only

MAC Industries
8125 South I-5
Oklahoma City, OK 73149
(405) 631-8553 or (800) 654-4970

Supplies
Offer **purple martin houses** in several styles, made of outdoor-sign plastic, which is easy to keep clean. They also sell several styles of birdfeeders.
❐ Catalog: $.50

MAN Productions
P.O. Box 577
Freeland, WA 98249
(206) 221-2191 or (800) 634-8675 TO/CC
Michael A. Nichols

Supplies
Offers **gardening and "chore" pants** called Kneez-eez, with padded knees and a drawstring waist, made from a polyester/cotton blend. Useful to gardeners, painters and carpenters, too. (1987)
❐ Catalog: Free, R&W, CAN/OV
⌂ Shop: All year, M-Sa, Harbor Village Square

Machin Designs

See The English Garden from Machin.

Maestro-Gro
P.O. Box 310
121 Lincoln Drive
Lowell, AR 72745
(501) 770-6154 TO/CC
Gary D. DeMasters & Jerry Carter

Supplies
Sells several **organic fertilizers**: Super-Plus, Pride-of-the-Bloom, Pride-of-the-Garden, Pride-of-the-Lawn, bone, blood, kelp, fish and feather meals, greensand, foscal rock phosphorus and agricultural limestone.
❐ Catalog: Free, R&W, CAN/OV
⌂ Shop: Daily, call ahead

Mainline of North America
P.O. Box 526
Junction of US 40 & State Route 38
London, OH 43140
(614) 852-9733
Paul A. Sullivan

Supplies
Offer **tillers, sickle-bar mowers, log splitters, snow throwers, rotary** and **power lawnmowers**. All are gear-driven -- no belts or chains; they say, "Entirely automotive in design"; thirty models to choose from.
❐ Catalog: Free, R&W, CAN/OV
⌂ Shop: All year, M-Sa

Malley Supply
7439 LaPalma Avenue, Suite 514
Buena Park, CA 90620-2698
Allan Garofalow

Supplies
A new supplier of round or square **plastic pots** in many sizes, flats and inserts for propagation and nursery containers for small trees and shrubs. They also sell white plastic plant labels. (1989)
❒ Catalog: $1d

Mantis Manufacturing Co.
1458 County Line Road
Huntingdon Valley, PA 19006
(215) 355-9700 or (800) 366-6268 TO/CC
HJS Enterprises, Inc.

Supplies
Offer a small, lightweight garden **tiller**, with attachments which convert it to a lawn dethatcher or aerator, edge-cutter or hedge-trimmer; both gas and electric models. They also sell a **portable power sprayer** and both small and large **chipper/shredders**.
❒ Catalog: Free, CAN/OV
⌂ Shop: All year, M-F

Max Marbles
1313 Mill Street S.E.
Salem, OR 97301
(503) 378-7166

Books
Offers a good selection of **rare and out-of-print books** about roses.
❒ Catalog: Free

The Matrix Group
P.O. Box 1176
Southport, CT 06490
James Orrico

Supplies
Sells **video cassettes** of "The Home Gardener," John Lenaton's popular series of 30 gardening programs organized by subject. Also offers a **videodisc**, "Gardening at Home," a complete A-to-Z of gardening basics coordinated with Lenaton's book, "The Home Gardener." He's lively and fun.
❒ Catalog: Free, R&W, CAN/OV, $30m

Don Mattern
267 Filbert Street
San Francisco, CA 94133
(415) 781-6066
Don Mattern

Supplies
Offers the HERRmidifier, a **humidifier with humidistat** for greenhouse and orchid growers, available in 110 or 220 volts.
❒ Catalog: Free, R&W, CAN/OV, $220m

Timothy Mawson
Main Street
New Preston, CT 06777
(212) 874-6839
Timothy Mawson

Books
Offers **used and out-of-print books** on gardening and other country pursuits.
❒ Catalog: $1

Maximum, Inc.
30 Samuel Barnet Boulevard
New Bedford, MA 02745
(508) 999-2226

Supplies
Offers **wind and weather instruments** in solid brass cases; catalog includes "complete weather stations" and wood panels on which to mount them.
❒ Catalog: Free

Emi Meade, Importer
16000 Fern Way
Guerneville, CA 95446
(707) 869-3218
Emi & Eugene Meade

Supplies
Offers two styles of Jollys, **waterproof garden clogs** from Europe in six colors; soft and comfortable, easy to rinse clean -- one of my good friends lives in them! The color now goes all the way through, so they don't show wear easily. Also sells replacement insoles. (1981)
❒ Catalog: Free, R&W, CAN/OV
⌂ Shop: By appointment only

Medina Agricultural Products Co.
P.O. Box 309
Highway 90 West
Hondo, TX 78861
(512) 426-3011
Arthur & Stuart Franke

Supplies
Sell the Medina **soil activator**, which they claim is like "yogurt for the soil," and Medina Plus, which contains micronutrients and growth hormones from seaweed extract for foliar feeding. They also offer HuMate humic acid to build soil, HastaGro fertilizers and other products. Informative flier.
❒ Catalog: Free, R&W

Micro Essential Laboratory, Inc.
4224 Avenue H
Brooklyn, NY 11210
(718) 338-3618 TO
Joel, Mark & Walter Florin

Supplies
Offer Hydrion **test papers for pH soil testing** and a kit for testing hydroponic solutions. They sell mostly to big operators; if you want small quantities, please tell them so when you request the catalog. (1935)
❒ Catalog: Free, R&W, CAN/OV, $25m

Mindsun
RD 2, Box 710
Andover, NJ 07821
(201) 398-9557
Edgar L. Owen

Services
"Gardenview" software for IBM and compatible computers: a **garden design program** in 136 colors which lets you see what your garden would actually look like every day of the year in a three-dimensional model. It can be rotated and viewed from any vantage point. Perfect for landscape architects and garden/computer fanatics!
❒ Catalog: Free, R&W, CAN/OV
⌂ Shop: Daily, call ahead

Mr. Birdhouse
2307B Highway 2 West
Grand Rapids, MN 55744
(218) 326-3044
Larry Lessin

Supplies
Martin houses made of riveted aluminum alloy for strength and carefree maintainance. Available in various sizes, well ventilated and easy to clean.
☐ Catalog: Free, R&W, CAN/OV
⌂ Shop: All year, M-Sa

Misti Maid, Inc.
5500 Boscell Common
Fremont, CA 94538-3143
(415) 656-5777 or (800) 634-2104 or 346-4784
John McNab

Supplies
Their Precision Watering **drip systems** feature individually adjustable drip emitters which can be used to mist, drip or sprinkle; nylon couplings are designed for standard household pressure use. They have a "how-to" video available for $5 (plus tax in CA) to help you get started. (1980)
☐ Catalog: Free, R&W, CAN/OV

Mitchells & Son
3857 - 25th Avenue West
Seattle, WA 98199
(206) 282-9708
Jeannine & Deryl Mitchell

Supplies
Small family business sells Rail-Rider **cedar planters** which fit onto railings up to six inches wide. They come in 24- or 30-inch lengths, with a planting depth of nearly 7 inches. The brackets are installed according to the width of your railing; also have a leveling bar to insure good drainage.
☐ Catalog: Free, R&W, CAN

Moss Products, Inc.
P.O. Box 72
Palmetto, FL 34220
(813) 729-5433
Graham Wilson

Supplies
Watering systems -- drip, sprinkler and mist sprayers -- very flexible and adaptable to many garden situations and types of plants.
☐ Catalog: Free, R&W, CAN

Mother Nature's Worm Castings
P.O. Box 1055
Avon, CT 06001
(203) 673-3029
Edward J. Saillant, Sr.

Supplies
Offers **worm castings**, an environmentally safe, nontoxic and organic fertilizer, high in phosphorus, potassium, magnesium, calcium and nitrate and low in ammonium. (1972)
☐ Catalog: Free, R&W, CAN/OV, $20m

Raoul Moxley Travel
76 Elmbourne Road
London, England SW17 8JJ
01-672-2437

Services
Offers **horticultural tours and treks** and archeology, history and culture tours all over the world. Write for information.

Multiple Concepts
P.O. Box 4248
Chattanooga, TN 37405
(615) 266-3967
Jim Crumley

Supplies
Sells Moisture Mizer **hydrogels** that slowly release water to potted and other plants. Available in several sizes; clubs could order larger sizes as a group and divide them among members.
☐ Catalog: Free

Nampara Gardens
2004 Golfcourse Road
Bayside, CA 95524
(707) 822-5744 TO/CC
Stefan & Rebecca Hall

Furniture ⚘ Ornaments
Redwood garden ornaments: **bridges, gates, benches and lanterns** in Japanese and Western styles. They will also do custom designs or build from yours. Products are elegant and made from rot-resistant redwood heartwood.
☐ Catalog: Free, R&W, CAN/OV

The Natural Gardening Company
217 San Anselmo Avenue
San Anselmo, CA 94960
(415) 456-5060 TO/CC
David Baldwin & Karin Kramer

Supplies ⚘ Tools ⚘ Books
Offers a nice selection of **imported garden tools**, books and supplies and a **copper snail barrier** which gives the little devils a mild shock -- they won't cross it. Also sells some birdhouses which mimic tree cavities for small garden birds, as well as organic "gourmet" seedlings. (1986)
☐ Catalog: Free, R&W, CAN
⌂ Shop: All year, daily

Natural Gardening Research Center
P.O. Box 149
Sunman, IN 47041
(812) 623-3800 TO/CC

Supplies
Natural insect and disease controls, supplies and equipment for organic gardening; all explained in an informative catalog. Offers organic insect controls, beneficial insects, fertilizers and drip irrigation systems. There are color pictures of insects and their damage in the catalog.
☐ Catalog: Free

Nature's Control
P.O. Box 35
Medford, OR 97501
(503) 899-8318
Don Jackson

Supplies
Predator mites, ladybugs, whitefly traps and parasites, mealybug predators and insecticidal soap for **natural pest control**; all especially useful for indoor or greenhouse growing. Stress helpful advice and fast service. (1980)
☐ Catalog: Free, R&W
⌂ Shop: All year, by appointment only

Necessary Trading Co.
P.O. Box 305
422 Salem Avenue
New Castle, VA 24127
(703) 864-5103 FAX 5186 TO/CC
Bill Wolf

Supplies ⬿ Tools ⬿ Books
Large selection of **organic insect controls, tools, books and soil amend-**
ments for "biological agriculture." The catalog's very informative; they
also offer organic pest controls for pets and traps for insect pests. (1979)
☐ Catalog: $2d, R&W, CAN/OV
⌂ Shop: All year, M-F; March-June, Sa

Nelson-Miller
318 Drummond Street
Nevada City, CA 95959
Todd Miller

Books
Here's another twist on old methods: **reviews of all the books available**
on a specific garden topic. The proprietors then print information in
their catalog on the books they consider the best and offer them for sale.
What are their qualifications to review books? Perhaps, like me, they just
love books and gardening. (1988)
☐ Catalog: Free, CAN

Nematec -- Biological Control Agents
P.O. Box 93
Lafayette, CA 94549-0093
(415) 866-2800
S. Paul Wilhelm

Supplies
Sells Bioquest, a **natural insecticide** of beneficial nematodes which
destroys weevils, cutworms, cabbage root maggots, wireworms and other insect
pests and lasts in the soil for several months, destroying new generations.
☐ Catalog: Free, $17m

Netafim Irrigation
10 E. Merrick Road
Valley Stream, NY 11580
(516) 561-6650
F. Harned

Supplies
Offers **drip irrigation supplies and drip irrigation kits** for home gardens,
as well as all the parts to create your own custom system. There are brief
instructions on how to install or design systems. (1968)
☐ Catalog: Free, R&W, CAN/OV, $25m

New England Garden Ornaments
38 E. Brookfield Road
North Brookfield, MA 01535
(508) 867-4474
Nancy Grimes & Humphrey Sutton

Furniture ⬿ Ornaments
Importers of many **garden ornaments** from England: Chilstone ornaments
in a variety of classic styles, lead statues, fountains and planters, architectural wooden trellises and much more. They will send you introductory
information for a long SASE.
☐ Catalog: $6.50, CAN, $30m
⌂ Shop: All year, Tu-Su

Nichols Industries

See Infopoint Software.

The Walt Nicke Company
P.O. Box 433
36 McLeod Lane
Topsfield, MA 01983
(508) 887-3388 TO/CC
Katrina Nicke

Supplies ⬿ Tools ⬿ Books
Garden tools, gadgets and supplies, many imported from Europe; a broad
selection. One of my favorite tools is a heavy-duty steel trowel with a long
handle which I bought from them years ago. There's much in the catalog which
is useful, decorative or just desirable for yourself or gifts.
☐ Catalog: Free, CAN
⌂ Shop: All year, M-F, call ahead

Nitron Industries, Inc.
P.O. Box 1447
4605 Johnson Road
Fayetteville, AR 72702
(501) 750-1777 or (800) 835-0123 TO/CC $15m
Frank & Gay E. Finger

Supplies
Offers a good selection of **organic growing supplies**: fertilizers, their own
Nitron soil amendment and others and Wet Flex porous hose. Catalog gives
good information on soil building, also offers composting supplies, water
purifiers, even a deodorizer for pets called Sweet Pea. (1977)
☐ Catalog: Free, R&W, CAN/OV
⌂ Shop: All year, M-F

North American Kelp
P.O. Box 279A
Cross Street
Waldoboro, ME 04572
(207) 832-7506
Robert C. Morse & George Seaver

Supplies
Offer Sea Crop, Sea Life Soil Conditioner and other **soil conditioners** made
from kelp; the only US manufacturer of seaplant products for gardening and
agriculture. Their catalog has detailed information on use, even as a
supplement to livestock feed. (1971)
☐ Catalog: Free, R&W, CAN, $10m

North Star Evergreens
P.O. Box 253
Eastwood Plaza Building
Park Rapids, MN 56470
(800) 732-5819 or 336-3361 TO/CC
Thom & Cathy Peterson

Supplies ⬿ Tools
Tools, supplies and equipment for foresters and Christmas tree growers,
but many items of use to serious gardeners and nurseries, too: sprayers,
hand tools and saws, safety equipment and insect and animal repellents.
A broad selection, including True Friends and Felco hand tools. (1964)
☐ Catalog: Free, R&W, CAN/OV
⌂ Shop: All year, M-Sa

Northern Greenhouse Sales
P.O. Box 42
Neche, ND 58265
(204) 327-5540
Bob Davis & Margaret Smith

Supplies
Offer **woven polyethylene** and other supplies for making your own greenhouse,
plus advice from the Far North on how to make it. The plastic poly is 9.5
mils thick and very strong, with an average life of 3 years; they will sell
small amounts. Canadian address: Box 1450, Altona, MB, R0G 0B0. (1979)
☐ Catalog: 3 FCS, R&W, CAN/OV
⌂ Shop: All year, daily, call ahead

Northwest Eden Sales, Inc.
15103 N.E. 68th Street
Redmond, WA 98052
(800) 545-3336 TO/CC $20m
Bruce Moulton

Supplies
Offers aluminum and glass **greenhouses and kits**, lean-tos, extensions and a selection of greenhouse accessories, from small home installations to huge commercial ranges. (1981)
❏ Catalog: Free, R&W, CAN/OV, $4m

Norway Industries
809 W. Main
Stoughton, WI 53589
(608) 873-8664 TO/CC
Brian Hanson

Supplies
Sells two models of **garden cart** -- the Carryall, 42 inches wide, and the Carryette, 32 inches wide for access through doorways; sold complete or as kits for you to put together with your own wood.
❏ Catalog: Free, R&W, CAN/OV
⌂ Shop: All year, M-F, call ahead

Nova Sylva, Inc.
C.P. 1624
1587 Rue Denault
Sherbrooke, PQ, Canada J1H 2R1
(819) 821-4617 FAX 4671
Pierre Roy

Supplies & Tools
Offers a good selection of **tools and equipment for foresters**: specialized tools and equipment for tree work and planting, pruning tools, sprayers, safety equipment, even cookshack and shower tents for forest camps.
❏ Catalog: Free, US/OV
⌂ Shop: All year, M-F

OFE International, Inc.
P.O. Box 161302
12100 S.W. 129th Court
Miami, FL 33186
(305) 253-7080 TO/CC
Jose Hortensi

Supplies & Tools
Offers **growing supplies for orchids and bromeliads**: clay orchid pots, wood and wire plant baskets, fertilizers, sprayers, watering accessories, growing media, plant labels, plant stands and books about orchids. (1980)
❏ Catalog: $2d, R&W, CAN/OV, $20m
⌂ Shop: All year, M-Sa, call ahead (closed December 24-31)

Odessa Natural Enterprises
P.O. Box 537
Odessa, FA 33556
(813) 920-4477
Tom Goldsworthy

Supplies
A wholesaler of Safer Products -- **insecticidal soap, fungicides, moss and algae killers, herbicides and flea and tick controls** -- all biodegradable. This is an opportunity for garden clubs and groups to get together and place larger orders for good savings.
❏ Catalog: Free

Ohio Earth Food, Inc.
13737 Duquette Avenue N.E.
Hartville, OH 44632
(216) 877-9356
Larry & Cynthia Ringer

Supplies & Services
Offer a broad selection of **natural soil conditioners and amendments**, including Erth-Rite and Maxicrop, insect controls and dormant oils; they also will do soil testing and make suggestions for which natural products to use. Farmers may request their quantity prices. (1972)
❏ Catalog: Free, R&W, CAN/OV
⌂ Shop: All year, M-Sa

Old-World Garden Troughs
P.O. Box 1253
Carmel, IN 46032
(317) 848-4490
Rod Butterworth & Ron Taylor

Ornaments
Offers hand-crafted garden **planters**, like old English garden sinks; useful for alpine and rock garden plants, herbs, bonsai groupings. They are available in several sizes and four colors and are shipped UPS. (1988)
❏ Catalog: Free, R&W, $25m

One Up Productions
P.O. Box 410777
San Francisco, CA 94141
(415) 558-8688 or (800) 331-6304 TO/CC
Hamilton V. Bryan

Supplies
Company specializing in **videos** for the gardener; they cover a number of subjects, from "how to" to landscaping and armchair tours of famous gardens. Adding new subjects all the time, such as vegetables, lawns, pests and diseases and pruning. (1982)
❏ Catalog: Free, R&W, CAN, $16m

Orchis Laboratories
86-F Mason Street
Burdett, NY 14818
(607) 546-2072

Services
Will do **virus testing and tissue culture on orchids**; also sell a home virus-testing kit and a home seed-sowing kit for orchid hobbyists.
❏ Catalog: Free, R&W, CAN/OV

Organic Control, Inc.
P.O. Box 781147
Los Angeles, CA 90016
(213) 937-7444
Steve Hazzard

Supplies
Suppliers of **beneficial insects** for nontoxic pest control and of organic pesticides and fungicides. They also sell worm castings. (1973)
❏ Catalog: Free, R&W, CAN/OV
⌂ Shop: All year, M-F

Organic Pest Management
P.O. Box 55267
Seattle, WA 98155
(206) 367-0707
David & Audrey Mirgon

Supplies
Sells **beneficial insects, bird repellents, earthworms and organic garden products**, including rodent and insect traps, humane live traps and pest controls for dogs and cats. (1979)
❏ Catalog: Free, R&W, CAN/OV, $25m
⌂ Shop: All year, M-F, call ahead

Original Home Gardener's Video Catalog See One Up Productions.

Orion Trading Company
1508 Posen Avenue
Albany, CA 94706
(415) 540-7136 FAX 528-0500 TO/CC $50m
Chris M. Hall

Ornaments
Sells bamboo stakes, poles, fencing and large-diameter **bamboo** for decorative uses such as gates and bridges. Also sells tropical thatching for the roofs of shelters and other decorative items for Japanese gardens.
❑ Catalog: $1, R&W, CAN, $25m

Ozark Handle & Hardware
P.O. Box 390
91 S. Main Street
Eureka Springs, AR 72632
(501) 423-6888 TO/CC
Eddie Silver

Supplies
Offers a very broad selection of **hardwood replacement handles** for tools of all sorts -- who else has wooden plow handles? Also has a space-age divining rod for finding cables and pipes and sells woven poly tarps. (1977)
❑ Catalog: $2d, R&W, CAN
⌂ Shop: All year, daily

P.L.A.N.T.S.
106 W. Pennsylvania, #1508
Redlands, CA 92374
(714) 792-9263
Michael G. Bacon

Services
A 1,100-plant **database** developed by a landscape architect which allows the selection of plants on maintainance requirements, flower color, heights, soil and water preferences, botanical name, many other headings. It runs on IBM compatibles, can be loaded onto a hard disk and printed out for reference. The $3 catalog charge brings you a demonstration disk. (1984)
❑ Catalog: $3, CAN/OV
⌂ Shop: All year, M-F, call ahead

Pacific Coast Greenhouse Manufacturing Co.
8360 Industrial Avenue
Cotati, CA 94931
(707) 795-2164 or (415) 492-8812 TO/CC
Bruce H. Noble, Mgr.

Supplies
Sell **greenhouses, greenhouse supplies and controls** and "residential sunspaces" (solariums). The greenhouses are free-standing or lean-to, made of redwood and come in sizes for home growers as well as large installations. Also make and sell Frisco Fog humidifiers. (1928)
❑ Catalog: $1, CAN/OV
⌂ Shop: All year, M-F; Sa, by appointment only

Pacific Garden Supply
P.O. Box 86606
Portland, OR 97286
(503) 655-9104 or (800) 833-GROW TO
C. E. Hilterbrand

Supplies
Offer a good selection of **indoor and hydroponic growing supplies** -- drip irrigation supplies, fertilizer, plant lights, beneficial insects, meters and instruments, greenhouse equipment and propagation supplies. They also have a growers' hotline for questions about hydroponics and indoor growing. (1988)
❑ Catalog: Free, R&W, CAN/OV
⌂ Shop: All year, daily

John Palmer Bonsai
P.O. Box 29
Sudbury, MA 01776
(617) 443-5084
W. John Palmer

Supplies ∾ Tools ∾ Books
Specializes in **bonsai books, tools, pots and supplies** -- with many books on Japanese gardens and bonsai techniques.
❑ Catalog: Free, CAN/OV
⌂ Shop: By appointment only

Pan Agro, Inc.
2084 N 1200 E
North Logan, UT 84321
(801) 752-5610
Nabil Youssef & Chris Gaddis, Mgrs.

Supplies
Offer Stretch-a-Pot, a sort of honeycomb **pot system** which comes in various sizes and depths up to 12 inches, made from polyethylene or durable paper; there are 300 to 800 cells per block. They also sell Continuem Nutra-Gel, a polymer with fertilizer included for slow release to plants. Specify which product you're interested in when you request information.
❑ Catalog: Free, R&W, CAN/OV, $50m

Paradise Information, Inc.
P.O. Box 1701
East Hampton, NY 11937
(800) 544-2721 TO/CC
Jim Owen

Services
Offers **databases** with over 5,000 plant descriptions; the program includes five databases, intended primarily for landscape architects; it will run on IBM and Macintosh computers. It will find plants by color, foliage, form, tolerances, height, zones, flowers, light, berries, wildlife, problems, etc.
❑ Catalog: Free, R&W, CAN/OV, $950m

Park Place
2251 Wisconsin Avenue N.W.
Washington, DC 20007
(202) 342-6294 TO/CC
C. Philip Mitchell & Charles H. Betts

Furniture ∾ Ornaments
Offers many types of **garden furniture, light fixtures, street lamps, urns, rockers, swings and gliders**; styles are elegant and the very thing for your stately home. (1979)
❑ Catalog: $2, R&W, CAN/OV
⌂ Shop: All year

Pat's "Mini-Pack" Labels
785 White Road
Watsonville, CA 95076
(408) 662-0551
Nick & Patty Russo

Supplies
Sell **plant markers and pot labels** in quantities of 100 or 300, packed with a permanent marking pen, available in white or yellow plastic. They have added modular plastic growing and potting benches and a fish-emulsion fertilizer in premeasured foil pouches. (1985)
❑ Catalog: Long SASE, R&W, CAN/OV, $12m

Patches and Pots
583 El Cajon Boulevard
El Cajon, CA 92020
(619) 442-7037 TO/CC $25m
Audrey Buchanan

Supplies
African violet growing supplies, including pots and saucers, Oyama Texas-style planters, reservoirs in many colors and support rings.
❑ Catalog: Free

Patio Pacific, Inc.
24433 Hawthorne Boulevard
Torrance, CA 90505-6506
(213) 378-9286 or (800) 826-2871 TO/CC
Alan Lethers

Supplies
Readers who pay close attention realize that Tusker was a favorite cat and that I'm partial to cats and dogs. This company carries nearly every brand of **pet doors**, both traditional flap models and panel pet doors which fit sliding glass doors; 79 models to fit gardeners' helpers of all sizes. (1972)
❑ Catalog: Free, R&W, CAN/OV
⌂ Shop: All year, M-Sa

Paw Paw Everlast Label Co.
P.O. Box 93
Paw Paw, MI 49079-0093
Arthur & Dorothy Arens

Supplies
Manufacture and sell **metal plant and garden labels** with zinc nameplates. They offer styles to put in the ground and to hang on the plant; also sell special marking pencils and crayons to write on the labels. (1962)
❑ Catalog: Free, R&W, CAN/OV

PeCo, Inc.
P.O. Box 1197
100 Airport Road
Arden, NC 28704
(704) 684-1234 or (800) 438-5823 TO/CC $10m
Peter & Brenda Hall

Supplies
Sell a completely self-contained **12-volt electric sprayer** which runs up to five hours on its rechargeable battery. It features a cart with big wheels to make it easy to move around and has a plug-in charger, an 8-foot hose and an opaque tank to keep track of fluid level. Also sell **lawn vacs**. (1971)
❑ Catalog: Free, R&W, CAN/OV

Peerless Products, Inc.
P.O. Box 2469
Shawnee Mission, MO 66201
(913) 432-2778
M. R. Welch, Retail Sales Mgr.

Supplies
Manufactures and sells aluminum **greenhouse windows** in eleven sizes, in bronze or white finishes.
❑ Catalog: Free

Phero Tech, Inc.
7572 Progress Way
Delta, BC, Canada V4G 1E1
(604) 255-7381
Stephen Burke, Sales Mgr.

Supplies
A source of state-of-the-art pheromone **insect traps** for garden, forest and agricultural applications; they are also doing research on animal repellents. Garden clubs or neighbors can band together to place orders. Americans write to 1816 - 35th Street, Missoula, MT 59801, or call (406) 549-1955. (1981)
❑ Catalog: Free, US, $100m

Phologistics
P.O. Box 1411
Ventura, CA 93002
(805) 658-0111 or (800) 541-5471 (CA) TO/CC
Florence Naylor

Supplies
Sells Nifty Scoops for transplanting African violets; also offers several brands of **water distillers** and other equipment for making and storing pure water, pH test papers -- and a cleaner to get label-gum off of glass, metal, etc. Hallelujah!
❑ Catalog: 2 FCS, R&W, CAN/OV
⌂ Shop: All year, M-F, 1860 Eastman Avenue, Suite 101

Pigeon Hill
94 Station Street, Suite 221
Hingham, MA 02043

Ornaments
Offer a variety of **sundials** from a little one to sit on your windowsill to outdoor models. They also sell herb markers, garden signs and two grand **boot scrapers**, one in the form of a cat which I really covet!
❑ Catalog: Free

Pine Garden Pottery
20331 State Route 530 N.E.
Arlington, WA 98223
(206) 435-5995
Max Braverman

Supplies
Offer hand-made wheel-thrown ceramic **bonsai containers** (glazed or unglazed, in many styles) -- their own cast containers in the Japanese style and low-cost imported containers from Southeast Asia. They also offer some tropical plants suitable for indoor bonsai; ask for plant list. (1971)
❑ Catalog: Free, R&W, CAN/OV, $50m
⌂ Shop: February-December, daily, call ahead

Plant Collectibles
103 Kenview Avenue
Buffalo, NY 14217
(716) 875-1221
Marseille Luxenberg

Supplies ⌁ Books
Growing and propagating supplies for indoors and out: pots in many sizes, fertilizers, potting soil, hanging baskets, peat pots and pellets, nozzles, plant lights and stands, Ortho and Sunset books and more.
❑ Catalog: $1, CAN/OV, $8m

Plastic Plumbing Products, Inc.
P.O. Box 186
17005 Manchester Road
Grover, MO 63040
(314) 458-2226
Bob Pisarkiewicz

Supplies
Sell Biwall and Rain Run kits for **drip and mist irrigation**, will develop custom-designed systems for customers in the Midwest. They also carry a large selection of parts and fittings for drip and mist irrigation systems and fountain heads and pond liners for ponds and pools. (1979)
❑ Catalog: $1, R&W, CAN/OV
⌂ Shop: All year, M-Sa, call ahead

Pleasant Hill Farm
20454 S. Springwater Road
Estacada, OR 97023
(503) 631-2918 TO/CC
Thomas C. Fedewa & Helene K. Fedewa

Ornaments
Offers wreaths and cuttings for **Christmas decorations**, Christmas trees, holly and aromatic decorations. Not really a garden supply, but some of you live in cities and need such good cheer! Nice gift, too. (1979)
❏ Catalog: $2, R&W, CAN/OV, SS:11-12
⌂ Shop: All year M-F; holiday season, Sa-Su, call ahead

The Plow & Hearth
301 Madison Road
Orange, VA 22960
(703) 672-1712 or (800) 527-5247 TO/CC
Peter G. Rice

Tools ✍ Furniture ✍ Ornaments
Color catalog offers **goods for home and garden**: tools, garden furniture, ornaments, birdhouses, fireplace accessories, pet supplies and other useful home goods -- even an "indestructible" rural mailbox. (1980)
❏ Catalog: Free, CAN
⌂ Shop: All year, daily (Route 250 West, Charlottesville)

Pomona Book Exchange
Rockton PO
Highway 52
Rockton, ON, Canada L0R 1X0
(519) 621-8897
Frederic & Walda Janson

Books ✍ Services
Offer **new, out-of-print and rare books** on plants, botany, gardening and horticulture, landscape design, fruit growing and related fields and will search for hard-to-find books. They also have a museum orchard and can supply propagation materials for several hundred varieties of apples to local Canadian collectors!
❏ Catalog: $1, US/OV
⌂ Shop: South of Wentworth Heritage Village, call ahead

Pompeian Studios
90 Rockledge Road
Bronxville, NY 10708
(914) 337-5595 FAX 337-5661 TO/CC
Pamela Humbert

Ornaments
Marble, bronze, limestone, mosaic and wrought iron **garden ornaments**, made to order in Italy and hand-carved or hand-finished; the styles are classic and charming. Prices are very upscale and vary with the exchange rate for the lira. Statues and fountains, mostly -- all very elegant and lovely.
❏ Catalog: $10d, R&W, CAN/OV

Popovitch Associates, Inc.
346 Ashland Avenue
Pittsburgh, PA 15228
(412) 344-6097
Don & Rose Popovitch

Ornaments
Sells eight **light fixtures** for gardens in natural styles, hand-crafted in copper and ceramic. Most of the styles are flower-shaped; one is shaped like a mushroom. All are elegant ornaments by day as well as functional at night.
❏ Catalog: Free, R&W

Pot Lock
1032 - 21st Street
Rock Island, IL 61201
(309) 786-5949
Charles J. White

Supplies
Offer a unique **device to lock bonsai and other pots** to your shelf -- good insurance for tempting or valuable specimens! They do not have a catalog; they charge $11 for six, including postage and handling. (1984)
❏ Catalog: See notes, R&W, CAN, $8m

Progressive Building Products
P.O. Box 453
Route 125 (Brentwood)
Exeter, NH 03833
(603) 679-1208 or (800) 776-2534
Robert Daley

Supplies
Sells **greenhouses and greenhouse building materials** for the hobbyist or the large commercial installation, as well as lean-to greenhouses and wooden solariums. Also offers greenhouse accessories and ventilation systems and controls in a well-illustrated catalog -- lots of construction details.
Formerly Greenhouse Builders Supply. (1986)
❏ Catalog: $2d, R&W, $10m
⌂ Shop: All year, M-Sa, by appointment only

Public Service Lamp Corp.
410 W. 16th Street
New York, NY 10011
(212) 989-5557 or (800) 221-4392 TO/CC $30m
Jack Howard, Sales Mgr.

Supplies
Sells Wonderlites, a self-ballasted **mercury vapor flood lamp** for any screw-socket -- excellent for growing plants indoors, even those with higher light requirements.
❏ Catalog: Free, R&W, CAN/OV, $10m

Putnam's
Main Street
Wilton, NH 03086
(603) 654-6564 TO/CC
Richard & Victoria Putnam

Supplies
Offers goatskin gardening **gloves**, a bug hat (veiled) for working outside under attack, overalls and other clothing in 100% cotton or wool.
❏ Catalog: Free, R&W, CAN
⌂ Shop: All year, M-Sa

Qualimetrics, Inc.
P.O. Box 230
Princeton, NJ 08542
(609) 924-4470 TO $50m
Thomas Tesauro

Supplies
Offers a large selection of **weather instruments**; those of special interest to gardeners are a temperature-time indicator, growing degree-day totalizers, humidity indicators and recorders for greenhouses, wind speed indicators, soil thermometers and rain gauges. Even sells complete weather stations.
❏ Catalog: $1d, CAN/OV, $50m
⌂ Shop: All year, by appointment only

Quest Rare Books
774 Santa Ynez
Stanford, CA 94305
(415) 324-3119
Gretl Meier

Books
A specialist in **old and rare books** on gardening, landscape design and history and botany; she will also search for books worldwide and buy collections or single volumes. (1986)
◻ Catalog: $3, CAN/OV
⌂ Shop: All year, by appointment only

RAM Log Splitters
1240 Harrison Avenue
Rockford, IL 61108-7292
(815) 963-0953 TO
Thomas D. Skibba & Michael L. Rohrbacher

Supplies ⟋ Tools
Make RAM Heavy Haulers -- **garden carts** with 20- or 26-inch wheels, and a model with a trailer hitch for pulling behind a garden tractor. They also sell RAM Log Splitters in various sizes; you can cut your wood and wheel it to the woodpile.
◻ Catalog: Free, R&W, CAN/OV, $25m

RNM Sales
P.O. Box 666
Jacksonville, OR 97530
(503) 899-7117 TO
Richard N. Maudlin

Tools
Offers a **stand-up weeder** called the Weed Twist which pulls weeds by the roots and can be used in lawns, as it leaves a small hole which quickly fills in with grass. A trigger releases the weeds. Saves sore backs and knees.
◻ Catalog: Free, R&W, CAN/OV, $20m

Rainbow Gardens Bookshop

See Rainbow Gardens Nursery & Bookshop in Section A.

Raindrip, Inc.
P.O. Box 2173
21305 Itasca Street
Chatsworth, CA 91313-2173
(800) 222-3747 or 367-3747 (CA) TO/CC
Barry Hanish

Supplies
Sell Raindrip **drip irrigation systems and supplies**; informative booklet tells you how to get started and what you'll need. They have a multiplex dripper which will go on the sprinkler fittings of existing underground systems. They also sell a video cassette on how to do it. (1975)
◻ Catalog: Free, R&W, CAN/OV, $10m

The Ram Company
RR 723, Box 16
Lowesville, VA 22951
(804) 277-8511
R. H. Fleming

Supplies
Sells the Fleming Hydro-Ram **pump**, which operates by using the energy of falling water rather than by electricity or gas. It can pump water uphill as much as ten times the downhill fall or drop of the water supply.
◻ Catalog: $3d, R&W, CAN/OV, $8m
⌂ Shop: All year, daily, call ahead

Bargyla Rateaver
9049 Covina Street
San Diego, CA 92126
(619) 566-9884
Dr. Bargyla Rateaver

Supplies
A source for **organic growing supplies and pest controls**: sabadilla dust, ryania, BT, fish meal, compost starter, BX, nematode remedy, Maxicrop seaweed powder and more. Also sells some organic gardening literature, including the second edition of his own "Organic Garden Primer." (1973)
◻ Catalog: Long SASE, CAN/OV, SS:W
⌂ Shop: Call ahead

Reed Bros.
Turner Station
Sebastopol, CA 95472
(707) 795-6261 FAX (707) 829-8620
Duncan Reed

Furniture ⟋ Ornaments
Makers of one-of-a-kind hand-carved **outdoor and indoor redwood furniture** and accessories; definitely "up-market" and very charming in a country-rustic style. They also do custom carving; ask for their retail price list.
◻ Catalog: $10, R&W, CAN/OV
⌂ Shop: All year, M-F, by appointment only

Joe Reed, Woodsmith
Georgetown, ME 04548

Supplies
Versailles boxes -- the classic **planter** -- wood finished with white polyurethane and equipped with plastic inserts; several sizes, several designs.
◻ Catalog: $1d

Peter Reimuller's Cart Warehouse
200 Center Street
Point Arena, CA 95468
Peter Reimuller

Supplies
Sells major brands of **garden carts** at a discount; brands include Garden Way, Stanley Forge, Foldit, Homestead and Carry-It. Price includes shipping. Carts really make country living easy! (1984)
◻ Catalog: Free, R&W, CAN

Ringer Corporation
9959 Valley View Road
Eden Prairie, MN 55344-3585
(612) 941-4180 or 829-5430 TO/CC

Supplies ⟋ Tools
A wide selection of **organic garden products**: soil amendments, potting soil boosters, insect controls, compost makers, lawn care products and various tools and irrigation equipment, all in an informative catalog. (1962)
◻ Catalog: Free, R&W, CAN
⌂ Shop: All year, M-F, call ahead

Robinson Iron
P.O. Drawer 1235
Robinson Road
Alexander City, AL 35010
(205) 329-8486

Furniture & Ornaments
Manufacture and sell **cast iron furniture, fountains, urns and statues** in a variety of classic styles. They will take orders for custom work and will sell direct to anyone in an area where they have no representative.
❏ Catalog: $3

Rocky Mountain Insectary
P.O. Box 152
Palisade, CO 81526
Linda Mowrer

Supplies
Sells **Pedio wasps** for control of the Mexican bean beetle; informative leaflet explains how to get them established. (1983)
❏ Catalog: Free, R&W, CAN, SS:4-10, $8m

Rodco Products Co., Inc.
P.O. Box 944
2565 - 16th Avenue
Columbus, NE 68601-0944
(402) 563-3596 or (800) 323 2799 TO/CC
Rodney F. Bahlen

Supplies
Computemp **temperature monitor and alarm**: takes Fahrenheit or Celcius readings, both indoors and out; records high and low of the day; will monitor air, soil or water at up to nine locations; will sound an alarm at a pre-set temperature -- does everything but get up to fix things! They are offering a new Rain-O-Matic electronic rain gauge, too. (1977)
❏ Catalog: Free, R&W, CAN/OV
⌂ Shop: All year, M-F

A. I. Root Company
P.O. Box 706
Medina, OH 44258-0706
(216) 725-6677 TO/CC $10m
Kim Flottum & Diana Sammataro

Supplies & Books
Everything for the home or commercial beekeeper and honey producer, even bee toys -- they've been in business since 1869 and have branches in three states. Also publish "Gleanings in Bee Culture," the monthly magazine of the beekeeping industry. (1869)
❏ Catalog: Free, R&W, CAN/OV
⌂ Shop: All year, M-Sa; branches listed in catalog

Rose & Gerard

See Smith & Hawken.

Rose Tender
1049 Mockingbird Lane
Van Wert, OH 45891
(419) 238-4851 TO
Jon Rhoades

Supplies
Offers a low-level **sprinkler to water roses below the leaves**, to reduce water spots and mildew; also a rose soaker and adapter heads which convert sprinklers for long narrow rose beds or regular lawn and garden use. (1962)
❏ Catalog: Free, R&W, CAN/OV, $10m

Royal Tidewater Collection, Inc.
P.O. Box 26
Main Street
Hillsboro, VA 22132-0026
(703) 668-6066 TO/CC
Tom Horvath

Ornaments
Pier and garden sculpture: original and limited editions by international artists, priced from $200 to $150,000. Works are generally realistic and dramatic in style, usually cast bronze. They will also do custom work and design consultation. (1978)
❏ Catalog: $4(3 IRC), R&W, CAN/OV
⌂ Shop: All year, M-Sa, by appointment only

Rudon International Trading Company
P.O. Box 331104
Ft. Worth, TX 76163
(817) 292-8485
John D. Croslin

Tools
Sells the EZ-Digger, a traditional **hand tool** from the Orient; it is a combination of weeder, hand hoe and trowel and can be used in vegetable and flower beds.
❏ Catalog: Free

© Bow House, Inc.
Artist: Charles Wilson

Ryans by Mail
23010 Lake Forest Drive, Suite D321
Laguna Hills, CA 92653
(800) 443-0100

Supplies
Catalog is for gadget-lovers; gardeners will be interested in GoPherIt II, a sound-emitting **gopher scarer** which runs on batteries. There are some other garden-related items as well as products for the home.
❒ Catalog: Free

St. Ann's Books
Rectory House
26, Priory Road
Great Malvern, Worcs, England WR14 3DR
(0684) 562818
Chris & Christine Johnson

Books
Rare and out-of-print books on natural history, including books on botany, floras and gardening books. Payment can be made by credit card -- easier and cheaper than paying the surcharge on US$ checks.
❒ Catalog: $1 (US bills)
⌂ Shop: By appointment only

Santa Barbara Greenhouses
1115-J Avenida Acaso
Camarillo, CA 93010
(805) 482-3765 TO/CC $50m
Robert Solakian

Supplies
Offer redwood and fiberglass prefabricated **greenhouses** in various sizes, as well as all of the accessories to fit them out, such as benches, mist systems, heaters and fans. They also have a line of deluxe redwood and glass greenhouses, which are shipped in preglazed sections.
❒ Catalog: Free, R&W, CAN/OV
⌂ Shop: All year, M-F, call ahead

Santa Barbara Orchid Garden & Library
1350 More Ranch Road
Santa Barbara, CA 93111
(805) 967-9798
Paul Gripp

Services
A retired orchid nurseryman who offers five-day **orchid study vacations** in Santa Barbara, with tours of nurseries, etc. Santa Barbara is a great orchid center, with many other attractions. He also provides an **orchid advice service and tours to orchid habitats**; write for details.
❒ Catalog: Free

Savoy Books
P.O. Box 271
Lanesboro, MA 01237
(413) 499-9968
Robert Fraker

Books
Specializes in American, English and French **books on agriculture and horticulture**, mostly fairly old and rare for collectors. Also old prints, nursery catalogs and other ephemera related to the history of gardening and agriculture. Material generally covers the 16th to 19th centuries. (1971)
❒ Catalog: Free, CAN/OV
⌂ Shop: By appointment only

Scanmask

See BioLogic.

Science Associates

See Qualimetrics, Inc.

Sculpture Cast Editions
P.O. Box 426
15 Tamara Drive
Roosevelt, NJ 08555
(609) 426-0942
James Mills

Ornaments
Cast stone or bronze statues for special gardens. Selection is small; most are charming young girls by well-known sculptors -- definitely upscale.
❒ Catalog: Free, R&W, CAN/OV
⌂ Shop: By appointment only

Seabright Enterprises
4026 Harlan Street
Emeryville, CA 94608
(415) 655-3126 or 3127 TO/CC $5m
Jim Wimberly, Mgr.

Supplies
Stickem Special is a **nonpoisonous compound** which traps flying and crawling pests and discourages cats. They also sell a "smart" and humane mouse trap, whitefly traps, a yellow jacket trap and Bird Begone, a colorless repellent.
❒ Catalog: Free, R&W, CAN/OV, $5m
⌂ Shop: All year, M-F

SeedScapes
P.O. Box 295
Edwardsburg, MI 49112
(616) 663-8601
Karen Tefft & Kathryn Alexander

Services
Offers **garden plans** for herb, vegetable and flower gardens; included with each design are growing tips for each plant, a general gardening manual, a monthly gardening calendar and sources of recommended seeds. Plans are based on your desires and situation. (1986)
❒ Catalog: $1d, CAN/OV, $8m

Seeker Press
P.O. Box 299
Battle Ground, IN 47920
(317) 567-2884
Laura Z. Clavio

Supplies
A source of **video cassettes** on many subjects, including herbs, gardening, flowers and flowercraft and tours of famous gardens; most are available in Beta and VHS format, and the narrator and contents are briefly summarized.
❒ Catalog: Free, R&W, CAN

Robert Shuhi -- Books
P.O. Box 268
Morris, CT 06763
(203) 567-5231 or 9384

Books
Offers an extensive list of **used and out-of-print books**, covering a broad selection in the fields of travel, archeology, nature, science and, of course, plants and gardening.
❒ Catalog: Free

Sidwell Enterprises

See Evans Biocontrol, Inc.

Signum Sign Systems
18531 S. Miles Road
Cleveland, OH 44128
(216) 475-5916
Debi Paschall, Mgr.

Supplies
Sell anodized aluminum **plant labels** with an outdoor life of 20 years, ideal for public gardens and those who grow very durable plants. They can be mounted or hung in several ways, come in several sizes with custom printing.
☐ Catalog: Free, CAN/OV

Simple's Creative Quality Trellises
RD 2, Box 69G
Honey Brook, PA 19344
(215) 273-3938

Ornaments
Suggested by a reader, this company offers **trellises** in several classic styles, made of cypress for long life; perfect for city terraces. Also sells houses for bluebirds, several types of **outdoor lights and mini-speakers** which look like birdhouses and a wooden doormat.
☐ Catalog: $1

Edward F. Smiley, Bookseller
43 Liberty Hill Road
Bedford, NH 03102
(603) 472-5800

Books ❧ Services
Offers **antiquarian and out-of-print books** on gardening and horticulture, including a few less-available new books. He also provides book search services for customers. (1977)
☐ Catalog: Free, CAN/OV

Smith & Hawken
25 Corte Madera
Mill Valley, CA 94941
(415) 383-8070 or 383-4415 TO/CC
Paul Hawken & Dave Smith

Tools ❧ Books ❧ Furniture ❧ Ornaments
Offer a very broad selection of **garden tools**, many imported from England or Japan, irrigation supplies, composting equipment, gardening clothing, books, gifts and garden furniture. They have added a bulb catalog and a new catalog from "Rose & Gerard" for household-oriented items. (1979)
☐ Catalog: Free
⌂ Shop: All year, daily

Solar Components Corporation
121 Valley Street
Manchester, NH 03103
(603) 668-8186 TO/CC
Scott F. Keller

Supplies
Everything for the **solar do-it-yourselfer**: solariums, greenhouses and greenhouse building materials, skylights, solar water heaters and hot air blowers, sun shades, solar-powered exhaust fans and photovoltaic modules.
☐ Catalog: $3
⌂ Shop: All year, M-F

Southern Statuary and Stone
3401 Fifth Avenue South
Birmingham, AL 35222
(205) 322-0379 or (800) 325-1253

Furniture ❧ Ornaments
Offers **statues, garden ornaments and light fixtures** of cast stone and cast lead, as well as Chippendale **garden furniture** American-made of cypress for durability.
☐ Catalog: $1 (furniture), $5 (furniture & garden ornaments)

Spalding Laboratories
760 Printz Road
Arroyo Grande, CA 93420
(805) 489-5946 TO/CC
Pat Spalding

Supplies
Sells Fly Predators, **beneficial insects** for fly control, and nontoxic Good-Bye-Fly traps, useful wherever flies are a problem -- around indoor plants, animals, farm buildings, greenhouses (who doesn't have flies?).
☐ Catalog: Free, R&W, CAN/OV, $10m

Spot Systems
A Division of Wisdom Industries, Inc.
5812 Machine Drive
Huntington Beach, CA 92649
(714) 891-1115 or (800) 854-7649 TO
W. R. Graziani

Supplies
Spot System **supplies for drip and mist irrigation** -- filters, separators, even Spot heaters; systems in kits for home gardeners. In addition to drip "vortex" emitters, they have Spot spray and Spot mist sprinklers. (1975)
☐ Catalog: Free, R&W, CAN/OV, $20m
⌂ Shop: All year, M-F

Spray-N-Grow, Inc.
P.O. Box 722038
8500 Commerce Park, #102
Houston, TX 77272
(713) 771-5760
Bill, Ethel & Natalie Muskopf

Supplies
Offer Spray-N-Grow, a **growth stimulant** which they say will make all plants grow better and have better and more fruit or flowers. Also sell Triple Action 20, a **fungicide** which controls bacteria and mildew as well.
☐ Catalog: Free, CAN/OV, $9m
⌂ Shop: All year, M-F

Standard Humidifier
P.O. Box 433
Pawtucket, RI 02861
(401) 722-8888 TO/CC
Thomas A. Barber

Supplies
Sells **humidifiers** in several sizes, both free-standing and overhead, available for 110 or 220-volt power, with various controls.
☐ Catalog: Free, R&W, CAN/OV
⌂ Shop: All year, M-F

The Stanley Forge Co., Inc.
1415 Guinotte
Kansas City, MO 64120
(816) 421-4265 TO/CC

Supplies
Sells two models of the Big Wheeler **garden cart**, one with 7-cubic-foot capacity, the other with 13-1/2-cubic-foot capacity; both are sold either as kits or assembled.
☐ Catalog: Free, CAN/OV

Starcross Community
P.O. Box 14279
Santa Rosa, CA 95402
(707) 526-0108 or 886-5446

Ornaments
Starcross Community is a lay Catholic monastery in Annapolis, CA, that has taken on the care of homeless children with AIDS. To raise money for their work, they sell **Christmas wreaths and trees**. Wreaths can be shipped anywhere in the US; trees can be shipped anywhere but HI or AK.
❐ Catalog: Free

Stuppy Greenhouse Manufacturing, Inc.
P.O. Box 12456
1212 Clay Street
North Kansas City, MO 64116
(800) 821-2132 or (800) 892-5044 (MO) TO/CC

Supplies
Everything for the commercial greenhouse grower, including the greenhouses: **shade cloth, drip irrigation supplies, greenhouse controls and equipment**. They will also sell to the home gardener. There is a $3.50 handling charge on orders less than $25 and a 3% discount for prepayment of your order.
❐ Catalog: Free, CAN/OV, $25m

Sturdi-Built Mfg. Co.
11304 S.W. Boones Ferry Road
Portland, OR 97219
(503) 244-4100
Bill Warner

Supplies
Offers redwood **greenhouses** in a number of styles, both free-standing and lean-to; also sells accessories and equipment. One model is round. They can be single or double-glazed and customized to fit your exact space. (1952)
❐ Catalog: $2, OV, $10m
⌂ Shop: All year, M-F, call ahead

Submatic Irrigation Systems
P.O. Box 246
Lubbock, TX 79408
(806) 747-9000 or (800) 858-4016 TO/CC
Gene Brown

Supplies
A broad selection of supplies for **drip and mist irrigation systems**, subsurface lawn irrigation and mini-sprinklers for a variety of uses -- both for home gardeners and commercial use. (1970)
❐ Catalog: Free, R&W, CAN/OV, $10m
⌂ Shop: All year, M-Sa

Sun Designs
P.O. Box 206
173 E. Wisconsin Avenue (Oconomowoc)
Delafield, WI 53018-0206
(414) 567-4255 TO/CC
Richard & Janet Strombeck

Ornaments
Publish several books of **garden structure designs** -- gazebos, bridges, privies, storage sheds, arbors -- and sell detailed plans for their construction. They have charming styles to fit almost any garden. The gazebo book is $9.45 ppd.; the garden structures books are $10.45 ppd. (1978)
❐ Catalog: See notes, R&W, CAN/OV
⌂ Shop: All year, M-Sa

Sunbird Products, Inc.
1191 Gambier Road
Mt. Vernon, OH 43050
(614) 397-6308 or (800) 445-5668 TO/CC
Daniel Breckenridge

Supplies
Offers the Sunbird **tiller/cultivator**, a lightweight machine which comes with a variety of labor-saving attachments: lawn dethatcher, snow thrower, brush cutter, string trimmer, water pump. The engine even comes off to make a hedge trimmer -- but you still have to get out of the hammock! (1985)
❐ Catalog: Free, CAN/OV
⌂ Shop: All year, call ahead

Suncraft, Inc.
414 South Street
Elmhurst, IL 60126
(312) 530-1552
Frederick Bach & Arthur Pudark

Supplies
Their trade name is Superior Greenhouses: several models of **aluminum greenhouses and lean-tos** with all necessary accessories -- exhaust fans, heaters and bench-frame fittings. Greenhouses have curved eaves, anodized aluminum frames and full-length roof vents. Also sell materials in kits for do-it-yourselfers. (1982)
❐ Catalog: $1d, R&W

Sunglo Solar Greenhouses
4441 - 26th Avenue West
Seattle, WA 98199
(206) 284-8900 or (800) 647-0606 TO/CC
Robert & Ron Goldsberry

Supplies
Manufacture and sell **greenhouses in kit form**, either freestanding or lean-to, with double or triple-wall construction; also offer greenhouse accessories.
❐ Catalog: Free, CAN/OV
⌂ Shop: All year, M-F

Sunstream Bee Supply
P.O. Box 225
Eighty Four, PA 15330
(412) 222-3330
Francis Yost

Supplies ⌘ Books
Offers a complete line of **beekeeping supplies and equipment**: bees, books, hives, honey-extracting equipment, clothing and gloves, even seeds of plants attractive to bees. You can buy a complete beginner's outfit -- with or without bees.
❐ Catalog: $1, CAN/OV, $10m
⌂ Shop: April-October, M,W,F,Su

Superior Autovents
17422 LaMesa Lane
Huntington Beach, CA 92647
(714) 848-0412

Supplies
Sells the Bayliss MK.7, a solar-powered **automatic vent opener** for greenhouses and coldframes; it can be set to open at temperatures between 55F and 75F and will lift a vent up to 32 pounds in weight.
❐ Catalog: Free, R&W, CAN, $40m
⌂ Shop: By appointment only

Superior Greenhouses   See Suncraft, Inc.

Jane Sutley Horticultural Books   See Flora & Fauna Books.

Sylvandale Gardens   See Full Circle Garden Products.

TFS Systems
P.O. Box 710038
8733 Magnolia, Suite 100
Santee, CA 92071
(619) 449-6408 FAX 449-2368 TO/CC
Trickle Soak Systems

Supplies
A broad selection of **supplies for drip irrigation systems** and free design advice for the customer; they sell a "Drip Irrigation Design Manual" for $3.95 ppd. -- 37 pages of practical advice. Also sell the Add-It fertilizer injector for drip systems or any garden faucet, as well as fertilizer, a soil wetting agent and drip system cleaner to use with the injector. (1977)
❑ Catalog: $2.50d, R&W, CAN/OV
⌂ Shop: All year, M-F

Taxonomic Computer
P.O. Box 12011
Raleigh, NC 27605

Services
Got their flier too late to contact them. They offer a **computer database** which runs on DBase or PC-File; it includes four "woody plant" modules which contain information on more than 5,000 plants. In addition, there are other modules for azaleas (450), tropical house plants (600) and bulbs (600 tender and hardy). You can search on many criteria, add your own comments, even add your own plants; annual updates are available. Write for information.
❑ Catalog: Free

Tec Laboratories, Inc.
P.O. Box 1958
Albany, OR 97321
(503) 926-4577 or (800) ITCHING TO/CC $7m

Supplies
Tecnu **Poison Oak-n-Ivy Cleanser** really works! I only have to look at poison oak or poison ivy to start scratching -- but if you wash at once you can avoid the rash, and if you're too late, it lessens the rash and itch; it sits on my kitchen sink. They also sell a venom remover for insect bites and stings and a 10-hour insect repellent which repels ticks. (1977)
❑ Catalog: Free, R&W, $5m

Terisan
1332 Jerome
Astoria, OR 97103
(503) 325-3765
Susan Schmieman

Services
Offer **plant selector software** (CAPS) with five regional databases, each with 400+ plants: Northeast/North Central, Southeast, Western, Northwest and temperate zones. Good information on each landscape plant, and you can add in plants, too; runs on IBM, Apple or Mackintosh. Also offer a **videodisc** with nearly 8,000 images of 900 species of woody landscape plants. (1982)
❑ Catalog: Free, CAN/OV, $15m

Terrace Software
P.O. Box 1236
Cambridge, MA 02238
(617) 491-4725
Roberta Norin

Services
"Mum's the Word" **integrated garden planning software** for the Mackintosh; it "combines object-oriented drawing tools with a horticultural database." Search the database for plants meeting your needs (or add your own plants), then "plant" it on your plan, automatically labeling the drawing. (1986)
❑ Catalog: Free, R&W, CAN/OV

Texas Greenhouse Co.
2524 White Settlement Road
Ft. Worth, TX 76107
(817) 335-5447 or (800) 227-5447 TO/CC
Jay Wallis, Mgr.

Supplies
Sells **greenhouses and lean-tos** with curved glass eaves, automatic venting and aluminum or redwood frames in a variety of sizes; also a complete line of greenhouse equipment and accessories. (1948)
❑ Catalog: $3, R&W, CAN/OV
⌂ Shop: All year, M-F

There's Always the Garden
32 W. Anapamu, #267
Santa Barbara, CA 93101
(805) 687-6478 TO/CC
Linda Cole

Supplies
Charming **tee-shirts, sweatshirts and totes**, silk-screened "There's Always the Garden" and in styles for flower or vegetable gardeners and bird lovers; new designs for herb and rose growers. Also adding notecards and rubber stamps with the same designs -- gardeners love to broadcast their passion.
❑ Catalog: Free, R&W, CAN/OV

Thurston Distributing, Inc.
914 Lee Street
Boise, ID 83702
(208) 342-1212
Bob Thurston

Supplies
Sell **diatomaceous earth** in a product called Darth, which kills many garden and agricultural pests but is harmless to pets and humans -- they claim you can even brush your teeth with it. A completely natural and nontoxic pest control.
❑ Catalog: Free, R&W, CAN/OV, $20m
⌂ Shop: All year, M-F

Tiny Trees Book Sales
P.O. Box 834
Hauppauge, NY 11788
T. T. Lee

Books
Offers a large selection of **books on bonsai**; some of the books described with quotations from reviews. Also bonsai notecards and Christmas cards.
❏ Catalog: Free, CAN/OV

Topiary, Inc.
41 Bering
Tampa, FL 33606
(813) 254-3229
Carole Guyton & Mia Hardcastle

Ornaments
Painted galvanized wire **topiary frames** in many animal and other shapes, many available already planted. They also sell "The Complete Book of Topiary," by Gallup & Reich, to help you get started.
❏ Catalog: Free, R&W

Touchwood Books
P.O. Box 610
Hastings, New Zealand
(070) 782872
Peter Arthur

Books
A broad selection of over 2,000 **new and used books** from all countries on plants, trees and gardening; they will search for books on request. (1987)
❏ Catalog: Free, US/OV

Trade-Wind Instruments
1076 Loraine Street
Enumclaw, WA 98022
(206) 825-2294 TO/CC
Ronald Tyler

Supplies
Weather instruments -- wind anemometers, wind odometers, rain gauge and tide clock. Useful to sailors, seaside dwellers, birdwatchers -- and gardeners, too. (1970)
❏ Catalog: Free, R&W, CAN/OV
⌂ Shop: All year, M-F

Trafalgar Designs

See Brandywine Garden Furniture.

Trans-Sphere Corp.

See Gothic Arch Greenhouses.

Trickle Soak Systems

See TFS Systems.

Trimit Sales Company
9 Granger Avenue
Saratoga Springs, NY 12866
(518) 587-2224 TO/CC
Robert G. Abbey

Supplies
Offers the Carry-It cart, a **garden cart** made of one piece of molded poly-ethylene which will not rust or rot and can carry liquids or wet materials without leaking. Extension sides are available to increase the capacity, and a hitch converts it to a trailer for a tractor. (1985)
❏ Catalog: Free, CAN/OV, $140m
⌂ Shop: All year, M-F

Tropexotic Growers, Inc.
708 - 60th Street N.W.
Bradenton, FL 34209
(813) 792-3574 TO $5m
Darwin Ralston

Supplies
Offers Superthrive, a **plant vitamin/hormone food** useful in transplanting and starting cuttings. One of life's mysteries is how customers are supposed to pour "one drop" out of a 1/2-inch-wide bottle mouth; put eyedropper tops on it, Superthrive!
❏ Catalog: SASE, R&W, OV
⌂ Shop: All year, M-Sa, by appointment only

Tropical Plant Products, Inc.
P.O. Box 547754
1715 Silver Star Road
Orlando, FL 32804
(407) 293-2451 or 2453
Kenneth & Janet Lewis

Supplies
Sells **orchid growing supplies**: fertilizers, wire hanging baskets, coconut fiber, fir bark, moss, tree fern baskets, sphagnum moss and osmunda fiber, totems and plaques for mounting bromeliads, fertilizers and more. (1974)
❏ Catalog: Long SASE, R&W, CAN/OV
⌂ Shop: All year, M-F

Turner Greenhouses
P.O. Box 1260
Highway 117 South
Goldsboro, NC 27530
(919) 734-8345 TO/CC
Gary Smithwick

Supplies ⚭ Books
Galvanized-steel-framed **greenhouses** in various sizes and configurations, available with fiberglass or polyethylene coverings, as well as a full line of equipment and accessories and books on propagation and gardening.
❏ Catalog: Free, CAN/OV, $10m
⌂ Shop: All year, M-F, call ahead

Twin Oaks Books
5446 W. Forest Home Avenue
Greenfield, WI 53220
(414) 546-3227 TO/CC
Les Miescke

Books
Specialize in **books about orchids** -- only orchids, but they have a broad selection, and each book is described in great detail; they will pay the book rate postage on purchases anywhere in the world. (1977)
❏ Catalog: Free, SASE, CAN/OV

Tyz-All Plastics, Inc.
240 Glen Head Road
Glen Head, NY 11545
(516) 676-2470
Gene Ballin, Pres.

Supplies
Manufacture and sell SuperTies, Aro-Ties and Tie-Strip adjustable **plastic ties and strapping**; these can be used to tie up plants and stake trees, bundle cut flowers, seal storage bags and for many other tasks.
❏ Catalog: Free, R&W

UPCO Irrigation
P.O. Box 206
Bouse, AZ 85325
(602) 851-2509 TO/CC $50m
Gregory Q. Upton

Supplies
Sells supplies and systems for **drip irrigation**; literature gives some
information on how to plan and install the system. (1982)
❐ Catalog: Free, R&W, CAN/OV
⌂ Shop: All year, M-F, by appointment only

Unipub
4611-F Assembly Drive
Lanham, MD 20706-4391
(301) 459-7666 or (800) 274-4888

Books
Source of US and British **government documents and international agency publications**, many having to do with agriculture, forestry and related fields,
some on historical gardens. Tell them which type of publication you want or
request a specific title. From Canada call (800) 233-0504; their FAX number
is (301) 459-0056.
❐ Catalog: Free

Unique Insect Control
5504 Sperry Drive
Citrus Heights, CA 95621
(916) 961-7945 or 967-7082
The Foley Family

Supplies
Offers several types of **beneficial insects**: ladybugs, green lacewings,
trichogramma wasps, praying mantids, fly parasites, white-fly parasites,
predatory mites, mealybug predators and earthworms. Their flier is very
informative. (1980)
❐ Catalog: Free, R&W, CAN/OV

F. R. Unruh
37 Oaknoll Road
Wilmington, DE 19808
(302) 994-2328
F. R. Unruh

Supplies
Wire and aluminum garden markers, either 4-1/2 or 11-1/2 inches high --
can be written on with wax pencil or stenciling tape; come in white, light
green or beige. (Garden markers are stuck in the ground next to the plant;
plant labels are attached to the plant.)
❐ Catalog: Free, R&W, $20m

The Urban Farmer Store
2833 Vicente Street
San Francisco, CA 94116
(415) 661-2204 FAX 7826 TO/CC
Tom Bressan & John Stokes

Supplies
Specialize in **drip and automatic irrigation systems**; catalog is a good
all-around introduction to the subject and offers all the necessary parts and
equipment. Carry products of several manufacturers and kits of their own.
❐ Catalog: $1d, R&W, CAN/OV
⌂ Shop: All year, M-Sa

VT Productions
P.O. Box 339
Soquel, CA 95073
(408) 438-3100
Monica Meyer

Supplies
Sells a **videodisc of exotic plants**, including a visual encyclopedia of
plant habitats and family groupings, time-lapse footage of flowering plants
and a computer-generated index to each frame. Produced for use in teaching botany, horticulture and landscaping at all levels. (1980)
❐ Catalog: Long SASE, CAN

Van Klassens Fine Garden Furniture
4619B Central Avenue Road
Knoxville, TN 37912
(615) 688-2565

Furniture
Sells classic **mahogany garden furniture**, solid and well-built: chairs,
swings, benches, lounges and tables. All can be given either a clear or a
white mahogany finish or your choice of 60 custom colors using a very durable paint. Available through designers or direct from the manufacturer.
❐ Catalog: $4

Vegetable Factory, Inc.
P.O. Box 2235
71 Vanderbilt Avenue
New York, NY 10163
(212) 867-0113 TO/CC
Dean Schwartz, Cust. Svs. Mgr.

Supplies
Sell a complete line of double-walled **greenhouses** in various sizes and
configurations. Their Sun-Porch (R) lean-to model converts to a screen
porch for summer use. Also offer insulated glazing panels for do-it-yourself
construction. (1972)
❐ Catalog: $2, R&W, CAN

Verilux, Inc.
P.O. Box 1512
Greenwich, CT 06836
(203) 869-3750 TO
H. Jackson Scott

Supplies
Verilux TruBloom **fluorescent plant lights** are balanced to promote normal,
compact growth -- long-lasting and available in various sizes for home or
commercial use. (1956)
❐ Catalog: Free, R&W, CAN/OV, $59m

Victory Garden Supply Co.
1428 E. High Street
Charlottesville, VA 22901
(804) 293-2298 TO/CC
Robert W. Sandow

Supplies
New company offers several models of aluminum **greenhouse**, benches,
vent openers, shades and ventilated shelving. (1987)
❐ Catalog: Free, CAN/OV, $5m
⌂ Shop: All year, M-F

Videodiscovery, Inc.
P.O. Box 85878
1515 Dexter Avenue North
Seattle, WA 98145
(206) 285-5400 TO/CC
Joe Clark

Supplies ◈ Services
Offers an "Encyclopedia of Landscape Horticulture" on **videodisc** -- over
7,000 still images of 1,000 woody landscape plants. Photos show full plant,
winter foliage, leaf, usage and identification characteristics; associated
database helps landscapers and students with plant selection. (1983)
❐ Catalog: Free, R&W, CAN/OV

Vine Arts
P.O. Box 83014
Portland, OR 97203-0014
(503) 289-7505
Janet Schuster

Ornaments
Topiary frames in various animal shapes; they will also do custom frames based on your suggestions. Frames are made of galvanized steel and treated with rust-proof paint; their life-size deer and foxes are popular.
☐ Catalog: $2d

Vintage Wood Works
P.O. Box 980
513 S. Adams
Fredericksburg, TX 78624
(512) 997-9513 TO/CC
Gregory Tatsch

Ornaments
Offers a charming Victorian **gazebo**, but also a broad selection of Victorian and period trim for houses, including porch turnings, gables, fret brackets, window cornices, shelves and more -- a terrific way to perk up a lackluster house or turn a shed into a decorative cottage!
☐ Catalog: $2, CAN/OV
⌂ Shop: All year, M-F

The Violet House
P.O. Box 1274
Gainesville, FL 32601
(904) 377-8465 or 378-4283 TO
Dick & Anne Maduro

Supplies
Offer **indoor growing supplies** -- plastic pots, wick-watering reservoirs, fertilizers, pesticides and potting materials for growing African violets and other houseplants. They also sell Nadeau sinningia and African violet seed. (1975)
☐ Catalog: Free, CAN/OV, $8m
⌂ Shop: All year, M-F, call ahead

Vixen Hill Gazebos
Main Street
Elverson, PA 19520
(215) 286-0909 FAX 2099
Douglas Jefferys & Christopher Peeples

Ornaments
Make easy-to-assemble **prefabricated gazebos**, available in four sizes, Victorian or Colonial in style, even glassed-in, made of cedar and assembled with brass acorn nuts. They also make benches and tables to fit.
☐ Catalog: $5d, CAN/OV

Voyages Jules Verne
10 Glentworth Street
London, England NW1 5PG
(01) 724-6624 FAX 723-5654

Services
An English tour operator specializing in **botanical tours** all over the world; also offers natural history and painting tours to many countries, even some which combine interests for couples with diverse hobbies.
☐ Catalog: Free

Warnico/USA, Inc.
619 Lake Avenue
Rochester, NY 14613
(716) 458-2840 TO/CC
Edward E. Warnick

Tools
Sells Easy Weeder and Roots 'n' All, **long-handled devices for cutting and lifting long-rooted weeds** without stooping -- great for gardeners with bad backs. They've just come out with the Big Boy professional model, with 400 pounds of pulling capacity. (1986)
☐ Catalog: Free, R&W, CAN/OV, $15m
⌂ Shop: All year, M-F, call ahead

WaterWorks West

See Hidden Garden Nursery, Inc., in Section A.

Gary Wayner -- Bookseller
Route 3, Box 18
Fort Payne, AL 35967-9501
(205) 845-5866 TO/CC $20m
Gary Wayner

Books
Specializes in scholarly **out-of-print books** on botany, gardening and natural history. (1976)
☐ Catalog: $1, CAN/OV

Weed Wizard, Inc.
P.O. Box 275
Dahlonega, GA 30533
(800) 262-5122

Tools
Sell a **permanent metal cutter** that replaces the monofilament line on rotary trimmers; they say it will fit almost any model.
☐ Catalog: Free

The Well-Furnished Garden
5635 West Boulevard
Vancouver, BC, Canada V6M 3W7
(604) 263-9424 or 2601
Thomas Hobbs or Brent Beattie

Ornaments
Importers of hand-made **Italian terra cotta pots**, a large and varied selection of many classic styles and sizes; all guaranteed to be frost-proof forever, anywhere. They also import antique garden furniture and ornaments from England, not shown in their literature; you could inquire about desired items to see what's available. (1986)
☐ Catalog: $3d, R&W, US/OV
⌂ Shop: All year, M-Sa

Wendelighting
2445 N. Naomi Street
Burbank, CA 91504
(818) 955-8066
Peter Jens Jacksen

Supplies
Offer a variety of **indoor and outdoor lighting systems**, aimed at the professional but available to anyone; they can also provide design services and consultation. Systems are low-voltage and inconspicuous, can be used in numerous configurations.
☐ Catalog: Free, R&W, CAN/OV
⌂ Shop: All year, M-F, by appointment only

West Coast Ladybug Sales
P.O. Box 903
Gridley, CA 95948
(916) 534-0840 or 846-2738
Russell E. Smith

Supplies & Services
Offers a selection of **beneficial insects** -- ladybugs, fly parasites, trichogramma parasitic wasps, cryptolaemus mealybug destroyers, green lacewings and praying mantis egg cases; informative leaflets on their benefits and how to release and establish them. (1968)
❑ Catalog: Free, R&W, CAN/OV, $3m
⌂ Shop: All year, call ahead

Wheelbarrow Books
22 Branswyn Avenue
Brighton, Sussex, England BN1 8XG

Books
Out-of-print, used and antiquarian gardening and botanical books.
❑ Catalog: Free

Wheeler Arts
66 Lake Park
Champaign, IL 61821-7101
(217) 359-6816 (2-5 pm weekdays)
Paula & Stephen Wheeler

Services
For those caught up in the home-publishing frenzy, here is a source of nice **horticultural clip art** called "Quick Art," both printed and on computer disk and CD-ROM. There is a nice variety of subjects, and they send a free sample with each catalog order. (1973)
❑ Catalog: $3d, R&W, CAN/OV, $2m

Wheldon & Wesley
Lytton Lodge, Codicote
Hitchin, Herts., England SG4 8TE
(0438) 820370 FAX 821478
Christopher K. Swann, Mgr.

Books
Dealers in **new, secondhand, old and rare books** on botany, flora of Britain and other countries and gardening books, as well as books in other fields of natural history. Books can be purchased with credit cards to save the hassle of exchange rates; catalogs available by Air Mail at UK6 per year.
❑ Catalog: Free
⌂ Shop: By appointment only

Wickatunk Marine, Inc.
P.O. Box 156
Wickatunk, NJ 07765
(201) 946-8326
Rosemarie & George Kopilak

Supplies
Supply PVC **pond liners** which are 20 mils thick and contoured to many shapes and sizes -- 60 designs in all. They claim that their system makes the liner cheaper because there is less waste than with flat sheets. (1982)
❑ Catalog: $1, CAN/OV

Wikco Industries, Inc.
Route 2, Box 154
Broken Bow, NE 68822
(308) 872-5327 or (800) 872-8864
Jackson M. Ideen

Tools & Furniture
Offer the Clear Creek **garden bench** in turn-of-the-century wrought iron style, with green, black or white enamel finish. Also sell the Super Spear Log Splitter for splitting firewood without an ax. They also have a "Grounds Maintenance Catalog" of tools and power equipment -- which I haven't seen; send $2 and ask for catalog #15.
❑ Catalog: Free, R&W, CAN

Wilkerson Books
31 Old Winter Street
Lincoln, MA 01773
(617) 259-1110
Robin Wilkerson

Books & Services
A good selection of **used and out-of-print books** on gardening and horticulture, herbs, plant exploration, garden history and design. Some are fairly recent; they will search for out-of-print titles. (1977)
❑ Catalog: $1d, R&W, CAN/OV
⌂ Shop: By appointment only

Willsboro Wood Products
P.O. Box 509
S. Ausable Street
Keesville, NY 12944
(518) 834-5200 or (800) 342-3373

Furniture
Adirondack-style **cedar furniture** -- chairs, chaises, settees, tables, picnic tables and benches.
❑ Catalog: Free, R&W, CAN/OV
⌂ Shop: All year, M-F

Wind & Weather
P.O. Box 2320
Albion Street Watertower
Mendocino, CA 95460
(707) 937-0323 TO/CC
Mary Latko

Supplies & Ornaments
Everything you need to enjoy and record the weather: **weather instruments**, shelters for weather stations, weathervanes, sundials and lots of books on weather -- even books for children. (1974)
❑ Catalog: Free, CAN/OV
⌂ Shop: All year, daily

Windleaves
7560 Morningside Drive
Indianapolis, IN 46240
(317) 251-1381 TO/CC
Bart & Marian Kister

Ornaments
Manufacture and sell **windvanes** sculpted in the shapes of leaves -- several styles, such as tuliptree, dogwood, ginkgo and mapleleaf; they can be stuck in the ground in the garden or mounted on a roof. Adding a sundial soon.
❑ Catalog: $1, R&W, CAN/OV
⌂ Shop: By appointment only

Winterthur Museum & Gardens
  Catalogue Division
102 Enterprise Place
Dover, DE 19735
(302) 678-9200 or (800) 767-0500 TO/CC $10m
Anne B. Coleman, Mgr.

Ornaments
Catalog from the Winterthur Museum & Gardens offers beautiful **reproductions** of items on display both in the gardens and in the house, as well as special plants from the gardens. A good selection of **gifts and garden ornaments** for any garden or gardener -- many tempting items.
❑ Catalog: Free
⌂ Shop: Museum shop, Tu-Su

Wisconsin Wagon Co.
507 Laurel Avenue
Janesville, WI 53545
(608) 754-0026 TO/CC
Albert & Lois Hough

Supplies
Make wooden children's toys, including **wheelbarrows**, sleds and great Janesville wagons. They also make an awning-covered **patio cart** useful as a bar or buffet and have added an adult-size wheelbarrow, probably because the little one is so cute that grown-ups had to have their own. (1979)
❑ Catalog: Free
⌂ Shop: February-Christmas, M-Sa, call ahead

Womanswork
P.O. Box 2547
Kennebunkport, ME 04046
(207) 967-8800
Karen Smiley

Supplies
Specialize in **gardening and work gloves** made to fit women's hands; they come in either supple suede pigskin or pigskin back and split-cowhide palms for heavy duty, in three sizes. They also make a practical work-apron with 15 pockets. (1985)
❑ Catalog: Free, R&W, CAN/OV, $8m

Wood Classics, Inc.
P.O. Box 455E
RD 1
High Falls, NY 12440
(914) 687-7288 TO/CC
Eric & Barbara Goodwin

Furniture
Nicely crafted American-made **wooden outdoor furniture** in rustic and classic styles -- tables, chairs, lounges, porch swings and rockers, made of mahogany or teak; all available finished or in kit form. They are adding planters and patio carts to their line.
❑ Catalog: $2, CAN/OV
⌂ Shop: All year, call ahead

The Wood Garden
11 Fitzrandolph Street
Green Brook, NJ 08812
(201) 968-4325
Alan J. Delage

Ornaments
Offers a wooden **wheelbarrow, planters**, some with attached trellises, and **barrels and tubs** made of chestnut wood. Also offers a kit for a small **trellis gazebo**. (1988)
❑ Catalog: Long SASE, R&W, CAN/OV

Wood Violet Books
3814 Sunhill Drive
Madison, WI 53704-6283
(608) 837-7207
Debra S. Cravens

Books & Services
New and used books, specializing in books on herbs and other garden subjects, including cookbooks for garden produce; they will search for hard-to-find books. (1983)
❑ Catalog: Free, CAN/OV
⌂ Shop: All year, call ahead

Elisabeth Woodburn
P.O. Box 398
Booknoll Farm
Hopewell, NJ 08525
(609) 466-0522
Elisabeth Woodburn

Books
A specialist in **horticultural books**, including new, used, out-of-print and very rare books for libraries and serious gardeners; separate catalogs for various categories are $2 each.
❑ Catalog: See notes, CAN/OV, $10m
⌂ Shop: By appointment only

Gary W. Woolson, Bookseller
RFD 1, Box 1576
Route 9 (Newburgh)
Hampden, ME 04444
(207) 234-4931 TO
Gary W. Woolson

Books
Specializes in **used and out-of-print books** on plants and gardening. (1967)
❑ Catalog: Free, R&W
⌂ Shop: By appointment only

Yonah Manufacturing Co.
P.O. Box 280
Airport Road
Cornelia, GA 30531
(404) 778-2126 TO/CC
James Bruce, Jr.

Supplies
Sell **shade cloth** providing from 30% to 92% actual shade -- used for greenhouses and shade structures, patio covers, etc. Sold with bindings and rust-proof brass grommets custom-sewn to your specifications. They also sell black fabric mulch in 100-foot rolls, 12 feet wide; call for a quote.
❑ Catalog: Free, R&W, CAN/OV
⌂ Shop: All year, M-F, call ahead

Zook & Ranck, Inc.
RD 1, Box 243
Gap, PA 17527
(717) 442-4171
Floyd H. Ranck, Gen. Mgr.

Supplies
Offers Erth-Rite **fertilizers and soil amendments** in several formulations for lawn and garden, roses, vegetables, trees, shrubs and bulbs; also greensand, bone meal, compost starter, diatomaceous earth, Maxicrop and other organic products. (1962)
❑ Catalog: Free, R&W, CAN/OV
⌂ Shop: All year, M-F, 9-5

Professional Societies and Trade Associations

Professional societies, trade associations and umbrella groups are listed alphabetically.

See the Index section for:

M. Magazine Index: an index to the titles of magazines offered by all societies and professional and trade associations, as well as those horticultural magazines and newsletters available by subscription.

Associations

Except where indicated, membership in these organizations is limited to those in specific trades or professions. Umbrella groups, although not open to general membership, can put you in touch with local affiliates.

Trade associations are listed because they are often excellent sources of information not available elsewhere. Many have useful promotional publications available to anyone; others have active public relations representatives who will field your questions. Dues are not listed because qualifications for membership do not include most people.

Professional societies are listed to help you connect with or get information from groups in fields of professional interest; inquire about membership and dues.

Some of the organizations listed here are groups formed to promote some particular conservation goal and are open to all; dues are listed for these groups.

A table of the symbols and abbreviations used
in this book appears on the bookmark.

All-America Selections
   National Garden Bureau, Inc.
Nona Wolfram-Koivula
1311 Butterfield Road, Suite 310
Downers Grove, IL 60515
(708) 963-0770

AAS tests new varieties of flowers and vegetables grown from seed, has test gardens located all over the US -- write for a list. NGB encourages home gardeners to grow plants from seed.

Alliance for Historic Landscape Preservation
82 Wall Street, Suite 1105
New York, NY 10005

Found too late to contact. Write for information.
❒ Annual Dues: in US: $20

American Association of Botanical Gardens
   & Arboreta
Susan Lathrop, Exec. Dir.
P.O. Box 206
Swarthmore, PA 19081
(215) 328-9145
The Public Garden (4)
AABGA Newsletter (12)

Professional association of botanical gardens, with regional meetings in various locations. Newsletter lists positions available in botanical gardens and they publish an annual Internship Directory; they also have a job hotline with recorded announcements -- call (215) 328-9146.
❒ Privileges: LIBRARY PLANTS TOURS

American Association of Nurserymen
Terri Gore
1250 I Street, # 500
Washington, DC 20005
(202) 789-2900
Discover the Pleasure of Gardening

Trade association providing services and information to nurserymen. Publish a directory of the nursery industry with a classified directory of goods and services; it includes many wholesale nurseries.

American Community Gardening Association
Vernon Bryant III, Co-op Ext.
4141 W. Belmont
Chicago, IL 60641
Journal of Community Gardening (4)
Newsletter (6)

Umbrella association for the community gardening movement; write for information.
❒ Privileges: CONVENTIONS

American Horticultural Therapy Association
Beverly Repe
9220 Wightman Road, Suite 300
Gaithersburg, MD 20879
(800) 634-1603
Journal of Therapeutic Horticulture (1)
People Plant Connection (11)

Professional association devoted to using horticulture to enhance the lives of special populations through therapy and vocational rehabilitation. The annual journal is available on subscription for US$15.
❒ Chapters: 11
❒ Privileges: CONVENTIONS

American Seed Trade Association
1030 - 15th Street Northwest, Suite 964
Washington, DC 20005
(202) 223-4080
ASTA Newsletter (12)

Trade association of seed companies; write for information.

American Society of Consulting Arborists
Jack Siebenthaler
700 Canterbury Road
Clearwater, FL 34624
(813) 446-3356
Arboriculture Consultant (6)

Trade association of qualified arborists; purpose is to educate the public on the value of trees and to refer them to members for consultation.
❒ Privileges: CONVENTIONS BOOKS

American Society of Landscape Architects
Edward Able, Jr., Exec. Dir.
1733 Connecticut Avenue Northwest
Washington, DC 20009
(202) 466-7730
Landscape Architecture (6)

Professional association; write for information.

Associated Landscape Contractors of America
Terry Peters
405 N. Washington Street
Falls Church, VA 22046
(703) 241-4004

Trade association devoted to exchange of business and technical information among its members; they have many educational programs and conferences.

**Association for Living History Farms
 & Agricultural Museums**
Robert Becker
P.O. Box 52
Rushville, NY 14544

Found too late to contact. Write for information.

Association for Zoological Horticulture
Pearl Pearson
c/o OKC Zoo, 2101 N.E. 50th
Oklahoma City, OK 73111
(405) 424-3344
Zoo Horticulture (4)

Group of horticulturists at zoos, promoting naturalistic landscaping and botanical collections which suit their animal exhibits.
❐ Chapters: 1
❐ Privileges: CONVENTIONS SEEDS TOURS

Association of Specialty Cut Flower Growers
Judy M. Laushman
155 Elm Street
Oberlin, OH 44074
(216) 774-2887
Cut Flower Quarterly

A new group dedicated to growing cut flowers for market; newsletter would be of interest to all who grow flowers for cutting.
❐ Privileges: CONVENTIONS

Canadian Horticultural Therapy Association
Brian Holley
c/o Royal Botanical Garden, Box 399
Hamilton, ON, Canada L8N 3H8
(416) 529-7618
CHTA Newsletter (4)

Society provides support and training for people in recreational and occupational therapy programs. It publishes a looseleaf informational guide which is updated with pages that come with the newsletter.
❐ Annual Dues: in CAN C$12; in US US$12
❐ Privileges: CONVENTIONS

Center for Plant Conservation
125 Arborway
Jamaica Plain, MA 02130
(617) 524-6988
Plant Conservation (4)
Bulletin Board (4)

Formed to create a systematic, comprehensive national program of conservation of endangered American plants, coordinates the programs of botanical gardens. Publishes "Plant Conservation Resource Book," $9.00 ppd.
❐ Garden: 19 gardens; write for list

**The Council on Botanical & Horticultural
 Libraries, Inc.**
John F. Reed
The New York Botanical Garden
Bronx, NY 10458
(212) 220-8728
Newsletter (3-4)
CBHL Plant Bibliography (occasional)

Association of libraries in the field of botany and horticulture.
❐ Privileges: CONVENTIONS

The Fertilizer Institute
H. William Hale
1015 - 18th Street Northwest
Washington, DC 20036
(202) 861-4934

Trade association; write for information.

Garden Centers of America
Patrick Redding
1250 I Street Northwest, Suite 500
Washington, DC 20005
(202) 789-2900
GCA Newsletter (10)

The trade association of the nursery/landscape industry; has over 3,500 member firms.

The Garden Club of America
Mrs. E. Murphy
598 Madison Avenue
New York, NY 10022
(212) 753-8287
GCA Bulletin (2)
Newsletter (6)

Umbrella organization for 185 local garden clubs; it has programs for awards and scholarships, civic improvement and education to promote the love of gardening.

Garden Clubs Canada
Mrs. J. D. Coons
P.O. Box 7094
Ancaster, ON, Canada L9G 3L3
Newsletter (2)

Umbrella organization for garden clubs all across Canada. Newsletter is available on subscription for C$3 in CAN, C$5 in US and overseas.

The Garden Conservancy
Antonia F. Adezio, Dir.
P.O. Box 219
Cold Spring, NY 10516
(914) 265-2045
Newsletter (2-3)

A new group devoted to preserving private gardens of particular interest. Membership open to all.
❒ Annual Dues: $25

Garden Writers Association of America
W. J. Jung
1218 Overlook Road
Eustis, FL 32726
(904) 589-8888
Quill & Trowel (6)
Directory (1)

Association of professional garden writers, dedicated to improving the standards of horticultural journalism in print and broadcast media.
❒ Privileges: CONVENTIONS

Historic Preservation Committee
  American Society of Landscape Architects
2425 Saugatuck Station
Westport, CT 06880
Landscapes

Found too late to contact. Write for information.
❒ Annual Dues: in US: $15

Horticultural Research Institute
1250 I Street Northwest, Suite 500
Washington, DC 20005
Journal of Environmental Horticulture (4)

Trade association; this is the research arm of the American Association of Nurserymen.

International Herb Growers & Marketers Assn.
P.O. Box 281
Silver Springs, PA 17575
(717) 285-4252

Group formed to unite those engaged in the production and marketing of herbs and to educate the public about herbs and herb-related products.
❒ Privileges: CONVENTIONS

International Plant Propagator's Society
Dr. John A. Wott, Sec.-Tres.
Center for Urban Hort., GF-15, Univ. of Wash.
Seattle, WA 98195
(206) 543-8602
Proceedings (1)

A professional group devoted to the art and science of plant propagation.

International Society of Arboriculture
Box 71-5, Lincoln Square Station
Urbana, IL 61801
(217) 328-2032
Journal of Arboriculture (12)

Write for information.

The Irrigation Association
Mark Williams
1911 N. Fort Myer Drive, Suite 1009
Arlington, VA 22209
(703) 524-1200
Irrigation News (12)

Trade association to promote the use of modern irrigation equipment and water and soil conservation.
❒ Privileges: CONVENTIONS LIBRARY BOOKS

Landscape Ontario Horticultural Trades
  Association
1293 Matheson Boulevard East
Mississauga, ON, Canada L4W 1R1
(416) 629-1184
Landscape Trades (12)

Association of Ontario nurserymen. Journal is available on subscription for C$30 in Canada, C$40 in the US and overseas.
❒ Privileges: CONVENTIONS EXHIBITS TOURS

The Lawn Institute
Beverly Roberts
P.O. Box 108
Pleasant Hill, TN 38578
(615) 277-3722
Harvests Newsletter (4)

Nonprofit trade association to enhance lawn grass research and education. Periodical is available on separate subscription.

Mailorder Association of Nurseries, Inc.
Camille G. Chioini, Exec. Dir.
8683 Doves Fly Way
Laurel, MD 20707
(301) 490-9143
Quarterly Newsletter

Trade association of larger mail-order nursery businesses.
❐ Privileges: CONVENTIONS

Master Gardeners, Cooperative Extension Service
Diane Relf or David McKissack
Dept. of Horticulture, Virginia Tech. Univ.
Blacksburg, VA 24061
(703) 231-6254

The Cooperative Extension Service of Virginia has served as a model for many states that use its concepts and training materials; it serves as a clearinghouse of information on programs in other states. There are now Master Gardeners active in 45 states; to locate a group in your area, or to start one, first contact the Cooperative Extension Service in your home county.

Men's Garden Clubs of America, Inc.
Nancy D. Gorden, Exec. Sec.
P.O. Box 241; 5560 Merle Hay Road
Johnston, IA 50131
(515) 278-0295
The Gardener (6)
MGCA Newsletter (6)

Umbrella organization for local men's garden clubs.
❐ Chapters: 150
❐ Privileges: CONVENTIONS LIBRARY BOOKS SEEDS

National Arbor Day Foundation
100 Arbor Avenue
Nebraska City, NE 68410
(402) 474-5655
Arbor Day (6)

A national nonprofit educational organization dedicated to tree planting and conservation; offers special trees to its members. Membership open to all.
❐ Annual Dues: $10

National Association of Women in Horticulture
Lori Anne Brown, Exec. Sec.
P.O. Box 1483
Mt. Dora, FL 32757-1483
(904) 383-8811
The Forum (12)
Directory of Women in Horticulture (1)

Recently formed group of women working in all branches of horticulture.
❐ Chapters: 4
❐ Privileges: CONVENTIONS

National Council of State Garden Clubs, Inc.
401 Magnolia Avenue
St. Louis, MO 63110
The National Gardener (6)

Umbrella group for state garden clubs, which in themselves are umbrella organizations for 11,000 local garden clubs.
❐ Chapters: 11,000

National Garden Bureau, Inc.

See All-America Selections.

National Junior Horticulture Association
Jan Hoffman
441 E. Pine Street
Fremont, MI 49412
(616) 924-5237
Going & Growing (3)

Umbrella organization for state and local chapters; students join chapters in their schools or through other local clubs.
❐ Privileges: CONVENTIONS

National Wildflower Research Center
Tony Martinez, Data Mgr.
2600 FM 973 North
Austin, TX 78725
(512) 929-3600
Wildflower Journal (2)
Wildflower Newsletter (6)

National group to promote conservation and use of native plants in public and private landscapes. Membership open to all.
❐ Annual Dues: in US, CAN, & OV US$25 (IMO)
❐ Garden: Display/research garden at the Center
❐ Privileges: CONVENTIONS LIBRARY BOOKS PLANTS EXHIBITS TRIPS TOURS

National Xeriscape Council, Inc.
Pat Miller, Exec. Dir.
940 E. 51st Street
Austin, TX 78751
(512) 454-8626

Nonprofit association devoted to "xeriscaping" -- landscaping to make gardens and plantings more water-efficient. Write for information.

Ontario Horticultural Association
Mrs. Bonnie Warner
RR #3
Englehart, ON, CANADA P0S 1H0
(705) 544-2474
Horticultural Societies Newsletter (4)

Umbrella organization for horticultural societies in Ontario; publishes a schedule of agricultural fairs and exhibitions and helps local groups with suggestions for programs and useful resources.
❐ Privileges: CONVENTIONS

Outdoor Power Equipment Institute
Dennis Dix
1901 L Street Northwest, Suite 700
Washington, DC 20036
(202) 296-3484

Trade association; write for information.

Perennial Plant Association
Steven M. Still
3383 Schirtzinger Road
Columbus, OH 43026
(614) 771-8431
Perennial Plant Symposium Proceedings (1)
Perennial Plants (4)

Trade association; promotes the development of the perennial plant industry, holds symposia and conferences.
❏ Privileges: CONVENTIONS

Regenerative Agriculture Association
Jim Morgan
222 Main Street
Emmaus, PA 18049
(215) 967-5171
The New Farm (7)

An association of commercial farmers using organic methods; has educational conferences. Membership open to all.
❏ Annual Dues: in US $15, in CAN US$19, OV US$21

Soil & Water Conservation Society
Ann Thornton
7515 N.E. Ankeny Road
Ankeny, IA 50021-9764
(515) 289-2331
Journal of Soil & Water Conservation (6)

Purpose is to advance the science and art of good land use. Periodical available on separate subscription for US$30 or US$35 overseas. Offers a list of native seed resources for US$3 ppd. Membership open to all.
❏ Annual Dues: in US & CAN US$44, OV US$50 (US bank draft)
❏ Chapters: 150
❏ Garden: Native grass meadow, 7515 N.E. Ankeny Road, Ankeny, IA
❏ Privileges: CONVENTIONS BOOKS

© Kimberly Garden of Oregon Hill
Artist: Lynn Adams

© Charley's Greenhouse Supply
Artist: Charley Yaw

D

Horticultural Societies

Horticultural societies are listed alphabetically.

See the Index section for:

L. Society Index: an index of horticultural societies listed by plant and/or other special interests.

M. Magazine Index: an alphabetical title index to magazines and other periodicals offered by societies, as well as horticultural and gardening magazines from other sources.

Societies

I have listed only societies that are of international, national or regional interest. There are also local garden clubs, regional chapters of national and state organizations and the "friends" groups at botanical gardens, any of which have activities and programs of interest. Ask at your favorite nursery, recreation department, or chamber of commerce or at the ornamental horticulture department of your local college to find out about local groups.

If you travel, consider the advantages of joining an international or foreign group a year or so before you go in order to find out about events and places you'd like to include in your plans.

I have to laugh now when I think how shy I was about daring to join the "experts." My experiences have been pure pleasure; I've learned a lot, volunteered time to useful projects, made many new friends — and I usually come home from meetings with a new plant. The gardener's greatest resource is other gardeners. The more you get into the network, the greater your pleasure will be!

Warning!

Nothing seems to change more quickly than the membership secretaries, addresses and membership dues of societies. I'd suggest that before you send off a check, write and ask for information about the society so that you'll know how much to send and where to send it.

Please see reverse side for society abbreviations and conventions used in this section.

A table of the symbols and abbreviations used
in this book appears on the bookmark.

Society Abbreviations and Conventions

Society publications are listed after the address with the number of issues per year indicated in parentheses — e.g. (6).

Available membership privileges are indicated as follows:

CONVENTIONS— conferences or annual meetings

LIBRARY — library for use of members

BOOKS — book sales to members

SEEDS — seed exchanges or sales to members

PLANTS — plant sales at meetings

EXHIBITS — plant shows or exhibits sponsored by society

TRIPS — local field trips for members

TOURS — tours or travel program for members

African Violet Society of America, Inc.
P.O. Box 3609
Beaumont, TX 77704
(409) 839-4725
African Violet Magazine (6)

❏ Annual Dues: in US $13.50, in CAN & OV $15.50
❏ Privileges: CONVENTIONS LIBRARY EXHIBITS

African Violet Society of Canada
1573 Arbordale Avenue
Victoria, BC, Canada V8N 5J1
(604) 477-7561
Chatter (4)

❏ Annual Dues: in US & CAN C$10, OV C$11

Alabama Wildflower Society
Mrs. Dottie Elam
240 Ivy Lane
Auburn, AL 36830
(205) 339-2541
Newsletter (2)

❏ Annual Dues: in US $5, in CAN & OV $8
❏ Chapters: 5
❏ Privileges: CONVENTIONS PLANTS TRIPS

Alaska Native Plant Society
Verna Pratt
P.O. Box 141613
Anchorage, AK 99514
(907) 333-8212
Newsletter (8)

❏ Annual Dues: in US $10, OV $12.50 (IMO)
❏ Privileges: SEEDS EXHIBITS TRIPS

Aloe, Cactus & Succulent Society of Zimbabwe
Rosemary Kimberley
P.O. Box 8514, Causeway
Harare, Zimbabwe
(263) (0) 39175
The INGENS Bulletin (2)
Excelsa (biennial)

Periodically holds major international conventions; also offers a quarterly
newsletter to members. Also publishes the Excelsa Taxonomic Series; write
for information.
❏ Annual Dues: US$10 or £5 (IMO)
❏ Privileges: CONVENTIONS BOOKS SEEDS PLANTS TRIPS TOURS

Alpine Garden Club of British Columbia
Erika Hobeck
13751, 56A Avenue
Surrey, BC, Canada V3W 1J4
Monthly Bulletin

One of the best and most extensive seed exchanges in the world!
❏ Annual Dues: in CAN C$13, C$15 family
❏ Privileges: CONVENTIONS LIBRARY BOOKS SEEDS PLANTS EXHIBITS TRIPS

Alpine Garden Society
E. Michael Upward
Lye End Link, St. John's
Woking, Surrey, England GU21 1SW
(04862) 69327
Quarterly Bulletin
Alpine Gardening (2)

Publishes a very interesting bulletin; also "Alpine Gardening," which is
aimed at inexperienced alpine gardeners. Also has an excellent seed exchange
and an extensive list of alpine and rock garden books for sale to members.
❏ Annual Dues: in US $24, in CAN C$26, OV £12 (IMO)
❏ Chapters: 50
❏ Privileges: CONVENTIONS LIBRARY BOOKS SEEDS PLANTS EXHIBITS TOURS

American Bamboo Society
Richard Haubrich
P.O. Box 640
Springville, CA 93265
(209) 539-2145
Journal (Irregular)
Newsletter (6)

❏ Annual Dues: in US, CAN & OV US$15
❏ Chapters: 5
❏ Garden: Quail Botanical Gardens, Encinitas, CA
❏ Privileges: CONVENTIONS LIBRARY BOOKS SEEDS PLANTS EXHIBITS TRIPS

American Begonia Society
John Ingles, Jr.
8922 Conway Drive
Riverside, CA 92503
(714) 687-3728
The Begonian (6)

There are sixty-four special interest round-robin letter "flights" -- members
meet at conventions. Has a seed exchange and seed sales.
❏ Annual Dues: in US & CAN US$15, OV US$19 (IMO)
❏ Chapters: 50
❏ Privileges: CONVENTIONS BOOKS SEEDS PLANTS EXHIBITS TOURS

American Bonsai Society
Anne D. Moyle
P.O. Box 358
Keene, NH 03431
(603) 352-9034
Bonsai Journal (4)
ABStracts (3)

❑ Annual Dues: in US $18, in CAN & OV US$22 (IMO)
❑ Privileges: CONVENTIONS LIBRARY

American Boxwood Society
Joan Butler
P.O. Box 85
Boyce, VA 22620
(703) 939-4646
The Boxwood Bulletin (4)

Another plant collection: National Arboretum, Washington, DC. Has "Boxwood Workshops" twice a year, annual tour in Mid-Atlantic states. The society's excellent "Buyers Guide," $3, is listed in the book section.
❑ Annual Dues: in US, CAN & OV US$15 (IMO)
❑ Garden: Blandy Experimental Farm, Boyce, VA
❑ Privileges: CONVENTIONS PLANTS TRIPS TOURS

American Calochortus Society
H. P. McDonald
260 Alden Road
Hayward, CA 94541
(415) 276-2414
Mariposa (4)

A brand-new society devoted to both botany and culture of the Western Mariposas and other Calochorti. Write for information.
❑ Annual Dues: $2

American Camellia Society
C. David Scheibert
P.O. Box 1217
Fort Valley, GA 31030-1217
(912) 967-2358
The Camellia Journal (4)
American Camellia Yearbook

Offers "Camellia Culture for Beginners" for $2 ppd. and "The Camellia" by Feathers & Brown (1978) for $12.50 ppd. in the United States.
❑ Annual Dues: in US $17.50, in CAN & OV US$19 (IMO)
❑ Chapters: 60
❑ Garden: Historic Massee Lane Gardens, Ft. Valley, GA
❑ Privileges: CONVENTIONS BOOKS PLANTS EXHIBITS

American Conifer Society
Mrs. Maxine Schwarz
P.O. Box 242
Severna Park, MD 21146
Bulletin (4)

❑ Annual Dues: $20
❑ Privileges: CONVENTIONS

American Daffodil Society, Inc.
Mary Lou Gripshover
1686 Grey Fox Trails
Milford, OH 45150
(513) 248-9137
The Daffodil Journal (4)

❑ Annual Dues: in US, CAN, & OV US$15 (IMO)
❑ Chapters: 35
❑ Garden: Whetstone Park, Columbus, OH
❑ Privileges: CONVENTIONS LIBRARY BOOKS PLANTS EXHIBITS

American Dahlia Society
Michael Martinolich
159 Pine Street
New Hyde Park, NY 11040
Bulletin (4)

❑ Annual Dues: in US $8, OV US$9
❑ Chapters: 6
❑ Privileges: EXHIBITS TOURS

American Fern Society, Inc.
James D. Caponetti, Treas.
Dept. of Botany, Univ. of Tennessee
Knoxville, TN 37996-1100
(615) 974-6219
American Fern Journal (4)
Fiddlehead Forum (6)

Membership does not include the more scholarly "American Fern Journal," which costs an extra $15 (plus $4 OV). Spore exchange has fresh spore available by exchange or at nominal cost to society members. Membership is by calendar year only. Also publishes "Pteridologia" (irregular); write for information.
❑ Annual Dues: in US $8, in CAN & OV US$10 (IMO)
❑ Chapters: 11
❑ Privileges: CONVENTIONS TRIPS

American Forestry Association
Kathy Amberger, Memb. Secy.
P.O. Box 2000
Washington, D.C. 20013
(202) 667-3300
American Forests (6)

The society, which was founded in 1875, is dedicated to balanced forest use. Co-sponsors "Global ReLeaf," an effort to plant one hundred million trees in the United States by 1992.
❑ Annual Dues: in US $24, in CAN & OV US$28 (IMO)
❑ Privileges: CONVENTIONS LIBRARY BOOKS

American Fuchsia Society
County Fair Building
9th Avenue at Lincoln Way
San Francisco, CA 94122
Monthly Bulletin

Has a number of chapters on the Pacific Coast.
❑ Annual Dues: in US $9, OV US$11 (PC or IMO)
❑ Privileges: CONVENTIONS LIBRARY BOOKS PLANTS EXHIBITS TRIPS

American Ginger Society
Tom Wood
P.O. Box 100
Archer, FL 32618
(904) 495-9168
Zingiber (2)

Display garden open by appointment only from July to September.
❏ Annual Dues: in US and CAN US$15, OV US$20 (IMO)
❏ Garden: Tom Wood Herb Farm, Archer, FL, by appointment only
❏ Privileges: CONVENTIONS LIBRARY SEEDS PLANTS EXHIBITS TRIPS

American Gloxinia & Gesneriad Society, Inc.
Ellen Todd, Memb. Secy.
P.O. Box 493
Beverly Farms, MA 01915
The Gloxinian (6)

Seeds are sold at a nominal cost to members.
❏ Annual Dues: in US $18, OV US$21
❏ Chapters: 42
❏ Privileges: CONVENTIONS LIBRARY SEEDS EXHIBITS

American Gourd Society
John Stevens
P.O. Box 274
Mount Gilead, OH 43338-0274
(419) 946-3302
The Gourd (4)

Annual meeting at Mt. Gilead Fairgrounds in July; annual show first full weekend in October, same location. Promotes the use of gourds for decorative and useful purposes; magazines show beautifully decorated gourds.
❏ Annual Dues: in US $5, in CAN & OV US$8 (IMO)
❏ Chapters: 6
❏ Privileges: CONVENTIONS BOOKS SEEDS

American Hemerocallis Society
Elly Launius, Exec. Secy.
1454 Rebel Drive
Jackson, MS 39211
(601) 366-4362
Daylily Journal (4)

Has a slide library for members; publishes an extensive source list; has many round-robins on topics of special interest. Also sells "Everything You've Always Wanted to Know about Daylilies" for $5 ppd.
❏ Annual Dues: $12.50 (IMO)
❏ Chapters: 15 US; 1 OV
❏ Garden: Many; see publications
❏ Privileges: CONVENTIONS PLANTS

American Herb Association
P.O. Box 353
Rescue, CA 95672
Quarterly Newsletter (4)

Publishes a directory of sources as well as a directory of herb gardens and one of herb schools. Emphasis is on medicinal herbs and the healing arts.
❏ Annual Dues: in US $20, in CAN US$28, OV US$30
❏ Privileges: BOOKS

American Hibiscus Society
Jeri Grantham, Exec. Secy.
P.O. Box 321540
Cocoa Beach, FL 32932-1540
(407) 783-2576
The Seed Pod (4)

Local chapters have shows, plant sales and exchange wood for grafting; they sell "What Every Hibiscus Grower Should Know" for $7.
❏ Annual Dues: in US $13, in CAN & OV US$23 (IMO)
❏ Chapters: 27
❏ Garden: Display gardens in S. FL, TX, CA
❏ Privileges: CONVENTIONS BOOKS SEEDS PLANTS EXHIBITS TRIPS TOURS

American Horticultural Society
Joseph M. Keyser
7931 E. Boulevard Drive
Alexandria, VA 22308
(703) 768-5700
American Horticulturist (6)
American Horticulturist News (6)

Has an extensive tour program, a gardener's information service for your problems and plant labels and books for members at special prices. Call toll-free at (800) 777-7931.
❏ Annual Dues: in US $35, in CAN & OV US$45 (IMO)
❏ Garden: River Farm, Mt. Vernon, VA
❏ Privileges: CONVENTIONS LIBRARY BOOKS SEEDS PLANTS EXHIBITS TOURS

American Hosta Society
Dennis Savory
5300 Whiting Avenue
Edina, MN 55435
Hosta Journal (2)

❏ Annual Dues: in US $12.50, in CAN & OV US$15 (IMO)
❏ Privileges: CONVENTIONS EXHIBITS

American Iris Society
Jeane Stayer
7414 E. 60th Street
Tulsa, OK 74145
Bulletin (4)

Has sections by types of iris; 24 regional affiliates and 127 chapters.
❏ Annual Dues: $9.50
❏ Garden: Many test gardens; see literature
❏ Privileges: CONVENTIONS PLANTS EXHIBITS

American Ivy Society
Elizabeth Carrick
P.O. Box 520
West Carrollton, OH 45449-0520
(513) 434-7069
The Ivy Journal (2)
Newsletter (2)

Regional display garden at Mendocino Coast Botanical Garden, Fort Bragg, CA. Ivy Research Center may be contacted at the society's address in West Carrollton, OH. They sell several books and pamphlets on ivy.
❏ Annual Dues: in US $15, in CAN C$20
❏ Chapters: 2
❏ Garden: AHS Garden, River Farm, Mt. Vernon, VA
❏ Privileges: CONVENTIONS LIBRARY BOOKS

American Orchid Society
Victoria Robb Creech
6000 S. Olive Avenue
West Palm Beach, FL 33405
(407) 585-8666
Bulletin (12)
AOS Awards Quarterly (4)

Has two meetings a year in different locations and publishes handbooks on various orchid subjects, including the "Handbook on Orchid Culture," $9 ppd. Also publishes "Lindleyana"; see Section E.
❏ Annual Dues: in US $28, in CAN & OV US$34 (IMO)
❏ Privileges: CONVENTIONS LIBRARY BOOKS

American Penstemon Society
Ann W. Bartlett, Memb. Secy.
1569 S. Holland Court
Lakewood, CO 80226
(303) 986-8096
Bulletin (2)

Publishes a very good "Manual for Beginners." Has another display collection at the Denver Botanical Garden. The society will accept membership payment either by personal check or International Money Order.
❒ Annual Dues: in US, CAN, & OV US$10 (in US$ only)
❒ Garden: Cox Arboretum, Dayton, OH
❒ Privileges: CONVENTIONS LIBRARY SEEDS PLANTS TRIPS

American Peony Society
Greta M. Kessenich
250 Interlachen Road
Hopkins, MN 55343
(612) 935-4706
Bulletin (4)

Write for list of publications.
❒ Annual Dues: in US, CAN & OV US$7.50 (IMO)
❒ Privileges: CONVENTIONS SEEDS

American Plant Life Society
R. Mitchel Beauchamp
P.O. Box 985
National City, CA 92050
(619) 474-3530
Herbertia (2)
Newsletter (4)

Devoted to the culture of, research on and preservation of bulbous plants, especially the Amaryllidaceae.
❒ Annual Dues: in US $20, in CAN & OV US$20 (IMO)
❒ Privileges: CONVENTIONS SEEDS

American Poinsettia Society
P.O. Box 706
Mission, TX 78572-1256
(512) 585-1256

Write for information.

American Pomological Society
Dr. R. M. Crassweller
103 Tyson Building
University Park, PA 16802
(814) 865-2571
Fruit Varieties Journal (4)

Promotes fruit variety and rootstock improvement through breeding and testing. Open to all; founded in 1848.
❒ Annual Dues: $16 (IMO or PC)
❒ Privileges: CONVENTIONS BOOKS

American Primrose Society
Jay G. Lunn
Route 5, Box 93
Hillsboro, OR 97124
(503) 640-4582
Primroses (4)

Has slide programs and round-robins, an interesting journal and excellent seed exchanges.
❒ Annual Dues: in US, CAN & OV US$10 (IMO)
❒ Chapters: 7
❒ Privileges: CONVENTIONS SEEDS PLANTS EXHIBITS

American Rhododendron Society
Barbara R. Hall, Exec. Secy.
P.O. Box 1380
Gloucester, VA 23061
(804) 693-4433
Journal (4)

Slide programs to rent, pollen bank, seed exchange. Local chapters have active programs and tours; some have libraries.
❒ Annual Dues: in US, CAN, & OV US$25 (IMO)
❒ Chapters: 60
❒ Garden: Some local chapters maintain gardens
❒ Privileges: CONVENTIONS BOOKS SEEDS PLANTS EXHIBITS TRIPS

American Rock Garden Society
Buffy Parker
15 Fairmead Road
Darien, CT 06820
Bulletin (4)

A very active society, with many local chapters. Winter study weekends -- one on the East Coast, one on the West Coast; annual spring meeting. Has an excellent bookstore for members.
❒ Annual Dues: in US, CAN & OV US$20 (IMO)
❒ Chapters: 29
❒ Privileges: CONVENTIONS LIBRARY BOOKS SEEDS PLANTS EXHIBITS TRIPS

American Rose Society
Membership Secretary
P.O. Box 30,000
Shreveport, LA 71130
(318) 938-5402
The American Rose Magazine (12)

❒ Annual Dues: in US & CAN US$25, OV US$40 (IMO)
❒ Garden: Shreveport, LA; call for directions
❒ Privileges: LIBRARY BOOKS TRIPS

American Willow Growers Network
Bonnie Gale
RD 1, Box 124A
South New Berlin, NY 13843
(607) 847-8264
Newsletter (1)

A new group sharing information and cuttings, developing new uses for the willow; holds basket-making workshops.
❒ Annual Dues: in US, CAN, & OV US$5 (IMO)
❒ Garden: South New Berlin, NY; call for information
❒ Privileges: CONVENTIONS LIBRARY PLANTS

Aril Society International
Donna Downey
5500 Constitution N.E.
Albuquerque, NM 87110
(505) 255-8207
Yearbook

A society of aril iris lovers; write for information.

Arizona Native Plant Society
David Ingram
P.O. Box 41206
Tucson, AZ 85717
Plant Press (4)

Has informal seed exchanges among members.
❐ Annual Dues: $15
❐ Chapters: 5
❐ Privileges: CONVENTIONS SEEDS EXHIBITS TRIPS TOURS

Arkansas Native Plant Society
Dr. James Gulden
Dept. of Forest Resources, UAM
Monticello, AR 71655
(501) 460-1049

Write for information.

Australian Fuchsia Society
Miss Rosalie Sharpe
P.O. Box 97, Norwood
Adelaide, SA, Australia 5062
08 2636077
Journal (4)

❐ Annual Dues: A$6 (IMO)
❐ Privileges: LIBRARY PLANTS EXHIBITS TRIPS

Australian Garden History Society
Diana Forrester, Exec. Off.
P.O. Box 972
Bowral, NSW, Australia 2576
(048) 871310
Australian Garden History (6)

Has garden tours, planning a plant collection.
❐ Annual Dues: in Australia A$20, OV A$25 (IMO)
❐ Privileges: CONVENTIONS BOOKS TRIPS TOURS

Australian Geranium Society
118 Thorney Road
Fairfield West, NSW, Australia 2165
Journal (4)

Write for information.

Australian Hibiscus Society
Miss J. Taylor, Memb. Secy.
8 Girraman Street
West Chermside, QLD, Australia 4032
(07) 3591569
The Hibiscus (6)

❐ Annual Dues: in US, CAN & OV A$20 (Air Mail) (IMO)
❐ Chapters: 6
❐ Privileges: CONVENTIONS LIBRARY BOOKS SEEDS PLANTS EXHIBITS TRIPS

The Australian Plant Society of California
Kathy Musial
P.O. Box 50722
Pasadena, CA 91115
Newsletter (4)
Australian Plants (4)

New society hopes to offer members a library, seed exchanges, tours and other privileges soon. Membership includes a subscription to "Australian Plants," published by the Society for Growing Australian Plants, also listed.
❐ Annual Dues: $18

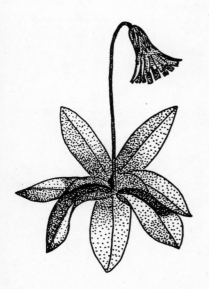

© We-Du Nurseries
Artist: Richard E. Weaver, Jr.

Australian Rhododendron Society
Miss L. Eaton
P.O. Box 21
Olinda, Victoria, Australia 3788
The Rhododendron (4)

Memberships commence on July 31st of each year.
❒ Annual Dues: A$15
❒ Chapters: 6
❒ Garden: Some local chapters have display gardens
❒ Privileges: CONVENTIONS SEEDS

Azalea Society of America, Inc.
Mrs. Marjorie Taylor
5203 Queensberry Avenue
Springfield, VA 22151
(703) 321-7053
The Azalean (4)

Local societies have plant shows and sales.
❒ Annual Dues: in US, CAN & OV US$15 (IMO)
❒ Chapters: 13
❒ Privileges: CONVENTIONS LIBRARY PLANTS EXHIBITS TRIPS

Bio-Dynamic Farming & Gardening Association
Roderick Shouldice
P.O. Box 550
Kimberton, PA 19442
(215) 935-7797
Bio-Dynamics (4)
Bio-Dynamics News & Events (6)

Promotes the bio-dynamic method of farming and gardening.
❒ Annual Dues: in US $35, in CAN US$42, OV US$48 (IMO)
❒ Chapters: 9
❒ Privileges: CONVENTIONS BOOKS

Bio-Integral Resource Center (BIRC)
P.O. Box 7414
Berkeley, CA 94707
(415) 524-2567
Common Sense Pest Control (4)

Group devoted to the least toxic methods of pest management. Members receive the non-technical "Common Sense Pest Control." Additional publication is "The IPM Practitioner," received by its professional members but also available on subscription. See Section E, Magazines.
❒ Annual Dues: in US $30, in CAN US$34, OV US$35 (IMO)
❒ Privileges: CONVENTIONS BOOKS

Biological Urban Gardening Services
Peggy Symonik, Exec. Secy.
P.O. Box 76
Citrus Heights, CA 95611-0076
(916) 726-5377
BUGS Flyer (4)

Organization devoted to reducing the use of pesticides. "BUGS" offers a professional category of membership for $15 a year, with additional services oriented toward horticultural professionals.
❒ Annual Dues: in US $10, in CAN & OV US$11.50

Bonsai Clubs International
Virginia Ellermann
2636 W. Mission Road, #277
Tallahassee, FL 32304
Bonsai Clubs International (6)

A large society, with many local chapters and activities.
❒ Annual Dues: in US $18, in CAN & OV US$18 (IMO)
❒ Chapters: 198
❒ Privileges: CONVENTIONS LIBRARY BOOKS

Botanical Club of Wisconsin
Rudy G. Koch, Dept. of Biology
Univ. of Wisconsin, La Crosse
LaCrosse, WI 54601

Write for information.

Botanical Society of South Africa
Diana Peters
Kirstenbosch
Claremont, Cape Town, South Africa 7735
(021) 797-2090
Veld & Flora (4)

Personal check in dollars may be sent; inquire first. In addition to Kirstenbosch, the society supports seven other botanical gardens, promotes the conservation and cultivation of the indigenous flora of South Africa. Also publishes wildflower guides.
❒ Annual Dues: in US $18, in CAN C$20
❒ Garden: Kirstenbosch Botanical Garden
❒ Privileges: LIBRARY BOOKS SEEDS PLANTS EXHIBITS TRIPS TOURS

British & European Geranium Society
Ray Plowright
1 Roslyn Road, Hathersage
Sheffield, England S30 1BY
Gazette (3)
Year Book

❒ Annual Dues: in US $5, in UK £2 (IMO)
❒ Chapters: 8
❒ Privileges: CONVENTIONS BOOKS PLANTS EXHIBITS TRIPS TOURS

The British Cactus & Succulent Society
c/o Miss W. E. Dunn
43 Dewer Drive
Sheffield, England S7 2GR
British Cactus and Succulent Journal (4)
Bradleya (1)

Members can send personal checks for dues; no seed exchange, but seeds are sold to members. "Bradleya" is available on separate subscription.
❒ Annual Dues: US$15 (PC)
❒ Chapters: 100
❒ Privileges: CONVENTIONS LIBRARY BOOKS SEEDS PLANTS EXHIBITS

British Columbia Fuchsia & Begonia Society
Mrs. P. Young
6773 Tyne Street
Vancouver, BC, Canada V5S 3M4

Write for information.

British Columbia Lily Society
Del Knowlton, Secy.-Treas.
5510 - 239th Street
Langley, BC, Canada V3A 7N6
(604) 534-4729

Discovered too late to contact; write for information.
☐ Annual Dues: C$5

British Fuchsia Society
Ron Ewart
29 Princes Crescent
Dollar, Scotland FK14 7BW
(0259) 43180
Bulletin (2)
Yearbook

Publishes a number of leaflets on fuchsia culture.
☐ Annual Dues: in US & CAN £5 (IMO)
☐ Privileges: CONVENTIONS BOOKS EXHIBITS

British Iris Society
Mrs. E. M. Wise
197 The Parkway, Iver Heath
Iver, Bucks., England SL0 0RQ
The Iris Year Book

Three shows a year at the RHS Hall in London; conventions every five years.
☐ Annual Dues: OV £7 (IMO)
☐ Privileges: CONVENTIONS LIBRARY BOOKS SEEDS PLANTS EXHIBITS

The British Ivy Society
Mr. W. F. Kennedy, Memb. Secy.
66 Corwall Road
Ruislip, Middlesex, England HA4 6AN
Journal (2)
Occasional Papers

Write for information.

British Pelargonium & Geranium Society
Mrs. Jan Taylor
23 Beech Crescent, Kidlington
Oxford, England OX5 1DW
Kidlington 5063
Pelargonium News (3)
Yearbook (1)

Has a Geraniaceae group for those interested in species geraniums.
☐ Annual Dues: £4 or US$10 (US bills or IMO)
☐ Privileges: CONVENTIONS BOOKS SEEDS PLANTS EXHIBITS TRIPS

Bromeliad Society, Inc.
2488 E. 49th Street
Tulsa, OK 74105
Journal (6)

Local affiliates have exhibits and plant sales, libraries and field trips.
☐ Annual Dues: in US $20, in CAN & OV US$25 (IMO)
☐ Chapters: 60
☐ Privileges: CONVENTIONS BOOKS SEEDS EXHIBITS TOURS

Bromeliad Study Group of Northern California
Daniel Arcos
1334 S. Van Ness Avenue
San Francisco, CA 94110
(415) 647-8114

Devoted to the cultivation, research and conservation of Bromeliads.
☐ Annual Dues: $10
☐ Privileges: LIBRARY PLANTS EXHIBITS TRIPS

Cactus & Succulent Society of America
Louise Lippold
P.O. Box 3010
Santa Barbara, CA 93130
Cactus & Succulent Journal (6)
CSSA Newsletter (6)

Subscription to the journal is separate from membership; see "Cactus & Succulent Journal" in Section E.
☐ Annual Dues: in US and CAN US$20, OV US$21 (IMO)
☐ Chapters: 50
☐ Privileges: CONVENTIONS LIBRARY EXHIBITS

California Horticultural Society
Mrs. Elsie Mueller
1847 - 34th Avenue
San Francisco, CA 94122
(415) 566-5222
Pacific Horticulture (4)
Monthly Bulletin (11)

General interest in ornamental horticulture. The society is active in the San Francisco Bay area; see also the Southern California Horticultural Institute and the Western Horticultural Society.
☐ Annual Dues: in US$25, in CAN US$30, OV US$32.50 (IMO)
☐ Privileges: LIBRARY SEEDS EXHIBITS TRIPS TOURS

California Native Plant Society
Kristina Schierenbeck
909 - 12th Street, #116
Sacramento, CA 95814
(916) 447-2677
Fremontia (4)
Bulletin (4)

Some local chapters have seed exchanges.
☐ Annual Dues: $18 (IMO)
☐ Chapters: 26
☐ Privileges: CONVENTIONS BOOKS SEEDS PLANTS EXHIBITS TRIPS

California Rare Fruit Growers, Inc.
Dianne M. Hand
California State Univ. Arboretum
Fullerton, CA 92634
The Fruit Gardener (4)
Journal (1)

For better understanding of growing subtropical fruits. Additional display gardens at the San Diego Zoo and at California Polytechnic in Pomona.
❐ Annual Dues: in US $12, in CAN & OV US$20 (IMO)
❐ Chapters: 14
❐ Garden: Fullerton Arboretum, Fullerton, CA
❐ Privileges: CONVENTIONS BOOKS SEEDS PLANTS TRIPS TOURS

Canadian Chrysanthemum & Dahlia Society
G. H. Lawrence
83 Aramaman Drive
Agincourt, ON, Canada M1T 2PM
(416) 293-6372

Write for information.
❐ Privileges: CONVENTIONS EXHIBITS

Canadian Geranium & Pelargonium Society
c/o Vandusen Botanical Gardens
5251 Oak Street
Vancouver, BC, Canada V6M 4H1
Storksbill (4)

❐ Annual Dues: C$7.50
❐ Garden: Display at Vandusen Botanical Gardens, Vancouver, BC
❐ Privileges: LIBRARY BOOKS SEEDS PLANTS EXHIBITS TRIPS

Canadian Gladiolus Society
P. Q. Drysdale
3770 Hardy Road, RR 1
Agassiz, BC, Canada V0M 1A0
(604) 796-2548
Canadian Gladiolus Annual
Fall Bulletin (1)

❐ Annual Dues: C$8
❐ Chapters: 15
❐ Privileges: CONVENTIONS

Canadian Iris Society
Mrs. Irene Specogna
RR 5
Bolton, ON, Canada L7E 5S1
(416) 880-4461
Newsletter (4)

Canadian members only. Iris shows and auctions, annual educational and awards program, regional activities.
❐ Annual Dues: C$5
❐ Garden: Laking Garden, Royal Botanical Gardens, Hamilton, ON
❐ Privileges: CONVENTIONS LIBRARY PLANTS EXHIBITS TRIPS

Canadian Orchid Society
President
128 Adelaide Street
Winnipeg, MB, Canada R3A 0W5
(204) 943-6870
The Canadian Orchid Journal (4)

Enthusiastic greenhouse growers, held together over long distances by an interesting magazine.
❐ Annual Dues: in US US$25, in CAN C$25, OV US$28 (IMO)
❐ Privileges: SEEDS PLANTS

Canadian Organic Growers
Kathy Lamarche, Memb. Secy.
P.O. Box 6408, Station J
Ottawa, ON, Canada K2A 3Y6
COGnition (4)

Hopes to develop a Heritage Garden.
❐ Annual Dues: in US, CAN and OV C$16 (IMO)
❐ Privileges: CONVENTIONS LIBRARY TRIPS

Canadian Prairie Lily Society
A. E. Delahay
RR 5
Saskatoon, SK, Canada S7K 3J8
Newsletter (3-4)

Concerned with growing the native prairie lilies of Canada.
❐ Annual Dues: in US or CAN $3
❐ Privileges: BOOKS PLANTS EXHIBITS TOURS

Canadian Rose Society
Dianne D. Lask
686 Pharmacy Avenue
Scarborough, ON, Canada M1L 3H8
The Rosarian (3)
Canadian Rose Annual

Promotes knowledge of rose-growing in northern climates; has a slide library and an annual garden tour.
❐ Annual Dues: C$15
❐ Chapters: 32
❐ Privileges: LIBRARY PLANTS EXHIBITS

The Canadian Wildflower Society
Tom Atkinson
75 Ternhill Crescent
North York, ON, Canada M3C E43
(416) 499-7907
Wildflower (4)

Society devoted exclusively to the wild flora of North America; interesting to beginners and experts alike; has a handsome magazine.
❐ Annual Dues: in US $20, in CAN C$20, OV C$25 (IMO)
❐ Privileges: CONVENTIONS BOOKS SEEDS PLANTS EXHIBITS TRIPS

Alan Chadwick Society
50 Oak Mountain Drive
San Rafael, CA 94903

Devoted to bio-dynamic organic gardening; write for information.

Colorado Native Plant Society
Myrna P. Steinkamp
P.O. Box 200
Fort Collins, CO 80522
Aquilegia (4-6)

Planning to have seed exchanges for members.
☐ Annual Dues: $8
☐ Chapters: 5
☐ Privileges: CONVENTIONS TRIPS

Cottage Garden Society
Mrs. C. Tordoff
5 Nixon Close, Thornhill
Dewsbury, W. Yorks., England WF12 0JA
0829 270120
Newsletter (4)

Purpose is to keep alive the tradition of gardening in the cottage style and the use of old-fashioned plants. Arranges garden visits in the summer.
☐ Annual Dues: in US and CAN US$20 (PC), in UK £5
☐ Privileges: SEEDS PLANTS EXHIBITS TRIPS

The Croft Institute
Jerry Chouinard
Route 3, Box 73
Stanley, WI 54768
(715) 644-2499
The Crofter (6)

Organization devoted to promoting small-scale organic food production for home and market gardeners.
☐ Annual Dues: in US $18, in CAN C$21, OV US$21 (IMO)

The Cryptanthus Society
Bob D. Whitman
2355 Rusk
Beaumont, TX 77702
(409) 835-0644
Journal (4)
Yearbook (1)

Send a first-class stamp for information or $2.50 for a sample issue of their journal.
☐ Annual Dues: in US $10, OV US$15 (IMO)
☐ Chapters: 35
☐ Garden: Marie Selby Botanic Garden, Sarasota, FL
☐ Privileges: CONVENTIONS BOOKS SEEDS PLANTS EXHIBITS TRIPS TOURS

The Cycad Society
David Mayo
1161 Phyllis Court
Mountain View, CA 94040
(415) 964-7898
The Cycad Newsletter (4)

Seed and pollen bank.
☐ Annual Dues: $15
☐ Privileges: SEEDS

Cyclamen Society
c/o Dr. David V. Bent
9 Tudor Drive
Otford, Kent, England TN14 5QP
(09592) 2322
Cyclamen Journal (2)

Society works to preserve and conserve wild species, has an exchange of viable seed in late summer, offers growing advice from experts.
☐ Annual Dues: OV £5.50 (IMO or US bills)
☐ Privileges: CONVENTIONS LIBRARY SEEDS EXHIBITS

Cymbidium Society of America
Mrs. Richard L. Johnston
6881 Wheeler Avenue
Westminster, CA 92683
(714) 894-5421
The Orchid Advocate (6)

☐ Annual Dues: $12.50
☐ Chapters: 4
☐ Privileges: EXHIBITS

The Daffodil Society (UK)
Ivor Fox
44 Wargrave Road, Twyford
Reading, Berks., England
Bulletin (2)

Write for information.
☐ Annual Dues: OV £3 (IMO)

The Delphinium Society
Mrs. Shirley E. Bassett
"Takakkaw," Ice House Wood
Oxted, Surrey, England RH8 9DW
Delphinium Year Book

Publishes a basic guide, "Delphiniums for All," US$4 (£1.50) ppd.
☐ Annual Dues: in US and CAN US$8, OV £4 or US$8 (IMO)
☐ Garden: Delphinium Trial Ground, RHS Garden, Wisley, Surrey
☐ Privileges: CONVENTIONS BOOKS SEEDS EXHIBITS

Desert Plant Society of Vancouver
2941 Parker Street
Vancouver, BC, Canada V5K 2T9
(604) 255-0606

Write for information.

Epiphyllum Society of America
Betty Berg
P.O. Box 1395
Monrovia, CA 91017
(818) 447-9688
The Bulletin (6)

☐ Annual Dues: in US & CAN US$6, OV Air Mail US$12
☐ Privileges: LIBRARY PLANTS EXHIBITS TRIPS

Eucalyptus Improvement Association
Jim Gunther
P.O. Box 1963
Diamond Springs, CA 95619
Newsletter (4)

New society; write for information.
❏ Annual Dues: $10

Federation of International Rose Exhibitors
Mrs. Susan Begg
Solis 1255, 186 Hurlingham
Buenos Aires, Argentina
(54) 1-665-2070
ARS Rosaceae (4)

A chapter of the American Rose Society. Promotes the skill and art of growing and exhibiting roses; exchanges information. Interested US residents may contact Vincent Gioia, P.O. Box 90970, Pasadena, CA 91109.
❏ Annual Dues: $15 (IMO)

Friends of the Trees
Michael Pilarski
P.O. Box 1466
Chelan, WA 98816
International Green Front Report (biennial)

The "International Green Front Report" is a wonderment! It's full of interest and information on conservation, permaculture and ecological living.
❏ Annual Dues: in US, CAN, & OV US$10 (IMO)

Garden History Society
Mrs. Anne Richards
5 The Knoll
Hereford, England HR1 1RU
0432-354479
Garden History (2)
Newsletter (3)

Has excellent tours in Europe and elsewhere.
❏ Annual Dues: in US & CAN US$30 (IMO), in UK £13.50
❏ Privileges: CONVENTIONS TRIPS TOURS

Gardenia Society of America
Lyman Duncan
P.O. Box 879
Atwater, CA 95301
(209) 385-4251
Gardenia Quarterly

❏ Annual Dues: $5

Georgia Botanical Society
Suzanne S. Jackson, Treas.
3461 Ashwood Lane
Chamblee, GA 30341

Write for information.

Gesneriad Hybridizers Association
Meg Stephenson
4115 Pillar Drive, Route 1
Whitmore Lake, MI 48189
Crosswords (3)

❏ Annual Dues: $5

Gesneriad Society International
2119 Pile Street
Clovis, NM 88101-3597
Gesneriad Journal (6)

❏ Annual Dues: in US $13.25 in CAN & OV US$16.25 (IMO)
❏ Privileges: CONVENTIONS BOOKS SEEDS PLANTS EXHIBITS

Hardy Plant Society (UK)
S. Wills
The Manor House, Walton-in-Gordano
Clevedon, Avon, England BS21 7AN
(01) 397-9923
The Hardy Plant (2)
Newsletter (3)

Offers seed exchanges, visits to members' gardens. See also Hardy Plant Society of Oregon and the Hardy Plant Society -- Mid-Atlantic Group (which offers joint membership).
❏ Annual Dues: OV £8.50 (IMO or US bills)
❏ Chapters: 20
❏ Garden: Wollaton Gardens, Nottingham, England
❏ Privileges: CONVENTIONS BOOKS SEEDS PLANTS EXHIBITS TRIPS

Hardy Plant Society -- Mid-Atlantic Group
Mrs. Peg Elliott
710 Hemlock Road
Media, PA 19063
(215) 566-0861
The Newsletter (4)

Promotes interest in hardy plants, particularly perennials. Offers membership in the HPS (UK) for an additional $11 a year, must receive application before November of each year.
❏ Annual Dues: in US $9, in CAN US$12
❏ Privileges: LIBRARY SEEDS PLANTS TRIPS TOURS

Hardy Plant Society of Oregon
Connie Hanni
33530 S.E. Bluff Road
Boring, OR 97009
(503) 663-9201
Bulletin (2)

Has a much-admired annual study weekend in the Northwest; the one I attended was an orgy of plant pleasure with super people!
❏ Annual Dues: $12
❏ Privileges: CONVENTIONS LIBRARY BOOKS SEEDS PLANTS EXHIBITS TRIPS

Hawaiian Botanical Society
Univ. of Hawaii, Botany Dept.
3190 Maile Way
Honolulu, HI 96822
Newsletter (3-4)

Not a plant or horticulture society as such; members are mostly botanists.
❏ Annual Dues: in US $7.50, $4 (student)

The Heather Society
Mrs. A. Small
Denbeigh, All Saints Road, Creeting St. Mary
Ipswich, Suffolk, England 1P6 8PJ
(0449) 711220
Bulletin (3)
Year Book

Has a slide library and a cultivar location service.
❏ Annual Dues: in US $16, in CAN C$20, in UK £6
❏ Garden: RHS Garden, Wisley; NHS Garden, Harlow Car, Harrogate
❏ Privileges: CONVENTIONS EXHIBITS TRIPS

The Hebe Society
Val Haywood
1 Woodpecker Drive
Hailsham, E. Sussex, England BN27 3E2
Hebe News

Found too late to contact. Write for information.
❏ Annual Dues: £4

Heliconia Society International
David Bar-Zvi
Flamingo Gardens, 3750 Flamingo Road
Ft. Lauderdale, FL 33330
(305) 473-2955
HSI Bulletin (4)

Plant collection centers: Flamingo Gardens, Fort Lauderdale, FL; Harold L. Lyon Arboretum, Honolulu, HI; Andromeda Gardens, Barbados, West Indies; National Tropical Botanical Garden, Kauai, HI.
❏ Annual Dues: in US, CAN, & OV US$20 (IMO)
❏ Chapters: 2
❏ Garden: See notes
❏ Privileges: CONVENTIONS EXHIBITS TRIPS TOURS

Herb Research Foundation
P.O. Box 2602
Longmont, CO 80501
(303) 449-2265
HerbalGram (4)

Formed to initiate, disseminate and publish research into common/uncommon herbs, primarily medicinal herbs. Offers botanical literature searches.
❏ Annual Dues: in US, CAN, & OV US$25 for individuals
❏ Privileges: CONVENTIONS BOOKS

Herb Society of America, Inc.
Leslie Rascan
9019 Kirtland Chardon Road
Mentor, OH 44060
(216) 256-0514
The Herbarist (1)

Society is not medically oriented. Membership is through sponsorship by a current member; write for information.
❏ Annual Dues: in US, CAN, & OV US$35 (IMO)
❏ Chapters: 31
❏ Garden: Herb Garden at The National Arboretum, Washington, DC
❏ Privileges: CONVENTIONS LIBRARY BOOKS SEEDS PLANTS EXHIBITS TRIPS TOURS

Heritage Rose Group
Miriam Wilkins
925 Galvin Drive
El Cerrito, CA 94530
(415) 526-6960
Heritage Rose Letter (4)

Local chapters have meetings and plant sales, help to organize Old Rose Symposia at the Huntington Library in San Marino, CA, and the University of California Botanical Garden, Berkeley, in alternate years. There is a $2.50 additional charge for First Class Air Mail overseas.
❏ Annual Dues: in US $5, in CAN & OV US$6 (US$ only)
❏ Chapters: 6
❏ Privileges: BOOKS SEEDS PLANTS EXHIBITS TRIPS

Heritage Seed Program
RR 3
Uxbridge, ONT, Canada L0C 1K0
Heritage Seed Program (3)

Canadian group interested in saving heirloom and endangered varieties of food crops to guard against the loss of genetic diversity.
❏ Annual Dues: in CAN C$10, in US & OV C$15
❏ Privileges: SEEDS

Historical Iris Preservation Society
Verona Weikhorst
4855 Santiago Way
Colorado Springs, CO 80917

Found too late to contact. Write for information.
❏ Annual Dues: $3

Hobby Greenhouse Association
HGA Membership
1432 Templeton Hills Road
Templeton, CA 93465
(805) 434-2692
Hobby Greenhouse (4)

❏ Annual Dues: in US $10, in CAN US$13, OV US$14 (IMO)
❏ Chapters: 7
❏ Privileges: BOOKS SEEDS

Holly Society of America, Inc.
Mrs. E. H. Richardson, Secy.
304 North Wind Road
Baltimore, MD 21204
(301) 825-8133
Holly Society Journal (4)

Has holly auctions and cutting exchanges, informative pamphlets, local chapters and annual meetings near notable holly collections.
❏ Annual Dues: in US, CAN, & OV US$15 (IMO)
❏ Chapters: 8
❏ Privileges: CONVENTIONS PLANTS TRIPS

Home Orchard Society
Winnifred M. Fisher
P.O. Box 776
Clackamas, OR 97015
(503) 630-3392
Pome News (4)

Has scion and rootstock exchanges, fruit exhibits. For members in the Northwest there are various other events.
❏ Annual Dues: in US, CAN, & OV US$10 (IMO)
❏ Chapters: 4
❏ Garden: HOS Arboretum, Clackamas Comm. Coll., Oregon City, OR
❏ Privileges: CONVENTIONS PLANTS EXHIBITS TRIPS

Horticultural Alliance of the Hamptons
Kate Tyree, Pres.
P.O. Box 202
Bridgehampton, NY 11932
(516) 267-6025
Newsletter (4)

A newly formed group; write for information.
❏ Annual Dues: $25 for individuals
❏ Privileges: LIBRARY PLANTS EXHIBITS TOURS

Horticultural Society of New York
Angela Gutierrez
128 W. 58th Street
New York, NY 10019
(212) 757-0915
HSNY Newsletter (4)

Sponsor of the New York Flower Show, held on the Hudson River Pier in March of every year.
❏ Annual Dues: $25
❏ Privileges: CONVENTIONS LIBRARY BOOKS PLANTS EXHIBITS TRIPS

The Hoya Society International
Christine M. Burton
P.O. Box 54271
Atlanta, GA 30308
The Hoyan (4)

Write for information.

Hydroponic Society of America
Gene Brisbon
P.O. Box 6067
Concord, CA 94553
(415) 682-4195
Hydroponic/Soilless Grower (6)
Annual Conference Proceedings (1)

Nonmembers may buy a copy of the Annual Conference Proceedings -- write for information.
❏ Annual Dues: in US & CAN US$25, OV US$35 (IMO)
❏ Chapters: 3
❏ Privileges: CONVENTIONS BOOKS TRIPS

Hydroponic Society of Victoria
Miss Eva Best
6/38 Maroo Street
Hughesdale, VIC, Australia 3166
(03) 729-5170
Newsletter (10)

Formed to encourage hobbyists and commercial growers.
❏ Annual Dues: A$15 (IMO)
❏ Privileges: CONVENTIONS LIBRARY TRIPS

Idaho Native Plant Society
P.O. Box 9451
Boise, ID 83707
Sage Notes (6)

❏ Annual Dues: $8
❏ Chapters: 3
❏ Privileges: CONVENTIONS TRIPS

Indigenous Bulb Growers Association of South Africa
Paul F. X. von Stein
3 The Bend
Edgemead, South Africa 7441
021 581 690
Bulletin (1)

Society devoted to the conservation of South African bulbous plants by means of cultivation and propagation.
❏ Annual Dues: in US, CAN, & OV US$10 (IMO or bank notes)
❏ Privileges: CONVENTIONS SEEDS EXHIBITS TRIPS

Indoor Citrus & Rare Fruit Society
176 Coronado Avenue
Los Altos, CA 94022
IC&RF Society Newsletter (4)

One of the very best newsletters, full of information and interest and letters from around the world. Will help members find information, seeds and plants of citrus and rare fruit.
❏ Annual Dues: in US $15, OV US$18 (IMO)
❏ Privileges: BOOKS SEEDS

Indoor Gardening Society of America
Robert D. Morrison
5305 S.W. Hamilton Street
Portland, OR 97221
(503) 292-9785
Indoor Garden (6)

Formerly the Indoor Light Gardening Society of America. Chapters have plant sales and exhibits; members grow plants under lights, on windowsills and in greenhouses.
❏ Annual Dues: in US & CAN US$15, OV US$17 (IMO)
❏ Chapters: 17
❏ Privileges: BOOKS SEEDS PLANTS

International Aroid Society
Bruce McManus
P.O. Box 43-1853
Miami, FL 33143
(305) 271-3767
Aroideana (4)
Newsletter (11)

Society devoted to members of the arum family (Araceae).
❏ Annual Dues: in US $15, in CAN & OV US$18 (IMO)
❏ Privileges: CONVENTIONS LIBRARY BOOKS TRIPS

International Asclepiad Society
Mrs. M. Thompson
10 Moorside Terrace, Driglington
Bradford, England BD11 1HX

☐ Annual Dues: £8

International Camellia Society
Thomas H. Perkins III
P.O. Box 750
Brookhaven, MS 39601-0750
(601) 833-7351
International Camellia Journal (1)
Mid-Year Newsletter (1)

Meets every other year in different host countries; dues may be paid in local currency through regional membership representatives.
☐ Annual Dues: $9
☐ Privileges: CONVENTIONS EXHIBITS

International Carnivorous Plant Society
Leo Song, Co-Editor
c/o Fullerton Arboretum, Calif. State Univ.
Fullerton, CA 92634
Carnivorous Plant Newsletter (4)

Has a very interesting magazine with color photographs and articles on plant hunting.
☐ Annual Dues: in US and CAN US$10, OV US$15 (IMO)
☐ Privileges: SEEDS

The International Clematis Society
Mrs. Hildegard Widman-Evison
Clematis Nursery, Domarie Vin., Les Sauvages
St. Sampson's, Channel Islands
Newsletter (2)

Has meetings in various countries. St. Sampson's is in Guernsey -- didn't have room to fit it in.
☐ Annual Dues: £5 + £2 entrance fee
☐ Privileges: CONVENTIONS SEEDS EXHIBITS

International Dwarf Fruit Tree Association
303 Dept. of Horticulture
Michigan State Univ.
East Lansing, MI 48824
(517) 355-5200

Write for information.

International Geranium Society
4610 Druid Street
Los Angeles, CA 90032-3202
Geraniums around the World (4)

☐ Annual Dues: $12.50
☐ Chapters: 8
☐ Privileges: CONVENTIONS BOOKS SEEDS

International Golden Fossil Tree Society
Clayton A. Fawkes, Pres.
201 W. Graham Avenue
Lombard, IL 60148
(708) 627-5636
Newsletter (irregular)

New society for lovers of ginkgo trees.
☐ Annual Dues: $2
☐ Privileges: CONVENTIONS

International Lilac Society
Walter W. Oakes
P.O. Box 315
Rumford, ME 04276
(207) 562-7453
Lilacs (4)
Proceedings (1)

Publishes a booklet on lilac culture, US$1 ppd.
☐ Annual Dues: in US & CAN US$10 (IMO or US bills)
☐ Privileges: CONVENTIONS PLANTS

International Oak Society
Steven Roesch
14870 Kingsway Drive
New Berlin, WI 53151
(414) 786-0383

A brand-new society formed to increase the number of oak species in cultivation and to encourage the hybridization of oaks. At present it functions mainly as a seed exchange.
☐ Annual Dues: No dues at present
☐ Garden: Collections in development
☐ Privileges: SEEDS

International Oleander Society
Elizabeth S. Head, Corr. Secy.
P.O. Box 3431
Galveston, TX 77552-0431
(409) 762-9334
Nerium News (4)

☐ Annual Dues: $5 (IMO)
☐ Garden: One is being planned in Galveston, TX
☐ Privileges: SEEDS TRIPS

International Ornamental Crabapple Society
Thomas L. Green
Morton Arboretum
Lisle, IL 60532
(312) 968-0074
Crab Gab (4)

☐ Annual Dues: $15
☐ Privileges: CONVENTIONS

The International Palm Society
Mrs. Lynn McKamey
P.O. Box 368
Lawrence, KS 66044
(913) 843-1235
Principes (4)

Members in seventy countries. Seeds sold to members at a nominal fee.
❏ Annual Dues: in US $20, in CAN & OV US$25 (IMO)
❏ Chapters: 16
❏ Privileges: CONVENTIONS BOOKS SEEDS PLANTS EXHIBITS TRIPS TOURS

International Tropical Fern Society
Elaine Spear
8720 S.W. 34th Street
Miami, FL 33165
(305) 221-0502
Chapter Bulletins

❏ Annual Dues: $6 to $10; varies by chapter
❏ Chapters: 21
❏ Garden: Emerald Forest, 8720 S.W. 34th Street, Miami, FL
❏ Privileges: CONVENTIONS LIBRARY BOOKS SEEDS PLANTS EXHIBITS TRIPS TOURS

International Water Lily Society
Charles B. Thomas
P.O. Box 104
Buckeystown, MD 21717
(301) 874-5373
Water Garden Journal (4)

❏ Annual Dues: $15
❏ Privileges: CONVENTIONS LIBRARY TOURS

Kansas Wildflower Society
Virginia Hocker
Mulvane Art Center, Washburn Univ.
Topeka, KS 66611
(913) 296-6324
Newsletter (4)

❏ Annual Dues: $15
❏ Privileges: CONVENTIONS BOOKS SEEDS TRIPS

The KUSA Society
Lorenz Schaller
P.O. Box 761
Ojai, CA 93023
The Cerealist (2)

A new society interested in the preservation of ancient seed crops and their potential for use as human food. Also sells ancient grain varieties through the KUSA Foundation; see Section A.
❏ Annual Dues: $25

Long Island Horticultural Society
Donald Brodman, Pres.
44 North Kings Avenue
Lindenhurst, NY 11757
(516) 884-1679
Newsletter (11)

Society has symposia for members, an annual picnic and plant sales and exhibits.
❏ Privileges: PLANTS EXHIBITS

Los Angeles International Fern Society
P.O. Box 90943
Pasadena, CA 91109-0943
LAIFS Journal
Monthly Fern Lesson

Has a spore store and round-robins on various subjects. Also holds educational programs.
❏ Annual Dues: $15
❏ Privileges: BOOKS

Louisiana Native Plant Society
Richard Johnson, Pres.
Route 1, Box 151
Saline, LA 71070

Write for information.
❏ Chapters: 2

The Magnolia Society, Inc.
Phelan A. Bright
907 S. Chestnut Street
Hammond, LA 70403-5102
(504) 542-9477
Magnolia (2)

The society will accept payment by International Money Order or bank draft in US dollars.
❏ Annual Dues: in US $15, in CAN & OV US$18
❏ Privileges: CONVENTIONS LIBRARY SEEDS TOURS

Manitoba Regional Lily Society
Jim Russell
P.O. Box 21
Winnipeg, MB, Canada R3C 2G1
(204) 453-7543

Discovered too late to contact; write for information.
❏ Privileges: PLANTS EXHIBITS

Marigold Society of America, Inc.
Jeannette Lowe
P.O. Box 112
New Britain, PA 18901
(215) 348-5273
Amerigold Newsletter (4)

❏ Annual Dues: in US, CAN, & OV US$12 (IMO, PC in US$)
❏ Garden: AHS Gardens, River Farm, Mt. Vernon, VA
❏ Privileges: CONVENTIONS

Massachusetts Horticultural Association
300 Massachusetts Avenue
Boston, MA 02115
(617) 536-9280
Horticulture (12)

Has sponsored the New England Spring Flower Show in Boston for 119 years.
❐ Annual Dues: in US $45
❐ Privileges: LIBRARY BOOKS EXHIBITS TRIPS

Master Gardeners International Corp. (MaGIC)
2904 Cameron Mills Road
Alexandria, VA 22302
(703) 683-6485
MaGIC Lantern (4)

New society for trained Master Gardeners, a fast-growing group. Hopes to offer many privileges to members, such as a library, book sales, seed exchanges, exhibits, field trips and horticultural tours. The newsletter will be a clearinghouse for information on groups nationwide.
❐ Annual Dues: in US, CAN, & OV US$10 (IMO)
❐ Privileges: CONVENTIONS TRIPS TOURS

Michigan Botanical Club
Mathaei Botanical Gardens
1800 Dixboro Road
Ann Arbor, MI 48105

Write for information.

Minnesota Native Plant Society
Robin Fox, Univ. of Minnesota
1445 Gortner Avenue, 220 BioSci Center - MNPS
St. Paul, MN 55108
Minnesota Plant Press (3)

Write for information.
❐ Annual Dues: in US, CAN, & OV US$8 (IMO)
❐ Privileges: CONVENTIONS SEEDS PLANTS TRIPS

Minnesota State Horticultural Society
161 Alderman Hall
Univ. of Minnesota, 1970 Folwell Avenue
St. Paul, MN 55108
(612) 624-7752
Minnesota Horticulturist (9)

Of interest to all Northern gardeners.
❐ Annual Dues: in US and CAN US$20, OV US$25 (IMO)
❐ Privileges: CONVENTIONS LIBRARY BOOKS PLANTS EXHIBITS TRIPS TOURS

Mississippi Native Plant Society
Victor A. Rudis
P.O. Box 2151
Starkville, MS 39759
(601) 324-0430
Newsletter (4)

❐ Annual Dues: $5
❐ Privileges: CONVENTIONS BOOKS SEEDS PLANTS TRIPS

Missouri Native Plant Society
John Darel, Treas.
P.O. Box 176, Dept. of Natural Resources
Jefferson City, MO 65102

Write for information.

National Auricula & Primula Society
Mr. B. Goalby
99 Somerfield Road, Bloxwich
Walsall, W. Midlands, England
Yearbook

Has three chapters, so I've given you the address of the one in the middle.
❐ Chapters: 3

© Siskiyou Rare Plant Nursery
Artist: Baldassare Mineo

National Chrysanthemum Society (UK)
H. B. Locke
2 Lucas House, Craven Road
Rugby, Warwicks., England CV21 3HY
(0788) 69039
Bulletin (3)

Has a second display garden at Brackenhill Park, Bradford (near Leeds).
❏ Annual Dues: £9 to all (IMO)
❏ Garden: RHS Gardens, Wisley, Surrey
❏ Privileges: CONVENTIONS BOOKS EXHIBITS

National Chrysanthemum Society, Inc. (USA)
Galen L. Goss
10107 Homar Pond Drive
Fairfax Station, VA 22039-1650
(703) 978-7951
The Chrysanthemum (4)

❏ Annual Dues: in US $12.50, in CAN & OV US$16.50 (IMO)
❏ Chapters: 52
❏ Privileges: CONVENTIONS BOOKS

National Fuchsia Society
11507 E. 187th Street
Artesia, CA 90701
Fuchsia Fan (12)

Write for information; dues in Canada and overseas are higher.
❏ Annual Dues: $12

National Gardening Association
Member Subscription Service
Depot Square
Peterborough, NH 03458
(802) 863-1308
National Gardening (12)

Dedicated to teaching people to grow food. Has a seed search service, a members' answer service, group insurance rates, new books at a discount and an interesting magazine for home food gardeners.
❏ Annual Dues: in US $18, in CAN & OV US$24 (IMO)
❏ Privileges: LIBRARY BOOKS SEEDS

National Sweet Pea Society
J. R. F. Bishop
3 Chalk Farm Road, Stokenchurch
High Wycombe, Bucks., England HP14 3TB
(024 026) 2153
Bulletin (2)
Annual

By paying £3 more, you can elect yourself a vice president. All societies should consider this!!
❏ Annual Dues: in UK £9, in US, CAN & OV £15
❏ Garden: Trial Grounds, RHS Garden, Wisley, Surrey
❏ Privileges: BOOKS SEEDS PLANTS EXHIBITS TRIPS

Native Plant Society of New Mexico
Jean Heflin
443 Live Oak Loop Northeast
Albuquerque, NM 87122
(505) 356-3942
Newsletter (6)

Seed exchange to be established soon.
❏ Annual Dues: in US $8, in CAN & OV US$25 (IMO)
❏ Chapters: 5
❏ Privileges: CONVENTIONS BOOKS SEEDS PLANTS EXHIBITS TRIPS

Native Plant Society of Oregon
Mary Falconer, Memb. Chair
1920 Engel Avenue Northwest
Salem, OR 97304
Bulletin (12)

❏ Annual Dues: $10
❏ Chapters: 10
❏ Privileges: TRIPS

Native Plant Society of Texas
Dana Tucker
P.O. Box 891
Georgetown, TX 78627
(512) 863-7794
Texas Native Plant Society News (6)

❏ Annual Dues: $15
❏ Chapters: 15
❏ Privileges: CONVENTIONS SEEDS PLANTS EXHIBITS TRIPS

New England Botanical Club
Botanical Museum
Oxford Street
Cambridge, MA 02138

Write for information.

New England Garden History Society
Walter Punch, Librarian MHS
300 Massachusetts Avenue
Boston, MA 02115
(617) 536-9280

Just getting organized: call or write for information.

New England Wild Flower Society
Bee Entwisle
Hemenway Road
Framingham, MA 01701
(508) 877-7630
Wildflower Notes (1)
Newsletter (2)

Chapters in each state in New England; seed exchanges with botanical gardens.
❏ Annual Dues: $30
❏ Chapters: 6
❏ Garden: Garden-in-the-Woods, Framingham, MA
❏ Privileges: CONVENTIONS LIBRARY BOOKS SEEDS PLANTS EXHIBITS TRIPS TOURS

New Jersey Native Plant Society
Frelinghuysen Arboretum
P.O. Box 1295 R
Morristown, NJ 07960

Write for information.

The New Zealand Alpine Garden Society
Mrs. Ann Lemon
17 Courage Road
Amberley, Canterbury, New Zealand
Christ Ch. 842-170
Bulletin (2)

❏ Annual Dues: NZ$12 (IMO)
❏ Privileges: CONVENTIONS LIBRARY SEEDS PLANTS EXHIBITS TRIPS TOURS

New Zealand Camellia Society
New Zealand Camellia Bulletin (4)

You can join through the Southern California Camellia Society, as US agent,
c/o M. Schmidt, 1523 Highland Oaks Drive, Arcadia, CA 91006.
❏ Annual Dues: NZ$10
❏ Chapters: 19
❏ Privileges: CONVENTIONS EXHIBITS

New Zealand Fuchsia Society, Inc.
Miss Joan Byres
P.O. Box 11-082
Ellerslie, Auckland, New Zealand 5
Auckland 872-118
Newsletter (11)

❏ Annual Dues: in US & CAN NZ$6 (IMO)
❏ Privileges: LIBRARY BOOKS PLANTS EXHIBITS TRIPS

Newfoundland Alpine & Rock Garden Club
Janet Story
c/o Memorial University Botanical Garden
St. John's, NF, Canada A1C 5S7
(709) 737-8590

A chapter of the American Rock Garden Society.
❏ Annual Dues: In Canada: $5
❏ Privileges: SEEDS TRIPS

North American Fruit Explorers
Jill Vorbeck, Memb. Chair
Route 1, Box 94
Chapin, IL 62628
(217) 245-7589
Pomona (4)

Dedicated fruit growers who locate, test and preserve special fruit and nut
varieties. New members receive the "Handbook for Fruit Explorers." Scion
and budstock exchanges, computer programs for test groups.
❏ Annual Dues: New members in US $11, in CAN & OV US$15
❏ Privileges: CONVENTIONS LIBRARY

North American Gladiolus Council
Peter Welcenbach
11102 W. Calumet Road
Milwaukee, WI 53224
(414) 354-7859
Bulletin (4)

❏ Annual Dues: in US & CAN US$8.50, OV US$11 (IMO)
❏ Chapters: 57
❏ Privileges: CONVENTIONS

North American Heather Society
Alice E. Knight
62 Elma-Monte Road
Elma, WA 98541
(206) 482-3258
Heather News (4)

❏ Annual Dues: in US $10, in CAN & OV US$10 (IMO)
❏ Chapters: 2
❏ Privileges: CONVENTIONS LIBRARY BOOKS PLANTS

North American Lily Society, Inc.
Dr. Robert Gilman, Secy-Treas.
P.O. Box 272
Owatonna, MN 55060
(507) 451-2170
Lily Yearbook (1)
Quarterly Bulletin (4)

❏ Annual Dues: $12.50 (IMO)
❏ Privileges: CONVENTIONS LIBRARY SEEDS EXHIBITS

**North Carolina Wild Flower
  Preservation Society**
Mrs. S. M. Cozart
900 W. Nash Street
Wilson, NC 27893
(919) 243-2048
Newsletter (2)

❏ Annual Dues: $7.50
❏ Garden: North Carolina Botanical Garden, Chapel Hill, NC
❏ Privileges: CONVENTIONS SEEDS TRIPS

Northern Horticultural Society
Harlow Car Gardens, Crag Lane
Harrowgate, England HG3 1QB
(0923) 65418
Northern Gardener (4)

Devoted to hardy plants. The Study Centre at Harlow Car includes a herbarium
and a reference collection of botanical specimens. The magazine would be of
interest to all in cold climates.
❏ Annual Dues: £5 (IMO)
❏ Garden: Harlow Car Gardens, Crag Lane, Harrowgate
❏ Privileges: LIBRARY SEEDS PLANTS EXHIBITS TOURS

Northern Nevada Native Plant Society
Loring Williams
P.O. Box 8965
Reno, NV 89507
(702) 358-7759
Newsletter (9)
Menzelia (irregular)

❏ Annual Dues: $7.50 (IMO)
❏ Privileges: LIBRARY BOOKS SEEDS PLANTS EXHIBITS TRIPS

Northern Nut Growers Association
Kenneth Bauman
9870 S. Palmer Road
New Carlisle, OH 45344
(513) 878-2610
Nutshell (4)
Annual Report

Publishes "Nut Tree Culture in North America," available for $17.50 ppd. in the US and Canada and $18.50 ppd. overseas.
❏ Annual Dues: in US & CAN US$15, OV US$17 (IMO)
❏ Privileges: CONVENTIONS BOOKS

Northwest Fuchsia Society
Joan Hampton
P.O. Box 33071
Seattle, WA 98133-0071
(206) 364-7735
The Fuchsia Flash (10)

❏ Annual Dues: in US $8, in CAN & OV US$10 (IMO)
❏ Chapters: 11
❏ Garden: Test Gardens at Marysville and Seattle, WA
❏ Privileges: CONVENTIONS LIBRARY BOOKS PLANTS EXHIBITS TRIPS

Northwest Horticultural Society
Mrs. Leo Cunningham
V. Isaacson Hall, Univ. of Washington, GF-15
Seattle, WA 98195
(206) 527-1794
Pacific Horticulture (4)

❏ Annual Dues: $20
❏ Privileges: SEEDS PLANTS EXHIBITS TRIPS TOURS

Northwest Perennial Alliance
Bob Lilly
P.O. Box 45574, University Station
Seattle, WA 98145
(206) 525-6245

❏ Annual Dues: in US & CAN US$10
❏ Privileges: CONVENTIONS PLANTS

Ohio Native Plant Society
A. K. Malmquist
6 Louise Drive
Chagrin Falls, OH 44022
(216) 338-6622
On the Fringe (6)

❏ Annual Dues: in US & CAN US$10
❏ Chapters: 8
❏ Privileges: CONVENTIONS BOOKS SEEDS PLANTS TRIPS

Ontario Regional Lily Society
Mrs. Gordon Brown
RR 1
Harley, ON, Canada N0E 1E0
Newsletter (3)

Has an annual garden picnic at the Royal Botanical Gardens, Hamilton, ON.
❏ Annual Dues: C$3
❏ Privileges: CONVENTIONS LIBRARY PLANTS EXHIBITS

Pacific Northwest Lily Society
Mary Hoffman
19766 S. Impala Lane
Oregon City, OR 97045
Bulletin (3 or 4)

❏ Annual Dues: in US, CAN, & OV US$5 (IMO)
❏ Privileges: CONVENTIONS LIBRARY BOOKS PLANTS EXHIBITS TRIPS

Pacific Orchid Society
Barbara Schafer
P.O. Box 1091
Honolulu, HI 96808
Na Okika O Hawaii/Hawaiian Orchid Journal (4)

❏ Annual Dues: in US $10, in CAN & OV US$15 (PC or IMO)
❏ Privileges: LIBRARY PLANTS EXHIBITS TRIPS

The Pennsylvania Horticultural Society
Elizabeth Gullan
325 Walnut Street
Philadelphia, PA 19106
(215) 625-8250
Green Scene (6)
PHS News (11)

Has a 14,000-volume horticultural library; offers workshops, lectures and other services. "Green Scene" is available on subscription for $8 a year.
❏ Annual Dues: $35 (IMO) for individuals
❏ Garden: 325 Walnut Street, Philadelphia, PA
❏ Privileges: LIBRARY EXHIBITS TRIPS TOURS

Pennsylvania Native Plant Society
1806 Commonwealth Building
316 Fourth Avenue
Pittsburgh, PA 15222

Write for information.

Peperomia Society International
5240 W. 20th Street
Vero Beach, FL 32960
The Gazette (4)

❏ Annual Dues: in US & CAN US$5, OV US$8
❏ Garden: Glasshouse Works, Stewart, OH
❏ Privileges: LIBRARY SEEDS

Permaculture Institute of North America
4649 Sunnyside North
Seattle, WA 98103
(206) 547-6838
The Permaculture Activist (4)

❏ Annual Dues: $25

Plant Amnesty
Cass Turnbull
906 N.W. 87th Street
Seattle, WA 98117
Newsletter (6)

A liberation group dedicated to freeing trees and shrubs from the mutilation
of poor pruning practices.
❏ Annual Dues: $10

The Plumeria Society of America, Inc.
P.O. Box 22791
Houston, TX 77227-2791
Newsletter (4)

Write for information.

Puget Sound Dahlia Association
Roger L. Walker
P.O. Box 5602
Bellevue, WA 98006
Bulletin (12)
Dahlias of Today (1)

This group's annual, "Dahlias of Today," is terrific; it is available from
Mrs. Dorothy Rasmussen, 14021 Sunnyside Avenue North, Seattle, WA 98133, for
$3 ppd., $1 more overseas, $3 more Air Mail. Also sold by dahlia nurseries.
❏ Annual Dues: $10 (members in WA and OR only)
❏ Garden: Volunteer Park in Seattle, WA
❏ Privileges: PLANTS

Rare Fruit Council International, Inc.
Carolyn Welch Betts
P.O. Box 561914
Miami, FL 33256
(305) 663-2852
Tropical Fruit News (12)
Yearbook

Has plant exchanges; publishes a cookbook for $10.95.
❏ Annual Dues: $25
❏ Chapters: 3
❏ Privileges: LIBRARY SEEDS PLANTS EXHIBITS

Rare Fruit Council of Australia
P.O. Box 707
Cairns, NQ, Australia 4870

Write for information.

Rare Pit & Plant Council
Debbie Peterson
251 W. 11th Street
New York, NY 10014
The Pits Newsletter

Society membership is strictly limited because members meet in each other's
living rooms; however, their lively newsletter, devoted to growing exotic
fruit and ornamentals indoors, is available by subscription.
❏ Annual Dues: $10

The Reblooming Iris Society
Howard L. Brookins
N75 W14257 North Point Road
Menomonee Falls, WI 53051
Bulletin (2)

A new section of the American Iris Society; members are encouraged to join
the AIS as well.
❏ Annual Dues: $3

Rhododendron Society of Canada
R. S. Dickhout
5200 Timothy Crescent
Niagara Falls, ON, Canada L2E 5G3
(416) 357-5981
Bulletin (2)

❏ Annual Dues: in US, CAN, & OV C$15 (IMO)
❏ Chapters: 3
❏ Privileges: CONVENTIONS LIBRARY BOOKS SEEDS PLANTS EXHIBITS

Rhododendron Species Foundation
Pam Elms
P.O. Box 3798
Federal Way, WA 98063-3798
(206) 661-9377
RSF Newsletter (4)

Offers classes, lectures and an independent study course by mail and has a
rhododendron library. Also has pollen distribution for hybridizers. It has
created a living collection of over 1,800 rhododendrons, and also displays
the Weyerhaeuser Pacific Rim Bonsai Collection.
❏ Annual Dues: $30 (IMO)
❏ Garden: Rhododendron Species Foundation, Federal Way, WA
❏ Privileges: CONVENTIONS LIBRARY BOOKS SEEDS PLANTS EXHIBITS TOURS

Rose Hybridizers Association
Larry D. Peterson
3245 Wheaton Road
Horseheads, NY 14845
(607) 562-8592
Newsletter (4)

☐ Annual Dues: in US & CAN US$7, OV US$7 (IMO)
☐ Garden: Test Garden, American Rose Center, Shreveport, LA
☐ Privileges: CONVENTIONS LIBRARY SEEDS

The Royal Horticultural Society
Membership Secretary
80 Vincent Square
London, England SW1P 2PE
The Garden (12)

Many plant and flower shows in London, including the granddaddy of them all, the Chelsea Flower Show. Also has a wonderful library at Vincent Square.
☐ Annual Dues: £19 (payment in US$ accepted)
☐ Garden: RHS Garden, Wisley, Surrey
☐ Privileges: LIBRARY BOOKS SEEDS PLANTS EXHIBITS TRIPS TOURS

The Royal National Rose Society
The Secretary
Chiswell Green
St. Albans, Herts., England AL2 3NR
(0727) 50461
The Rose (4)

Claims to be one of the oldest, largest and friendliest plant societies in the world.
☐ Annual Dues: £8 (IMO)
☐ Garden: The Gardens of the Rose, St. Albans
☐ Privileges: CONVENTIONS LIBRARY BOOKS EXHIBITS TOURS

Sacramento Perennial Garden Club
Betty Morris
2833 Ione Street
Sacramento, CA 95821
(916) 487-7662

☐ Annual Dues: $5
☐ Privileges: BOOKS SEEDS PLANTS EXHIBITS TRIPS

The Saintpaulia and Houseplant Society
Miss N. Tanburn
82 Rossmore Court, Park Road
London, England NW1 6XY
Quarterly Bulletin

Found too late to contact; write for information.
☐ Annual Dues: in US & CAN, £3, Airmail £4; in UK, £2

Saintpaulia International
Roberta M. Hale
1650 Cherry Hill Road
State College, PA 16803
Saintpaulia International News (6)

☐ Annual Dues: in US $11, in CAN & OV US$13.50
☐ Privileges: CONVENTIONS SEEDS PLANTS EXHIBITS

San Diego Historical Society
    Horticultural Heritage Committee
P.O. Box 81825
San Diego, CA 92138
Trellis

Active historical garden restoration group.
☐ Annual Dues: in US: $6

Saskatchewan Orchid Society
Paul Junk
P.O. Box 411
Saskatoon, SK, Canada SFK 3L3
(306) 374-2978
Newsletter (6)

☐ Annual Dues: C$10
☐ Privileges: LIBRARY BOOKS PLANTS TRIPS TOURS

Scottish Rock Garden Club
Miss K. M. Gibb
21 Merchiston Park
Edinburgh, Scotland EH10 4PW
031-229-8138
The Rock Garden (2)
Year Book

Has a very extensive seed exchange.
☐ Annual Dues: in US $20, in CAN & OV £9 (IMO or PC)
☐ Privileges: CONVENTIONS LIBRARY BOOKS SEEDS PLANTS EXHIBITS TRIPS TOURS

Seattle Tilth Association
4649 Sunnyside Avenue North
Seattle, WA 98115
(206) 633-0451
Sea-Tilth (12)

Part of a regional association in Pacific Northwest, promoting sustainable regional agriculture; may be able to put you in touch with groups in your part of the Northwest. Also has a Tilth Placement Service to place workers on organic farms (P.O. Box 95261, Seattle, WA 98145-2261). Local members only; no membership services by mail.
☐ Annual Dues: $12
☐ Garden: Urban Agricultural Center, 4649 Sunnyside Avenue North
☐ Privileges: CONVENTIONS LIBRARY BOOKS SEEDS PLANTS EXHIBITS TRIPS

The Sedum Society
Micki Crozier
Route 2, Box 130
Sedgwick, KS 67135
(316) 796-0496
Newsletter (4)

A new group; has seed and cutting exchanges. Write for information.
☐ Garden: Northumberland, England
☐ Privileges: SEEDS

Seed Savers Exchange
c/o Kent Whealy
Rural Route 3, Box 239
Decorah, IA 52101
(319) 382-5990
Winter Yearbook
Newsletter (2)

Sells the "Garden Seed Inventory" ($17.50 ppd.) and the "Fruit, Berry and Nut Inventory" ($19.00 ppd.), which are excellent source books for heirloom varieties. Is also planning a Heritage Farm near Decorah, IA.
❏ Annual Dues: in US $15, in CAN US$20, OV US$30 (IMO)
❏ Privileges: BOOKS SEEDS

Sempervivum Fanciers Association
Dr. C. William Nixon
37 Oxbow Lane
Randolph, MA 02368
(617) 963-6737
Newsletter (4)

Largely the effort of Dr. Nixon; not a formal "association."
❏ Annual Dues: in US$14; in CAN & OV US$15 (IMO)

The Sempervivum Society
Peter J. Mitchell
11 Wingle Tye Road
Burgess Hill, W. Sussex, England RH15 9HR
(0444) 236848
Newsletter (3)

Sells a cultural guide, "Houseleeks -- An Introduction," for £1.
❏ Annual Dues: in US & OV, £2.50 (IMO)
❏ Garden: Burgess Hill, West Sussex, England
❏ Privileges: CONVENTIONS LIBRARY BOOKS PLANTS EXHIBITS

The Society for Growing Australian Plants
Glen Harvey
5 Ellesmere Road
Crymea Bay, NSW, Australia 2227
Australian Plants (4)

Magazine available on separate subscription for US$9 a year; send an International Money Order.
❏ Annual Dues: OV US$15 (IMO)
❏ Privileges: CONVENTIONS LIBRARY BOOKS SEEDS PLANTS EXHIBITS TRIPS TOURS

The Society for Japanese Irises
Mrs. Andrew C. Warner
16815 Falls Road
Upperco, MD 21155
(301) 374-4788
The Review (2)

A section of the American Iris Society. Private gardens are open for display to members to show well-grown plants and newer varieties.
❏ Annual Dues: $3.50
❏ Privileges: CONVENTIONS BOOKS PLANTS EXHIBITS TRIPS TOURS

Society for Louisiana Irises
P.O. Box 40175
Lafayette, LA 70504
(318) 264-6203
Newsletter (4)
Special Bulletins (occasional)

Established in 1941, the society meets each April in Lafayette, LA, and has published a book on Louisiana irises.
❏ Annual Dues: in US $7.50
❏ Privileges: CONVENTIONS BOOKS EXHIBITS TRIPS

Society for Pacific Coast Native Iris
c/o Mrs. Dorothy Foster
977 Meredith Court
Sonoma, CA 95476
SPCNI Almanac (2)

A section of the American Iris Society.
❏ Annual Dues: $4
❏ Privileges: SEEDS

Solanaceae Enthusiasts
John M. Riley
3370 Princeton Court
Santa Clara, CA 95051
(408) 241-9440
Solanaceae Quarterly (4)

Group is devoted to edible members of the Solanaceae family, for growers of rare fruit.
❏ Annual Dues: in US $10, in CAN US$12, OV US$15 (PC)
❏ Privileges: BOOKS SEEDS

South African Fuchsia Society
P.O. Box 193
Hilton, South Africa 3245
(011) 869-7697 RSA
The South African Fuchsia Fanfare (3)

❏ Annual Dues: R10 (IMO)
❏ Chapters: 5
❏ Privileges: LIBRARY PLANTS EXHIBITS TRIPS

Southern California Botanists
Alan Romspert
Dept. of Biology, Fullerton State Univ.
Fullerton, CA 92634
(714) 449-7034
Crossosoma (6)

Devoted to the study, preservation and conservation of native plants of California. Has an annual symposium and pot luck.
❏ Annual Dues: Individuals in US, CAN, & OV US$8 (PC or IMO)
❏ Privileges: CONVENTIONS BOOKS PLANTS TRIPS

Southern California Horticultural Institute
Joan DeFato
P.O. Box 49798, Barrington Station
Los Angeles, CA 90049-0798
(818) 567-1496
Pacific Horticulture (4)
Monthly Bulletin

❏ Annual Dues: $18
❏ Privileges: BOOKS PLANTS EXHIBITS TRIPS

Southern Fruit Fellowship
David E. Ulmer
Route 3, Box 268
Columbus, MS 39701
(601) 328-2189
Newsletter (4)

☐ Annual Dues: in US $5
☐ Privileges: CONVENTIONS SEEDS PLANTS EXHIBITS TRIPS

Southern Garden History Society
Mrs. Zachary T. Bynum, Jr.
Old Salem, Inc., Box F, Salem Station
Winston-Salem, NC 27101
(919) 724-3125
News Bulletin (4)

☐ Annual Dues: $15 (IMO)
☐ Privileges: CONVENTIONS PLANTS

Southern Illinois Native Plant Society
Dr. Robert Mohlenbrock
Botany Dept., Southern Illinois Univ.
Carbondale, IL 52901

Write for information.

Species Iris Group of North America
Florence E. Stout
150 N. Main Street
Lombard, IL 60148
(312) 627-1421
SIGNA (2)

Has an excellent seed exchange.
☐ Annual Dues: in US, CAN, & OV US$3.50 (PC or IMO)
☐ Privileges: CONVENTIONS SEEDS EXHIBITS TRIPS TOURS

Tennessee Native Plant Society
Dept. of Botany
Univ. of Tennessee
Knoxville, TN 37996
(615) 974-2256
Newsletter (6)

☐ Annual Dues: $5
☐ Privileges: CONVENTIONS SEEDS TRIPS TOURS

The Terrarium Association
Robert C. Baur
P.O. Box 276
Newfane, VT 05345
(802) 365-4721

Not really a society, but a source of information and literature on terrarium growing.

Texas State Horticultural Society
Norman Winter
4348 Carter Creek, Suite 101
Bryan, TX 77802
(409) 846-1752
Texas Horticulturist (12)

☐ Annual Dues: $10
☐ Privileges: CONVENTIONS

The Toronto Bonsai Society
495 Deloraine Avenue
Toronto, ON, Canada M5M 2C1
(416) 782-2403

Write for information.

The Toronto Cactus & Succulent Club
Betty Naylor
P.O. Box 334
Brampton, ON, Canada L6V 2L3
(416) 767-6433
Cactus Factus (8)

☐ Annual Dues: C$15
☐ Privileges: CONVENTIONS LIBRARY SEEDS PLANTS EXHIBITS TRIPS

Toronto Gesneriad Society
70 Enfield Road
Etabicoke, ON, Canada M8W 1T9

Write for information.

Tropical Flowering Tree Society
Dolores Fugina
Fairchild Trop. Garden, 10901 Old Cutler Road
Miami, FL 33156
(305) 248-0818
Quarterly Bulletin

A new society; write for information.
☐ Annual Dues: in US $10, OV US$20

Tubers
Steve Neal
HCR 4, Box 169-D
Gainesville, MO 65655-9729
Tater Talk (2)

Group dedicated to lovers of the potato -- and who isn't!
❏ Annual Dues: $10

Utah Native Plant Society
Pam Poulsen, Treas.
3631 S. Carolyn Street
Salt Lake City, UT 84106
Sego Lily (12)

Has an annual mushroom hunt.
❏ Annual Dues: $10
❏ Privileges: SEEDS PLANTS TRIPS

Victoria Orchid Society
Rona Chalmers
P.O. Box 337
Victoria, BC, Canada V8W 2N2
(604) 656-3094
Bulletin (10)

❏ Annual Dues: C$12
❏ Privileges: CONVENTIONS LIBRARY BOOKS PLANTS EXHIBITS TRIPS

Vinifera Wine Growers Association
Mrs. Juanita Swedenburg
P.O. Box P
The Plains, VA 22171
(703) 754-8564
Journal (4)

Has an annual seminar at Middleburg, VA, at the Virginia Wine Festival, the last Saturday in August. Open to anyone interested in home or commercial viticulture and enology.
❏ Annual Dues: $17
❏ Privileges: CONVENTIONS LIBRARY BOOKS

Virginia Native Plant Society
P. H. White
P.O. Box 844
Annandale, VA 22003
Bulletin (4)

Has a good book and gift sales list for members. Publishes several cultural guides, offers a list of sources free with a long SASE.
❏ Annual Dues: US$10
❏ Chapters: 8
❏ Privileges: CONVENTIONS BOOKS PLANTS TRIPS

Washington Native Plant Society
Department of Botany, KB-15
Univ. of Washington
Seattle, WA 98195
(206) 543-1942
Douglasia (4)
Occasional Papers

Has annual backpack trips and study weekends.
❏ Annual Dues: in US, CAN, & OV US$10
❏ Chapters: 6
❏ Privileges: CONVENTIONS BOOKS PLANTS TRIPS

Western Horticultural Society
Robert Young
P.O. Box 60507
Palo Alto, CA 94306
(415) 369-2358
Pacific Horticulture (4)
Newsletter (10)

Has plant raffles at every meeting.
❏ Annual Dues: $20
❏ Privileges: BOOKS PLANTS EXHIBITS TRIPS

Woody Plant Society
Betty Ann Mech
1315 - 66th Avenue Northeast
Minneapolis, MN 55432
(612) 574-1197
Bulletin (2)

Devoted to "underused, rare and superior plants" hardy in Zone 4. Membership includes both amateurs and professional plantsmen.
❏ Annual Dues: in US & CAN $15 (North America only)
❏ Privileges: BOOKS SEEDS PLANTS TRIPS

Worcester County Horticultural Society
Virginia Rich
30 Tower Hill Road
Boylston, MA 01505
(508) 869-6111
Grow with Us (6)

The society maintains a display garden and sponsors the Worcester Spring Flower Show annually.
❏ Annual Dues: $25
❏ Garden: Tower Hill Botanic Garden, Boylston, MA
❏ Privileges: LIBRARY BOOKS PLANTS EXHIBITS TRIPS TOURS

World Pumpkin Confederation
Ray Waterman, V. Pres.
14050 Gowanda State Road
Collins, NY 14034
(716) 532-5995
Newsletter (4)

Promotes the sport/hobby of growing giant pumpkins on a worldwide level.
❏ Annual Dues: in US, CAN, & OV US$10 (IMO or bank draft)
❏ Garden: Giant Pumpkin Gardens at Collins, NY
❏ Privileges: CONVENTIONS

Wyoming Native Plant Society
Robert Dorn
P.O. Box 1471
Cheyenne, WY 82003
Newsletter (3)

Annual meeting is usually a field trip.
❏ Annual Dues: in US, CAN, & OV US$7 (IMO)
❏ Privileges: CONVENTIONS TRIPS

© Maryland Aquatic Nurseries
Artist: Anne Gaver

$$\boxed{E}$$

Magazines

Horticultural magazines and newsletters published in English and available by subscription from all over the world are listed alphabetically by title.

See the Index section for:

M. Magazine Index: an alphabetical title index to horticultural and gardening magazines and newsletters available by subscription, as well as those issued by societies.

Since subscription rates are subject to change, I'd suggest that you write for information before sending payment for a subscription.

The true gardener pulls the gardening magazines out of the mail and flops right down to read them first. They have an alarming way of multiplying — they must have invasive root systems. At any rate, they are very difficult to weed!

Be sure to notice the annual *Gardener's Index* listed in this section. It currently indexes the seven most popular gardening magazines, and does so very thoroughly, making it easy to find vaguely remembered articles, articles about particular plants and cultivars, book reviews, comparisons of garden equipment, descriptions of famous gardens and gardeners, and much more. More magazines will be added. As soon as you find you can't throw out aging magazines, you'll have to have it, and you'll wonder how you ever got along without it. Back issues are available.

A table of the symbols and abbreviations used
in this book appears on the bookmark.

Agricultural Review
North Carolina Dept. of Agriculture
P.O. Box 27647
Raleigh, NC 27611

Market bulletin.
❏ Price: Free in NC
❏ Issues/Year: 24
❏ Region: North Carolina

Agriculture -- Kentucky's Pride
Kentucky Dept. of Agriculture
Div. of Comm., 7th Floor, Capital Plaza Tower
Frankfort, KY 40601

Market bulletin.
❏ Price: Free in US
❏ Issues/Year: 4
❏ Region: Southeast, Midwest

Alabama Farmers' Bulletin
Alabama Dept. of Agriculture & Industries
P.O. Box 3336
Montgomery, AL 36193-0001

Market bulletin.
❏ Price: $5 for nonresidents of Alabama
❏ Issues/Year: 12
❏ Region: Alabama

Amaranth Today
Rodale Press, Inc.
33 E. Minor Street
Emmaus, PA 18049

Focus is on developing Amaranth as a commercial crop, as well as on its nutritional qualities.
❏ Price: in US $15, in CAN C$21, OV US$25 (IMO)
❏ Issues/Year: 4

Arnoldia
Harvard Univ., The Arnold Arboretum
The Arborway
Jamaica Plain, MA 02130

Devoted to all aspects of plants.
❏ Price: in US $12
❏ Issues/Year: 4

Australian Garden Journal
Australian Garden Journal Pty., Ltd.
P.O. Box 588
Bowral, NSW, Australia 2576

A general-interest magazine on plants, garden design and garden history.
❏ Price: in US, CAN & OV A$30 (in Australia A$18)
❏ Issues/Year: 6

Australian Orchid Review
14 McGill Street
Lewisham, NSW, Australia 2049

Back issues available for US$7.50 each; send long SASE for list.
❏ Price: in US $22 surface, $33 Air Mail
❏ Issues/Year: 4

The Avant Gardener
Horticultural Data Processors
P.O. Box 489
New York, NY 10028

Summarizes new information on all phases of gardening. Lists new sources of garden materials, sometimes has special-interest issues.
❏ Price: in US $18, in CAN & OV US$20 (IMO)
❏ Issues/Year: 12

Backyard Gardener Idea-Letter
James J. Martin
P. O. Box 605
Winfield, IL 60190

Aimed at gardeners with small vegetable, herb or flower gardens; gardening advice and related garden crafts and projects.
❏ Price: in US $15, in CAN US$16
❏ Issues/Year: 6
❏ Region: Midwest & Northern states

Baer's Garden Newsletter
John Baer's Sons
P.O. Box 328
Lancaster, PA 17603

Folksy newsletter from the editors of Baer's Agricultural Almanac; they say it's for the lively, intelligent gardener -- but aren't we all?
❏ Price: in US $4, in CAN US$5
❏ Issues/Year: 4

Bonsai Today
Stone Lantern Publishing Company
P.O. Box 816
Sudbury, MA 01776

New and attractive bonsai magazine.
❏ Price: in US $42, in CAN US$48, OV US$54
❏ Issues/Year: 6

Botanical & Herb Reviews
Steven Foster
P.O. Box 106
Eureka Springs, AR 72632

Reviews of books, periodicals and software related to botany, ethnobotany, taxonomy and herbs.
❏ Price: in US & CAN US$8, OV US$10 (IMO)
❏ Issues/Year: 4

John E. Bryan Gardening Newsletter
John E. Bryan, Inc.
300 Valley Street, Suite 206
Sausalito, CA 94965

A gardening newsletter which focuses on northern California growing conditions, but contains a lot of general information and musings as well.
❏ Price: in US & CAN US$30, OV £16 (PC)
❏ Issues/Year: 12
❏ Region: Northern California

The Bu$iness of Herbs
Northwind Farm Publications
Route 2, Box 246
Shevlin, MN 56676

Newsletter for the small herb grower and seller, expanding into more general articles about herbs of "more lasting significance."
❑ Price: in US $20, CAN US$23, OV US$28 (IMO)
❑ Issues/Year: 6

Cacti & Other Succulents
Marina J. Welham
8591 Lochside Drive
Sidney, BC, Canada V8L 1M5

Replaces the now defunct "Cactus & Succulent Information Exchange."
❑ Price: in US & CAN US$11, OV US$13 (IMO)
❑ Issues/Year: 6

Cactus & Succulent Journal
Allen Press
P.O. Box 368
Lawrence, KS 66044

Journal of the Cactus & Succulent Society available only by subscription.
❑ Price: individuals in US & CAN US$22, OV US$24 (IMO)
❑ Issues/Year: 6

California Garden
San Diego Floral Association
Caso del Prado, Balboa Park
San Diego, CA 92101-1619

For gardeners in Mediterranean climates, particularly southern California; information on garden events in the San Diego area.
❑ Price: in US $5, in CAN & OV US$8
❑ Issues/Year: 6
❑ Region: Southern California

Canadian Horticultural History
Royal Botanical Gardens (CCHHS)
P.O. Box 399
Hamilton, ON, Canada L8N 3H8

New journal will feature Canadian gardens, historical restorations, plant collectors, early nurseries, etc. Subscription is for 4 issues.
❑ Price: in US $22, in CAN C$20, OV US$22
❑ Issues/Year: Irregular

Carolina Gardener
Tri-Star Communications Inc.
P.O. Box 13269
Greensboro, NC 27415

Regional gardening suggestions and information on garden events.
❑ Price: in US $10
❑ Issues/Year: 8
❑ Region: North and South Carolina

Chestnutworks
Chestnut Growers Exchange
Route 1, Box 341
Alachua, FL 32615

Periodical devoted wholly to the chestnut: culture, propagation, research, history, recipes and sources of these magnificent trees.
❑ Price: in US $10, in CAN US$15, OV US$20 (IMO)
❑ Issues/Year: 2

Connecticut Market Bulletin
Connecticut Dept. of Agriculture
Room 234, State Office Building
Hartford, CT 06106

❑ Price: in US $7
❑ Issues/Year: 50
❑ Region: Connecticut

Country Journal
Cowles Magazines
P.O. Box 392
Mt. Morris, IL 61054

Generally a magazine on country living, but it has many articles on gardening and fruit growing. For "the person who lives in the country or wishes that they did."
❑ Price: in US $16.95, in CAN & OV US$22.95
❑ Issues/Year: 6

The Cultivar
UCSC Agroecology Program
Univ. of California
Santa Cruz, CA 95064

Newsletter for researchers, farmers and gardeners interested in agro-ecological approaches to farming and gardening.
❑ Price: Free
❑ Issues/Year: 2

Desert Plants
Boyce Thompson Southwestern Arboretum
P.O. Box AB
Superior, AZ 85273

Devoted to cultivated and wild desert plants; quite scholarly.
❑ Price: in US & CAN US$15, OV US$20
❑ Issues/Year: 4
❑ Region: Southwest

Bev Dobson's Rose Letter
Beverly R. Dobson
215 Harriman Road
Irvington, NY 10533

Newsletter for the enthusiastic rose lover, full of rose news. Updates her annual "Combined Rose List" (see book list).
❑ Price: in US & CAN US$12, OV US$18
❑ Issues/Year: 6

Dwarf Conifer Notes
Theophrastus
P.O. Box 458
Little Compton, RI 02837-0458

Theophrastus publishes books on conifers and other subjects and reprints of garden classics, will send Dwarf Conifer Notes to book buyers if they ask.
❑ Price: Sent free to buyers of books
❑ Issues/Year: Irregular

Elizabeth
Elizabeth Harris
Route 1, Box 1746AA
Davidson, NC 28036

Newsletter for North Carolina gardeners, charmingly personal in tone.
❑ Price: in US $6
❑ Issues/Year: 6
❑ Region: North Carolina

Fine Gardening
The Taunton Press
P.O. Box 355, 63 S. Main Street
Newtown, CT 06470

One of the best general-interest gardening magazines.
❑ Price: in US $22, in CAN & OV US$27 (IMO)
❑ Issues/Year: 6

Flower & Garden
Modern Handcraft, Inc.
4251 Pennsylvania
Kansas City, MO 64111

A good general-interest gardening magazine, with articles on all phases of
home gardening, regional reports and reports on new cultivars and products.
❑ Price: in US $8, in CAN & OV US$11 (IMO)
❑ Issues/Year: 6

The Four Seasons
Regional Parks Botanic Garden
Tilden Regional Park, Botanic Garden
Berkeley, CA 94708-1199

Magazine covering all aspects of California native plants, both technical and
semipopular articles. For the experienced enthusiast and botanists.
❑ Price: US$10 (IMO)
❑ Issues/Year: 4
❑ Region: California (native plants)

Garden
The Garden Society
New York Botanical Garden
Bronx, NY 10458

Published by a consortium of horticultural societies. Covers the plant
world: gardening, botany, plant sciences, art, agriculture and history; not
oriented to practical gardening.
❑ Price: in US $12.95, in CAN & OV US$15.45 (IMO)
❑ Issues/Year: 6

The Garden
Home & Law Publishing, Ltd.
Greater London House, Hampstead Road
London, England NW1 7QP

The Journal of the Royal Horticultural Society, available by subscription to
those who want it without becoming a fellow of the society.
❑ Price: £17.50 surface mail
❑ Issues/Year: 12

Garden Design
American Society of Landscape Architects
1733 Connecticut Avenue N.W.
Washington, DC 20009

The only periodical I'm aware of that concentrates on residential garden
design -- domestic, international and historical.
❑ Price: in US & CAN US$20, OV US$25
❑ Issues/Year: 4

Garden Network Monthly
Benedyk and Gabella
P.O. Box 302
Villa Park, IL 60181-0302

General-interest newsletter, consumer-oriented.
❑ Price: Write for information
❑ Issues/Year: 12
❑ Region: Harsh North Central climate

Garden Railways
Sidestreet Bannerworks, Inc.
P.O. Box 61461
Denver, CO 80206

Overseas customers may receive their issues via air mail for US$50. Magazine
for gardening railroaders -- or railroading gardeners! Emphasis is on
railroading, but it's delightful.
❑ Price: in US $18, in CAN & OV US$24 (IMO)
❑ Issues/Year: 6

The Gardener's Eye
Harvey Childs, Hurricane Publishing Company
P. O. Box 22382
Denver, CO 80222

A general-interest newletter on gardening; each issue has a pull-out calendar
to post on the wall and a feature for travelling gardeners, and offers various tools and equipment for sale.
❑ Price: in US $24, in CAN US$28, OV US$30 (IMO)
❑ Issues/Year: 12

Gardener's Guide
Carol Honey, Wayne Newell
6111 N. Marina Pacifica Drive, Key 15
Long Beach, CA 90803

A tabloid garden magazine for gardeners in southern California; contains a
calendar of events.
❑ Price: in US $12
❑ Issues/Year: 12

Gardener's Index
CompuDex Press
P. O. Box 27041
Kansas City, MO 64110

A terrific combined annual index to "American Horticulturist," "Fine
Gardening," "Flower & Garden," "Garden," "Horticulture," "National Gardening"
and "Organic Gardening" -- very thorough and useful -- a must! Available for
1986, 1987 and 1988. Additional magazines will be added for 1989.
❑ Price: in US $12
❑ Issues/Year: 1

Gardeners Share
Peggy Byers
P.O. Box 243
Columbus, IN 47273

Newsletter for gardeners with information on sources, plants and seeds for
trade, gardening hints, comparisons between catalogs. Because of the possibility of pests traveling to and fro, does not encourage subscribers outside
the US, but will send the newsletter to Canada for $20 and overseas for $30.
❑ Price: in US $15 (see notes)
❑ Issues/Year: 6

Gardening from the Heartland
Karen Johnson
P.O. Box 57
Taylor Ridge, IL 61284

A general-interest newsletter for gardeners in the Midwest, including
information on gardens to visit and gardening events.
❑ Price: $10
❑ Issues/Year: 6
❑ Region: Midwest

Gardening Newsletter by Bob Flagg
Morningside Associates
P.O. Box 2306
Houston, TX 77001

A general gardening newsletter oriented to the Sun Belt and Gulf Coast South.
☐ Price: in US $14.95
☐ Issues/Year: 12
☐ Region: Gulf Coast & Sun Belt South

Gil's Garden
Gil Whitton
1300 Casa Vista Drive
Palm Harbor, FL 34683

Includes information on tropical plants, questions and answers, gardening suggestions for each month.
☐ Price: in US $18, OV US$25
☐ Issues/Year: 12
☐ Region: Florida & Gulf Coast

The Green Thumb Companion
Robin Patten
P. O. Box 67
Prescott, IA 50859

Bimonthly newsletter about houseplants.
☐ Price: in US & CAN US$12.75, OV US$16.75 (IMO)
☐ Issues/Year: 6

Greener Gardening, Easier
E. Dexter Davis, Horticulturist
26 Norfolk Street
Holliston, MA 01746

A gardening newsletter oriented to New England; good information on gardening events in the area, book reviews, seasonal gardening advice.
☐ Price: in US $13
☐ Issues/Year: 12
☐ Region: New England

The Growing Edge Magazine
Tom Alexander & Nancy Votrain
P.O. Box 1027
Corvallis, OR 97339

"Indoor and outdoor gardening for today's high tech grower." New magazine concerned primarily with hydroponic and greenhouse growing.
☐ Price: in US $14.95, in CAN US$24.95
☐ Issues/Year: 4

Growing from Seed
Thompson & Morgan
P.O. Box 1308
Jackson, NJ 08527

Magazine on growing all types of ornamentals from seed. Nice feature is an A-to-Z Seed Raiser's Directory, giving details on germination of many seeds.
☐ Price: in US $9.95
☐ Issues/Year: 4

Hardy Enough
Joe Hebert
351 Pleasant Street, Suite 259
Northampton, MA 01060

A newsletter for adventurous gardeners who are trying to grow subtropical plants north of their usual hardiness range.
☐ Price: in US & CAN US$24, OV US$30 (IMO)
☐ Issues/Year: 5
☐ Region: USDA Zones 5 to 8

Harrowsmith (Canada)
Camden House Publishing
7 Queen Victoria Road
Camden East, ON, Canada K0K 1J0

Originated in Canada, Harrowsmith covers all phases of country living in the North.
☐ Price: in CAN C$16
☐ Issues/Year: 6

Harrowsmith (US)
Camden House Publishing
Ferry Road
Charlotte, VT 05445

Magazine on all phases of country living; quite a lot of articles on gardening, particularly growing vegetables and fruit. Northeastern emphasis.
☐ Price: in US $24, OV US$30 (IMO)
☐ Issues/Year: 6

The Herb Companion
Interweave Press, Inc.
306 N. Washington Avenue
Loveland, CO 80537

Fairly new and very attractive magazine on herbs: growing, history, cooking and crafts.
☐ Price: in US $21, in CAN & OV US$26 (IMO)
☐ Issues/Year: 6

The Herb Quarterly
Long Mountain Press, Inc.
P.O. Box 548
Boiling Springs, PA 17007

Fine publication devoted to herbs: their culture, history, use and recipes.
☐ Price: in US $24, in CAN US$27, OV US$29 (IMO)
☐ Issues/Year: 4

The Herb, Spice and Medicinal Plant Digest
Univ. of Massachusetts
Dept. of Plant & Soil Sci., Stockbridge Hall
Amherst, MA 01003

Quarterly for herb growers and those interested in uses of herbs; issues have surveys of recent literature, some technical material -- not for beginners.
☐ Price: in US, CAN & OV US$6 (PC or IMO)
☐ Issues/Year: 4

The Herbal Kitchen
Diane Lea Mathews
Box 134
Salisbury Center, NY 13454

Gardening and culinary information on herbs, herb sources and herbal lore.
☐ Price: in US $15, in CAN & OV US$18 (IMO)
☐ Issues/Year: 5

The Herbalist
1 Station Road, Foxton
Cambridge, England

English herb magazine; write for information.
☐ Issues/Year: 6

Herban Lifestyles
Stone Acre Press
84 Carpenter Road
New Hartford, CT 06057

Newsletter on "how we live, work & play with herbs." General interest.
❑ Price: in US $18, CAN US$20, OV US$30
❑ Issues/Year: 6

Himalayan Plant Journal
Primulaceae Books
Abhijit Villa, BPO Ecchey Kalimpong-734301
Darjeeling, WB, India 734301

Deals with conservation, culture, history, hybridization and identification
of Himalayan flora. Send subscription money by bank draft drawn on New York
via registered air mail.
❑ Price: in US, CAN & OV US$25 Air Mail
❑ Issues/Year: 2 or 4
❑ Region: Himalayas

Horticulture
Horticulture Limited Partnership
P.O. Box 2595
Boulder, CO 80323

A fine general-interest magazine devoted to all aspects of gardening and
horticulture.
❑ Price: in US $24, in CAN & OV US$30
❑ Issues/Year: 12

HortIdeas
HortIdeas Publishing
Route 1, Box 302
Gravel Switch, KY 40328

A gardeners' "digest": the latest research, new sources of plants and
supplies, book reviews...a tour of the home gardening world. Among the best
of current reading for all gardeners.
❑ Price: in US $15, in CAN US$17.50, OV US$20 (IMO)
❑ Issues/Year: 12

Hortus
David Wheeler, Editor
The Neuadd, Rhayader
Powys, Wales, UK LD6 5HH

Quarterly devoted to writings by distinguished British gardeners, with a
sprinking of American writers; enough reading for several evenings.
❑ Price: in US, CAN & OV US$50 (IMO, PC)
❑ Issues/Year: 4

Houseplant Forum
  A Fleur de Pot (French edition)
HortiCom, Inc.
1449 William
Sillery, PQ, Canada G1S 4G5

Newsletter well illustrated by drawings, with in-depth information on indoor
plants; helpful to beginners and those looking for new challenges.
❑ Price: in US & OV US$12.50, in CAN C$12.50 (IMO)
❑ Issues/Year: 6

The IPM Practitioner
Bio-Integral Resource Center
P.O. Box 7414
Berkeley, CA 94707

Journal covers the field of integrated pest management: research, new devel-
opments, products and publications -- oriented to professionals. Subscription rates for institutions are: in US $50, in CAN & OV US$60.
❑ Price: in US $25, in CAN & OV US$35 for individuals (IMO)
❑ Issues/Year: 10

Indian Orchid Journal
Ganesh Mani Pradhan & Udai C. Pradhan
Ganesh Villa
Kalimpong 734-301, WB, India

❑ Price: in US $15 (US$20 for Air Mail)
❑ Issues/Year: 4

International Bonsai
International Bonsai Arboretum
1070 Martin Road
West Henrietta, NY 14586-9623

Quarterly for the serious bonsai enthusiast. Add US$10 to the subscription
price for overseas air mail. They also sell video tapes and have a bonsai
arboretum; call (716) 334-2595 to arrange a visit.
❑ Price: in US & CAN US$24, OV US$30 (IMO)
❑ Issues/Year: 4

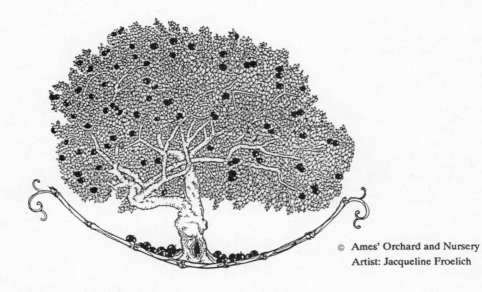

© Ames' Orchard and Nursery
Artist: Jacqueline Froelich

The Island Grower
Greenheart Publications
RR 4
Sooke, BC, Canada V0S 1N0

For all types of gardeners, especially ornamental; written by many of the garden experts of British Columbia.
❏ Price: in US $19, in CAN C$12, OV C$19 (IMO)
❏ Issues/Year: 11
❏ Region: Pacific Northwest

Journal of Garden History
Taylor & Francis, Inc.
242 Cherry Street
Philadelphia, PA 19106-1906

Write for information.
❏ Price: in US & CAN US$48
❏ Issues/Year: 4

The Kew Magazine
Basil Blackwell, Ltd.
2 Cambridge Center
Cambridge, MA 02142

Devoted to plants, with beautiful illustrations. Articles are scientific but understandable, deal with plant habitats and taxonomy. Address for UK and foreign subscriptions: 108 Cowley Road, Oxford, OX4 1JF, UK.
❏ Price: in US $47.50, in CAN £27.50, OV £32.75
❏ Issues/Year: 4

Kiwifruit Enthusiasts Journal
Friends of the Trees Society
P.O. Box 1466
Chelan, WA 98816

Issued by Friends of the Trees, sold by the issue. Information on available kiwi species, growing suggestions, sources, propagation and more.
❏ Price: in US $10, in CAN & OV US$12 (IMO)
❏ Issues/Year: 1

Lindleyana
American Orchid Society
6000 S. Olive Avenue
West Palm Beach, FL 33405

The scientific journal of the American Orchid Society.
❏ Price: in US $20, in CAN & OV US$22 (PC or IMO)
❏ Issues/Year: 4

Living Off the Land, Subtropic Newsletter
Geraventure
P.O. Box 2131
Melbourne, FL 32902-2131

A newsletter oriented toward growing edibles, particularly tropical fruits and crops; list of seeds wanted and available in each issue.
❏ Price: in US & CAN US$12, OV US$15 (IMO)
❏ Issues/Year: 5

The Maine Organic Farmer & Gardener
Maine Organic Farmers & Gardeners Association
P.O. Box 2176
Augusta, ME 04330

Tabloid periodical for organic gardeners and market farmers, lists gardens to visit, has a calendar of events.
❏ Price: in US & CAN US$8, OV US$14
❏ Issues/Year: 6

The Market Bulletin
West Virginia Dept. of Agriculture
State Capitol
Charleston, WV 25305

Subscriptions are free to West Virginia, Virginia, Ohio, Pennsylvania, Kentucky, Maryland and Washington, DC. Advertising is free to West Virginia residents only.
❏ Price: See notes
❏ Issues/Year: 12

The Metropolitan Gardener
Karen Fausch
P.O. Box 20120, London Terrace Station
New York, NY 10011

New newsletter for city gardeners, especially in the Northeast.
❏ Price: in US $16, in CAN US$18, OV US$25 (IMO)
❏ Issues/Year: 6

**New England Farm Bulletin
& Garden Gazette**
Jacob' Meadow, Inc.
P.O. Box 147
Cohasset, MA 02025

For small farmers and market gardeners; questions and answers, ads for the sale and exchange of farming equipment, animals and plants, calendar of events.
❏ Price: in US $15
❏ Issues/Year: 24
❏ Region: New England

The New England Gardener
New England Horticultural Services, Inc.
P.O. Box 2699
Nantucket, MA 02584

Newsletter on gardening in New England, "how to" and "when to," with longer articles on plants and special projects. Also covers gardening events.
❏ Price: in US $14.95, in CAN C$17.95, OV US$17.95
❏ Issues/Year: 12
❏ Region: New England

Northland Berry News
Minnesota Berry Growers Association
19060 Manning Trail North
Marine on St. Croix, MN 55047

Of interest to all who grow more than a few raspberries, strawberries or blueberries, especially "pick-your-own" operations and market gardeners.
❏ Price: $15
❏ Issues/Year: 6

The Orchid Digest
Mrs. N. H. Atkinson, Memb. Secy.
P.O. Box 916
Carmichael, CA 95609-0916

A quarterly magazine for orchid growers; many color photographs.
❏ Price: in US $18, OV US$33
❏ Issues/Year: 4

The Orchid Hunter
Terry Ferraro, Editor
2250 Beulah Road
Pittsburgh, PA 15235

New newsletter for orchid hobbyists and professionals.
❏ Price: in US $15, OV US$21
❏ Issues/Year: 12

Orchid Information Exchange
Doreen Vander Tuin
1230 Plum Avenue
Simi Valley, CA 93065

A newsletter/round-robin for orchid enthusiasts of all levels of expertise.
❏ Price: in US & CAN US$10, OV US$15 (IMO)
❏ Issues/Year: 12

The Orchid Review
The Orchid Review, Ltd.
New Gate Farm, Scotchey Lane, Stour Provost
Gillingham, Dorset, UK SP8 5LT

The orchid journal of the Royal Horticulture Society; international in scope.
❏ Price: £21.50, is US & OV US$36.50 or £23.50
❏ Issues/Year: 12

Organic Gardening
Rodale Press, Inc.
33 East Minor Street
Emmaus, PA 18098

The "old standby" has been upsized, updated and upscaled; I miss the homey touch, myself.
❏ Price: in US $18, in CAN US$23, OV US$28
❏ Issues/Year: 12

Pacific Horticulture
Pacific Horticultural Foundation
P.O. Box 680
Berkeley, CA 94701

Published by a consortium of Pacific Coast horticultural societies; a very interesting and beautiful magazine with worldwide readership.
❏ Price: in US $12, in CAN US$14, OV US$16
❏ Issues/Year: 4

The Palm Quarterly
Temperate Zone Chapter, IPS
6303 Hallwood Avenue
Verona, PA 15147

Published by the Temperate Zone Chapter of the International Palm Society; a "how-to" newsletter for the adventurous gardener growing palms outdoors in cold climates.
❏ Price: In US & CAN US$8, OV $10 (IMO)
❏ Issues/Year: 4

Permaculture with Native Plants
Curtin Mitchell
P.O. Box 38
Lorane, OR 97451

Newsletter devoted to growing and using edible and useful native plants of Pacific Northwest. Informative; carries seed exchange offers and sources.
❏ Price: Free; donation appreciated
❏ Issues/Year: 3 to 4
❏ Region: Pacific Northwest

Phalaenopsis Fancier
Doreen Vander Tuin
1230 Plum Avenue
Simi Valley, CA 93065

A new newsletter/round-robin for fanciers of Phalaenopsis orchids.
❏ Price: in US & CAN US$10, OV US$15 (IMO)
❏ Issues/Year: 12

Plants & Gardens
  Plants & Gardens News
Brooklyn Botanic Garden
1000 Washington Avenue
Brooklyn, NY 11225

Each very informative issue covers one subject in depth: herbs, rock gardens, propagation, shade gardening or other garden subjects. Very good value!
❏ Price: in US $20, in CAN & OV US$35
❏ Issues/Year: 4

The Plantsman
The Royal Horticultural Society
80 Vincent Square
London, England SW1P 2PE

Fairly scholarly coverage of all types of plants in garden use. Several well-illustrated articles in each issue; scope is international.
❏ Price: US & OV £13.50, in UK £12
❏ Issues/Year: 4

Play Dirt
Russell Webber
1102 Floradale Drive
Austin, TX 78753-3924

New newsletter "for gardeners with a sense of humor"; starts publication in spring 1990.
❏ Price: $12
❏ Issues/Year: 12

Potpourri from Herbal Acres
Pinerow Publications
P.O. Box 428
Washington Crossing, PA 18977

An herb newsletter from Phyllis Shaudys, author of "The Pleasure of Herbs." It covers all aspects of the herbal life.
❏ Price: in US & CAN $18
❏ Issues/Year: 4

Potpourri Party-Line
Berry Hill Press
7336 Berry Hill
Palos Verdes Penins., CA 90274

Newsletter with emphasis on the how-to of herbal crafts and fragrance.
❏ Price: in US $12.50
❏ Issues/Year: 4

Rosy Outlook Magazine
"Rosy" McKenney
1014 Enslen Street
Modesto, CA 95350

An independent quarterly magazine for rose lovers, very enjoyable.
❏ Price: in US & CAN US$10
❏ Issues/Year: 4

San Diego Garden Digest
Ralph Garcia
1516 W. Redwood Street, Suite 106
San Diego, CA 92101

New magazine starting too late for me to see and describe; purpose is to inform gardeners on gardening conditions in San Diego County.
❑ Price: in US $9
❑ Issues/Year: 12
❑ Region: Southern California

Small Farm News
Small Farm Center, Cooperative Extension
Univ. of California
Davis, CA 95616

A newsletter for the small market gardener. The Small Farm Center also has free and sale publications on many topics of interest to market gardeners; the list is free.
❑ Price: Free
❑ Issues/Year: 6
❑ Region: California

Solanaceae Quarterly
3370 Princeton Court
Santa Clara, CA 95051

Devoted to edible members of the Solanaceae family.
❑ Price: in US $3
❑ Issues/Year: 4

Southern Living
H. B. Flora
P.O. Box 523
Birmingham, AL 35201

Magazine has frequent articles on gardening in the South. Overseas subscription rate may be paid by check in US currency.
❑ Price: in US $21.95, in CAN & OV US$24
❑ Issues/Year: 12
❑ Region: Southeast, TX, OK, MO, DC

Spice & Herb Arts
Kaye Cude
5091 Muddy Lane
Buckingham, FL 33905

Mentioned in Living Off the Land # 76
❑ Price: in US $10
❑ Issues/Year: 6

Sunset Magazine
Lane Publishing Co.
80 Willow Road
Menlo Park, CA 94025-3691

Familiar to all in the 13 Western states; there are four regional editions, and each issue carries gardening features customized by region.
❑ Price: $14 in 13 Western states
❑ Issues/Year: 12
❑ Region: Western states

TLC ... for plants
Gardenvale Publishing Company, Ltd.
1 Pacifique
Ste Anne de Bellevue, PQ, Canada H9X 1C5

Very nice Canadian garden magazine; includes articles on both indoor and outdoor gardening and plants.
❑ Price: in US $12.95, in CAN C$12.95
❑ Issues/Year: 4
❑ Region: Canada

The Twenty-First Century Gardener
Growers Press, Inc.
P.O. Box 189
Princeton, BC, Canada V0X 1W0

For greenhouse and hydroponic growers. Foreign subscribers may receive their issues via air mail for US$10 extra. Back issues available.
❑ Price: in US $15, in CAN C$15, OV US$20
❑ Issues/Year: 4

Urban Forest Forum
American Forestry Association
P.O. Box 2000
Washington, DC 20013

For those concerned with public tree-planting policy as well as with city beautification and appropriate use of trees.
❑ Price: in US free, OV US$10 (IMO)
❑ Issues/Year: 6

The Weekend Garden Journal
Jim Bennett
P.O. Drawer 1607
Aiken, SC 29802

General-interest magazine, with articles stressing practical gardening.
❑ Price: in US $11.95, in CAN US$15.95
❑ Issues/Year: 7

Weekly Market Bulletin
New Hampshire Dept. of Agriculture
Caller Box 2042
Concord, NH 03302-2042

❑ Price: in US & CAN US$10
❑ Issues/Year: 52

The Whole Chili Pepper
Out West Publishing Company
P.O. Box 4278
Albuquerque, NM 87196

Magazine devoted to spicy foods and to growing and cooking with peppers.
❑ Price: Write for information
❑ Issues/Year: 12

© Prairie Moon Nursery
Artist: Yarrow

F

Libraries

Libraries with special horticultural collections are listed by state or province and then alphabetically by city.

Many public libraries have good collections of books on plants and gardening and will try to borrow books they don't have through interlibrary loan. Some cities, such as Philadelphia (the Library Company of Philadelphia) and San Francisco (the Mechanics Institute), have membership libraries with good horticultural collections. Some colleges and universities will allow alumni and local residents to use their libraries for an annual fee, or you can sign up for a horticultural course and get library privileges for a semester.

Many of the libraries listed, particularly those at botanical gardens, are supported by very active membership groups, horticultural societies or "friends" groups. It is well worth joining such a group to have the use of a good library, to say nothing of all the other interesting activities these groups offer.

Library Abbreviations and Conventions

Available library services are indicated as follows:

MEMBERS ONLY — only members may borrow books

REFERENCE ONLY — books do not circulate

INTERLIBRARY LOANS — other libraries may borrow books

LOANS TO PUBLIC — public may borrow books, subject to library rules

A table of the symbols and abbreviations used
in this book appears on the bookmark.

ALABAMA

Horace Hammond Memorial Library
Birmingham Botanical Gardens
2612 Lane Park Road
Birmingham, AL 35223
(205) 879-1227
Ida Burns

☐ Open: M-F 8-5
☐ Number of Books: 3,600
☐ Periodical Titles: 150
☐ Services: LOANS TO PUBLIC

ALASKA

Library
University of Alaska Museum Herbarium
907 Yukon Drive
Fairbanks, AL 99701
(907) 479-7108

Call or write for information.

ALBERTA, CANADA

Library
Faculty of Environmental Design
University of Calgary
Calgary, AB, Canada T2N 1N4

Call or write for information.

ARIZONA

Richter Memorial Library
Desert Botanical Garden
1201 N. Galvin Parkway
Phoenix, AZ 85008
(602) 941-1225
Jane B. Cole

Particularly strong collection on desert plants; also has a collection of garden catalogs.
☐ Open: M-F
☐ Number of Books: 10,000
☐ Periodical Titles: 126
☐ Services: REFERENCE ONLY INTERLIBRARY LOANS

Boyce Thompson Southwestern Arboretum Library
Boyce Thompson Southwestern Arboretum
US Highway 60, east of Superior
Superior, AZ 85273
(602) 689-2723
Carole Crosswhite

Researchers may make an appointment to use the library; call or write for information.
☐ Services: REFERENCE ONLY

BRITISH COLUMBIA, CANADA

Library
University of British Columbia Botanical Gdn.
6501 N.W. Marine Drive
Vancouver, BC, Canada V6T 1W5
(604) 228-4779
Dr. Gerald B. Straley

☐ Open: M-F 8-4:30
☐ Number of Books: 1,500
☐ Periodical Titles: 200
☐ Services: REFERENCE ONLY

VanDusen Gardens Library
Vancouver Botanical Gardens Association
5251 Oak Street
Vancouver, BC, Canada V6M 4H1
(604) 266-7194
Barbara Fox

Tu-F 10am-3pm; September to June only, W 7pm-9pm, Su 1pm-4pm; closed August. Best to call for information, as times may vary in future.
☐ Open: See notes
☐ Number of Books: 3,100
☐ Periodical Titles: 50
☐ Services: REFERENCE ONLY

CALIFORNIA

Plant Science Library
Los Angeles State & County Arboretum
301 N. Baldwin Avenue
Arcadia, CA 91007-2697
(818) 446-8251, ext. 3
Joan DeFato

❑ Open: M-F 9-5
❑ Number of Books: 13,000
❑ Periodical Titles: 175
❑ Services: REFERENCE ONLY INTERLIBRARY LOANS

Rancho Santa Ana Botanic Garden Library
1500 N. College Avenue
Claremont, CA 91711
(714) 625-8767
Beatrice M. Beck

Researchers may make special appointments. Collection strong in publications on drought-tolerant plants and water-saving concepts.
❑ Open: M-F 8-12, 1-5
❑ Number of Books: 35,000
❑ Services: REFERENCE ONLY

Fullerton Arboretum Library
Fullerton Arboretum
California State University
Fullerton, CA 92634
(714) 773-3579
Celia Kutcher

Located at the corner of Yorba Linda Boulevard and Associated Road.
❑ Open: Th 12-3; Sa 1-4
❑ Number of Books: 1,000
❑ Periodical Titles: 20
❑ Services: REFERENCE ONLY INTERLIBRARY LOANS

South Coast Plant Science Library
South Coast Botanic Garden
26300 Crenshaw Boulevard
Palos Verdes Penin., CA 90274
(213) 377-0468
Virginia Gardner

❑ Open: W 12:30-3:30, Su 1-4
❑ Number of Books: 500
❑ Periodical Titles: 10
❑ Services: MEMBERS ONLY REFERENCE ONLY

Library & Information Center
San Diego Floral Association
Room 105, Casa del Prado, Balboa Park
San Diego, CA 92103-1619
(619) 232-5762
Elsie M. Topham

Call ahead to see whether the library is open if you are coming from a distance.
❑ Open: M-F 10-3
❑ Number of Books: 3,325
❑ Periodical Titles: 35
❑ Services: REFERENCE ONLY

Helen Crocker Russell Library of Horticulture
Strybing Arboretum Society
Ninth Avenue at Lincoln Way
San Francisco, CA 94122
(415) 661-1514
Barbara M. Pitschel

❑ Open: Daily 10-4
❑ Number of Books: 14,000
❑ Periodical Titles: 300
❑ Services: REFERENCE ONLY

Botanical Library
Huntington Botanical Gardens
1151 Oxford Road
San Marino, CA 91108
(818) 405-2160
Danielle Rudeen

For the use of "qualified researchers, by appointment only."
❑ Open: M-F 8-5 by appointment
❑ Number of Books: 8,000
❑ Periodical Titles: 150
❑ Services: MEMBERS ONLY

Library
Santa Barbara Botanic Garden
1212 Mission Canyon Road
Santa Barbara, CA 93105
(805) 682-4726
Rebecca J. Eldridge

Collection strong in California native plants; members may use library for reference, general public must make appointments in advance.
❑ Open: M-F 9-5
❑ Number of Books: 7,000
❑ Periodical Titles: 150
❑ Services: REFERENCE ONLY

Wallace Sterling Library of Landscape Arch.
Filoli Center & Friends of Filoli
Canada Road
Woodside, CA 94062
(415) 364-8300
Tom Rogers

Collection in landscape architecture and garden design; researchers may call or write for an appointment.
❑ Open: By appointment only
❑ Number of Books: 3,000
❑ Services: REFERENCE ONLY

COLORADO

Helen Fowler Library
Denver Botanic Gardens
909 York Street
Denver, CO 80206
(303) 331-4000
Solange G. Gignac (ext. 32 or 33)

Members of the botanic garden get in free, may borrow from the library. Public entry fee to the garden is $3.
❑ Open: M-Sun 10-4
❑ Number of Books: 17,500
❑ Periodical Titles: 400
❑ Services: MEMBERS ONLY INTERLIBRARY LOANS

CONNECTICUT

Library
The Greenwich Garden Center
Bible Street
Cos Cob, CT 06807
(203) 869-9242
Mrs. D. M. McAvity

Call or write for information.

Bartlett Arboretum Library
Univ. of Connecticut, Dept. of Plant Science
151 Brookdale Road
Stamford, CT 06903-4199
(203) 322-6971
Gaye P. Mote

❑ Open: M-F 8:30-4
❑ Number of Books: 2,500
❑ Periodical Titles: 35
❑ Services: LOANS TO PUBLIC

DELAWARE

Wilmington Garden Center Library
Wilmington Garden Center
503 Market Street Mall
Wilmington, DE 19801
(302) 658-1913

❑ Open: M-F 10-3
❑ Number of Books: 2,000+
❑ Periodical Titles: 20
❑ Services: REFERENCE ONLY

DISTRICT OF COLUMBIA

Library
Society of American Foresters
5400 Grosvenor Lane
Washington, DC 20014
(301) 897-8720
Barry Walsh

Call or write for information.

Library
Dumbarton Oaks Garden
1703 - 32nd Street N.W.
Washington, DC 20007
(202) 342-3280
Laura Byers

Call or write for information.

Library
Landscape Architecture Foundation
1733 Connecticut Avenue N.W.
Washington, DC 20015
(202) 233-6229

Small collection focused on landscape architecture and design.
❑ Open: M-F 9-5
❑ Services: MEMBERS ONLY REFERENCE ONLY

US National Arboretum Library
USDA, Agricultural Research Service
3501 New York Avenue N.E.
Washington, DC 20002
(202) 475-4815
Robert Anderson

❑ Open: Tu, Th or by appointment
❑ Number of Books: 7,000
❑ Periodical Titles: 200
❑ Services: REFERENCE ONLY INTERLIBRARY LOANS

Office of Horticulture Branch Library
Smithsonian Institution
Arts & Industries Building, Room 2401
Washington, DC 20560
(202) 357-1544
Susan Gurney or Marca Woodhams

Library has 15,000 nursery and seed catalogs; focus is garden history and design. Also an excellent Botany Library in the Natural History Museum. Researchers may make an appointment to use the library.
❑ Open: M-F 10-5 by appointment
❑ Number of Books: 3,500
❑ Periodical Titles: 250
❑ Services: INTERLIBRARY LOANS

FLORIDA

Library
Rare Fruit & Vegetable Council
3245 College Avenue
Davie, FL 33314
(305) 942-4493
Jayne H. Morgenstern

Collection on the use of food-producing plants for permaculture.
❑ Open: Open before meetings
❑ Number of Books: 500
❑ Periodical Titles: 3
❑ Services: MEMBERS ONLY

(continued next page)

FLORIDA (continued)

Montgomery Library
Fairchild Tropical Garden
10901 Old Cutler Road
Miami, FL 33156
(305) 667-1651

❒ Open: Daily 9:30-4:30
❒ Number of Books: 7,000
❒ Services: MEMBERS ONLY REFERENCE ONLY

Research Library
Marie Selby Botanical Gardens
811 S. Palm Avenue
Sarasota, FL 33577
(813) 366-5730, ext. 39
Janet Kuhn

Members may use the library for reference by appointment.
❒ Open: By appointment only
❒ Number of Books: 4,500
❒ Periodical Titles: 140
❒ Services: MEMBERS ONLY

GEORGIA

Sheffield Botanical Library
Atlanta Botanical Garden
Piedmont Park at The Prado
Atlanta, GA 30309
(404) 876-5859
Lu Ann Schwarz, Miriam Boland

❒ Open: Tu-Sa 10-4, Su 12-5
❒ Number of Books: 1,300
❒ Periodical Titles: 25
❒ Services: REFERENCE ONLY

Cherokee Garden Library
Cherokee Garden Club
3101 Andrews Drive N.W.
Atlanta, GA 30305
(404) 261-1837
Sara Dietch

❒ Open: M-Sa 9-5
❒ Number of Books: 3,500
❒ Periodical Titles: 50
❒ Services: REFERENCE ONLY

Fernbank Science Center Library
156 Heaton Park Drive N.E.
Atlanta, GA 30307
(404) 378-4311
Mary Larsen or Shirley Brown

Hours are M 8am-5pm; Tu-Th 8am-9pm; F 8am-5pm; Sa 10am-5pm.
❒ Open: See notes
❒ Number of Books: 18,500
❒ Periodical Titles: 355
❒ Services: REFERENCE ONLY

Library
American Camellia Society
P. O. Box 1217
Fort Valley, GA 31030
(912) 967-2358
Joseph H. Pyron

Collection of books available to members or researchers by
appointment; books do not circulate.
❒ Services: REFERENCE ONLY

HAWAII

Waimea Arboretum Foundation Library
Waimea Arboretum Foundation
59-864 Kamehameha Highway
Haleiwa, HI 96712
(808) 638-8655
Shirley B. Gerum

Call to find out which days they're open; they did not specify.
❒ Open: 8-4
❒ Number of Books: 500
❒ Periodical Titles: 30
❒ Services: REFERENCE ONLY

Bishop Museum Library
Bernice Pauani Bishop Museum
1525 Bernice Street (P.O. Box 19000-A)
Honolulu, HI 96817-0916
(808) 848-4148
Marguerite K. Ashford

Library includes a horticultural collection.
❒ Open: T-F 10-3; Sat 9-12
❒ Number of Books: 90,000
❒ Periodical Titles: 2,500
❒ Services: REFERENCE ONLY INTERLIBRARY LOANS

Lyon Arboretum Reference Collection
Harold L. Lyon Arboretum
3860 Manoa Road
Honolulu, HI 96822
(808) 988-3177
Dr. Y. Sagawa, Director

Open to researchers only by prior appointment; write for information.
❒ Open: M-F 9-3, Sa 9-12
❒ Services: REFERENCE ONLY

(continued next page)

HAWAII (continued)

National Tropical Botanic Garden Library
Papalina Road, Kalaheo (P.O. Box 340, Lawai)
Kauai, HI 96765
(808) 332-7324 or 7325
Lynwood M. Hume

A strong collection on tropical plants. Members may use the library for research; visiting researchers should write ahead to make arrangements.
❒ Open: M-F 7-3:30
❒ Number of Books: 3,000
❒ Periodical Titles: 875
❒ Services: REFERENCE ONLY

ILLINOIS

Library
Field Museum of Natural History
Roosevelt Road & Lake Shore Drive
Chicago, IL 60605
(312) 922-9410

General public may use botanical and horticultural books for reference in the Reading Room.
❒ Open: M-F 9-4:30
❒ Number of Books: 40,000
❒ Services: REFERENCE ONLY INTERLIBRARY LOANS

Chicago Botanic Garden Library
Chicago Horticultural Society
Lake-Cook Road
Glencoe, IL 60022
(708) 835-8200
Virginia Henrichs

Hours are M-Sa 9am-4pm; from May to September also open Su 1pm-4pm.
❒ Open: See notes
❒ Number of Books: 10,000
❒ Periodical Titles: 200
❒ Services: MEMBERS ONLY REFERENCE ONLY

Sterling Morton Library
Morton Arboretum
Route 53
Lisle, IL 60532
(708) 719-2430
Rita M. Hassert

❒ Open: M-F 9-5, Sa 10-4
❒ Number of Books: 23,000
❒ Periodical Titles: 400
❒ Services: REFERENCE ONLY INTERLIBRARY LOANS

Agricultural Library
University of Illinois
1301 W. Gregory Drive (226 Mumford)
Urbana, IL 61801
(217) 333-2416
Carol Boast or Maria Porta

Hours M-Th 8am-10pm; F-Sa 8am-5pm; Su 1pm-10pm.
❒ Open: See notes
❒ Number of Books: 200,000
❒ Periodical Titles: 3,000
❒ Services: REFERENCE ONLY INTERLIBRARY LOANS

INDIANA

Library
Indianapolis Museum of Art Horticultural Soc.
1200 W. 38th Street
Indianapolis, IN 46208

Call or write for information.

(continued next page)

INDIANA (continued)

The Hayes Regional Arboretum Library
801 Elks Road
Richmond, IN 47374
(317) 962-3745

Please call and make an appointment to use the library.
☐ Open: Tu-Sa 1-5
☐ Number of Books: 1,000
☐ Services: REFERENCE ONLY

IOWA

Library
Bickelhaupt Arboretum
340 S. 14th Street
Clinton, IA 52732
(319) 242-4771
F. K. Bickelhaupt

☐ Open: Daily 9-6
☐ Number of Books: 800
☐ Periodical Titles: 10
☐ Services: LOANS TO PUBLIC

**Men's Garden Clubs of America, Inc.
Lending Library**
5560 Merle Hay Road
Johnston, IA 50131
(515) 278-0295
Nancy D. Gorden, Exec. Secy.

☐ Open: M-F 9-4
☐ Number of Books: 500
☐ Services: LOANS TO PUBLIC

KANSAS

Frank Good Library
Botanica, The Wichita Gardens
701 N. Amidon
Wichita, KS 67203
(316) 264-0448
Amy Kaspar Wolf

☐ Open: MWF 9-5:30; TuThS 9-12
☐ Number of Books: 2,500
☐ Periodical Titles: 30
☐ Services: REFERENCE ONLY

LOUISIANA

Library
R. S. Barnwell Memorial Gardens & Art Center
501 Clyde Fant Parkway
Shreveport, LA 71101
(318) 226-6495
Sheila Nuttall

Call or write for information.

MAINE

Thuya Lodge Library
Asticou Terraces
Northeast Harbor, ME 04662
(207) 276-5456

Call or write for information.

MARYLAND

The Cylburn Horticultural Library
Cylburn Park Mansion
4915 Greenspring Avenue
Baltimore, MD 21209
(301) 367-2217
Adelaide C. Rackemann

Call to find out dates of Open House Sundays.
☐ Open: Th 1-3, some Su 2-4
☐ Number of Books: 1,600
☐ Periodical Titles: 4
☐ Services: MEMBERS ONLY REFERENCE ONLY

National Agricultural Library
US Department of Agriculture
10301 Baltimore Boulevard
Beltsville, MD 20705
(301) 344-3755

Probably the largest of all the libraries -- the public may use it for reference only. There is a branch reading room in DC, at USDA South, Room 1052; for information call (202) 447-3434.
☐ Open: M-F 8-4:30
☐ Services: REFERENCE ONLY

(continued next page)

MARYLAND (continued)

Brookside Gardens Library
Maryland-National Capital Park & Plan. Comm.
1500 Glenallan Avenue
Wheaton, MD 20902
(301) 949-8231
Rebecca Zastrow

❑ Open: M-F 9-5; Sa-Su 12-5
❑ Number of Books: 2,000
❑ Periodical Titles: 20
❑ Services: REFERENCE ONLY

MASSACHUSETTS

Massachusetts Horticultural Society Library
The Massachusetts Horticultural Society
300 Massachusetts Avenue
Boston, MA 02115
(617) 536-9280
Walter T. Punch

Open M-Tu, Th-F 8:30am-4:30pm; W 8:30am-8 pm; Sa l0am-2pm.
❑ Open: See notes
❑ Number of Books: 35,000
❑ Periodical Titles: 320
❑ Services: REFERENCE ONLY INTERLIBRARY LOANS

Library
Worcester County Horticultural Society
30 Tower Hill Road
Boylston, MA 01505
(508) 869-6111
Margot K. Wallin

Hours are M-F 8:30am-5pm; open Sa-Su 10am-4pm May to October only.
❑ Open: See notes
❑ Number of Books: 7,000
❑ Periodical Titles: 45
❑ Services: MEMBERS ONLY REFERENCE ONLY

The Botany Libraries
Harvard University Herbaria Building
22 Divinity Avenue
Cambridge, MA 02138
(617) 495-2366
Barbara A. Callahan

Library of the Gray Herbarium, Arnold Arboretum, Economic Botany
Library and Oakes Ames Orchid Library; available to serious users
and researchers by appointment. Call or write for information.
❑ Open: M-F 9-5
❑ Number of Books: 250,000
❑ Periodical Titles: 1,500
❑ Services: REFERENCE ONLY INTERLIBRARY LOANS

Lawrence Necomb Library
New England Wild Flower Society
Hemenway Road
Framingham, MA 01701
(508) 877-7630
Mary M. Walker

❑ Open: Tu-F 9-4
❑ Number of Books: 3,500
❑ Periodical Titles: 10
❑ Services: MEMBERS ONLY REFERENCE ONLY INTERLIBRARY LOANS

Berkshire Garden Center Library
Berkshire Garden Center -- Botanical Garden
Stockbridge, MA 01262
(413) 298-3926

Call or write for information.
❑ Open: 9-4
❑ Number of Books: 1,500
❑ Services: MEMBERS ONLY

MICHIGAN

The Detroit Garden Center Library
The Detroit Garden Center
1460 E. Jefferson Avenue
Detroit, MI 48207
(313) 259-6363
Margaret H. Grazier

❑ Open: Tu-Th 9:30-3:30
❑ Number of Books: 5,800
❑ Periodical Titles: 15
❑ Services: MEMBERS ONLY REFERENCE ONLY

Detroit Public Library
5201 Woodward Avenue
Detroit, MI 48202
(313) 833-1400 or 1450

Has a collection on gardening, botany and agriculture.
❑ Open: Call for information
❑ Number of Books: 5,500
❑ Periodical Titles: 61
❑ Services: INTERLIBRARY LOANS LOANS TO PUBLIC

Library
Chippewa Nature Center
400 S. Badour Road, Route 9
Midland, MI 48640
(517) 631-0803
Meg Ulery

Librarian on duty M, W, Th 8am-3pm.
❑ Open: M-F 8-5, Sa 9-5, Su 1-5
❑ Number of Books: 2,500
❑ Periodical Titles: 86
❑ Services: MEMBERS ONLY REFERENCE ONLY

(continued next page)

MICHIGAN (continued)

The Dow Gardens Library
The Dow Gardens
1018 W. Main Street
Midland, MI 48640
(517) 631-2677
Amy Hurlbert

Entrance to the library is through the Information Center, located at the corner of West Saint Andrews & Eastman Roads.
❑ Open: M-F 10-4
❑ Number of Books: 1,100
❑ Periodical Titles: 33
❑ Services: REFERENCE ONLY

The Fernwood Botanic Garden Library
Fernwood Botanic Garden
13988 Range Line Road
Niles, MI 49120
(616) 695-6491
R. Hines

Has a collection of garden catalogs.
❑ Open: M-F 9-5
❑ Number of Books: 3,000
❑ Periodical Titles: 45
❑ Services: MEMBERS ONLY REFERENCE ONLY

Hidden Lake Gardens Library
Michigan State University
Tipton, MI 49287
(517) 431-2060
Laura Furgason

❑ Open: Call for hours
❑ Number of Books: 3,000
❑ Periodical Titles: 8
❑ Services: REFERENCE ONLY

Library, Matthaei Botanical Gardens
The University of Michigan
1800 N. Dixboro Road
Ypsilanti, MI 48105
(313) 763-7060
Mrs. Annie Hannan

Members may use the library for reference.
❑ Open: M-F 8-5
❑ Number of Books: 1,700
❑ Periodical Titles: 30
❑ Services: MEMBERS ONLY REFERENCE ONLY

MINNESOTA

Anderson Horticultural Library
Minnesota Landscape Arboretum, Univ. of Minn.
3675 Arboretum Drive, P.O. Box 39
Chanhassen, MN 55317
(612) 443-2460
Richard T. Isaacson

❑ Open: M-F 8-4:30; Sa-Su 11-4:30
❑ Number of Books: 9,500
❑ Periodical Titles: 375
❑ Services: REFERENCE ONLY

MISSOURI

St. Louis Parks Department Library
The Jewel Box Conservatory
5600 Clayton Road
St. Louis, MO 63110
(316) 535-0400
Susan Baker

Call or write for information.

Missouri Botanical Garden Library
P.O. Box 299
St. Louis, MO 63109
(314) 577-5155
Constance Wolf

Researchers must make special appointments.
❑ Open: M-F 8:30-5
❑ Number of Books: 110,000
❑ Periodical Titles: 1,500

NEW JERSEY

Elvin McDonald Horticultural Library
Monmouth County Park System
Deep Cut Park, 352 Red Hill Road
Middletown, NJ 07748
(201) 671-6050
Mae H. Fisher

❑ Open: Daily 9-4:30
❑ Number of Books: 1,950
❑ Periodical Titles: 24
❑ Services: REFERENCE ONLY

Elizabeth Donnell Kay Botanical Library
George Griswold Frelinghuysen Arboretum
P.O. Box 1295R, 53 East Hanover Avenue
Morristown, NJ 07960
(201) 285-6166
Helen Hesselgrave

Call or write for information.

NEW YORK

The New York Botanical Garden Library
The New York Botanical Garden
200th Street & Kazimiroff Boulevard
Bronx, NY 10458
(212) 220-8751
John F. Reed, Bernadette Callery

Academic year hours are M-Th 11am-6pm, F-Sa 11am-4pm.
Call for summer hours.
❏ Open: See notes
❏ Number of Books: 187,000
❏ Periodical Titles: 2,000
❏ Services: REFERENCE ONLY INTERLIBRARY LOANS

The Library
Brooklyn Botanic Garden
1000 Washington Avenue
Brooklyn, NY 11225-1099
(718) 622-4433
Brenda Weisman

❏ Open: Tu-F 9:30-4:30
❏ Number of Books: 40,000
❏ Periodical Titles: 500
❏ Services: REFERENCE ONLY

George Landis Arboretum Library
Esperance, NY 12066
(518) 875-6935
Fred Lape

Call or write for information.

Library
Queens Botanical Garden
43-50 Main Street
Flushing, NY 11355

Call or write for information.

Library
Liberty Hyde Bailey Hortorium
467 Mann Library, Cornell University
Ithaca, NY 14853
(607) 255-2131
Dr. Jerrold Davis

Collection in taxonomic botany, open to qualified researchers only; call to
make arrangements in advance. Similar collection in Mann Library.
❏ Open: M-F 8-5
❏ Number of Books: 10,000
❏ Periodical Titles: 350
❏ Services: MEMBERS ONLY REFERENCE ONLY

Library
The Cary Arboretum
P.O. Box AB
Millbrook, NY 12545
(914) 677-5343
Betsy Calvin

Call or write for information.

Garden Club of America Library
598 Madison Avenue
New York, NY 10022
(212) 753-8287
Anne C. Shomer

Members must pay a fee of $1 to borrow a book.
❏ Open: M-F 9-4:30
❏ Number of Books: 3,000
❏ Services: MEMBERS ONLY REFERENCE ONLY

Horticultural Society of New York Library
Horticultural Society of New York
128 W. 58th Street
New York, NY 10019
(212) 757-0915
Katherine Powis

Large collection of seed and nursery catalogs.
❏ Open: M-F 10-6
❏ Number of Books: 18,000
❏ Periodical Titles: 90
❏ Services: MEMBERS ONLY REFERENCE ONLY

Garden Library
Planting Fields Arboretum
Oyster Bay, NY 11771
(516) 922-9024
Elizabeth Reilley

❏ Open: W 11-4, Sa 10-3
❏ Number of Books: 5,700
❏ Periodical Titles: 40
❏ Services: MEMBERS ONLY REFERENCE ONLY

Herbarium Library
Monroe County Parks Arboretum
180 Reservoir Avenue
Rochester, NY 14620
(716) 244-9023
James W. Kelly

❏ Open: T-F 10-6
❏ Number of Books: 497
❏ Periodical Titles: 23
❏ Services: REFERENCE ONLY

Library
Garden Center of Rochester
5 Castle Park
Rochester, NY 14620
(716) 473-5130
Regina Campbell

Also open from October to June on the first Saturday of the month
from 9:30 to 12:30.
❏ Open: Tu-Th 9:30-3:30
❏ Number of Books: 4,000
❏ Periodical Titles: 24
❏ Services: MEMBERS ONLY REFERENCE ONLY

NORTH CAROLINA

Totten Library
North Carolina Botanical Garden -- UNC
Box 3375, Totten Center
Chapel Hill, NC 27599-3375
(919) 967-2246
Barbara Emerson

Totten Center is located just off 15-501/54 Bypass on Laurel Hill Road.
❏ Open: M-F 8-5
❏ Number of Books: 1,500
❏ Periodical Titles: 30
❏ Services: REFERENCE ONLY

OHIO

Library
Civic Garden Center of Greater Cincinnati
2715 Reading Road
Cincinnati, OH 45206
(513) 221-0981
Jeanne Bridewell

Call or write for information.

Lloyd Library
917 Plum Street
Cincinnati, OH 45202
(513) 721-3707
Rebecca A. Perry

Open the first and third Saturdays of the month 9am-4pm.
❏ Open: M-F 8:30-4; see notes
❏ Number of Books: 65,000
❏ Periodical Titles: 500
❏ Services: REFERENCE ONLY

Eleanor Squire Library
The Garden Center of Greater Cleveland
11030 East Boulevard
Cleveland, OH 44106
(216) 721-1600
Joanna C. Bristol

❏ Open: M-F 9-5, Su 2-5
❏ Number of Books: 14,700
❏ Periodical Titles: 200
❏ Services: MEMBERS ONLY REFERENCE ONLY INTERLIBRARY LOANS

Biological Sciences Library
Ohio State University
1735 Neil Avenue
Columbus, OH 43210
(614) 422-1744

Call or write for information.

Cox Arboretum Library
Montgomery County Park District
6733 Springboro Pike
Dayton, OH 45449
(513) 434-9005
Ruth McManis

❏ Open: M-F 10-4
❏ Number of Books: 2,200
❏ Periodical Titles: 16
❏ Services: MEMBERS ONLY REFERENCE ONLY

Kingwood Center Library
Kingwood Center
900 Park Avenue West
Mansfield, OH 44906
(419) 522-0211
William W. Collins

Residents of Richland and five surrounding counties may borrow books.
❏ Open: Tu-Sa 9-5
❏ Number of Books: 8,000
❏ Periodical Titles: 125
❏ Services: INTERLIBRARY LOANS LOANS TO PUBLIC

Library
Herb Society of America
9019 Kirtland-Chardon Road
Mentor, OH 44060
(216) 256-0514
Martha Boice

Has slide lectures for rent on many aspects of herb history and culture.
❏ Open: M-F 9-5
❏ Number of Books: 600
❏ Periodical Titles: 4
❏ Services: MEMBERS ONLY REFERENCE ONLY

Warren H. Corning Library
The Holden Arboretum
9500 Sperry Road
Mentor, OH 44060
(216) 946-4400, ext. 225
Nadia Aufderheide

❏ Open: Tu-F 10-5, Sa-Su 1-4
❏ Number of Books: 6,000
❏ Periodical Titles: 140
❏ Services: REFERENCE ONLY INTERLIBRARY LOANS

The Dawes Arboretum Library
The Dawes Arboretum
7770 Jacksontown Road S.E.
Newark, OH 43055
(614) 323-2355
Linda Milligan

Members may use the library for reference; researchers should make an appointment.
❏ Open: M-F 8-4:30
❏ Number of Books: 3,000
❏ Periodical Titles: 30

(continued next page)

OHIO (continued)

Library
Gardenview Horticultural Park
16711 Pearl Road
Strongsville, OH 44136
(216) 238-6653
Henry A. Ross

Library open to members only; they may use it at any time.
☐ Open: See notes.
☐ Number of Books: 4,000
☐ Services: MEMBERS ONLY

Environmental Library
George P. Crosby Gardens
5403 Elmer Drive
Toledo, OH 43651
(419) 536-8365
Mary Tucker

Call or write for information.

Horticultural Library
Toledo Botanical Garden
5403 Elmer Drive
Toledo, OH 43615
(419) 536-8365
Jay Brewster

Call or write for information on hours.
☐ Open: By appointment only
☐ Number of Books: n/a
☐ Periodical Titles: n/a
☐ Services: REFERENCE ONLY

OKLAHOMA

Tulsa Garden Center Library
2453 S. Peoria
Tulsa, OK 74114
(918) 749-6401
Mrs. Donald Ross

Call or write for information.

ONTARIO, CANADA

Royal Botanical Gardens Library
Royal Botanical Gardens
680 Palins Road West
Burlington, ON, Canada L7 7T 4H4
(416) 527-1158, ext. 159
Ina Vrugtman

Open Sa 9am-12pm in winter only.
☐ Open: M-F 9-5, see notes
☐ Number of Books: 7,500
☐ Periodical Titles: 450
☐ Services: MEMBERS ONLY INTERLIBRARY LOANS

Library
The Civic Garden Centre, Ontario, Canada
777 Lawrence Avenue East
Don Mills, ON, Canada M3C 1P2
(416) 445-1552
Pamela Mackenzie

☐ Open: M-F 9:30-5, Sa-Su 12-5
☐ Number of Books: 6,000
☐ Periodical Titles: 40
☐ Services: REFERENCE ONLY INTERLIBRARY LOANS

School of Horticulture Library
Niagara Parks Commission
Niagara Parkway North (P.O. Box 150)
Niagara Falls, ON, Canada L2E 6T2
(416) 356-8554
Shirley Stoner

Open to staff and students daily; researchers may use the library
by appointment.
☐ Open: See notes
☐ Number of Books: 3,000
☐ Periodical Titles: 65
☐ Services: MEMBERS ONLY REFERENCE ONLY

Ottawa Research Station Library
Agriculture Canada
Central Experimental Farm, Building 75
Ottawa, ON, Canada K1A OC6
(613) 995-9428, ext. 30
Gail A. Waters

☐ Open: M-F 8-4
☐ Number of Books: 25,000
☐ Periodical Titles: 250
☐ Services: MEMBERS ONLY REFERENCE ONLY INTERLIBRARY LOANS

OREGON

Library
Berry Botanic Garden
11505 S.W. Summerville Road
Portland, OR 97219
(503) 636-4112
Myrtle R. Snyder

Members may use the library and borrow books.
☐ Open: M-F 8-5
☐ Number of Books: 600
☐ Services: MEMBERS ONLY

PENNSYLVANIA

Joseph Krauskopf Library
Delaware Valley College
Route 202
Doylestown, PA 18901
(215) 345-1500
C. Shook, Director

Open M-Th 8:30am-midnight, F 8am-9:30pm, Sa 12pm-5pm, Su 2pm-11pm.
Building a collection of current seed and nursery catalogs; specializes in
science and agriculture.
❑ Open: See notes
❑ Number of Books: 50,300
❑ Periodical Titles: 662
❑ Services: REFERENCE ONLY INTERLIBRARY LOANS

Longwood Gardens Library
Longwood Gardens, Inc.
Kennett Square, PA 19348
(215) 388-6741, ext. 501
Enola J. N. Teeter

To use the library you must pay the entrance fee to the gardens.
❑ Open: M-F 7:30-4:30
❑ Number of Books: 18,000
❑ Periodical Titles: 280
❑ Services: REFERENCE ONLY

Academy of Natural Sciences Library
Academy of Natural Sciences of Philadelphia
19th Street & The Parkway
Philadelphia, PA 19103
(215) 299-1140
Linda Rossi

Large botanical research collection. Horticultural collection focuses on
pre-1860 American imprints.
❑ Open: M-F 9-5
❑ Number of Books: 190,000
❑ Periodical Titles: 3,200
❑ Services: REFERENCE ONLY INTERLIBRARY LOANS

Pennsylvania Horticultural Society Library
325 Walnut Street
Philadelphia, PA 19106
(215) 625-8261
Janet Evans

❑ Open: M-F 9-5
❑ Number of Books: 14,000
❑ Periodical Titles: 200
❑ Services: MEMBERS ONLY REFERENCE ONLY

Morris Arboretum Library
University of Pennsylvania
9414 Meadowbrook Avenue
Philadelphia, PA 19118
(215) 247-5777
Ann F. Rhoads

❑ Open: M-F 9-5
❑ Number of Books: 6,000
❑ Periodical Titles: 60
❑ Services: REFERENCE ONLY INTERLIBRARY LOANS

Library
Carnegie Museum of Natural History
4400 Forbes Avenue
Pittsburgh, PA 15213
(412) 622-3264

Very large collection; number of books cited are just the botanical books.
❑ Open: Daily 8:30-5
❑ Number of Books: 2,800
❑ Periodical Titles: 200
❑ Services: REFERENCE ONLY INTERLIBRARY LOANS

Hunt Botanical Library
Hunt Institute for Botanical Documentation
Carnegie Mellon University
Pittsburgh, PA 15213
(412) 268-2436
Charlotte Tancin

❑ Open: M-F 1-5
❑ Number of Books: 24,000
❑ Periodical Titles: 650
❑ Services: REFERENCE ONLY INTERLIBRARY LOANS

Pittsburgh Civic Garden Center Library
Pittsburgh Civic Garden Center
1059 Shady Lane
Pittsburgh, PA 15232
(412) 441-4442
Jean Aiken

❑ Open: M-Sa 10-4
❑ Number of Books: 2,200
❑ Periodical Titles: 15
❑ Services: MEMBERS ONLY REFERENCE ONLY

Barbara Spaulding Cramer Library
The Scott Arboretum of Swarthmore College
500 College Avenue
Swarthmore, PA 19081
(215) 328-8025
Erica Glasener

❑ Open: M-F 8:30-4:30
❑ Number of Books: 800
❑ Periodical Titles: 45
❑ Services: MEMBERS ONLY REFERENCE ONLY

QUEBEC, CANADA

Montreal Botanical Garden Library
Jardin Botanique de la Ville de Montreal
4101 rue Sherbrooke est
Montreal, PQ, Canada H1X 2B2
(514) 872-1824
Celine Arseneault

Open M,W,F 8:30am-12pm, 1:15pm-4:30pm; Tu 8:30am-4:30pm.
❑ Open: See notes
❑ Number of Books: 10,000
❑ Periodical Titles: 245
❑ Services: REFERENCE ONLY INTERLIBRARY LOANS

SOUTH CAROLINA

Orangeberg County Library
P. O. Box 1367
Orangeberg, SC 29115
(803) 531-4636

Call or write for information.

TENNESSEE

Library
Dixon Gallery & Gardens
4339 Park Avenue
Memphis, TN 38117
(901) 761-5250
Carol Griffin

Library may be used by members of the sponsoring organization.
❑ Open: Tu-Sa 11-5, Su 1-5
❑ Number of Books: 1,000
❑ Periodical Titles: 40

Sybil G. Malloy Memorial Library
Memphis Botanic Garden
750 Cherry Road
Memphis, TN 38117
(901) 685-1566
Ruth Cobb

❑ Open: Daily 9-4:30
❑ Number of Books: 1,000
❑ Periodical Titles: 25
❑ Services: REFERENCE ONLY

The Botanical Gardens Library
Cheekwood
Forrest Park Drive
Nashville, TN 37205
(615) 353-2148
Muriel H. Connell

Members may borrow books; the general public may use materials there.
❑ Open: T-Sa 9-5, Su 1-5
❑ Number of Books: 4,500
❑ Periodical Titles: 60
❑ Services: MEMBERS ONLY REFERENCE ONLY INTERLIBRARY LOANS

TEXAS

**National Wildflower Research Center
   Clearinghouse**
2600 FM 973 North
Austin, TX 78725-4201
(512) 929-3600
Annie Gillespie, Beth Anderson

❑ Open: M-F 9-4
❑ Number of Books: 500
❑ Periodical Titles: 60
❑ Services: REFERENCE ONLY

W. J. Rogers Memorial Library
The Beaumont Council of Garden Clubs
The Garden Center in Tyrrell Park
Beaumont, TX 77705
(409) 842-3135
Myra Clay

Collection related to plants which thrive on the Gulf Coast.
❑ Open: Daily by appointment
❑ Number of Books: 1,200
❑ Services: MEMBERS ONLY INTERLIBRARY LOANS

Mary Daggett Lake Library
Fort Worth Botanic Garden
3220 Botanic Garden Drive North
Fort Worth, TX 76107
(817) 870-7687
Jana Johnson

❑ Open: M-F 8-5, Sa 9-4, Su 1-4
❑ Number of Books: 3,000
❑ Periodical Titles: 15
❑ Services: MEMBERS ONLY REFERENCE ONLY

VIRGINIA

Harold B. Tukey Memorial Library
American Horticultural Society
7931 E. Boulevard Drive
Alexandria, VA 22308
(703) 768-5700
Raymond J. Rogers

Members may use the library for reference.
❑ Open: M-F 8:30-5
❑ Number of Books: 2,500
❑ Periodical Titles: 200

Crawford Reid Memorial Library
The Irrigation Association
1911 N. Fort Myer, Suite 1009
Arlington, VA 22209
(703) 524-1200
R. L. "Bob" Sears

Call for information on the collection.
❑ Open: M-F 8-5
❑ Number of Books: 700
❑ Periodical Titles: 25
❑ Services: REFERENCE ONLY

(continued next page)

VIRGINIA (continued)

Blandy Experimental Farm Library
University of Virginia
Route 50 (1-1/2 miles east of Route 340)
Boyce, VA 22620
(703) 837-1758
Christopher F. Sacchi

❏ Open: By appointment
❏ Number of Books: 1,200
❏ Periodical Titles: 20
❏ Services: REFERENCE ONLY

Library
Norfolk Botanical Garden
Norfolk, VA 23518
(804) 441-5386
Debbi Haddaway

You must pay the entrance fee to the garden; members may borrow from the library.
❏ Open: M-F 8:30-5
❏ Number of Books: 1,950
❏ Periodical Titles: 13
❏ Services: MEMBERS ONLY REFERENCE ONLY

Library
Rose Hybridizers Association
2609 Royal Palm Arch
Virginia Beach, VA 23452
James Selby

For use by members only; write for information.
❏ Number of Books: 300
❏ Services: MEMBERS ONLY

WASHINGTON

Rhododendron Reference Library
Rhododendron Species Foundation
P.O. Box 3798
Federal Way, WA 98003
(206) 927-6960
Mrs. Richard B. Johnson

Call or write for information.

Elisabeth C. Miller Horticultural Library
Center for Urban Horticulture
University of Washington, GF-15
Seattle, WA 98195
(206) 543-8616
Laura Lipton, Valerie Easton

❏ Open: M-F 9-5
❏ Number of Books: 6,000
❏ Periodical Titles: 200
❏ Services: REFERENCE ONLY

Graham Visitor Collection
Arboretum Foundation
Washington Park Arboretum
Seattle, WA 98195
(206) 325-4510
Nancy Ballard

A reference library only for the use of members of the Arboretum Foundation.
❏ Open: M-F 10-3:45, Sa-Su 12-4
❏ Number of Books: 500
❏ Services: MEMBERS ONLY

Library
University of Washington Arboretum
East Madison & Lake Washington Boulevard East
Seattle, WA 98195
(206) 543-8800

Call or write for information.

WEST VIRGINIA

Library
Wheeling Garden Center
Oglebay Park
Wheeling, WV 26003
(304) 242-0665

Call or write for information.

WISCONSIN

Reference Library
Boerner Botanical Gardens
5879 S. 92nd Street
Hales Corners, WI 53130
(414) 425-1131

Hours are March to October, daily, 8am-sunset; November and December, daily, 8am-4pm; January and February, M-F, 8am-4pm.
❏ Open: See notes
❏ Number of Books: 2,000
❏ Services: REFERENCE ONLY

G

Books

Useful books on plants and gardening, for reference and daily use as well as for pleasure, are grouped into general categories by plant groups or plant uses. At the end of the list are "good reads," guidebooks of gardens to visit, and plant-finding source books.

The books listed in this section are all books I consider worthwhile. It is agony to pare down the list to roughly 200 books; I always leave it until last and approach the task with dread. The notes are my own opinions, except as noted, based on general garden and plant knowledge but no great expertise in any one field.

Most of the books are fairly recent and should be available in public libraries, bookstores, from secondhand bookshops or on remainder tables. However, I resent the idea that the newest books are always the best; it strikes me that the most quoted garden writer in America seems to be Louise Beebe Wilder, whose books are now thirty and forty years old (some available in Dover Press reprints).

Books have been listed on merit without regard to price. Garden books are fairly expensive, and you might want to examine the books in a library or bookstore before ordering them; sometimes there are books of equal merit for your purposes at vastly different prices. Prices and availability can be checked in *Books in Print*.

The most encouraging development is the recent surge of good American gardening and plant books and regional gardening guides. What we should admire in others is their love for and knowledge of plants; we should spend our limited book budgets on books written for our own unique gardening conditions and recommending the plants most available to us.

Mail-order sources of new, used and rare books are listed in the Garden Suppliers and Services section. Books on specific plants or areas of horticultural interest are often available from specialist nurseries and seed companies. In addition, many societies sell books to their members, often at special prices; some sell to nonmembers as well.

You should ask horticultural book suppliers for books not commonly found in local bookstores; bookstores can also special-order such books if they are still in print. Addresses of publishers not given can be found in *Books in Print* or *Forthcoming Books*, available in public libraries and most bookstores. Society addresses not given are listed in the Horticultural Societies section of this book.

A table of the symbols and abbreviations used
in this book appears on the bookmark.

USEFUL REFERENCE BOOKS

Hortus Third. New York, Macmillan, 1976. A dictionary of plants cultivated in the U.S. and Canada — which means a very great many! It is the standard North American reference and should be in almost any library.

Flowering Plant Index of Illustration and Information. The Garden Center of Greater Cleveland. Boston, G. K. Hall, 1979. 2 v. Supplement, 1982. 2 v. Only available in large horticultural libraries; very useful if you need to locate color illustrations of unusual plants. Each entry indicates if the illustration is of flower, fruit or general plant habit; there are 55,000 entries in the first two volumes. The two-volume supplement, equally thick, covers books published from 1965 through 1977.

The Illustrated Encyclopedia of Horticulture. Thomas Everett. New York, Garland, 1982. This 10-volume work is monumental; descriptions are more complete and easier to read than *Hortus Third*. Quite a bit of cultural information; most of the photographs are in black and white.

The Royal Horticultural Society Dictionary of Gardening. Patrick Synge, ed. Oxford, Clarendon Press, 1974. This work, in 4 volumes with a supplement, covers plants cultivated in Great Britain — also a very great many. Now being revised for republication in the 1990s.

The European Garden Flora. Cambridge University Press, 1984. Recommended by a very knowledgeable reader, who says it will become the standard reference for identification of cultivated ornamental plants. Expensive and technical; you might try to get your library interested.

The Seedlist Handbook. Mabel G. Harkness. 4th ed. Portland, OR, Timber Press, 1986. Originally for people requesting unfamiliar seeds from seed exchange lists, it briefly describes a huge variety of plants by type, size, flower color and place of origin and gives references to information and illustrations of each plant in more than 300 authoritative books and many magazine articles.

Dictionary of Plant Names. Allen J. Coombes. Portland, OR, Timber Press, 1985. Handy small book with information on pronunciation and derivation in concise entries.

Plant Names Simplified. A. T. Johnson & H. A. Smith. London, Hamlyn, 1972. Pocket-sized; gives pronunciation and derivation of plant names and very brief plant descriptions.

North American Horticulture: A Reference Guide. American Horticultural Society. Rev. ed. New York, Macmillan, 1990. A directory of horticultural societies and organizations, educational institutions and programs, botanical gardens, periodicals, journals and much more.

Directory of Regional Gardening Resources. New York, Garden Club of America, 1987. This is a gem! It covers the country by regions, giving a bibliography of books on regional gardening, lists (by state) of plants, nurseries and gardens to visit and lists of regional gardening books. It's $5.50 ppd., which includes the 1989 supplement, from the Garden Club of America — a steal for so much information.

Healthy Harvest III: A Directory of Sustainable Agriculture & Horticultural Organizations, 1989-1990. Deborah Preston, ed. Washington, DC, Potomac Valley Press, 1989. Lists more than 1,000 organizations and sources, with subject and geographical indexes and a description of each. Includes apprenticeships and internships, consultants, courses, development organizations, marketing cooperatives, newsletters, volunteer programs and much more. An excellent reference. (1424 16th Street N.W., Washington, DC 20036.)

Growing with Gardening: A Twelve-Month Guide for Therapy, Recreation, and Education. Bibby Moore. Chapel Hill, University of North Carolina Press, 1989. A week-by-week guide to horticultural projects for anyone using horticulture in teaching or therapy. Advice on how to develop and budget a program and how to find volunteers, lists of references and sources. A wonderful book.

GARDENING ENCYCLOPEDIAS

The Gardening Encyclopedia. Donald Wyman. Updated ed. New York, Macmillan, 1987. My favorite of the popular gardening encyclopedias; easy to read and use, but with a northeastern point of view.

Taylor's Encyclopedia of Gardening. Norman Taylor. 4th ed. Boston, Houghton Mifflin, 1961. Another northeastern gardening guide, which sometimes has things I can't find in Wyman. Good guide to gardening specifics by state.

America's Garden Book. James & Louise Bush-Brown. Rev. ed. New York, Scribner, 1980. Highly recommended by a reader.

Sunset Western Garden Book. 5th ed. Menlo Park, CA, Lane Publishing Co., 1988. An excellent guide to gardening anywhere in the western U.S. The West is divided into 24 climate zones, and the plant encyclopedia indicates in which zones each plant will grow — very useful for choosing plants. This very fine book turns up on lists of favorite books from people all over the country.

The Garden Primer. Barbara Damrosch. New York, Workman, 1988. An excellent basic gardening book, dealing with all aspects of gardening in a sensible and very easy-to-understand manner. Damrosch tells you how to adapt advice to your climate and introduces many useful plants. The perfect gift for a new gardener and useful as a reference to any gardener.

Reader's Digest Illustrated Guide to Gardening. Pleasantville, NY, Reader's Digest Assn., 1981. Still one of the best how-to gardening guides, with lots of illustrations and extensive sections on choosing appropriate plants.

The Complete Book of Gardening. Richard Ray, Derek Fell & Michael MacCaskey. Los Angeles, Oracle Books, 1987. A collection of materials from many of the excellent HP gardening books. It covers all the basics.

The Complete Book of Gardening. Michael Wright. New York, Warner, 1989. This is a fine over-all guide to gardening; I haven't seen the updated edition to check what changes have been made.

The Encyclopedia of Organic Gardening. New rev. ed. Emmaus, PA, Rodale Press, 1978. Comprehensive beginner's guide to organic gardening, methods and crops, easy to read and use.

The Ortho Problem Solver. Michael Smith, ed. 2nd ed. San Ramon, CA, Ortho Books, 1982. A color encyclopedia of plant diseases and pest problems, with color photographs of the problem, a discussion of the conditions that cause it and suggested solutions. Includes some cultural information and suggestions. Problems are entered by plant, making them fairly easy to locate. Available for reference in most garden centers.

The Practical Gardener: A Guide to Breaking New Ground. Roger B. Swain. Boston, Little, Brown, 1989. Not an encyclopedia, but good basic information for every gardener on a myriad of subjects, with a northeastern focus (e.g., how to make maple syrup).

Rodale's Garden Insect, Disease & Weed Identification Guide. Miranda Smith & Anna Carr. Emmaus, PA, Rodale Press, 1988. Gives illustrations, descriptions, life cycles and organic prevention and controls of common garden pests, diseases and weeds.

Rodale's Garden Problem Solver: Vegetables, Fruits, and Herbs. Jeff Ball. Emmaus, PA, Rodale Press, 1988. Problems are listed by plant host, so it's easy to find the problem and suggestions for an organic method of control. Also general suggestions for controlling insect and animal pests and diseases.

Controlling Lawn and Garden Insects. L. Patricia Kite. San Ramon, CA, Ortho Books, 1987. Offers good color pictures of the pests, advice on chemical and nontoxic methods of control.

Pruning Simplified. Lewis Hill. Updated ed. Pownal, VT, Storey Communications, 1986. A good, easy-to-understand introduction to the principles of pruning.

Sunset Pruning Handbook. Menlo Park, CA, Lane Publishing Co., 1983. A good introduction, with basic principles explained, and an encyclopedia of how to prune many common garden plants.

ILLUSTRATED BOOKS USEFUL FOR FINDING AND IDENTIFYING PLANTS

American Horticultural Society Encyclopedia of Garden Plants. Christopher Brickell, ed. New York, Macmillan, 1989. A joint effort of the AHS and the RHS, it lists 8,000 garden plants of all types, with color photographs of 4,000. Plants listed by type, size, season of interest and color of flowers, but indexed by botanical name with cross-references to the photographs.

Reader's Digest Encyclopedia of Garden Plants and Flowers. London, Reader's Digest Assn., 1975. My copy of this is nearly worn out. It has small color pictures of a great variety of plants, with good descriptions and some information on growing.

The Complete Handbook of Garden Plants. Michael Wright. New York, Facts on File, 1984. A concise guide to popular garden trees, shrubs and flowers, with color paintings of many.

Prentice-Hall Encyclopedia of Garden Plants. Anita Pereire. New York, Prentice-Hall, 1989. A reference to many popular garden plants; each is shown in color and briefly described.

Right Plant, Right Place. Nicola Ferguson. New York, Summit, 1984. A good illustrated guide to popular garden plants, organized by garden and growing conditions.

The Concise Encyclopedia of Garden Plants. Kenneth A. Beckett. Topsfield, MA, Salem House, 1983. More than 2,000 color photographs of popular garden plants, with brief plant descriptions and growing requirements.

The Gardener's Illustrated Encyclopedia of Trees & Shrubs. Brian Davis. Emmaus, PA, Rodale Press, 1987. Concise information; color photos are mostly close-ups, with black & white silhouettes of plants. One of my favorites; a good companion to Dirr's *Manual of Woody Landscape Plants* (see Trees and Shrubs, below).

Exotica 4. Alfred B. Graf. East Rutherford, NJ, Roehrs, 1985. 2 v. A pictorial encyclopedia of exotic and tropical plants, including most plants that are grown indoors or in greenhouses.

Tropica. Alfred B. Graf. East Rutherford, NJ, Roehrs, 1986. 3rd ed. A color encyclopedia of tropical and subtropical plants of all kinds.

The Illustrated Book of Food Plants: A Guide to the Fruit, Vegetables, Herbs & Spices of the World. S. G. Harrison, G. B. Masefield, & Michael Wallis. London, Peerage Books, 1985. Illustrated by color paintings, it will show you what almost any edible looks like and usually includes both leaves and fruit.

Reader's Digest Guide to Creative Gardening. London, Reader's Digest Assn., 1984. A guide to choosing garden plants which is lavishly and romantically illustrated; more than most of the books of this kind, it shows plants in association and something of the habit of the whole plant. Not strong on plant descriptions and growing requirements, more a "looker."

Poisonous Plants: A Color Field Guide. Lucia Woodward. New York, Hippocrene Books, 1985. Color photos, descriptions, symptoms, treatment and tables of season and types of danger.

Weeds of the United States and Their Control. Harri J. Lorenzi & Larry S. Jeffery. New York, AVI (Van Nostrand Reinhold), 1987. Color photos, maps, descriptions, habitat and suggested controls.

BOOKS IN SERIES

A number of publishers issue books on basic gardening and plants, all of which offer good information and value. Some of these books are listed individually here; all are well worth consideration. The publishers include Ortho Books, Sunset (Lane Publishing), HP Books (Price Stern Sloan), Harrowsmith and Garden Way (Storey Communications). Slightly more expensive but also very good are the Taylor's Guides of Houghton Mifflin and the Time-Life books. All have good color illustrations and contain the basic information that gardeners want at reasonable prices; most are readily available in bookstores.

PROPAGATION

Secrets of Plant Propagation. Lewis Hill. Pownal, VT, Storey Communications, 1985. Good overview of the subject, easy to understand.

The New Seed Starter's Handbook. Nancy Bubel. Emmaus, PA, Rodale Press, 1988. Good information on starting vegetables and some trees, shrubs and garden flowers from seed, with tips on seed saving.

Park's Success with Seeds. Ann Reilly. Greenwood, SC, Park Seed Co., 1978. Brief information on habit, uses, germination and culture; very useful color photos of the seedlings. (See Park Seed Co., Section A.)

Growing Plants from Seed. Richard Gorer. Boston, Faber and Faber, 1978. Concise information; section on special treatments.

BOOKS ON PLANTS FOR SPECIFIC CONDITIONS & EFFECTS

Scented Flora of the World. Roy Genders. New York, St. Martin's, 1977. A very interesting and readable book on scented plants — the author's nose is very lenient and coverage is broad. There are newer books, but this one's my favorite.

The Fragrant Garden: A Book About Sweet Scented Flowers and Leaves. Louise Beebe Wilder. New York, Dover, 1974. Here's a delightful chance to see why Mrs. Wilder is so often quoted by other garden writers.

The Complete Shade Gardener. George Schenk. Boston, Houghton Mifflin, 1984. Written by an experienced plantsman whose style and humor put him high on my list of "good reads."

Shade Gardening. A. Cort Sinnes. San Francisco, Ortho Books, 1982. Good illustrations and plant directory; plenty of help with creative and practical aspects.

Landscaping with Container Plants. Jim Wilson. Boston, Houghton Mifflin, 1990. If you know Jim Wilson from the *Victory Garden* show, you'll feel as if you're visiting with him — his book is full of inspirational pictures and practical advice based on new types of planting media.

The Terrace Gardener's Handbook. Linda Yang. Rev. ed. New York, Random House, 1990. Everything you need to know, from hauling things up to the roof to analyzing exposures and growing conditions, planting and aftercare; very useful and sensible advice.

The Water Garden. Anthony Paul & Yvonne Rees. New York, Viking Penguin, 1986. Not as practical as the books below, but full of inspirational photos which will spark design ideas.

Water Gardening Basics. William C. Uber. Upland, CA, Dragonflyer Press, 1988. Written by the proprietor of Van Ness Water Gardens for home gardeners and garden designers; a beautiful book that covers all the basics. (See Van Ness Water Gardens, Section A.)

Water Gardens for Plants and Fish. Charles B. Thomas. Neptune City, NJ, TFH Publications, 1988. Written by the proprietor of Lilypons Water Gardens, this book covers everything you need to know to get started and to care for your plants and fish. (See Lilypons Water Gardens, Section A.)

Hedges, Screens and Espaliers. Susan Chamberlin. Los Angeles, Price Stern Sloan, 1982. Well-illustrated guide to choosing and caring for hedges, screens and espaliered shrubs and fruit trees.

Gardening with the New Small Plants. Oliver E. Allen. Boston, Houghton Mifflin, 1987. I don't know how "new" these plants are, but it's a good guide to small plants for tight spaces.

Taylor's Guide to Ground Covers, Vines & Grasses. Boston, Houghton Mifflin, 1987. An excellent introduction to plants used for ground covers, as well as to vines for walls and trellises.

REGIONAL GARDENING BOOKS

Successful Southern Gardening: A Practical Guide for Year-Round Beauty. Sandra F. Ladendorf. Chapel Hill, University of North Carolina Press, 1989. A fine modern guide to gardening in the hot and humid climate of the South. She offers good practical advice, lists recommended plants and suggests further reading and sources. Her lengthy credits are testimony to the joy of gardening friends.

Southern Gardens, Southern Gardening. William L. Hunt. Durham, NC, Duke University Press, 1982. This book is full of good advice on how to grow plants under southern growing conditions.

A Southern Garden: A Handbook for the Middle South. Elizabeth Lawrence. Rev. ed. Chapel Hill, University of North Carolina Press, 1984. I've only recently discovered Lawrence, a regional writer who gives great pleasure with her information. I also enjoyed her *Gardening for Love: the Market Bulletins*. Allen Lacy, ed. Durham, NC, Duke University Press, 1987.

Perennial Garden Color for Texas and the South. William C. Welch. Dallas, Taylor Publishing, 1989. A very fine book for gardeners in difficult garden climates of the South, with good suggestions for plant selection, culture and garden design.

Neil Sperry's Complete Guide to Texas Gardening. Dallas, Taylor Publishing, 1982. From the flowery cowboy boots on the cover to the last page, it covers everything: it's comprehensive, anticipates every question and recommends suitable plants and landscaping solutions — all in an easy and friendly manner.

Cold Climate Gardening: How to Extend Your Growing Season by at Least 30 Days. Lewis Hill. Pownal, VT, Storey Communications, 1987. A guide to "defensive" gardening for cold climates, written with humor and good hard-won advice.

The Best of the Hardiest. John J. Sabuco. 2nd ed. Flossmoor, IL, Good Earth Publishing, 1987. Essential to the cold-climate gardener; covers many types of plants, source lists.

Trees and Shrubs for Northern Gardens and *Gardening in the Upper Midwest*. Leon Snyder, University of Minnesota Press, 1980 and 1985. Suggested by a reader in Wisconsin; I haven't seen these books.

The Year in Bloom: Gardening for all Seasons in the Pacific Northwest. Ann Lovejoy. Seattle, Sasquatch Books, 1987. Ann Lovejoy writes so well that if her name was Vita she'd be the rage. If you don't live in the Northwest, read her just for the fun of it; after all, Vita was a "local" writer, too.

Plants for Dry Climates: How to Select, Grow and Enjoy. Mary Rose Duffield & Warren D. Jones. Los Angeles, Price Stern Sloan, 1981. Plants for very dry conditions, especially the southwestern deserts.

Gardening in Dry Climates. Scott Millard. San Ramon, CA, Ortho Books, 1989. We're all learning to get along with less water; this book offers good advice on garden strategy and plant selection in dry climates.

Waterwise Gardening: Beautiful Gardens with Less Water. Menlo Park, CA, Lane Publishing Co., 1989. Landscaping ideas, irrigation systems and plant selection for gardens that use less water. Before long this won't apply just to western gardeners.

TREES AND SHRUBS

Flowering Plants in the Landscape. Mildred E. Mathias, ed. Berkeley, University of California Press, 1982. Excellent color photographs of trees, shrubs and vines for subtropical climates, with hardiness indicated.

Trees and Shrubs for Dry California Landscapes. Bob Perry. San Dimas, CA, Land Design Publications, 1981. This book has become a standard in California. Good discussion of planting for erosion and fire control and an excellent section on selecting appropriate plants.

Tropicals. Gordon Courtright. Portland, OR, Timber Press, 1988. A "visual dictionary" of plants that will grow well in zones 9 and 10; each is well described and shown in a color photograph. His similar *Trees and Shrubs for Temperate Climates* (also Timber Press, 1988) is a standard in the West, now in its third edition; the quality of the photographs is quite uneven.

Manual of Woody Landscape Plants: Their Identification, Ornamental Characteristics, Culture, Propagation and Uses. Michael A. Dirr. Champaign, IL, Stipes Publishing Co., 1983. I keep this one next to my bed — it's one of my all-time favorites! Full of excellent information (the title says it all), but also wittily written; until an edition with good color photographs is published, I use it with Brian Davis's excellent book on trees and shrubs (see "Illustrated Books") or the new one by Phillips & Rix.

Shrubs. Roger Phillips & Martyn Rix. New York, Random House, 1989. Like their excellent photographic books on roses and bulbs, this book will help you identify and choose among over 1,900 shrubs; the authors are British, and so are many of the cultivars shown. Even J. C. Raulston liked it and could find only two errors!

Trees & Shrubs Hardy in the British Isles. W. J. Bean. 8th ed. rev. London, John Murray, 1976-1980. This is the British standard for looking up trees and shrubs; it lists almost any woody plant hardy enough to grow in some part of Britain, no matter what the origin. Plant descriptions are exhaustive, but there are all too few illustrations. A supplement was published in 1988.

Trees of North America. Alan Mitchell. New York, Facts on File, 1987. Shoot me if I'm wrong, but I think this Englishman's book is called "Trees of Britain & Europe" on the other side of the pond! At any rate, it's a good all-round treatment of trees that grow well in our gardens, with color illustrations and tree profiles.

Trees for American Gardens and *Shrubs & Vines for American Gardens*. Donald Wyman. New York, Macmillan, 1965 and 1969. Two excellent books for choosing garden trees, shrubs and vines.

Plants that Merit Attention: V. 1, Trees. Janet Poor, ed. Portland, OR, Timber Press, 1984. Suggests the use of many beautiful trees not well known or widely used in the past.

100 Great Garden Plants. William H. Frederick, Jr. Portland, OR, Timber Press, 1986. Like the book above, this one draws attention to all types of woody plants off the beaten path.

Manual of Cultivated Broad-Leaved Trees & Shrubs. Gerd Krussmann. Portland, OR, Timber Press, 1985-. Multivolume set giving great detail; a challenge to Bean's work.

Conifers. D. M. Van Gelderen & J. R. P. van Hoey Smith. Portland, OR, Timber Press, 1986. A good companion to the book above; many color photographs showing trees in gardens and in their natural habitats. Many cultivars illustrated.

Ornamental Conifers. Charles R. Harrison. New York, Hafner Press, 1975. A very good treatment of conifers, both large and dwarf; good color photographs and plant descriptions, with notes on hardiness.

Japanese Maples. J. D. Vertrees. Portland, OR, Timber Press, 1987. Certainly the definitive book on Japanese maples — at least in English. Well illustrated in color, with excellent plant descriptions and information on culture. A beautiful book in itself, updated from the 1978 edition.

Palms. Alec Blombery and Tony Rodd. Topsfield, MA, Salem House, 1983. Good color photographs and plant descriptions of palms from all over the world. There is some cultural and propagation information in a separate section.

The Color Dictionary of Camellias. Stirling Macoboy. Topsfield, MA, Merrimack Pub. Circle, 1983. Good color photographs of many cultivars, good introductory treatment.

The Book of Bamboo. David Farrelly. San Francisco, Sierra Club Books, 1984. A very lovely book, giving an inspiring introduction to bamboo and its many uses.

Azaleas. Fred Galle. Portland, OR, Timber Press, 1987. According to azalea lovers, this is the bible; it is a monumental work.

Greer's Guidebook to Available Rhododendrons, Species & Hybrids. Harold E. Greer. Rev. ed. Eugene, OR, Offshoot Pub., 1987. An overview of rhododendrons available in commerce, with some information on growing and a number of color photographs. Available from Greer Gardens (see Section A.)

Magnolias. James M. Gardiner. Chester, CT, Globe Pequot, 1989. An introduction to the fabulous magnolias, with cultural information and descriptions of many species and varieties.

ALPINE & ROCK GARDEN PLANTS

Alpines for Your Garden. Alan Bloom. Chicago, Floraprint, 1981. Many color photographs, brief information on growing.

Rock Gardening: A Guide to Growing Alpines & Other Wildflowers in the American Garden. H. Lincoln Foster. Portland, OR, Timber Press, 1982. Remains the standard; it has recently been reissued.

BULBS

All About Bulbs. Rev. ed. San Ramon, CA, Ortho Books, 1986. Color guide to growing bulbs; good cultural advice, broad coverage of Dutch and species bulbs.

Bulbs: How To Select, Grow and Enjoy. George H. Scott. Los Angeles, Price Stern Sloan, 1982. A fine color-illustrated introduction to bulbs of all types and seasons.

The Bulb Book: A Photographic Guide to Over 800 Hardy Bulbs. Martin Rix & Roger Phillips. London, Pan Books, 1981. Good for identification of both plants and bulbs; mostly species bulbs.

The Little Bulbs. Elizabeth Lawrence. Durham, NC, Duke University Press, 1986. A "good read" that contains good information on species bulbs, especially narcissus.

Modern Miniature Daffodils: Species and Hybrids. James S. Wells. Portland, OR, Timber Press, 1989. These charming little bulbs may not be everybody's cup of tea, but I absolutely fell in love with them when I opened this book and so will you; they make 'King Alfred' look like Hulk Hogan.

FERNS

Ferns to Know and Grow. F. Gordon Foster. 3rd ed. Portland, OR, Timber Press, 1984. A practical guide to choosing and growing ferns in the home garden.

Fern Growers Manual. Barbara Joe Hoshizaki. New York, Knopf, 1979. Another fine book on ferns; practical advice.

Encyclopedia of Ferns. David L. Jones. Portland, OR, Timber Press, 1987. Growing, propagation, disease control, good descriptions and color and black and white photos.

FLOWER ARRANGING & PRESERVING

The Flower Arranger's Garden. Rosemary Verey. Boston, Little, Brown, 1989. The inspiration in this book comes from the arrangements themselves, which use a variety of unusual plants and containers to create charming results.

The Scented Room: Cherchez's Book of Dried Flowers, Fragrance and Potpourri. Barbara Orbach. New York, Clarkson Potter, 1986. Practical advice for preserving flowers for decoration and scent.

Everlasting Design: Ideas and Techniques for Dried Flowers. Diana Penzner & Mary Forsell. Boston, Houghton Mifflin, 1988. Suggestions for preserving and arranging garden flowers.

Flowers that Last Forever: Growing, Harvesting and Preserving. Betty M. Jacobs. Pownal, VT, Storey Communications, 1988. Suggestions for many flower crafts.

HERBS

Herb Gardening at its Best. Sal Gilbertie & Larry Sheehan. New York, Macmillan, 1980. A nice introduction, interesting and well illustrated.

Herbs: Gardens, Decorations & Recipes. Emelie Tolley & Chris Mead. New York, Crown, 1985. A very beautiful book with many color photographs; herb garden design and plant selection, how to make decorations with herbs and using herbs in cooking. A real feast for the eyes — full of inspiration.

Rodale's Illustrated Encyclopedia of Herbs. C. Kowalchik & William H. Hylton, eds. Emmaus, PA, Rodale Press, 1987. Color photos and drawings; history, uses and cultivation, index of botanical names and medicinal uses, bibliography of books and newsletters.

Herb Garden Design. Faith Swanson & Virginia Rady. Hanover, NH, University Press of New England, 1984. Full of plans and suggestions for planting herb gardens of all kinds and styles.

Landscaping with Herbs. James Adams. Portland, OR, Timber Press, 1987. Good advice on choosing and using herbs as garden plants; well written and interesting. I find the diagrams confusing, but the photographs are good. Recipes scattered throughout.

The Pleasure of Herbs: A Month-by-Month Guide to Growing, Using, and Enjoying Herbs. Phyllis Shaudys. Pownal, VT, Storey Communications, 1986. A basic guide to herbs, covering a lot of vital information in a charming manner; an ideal first herb book.

Southern Herb Growing. Madalene Hill, Gwen Barclay & Jean Hardy. Fredericksburg, TX, Shearer Publishing, 1987. Not all herbs like the hot climate of the South, but this book will prove that it can be done, and very beautifully. Good information on culture, culinary and other uses and a good selection of recipes. (406 Post Oak Road, Fredericksburg, TX 78624.)

HOUSE & GREENHOUSE PLANTS

Reader's Digest Success with Houseplants. New York, Random House, 1979. Very good information on plants and their cultural requirements, with nice color paintings throughout.

Essential Guide to Perfect House Plants. George Seddon. New York, Summit Books, 1985. By the author of my old favorite, *The Best Plant Book Ever.*

How to Select and Grow African Violets and Other Gesneriads. Theodore James, Jr. Los Angeles, Price Stern Sloan, 1983. A nice introduction to what seem to be the most popular plants in America.

How to Grow Healthy Houseplants. Rob Herwig. Los Angeles, Price Stern Sloan, 1979. Descriptions, color photographs and information on care of many popular houseplants.

Foliage Plants for Decorating Indoors. Virginie & George Elbert. Portland, OR, Timber Press, 1989. Of interest to both indoor plant professionals and hobbyists, this book is packed with essential information and includes an excellent indoor plant encyclopedia; it will be a standard for years to come.

The Miracle House Plants: African Violets and Other Easy-to-Bloom Plants in the Gesneriad Family. Virginie & George Elbert. New York, Crown, 1976. A more detailed study of gesneriads and their care.

The Bromeliads. Victoria Padilla. New York, Crown, 1986. A good, well-illustrated introduction.

The Illustrated Encyclopedia of Succulents: A Guide to the Natural History and Cultivation of Cactus and Cactus-Like Plants. Gordon Rowley. New York, Crown, 1978. Enter at your peril; you'll fall in love and want every plant you see! Good color photographs.

All About Growing Orchids. Rick Bond. San Ramon, CA, Ortho Books, 1988. There are zillions of orchid books — this is a good place to start learning the basics.

Orchids as House Plants Rebecca Northen. Rev. ed. New York, Dover, 1976. Northen's book comes highly recommended by several orchid nurseries, as does her *Home Orchid Growing*, 4th ed., published in 1990.

PERENNIALS

Perennials for American Gardens. Ruth Rogers Clausen & Nicolas H. Ekstrom. New York, Random House, 1989. A wonderful encyclopedia of perennial plants, including many that are too little known, with good general cultural information and many excellent color photographs. It has an extensive bibliography.

Herbaceous Perennial Plants: A Treatise on Their Identification, Culture and Garden Attributes. Allen M. Armitage. Athens, GA, Varsity Press, 1989. This excellent book should be on every perennial gardener's shelf — it's beautifully written, has special features such as keys to species for quick identification, information on propagation and references to further reading on many plants. Line drawings, some color photographs.

Manual of Herbaceous Ornamental Plants. Steven M. Still. 3rd ed. Champaign, IL, Stipes Publishing Co., 1988. Really a college text, this gives good information on plant selection and culture, notes on propagation, diseases and pests and has a good drawing of each plant.

The Perennial Gardener. Frederick McGourty. Boston, Houghton Mifflin, 1989. This book's a combination of practical gardening advice for northeasterners and a delightful "read" for everybody else. The descriptions of the plants and their habits, both good and bad, are frequently hilarious and always right on.

Perennial Garden Plants or the Modern Florilegium. Graham Stuart Thomas. 2nd ed. London, Dent, 1982. Written by one of the great English plantsmen, this is a "good read," with sound advice on plant selection. See also his excellent *The Art of Planting* (Boston, Godine, 1984). He has also written three much-admired books on old roses.

Perennials: How to Select, Grow & Enjoy. Pamela Harper & Frederick McGourty. Los Angeles, Price Stern Sloan, 1985. An excellent joint effort by two experts, with situation and growing well covered; beautiful color photographs.

All About Perennials. A. Cort Sinnes. San Ramon, CA, Ortho Books, 1981. Another well-written and -illustrated guide to choosing perennials — good color photographs, ideas for planting perennial borders, plant descriptions and cultural requirements.

Color in Your Garden. Penelope Hobhouse. Boston, Little, Brown, 1985. Extending your garden pleasure through the use of plants to provide interest at different seasons of the year. Worth study.

The Well-Chosen Garden. Christopher Lloyd. New York, Harper & Row, 1984. Advice on choosing garden plants from a well-known British plantsman. See also his *The Well-Tempered Gardener* and *The Adventurous Gardener* (both New York, Random House, 1985).

The Green Tapestry: Choosing and Growing the Best Perennial Plants for your Garden. Beth Chatto. New York, Simon & Schuster, 1989. This is the sort of book I love, showing how plants look in combination. This book is full of inspiring ideas and color photographs. What an eye she has!

Clematis. Barry Fretwell. Deer Park, WI, Capability's Books, 1989. Clematis has been underused in American gardens and our choice of plants has been limited, but the rash of books on clematis will soon change all that. This one has good descriptions and many good color photographs. (See Section B.)

The Hosta Book. Paul Aden. Portland, OR, Timber Press, 1988. Written by hosta experts, this book will give you a new appreciation of the diversity and usefulness of this popular plant.

The Daylily Encyclopedia. Steve Webber, ed. Damascus, MD, Webber Gardens, 1988. Lists over a thousand daylily cultivars, with good brief descriptions and cultural information. Also gives information on bloom period in various zones and lists of awards, favorites and suppliers. Only a few color photographs. (9180 Main Street, Damascus, MD 20872.)

The World of Irises. Wichita, KS, American Iris Society, 1978. A very thorough treatment of a very popular group of plants; it should make all of the confusing categories clear.

Ornamental Grass Gardening: Design Ideas, Functions and Effects. Thomas Reinhardt, Martina Reinhardt & Mark Moskowitz. Los Angeles, Price Stern Sloan, 1989. The use of ornamental grasses has become very popular. This book is full of good ideas and plant choices.

ROSES

Roses: How to Select, Grow and Enjoy. Richard Ray and Michael McCaskey. Rev. ed. Los Angeles, Price Stern Sloan, 1981. A good general introduction to roses and rose growing, full of general information and color photographs and descriptions of many popular roses.

All About Roses. Rex Wolf & James McNair. San Ramon, CA, Ortho Books, 1983. A good introductory treatment of rose growing, with color photographs of many roses; information on pruning, propagating and treating problems.

Growing Good Roses. Rayford C. Reddell. New York, Harper & Row, 1988. Good growing advice from a professional rose grower; he gives specifics on particular cultivars, steering the new grower away from those that are fussy or don't perform well.

My World of Old Roses. Trevor Griffiths. Christchurch, Whitcoulls Publishers, 1983. By a jolly New Zealander besotted with old garden roses, this book is both a good read and a feast for the eyes. *The Book of Classic Old Roses* followed (New York, Penguin USA, 1987).

Classic Roses. Peter Beales. New York, Holt, Reinhart & Winston, 1985. Another book on old roses; comprehensive coverage with hundreds of color photographs; it is one of my bedside winter-dreaming books. The author is a British rose grower and expert. See also his *Twentieth Century Roses*. New York, Harper & Row, 1989.

Roses. Roger Phillips & Martyn Rix. New York, Random House, 1988. If I only had a dollar for every time I've looked longingly through this book! It is an absolute must for lovers of roses, with good coverage of the very popular old roses. The treatment of the modern hybrids is biased toward English varieties.

VEGETABLE & FRUIT GROWING

Field and Garden Vegetables of America. Fearing Burr. Chillicothe, IL, American Botanist, 1988. Originally published in 1863, this book describes nearly 1,100 vegetable varieties in cultivation at that time; it is an invaluable source of information to those interested in identifying and preserving heirloom vegetables. Beautifully reprinted, fun to read! (See Section B.)

High-Yield Gardening: How to Get More From Your Garden Space and More From Your Garden Season. Marjorie B. Hunt & Brenda Bortz. Emmaus, PA, Rodale Press, 1986. A very practical guide, with sources and reading lists.

Gardening: The Complete Guide to Growing America's Favorite Fruits and Vegetables. National Gardening Assn. Reading, MA, Addison-Wesley, 1986. A beautiful and basic introduction to the food garden.

How to Grow More Vegetables Than You Ever Thought Possible on Less Land Than You Can Imagine. John Jeavons. Rev. ed. Berkeley, CA, Ten Speed Press, 1982. Good book on the bio- dynamic or French intensive method of organic growing by a disciple of Alan Chadwick.

Growing Vegetables West of the Cascades. Steve Solomon. Seattle, Sasquatch Books, 1989. Essential to the northwestern vegetable gardener; everything from start to finish.

Winter Gardening in the Maritime Northwest: Cool-Season Crops For the Year-Round Gardener. Binda Colebrook. Seattle, Sasquatch Books, 1989. How to keep the vegetable plot going; I think they use the term "year-round" just to rile easterners.

Growing Vegetables California Styls. Marsha Prillwitz. Sacramento, CA, Poppy Press, 1988. Advice for Californians, particularly those in the hot central valley and foothills. (P.O. Box 215485, Sacramento, CA 95821.)

Fruits & Berries for the Home Garden. Lewis Hill. Pownal, VT, Storey Communications, 1977. Practical advice on growing all sorts of fruits, including pruning and controlling diseases and insects; even some recipes.

Register of New Fruit & Nut Varieties. Brooks & Olmo. Berkeley, University of California Press, 1972. Varieties are new since 1920. Suggested by a reader who says it's the best book on hardy fruit and nuts.

Citrus — How to Select, Grow, and Enjoy. Richard Ray and Lance Walheim. Los Angeles, Price Stern Sloan, 1980. An informative and well-illustrated book on growing all sorts of citrus, including unusual kinds.

All About Citrus & Subtropical Fruits. San Ramon, CA, Ortho, 1985. A book that covers citrus and other fruit for warmer climates.

A Guide to Tropical and Subtropical Vvegetables. Nick Acrivos. Melbourne, FL, Brevard Rare Fruit Council, 1988. An excellent guide to vegetables for hot climates, including many favorites of the Orient, Africa, Central and South America. Available for $6 ppd. from Southern Seeds, Melbourne, FL (See Section A).

A Guide to Tropical Fruit Trees and Vines. Nick Acrivos. Melbourne, FL, Brevard Rare Fruit Council, 1987. A companion to the book above, describing many tropical fruits. Same source and price.

WILDFLOWERS

Growing and Propagating Wildflowers. Harry R. Phillips. Chapel Hill, University of North Carolina Press, 1985. Advice on growing wildflowers, including seed collecting and germination methods, cultivation and use in a garden setting.

The Wildflower Meadow Book: A Gardener's Guide. Laura C. Martin. Chester, CT, Globe Pequot, 1986. There's more to planting a meadow than sprinkling wildflower seeds and hoping — here's practical step-by-step information on how to do it successfully.

A Garden of Wildflowers: 101 Native Species and How to Grow Them. Henry W. Art. Pownal, VT, Storey Communications, 1986. National in scope; maps, culture and propagation, list of sources and botanical gardens with native plant collections. See also his *The Wildflower Gardener's Guide* from the same publisher; specifically for the Northeast, Great Lakes and Mid- Atlantic regions.

Growing California Native Plants. Marjorie G. Schmidt. Berkeley, University of California Press, 1980. The definitive book on growing California natives, which are different in most respects from wildflowers in the rest of the country.

LANDSCAPE HISTORY AND DESIGN

The Principles of Gardening. Hugh Johnson. New York, Simon & Schuster, 1984. This is one of my very favorite books — an all-round discussion of gardening in all aspects, it will open your eyes to the look of a garden and everything that goes into making one. I wish he'd write more gardening books.

Visions of Paradise: Themes and Variations on the Garden. Marina Schinz. New York, Stewart, Tabori & Chang, 1985. A terrific companion to Hugh Johnson's book; a feast for the eyes and the imagination.

The Education of a Gardener. Russell Page. New York, Random House, 1985. Again, not a how-to book but a thoughtful discussion of making gardens by a master. It will repay reading many times over; my copy is heavily marked up so I can find points that struck my fancy.

The Quest for Paradise: A History of the World's Gardens. Ronald King. New York, W. H. Smith, 1979. This is the best one-volume introduction to garden history that I have found, covering major gardens the world over, with good color illustrations.

The House of Boughs. Elizabeth Wilkinson & Marjorie Henderson. New York, Viking, 1985. A very interesting compendium of garden ornament in many periods and garden styles — well worth studying, especially for creating period gardens, full of ideas to trigger your creativity.

Garden Furniture and Ornament. Poughkeepsie, NY, Apollo Books, 1987. A reprint of the 1910 catalog of J. P. White's Pyghtle Works in Bedford, England, it is a gold mine of design ideas for gates, benches, arbors and treillage, pergolas, etc. The prices will make you weep; £5 for a teak bench of elaborate design!

The Oxford Companion to Gardens. Geoffrey & Susan Jellicoe, Patrick Goode, Michael Lancaster. New York, Oxford University Press, 1986. An encyclopedic reference to garden history, design and ornament; European in emphasis.

The Garden Book: Designing, Creating and Maintaining Your Garden. John Brookes. New York, Crown, 1984. A very practical and interesting guide to achieving the garden effects you want, well illustrated with contruction and planting details. See also his *The Small Garden* (New York, Crown, 1989) and *The Country Garden* (New York, Crown, 1987).

Gardens are for People. Thomas Church. 2nd ed. New York, McGraw-Hill, 1983. A treatise on creating gardens by a celebrated California landscape architect, illustrated primarily with photographs of gardens he designed.

Taylor's Guide to Garden Design. Boston, Houghton Mifflin, 1988. Thoughtful essays by experts in many types of gardens, with guides to plants for various uses; this book repays careful reading.

The New American Landscape Gardener. Phebe Leighton & Calvin Simonds. Emmaus, PA, Rodale Press, 1987. A somewhat pretentious title for a practical book that takes you through the steps of turning a plain yard into an attractive garden.

Personal Landscapes. Jerome Malitz. Portland, OR, Timber Press, 1989. It's hard to know where to list this book. It's an interesting read, but also gives forceful and witty personal opinions about garden designs that reflect natural landscapes in feeling if not in scale.

The Complete Book of Edible Landscaping. Rosalind Creasy. San Francisco, Sierra Club Books, 1982. An inspiring book which makes you think twice about plant choices for your garden! She gives lots of information on mixing edibles with ornamentals and choosing the right edibles for your garden, with detailed information on the plants.

Designing and Maintaining Your Edible Landscape Naturally. Robert Kourik. Santa Rosa, CA, Metamorphic Press, 1986. Everything there is to know about growing vegetables and fruit to make your food garden attractive as well. More "nuts and bolts" than the book above. (P.O. Box 1841, Santa Rosa, CA 95402.)

GOOD READS

The Essential Earthman: Henry Mitchell on Gardening. New York, Farrar, Straus & Giroux, 1983. This book is so full of plant love and humor that you'll want to start over again when you finish.

Onward and Upward in the Garden. Katharine S. White. New York, Farrar, Straus & Giroux, 1979. A book full of vinegary opinions; and good reading, but if you don't live in New England, you'll get no sympathy from her!

Green Thoughts: A Writer in the Garden. Eleanor Perenyi. New York, Random House, 1981. Another New Englander writing well about gardening — but honestly, it's possible to live and garden in mild climates; you don't have to freeze to be happy.

V. Sackville-West's Garden Book. New York, Macmillan, 1979. Excerpts from Vita Sackville-West's garden books and columns, organized by the months of the year. Her love of plants and ideas for plantings bubble out of the pages. A visit to Sissinghurst Castle proves that she knew her stuff.

The Illustrated Garden Book: A New Anthology. Robin Lane Fox, ed. New York, Atheneum, 1986. Mostly new excerpts from the London *Observer* garden columns of Vita Sackville-West. Nice illustrations, pictures of Sissinghurst Castle in all seasons.

Home Ground: A Gardener's Miscellany. Allen Lacy. New York, Farrar, Straus & Giroux, 1985. A collection of essays by one of our very best garden writers. See also his *Further Afield: A Gardener's Excursions* (New York, Farrar, Straus & Giroux, 1986).

The Opinionated Gardener: Random Offshoots From an Alpine Garden. Geoffrey B. Charlesworth. Boston, Godine, 1988. Very amusing essays on gardening, not just of alpines, by a man who admits that he loves to weed. He can also write with the best of them.

Thyme on my Hands. Eric Grissell. Portland, OR, Timber Press, 1987. The trials and travails of a garden maker, amusingly written and well worth his trouble if the photo on the cover is any proof. Well-developed appreciation of the garden cat, but you begin to wonder why he gardens if his back is that bad — he could take up birdwatching with his cats.

The Gardener's Year. Karel Capek. Madison, University of Wisconsin, 1984. Proof that gardening knows no boundaries, this little book written in Prague in the 1930s will make you laugh out loud — his wry observations are timeless.

Gertrude Jekyll on Gardening. Penelope Hobhouse. New York, Random House, 1985. Do I have to admit that Jekyll puts me right to sleep? Apparently Hobhouse had the same problem, so she made excerpts of the books for readers like me.

The American Gardener: A Sampler. Allen Lacy, ed. New York, Farrar, Straus & Giroux, 1988. A wonderful way to become acquainted with good garden writers. The selections are loosely arranged by subject and date from the nineteenth and twentieth centuries.

American Garden Writing: Gleanings From Garden Lives Then and Now. Bonnie Marranca, ed. New York, PAJ Publications, 1988. Another omnibus of garden writing. Her selections differ from Lacy's, so you can profitably read both.

The Gardener's Bed-Book. Richardson Wright. New York, PAJ Publications, 1988. I picked up a copy of this years ago and loved it! Humorous short essays make it perfect for the bedside table.

Ruth Page's Gardening Journal. Boston, Houghton Mifflin, 1989. Short essays taken from the popular radio programs of Ruth Page; written with good humor and offering good advice. I wish I were within the sound of her voice!

GUIDES TO GARDENS

Handbook on American Gardens: A Traveler's Guide. Brooklyn, NY, Brooklyn Botanic Garden, 1986. Gives good concise coverage of gardens in the United States. BBG Handbook #111.

The Traveler's Guide to American Gardens. Mary Helen Ray & Robert P. Nicholls, eds. Chapel Hill, University of North Carolina Press, 1988. A state-by-state guide to gardens of interest; each is briefly described, those of special merit are starred.

Gardens of North America and Hawaii: A Traveler's Guide. Irene & Walter Jacob. Portland, OR, Timber Press, 1986. Very useful; small enough to take with you on a trip; rates the gardens.

Collins Book of British Gardens: A Guide To 200 Gardens in England, Scotland & Wales. George Plumptre. London, Collins, 1985. Organized by region, then by county; black and white photos, regional maps, a page or two on each garden. The *Shell Guide to the Gardens of England and Wales* has been recently updated, too. It's distributed in this country by David & Charles.

The Rose Gardens of England. Michael Gibson. Chester, CT, Globe Pequot, 1988. Guide to English gardens with fine rose collections.

Guide to Herb Gardens. Herb Society of America. A guide to 480 herb gardens to visit in the US and Canada. $3.75 ppd.

PLANT-FINDING SOURCEBOOKS

One would think that through the magic of computers, it would be easy to compile directories of sources by botanical name. Au contraire! Such magic takes endless hours of inputting and checking; sources come and go, catalogs change every year; people spending endless hours at the computer turn to stone as their tempers grow very short! It seems to me that the best solution is to divide the job into much smaller, specialized pieces; an ideal project for plant societies. Listed below are some fine efforts.

Anderson Horticultural Library's Source List of Plants and Seeds. 1989. Completely indexes over 400 retail and wholesale catalogs; lists over 40,000 plants by botanical name. $29.95 ppd. Minnesota Landscape Arboretum, Box 39, Chanhassen, MN 55317.

The Plant Finder: 22,000 Plants and Where to Buy Them. Chris Philip. 1987. Wait a minute! This is published by the Hardy Plant Society of Great Britain, and many of the nurseries do not ship overseas (the book does not indicate which do). It's a fine effort and worth buying if you are searching for plants that are very rare in North America. $16 ppd. from HPS, 539 Woodland Ave., Media, PA 19063.

Nursery Source Manual: A Handbook. Brooklyn, NY, Brooklyn Botanic Garden, 1987. Lists 1,200 trees and shrubs by botanical name, with retail and wholesale sources. Handbook #99.

Woody Plant Source List, 1987. Ottawa, Agriculture Canada, 1987. Trevor Cole. A guide to sources of hardy plants in Canada, listed by botanical name. Lists both wholesale and retail sources.

Perennials: A Nursery Source Manual. Brooklyn, NY, Brooklyn Botanic Garden, 1989. Like their earlier "Nursery Source Manual," this guide lists many hundreds of perennials by botanical name, gives brief descriptions and indexes the plants to 60 wholesale and retail sources. Other specialist nurseries are listed as well. Handbook #118.

The Combined Rose List. Irvington NY, Beverly Dobson, annual. This is a tour de force: Beverly Dobson compiles a list every year of every species and hybrid rose cultivar listed by dozens of rose nurseries in the US, Canada and overseas. They are listed by cultivar name, with brief information on year of introduction, breeder, color of flower and where you can get it. You can't grow roses and not have it! Current issue is US$15 ppd. ($20 overseas); write to 215 Harriman Road, Irvington, NY 10533.

Longwood Gardens Plant and Seed Sources. Kennett Square, PA, Longwood Gardens, 1987. Lists mail-order sources for hundreds of plants grown in the Gardens, from trees to vegetables. Plants listed by botanical, common and cultivar names, with nursery sources. US$4.50 ppd; write to Longwood Gardens, P.O. Box 501, Kennett Square, PA 19348-0501.

Nursery Sources, Native Plants and Wild Flowers. Framingham, MA, New England Wild Flower Society, 1987. A list of wholesale and retail nurseries that specialize in native plants and wild flowers, listed by region, with notes as to plant and seed sources. US$3.50 ppd.

Sources of Native Seeds and Plants. Ankeny, IA, Soil and Water Conservation Society, 1987. A sourcebook for plants to use in conservation and restoration work — native plants, grasses and trees, both seed and plants. Sources listed by state. US$3 ppd.

Hortus Northwest: A Pacific Northwest Native Plant Directory. Dale Shank, ed. 1989. Lists 68 native plant nurseries in the northwest and northern California. $8ppd. from Hortus Northwest, P.O. Box 955, Canby, OR 97013.

Graham Center Seed and Nursery Directory. Pittsboro, NC, Rural Advancement Fund, 1988. They call it "a gardener's and farmer's guide to sources of traditional, old-timey vegetables, fruit and nut varieties, herbs and native plants." It lists sources by plant type, gives information on saving seed. Send a self-addressed stamped envelope for information to RAF, Box 1029, Pittsboro, NC 27312.

Garden Seed Inventory. Kent Whealy, ed. 2d ed. Decorah, IA, Seed Savers Publications, 1988. Lists every nonhybrid vegetable variety available from seed companies in the U.S. and Canada, with descriptions and sources for each. One of those wonderful original ideas, laboriously and lovingly compiled and extremely useful to the whole world of horticulture. Bravo! (See Seed Savers Exchange, Section D.)

Fruit, Berry and Nut Inventory. Kent Whealy, ed. Decorah, IA, Seed Saver Publications, 1989. Like their *Garden Seed Inventory*; this book lists fruit and nut varieties, with plant descriptions and sources.

Boxwood Buyer's Guide. American Boxwood Society. Boyce, VA, no date. A guide to retail, mail order and wholesale sources of boxwood. Approximately 40 species and cultivars. A model for society plant source lists, indexed by cultivar and location of source. US$3 ppd.

Herb Gardener's Resource Guide. 3rd ed. 1990. Nearly a thousand sources of herbs, herb supplies and products, herb gardens and more. Available from Northwind Farm, Route 2, Box 246, Shevlin, MN 56676. Write for price.

The American Association of Nurserymen has compiled a list of commercial plant-locating services and state commercial nursery source publications; send a long SASE for its *Plant Locators* list.

There — that's over two hundred useful and informative books, many of which are also interesting and amusing to read. And yet ... and yet ... I still haven't told you about all the books I think are wonderful: the beautiful *Euphorbia Journals* and *Caudiciform* book from Strawberry Press in Mill Valley, *Down the Garden Path* by Beverly Nichols and the equally funny *The Gardener's Friend and Other Pests* by Americans George S. Chappell and Ridgely Hunt, and what about Peter Loewer, Thalassa Cruso, Hillier's *Manual*, J.C. Raulston's *Newsletter* from the North Carolina State University Arboretum, the Good Earth Forum on Compuserve? I still think there are things I should have remembered to tell you, but it's time for you to escort me to the door and say very firmly *"Goodnight, Barbara!"*

© Sandy Mush Herb Nursery
Artist: Dorothy Lee

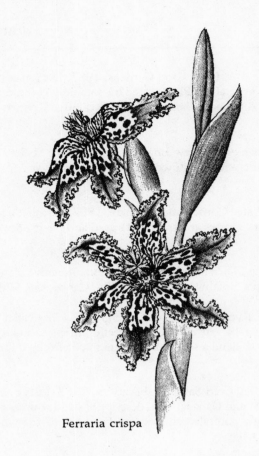

Ferraria crispa

Crocosmia

Gloriosa superba

© Bio-Quest International
Artist: Shari Smith

Indexes

H. Plant Sources Index: an index of plant and seed sources by plant specialties. Two-letter geographical codes are included to help you find the closest source or a source in a similar climate.

J. Geographical Index: an index of plant and seed sources by location. U.S. and Canadian sources are listed by state or province. Overseas sources are listed by country. Within each primary location, cities or post offices are listed alphabetically. Symbols indicate which sources have nurseries or shops and which have plant displays or display gardens to visit.

K. Product Sources Index: an index of suppliers and services listed by specialty. Within categories, sources are listed by location, and a symbol indicates whether they have a shop to visit.

L. Society Index: an index of horticultural societies listed by plant and/or other special interests.

M. Magazine Index: an alphabetical title index of magazines offered by societies, as well as other horticultural and gardening magazines, newsletters and other occasional publications. If a magazine is issued by a society, a symbol indicates whether it is available to members only.

Notes on Indexing

Each plant source or supplier is indexed for up to twelve specialties and/or trade names. When a source didn't indicate which specialties it preferred, I have chosen for them from a study of its catalog. The companies vary from small to large, and their specialties from narrow to very broad.

For those with few specialties, the indexing is very specific, but as offerings become greater, the indexing becomes broader. A small nursery that offers only ivy is listed under "Ivy," but a large nursery that includes ivy as one of its many offerings is listed under "Ground Covers." Similarly, "Sundials" is a specific category, versus the more general "Garden Ornaments."

You should check both the specific category and the general category to be sure you find all possible sources. Where specific plants are indexed — for instance, crabapples — it is because I have found a better-than-usual selection offered by that source.

The notes on catalogs in the alphabetical listings include some specialties that I was unable to index because each "listee" was limited to twelve categories. To jog your memory, you could jot the company name into the index next to the appropriate category.

A table of the symbols and abbreviations used
in this book appears on the bookmark.

PAGE SOURCE

ACACIAS
A 14   Bushland Flora (Australian Seed Specialists), Au
A 17   Carter Seeds, CA
A 22   Copacabana Gardens, CA
A 50   International Seed Supplies, Au
A 73   Nindethana Seed Service, Au
A 77   D. Orriell -- Seed Exporters, Au

ACHIMENES
A 13   Buell's Greenhouse, Inc., CT
A 42   Robert B. Hamm, CA
A 54   Karleens Achimenes, GA
A 60   Les Violettes Natalia, PQ
A 101   Sunshine Violets & Gesneriads, MA
A 103   Tiki Nursery, NC

ADENIUMS
A 13   John Brudy Exotics, FL
A 48   Jerry Horne -- Rare Plants, FL

ADROMISCHUS
A 88   Grace Rollerson, BC

AECHMEAS
A 26   Dane Company, TX
A 47   Holladay Jungle, CA
A 94   Shelldance Nursery, CA

AESCHYNANTHUS
A 47   Hill 'n dale, CA
A 52   Jeannette's Jesneriads, LA
A 60   Les Violettes Natalia, PQ
A 64   McKinney's Glasshouse, KS
A 81   Plant Villa, IL
A 81   Pleasant Hill African Violets, TX
A 92   Sedona Gardens, BC
A 101   Sunshine State Tropicals, FL
A 101   Sunshine Violets & Gesneriads, MA
A 103   Tiki Nursery, NC
A 114   Wilson's Violet Haven, TX

AFRICAN VIOLET LEAVES
A 2   Alice's Violet Room, MO
A 13   Elizabeth Buck African Violets, MI
A 16   Cape Cod Violetry, MA
A 48   Hortense's African Violets, TX
A 50   Inland African Violets, AB
A 53   JoS Violets, TX
A 55   Kent's Flowers, NE
A 60   Les Violettes Natalia, PQ
A 62   Lloyd's African Violets, NY
A 66   Marvelous Minis, MI
A 68   Mighty Minis, CA
A 81   Plant Villa, IL
A 81   Pleasant Hill African Violets, TX
A 103   Tiki Nursery, NC
A 105   Travis' Violets, GA
A 109   The Violet Showcase, CO
A 109   Violets Collectible, CA
A 114   Wilson's Violet Haven, TX
A 117   Zaca Vista Nursery, CA

AFRICAN VIOLETS
A 2   Alice's Violet Room, MO
A 13   Buell's Greenhouse, Inc., CT
A 16   Cape Cod Violetry, MA
A 26   Davidson-Wilson Greenhouses, IN
A 32   Fischer Greenhouses, NJ
A 36   Lorine Friedrich, TX
A 48   Hortense's African Violets, TX
A 50   Inland African Violets, AB
A 52   Jeannette's Jesneriads, LA
A 53   JoS Violets, TX
A 54   Kartuz Greenhouses, CA
A 55   Kent's Flowers, NE
A 63   Lyndon Lyon Greenhouses, Inc., NY
A 64   McKinney's Glasshouse, KS
A 66   Marvelous Minis, MI
A 68   Mighty Minis, CA
A 81   Plant Factory, NJ
A 81   Plant Villa, IL
A 81   Pleasant Hill African Violets, TX
A 92   Sedona Gardens, BC
A 101   Sunshine Violets & Gesneriads, MA
A 103   Tinari Greenhouses, PA
A 105   Travis' Violets, GA
A 109   The Violet Showcase, CO
A 109   Violets Collectible, CA
A 109   Volkmann Bros. Greenhouses, TX
A 109   Volkmann Gardens, TX
A 111   West Coast Violets, BC
A 114   Wilson's Violet Haven, TX
A 117   Zaca Vista Nursery, CA

AGAPANTHUS
A 3   Amaryllis, Inc., LA
A 9   Bio-Quest International, CA
A 28   Dunford Farms, WA

AGAVES
A 5   Apacha Cactus, CA
A 15   Cactus Gem Nursery, AR
A 19   Christa's Cactus, AZ
A 46   Highland Succulents, OH
A 56   Gerhard Koehres Cactus & Succulent Nursery, We
A 66   Marilynn's Garden, CA
A 67   Mesa Garden, NM
A 72   Neon Palm Nursery, CA
A 72   New Mexico Cactus Research, NM
A 100   Succulent Plants, MN
A 101   Sunnyvale Cactus Nursery, MA
A 117   Yucca Do Nursery, TX

AJUGAS
A 83   Prentiss Court Ground Covers, SC
A 103   Ter-El Nursery, PA
A 106   Turnipseed Nursery Farms, GA

ALLIUMS
A 6   Avon Bulbs, En
A 12   Broadleigh Gardens, En
A 13   Bundles of Bulbs, MD
A 19   Paul Christian -- Rare Plants, Wa
A 25   The Daffodil Mart, VA

PAGE SOURCE

ALLIUMS (continued)
A 26   Peter De Jager Bulb Co., MA
A 36   Frosty Hollow Nursery, WA
A 42   Dr. Joseph C. Halinar, OR
A 48   Honeywood Lilies, SK
A 67   Messelaar Bulb Co., MA
A 69   Monashee Gardens, BC
A 82   Potterton & Martin, En
A 88   Robinett Bulb Farm, CA
A 108   Van Engelen, Inc., CT
A 108   Veldheer Tulip Gardens, MI

ALOES
A 1   Abbey Gardens, CA
A 5   Apacha Cactus, CA
A 15   Cactus by Mueller, CA
A 15   Cactus Gem Nursery, AR
A 19   Christa's Cactus, AZ
A 27   Desert Theatre, CA
A 41   Grigsby Cactus Gardens, CA
A 46   Highland Succulents, OH
A 56   Gerhard Koehres Cactus & Succulent Nursery, We
A 66   Marilynn's Garden, CA
A 67   Mesa Garden, NM
A 72   Neon Palm Nursery, CA
A 78   The PanTree, CA
A 100   Succulent Plants, MN
A 100   Succulenta, CA

ALPINE PLANTS
See also specific plants
A 2   Albiflora, Inc., Ja
A 3   Alpenflora Gardens, BC
A 3   Alpine Gardens & Calico Shop, WI
A 9   Birch Farm Nursery, En
A 10   Bluestone Perennials, OH
A 16   Callahan Seeds, OR
A 18   Chadwell Himalayan Seed, En
A 19   Chehalis Rare Plant Nursery, WA
A 19   Chiltern Seeds, En
A 21   Colorado Alpines, Inc., CO
A 26   Daystar, ME
A 36   Frosty Hollow Nursery, WA
A 46   High Altitude Gardens, ID
A 49   J. L. Hudson, Seedsman, CA
A 52   Klaus R. Jelitto, We
A 57   P. Kohli & Co., In
A 57   L. Kreeger, En
A 61   Life-Form Replicators, MI
A 70   Mt. Tahoma Nursery, WA
A 72   Nature's Garden Nursery, OR
A 87   Rice Creek Gardens, MN
A 90   Jim & Irene Russ Quality Plants, CA
A 93   The Seed Source, NC
A 93   Seedalp, Sw
A 96   Siskiyou Rare Plant Nursery, OR
A 96   Skyline Nursery, WA
A 97   Solar Green, Ltd., ID
A 98   Southern Seeds, Ne
A 98   Southwestern Native Seeds, AZ
A 99   Springvale Farm Nursery, IL
A 102   Surry Gardens, ME
A 104   Torbay's Plant World, En
A 107   Twombly Nursery, CT

ALSTROEMERIAS
A 3   Alpine Valley Gardens, CA
A 6   B & D Lilies, WA
A 28   Dunford Farms, WA
A 80   Pine Heights Nursery, Au

PAGE SOURCE

ALSTROEMERIAS
A 88   Robinett Bulb Farm, CA

AMARANTH
A 24   Cross Seed Company, KS
A 39   The Grain Exchange, KS
A 60   Le Champion Heritage Seeds, CA
A 71   Native Seeds/SEARCH, AZ
A 81   Plants of the Southwest, NM
A 98   Southern Seeds, FL
A 102   Talavaya Seeds, NM

AMARYLLIS
A 3   Amaryllis, Inc., LA
A 9   Bio-Quest International, CA
A 25   The Daffodil Mart, VA
A 26   Peter De Jager Bulb Co., MA
A 28   Dutch Gardens, Inc., NJ
A 38   Gladside Gardens, MA
A 54   Kelly's Plant World, CA
A 67   Messelaar Bulb Co., MA
A 80   Pine Heights Nursery, Au
A 84   Quality Dutch Bulbs, NJ
A 107   TyTy Plantation, GA
A 107   Van Bourgondien Bros., Inc., NY
A 108   Van Engelen, Inc., CT

ANNUALS
See also Flowers, Heirloom
A 1   Abundant Life Seed Foundation, WA
A 2   Alberta Nurseries & Seed Company, AB
A 2   Allen, Sterling & Lothrop, ME
A 6   Archias' Seed Store, MO
A 11   Bountiful Gardens, CA
A 14   W. Atlee Burpee Company, PA
A 14   D. V. Burrell Seed Growers Co., CO
A 14   Bushland Flora (Australian Seed Specialists), Au
A 14   The Butchart Gardens, BC
A 17   Carter Seeds, CA
A 19   Chiltern Seeds, En
A 21   Comstock, Ferre & Co., CT
A 23   The Country Garden, WI
A 24   Crosman Seed Corp., NY
A 25   William Dam Seeds, ON
A 26   Dan's Garden Shop, MD
A 27   DeGiorgi Seed Company, NE
A 27   Dominion Seed House, ON
A 28   E & H Products, CA
A 28   Early's Farm & Garden Centre, Inc., SK
A 31   F W H Seed Exchange, CA
A 31   Fedco Seeds, ME
A 32   Henry Field Seed & Nursery Co., IA
A 35   Fox Hollow Herbs, PA
A 35   The Fragrant Path, NE
A 36   Garden City Seeds, MT
A 37   Gardenimport, Inc., ON
A 40   Green Horizons, TX
A 41   Grianan Gardens, CA
A 41   Gurney Seed & Nursery Co., SD
A 43   Harris Seeds, NY
A 43   Hastings, GA
A 43   Havasu Hills Herbs, CA
A 46   High Altitude Gardens, ID
A 49   J. L. Hudson, Seedsman, CA
A 49   Ed Hume Seeds, Inc., WA
A 50   Intermountain Seeds, ID
A 51   Island Seed Mail Order, BC
A 52   Johnny's Selected Seeds, ME
A 53   J. W. Jung Seed Co., WI
A 55   Kilgore Seed Company, FL
(continued next page)

PAGE SOURCE

ANNUALS (continued)
A 56   Kings Herb Seeds, Au
A 58   D. Landreth Seed Company, MD
A 60   Orol Ledden & Sons, NJ
A 61   Liberty Seed Company, OH
A 64   McFayden Seeds, MB
A 67   Earl May Seed & Nursery Co., IA
A 68   Meyer Seed Co., MD
A 70   Mountain Valley Seeds & Nursery, UT
A 71   National Heirloom Flower Seed Exchange, MA
A 72   Nichols Garden Nursery, Inc., OR
A 73   Northplan/Mountain Seed, ID
A 75   Ontario Seed Company, Ltd., ON
A 77   Ozark National Seed Order, NY
A 78   Park Seed Company, Inc., SC
A 80   Pinetree Garden Seeds, ME
A 82   Pony Creek Nursery, WI
A 84   Putney Nursery, Inc., VT
A 85   Ravenswood Seeds, WI
A 89   Roswell Seed Co., NM
A 90   SPB Sales, TX
A 92   Seed Centre, Ltd., AB
A 93   Seeds Blum, ID
A 93   Seedway, Inc., NY
A 93   Select Seeds, CT
A 95   Shepherd's Garden Seeds, CA
A 95   R. H. Shumway Seedsman, SC
A 95   Siegers Seed Co., MI
A 98   Specialty Seeds, Au
A 100   Stokes Seed Company, NY
A 102   T & T Seeds, Ltd., MB
A 103   Territorial Seed Company, OR
A 103   Thompson & Morgan, NJ
A 105   Tregunno Seeds, ON
A 106   Otis Twilley Seed Co., PA
A 108   Vermont Bean Seed Co., VT
A 109   Vesey's Seeds, Ltd., PE
A 112   Westwind Seeds, AZ
A 113   Wild Seeds, Wa
A 116   Wyatt-Quarles Seed Co., NC

ANTHURIUMS
A 17   Carter & Holmes, Inc., SC
A 20   City Gardens, MI
A 30   Exotics Hawaii, Ltd., HI
A 35   Fox Orchids, Inc., AR
A 48   Jerry Horne -- Rare Plants, FL
A 66   Marilynn's Garden, CA
A 106   Tropicals Unlimited, HI

APPLES
A 1   Adams County Nursery, Inc., PA
A 4   Ames' Orchard and Nursery, AR
A 13   Buckley Nursery, WA
A 13   Burford Brothers, VA
A 20   Cloud Mountain Nursery, WA
A 29   Emlong Nurseries, MI
A 31   Farmer Seed & Nursery, MN
A 40   Greenmantle Nursery, CA
A 52   Johnson Nursery, GA
A 58   LBG Nursery, MN
A 62   Long Hungry Creek Nursery, TN
A 70   Moosebell Flower, Fruit & Tree Co., ME
A 72   New York State Fruit Testing Coop. Assn., NY
A 82   Pony Creek Nursery, WI
A 88   Rocky Meadow Orchard & Nursery, IN
A 90   St. Lawrence Nurseries, NY
A 99   Stark Bro's Nurseries & Orchards Co., MO
A 107   TyTy South Orchards, GA
A 108   VanWell Nursery, Inc., WA

PAGE SOURCE

APPLES
A 115   Windy Ridge Nursery, AB
A 115   Womack's Nursery Co., TX

APPLES, ANTIQUE
A 4   Ames' Orchard and Nursery, AR
A 5   Arbor & Espalier, CA
A 8   Bear Creek Nursery, WA
A 13   Burford Brothers, VA
A 29   Edible Landscaping, VA
A 38   Golden Bough Tree Farm, ON
A 40   Greenmantle Nursery, CA
A 46   Hidden Springs Nursery -- Edible Landscaping, TN
A 59   Lawson's Nursery, GA
A 62   Living Tree Centre, CA
A 62   Long Hungry Creek Nursery, TN
B 33   Pomona Book Exchange, ON
A 97   Sonoma Antique Apple Nursery, CA
A 98   Southern Exposure Seed Exchange, VA
A 98   Southmeadow Fruit Gardens, MI
A 104   Tolowa Nursery, OR
A 106   Tsolum River Fruit Trees, BC

APPLES, ANTIQUE (SAMPLES TO TASTE)
A 5   Applesource, IL
A 97   Sonoma Antique Apple Nursery, CA

APPLES, LOW-CHILL
A 24   Cumberland Valley Nurseries, Inc., TN
A 30   Exotica Rare Fruit Nursery, CA
A 51   Ison's Nursery, GA
A 62   Long Hungry Creek Nursery, TN
A 76   Oregon Exotica Nursery, OR
A 97   Sonoma Antique Apple Nursery, CA

APRICOTS
A 1   Adams County Nursery, Inc., PA
A 13   Buckley Nursery, WA
A 24   Cumberland Valley Nurseries, Inc., TN
A 29   Emlong Nurseries, MI
A 38   Golden Bough Tree Farm, ON
A 41   Grimo Nut Nursery, ON
A 46   Hidden Springs Nursery -- Edible Landscaping, TN
A 51   Ison's Nursery, GA
A 62   Living Tree Centre, CA
A 72   New York State Fruit Testing Coop. Assn., NY
A 115   Womack's Nursery Co., TX

AQUATIC PLANTS
See also Bog Plants
See also specific plants
A 9   Kurt Bluemel, Inc., MD
A 20   Coastal Gardens & Nursery, SC
A 23   Country Wetlands Nursery, WI
A 29   Eco-Gardens, GA
A 40   Greenlee Nursery, CA
A 41   Gurney Seed & Nursery Co., SD
A 55   Kester's Wild Game Food Nurseries, WI
A 59   Laurie's Garden, OR
A 61   Lilypons Water Gardens, MD
A 66   Maryland Aquatic Nurseries, MD
A 70   Moore Water Gardens, ON
A 78   Paradise Water Gardens, MA
A 79   Perry's Water Gardens, NC
A 91   Santa Barbara Water Gardens, CA
A 91   S. Scherer & Sons, NY
A 96   Slocum Water Gardens, FL
A 97   South Florida Seed Supply, FL
A 103   Tilley's Nursery/The WaterWorks, PA
A 105   William Tricker, Inc., OH
(continued next page)

PAGE SOURCE

AQUATIC PLANTS (continued)

A 108   Van Ness Water Gardens, CA
A 110   Water Ways Nursery, VA
A 110   Waterford Gardens, NJ
A 112   Wicklein's Aquatic Farm & Nursery, Inc., MD
A 113   Wildlife Nurseries, WI

AQUILEGIAS

A 9   Blackmore & Langdon, En
A 16   Canyon Creek Nursery, CA
A 21   Colorado Alpines, Inc., CO
A 24   Cricklewood Nursery, WA
A 24   Crownsville Nursery, MD
A 28   Donaroma's Nursery, MA
A 35   The Fragrant Path, NE
A 43   Hauser's Superior View Farm, WI
A 57   L. Kreeger, En
A 61   Life-Form Replicators, MI
A 61   Linn Farm Perennials, VA
A 69   Montrose Nursery, NC
A 93   The Seed Source, NC
A 93   Seedalp, Sw
A 93   Select Seeds, CT
A 104   Torbay's Plant World, En
A 112   Whayes End Nursery, VA

AROIDS

A 13   John Brudy Exotics, FL
A 30   Exotics Hawaii, Ltd., HI
A 37   Garden World, TX
A 38   Gladside Gardens, MA
A 38   Glasshouse Works, OH
A 41   Gulf Coast Plantsmen, LA
A 44   Heliconia Haus, FL
A 48   Jerry Horne -- Rare Plants, FL
A 65   Ann Mann's Orchids, FL
A 81   The Plant Shop's Botanical Gardens, CA
A 98   Southern Exposure, TX

ASPARAGUS

A 1   Ahrens Nursery & Plant Labs, IN
A 2   Allen Company, MD
A 9   Blue Star Lab, NY
A 12   Brittingham Plant Farms, MD
A 52   Jackson & Perkins Co., OR
A 57   Krohne Plant Farms, MI
A 58   D. Landreth Seed Company, MD
A 74   Nourse Farms, Inc., MA
A 86   Rayner Bros., MD
A 87   Rider Nurseries, IA

ASTERS, PERENNIAL

A 33   Flora Favours, WI
A 50   Indigo Knoll Perennials, MD
A 58   Lamb Nurseries, WA
A 102   Surry Gardens, ME

ASTILBES

A 14   Busse Gardens, MN
A 28   Donaroma's Nursery, MA
A 33   Flora Favours, WI
A 94   Shady Oaks Nursery, MN
A 109   Andre Viette Farm & Nursery, VA

AVOCADOS

A 16   California Nursery Co., CA
A 22   Copacabana Gardens, CA
A 98   South Seas Nursery, CA

PAGE SOURCE

AZALEAS, DECIDUOUS

A 6   B & B Laboratories, WA
A 17   Carlson's Gardens, NY
A 24   The Cummins Garden, NJ
A 33   Flora Lan Nursery, OR
A 38   Girard Nurseries, OH
A 42   Hammond's Acres of Rhodys, WA
A 47   Hillhouse Nursery, NJ
A 72   E. B. Nauman, Nurseryman, NY
A 74   Oak Hill Farm, SC
A 89   Roslyn Nursery, NY
A 103   Thomasville Nurseries, GA
A 105   Transplant Nursery, GA
A 112   Westgate Garden Nursery, CA
A 112   Whitney Gardens, WA

AZALEAS, EVERGREEN

A 17   Carlson's Gardens, NY
A 24   The Cummins Garden, NJ
A 33   Flora Lan Nursery, OR
A 38   Girard Nurseries, OH
A 40   The Greenery, WA
A 41   Gulf Coast Plantsmen, LA
A 42   Hammond's Acres of Rhodys, WA
A 43   James Harris Hybrid Azaleas, GA
A 47   Hillhouse Nursery, NJ
A 47   Holly Hills, Inc., IN
A 65   Magnolia Nursery & Display Garden, AL
A 69   Miniature Plant Kingdom, CA
A 71   Musser Forests Inc., PA
A 74   Oak Hill Farm, SC
A 77   Owen Farms, TN
A 89   Roslyn Nursery, NY
A 97   Sorum's Nursery, OR
A 100   Stubbs Shrubs, OR
A 103   Thomasville Nurseries, GA
A 105   Transplant Nursery, GA
A 112   Westgate Garden Nursery, CA
A 112   Whitney Gardens, WA

AZALEAS, HYBRIDS

A 5   Appalachian Gardens, PA
A 11   The Bovees Nursery, OR
A 17   Carlson's Gardens, NY
A 18   Chambers Nursery, OR
A 24   Crownsville Nursery, MD
A 27   DeGrandchamp's Blueberry Farm, MI
A 41   Greer Gardens, OR
A 42   Hall Rhododendrons, OR
A 42   Hammond's Acres of Rhodys, WA
A 43   James Harris Hybrid Azaleas, GA
A 43   Hass Nursery, OR
A 47   Hillhouse Nursery, NJ
A 47   Holly Hills, Inc., IN
A 53   Justice Gardens, GA
A 74   Nuccio's Nurseries, CA
A 103   Thomasville Nurseries, GA
A 105   Transplant Nursery, GA
A 107   Twombly Nursery, CT
A 112   Frank B. White, Jr., MD
A 112   Whitney Gardens, WA
B 43   Winterthur Museum & Gardens, DE

AZALEAS, SPECIES

A 11   The Bovees Nursery, OR
A 16   Camellia Forest Nursery, NC
A 17   Carlson's Gardens, NY
A 29   Eco-Gardens, GA
A 42   Hammond's Acres of Rhodys, WA
A 43   James Harris Hybrid Azaleas, GA

(continued next page)

PAGE SOURCE

AZALEAS, SPECIES (continued)
A 47　　Holly Hills, Inc., IN
A 58　　Lamtree Farm, NC
A 63　　The Lowrey Nursery, TX
A 65　　Magnolia Nursery & Display Garden, AL
A 65　　Maple Leaf Nursery, CA
A 74　　Northwest Biological Enterprises, OR
A 74　　Oak Hill Farm, SC
A 92　　F. W. Schumacher Co., MA
A 105　　Transplant Nursery, GA
A 112　　Whitney Gardens, WA

BAMBOO
A 7　　A Bamboo Shoot, CA
A 7　　Bamboo Sourcery, CA
A 9　　Kurt Bluemel, Inc., MD
A 10　　Bonsai of Georgia, GA
A 16　　California Nursery Co., CA
A 29　　Endangered Species, CA
A 38　　Glasshouse Works, OH
A 72　　Neon Palm Nursery, CA
A 99　　Stallings Exotic Nursery, CA
A 104　　Tradewinds Nursery, CA
A 107　　Upper Bank Nurseries, PA

BAMBOO, HARDY
A 4　　American Bamboo Company, OH
A 7　　A Bamboo Shoot, CA
A 7　　Bamboo Sourcery, CA
A 9　　Kurt Bluemel, Inc., MD
A 21　　Colvos Creek Nursery & Landscaping, WA
A 29　　Endangered Species, CA
A 41　　Gulf Coast Plantsmen, LA
A 63　　Louisiana Nursery, LA
A 84　　Raintree Nursery, WA
A 86　　Steve Ray's Bamboo Gardens, AL
A 104　　Tradewinds Nursery, CA
A 106　　Tripple Brook Farm, MA
A 107　　Upper Bank Nurseries, PA

BANANAS
A 7　　The Banana Tree, PA
A 22　　Copacabana Gardens, CA
A 30　　Exotica Rare Fruit Nursery, CA
A 37　　Garden World, TX
A 60　　W. O. Lessard Nursery, FL
A 87　　Richardson's Seaside Banana Garden, CA
A 98　　Southern Seeds, FL
A 99　　Stallings Exotic Nursery, CA
A 107　　TyTy South Orchards, GA

BANKSIAS
A 14　　Bushland Flora (Australian Seed Specialists), Au
A 50　　International Seed Supplies, Au
A 73　　Nindethana Seed Service, Au
A 77　　D. Orriell -- Seed Exporters, Au
A 84　　Protea Seed & Nursery Suppliers, So
A 105　　Trans Pacific Nursery, OR

BASILS
A 109　　Village Arbors, AL

BEANS
A 24　　Cross Seed Company, KS
A 30　　Evergreen Y. H. Enterprises, CA
A 32　　Fern Hill Farm, NJ
A 36　　Garden City Seeds, MT
A 39　　Good Seed Co., WA
A 44　　Heirloom Seeds, PA
A 46　　High Altitude Gardens, ID

BEANS
A 60　　Le Champion Heritage Seeds, CA
A 62　　Lockhart Seeds, CA
A 69　　Miller-Bowie County Farmers Assn., TX
A 70　　Mountain Valley Seeds & Nursery, UT
A 71　　Native Seeds/SEARCH, AZ
A 108　　Vermont Bean Seed Co., VT
A 112　　Westwind Seeds, AZ
A 114　　Willhite Seed Co., TX

BEE PLANTS
A 1　　Abundant Life Seed Foundation, WA
A 12　　Joseph Brown, Native Seeds, VA
A 18　　John Chambers, En
A 21　　Companion Plants, OH
A 28　　Dutch Mill Herb Farm, OR
A 29　　Earthstar Herb Gardens, AZ
A 35　　Fox Hill Farm, MI
A 39　　Good Hollow Greenhouse & Herbarium, TN
A 39　　Goodwin Creek Gardens, OR
A 42　　Halcyon Gardens, PA
A 43　　Havasu Hills Herbs, CA
A 44　　The Herbfarm, WA
A 45　　Herbs-Liscious, IA
A 56　　Kimberly Garden on Oregon Hill, NY
A 73　　Northplan/Mountain Seed, ID
A 79　　Theodore Payne Foundation, CA
A 83　　Prairie Nursery, WI
A 85　　Rasland Farm, NC
A 91　　Sandy Mush Herb Nursery, NC
A 93　　Select Seeds, CT
B 38　　Sunstream Bee Supply, PA
A 102　　Taylor's Herb Gardens, CA

BEECHES
A 14　　Burnt Ridge Nursery, WA
A 20　　Coenosium Gardens, OR
A 35　　Foxborough Nursery, Inc., MD
A 49　　Hughes Nursery, WA
A 57　　Michael & Janet Kristick, PA
A 107　　Twombly Nursery, CT
A 112　　Whitman Farms, OR

BEGONIAS, FOLIAGE
A 38　　Glasshouse Works, OH
A 42　　Robert B. Hamm, CA
A 54　　Kartuz Greenhouses, CA
A 54　　Kay's Greenhouses, TX
A 59　　Lauray of Salisbury, CT
A 62　　Logee's Greenhouses, CT
A 63　　Paul P. Lowe, FL
A 66　　Marvelous Minis, MI
A 68　　Mighty Minis, CA
A 81　　Plant Factory, NJ
A 81　　The Plant Shop's Botanical Gardens, CA
A 92　　Sedona Gardens, BC
A 101　　Sunshine State Tropicals, FL
A 101　　Sunshine Violets & Gesneriads, MA
A 103　　Tiki Nursery, NC

BEGONIAS, TUBEROUS
A 5　　Antonelli Brothers, Inc., CA
A 9　　Blackmore & Langdon, En
A 11　　Breck's, IL
A 24　　Cruickshank's, Inc., ON
A 28　　Dutch Gardens, Inc., NJ
A 31　　Fairyland Begonia & Lily Garden, CA
A 36　　G & G Gardens and Growers, CA
A 37　　Gardenimport, Inc., ON
A 50　　Inter-State Nurseries, IA
(continued next page)

PAGE SOURCE

PAGE SOURCE

BEGONIAS, TUBEROUS (continued)

A 91   John Scheepers, Inc., NY
A 99   Stanek's Garden Center, WA
A 107 Van Bourgondien Bros., Inc., NY
A 108 Veldheer Tulip Gardens, MI

BERBERIS

A 45   Heronswood Nursery, WA
A 97   Smith Nursery Co., IA
A 110 Wavecrest Nursery & Landscaping Co., MI
A 117 Yucca Do Nursery, TX

BERRIES, MIXED

See also specific berries

A 4   Ames' Orchard and Nursery, AR
A 8   Vernon Barnes & Son Nursery, TN
A 10   Boston Mountain Nurseries, AR
A 12   Brittingham Plant Farms, MD
A 20   Cloud Mountain Nursery, WA
A 27   Dominion Seed House, ON
A 31   Farmer Seed & Nursery, MN
A 31   Fedco Seeds, ME
A 35   Fowler Nurseries, Inc., CA
A 36   Garden of Delights, FL
A 43   Hastings, GA
A 52   Johnson Nursery, GA
A 53   J. W. Jung Seed Co., WI
A 54   Kelly Nurseries, NY
A 57   V. Kraus Nurseries, Ltd., ON
A 60   Henry Leuthardt Nurseries, Inc., NY
A 64   McConnell Nurseries, Inc., ON
A 69   J. E. Miller Nurseries, Inc., NY
A 70   Morden Nurseries, Ltd., MB
A 74   Northwoods Nursery, OR
A 77   Pacific Berry Works, WA
A 78   Pacific Tree Farms, CA
A 79   Pense Nursery, AR
A 82   Pony Creek Nursery, WI
A 84   Raintree Nursery, WA
A 86   Rayner Bros., MD
A 91   Savage Farms Nursery, TN
A 95   R. H. Shumway Seedsman, SC
A 99   Stanek's Garden Center, WA
A 99   Stark Bro's Nurseries & Orchards Co., MO
A 102 T & T Seeds, Ltd., MB
A 104 Tolowa Nursery, OR
A 107 TyTy South Orchards, GA
A 108 VanWell Nursery, Inc., WA

BILLBERGIAS

A 26   Dane Company, TX
A 38   Golden Lake Greenhouses, CA
A 47   Holladay Jungle, CA
A 94   Shelldance Nursery, CA

BLACKBERRIES

A 1   Ahrens Nursery & Plant Labs, IN
A 2   Allen Company, MD
A 10   Boston Mountain Nurseries, AR
A 12   Brittingham Plant Farms, MD
A 13   Buckley Nursery, WA
A 28   Dyke Bros. Nursery, OH
A 30   Enoch's Berry Farm, AR
A 51   Ison's Nursery, GA
A 65   Makielski Berry Farm & Nursery, MI
A 70   Mt. Leo Nursery, TN
A 74   Nourse Farms, Inc., MA
A 79   Pense Nursery, AR
A 86   Rayner Bros., MD

BLUEBERRIES, HARDY

A 2   Allen Company, MD
A 4   Ames' Orchard and Nursery, AR
A 8   Bear Creek Nursery, WA
A 9   Blue Star Lab, NY
A 9   Blueberry Hill, ON
A 10   Boston Mountain Nurseries, AR
A 12   Brittingham Plant Farms, MD
A 20   Cloud Mountain Nursery, WA
A 27   DeGrandchamp's Blueberry Farm, MI
A 28   Dyke Bros. Nursery, OH
A 29   Edible Landscaping, VA
A 43   Hartmann's Plantation, Inc., MI
A 46   Highlander Nursery, AR
A 65   Makielski Berry Farm & Nursery, MI
A 69   J. E. Miller Nurseries, Inc., NY
A 86   Rayner Bros., MD
A 90   St. Lawrence Nurseries, NY
A 115 Windy Ridge Nursery, AB

BLUEBERRIES, RABBITEYE (LOW-CHILL)

A 32   Finch Blueberry Nursery, NC
A 43   Hartmann's Plantation, Inc., MI
A 46   Highlander Nursery, AR
A 51   Ison's Nursery, GA
A 59   Lawson's Nursery, GA
A 77   Owen's Vineyard & Nursery, GA

BOG PLANTS

See also Aquatic Plants

A 10   Boehlke's Woodland Gardens, WI
A 17   Carolina Exotic Gardens, NC
A 20   Coastal Gardens & Nursery, SC
A 23   Country Wetlands Nursery, WI
A 60   Lee's Botanical Gardens, FL
A 61   Life-Form Replicators, MI
A 61   Lilypons Water Gardens, MD
A 61   Limerock Ornamental Grasses, PA
A 66   Maryland Aquatic Nurseries, MD
A 70   Moore Water Gardens, ON
A 72   Niche Gardens, NC
A 75   Oakridge Nurseries, NH
A 75   Orchid Gardens, MN
A 79   Perry's Water Gardens, NC
A 79   Peter Pauls Nurseries, NY
A 83   Prairie Ridge Nursery/CRM Ecosystems, Inc., WI
A 87   Rice Creek Gardens, MN
A 91   Santa Barbara Water Gardens, CA
A 91   S. Scherer & Sons, NY
A 96   Slocum Water Gardens, FL
A 97   South Florida Seed Supply, FL
A 103 Tilley's Nursery/The WaterWorks, PA
A 105 William Tricker, Inc., OH
A 106 Tripple Brook Farm, MA
A 107 Twombly Nursery, CT
A 108 Van Ness Water Gardens, CA
A 110 Waterford Gardens, NJ
A 112 Wicklein's Aquatic Farm & Nursery, Inc., MD
A 113 Wild Seeds, Wa
A 113 Wildflower Nursery, NC

BONSAI, FINISHED

B 6   Bonsai Creations, FL
A 10   Bonsai of Georgia, GA
A 10   The Bonsai Shop, NY
A 13   Brussel's Bonsai Nursery, MS
A 20   City Gardens, MI
A 66   Matsu-Momiji Nursery, PA
A 69   Miniature Plant Kingdom, CA
A 81   Plant City Bonsai, GA
(continued next page)

PAGE SOURCE

BONSAI, FINISHED (continued)
A 94   Shanti Bithi Nursery, CT
A 114   Wildwood Gardens, OH

BONSAI, PLANTS FOR
See also specific plants
A 6   Artistic Plants, TX
B 6   Bonsai Associates, Inc., MD
B 6   Bonsai Creations, FL
A 10   Bonsai Farm, TX
A 10   Bonsai of Georgia, GA
A 13   Brussel's Bonsai Nursery, MS
A 20   City Gardens, MI
A 20   Coenosium Gardens, OR
A 24   The Cummins Garden, NJ
A 27   Del's Japanese Maples, OR
A 34   Forestfarm, OR
A 35   Foxborough Nursery, Inc., MD
A 38   Girard Nurseries, OH
A 38   Glasshouse Works, OH
A 40   Greenlife Gardens Greenhouses, GA
A 48   Jerry Horne -- Rare Plants, FL
A 57   Michael & Janet Kristick, PA
A 63   Loucks Nursery, OR
A 65   Maple Leaf Nursery, CA
A 65   Maplewood Seed Company, OR
A 66   Marrs Tree Farm, WA
A 66   Matsu-Momiji Nursery, PA
A 69   Miniature Plant Kingdom, CA
A 70   Mt. Tahoma Nursery, WA
A 77   Owen Farms, TN
B 32   Pine Garden Pottery, WA
A 81   Plant City Bonsai, GA
A 86   Rhapis Gardens, TX
A 88   Grace Rollerson, BC
A 94   Shanti Bithi Nursery, CT
A 96   Singers' Growing Things, CA
A 97   South Florida Seed Supply, FL
A 98   Southern Seeds, Ne
A 99   Springvale Farm Nursery, IL
A 99   Stallings Exotic Nursery, CA
A 100   Succulent Plants, MN
A 101   Sunnyslope Gardens, CA
A 105   Trans Pacific Nursery, OR
A 105   Transplant Nursery, GA
A 114   Wildwood Gardens, OH

BOUGAINVILLEA
A 26   Davidson-Wilson Greenhouses, IN
A 82   The Plumeria People, TX
A 92   Sedona Gardens, BC
A 99   Stallings Exotic Nursery, CA
A 101   Sunshine State Tropicals, FL

BOX
A 5   Appalachian Gardens, PA
A 17   Carroll Gardens, MD
A 24   The Cummins Garden, NJ
A 26   Daystar, ME
A 35   Foxborough Nursery, Inc., MD
A 45   Heronswood Nursery, WA

BRODIAEAS
A 88   Robinett Bulb Farm, CA

BROMELIADS
See also specific plants
A 2   Alberts & Merkel Bros., Inc., FL
A 10   Arthur Boe Distributor, LA
A 20   City Gardens, MI

BROMELIADS
A 26   Dane Company, TX
A 30   Exotics Hawaii, Ltd., HI
A 34   Fort Caroline Orchids, FL
A 35   Fox Orchids, Inc., AR
A 38   Glasshouse Works, OH
A 38   Golden Lake Greenhouses, CA
A 47   Holladay Jungle, CA
A 63   Paul P. Lowe, FL
A 65   Ann Mann's Orchids, FL
A 66   Marilynn's Garden, CA
A 72   Neon Palm Nursery, CA
A 74   Oak Hill Gardens, IL
A 81   The Plant Shop's Botanical Gardens, CA
A 84   Rainforest Flora, Inc., CA
A 94   Shelldance Nursery, CA
A 98   Southern Exposure, TX
A 101   W. K. Quality Bromeliads, CA

BUCKWHEAT
A 24   Cross Seed Company, KS
A 39   The Grain Exchange, KS
A 55   Kester's Wild Game Food Nurseries, WI
A 83   Prairie State Commodities, IL

BULBS, SPECIES
See also specific plants
A 6   Avon Bulbs, En
A 6   B & B Laboratories, WA
A 9   Bio-Quest International, CA
A 12   Broadleigh Gardens, En
A 13   Bundles of Bulbs, MD
A 16   Cape Seed & Bulb, So
A 18   Chadwell Himalayan Seed, En
A 19   Paul Christian -- Rare Plants, Wa
A 21   Conley's Garden Center, ME
A 24   Cricklewood Nursery, WA
A 24   Cruickshank's, Inc., ON
A 25   The Daffodil Mart, VA
A 29   Eco-Gardens, GA
A 39   Russell Graham, Purveyor of Plants, OR
A 48   Honeywood Lilies, SK
A 56   Kline Nursery Co., OR
A 57   P. Kohli & Co., In
A 63   McClure & Zimmerman, WI
A 64   Mad River Imports, VT
A 67   Messelaar Bulb Co., MA
A 80   Pine Heights Nursery, Au
A 81   The Plant Shop's Botanical Gardens, CA
A 82   Potterton & Martin, En
A 84   Quality Dutch Bulbs, NJ
A 88   Robinett Bulb Farm, CA
A 90   Rust-En-Vrede Nursery, So
A 96   Siskiyou Rare Plant Nursery, OR
A 96   Anthony J. Skittone, CA
A 98   Southwest Seeds, En
A 105   Trans Pacific Nursery, OR
A 108   Van Engelen, Inc., CT
A 112   White Flower Farm, CT
A 113   Wild Seeds, Wa
A 113   Wildflower Nursery, NC
A 116   Guy Wrinkle Exotic Plants, CA

BULBS, SPRING BLOOMING
See also specific plants
A 3   Jacques Amand, Ltd., En
A 3   Amaryllis, Inc., LA
A 6   Archias' Seed Store, MO
A 6   Avon Bulbs, En
A 7   Bakker of Holland, MO
(continued next page)

PAGE SOURCE

BULBS, SPRING BLOOMING (continued)
A 11 Breck's, IL
A 12 Broadleigh Gardens, En
A 13 The Bulb Crate, IL
A 13 Bundles of Bulbs, MD
A 14 W. Atlee Burpee Company, PA
A 19 Paul Christian -- Rare Plants, Wa
A 24 Cruickshank's, Inc., ON
A 25 The Daffodil Mart, VA
A 26 Peter De Jager Bulb Co., MA
A 28 Dutch Gardens, Inc., NJ
A 37 Gardenimport, Inc., ON
A 53 J. W. Jung Seed Co., WI
A 54 Kelly Nurseries, NY
A 63 McClure & Zimmerman, WI
A 64 McConnell Nurseries, Inc., ON
A 64 McFayden Seeds, MB
A 64 Mad River Imports, VT
A 67 Earl May Seed & Nursery Co., IA
A 67 Messelaar Bulb Co., MA
A 78 Park Seed Company, Inc., SC
A 79 Peaceful Valley Farm Supply, CA
A 80 Pine Heights Nursery, Au
A 82 Potterton & Martin, En
A 84 Quality Dutch Bulbs, NJ
A 91 John Scheepers, Inc., NY
B 37 Smith & Hawken, CA
A 103 Territorial Seed Company, OR
A 108 Van Engelen, Inc., CT
A 108 Mary Mattison van Schaik, VT
A 108 Vandenberg, NY
A 108 Veldheer Tulip Gardens, MI
A 111 Weiss Brothers Nursery, CA
A 112 White Flower Farm, CT

BULBS, SUMMER BLOOMING
See also specific plants
A 2 Alberta Nurseries & Seed Company, AB
A 3 Jacques Amand, Ltd., En
A 5 Antonelli Brothers, Inc., CA
A 6 Avon Bulbs, En
A 7 Bakker of Holland, MO
A 9 Bio-Quest International, CA
A 11 Breck's, IL
A 13 The Bulb Crate, IL
A 14 W. Atlee Burpee Company, PA
A 17 Carroll Gardens, MD
A 24 Cruickshank's, Inc., ON
A 25 William Dam Seeds, ON
A 26 Peter De Jager Bulb Co., MA
A 27 Dominion Seed House, ON
A 28 Dutch Gardens, Inc., NJ
A 31 Fairyland Begonia & Lily Garden, CA
A 37 Gardenimport, Inc., ON
A 45 Heritage Gardens, IA
A 52 Jackson & Perkins Co., OR
A 53 J. W. Jung Seed Co., WI
A 54 Kelly's Plant World, CA
A 61 Lindel Lilies, BC
A 63 McClure & Zimmerman, WI
A 64 McConnell Nurseries, Inc., ON
A 67 Earl May Seed & Nursery Co., IA
A 67 Messelaar Bulb Co., MA
A 68 Meyer Seed Co., MD
A 78 Park Seed Company, Inc., SC
A 79 Peaceful Valley Farm Supply, CA
A 80 Pine Heights Nursery, Au
A 84 Quality Dutch Bulbs, NJ
A 90 Salter Tree Farm, FL
A 91 John Scheepers, Inc., NY

BULBS, SUMMER BLOOMING
A 96 Anthony J. Skittone, CA
A 96 Skolaski's Glads & Field Flowers, WI
B 37 Smith & Hawken, CA
A 99 Spring Hill Nurseries Co., IL
A 102 T & T Seeds, Ltd., MB
A 103 Territorial Seed Company, OR
A 107 TyTy Plantation, GA
A 107 Van Bourgondien Bros., Inc., NY
A 108 Veldheer Tulip Gardens, MI
A 110 Mary Walker Bulb Company, GA
A 110 The Waushara Gardens, WI
A 110 Wayside Gardens, SC
A 112 White Flower Farm, CT

BULBS, TENDER
See also specific plants
A 9 Bio-Quest International, CA
A 25 The Daffodil Mart, VA
A 38 Gladside Gardens, MA
A 54 Kelly's Plant World, CA
A 67 Messelaar Bulb Co., MA
A 82 The Plumeria People, TX
A 107 TyTy Plantation, GA
A 107 Van Bourgondien Bros., Inc., NY
A 110 Mary Walker Bulb Company, GA

BUTTERNUTS
A 32 Fernald's Hickory Hill Nursery, IL
A 41 Grimo Nut Nursery, ON
A 73 Nolin River Nut Tree Nursery, KY
A 90 Saginaw Valley Nut Nursery, MI

CACTUS
See also specific plants
A 1 Abbey Gardens, CA
A 5 Apacha Cactus, CA
A 6 Aztekakti/Desertland Nursery, TX
A 6 B & T Associates, En
A 15 Cactus by Dodie, CA
A 15 Cactus by Mueller, CA
A 15 Cactus Gem Nursery, AR
A 19 Christa's Cactus, AZ
A 27 Desert Nursery, NM
A 27 Desert Theatre, CA
A 37 Garden World, TX
A 41 Grigsby Cactus Gardens, CA
A 44 Henrietta's Nursery, CA
A 54 K & L Cactus Nursery, CA
A 56 Gerhard Koehres Cactus & Succulent Nursery, We
A 59 Lauray of Salisbury, CT
A 67 Mesa Garden, NM
A 72 New Mexico Cactus Research, NM
A 81 The Plant Shop's Botanical Gardens, CA
A 81 Plants of the Southwest, NM
A 84 Rainbow Gardens Nursery & Bookshop, CA
A 86 Redlo Cacti, OR
A 88 Grace Rollerson, BC
A 84 Sand Ridge Greenhouse, OK
A 92 Schulz Cactus Gardens, CA
A 92 Scotty's Desert Plants, CA
A 93 The Seed Shop, MT
A 94 Shein's Cactus, CA
A 98 Southwest Seeds, En
A 103 Thompson & Morgan, NJ
A 116 Roy Young, Seedsman, En

CACTUS, WINTER HARDY
See also specific plants
A 15 The Cactus Patch, KS

(continued next page)

PAGE SOURCE

CACTUS, WINTER HARDY (continued)
A 19   Christa's Cactus, AZ
A 21   Colvos Creek Nursery & Landscaping, WA
A 27   Desert Nursery, NM
A 50   Intermountain Cactus, UT
A 56   Gerhard Koehres Cactus & Succulent Nursery, We
A 67   Mesa Garden, NM
A 68   Midwest Cactus, MO
A 72   Neon Palm Nursery, CA
A 72   New Mexico Cactus Research, NM
A 76   Oregon Exotica Nursery, OR
A 86   Redlo Cacti, OR
A 88   Grace Rollerson, BC
A 101   Sunnyvale Cactus Nursery, MA

CALADIUMS
A 15   Caladium World, FL
A 101   Sunshine Caladium Farms, FL
A 107   Van Bourgondien Bros., Inc., NY

CALLA LILIES
A 31   Fairyland Begonia & Lily Garden, CA

CALLISTEMONS
A 14   Bushland Flora (Australian Seed Specialists), Au
A 105   Trans Pacific Nursery, OR

CALLUNAS
A 29   Eastern Plant Specialties, ME
A 44   Heaths and Heathers, WA
A 88   Rock Spray Nursery, MA

CALOCHORTUS
A 88   Robinett Bulb Farm, CA

CAMELLIAS
A 11   The Bovees Nursery, OR
A 16   Camellia Forest Nursery, NC
A 33   Flora Lan Nursery, OR
A 64   Ma-Dot-Cha Hobby Nursery, AL
A 65   Magnolia Nursery & Display Garden, AL
A 74   Nuccio's Nurseries, CA

CAMPANULAS
A 16   Canyon Creek Nursery, CA
A 28   Donaroma's Nursery, MA
A 31   Far North Gardens, MI
A 32   Fieldstone Gardens, Inc., ME
A 33   Flora Favours, WI
A 41   Grianan Gardens, CA
A 52   Klaus R. Jelitto, We
A 57   L. Kreeger, En
A 61   Linn Farm Perennials, VA
A 70   Mt. Tahoma Nursery, WA
A 83   The Primrose Path, PA
A 87   Rice Creek Gardens, MN
A 93   The Seed Source, NC
A 93   Seedalp, Sw
A 93   Select Seeds, CT
A 96   Skyline Nursery, WA
A 102   Surry Gardens, ME
A 112   Whayes End Nursery, VA
A 115   Winter Greenhouse, WI

CANNAS
A 4   American Daylily & Perennials, MO
A 28   Dutch Gardens, Inc., NJ
A 38   Gladside Gardens, MA
A 44   Heliconia Haus, FL
A 54   Kelly's Plant World, CA

PAGE SOURCE

CANNAS
A 56   Kinder Canna Farm, OK
A 60   Orol Ledden & Sons, NJ
A 91   Santa Barbara Water Gardens, CA
A 101   Sunshine State Tropicals, FL
A 107   TyTy Plantation, GA
A 110   Mary Walker Bulb Company, GA
A 110   The Waushara Gardens, WI
A 116   Wright Iris Nursery, CA

CANTALOUPES
A 14   D. V. Burrell Seed Growers Co., CO
A 53   Jordan Seeds, MN
A 62   Lockhart Seeds, CA
A 69   Miller-Bowie County Farmers Assn., TX
A 82   Porter & Son, TX
A 89   Roswell Seed Co., NM
A 108   Vermont Bean Seed Co., VT
A 114   Willhite Seed Co., TX

CARAMBOLA
A 68   Roger & Shirley Meyer, CA

CARNATIONS
A 3   Allwood Bros., En
A 23   The Country Garden, WI
A 101   Sunnyslope Gardens, CA

CARNIVOROUS PLANTS
See also specific plants
A 2   Allgrove Farm, Inc., MA
A 5   Armstrong Roses, CA
A 9   Black Copper Kits, NJ
A 17   Carolina Exotic Gardens, NC
A 18   Cedar Ridge Nurseries, PA
A 60   Lee's Botanical Gardens, FL
A 66   Marston Exotics, En
A 77   Orgel's Orchids, FL
A 79   Peter Pauls Nurseries, NY
A 81   The Plant Shop's Botanical Gardens, CA
A 98   Southwest Seeds, En

CAUDICIFORMS
A 1   Abbey Gardens, CA
A 6   Artistic Plants, TX
A 7   The Banana Tree, PA
A 15   Cactus by Mueller, CA
A 19   Christa's Cactus, AZ
A 48   Jerry Horne -- Rare Plants, FL
A 54   K & L Cactus Nursery, CA
A 86   Redlo Cacti, OR
A 96   Singers' Growing Things, CA
A 100   Succulent Plants, MN
A 100   Succulenta, CA
A 116   Guy Wrinkle Exotic Plants, CA

CEANOTHUS
A 59   Las Pilitas Nursery, CA

CHERIMOYAS
A 36   Fruit Spirit Botanical Gardens, Au
A 36   Garden of Delights, FL
A 68   Roger & Shirley Meyer, CA
A 98   South Seas Nursery, CA

CHERRIES
A 1   Adams County Nursery, Inc., PA
A 13   Buckley Nursery, WA
A 20   Cloud Mountain Nursery, WA
A 24   Cumberland Valley Nurseries, Inc., TN
(continued next page)

PAGE	SOURCE

CHERRIES (continued)
A 38   Golden Bough Tree Farm, ON
A 40   Greenmantle Nursery, CA
A 52   Johnson Nursery, GA
A 58   LBG Nursery, MN
A 72   New York State Fruit Testing Coop. Assn., NY
A 88   Rocky Meadow Orchard & Nursery, IN
A 90   St. Lawrence Nurseries, NY
A 97   Sonoma Antique Apple Nursery, CA
A 104   Tolowa Nursery, OR
A 108   VanWell Nursery, Inc., WA

CHESTNUTS, HYBRID
A 8   Bear Creek Nursery, WA
A 14   Burnt Ridge Nursery, WA
A 19   Chestnut Hill Nursery, Inc., FL
A 35   Fowler Nurseries, Inc., CA
A 37   Louis Gerardi Nursery, IL
A 39   John H. Gordon, Jr., Grower, NY
A 40   Greenmantle Nursery, CA
A 41   Grimo Nut Nursery, ON
A 73   Nolin River Nut Tree Nursery, KY
A 75   Oikos Tree Crops, MI
A 90   Saginaw Valley Nut Nursery, MI
A 114   Wiley's Nut Grove, OH

CHRISTMAS TREES, LIVING
A 12   Brookfield Nursery & Tree Plantation, VA

CHRYSANTHEMUMS
A 4   American Daylily & Perennials, MO
A 10   Bluestone Perennials, OH
A 28   Dooley Gardens, MN
A 43   Hauser's Superior View Farm, WI
A 45   Heritage Gardens, IA
A 49   Huff's Garden Mums, KS
A 50   Indigo Knoll Perennials, MD
A 56   King's Mums, CA
A 58   Lamb Nurseries, WA
A 68   Milaeger's Gardens, WI
A 71   Mums by Paschke, PA
A 101   Sunnyslope Gardens, CA
A 103   Ter-El Nursery, PA
A 115   Winter Greenhouse, WI

CITRANGES
A 76   Oregon Exotica Nursery, OR

CITRUS
A 16   California Nursery Co., CA
A 30   Exotica Rare Fruit Nursery, CA
A 37   Garden World, TX
A 62   Logee's Greenhouses, CT
A 76   Oregon Exotica Nursery, OR
A 84   Raintree Nursery, WA
A 95   Sherwood's Greenhouses, LA

CITRUS, DWARF
A 34   Four Winds Growers, CA
A 76   Oregon Exotica Nursery, OR
A 78   Pacific Tree Farms, CA

CITRUS, HARDY
A 76   Oregon Exotica Nursery, OR

CLEMATIS
A 17   Carroll Gardens, MD
A 18   Chadwell Himalayan Seed, En
A 20   Clifford's Perennial & Vine, WI
A 24   Cruickshank's, Inc., ON

PAGE	SOURCE

CLEMATIS
A 32   Fieldstone Gardens, Inc., ME
A 35   The Fragrant Path, NE
A 66   Maroushek Gardens, MN
A 68   Milaeger's Gardens, WI
A 78   Park Seed Company, Inc., SC
A 98   Southern Seeds, Ne
A 99   Arthur H. Steffen, Inc., NY
A 112   Whayes End Nursery, VA

COLCHICUMS
A 3   Jacques Amand, Ltd., En
A 26   Peter De Jager Bulb Co., MA
A 63   McClure & Zimmerman, WI

COLEUS
A 21   Color Farm Growers, FL

COLUMNEAS
A 36   Lorine Friedrich, TX
A 52   Jeannette's Jesneriads, LA
A 60   Les Violettes Natalia, PQ
A 63   Lyndon Lyon Greenhouses, Inc., NY
A 64   McKinney's Glasshouse, KS
A 74   Oak Hill Gardens, IL
A 81   Plant Villa, IL
A 81   Pleasant Hill African Violets, TX
A 92   Sedona Gardens, BC
A 101   Sunshine State Tropicals, FL
A 101   Sunshine Violets & Gesneriads, MA
A 103   Tiki Nursery, NC
A 109   The Violet Showcase, CO
A 114   Wilson's Violet Haven, TX

CONIFERS
A 5   Appalachian Gardens, PA
A 11   Botanicals, MA
A 16   Callahan Seeds, OR
A 16   Camellia Forest Nursery, NC
A 17   Carter Seeds, CA
A 17   Cascade Forestry Nursery, IA
A 18   Catalpa Nursery, MD
A 19   Chiltern Seeds, En
A 20   Clargreen Gardens, Ltd., ON
A 20   Coenosium Gardens, OR
A 34   Forestfarm, OR
A 38   Girard Nurseries, OH
A 38   Golden Bough Tree Farm, ON
A 48   Hortico, Inc., ON
A 54   Kelly Nurseries, NY
A 57   V. Kraus Nurseries, Ltd., ON
A 57   Michael & Janet Kristick, PA
A 70   Mt. Leo Nursery, TN
A 71   Musser Forests Inc., PA
A 71   Native Seed Foundation, ID
A 72   Neon Palm Nursery, CA
A 74   Northwest Biological Enterprises, OR
A 77   Owen Farms, TN
A 78   Pacific Tree Farms, CA
A 86   Recor Tree Seed, CO
A 91   Savage Farms Nursery, TN
A 92   F. W. Schumacher Co., MA
A 93   The Seed Source, NC
A 94   Sheffield's Seed Co., NY
A 96   Silvaseed Company, Inc., WA
A 96   Silver Springs Nursery, ID
A 107   Valley Nursery, MT

CONIFERS, DWARF
A 16   Camellia Forest Nursery, NC
(continued next page)

PAGE SOURCE

CONIFERS, DWARF (continued)
A 20   Coenosium Gardens, OR
A 24   The Cummins Garden, NJ
A 26   Daystar, ME
A 29   Eastern Plant Specialties, ME
A 35   Foxborough Nursery, Inc., MD
A 38   Girard Nurseries, OH
A 41   Greer Gardens, OR
A 47   Holly Hills, Inc., IN
A 57   Michael & Janet Kristick, PA
A 66   Marrs Tree Farm, WA
A 66   Matsu-Momiji Nursery, PA
A 69   Miniature Plant Kingdom, CA
A 70   Mt. Tahoma Nursery, WA
A 83   Powell's Gardens, NC
A 87   Rice Creek Gardens, MN
A 88   Rocknoll Nursery, OH
A 89   Roslyn Nursery, NY
A 96   Siskiyou Rare Plant Nursery, OR
A 99   Springvale Farm Nursery, IL
A 107 Twombly Nursery, CT
A 110 Washington Evergreen Nursery, NC
A 114 Wildwood Gardens, OH

CONIFERS, SEEDLING
A 7   Barber Nursery, OR
A 17   Carino Nurseries, PA
A 21   Cold Stream Farm, MI
A 33   Flickingers' Nursery, PA
A 38   Girard Nurseries, OH
A 45   Heronswood Nursery, WA
A 58   Lamtree Farm, NC
A 59   Lawyer Nursery, Inc., MT
A 66   Marrs Tree Farm, WA
A 71   Musser Forests Inc., PA
A 81   Plants of the Wild, WA
A 84   Qualitree Nursery, OR
A 96   Silvaseed Company, Inc., WA
A 97   Smith Nursery Co., IA
A 112 Whitman Farms, OR

CORN
A 24   Cross Seed Company, KS
A 50   Illinois Foundation Seeds, Inc., IL
A 53   Jordan Seeds, MN
A 61   Liberty Seed Company, OH
A 62   Lockhart Seeds, CA
A 70   Mountain Valley Seeds & Nursery, UT
A 83   Prairie State Commodities, IL
A 89   Rupp Seeds, Inc., OH
A 90   SPB Sales, TX
A 93   Seedway, Inc., NY
A 95   Shissler Seed Company, IL
A 100 Stokes Seed Company, NY
A 114 Willhite Seed Co., TX

CORN, HEIRLOOM
A 3   Alston Seed Growers, NC
A 22   Corns, OK
A 33   Floating Mountain Seeds, WA
A 39   Good Seed Co., WA
A 39   The Grain Exchange, KS
A 60   Le Champion Heritage Seeds, CA
A 71   Native Seeds/SEARCH, AZ
A 78   Paul's Premium Seeds, CA
A 95   R. H. Shumway Seedsman, SC
A 98   Southern Exposure Seed Exchange, VA
A 102 Talavaya Seeds, NM
A 112 Westwind Seeds, AZ

CORYPHANTHAS
A 15   The Cactus Patch, KS
A 67   Mesa Garden, NM
A 84   Sand Ridge Greenhouse, OK
A 92   Schulz Cactus Gardens, CA
A 93   The Seed Shop, MT
A 94   Shein's Cactus, CA

CRABAPPLES
A 7   Barber Nursery, OR
A 44   Heard Gardens, Ltd., IA
A 58   LBG Nursery, MN
A 66   Mary's Plant Farm, OH
A 70   Moosebell Flower, Fruit & Tree Co., ME
A 70   Morden Nurseries, Ltd., MB
A 92   F. W. Schumacher Co., MA
A 107 Twombly Nursery, CT

CRANBERRIES
A 90   St. Lawrence Nurseries, NY

CRAPE MYRTLES
A 8   Beaver Creek Nursery, TN
A 19   David Chopin Nursery, LA
A 40   Greenlife Gardens Greenhouses, GA
A 41   Gulf Coast Plantsmen, LA
A 53   Justice Gardens, GA

CRASSULAS
A 1   Abbey Gardens, CA
A 15   Cactus by Dodie, CA
A 46   Highland Succulents, OH
A 59   Lauray of Salisbury, CT
A 67   Mesa Garden, NM
A 78   Parsley's Cape Seeds, So
A 86   Redlo Cacti, OR
A 88   Grace Rollerson, BC

CRINUMS
A 38   Gladside Gardens, MA
A 41   Gulf Coast Plantsmen, LA
A 54   Kelly's Plant World, CA
A 63   Louisiana Nursery, LA
A 80   Pine Heights Nursery, Au
A 107 TyTy Plantation, GA
A 110 Mary Walker Bulb Company, GA

CROCUS
A 3   Jacques Amand, Ltd., En
A 7   Bakker of Holland, MO
A 12   Broadleigh Gardens, En
A 19   Paul Christian -- Rare Plants, Wa
A 64   Mad River Imports, VT
A 67   Messelaar Bulb Co., MA
A 82   Potterton & Martin, En
A 108 Van Engelen, Inc., CT
A 108 Mary Mattison van Schaik, VT

CROWN VETCH
A 30   Ernst Crownvetch Farms, PA
A 55   Kester's Wild Game Food Nurseries, WI

CRYPTANTHUS
A 26   Dane Company, TX
A 38   Golden Lake Greenhouses, CA
A 63   Paul P. Lowe, FL
A 98   Southern Exposure, TX

CURRANTS
A 8   Bear Creek Nursery, WA
(continued next page)

PAGE SOURCE

CURRANTS (continued)
A 20   Cloud Mountain Nursery, WA
A 46   Hidden Springs Nursery -- Edible Landscaping, TN
A 65   Makielski Berry Farm & Nursery, MI
A 70   Moosebell Flower, Fruit & Tree Co., ME
A 82   Plumtree Nursery, NY
A 98   Southmeadow Fruit Gardens, MI
A 104   Tolowa Nursery, OR
A 112   Whitman Farms, OR
A 115   Windy Ridge Nursery, AB

CYCADS
See also specific plants
A 7   The Banana Tree, PA
A 24   Cycad Gardens, CA
A 29   Endangered Species, CA
A 30   Exotic Seeds, Lothar Seik, We
A 48   Jerry Horne -- Rare Plants, FL
A 72   Neon Palm Nursery, CA
A 77   D. Orriell -- Seed Exporters, Au
A 84   Rainforest Flora, Inc., CA
A 86   Rhapis Gardens, TX
A 116   Guy Wrinkle Exotic Plants, CA

CYCLAMEN, HARDY
A 3   Jacques Amand, Ltd., En
A 6   Avon Bulbs, En
A 31   Far North Gardens, MI
A 39   Russell Graham, Purveyor of Plants, OR
A 56   Kline Nursery Co., OR
A 69   Montrose Nursery, NC
A 82   Potterton & Martin, En
A 103   Tile Barn Nursery, En

DABOECIAS
A 44   Heaths and Heathers, WA

DAFFODILS
A 7   Bakker of Holland, MO
A 11   Breck's, IL
A 12   Brooksfield Farm, WA
A 21   Comanche Acres Iris Gardens, MO
A 22   Cooper's Garden, MN
A 28   Dutch Gardens, Inc., NJ
A 67   Maxim's Greenwood Gardens, CA
A 67   Messelaar Bulb Co., MA
A 82   Potterton & Martin, En
A 84   Quality Dutch Bulbs, NJ
A 84   Ramona Gardens, CA
A 91   John Scheepers, Inc., NY
A 103   Territorial Seed Company, OR
A 107   Van Bourgondien Bros., Inc., NY
A 108   Van Engelen, Inc., CT
A 108   Mary Mattison van Schaik, VT
A 108   Vandenberg, NY
A 108   Veldheer Tulip Gardens, MI
A 110   Wayside Gardens, SC
A 114   Nancy Wilson Species & Miniature Narcissus, CA

DAFFODILS, NOVELTY
A 3   Jacques Amand, Ltd., En
A 6   Avon Bulbs, En
A 10   Bonnie Brae Gardens, OR
A 12   Broadleigh Gardens, En
A 13   Bundles of Bulbs, MD
A 17   Carncairn Daffodils, Ltd., No
A 18   Cascade Daffodils, MN
A 25   The Daffodil Mart, VA
A 26   Peter De Jager Bulb Co., MA
A 39   Russell Graham, Purveyor of Plants, OR

PAGE SOURCE

DAFFODILS, NOVELTY
A 43   Hatfield Gardens, OH
A 63   McClure & Zimmerman, WI
A 64   Mad River Imports, VT
A 69   Grant Mitsch Novelty Daffodils, OR
A 77   Oregon Trail Daffodils, OR

DAHLIAS
A 3   Alpen Gardens, MT
A 5   Antonelli Brothers, Inc., CA
A 8   Bedford Dahlias, OH
A 9   Blue Dahlia Gardens, IL
A 11   Breck's, IL
A 21   Connell's Dahlias, WA
A 24   Cruickshank's, Inc., ON
A 25   Dahlias by Phil Traff, WA
A 28   Dutch Gardens, Inc., NJ
A 30   Evergreen Acres Dahlia Gardens, NY
A 37   Garden Valley Dahlias, OR
A 38   Gladside Gardens, MA
A 48   Hookland's Dahlias, OR
A 49   Ed Hume Seeds, Inc., WA
A 57   Kordonowy's Dahlias, WA
A 72   Nicholls Gardens, VA
A 81   Pleasant Valley Glads, MA
A 86   Rex Bulb Farms, WA
A 91   John Scheepers, Inc., NY
A 92   Sea-Tac Gardens, WA
A 94   Shackleton's Dahlias, OR
A 102   Swan Island Dahlias, OR
A 107   Van Bourgondien Bros., Inc., NY
A 108   Veldheer Tulip Gardens, MI

DAPHNES
A 33   Flora Lan Nursery, OR
A 45   Heronswood Nursery, WA
A 70   Mt. Tahoma Nursery, WA
A 88   Rose Acres, CA
A 96   Siskiyou Rare Plant Nursery, OR

DAYLILIES
A 1   Adamgrove, MO
A 3   Alpine Valley Gardens, CA
A 3   Amaryllis, Inc., LA
A 3   Ambergate Gardens, MN
A 4   American Daylily & Perennials, MO
A 8   Barnee's Garden, TX
A 10   Borbeleta Gardens, MN
A 12   Lee Bristol Nursery, CT
A 14   Busse Gardens, MN
A 16   Caprice Farm, OR
A 18   Champlain Isle Agro Associates, VT
A 20   Clifford's Perennial & Vine, WI
A 20   Coastal Gardens & Nursery, SC
A 20   Coburg Planting Fields, IN
A 21   Comanche Acres Iris Gardens, MO
A 22   Cooper's Garden, MN
A 22   Cordon Bleu Farms, CA
A 23   Country View Gardens, MI
A 24   Cruickshank's, Inc., ON
A 26   Daylily World, FL
A 26   Daylily Discounters, FL
A 27   Don's Daylily Garden, MO
A 29   Englerth Gardens, MI
A 31   Fairway Enterprises, MN
A 34   Floyd Cove Nursery, NY
A 37   Garden Perennials, NE
A 41   Greenwood Daylily Gardens, CA
A 42   Hahn's Rainbow Iris Garden, MO
A 42   Dr. Joseph C. Halinar, OR
(continued next page)

PAGE SOURCE

DAYLILIES (continued)
A 43   Hatfield Gardens, OH
A 46   Hickory Hill Gardens, PA
A 47   Holbrook Farm & Nursery, NC
A 48   Homestead Division of Sunnybrook Farms, OH
A 48   Honeywood Lilies, SK
A 50   Inter-State Nurseries, IA
A 52   Jernigan Gardens, NC
A 56   Kimberly Garden on Oregon Hill, NY
A 56   Klehm Nursery, IL
A 63   Louisiana Nursery, LA
A 63   McClure & Zimmerman, WI
A 64   McMillen's Iris Garden, ON
A 65   Maple Tree Gardens, NE
A 67   Maxim's Greenwood Gardens, CA
A 67   Meadowlake Gardens, SC
A 69   Miller's Manor Gardens, IN
A 69   Monashee Gardens, BC
A 72   Nicholls Gardens, VA
A 74   Oakes Daylilies, TN
A 80   Pinecliffe Daylily Gardens, IN
A 82   Pollen Bank, CA
A 83   Powell's Gardens, NC
A 83   Prentiss Court Ground Covers, SC
A 84   Ramona Gardens, CA
A 88   Robyn's Nest Nursery, WA
A 88   Rocknoll Nursery, OH
A 91   Saxton Gardens, NY
A 92   Seawright Gardens, MA
A 94   Shady Oaks Nursery, MN
A 97   Solomon Daylilies, VA
A 100 Stoecklein's Nursery, PA
A 102 Dave Talbott Nursery, FL
A 103 Ter-El Nursery, PA
A 103 Thomasville Nurseries, GA
A 104 Tranquil Lake Nursery, MA
A 107 Valente Gardens, ME
A 107 Van Bourgondien Bros., Inc., NY
A 108 Vandenberg, NY
A 109 Andre Viette Farm & Nursery, VA
A 113 Gilbert H. Wild & Son, Inc., MO
A 114 Wimberlyway Gardens, FL
A 116 Worel's Iris Gardens, MN

DELPHINIUMS
A 9   Blackmore & Langdon, En
A 27   DeGiorgi Seed Company, NE
A 28   Donaroma's Nursery, MA
A 32   Fieldstone Gardens, Inc., ME
A 43   Hauser's Superior View Farm, WI
A 61   Life-Form Replicators, MI
A 68   Milaeger's Gardens, WI
A 93   Select Seeds, CT
A 115 Winter Greenhouse, WI

DESERT PLANTS
See also specific plants
A 6   Aztekakti/Desertland Nursery, TX
A 8   Bernardo Beach Native Plant Farm, NM
A 15   Cactus Gem Nursery, AR
A 25   The Nursery at the Dallas Nature Center, TX
A 27   Desert Nursery, NM
A 49   J. L. Hudson, Seedsman, CA
A 50   Intermountain Cactus, UT
A 54   K & L Cactus Nursery, CA
A 68   Midwest Cactus, MO
A 71   Native Seeds/SEARCH, AZ
A 73   Nindethana Seed Service, Au
A 77   D. Orriell -- Seed Exporters, Au
A 78   The PanTree, CA

DESERT PLANTS
A 79   Theodore Payne Foundation, CA
A 84   Sand Ridge Greenhouse, OK
A 92   Schulz Cactus Gardens, CA
A 92   Scotty's Desert Plants, CA
A 93   The Seed Shop, MT
A 98   Southwest Seeds, En
A 98   Southwestern Native Seeds, AZ
A 100 Succulenta, CA
A 102 Talavaya Seeds, NM
A 114 Wildwood Nursery, CA
A 116 Guy Wrinkle Exotic Plants, CA

DIANTHUS
A 3   Allwood Bros., En
A 5   Appalachian Wildflower Nursery, PA
A 6   B & B Laboratories, WA
A 10   Bluestone Perennials, OH
A 14   Busse Gardens, MN
A 16   Canyon Creek Nursery, CA
A 21   Colorado Alpines, Inc., CO
A 23   The Country Garden, WI
A 27   DeGiorgi Seed Company, NE
A 28   Donaroma's Nursery, MA
A 31   Far North Gardens, MI
A 33   Flora Favours, WI
A 35   The Fragrant Path, NE
A 37   Garden Place, OH
A 41   Grianan Gardens, CA
A 47   Holbrook Farm & Nursery, NC
A 50   Indigo Knoll Perennials, MD
A 52   The Thomas Jefferson Center, VA
A 52   Klaus R. Jelitto, We
A 53   Joyce's Garden, OR
A 57   L. Kreeger, En
A 58   Lamb Nurseries, WA
A 61   Life-Form Replicators, MI
A 61   Linn Farm Perennials, VA
A 83   Powell's Gardens, NC
A 87   Rice Creek Gardens, MN
A 88   Robyn's Nest Nursery, WA
A 88   Rocknoll Nursery, OH
A 93   Seedalp, Sw
A 93   Select Seeds, CT
A 102 Surry Gardens, ME
A 104 Torbay's Plant World, En
A 112 Whayes End Nursery, VA
A 115 Winter Greenhouse, WI

DIGITALIS
A 43   Hauser's Superior View Farm, WI

DISCHIDIAS
A 38   Golden Lake Greenhouses, CA
A 40   Green Plant Research, HI
A 47   Hill 'n dale, CA

DOGWOODS
A 5   Appalachian Gardens, PA
A 7   Barber Nursery, OR
A 17   Carroll Gardens, MD
A 35   Foxborough Nursery, Inc., MD
A 38   Girard Nurseries, OH
A 41   Greer Gardens, OR
A 81   Plants of the Wild, WA
A 94   Sheffield's Seed Co., NY
A 97   Smith Nursery Co., IA

DROSERAS
A 66   Marston Exotics, En

PAGE SOURCE

DROUGHT-TOLERANT PLANTS
See also specific plants
A 1   Abbey Gardens, CA
A 3   Ambergate Gardens, MN
A 5   Apacha Cactus, CA
A 6   Aztekakti/Desertland Nursery, TX
A 7   Bamboo Sourcery, CA
A 8   Bernardo Beach Native Plant Farm, NM
A 11   Botanicals, MA
A 12   Brookside Wildflowers, NC
A 12   Joseph Brown, Native Seeds, VA
A 14   Bushland Flora (Australian Seed Specialists), Au
A 16   Callahan Seeds, OR
A 19   Christa's Cactus, AZ
A 22   Copacabana Gardens, CA
A 25   The Nursery at the Dallas Nature Center, TX
A 27   Desert Nursery, NM
A 28   Dutch Mill Herb Farm, OR
A 36   Frosty Hollow Nursery, WA
A 36   Garden of Delights, FL
A 37   Garden Perennials, NE
A 39   Good Hollow Greenhouse & Herbarium, TN
A 40   Greenlee Nursery, CA
A 41   Grigsby Cactus Gardens, CA
B 19   Harmony Farm Supply, CA
A 43   Havasu Hills Herbs, CA
A 45   Heymaqua Seed Service, CA
A 49   J. L. Hudson, Seedsman, CA
A 53   Joyce's Garden, OR
A 59   Landscape Alternatives, Inc., MN
A 59   Larner Seeds, CA
A 59   Las Pilitas Nursery, CA
A 62   Little Valley Farm, WI
A 65   Maple Leaf Nursery, CA
A 66   Marilynn's Garden, CA
A 68   Midwest Cactus, MO
A 70   Moon Mountain Wildflowers, CA
A 71   Native Seed Foundation, ID
A 71   Native Seeds, Inc., MD
A 71   Native Seeds/SEARCH, AZ
A 71   Natural Gardens, TN
A 72   Neon Palm Nursery, CA
A 72   Niche Gardens, NC
A 73   Nindethana Seed Service, Au
A 73   Northplan/Mountain Seed, ID
A 75   Old Farm Nursery, CO
A 77   D. Orriell -- Seed Exporters, Au
A 78   The PanTree, CA
A 79   Theodore Payne Foundation, CA
A 81   Plants of the Southwest, NM
A 81   Plants of the Wild, WA
A 83   Prairie Nursery, WI
A 83   Prairie Ridge Nursery/CRM Ecosystems, Inc., WI
A 86   Redwood City Seed Co., CA
A 88   Rock Spray Nursery, MA
A 84   Sand Ridge Greenhouse, OK
A 93   The Seed Shop, MT
A 98   Southwest Seeds, En
A 98   Southwestern Native Seeds, AZ
A 100 Succulent Plants, MN
A 100 Succulenta, CA
A 101 Sunlight Gardens, TN
A 102 Talavaya Seeds, NM
A 112 Whayes End Nursery, VA
A 113 Wildflower Seed Company, CA
A 114 Wildwood Nursery, CA

DRYANDRAS
A 73   Nindethana Seed Service, Au
A 77   D. Orriell -- Seed Exporters, Au

DRYANDRAS
A 105 Trans Pacific Nursery, OR

DYE PLANTS
See also Herbs
A 17   Casa Yerba Gardens, OR
A 21   Companion Plants, OH
A 23   Cricket Hill Herb Farm, Ltd., MA
A 35   Fox Hill Farm, MI
A 39   Goodwin Creek Gardens, OR
A 43   Havasu Hills Herbs, CA
A 44   The Herbfarm, WA
A 45   Herbs-Liscious, IA
A 49   J. L. Hudson, Seedsman, CA
A 63   Lost Prairie Herb Farm, MT
A 71   Native Seeds/SEARCH, AZ
A 85   Rasland Farm, NC
A 87   Richters, ON
A 89   The Rosemary House, PA
A 91   Sandy Mush Herb Nursery, NC
A 110 Wyrttun Ward, MA

ECHEVERIAS
A 1   Abbey Gardens, CA
A 15   Cactus by Mueller, CA
A 15   Cactus Gem Nursery, AR
A 46   Highland Succulents, OH
A 54   K & L Cactus Nursery, CA
A 59   Lauray of Salisbury, CT
A 88   Grace Rollerson, BC
A 92   Scotty's Desert Plants, CA
A 100 Succulent Plants, MN

ECHINACEAS
A 12   Joseph Brown, Native Seeds, VA
A 29   Earthstar Herb Gardens, AZ
A 83   Prairie Ridge Nursery/CRM Ecosystems, Inc., WI
A 112 Whayes End Nursery, VA

ECHINOCEREUS
A 6   Aztekakti/Desertland Nursery, TX
A 15   The Cactus Patch, KS
A 27   Desert Nursery, NM
A 44   Henrietta's Nursery, CA
A 50   Intermountain Cactus, UT
A 67   Mesa Garden, NM
A 72   New Mexico Cactus Research, NM
A 86   Redlo Cacti, OR
A 84   Sand Ridge Greenhouse, OK
A 92   Schulz Cactus Gardens, CA
A 93   The Seed Shop, MT
A 98   Southwest Seeds, En
A 101 Sunnyvale Cactus Nursery, MA

ELDERBERRIES
A 46   Hidden Springs Nursery -- Edible Landscaping, TN

EPIMEDIUMS
A 3   Ambergate Gardens, MN
A 16   Canyon Creek Nursery, CA
A 29   Eco-Gardens, GA
A 32   Fieldstone Gardens, Inc., ME
A 48   Homestead Division of Sunnybrook Farms, OH
A 88   Rocknoll Nursery, OH
A 94   Shady Oaks Nursery, MN
A 96   Skyline Nursery, WA
A 96   Sleepy Hollow Herb Farm, KY

EPIPHYLLUMS
A 7   Fred Bach Epiphyllums, IL
(continued next page)

PAGE SOURCE

EPIPHYLLUMS (continued)
A 15   Cactus Gem Nursery, AR
A 34   Fort Caroline Orchids, FL
A 38   Golden Lake Greenhouses, CA
A 40   Greenlife Gardens Greenhouses, GA
A 44   Henrietta's Nursery, CA
A 59   Lauray of Salisbury, CT
A 66   Marilynn's Garden, CA
A 84   Rainbow Gardens Nursery & Bookshop, CA
A 92   Scotty's Desert Plants, CA
A 92   Sedona Gardens, BC

EPISCIAS
A 13   Buell's Greenhouse, Inc., CT
A 16   Cape Cod Violetry, MA
A 36   Lorine Friedrich, TX
A 37   Georgetown Greenhouse & Nursery, PA
A 60   Les Violettes Natalia, PQ
A 63   Lyndon Lyon Greenhouses, Inc., NY
A 64   McKinney's Glasshouse, KS
A 81   Plant Villa, IL
A 81   Pleasant Hill African Violets, TX
A 92   Sedona Gardens, BC
A 101   Sunshine State Tropicals, FL
A 101   Sunshine Violets & Gesneriads, MA
A 103   Tiki Nursery, NC
A 109   The Violet Showcase, CO
A 109   Volkmann Gardens, TX
A 114   Wilson's Violet Haven, TX

ERICAS
A 16   Cape Seed & Bulb, So
A 20   Clargreen Gardens, Ltd., ON
A 21   Colvos Creek Nursery & Landscaping, WA
A 26   Daystar, ME
A 44   Heaths and Heathers, WA
A 78   Parsley's Cape Seeds, So
A 84   Protea Seed & Nursery Suppliers, So

ERIGERONS
A 57   L. Kreeger, En

ERIOGONUMS
A 57   L. Kreeger, En
A 59   Las Pilitas Nursery, CA

ERYTHRONIUMS
A 19   Paul Christian -- Rare Plants, Wa
A 88   Robinett Bulb Farm, CA

EUCALYPTUS
A 16   Callahan Seeds, OR
A 17   Carter Seeds, CA
A 21   Companion Plants, OH
A 22   Copacabana Gardens, CA
A 50   International Seed Supplies, Au
A 73   Nindethana Seed Service, Au
A 77   D. Orriell -- Seed Exporters, Au

EUCALYPTUS, HARDY
A 14   Bushland Flora (Australian Seed Specialists), Au
A 21   Colvos Creek Nursery & Landscaping, WA
A 34   Forestfarm, OR
A 73   Nindethana Seed Service, Au

EUCODONIAS
A 54   Karleens Achimenes, GA

EUPHORBIAS
A 1   Abbey Gardens, CA

EUPHORBIAS
A 15   Cactus by Dodie, CA
A 15   Cactus by Mueller, CA
A 19   Christa's Cactus, AZ
A 27   Desert Theatre, CA
A 38   Glasshouse Works, OH
A 41   Grigsby Cactus Gardens, CA
A 44   Henrietta's Nursery, CA
A 46   Highland Succulents, OH
A 54   K & L Cactus Nursery, CA
A 56   Gerhard Koehres Cactus & Succulent Nursery, We
A 66   Marilynn's Garden, CA
A 72   New Mexico Cactus Research, NM
A 78   The PanTree, CA
A 86   Redlo Cacti, OR
A 92   Scotty's Desert Plants, CA
A 96   Singers' Growing Things, CA
A 100   Succulent Plants, MN
A 100   Succulenta, CA
A 116   Guy Wrinkle Exotic Plants, CA

EVERLASTING FLOWERS
A 16   Camelot North, MN
A 18   Catnip Acres Herb Nursery, CT
A 21   Companion Plants, OH
A 21   Comstock, Ferre & Co., CT
A 23   The Country Garden, WI
A 23   Cricket Hill Herb Farm, Ltd., MA
A 25   Dacha Barinka, BC
A 27   DeGiorgi Seed Company, NE
A 31   Fedco Seeds, ME
A 35   Fox Hill Farm, MI
A 39   Goodwin Creek Gardens, OR
A 41   Grianan Gardens, CA
A 44   Herb Gathering, Inc., MO
A 56   Kings Herb Seeds, Au
A 72   Nichols Garden Nursery, Inc., OR
A 73   Nindethana Seed Service, Au
A 73   Northplan/Mountain Seed, ID
A 77   D. Orriell -- Seed Exporters, Au
A 80   Pinetree Garden Seeds, ME
A 85   Rasland Farm, NC
A 87   Richters, ON
A 89   Rose Hill Herbs and Perennials, VA
A 91   Sandy Mush Herb Nursery, NC
A 95   Shepherd's Garden Seeds, CA
A 96   Sleepy Hollow Herb Farm, KY
A 98   Specialty Seeds, Au
A 100   Stokes Seed Company, NY
A 106   Otis Twilley Seed Co., PA
A 111   Well-Sweep Herb Farm, NJ

FERNS
A 9   Kurt Bluemel, Inc., MD
A 17   Carter & Holmes, Inc., SC
A 20   City Gardens, MI
A 20   Coastal Gardens & Nursery, SC
A 30   Exotic Seeds, Lothar Seik, We
A 34   Foliage Gardens, WA
A 34   Fort Caroline Orchids, FL
A 48   Jerry Horne -- Rare Plants, FL
A 49   Huronview Nurseries & Garden Centre, ON
A 62   Logee's Greenhouses, CT
A 66   Marvelous Minis, MI
A 72   Neon Palm Nursery, CA
A 108   Varga's Nursery, PA

FERNS, HARDY
A 9   Kurt Bluemel, Inc., MD
A 10   Boehlke's Woodland Gardens, WI
(continued next page)

PAGE SOURCE

FERNS, HARDY (continued)
A 12 Brookside Wildflowers, NC
A 14 Busse Gardens, MN
A 21 Conley's Garden Center, ME
A 24 Crownsville Nursery, MD
A 26 Daystar, ME
A 29 Eco-Gardens, GA
A 31 Fancy Fronds, WA
A 33 Flowerland, NE
A 34 Foliage Gardens, WA
A 37 Gardens of the Blue Ridge, NC
A 39 Russell Graham, Purveyor of Plants, OR
A 47 Holbrook Farm & Nursery, NC
A 48 Homestead Division of Sunnybrook Farms, OH
A 48 Hortico, Inc., ON
A 56 Kline Nursery Co., OR
A 58 Lamtree Farm, NC
A 72 Nature's Garden Nursery, OR
A 74 Northwest Biological Enterprises, OR
A 74 Novelty Nurseries, OH
A 75 Oakridge Nurseries, NH
A 75 Orchid Gardens, MN
A 77 Owen Farms, TN
A 80 Piedmont Gardens, CT
A 83 The Primrose Path, PA
A 94 Shady Oaks Nursery, MN
A 96 Siskiyou Rare Plant Nursery, OR
A 99 Squaw Mountain Gardens, OR
A 101 Sunlight Gardens, TN
A 107 TyTy Plantation, GA
A 108 Varga's Nursery, PA
A 113 Wildflower Nursery, NC
A 113 The Wildflower Source, IL
A 113 Wildginger Woodlands, NY
A 113 The Wildwood Flower, NC
A 115 Woodlanders, Inc., SC

FIGS
A 14 Burnt Ridge Nursery, WA
A 29 Edible Landscaping, VA
A 30 Exotica Rare Fruit Nursery, CA
A 32 The Fig Tree Nursery, FL
A 36 Garden of Delights, FL
A 46 Hidden Springs Nursery -- Edible Landscaping, TN
A 51 Ison's Nursery, GA
A 74 Northwoods Nursery, OR
A 76 Oregon Exotica Nursery, OR
A 97 Sonoma Antique Apple Nursery, CA
A 97 Sorum's Nursery, OR
A 104 Tolowa Nursery, OR

FILBERTS
A 8   Bear Creek Nursery, WA
A 38 Golden Bough Tree Farm, ON
A 39 John H. Gordon, Jr., Grower, NY
A 58 LBG Nursery, MN
A 75 Oikos Tree Crops, MI
A 90 Saginaw Valley Nut Nursery, MI
A 114 Wiley's Nut Grove, OH

FLOWERS, HEIRLOOM
A 21 Color Farm Growers, FL
A 23 The Country Garden, WI
A 31 F W H Seed Exchange, CA
A 33 Floating Mountain Seeds, WA
A 33 The Flower & Herb Exchange, IA
A 35 Fox Hollow Herbs, PA
A 35 The Fragrant Path, NE
A 44 Heirloom Garden Seeds, CA
A 44 Heirloom Seeds, PA

FLOWERS, HEIRLOOM
A 52 The Thomas Jefferson Center, VA
A 56 Kings Herb Seeds, Au
A 71 National Heirloom Flower Seed Exchange, MA
A 93 Select Seeds, CT
A 103 Thompson & Morgan, NJ
A 113 Wild Seeds, Wa

FRAGRANT PLANTS
A 16 Canyon Creek Nursery, CA
A 16 Cape Seed & Bulb, So
A 18 Catnip Acres Herb Nursery, CT
A 21 Companion Plants, OH
A 23 The Cottage Herb Farm Shop, NY
A 23 Cricket Hill Herb Farm, Ltd., MA
A 25 Dabney Herbs, KY
A 29 Earthstar Herb Gardens, AZ
A 30 Exotica Rare Fruit Nursery, CA
A 34 Forestfarm, OR
A 35 Fox Hill Farm, MI
A 35 The Fragrant Path, NE
A 39 Good Hollow Greenhouse & Herbarium, TN
A 39 Goodwin Creek Gardens, OR
A 41 Grianan Gardens, CA
A 42 Halcyon Gardens, PA
A 43 Hartman's Herb Farm, MA
A 44 The Herbfarm, WA
A 52 The Thomas Jefferson Center, VA
A 61 Linn Farm Perennials, VA
A 62 Logee's Greenhouses, CT
A 63 Lost Prairie Herb Farm, MT
A 61 Meadowbrook Herb Garden, RI
A 72 Niche Gardens, NC
A 82 The Plumeria People, TX
A 85 Rasland Farm, NC
A 87 Richters, ON
A 89 The Rosemary House, PA
A 89 Roses of Yesterday & Today, CA
A 91 Sandy Mush Herb Nursery, NC
A 93 Seeds Blum, ID
A 93 Select Seeds, CT
A 94 Shady Hill Gardens, IL
A 95 Shepherd's Garden Seeds, CA
A 99 Stallings Exotic Nursery, CA
A 102 Taylor's Herb Gardens, CA
A 104 Tinmouth Channel Farm, VT
A 106 Triple Oaks Nursery, NJ
A 115 Winter Greenhouse, WI

FRANKLINIA
A 5   Appalachian Gardens, PA
A 6   B & B Laboratories, WA
A 39 Gossler Farms Nursery, OR
A 53 Justice Gardens, GA
A 58 Lamtree Farm, NC
A 112 Whitman Farms, OR

FRITILLARIAS
A 3   Jacques Amand, Ltd., En
A 6   Avon Bulbs, En
A 12 Broadleigh Gardens, En
A 19 Paul Christian -- Rare Plants, Wa
A 26 Peter De Jager Bulb Co., MA
A 39 Russell Graham, Purveyor of Plants, OR
A 82 Potterton & Martin, En
A 84 Quality Dutch Bulbs, NJ
A 88 Robinett Bulb Farm, CA

FRUIT TREES
See also specific fruits
(continued next page)

PAGE SOURCE

FRUIT TREES (continued)
A 1   Ahrens Nursery & Plant Labs, IN
A 8   Vernon Barnes & Son Nursery, TN
A 24 Cumberland Valley Nurseries, Inc., TN
A 29 Emlong Nurseries, MI
A 35 Fowler Nurseries, Inc., CA
A 37 Louis Gerardi Nursery, IL
A 57 V. Kraus Nurseries, Ltd., ON
A 59 Lawson's Nursery, GA
A 70 Mt. Leo Nursery, TN
A 74 Northwoods Nursery, OR
A 82 Pony Creek Nursery, WI
A 84 Raintree Nursery, WA
A 87 Rider Nurseries, IA
A 91 Savage Farms Nursery, TN
A 99 Stark Bro's Nurseries & Orchards Co., MO
A 108 VanWell Nursery, Inc., WA

FRUIT TREES, ANTIQUE
A 4   Ames' Orchard and Nursery, AR
A 40 Greenmantle Nursery, CA
A 52 The Thomas Jefferson Center, VA
A 58 LBG Nursery, MN
A 59 Lawson's Nursery, GA
A 60 Henry Leuthardt Nurseries, Inc., NY
A 98 Southmeadow Fruit Gardens, MI

FRUIT TREES, DWARF
A 4   Ames' Orchard and Nursery, AR
A 34 Four Winds Growers, CA
A 54 Kelly Nurseries, NY
A 60 Henry Leuthardt Nurseries, Inc., NY
A 86 Rayner Bros., MD
A 98 Southmeadow Fruit Gardens, MI
A 108 VanWell Nursery, Inc., WA

FRUIT TREES, ESPALIERED
A 5   Arbor & Espalier, CA
A 60 Henry Leuthardt Nurseries, Inc., NY
A 62 Long Hungry Creek Nursery, TN

FRUIT TREES, HARDY
See also specific fruits
A 1   Adams County Nursery, Inc., PA
A 8   Bear Creek Nursery, WA
A 8   Beaverlodge Nursery, AB
A 31 Farmer Seed & Nursery, MN
A 31 Fedco Seeds, ME
A 38 Golden Bough Tree Farm, ON
A 53 J. W. Jung Seed Co., WI
A 58 LBG Nursery, MN
A 58 Lakeshore Tree Farms, Ltd., SK
A 59 Lawyer Nursery, Inc., MT
A 64 McConnell Nurseries, Inc., ON
A 65 Makielski Berry Farm & Nursery, MI
A 69 J. E. Miller Nurseries, Inc., NY
A 70 Moosebell Flower, Fruit & Tree Co., ME
A 70 Morden Nurseries, Ltd., MB
A 72 New York State Fruit Testing Coop. Assn., NY
A 90 St. Lawrence Nurseries, NY
A 99 Stanek's Garden Center, WA
A 102 T & T Seeds, Ltd., MB

FRUIT TREES, LOW-CHILL
A 63 The Lowrey Nursery, TX
A 78 Pacific Tree Farms, CA
A 98 South Seas Nursery, CA

FRUIT TREES, WIDE ASSORTMENT
A 1   Ahrens Nursery & Plant Labs, IN

FRUIT TREES, WIDE ASSORTMENT
A 41 Gurney Seed & Nursery Co., SD
A 57 V. Kraus Nurseries, Ltd., ON

FRUIT, NEW VARIETIES
See also specific fruits
A 4   Ames' Orchard and Nursery, AR
A 36 Garden of Delights, FL
A 40 Greenmantle Nursery, CA
A 72 New York State Fruit Testing Coop. Assn., NY
A 84 Raintree Nursery, WA
A 95 Sherwood's Greenhouses, LA

FRUIT, TROPICAL
See also specific fruits
A 6   B & T Associates, En
A 7   The Banana Tree, PA
A 13 John Brudy Exotics, FL
A 22 Copacabana Gardens, CA
A 30 Exotica Rare Fruit Nursery, CA
A 36 Fruit Spirit Botanical Gardens, Au
A 36 Garden of Delights, FL
A 37 Garden World, TX
A 38 Global Seed Exchange, WA
A 68 Roger & Shirley Meyer, CA
A 78 Pacific Tree Farms, CA
A 82 Possum Trot Tropical Fruit Nursery, FL
A 98 South Seas Nursery, CA
A 106 Tropicals Unlimited, HI

FUCHSIAS
A 4   Annabelle's Fuchsia Garden, CA
A 36 G & G Gardens and Growers, CA
A 46 Hidden Springs Herb and Fuchsia Farm, TN
A 67 Merry Gardens, ME
A 98 Southern Seeds, Ne
A 101 Sunshine Violets & Gesneriads, MA
A 103 Tiki Nursery, NC

FUCHSIAS, HARDY
A 4   Annabelle's Fuchsia Garden, CA
A 46 Hidden Springs Herb and Fuchsia Farm, TN
A 58 Lamb Nurseries, WA
A 102 A. P. & E. V. Tabraham, En

GARDENIAS
A 74 Nuccio's Nurseries, CA

GARLIC
A 17 Casa Yerba Gardens, OR
A 25 Dacha Barinka, BC
A 27 Delegeane Garlic Farms, CA
A 29 Earthstar Herb Gardens, AZ
A 35 Fox Hollow Herbs, PA
A 36 Garden City Seeds, MT
A 39 Good Seed Co., WA
A 54 Kalmia Farm, VA
A 72 Nichols Garden Nursery, Inc., OR
A 79 Peaceful Valley Farm Supply, CA
A 90 S & H Organic Acres, CA
A 98 Southern Exposure Seed Exchange, VA

GARLIC, SKINLESS
A 82 Plumtree Nursery, NY

GASTERIAS
A 14 Burk's Nursery, AR
A 100 Succulenta, CA

PAGE SOURCE

GENERAL NURSERY STOCK
See also specific plants
A 2   Alberta Nurseries & Seed Company, AB
A 4   Ames' Orchard and Nursery, AR
A 8   Vernon Barnes & Son Nursery, TN
A 13   Buckley Nursery, WA
A 14   W. Atlee Burpee Company, PA
A 29   Emlong Nurseries, MI
A 31   Farmer Seed & Nursery, MN
A 32   Henry Field Seed & Nursery Co., IA
A 35   Fowler Nurseries, Inc., CA
A 38   Girard Nurseries, OH
A 41   Gurney Seed & Nursery Co., SD
A 43   Hastings, GA
A 49   Huronview Nurseries & Garden Centre, ON
A 50   Inter-State Nurseries, IA
A 52   Jackson & Perkins Co., OR
A 52   Johnson Nursery, GA
A 53   J. W. Jung Seed Co., WI
A 54   Kelly Nurseries, NY
A 57   V. Kraus Nurseries, Ltd., ON
A 58   Lakeshore Tree Farms, Ltd., SK
A 59   Lawson's Nursery, GA
A 59   Lawyer Nursery, Inc., MT
A 64   McFayden Seeds, MB
A 67   Earl May Seed & Nursery Co., IA
A 67   Mellinger's, Inc., OH
A 69   J. E. Miller Nurseries, Inc., NY
A 70   Morden Nurseries, Ltd., MB
A 82   Pony Creek Nursery, WI
A 87   Rider Nurseries, IA
A 92   Seed Centre, Ltd., AB
A 95   R. H. Shumway Seedsman, SC
A 99   Stark Bro's Nurseries & Orchards Co., MO
A 102 T & T Seeds, Ltd., MB
A 108 VanWell Nursery, Inc., WA

GENTIANS
A 5   Appalachian Wildflower Nursery, PA
A 12   Brookside Wildflowers, NC
A 52   Klaus R. Jelitto, We
A 72   Nature's Garden Nursery, OR
A 83   Prairie Moon Nursery, MN
A 93   The Seed Source, NC
A 93   Seedalp, Sw
A 102 Surry Gardens, ME
A 104 Torbay's Plant World, En

GERANIUMS
A 22   Cook's Geranium Nursery, KS
A 26   Davidson-Wilson Greenhouses, IN
A 58   Lake Odessa Greenhouse, MI
A 92   Sedona Gardens, BC
A 94   Shady Hill Gardens, IL
A 116 Young's Mesa Nursery, CA

GERANIUMS, MINIATURE
A 22   Cook's Geranium Nursery, KS
A 26   Davidson-Wilson Greenhouses, IN
A 67   Merry Gardens, ME
A 94   Shady Hill Gardens, IL
A 116 Young's Mesa Nursery, CA

GERANIUMS, SCENTED
A 22   Cook's Geranium Nursery, KS
A 23   Cricket Hill Herb Farm, Ltd., MA
A 25   Dabney Herbs, KY
A 26   Davidson-Wilson Greenhouses, IN
A 28   Dutch Mill Herb Farm, OR
A 29   Earthstar Herb Gardens, AZ

GERANIUMS, SCENTED
A 35   Fox Hill Farm, MI
A 39   Good Hollow Greenhouse & Herbarium, TN
A 42   Robert B. Hamm, CA
A 43   Hartman's Herb Farm, MA
A 44   The Herb Barn, PA
A 45   Herbs-Liscious, IA
A 46   Hidden Springs Herb and Fuchsia Farm, TN
A 47   Hilltop Herb Farm, TX
A 58   Lake Odessa Greenhouse, MI
A 62   Logee's Greenhouses, CT
A 63   Lost Prairie Herb Farm, MT
A 64   McCrory's Sunny Hill Herb Farm, FL
A 67   Merry Gardens, ME
A 85   Rasland Farm, NC
A 87   Richters, ON
A 89   Rose Hill Herbs and Perennials, VA
A 89   The Rosemary House, PA
A 91   Sandy Mush Herb Nursery, NC
A 94   Shady Hill Gardens, IL
A 96   Sleepy Hollow Herb Farm, KY
A 101 Sunnybrook Farms Nursery, OH
A 106 Triple Oaks Nursery, NJ
A 109 Village Arbors, AL
A 111 Well-Sweep Herb Farm, NJ
A 116 Wrenwood of Berkeley Springs, WV
A 116 Young's Mesa Nursery, CA

GERANIUMS, SPECIES
A 14   Busse Gardens, MN
A 16   Canyon Creek Nursery, CA
A 20   Clifford's Perennial & Vine, WI
A 24   Cricklewood Nursery, WA
A 32   Fieldstone Gardens, Inc., ME
A 33   Flora Favours, WI
A 37   Garden Place, OH
A 47   Holbrook Farm & Nursery, NC
A 56   Kimberly Garden on Oregon Hill, NY
A 58   Lamb Nurseries, WA
A 68   Milaeger's Gardens, WI
A 83   Powell's Gardens, NC
A 83   The Primrose Path, PA
A 94   Shady Hill Gardens, IL
A 98   Southern Seeds, Ne
A 116 Young's Mesa Nursery, CA

GESNERIADS
See also specific plants
A 13   Buell's Greenhouse, Inc., CT
A 26   Davidson-Wilson Greenhouses, IN
A 32   Fischer Greenhouses, NJ
A 38   Glasshouse Works, OH
A 42   Robert B. Hamm, CA
A 52   Jeannette's Jesneriads, LA
A 54   Karleens Achimenes, GA
A 54   Kartuz Greenhouses, CA
A 59   Lauray of Salisbury, CT
A 60   Les Violettes Natalia, PQ
A 62   Logee's Greenhouses, CT
A 63   Lyndon Lyon Greenhouses, Inc., NY
A 64   McKinney's Glasshouse, KS
A 66   Marvelous Minis, MI
A 68   Mighty Minis, CA
A 81   Plant Villa, IL
A 81   Pleasant Hill African Violets, TX
A 101 Sunshine State Tropicals, FL
A 101 Sunshine Violets & Gesneriads, MA
A 114 Wilson's Violet Haven, TX
A 117 Zaca Vista Nursery, CA

PAGE SOURCE

GINGERS
A 38 Glasshouse Works, OH
A 41 Gulf Coast Plantsmen, LA
A 44 Heliconia Haus, FL
A 63 Louisiana Nursery, LA
A 80 Pine Heights Nursery, Au
A 99 Stallings Exotic Nursery, CA
A 101 Sunshine State Tropicals, FL
A 107 TyTy Plantation, GA
A 110 Mary Walker Bulb Company, GA
A 115 Tom Wood, Nurseryman, FL

GINSENG
A 21 Companion Plants, OH
A 25 Dabney Herbs, KY
A 80 Pick's Ginseng, KY

GLADIOLUS
A 5 Antonelli Brothers, Inc., CA
A 11 Breck's, IL
A 21 Connell's Dahlias, WA
A 24 Cruickshank's, Inc., ON
A 28 Dutch Gardens, Inc., NJ
A 28 Early's Farm & Garden Centre, Inc., SK
A 38 Gladside Gardens, MA
A 49 Ed Hume Seeds, Inc., WA
A 50 Inter-State Nurseries, IA
A 59 Lazarus Enterprises, OR
A 61 Michigan Bulb Co., MI
A 81 Pleasant Valley Glads, MA
A 91 John Scheepers, Inc., NY
A 96 Skolaski's Glads & Field Flowers, WI
A 99 Stanek's Garden Center, WA
A 101 Alex Summerville, NJ
A 107 Van Bourgondien Bros., Inc., NY
A 108 Veldheer Tulip Gardens, MI
A 110 Mary Walker Bulb Company, GA
A 110 The Waushara Gardens, WI

GLADIOLUS, SPECIES
A 6 Avon Bulbs, En
A 9 Bio-Quest International, CA
A 12 Broadleigh Gardens, En
A 16 Cape Seed & Bulb, So
A 78 Parsley's Cape Seeds, So
A 90 Rust-En-Vrede Nursery, So
A 96 Anthony J. Skittone, CA

GLOXINIAS
A 5 Antonelli Brothers, Inc., CA
A 9 Blackmore & Langdon, En
A 13 Buell's Greenhouse, Inc., CT
A 54 Karleens Achimenes, GA
A 81 Plant Villa, IL

GOOSEBERRIES
A 8 Bear Creek Nursery, WA
A 29 Edible Landscaping, VA
A 65 Makielski Berry Farm & Nursery, MI
A 70 Moosebell Flower, Fruit & Tree Co., ME
A 79 Pense Nursery, AR
A 98 Southmeadow Fruit Gardens, MI
A 112 Whitman Farms, OR

GOURDS
A 3 Alston Seed Growers, NC
A 27 DeGiorgi Seed Company, NE
A 55 Kilgore Seed Company, FL
A 62 Lockhart Seeds, CA
A 64 Boris McCubbin, TN

GOURDS
A 68 Meta Horticultural Labs, KY
A 71 Native Seeds/SEARCH, AZ
A 87 Ripley's Believe It or Not Seed Catalog, CT
A 90 SPB Sales, TX
A 98 Southern Seeds, FL
A 101 Sunrise Oriental Seed Co., CT
A 102 Talavaya Seeds, NM
A 114 Willhite Seed Co., TX

GRAINS
A 1 Abundant Life Seed Foundation, WA
A 11 Bountiful Gardens, CA
A 24 Cross Seed Company, KS
A 30 Ernst Crownvetch Farms, PA
A 39 The Grain Exchange, KS
A 55 Kester's Wild Game Food Nurseries, WI
A 57 Kusa Research Foundation, CA
A 89 Roswell Seed Co., NM
A 98 Southern Exposure Seed Exchange, VA

GRAPE SCIONS
A 62 Lon's Oregon Grapes, OR
A 97 Sonoma Grapevines, CA

GRAPES, TABLE
A 10 Boordy Nursery, MD
A 10 Boston Mountain Nurseries, AR
A 12 Brittingham Plant Farms, MD
A 13 Buckley Nursery, WA
A 16 California Nursery Co., CA
A 18 Champlain Isle Agro Associates, VT
A 20 Cloud Mountain Nursery, WA
A 29 Edible Landscaping, VA
A 32 The Fig Tree Nursery, FL
A 34 Foster Nurseries, NY
A 35 Fowler Nurseries, Inc., CA
A 38 Golden Bough Tree Farm, ON
A 43 Hastings, GA
A 48 Hollydale Nursery, TN
A 51 Ison's Nursery, GA
A 52 Johnson Nursery, GA
A 54 Kelly Nurseries, NY
A 59 Lawson's Nursery, GA
A 60 Henry Leuthardt Nurseries, Inc., NY
A 62 Lon's Oregon Grapes, OR
A 65 Makielski Berry Farm & Nursery, MI
A 69 J. E. Miller Nurseries, Inc., NY
A 72 New York State Fruit Testing Coop. Assn., NY
A 77 Owen's Vineyard & Nursery, GA
A 79 Pense Nursery, AR
A 87 Rider Nurseries, IA
A 90 St. Lawrence Nurseries, NY
A 91 Savage Farms Nursery, TN
A 97 Sonoma Grapevines, CA
A 98 Southmeadow Fruit Gardens, MI
A 99 Stanek's Garden Center, WA
A 99 Stark Bro's Nurseries & Orchards Co., MO
A 107 TyTy South Orchards, GA
A 108 VanWell Nursery, Inc., WA
A 112 Whitman Farms, OR
A 115 Womack's Nursery Co., TX

GRAPES, WINE
A 10 Boordy Nursery, MD
A 13 Buckley Nursery, WA
A 16 California Nursery Co., CA
A 20 Cloud Mountain Nursery, WA
A 34 Foster Nurseries, NY
A 35 Fowler Nurseries, Inc., CA
(continued next page)

PAGE SOURCE

GRAPES, WINE (continued)
A 46   Hidden Springs Nursery -- Edible Landscaping, TN
A 51   Ison's Nursery, GA
A 58   LBG Nursery, MN
A 60   Henry Leuthardt Nurseries, Inc., NY
A 62   Lon's Oregon Grapes, OR
A 72   New York State Fruit Testing Coop. Assn., NY
A 77   Owen's Vineyard & Nursery, GA
A 97   Sonoma Grapevines, CA
A 115   Womack's Nursery Co., TX

GRASSES, LAWN AND TURF
A 2   Allen, Sterling & Lothrop, ME
A 6   Archias' Seed Store, MO
A 28   Early's Farm & Garden Centre, Inc., SK
A 58   D. Landreth Seed Company, MD
A 60   Orol Ledden & Sons, NJ
A 83   Prairie State Commodities, IL
A 89   Roswell Seed Co., NM
A 92   Seed Centre, Ltd., AB
A 105   Tregunno Seeds, ON

GRASSES, ORNAMENTAL
A 8   Beaver Creek Nursery, TN
A 9   Kurt Bluemel, Inc., MD
A 17   Carroll Gardens, MD
A 17   Carter Seeds, CA
A 20   Clifford's Perennial & Vine, WI
A 23   The Country Garden, WI
A 24   Crownsville Nursery, MD
A 29   Endangered Species, CA
A 34   Flowerplace Plant Farm, MS
A 37   Garden Place, OH
A 37   Gardenimport, Inc., ON
A 39   Russell Graham, Purveyor of Plants, OR
A 40   Greenlee Nursery, CA
A 41   Gulf Coast Plantsmen, LA
A 43   Hatfield Gardens, OH
A 46   High Altitude Gardens, ID
A 52   Klaus R. Jelitto, We
A 53   Johnson Seed Company, CA
A 56   Klehm Nursery, IL
A 57   Kusa Research Foundation, CA
A 59   Landscape Alternatives, Inc., MN
A 61   Limerock Ornamental Grasses, PA
A 66   Maryland Aquatic Nurseries, MD
A 75   Old Farm Nursery, CO
A 80   Piccadilly Farm, GA
A 83   Powell's Gardens, NC
A 88   Robyn's Nest Nursery, WA
A 91   Sandy Mush Herb Nursery, NC
A 93   The Seed Source, NC
A 94   Shady Oaks Nursery, MN
A 96   Skyline Nursery, WA
A 99   Stallings Exotic Nursery, CA
A 100   Stoecklein's Nursery, PA
A 105   Trans Pacific Nursery, OR
A 107   Twombly Nursery, CT
A 109   Andre Viette Farm & Nursery, VA
A 112   White Flower Farm, CT
A 114   Wildwood Nursery, CA

GRASSES, PRAIRIE
A 25   The Nursery at the Dallas Nature Center, TX
A 58   LaFayette Home Nursery, Inc., IL
A 59   Larner Seeds, CA
A 62   Little Valley Farm, WI
A 68   Milaeger's Gardens, WI
A 69   Miller Grass Seed Company, TX
A 83   Prairie Moon Nursery, MN

PAGE SOURCE

GRASSES, PRAIRIE
A 83   Prairie Nursery, WI
A 83   Prairie Ridge Nursery/CRM Ecosystems, Inc., WI
A 83   Prairie Seed Source, WI
A 100   Stock Seed Farms, Inc., NE
A 106   Turner Seed Company, TX

GRASSES, RANGE AND RECLAMATION
A 4   Amenity Plant Products, PA
A 28   Early's Farm & Garden Centre, Inc., SK
A 30   Ernst Crownvetch Farms, PA
A 53   Johnson Seed Company, CA
A 59   Larner Seeds, CA
A 69   Miller Grass Seed Company, TX
A 73   Northplan/Mountain Seed, ID
A 79   Peaceful Valley Farm Supply, CA
A 81   Plants of the Southwest, NM
A 83   Prairie State Commodities, IL
A 86   Redwood City Seed Co., CA
A 89   Roswell Seed Co., NM
A 97   South Florida Seed Supply, FL
A 100   Stock Seed Farms, Inc., NE
A 106   Turner Seed Company, TX

GREEN MANURE CROPS
A 11   Bountiful Gardens, CA
A 37   Garden World, TX
A 39   Good Seed Co., WA
B 18   Green Earth Organics, WA
B 19   Harmony Farm Supply, CA
A 52   Johnny's Selected Seeds, ME
A 60   Orol Ledden & Sons, NJ
B 29   Necessary Trading Co., VA
A 79   Peaceful Valley Farm Supply, CA
A 83   Prairie State Commodities, IL
A 95   R. H. Shumway Seedsman, SC
A 103   Territorial Seed Company, OR

GREENHOUSE/TROPICAL PLANTS
See also specific plants
A 2   Alberts & Merkel Bros., Inc., FL
A 4   Annabelle's Fuchsia Garden, CA
A 6   B & T Associates, En
A 7   The Banana Tree, PA
A 9   Bird Rock Tropicals, CA
A 10   Arthur Boe Distributor, LA
A 13   John Brudy Exotics, FL
A 17   Carter & Holmes, Inc., SC
A 17   Carter Seeds, CA
A 18   Cedar Ridge Nurseries, PA
A 18   Chadwell Himalayan Seed, En
A 20   City Gardens, MI
A 20   Clargreen Gardens, Ltd., ON
A 26   Dane Company, TX
A 26   Davidson-Wilson Greenhouses, IN
A 27   DeGiorgi Seed Company, NE
A 29   Endangered Species, CA
A 30   Exotica Rare Fruit Nursery, CA
A 30   Exotics Hawaii, Ltd., HI
A 32   Fischer Greenhouses, NJ
A 34   Foliage Gardens, WA
A 34   Fort Caroline Orchids, FL
A 35   The Fragrant Path, NE
A 36   Fruit Spirit Botanical Gardens, Au
A 36   G & B Orchid Lab & Nursery, CA
A 36   Garden of Delights, FL
A 37   Garden World, TX
A 38   Glasshouse Works, OH
A 38   Global Seed Exchange, WA
A 38   Golden Lake Greenhouses, CA
(continued next page)

PAGE SOURCE

GREENHOUSE/TROPICAL PLANTS (continued)

A 40   Green Plant Research, HI
A 42   Robert B. Hamm, CA
A 44   Heliconia Haus, FL
A 47   Holladay Jungle, CA
A 48   Jerry Horne -- Rare Plants, FL
A 49   J. L. Hudson, Seedsman, CA
A 54   Kartuz Greenhouses, CA
A 60   W. O. Lessard Nursery, FL
A 62   Logee's Greenhouses, CT
A 65   Ann Mann's Orchids, FL
A 67   Merry Gardens, ME
A 74   Oak Hill Gardens, IL
A 76   Orchids Royale, CA
A 78   Pacific Tree Farms, CA
A 78   Palms for Tropical Landscaping, FL
A 81   The Plant Shop's Botanical Gardens, CA
A 82   The Plumeria People, TX
A 84   Rainforest Flora, Inc., CA
A 84   Rainforest Plantes et Fleurs, Inc., HI
A 86   Rhapis Gardens, TX
A 87   Rhapis Palm Growers, CA
A 90   SLO Gardens, CA
A 92   Sedona Gardens, BC
A 94   Shelldance Nursery, CA
A 97   South Florida Seed Supply, FL
A 98   South Seas Nursery, CA
A 101   Sunshine State Tropicals, FL
A 103   Thompson & Morgan, NJ
A 106   Tropicals Unlimited, HI
A 112   Westside Exotics Palm Nursery, CA
A 115   Tom Wood, Nurseryman, FL
A 116   Guy Wrinkle Exotic Plants, CA

GROUND COVERS
See also specific plants

A 2   Allen, Sterling & Lothrop, ME
A 3   Alpenflora Gardens, BC
A 3   Ambergate Gardens, MN
A 7   Bamboo Sourcery, CA
A 9   Kurt Bluemel, Inc., MD
A 10   Bluestone Perennials, OH
A 11   Botanicals, MA
A 16   Camelot North, MN
A 20   Clifford's Perennial & Vine, WI
A 21   Conley's Garden Center, ME
A 26   Daylily Discounters, FL
A 29   Eastern Plant Specialties, ME
A 30   Ernst Crownvetch Farms, PA
A 32   Henry Field Seed & Nursery Co., IA
A 37   Garden Perennials, NE
A 37   Garden Place, OH
A 38   Gilson Gardens, OH
A 41   Gurney Seed & Nursery Co., SD
A 44   The Herbfarm, WA
A 45   Heritage Gardens, IA
A 48   Homestead Division of Sunnybrook Farms, OH
A 51   Ivies of the World, FL
A 53   Joyce's Garden, OR
A 53   J. W. Jung Seed Co., WI
A 59   Landscape Alternatives, Inc., MN
A 61   Limerock Ornamental Grasses, PA
A 63   The Lowrey Nursery, TX
A 66   Mary's Plant Farm, OH
A 71   Musser Forests Inc., PA
A 71   Native Gardens, TN
A 79   Peekskill Nurseries, NY
A 81   Plant World, TN
A 81   Plants of the Wild, WA
A 83   Powell's Gardens, NC

GROUND COVERS

A 83   Prentiss Court Ground Covers, SC
A 84   Putney Nursery, Inc., VT
A 90   Salter Tree Farm, FL
A 96   Silver Springs Nursery, ID
A 96   Siskiyou Rare Plant Nursery, OR
A 99   Spring Hill Nurseries Co., IL
A 99   Springvale Farm Nursery, IL
A 99   Squaw Mountain Gardens, OR
A 100   Stoecklein's Nursery, PA
A 103   Ter-El Nursery, PA
A 106   Tripple Brook Farm, MA
A 106   Turnipseed Nursery Farms, GA
A 110   Wayside Gardens, SC
A 113   Wildflower Nursery, NC
A 113   The Wildflower Source, IL
A 114   Wildwood Gardens, OH
A 115   Winter Greenhouse, WI
A 116   Wrenwood of Berkeley Springs, WV

GUZMANIAS

A 38   Golden Lake Greenhouses, CA
A 47   Holladay Jungle, CA
A 63   Paul P. Lowe, FL
A 94   Shelldance Nursery, CA

GYMNOCALYCIUMS

A 6   Aztekakti/Desertland Nursery, TX
A 15   Cactus by Dodie, CA
A 27   Desert Theatre, CA
A 84   Sand Ridge Greenhouse, OK
A 92   Schulz Cactus Gardens, CA
A 94   Shein's Cactus, CA
A 100   Succulenta, CA

HAWORTHIAS

A 1   Abbey Gardens, CA
A 14   Burk's Nursery, AR
A 15   Cactus by Dodie, CA
A 27   Desert Nursery, NM
A 41   Grigsby Cactus Gardens, CA
A 46   Highland Succulents, OH
A 54   K & L Cactus Nursery, CA
A 84   Rainbow Gardens Nursery & Bookshop, CA
A 86   Redlo Cacti, OR
A 88   Grace Rollerson, BC
A 92   Scotty's Desert Plants, CA
A 94   Shein's Cactus, CA
A 100   Succulent Plants, MN
A 100   Succulenta, CA
A 116   Guy Wrinkle Exotic Plants, CA

HAZELNUTS

A 14   Burnt Ridge Nursery, WA
A 32   Fernald's Hickory Hill Nursery, IL
A 39   John H. Gordon, Jr., Grower, NY
A 41   Grimo Nut Nursery, ON
A 97   Smith Nursery Co., IA

HEATHERS
See also specific plants

A 24   The Cummins Garden, NJ
A 26   Daystar, ME
A 27   DeGrandchamp's Blueberry Farm, MI
A 29   Eastern Plant Specialties, ME
A 35   Foxborough Nursery, Inc., MD
A 44   Heaths and Heathers, WA
A 47   Holbrook Farm & Nursery, NC
A 88   Rock Spray Nursery, MA
A 91   Sandy Mush Herb Nursery, NC

PAGE SOURCE

HELICONIAS
A 7   The Banana Tree, PA
A 44   Heliconia Haus, FL
A 82   The Plumeria People, TX

HELLEBORES
A 5   Appalachian Wildflower Nursery, PA
A 16   Camellia Forest Nursery, NC
A 39   Gossler Farms Nursery, OR
A 47   Holbrook Farm & Nursery, NC
A 58   Lamb Nurseries, WA
A 69   Montrose Nursery, NC
A 72   Nature's Garden Nursery, OR
A 80   Piccadilly Farm, GA
A 93   Seedalp, Sw

HERBS
A 1   Abundant Life Seed Foundation, WA
A 1   Ahrens Nursery & Plant Labs, IN
A 2   Allen, Sterling & Lothrop, ME
A 10   Bluestone Perennials, OH
A 11   Bountiful Gardens, CA
A 16   Camelot North, MN
A 17   Carroll Gardens, MD
A 17   Casa Yerba Gardens, OR
A 18   Catnip Acres Herb Nursery, CT
A 18   John Chambers, En
A 18   Champlain Isle Agro Associates, VT
A 21   Companion Plants, OH
A 22   The Cook's Garden, VT
A 23   The Cottage Herb Farm Shop, NY
A 23   Cricket Hill Herb Farm, Ltd., MA
A 24   Crosman Seed Corp., NY
A 24   Crownsville Nursery, MD
A 25   Dabney Herbs, KY
A 25   Dacha Barinka, BC
A 25   William Dam Seeds, ON
A 26   T. DeBaggio Herbs by Mail, VA
A 27   DeGiorgi Seed Company, NE
A 28   Dutch Mill Herb Farm, OR
A 28   E & H Products, CA
A 29   Earthstar Herb Gardens, AZ
A 31   Fedco Seeds, ME
A 33   Floating Mountain Seeds, WA
A 33   The Flower & Herb Exchange, IA
A 34   Flowerplace Plant Farm, MS
A 35   Fox Hill Farm, MI
A 35   Fox Hollow Herbs, PA
A 35   The Fragrant Path, NE
A 36   Garden City Seeds, MT
A 37   Garden Place, OH
A 39   Good Hollow Greenhouse & Herbarium, TN
A 39   Good Seed Co., WA
A 39   Goodwin Creek Gardens, OR
A 42   Halcyon Gardens, PA
A 43   Harris Seeds, NY
A 43   Hartman's Herb Farm, MA
A 43   Hastings, GA
A 43   Havasu Hills Herbs, CA
A 44   Heirloom Garden Seeds, CA
A 44   The Herb Barn, PA
A 44   Herb Gathering, Inc., MO
A 44   The Herbfarm, WA
A 45   Herbs-Liscious, IA
A 45   Heymaqua Seed Service, CA
A 46   Hidden Springs Herb and Fuchsia Farm, TN
A 47   Hilltop Herb Farm, TX
A 51   Island Seed Mail Order, BC
A 52   Johnny's Selected Seeds, ME
A 53   Johnson Seed Company, CA

HERBS
A 53   Joyce's Garden, OR
A 55   Kilgore Seed Company, FL
A 56   Kings Herb Seeds, Au
A 58   Lagomarsino Seeds, CA
A 58   D. Landreth Seed Company, MD
A 62   Logee's Greenhouses, CT
A 63   Lost Prairie Herb Farm, MT
A 63   The Lowrey Nursery, TX
A 64   McCrory's Sunny Hill Herb Farm, FL
A 66   Mary's Plant Farm, OH
A 61   Meadowbrook Herb Garden, RI
A 67   Merry Gardens, ME
A 68   Meyer Seed Co., MD
A 70   Mountain Valley Seeds & Nursery, UT
A 72   Nichols Garden Nursery, Inc., OR
A 77   Ozark National Seed Order, NY
A 79   Peace Seeds, OR
A 80   Pinetree Garden Seeds, ME
A 84   Putney Nursery, Inc., VT
A 85   Rasland Farm, NC
A 85   Ravenswood Seeds, WI
A 85   Rawlinson Garden Seed, NS
A 87   Richters, ON
A 89   Rose Hill Herbs and Perennials, VA
A 89   The Rosemary House, PA
A 91   Sanctuary Seeds/Folklore Herb Co., Ltd., BC
A 91   Sandy Mush Herb Nursery, NC
A 93   Seeds Blum, ID
A 95   Shepherd's Garden Seeds, CA
A 96   Sleepy Hollow Herb Farm, KY
A 98   Southern Exposure Seed Exchange, VA
A 98   Specialty Seeds, Au
A 101 Sunnybrook Farms Nursery, OH
A 102 Taylor's Herb Gardens, CA
A 103 Territorial Seed Company, OR
A 104 Tinmouth Channel Farm, VT
A 105 Tregunno Seeds, ON
A 106 Triple Oaks Nursery, NJ
A 108 Vermont Bean Seed Co., VT
A 109 Village Arbors, AL
A 110 Wyrttun Ward, MA
A 111 Weiss Brothers Nursery, CA
A 111 Well-Sweep Herb Farm, NJ
A 112 Westwind Seeds, AZ
A 112 White Flower Farm, CT
A 116 Wrenwood of Berkeley Springs, WV

HERBS, ORIENTAL
A 6   B & T Associates, En
A 18   Catnip Acres Herb Nursery, CT
A 21   Companion Plants, OH
A 28   Dutch Mill Herb Farm, OR
A 30   Evergreen Y. H. Enterprises, CA
A 39   Goodwin Creek Gardens, OR
A 45   Herbs-Liscious, IA
A 87   Richters, ON
A 101 Sunrise Oriental Seed Co., CT

HEUCHERAS
A 10   Bluestone Perennials, OH
A 14   Busse Gardens, MN
A 37   Garden Place, OH
A 43   Hauser's Superior View Farm, WI
A 61   Linn Farm Perennials, VA
A 69   Montrose Nursery, NC
A 83   The Primrose Path, PA

HIBISCUS
A 1   Air Expose, TX
(continued next page)

PAGE SOURCE

HIBISCUS (continued)
A 33   Florida Colors Nursery, FL
A 74   Oak Hill Gardens, IL
A 82   The Plumeria People, TX
A 86   Reasoner's, Inc., FL
A 99   Stallings Exotic Nursery, CA

HIBISCUS, HARDY
A 1   Air Expose, TX
A 20   Clifford's Perennial & Vine, WI
A 41   Gulf Coast Plantsmen, LA
A 65   Magnolia Nursery & Display Garden, AL
A 112   Whayes End Nursery, VA

HICKORY NUTS
A 37   Louis Gerardi Nursery, IL
A 41   Grimo Nut Nursery, ON
A 73   Nolin River Nut Tree Nursery, KY
A 114   Wiley's Nut Grove, OH

HOLLY
A 5   Appalachian Gardens, PA
A 8   Beaver Creek Nursery, TN
A 13   Bull Valley Rhododendron Nursery, PA
A 16   Camellia Forest Nursery, NC
A 21   Colvos Creek Nursery & Landscaping, WA
A 27   DeGrandchamp's Blueberry Farm, MI
A 29   Eastern Plant Specialties, ME
A 35   Foxborough Nursery, Inc., MD
A 38   Girard Nurseries, OH
A 45   Heronswood Nursery, WA
A 47   Holly Hills, Inc., IN
A 48   Hollyvale Farm, WA
A 65   Magnolia Nursery & Display Garden, AL
A 89   Roslyn Nursery, NY
A 90   Salter Tree Farm, FL
A 92   F. W. Schumacher Co., MA
A 110   Wavecrest Nursery & Landscaping Co., MI

HORSERADISH
A 74   Nourse Farms, Inc., MA

HOSTAS
A 3   Ambergate Gardens, MN
A 4   American Daylily & Perennials, MO
A 14   Busse Gardens, MN
A 16   Caprice Farm, OR
A 20   Clifford's Perennial & Vine, WI
A 20   Coastal Gardens & Nursery, SC
A 22   Cooper's Garden, MN
A 24   Crownsville Nursery, MD
A 28   Donnelly's Nursery, NC
A 29   Englerth Gardens, MI
A 31   Fairway Enterprises, MN
A 33   Flowerland, NE
A 43   Hatfield Gardens, OH
A 46   Hickory Hill Gardens, PA
A 46   Hildenbrandt's Iris Gardens, NE
A 48   Homestead Division of Sunnybrook Farms, OH
A 50   Inter-State Nurseries, IA
A 52   Jernigan Gardens, NC
A 56   Kimberly Garden on Oregon Hill, NY
A 56   Klehm Nursery, IL
A 66   Maroushek Gardens, MN
A 67   Meadowlake Gardens, SC
A 68   Milaeger's Gardens, WI
A 77   Owen's Vineyard & Nursery, GA
A 80   Piccadilly Farm, GA
A 80   Piedmont Gardens, CT
A 83   Powell's Gardens, NC

PAGE SOURCE

HOSTAS
A 86   Reath's Nursery, MI
A 88   Robyn's Nest Nursery, WA
A 88   Rocknoll Nursery, OH
A 91   Savory's Gardens, Inc., MN
A 91   Saxton Gardens, NY
A 94   Shady Oaks Nursery, MN
A 96   Skyline Nursery, WA
A 100   Stoecklein's Nursery, PA
A 101   Sunnybrook Farms Nursery, OH
A 107   Van Bourgondien Bros., Inc., NY
A 108   Vandenberg, NY
A 109   Andre Viette Farm & Nursery, VA
A 109   Walden -- West, OR
A 116   Worel's Iris Gardens, MN

HOUSEPLANTS
See also specific plants
A 6   B & T Associates, En
A 9   Betsy's Brierpatch, NY
A 13   John Brudy Exotics, FL
A 21   Color Farm Growers, FL
A 25   William Dam Seeds, ON
A 26   Davidson-Wilson Greenhouses, IN
A 29   Endangered Species, CA
A 32   Henry Field Seed & Nursery Co., IA
A 38   Glasshouse Works, OH
A 40   Greenlife Gardens Greenhouses, GA
A 41   Gurney Seed & Nursery Co., SD
A 42   Robert B. Hamm, CA
A 47   Holladay Jungle, CA
A 48   Jerry Horne -- Rare Plants, FL
A 54   Karleens Achimenes, GA
A 54   Kartuz Greenhouses, CA
A 54   Kay's Greenhouses, TX
A 58   Lake Odessa Greenhouse, MI
A 59   Lauray of Salisbury, CT
A 63   Lyndon Lyon Greenhouses, Inc., NY
A 64   McConnell Nurseries, Inc., ON
A 67   Mellinger's, Inc., OH
A 67   Merry Gardens, ME
A 74   Oak Hill Gardens, IL
A 75   Orchibec, PQ
A 79   Peter Pauls Nurseries, NY
A 81   Pleasant Hill African Violets, TX
A 86   Rhapis Gardens, TX
A 92   Sedona Gardens, BC
A 99   Spring Hill Nurseries Co., IL
A 100   Stokes Seed Company, NY
A 101   Sunnybrook Farms Nursery, OH
A 101   Sunshine State Tropicals, FL
A 101   Sunshine Violets & Gesneriads, MA

HOYAS
A 1   Abbey Gardens, CA
A 38   Golden Lake Greenhouses, CA
A 40   Green Plant Research, HI
A 47   Hill 'n dale, CA
A 54   Kartuz Greenhouses, CA
A 59   Lauray of Salisbury, CT
A 65   Ann Mann's Orchids, FL
A 66   Marilynn's Garden, CA
A 84   Rainbow Gardens Nursery & Bookshop, CA
A 84   Rainforest Plantes et Fleurs, Inc., HI
A 90   SLO Gardens, CA
A 92   Sedona Gardens, BC

HUMMINGBIRD PLANTS
A 49   Hummingbird Gardens, CA

PAGE SOURCE

HYACINTHS
A 25   The Daffodil Mart, VA
A 26   Peter De Jager Bulb Co., MA
A 67   Messelaar Bulb Co., MA
A 84   Quality Dutch Bulbs, NJ
A 108   Van Engelen, Inc., CT
A 108   Mary Mattison van Schaik, VT
A 108   Veldheer Tulip Gardens, MI

HYDRANGEAS
A 5   Appalachian Gardens, PA
A 45   Heronswood Nursery, WA
A 63   Louisiana Nursery, LA
A 66   Mary's Plant Farm, OH
A 77   Owen Farms, TN
A 113   The Wildwood Flower, NC

IRIS, ARIL
A 56   Kirkland Iris Garden, WA
A 65   Maple Tree Gardens, NE
A 67   Maxim's Greenwood Gardens, CA
A 69   Miller's Manor Gardens, IN
A 82   Pleasure Iris Gardens, NM
A 95   Shepard Iris Garden, AZ
A 116   Worel's Iris Gardens, MN

IRIS, BEARDED (VARIOUS TYPES)
See also specific type
A 1   Adamgrove, MO
A 2   Aitken's Salmon Creek Garden, WA
A 13   The Bulb Crate, IL
A 21   Comanche Acres Iris Gardens, MO
A 23   Country View Gardens, MI
A 24   C. Criscola Iris Garden, WA
A 28   Dutch Gardens, Inc., NJ
A 37   Gardenimport, Inc., ON
A 42   Hahn's Rainbow Iris Garden, MO
A 51   Iris Acres, IN
A 56   Kirkland Iris Garden, WA
A 63   Long's Gardens, CO
A 64   McMillen's Iris Garden, ON
A 65   Maple Tree Gardens, NE
A 66   Mary's Plant Farm, OH
A 66   Maryott's Gardens, CA
A 67   Maxim's Greenwood Gardens, CA
A 68   Mid-America Iris Gardens, OK
A 69   Miller's Manor Gardens, IN
A 70   Moonshine Gardens, CA
A 72   Nicholls Gardens, VA
A 73   North Pine Iris Gardens, NE
A 82   Pleasure Iris Gardens, NM
A 83   Powell's Gardens, NC
A 84   Ramona Gardens, CA
A 92   Schreiner's Gardens, OR
A 95   Shepard Iris Garden, AZ
A 99   Spruce Gardens, NE
A 106   21st Century Gardens, AZ
A 116   Worel's Iris Gardens, MN

IRIS, BULBOUS
A 21   Comanche Acres Iris Gardens, MO
A 26   Peter De Jager Bulb Co., MA
A 108   Van Engelen, Inc., CT

IRIS, CRESTED
A 1   Adamgrove, MO
A 59   Laurie's Garden, OR

IRIS, DWARF BEARDED
A 1   Adamgrove, MO

IRIS, DWARF BEARDED
A 2   Aitken's Salmon Creek Garden, WA
A 21   Comanche Acres Iris Gardens, MO
A 23   Country View Gardens, MI
A 24   C. Criscola Iris Garden, WA
A 42   Hahn's Rainbow Iris Garden, MO
A 43   Hatfield Gardens, OH
A 46   Hildenbrandt's Iris Gardens, NE
A 49   Huggins Farm Irises, TX
A 51   Iris Acres, IN
A 51   Iris Gardens, MT
A 51   Iris Test Gardens, WA
A 56   Kirkland Iris Garden, WA
A 63   Long's Gardens, CO
A 64   McMillen's Iris Garden, ON
A 65   Maple Tree Gardens, NE
A 66   Maryott's Gardens, CA
A 68   Mid-America Iris Gardens, OK
A 69   Miller's Manor Gardens, IN
A 69   Monashee Gardens, BC
A 70   Moonshine Gardens, CA
A 72   Nicholls Gardens, VA
A 73   North Pine Iris Gardens, NE
A 82   Pleasure Iris Gardens, NM
A 85   Randy's Iris Garden, UT
A 92   Schreiner's Gardens, OR
A 99   Spruce Gardens, NE
A 106   21st Century Gardens, AZ
A 116   Worel's Iris Gardens, MN
A 116   Wright Iris Nursery, CA

IRIS, HORNED
A 2   Aitken's Salmon Creek Garden, WA
A 21   Comanche Acres Iris Gardens, MO
A 49   Huggins Farm Irises, TX
A 64   McMillen's Iris Garden, ON
A 67   Maxim's Greenwood Gardens, CA
A 68   Mid-America Iris Gardens, OK
A 70   Moonshine Gardens, CA
A 95   Shepard Iris Garden, AZ
A 106   21st Century Gardens, AZ

IRIS, JAPANESE
A 2   Aitken's Salmon Creek Garden, WA
A 16   Caprice Farm, OR
A 20   Coastal Gardens & Nursery, SC
A 29   Englerth Gardens, MI
A 30   Ensata Gardens, MI
A 32   Fieldstone Gardens, Inc., ME
A 38   Gladside Gardens, MA
A 51   The Iris Pond, VA
A 59   Laurie's Garden, OR
A 61   Lilypons Water Gardens, MD
A 65   Magnolia Nursery & Display Garden, AL
A 66   Maryland Aquatic Nurseries, MD
A 67   Maxim's Greenwood Gardens, CA
A 67   Meadowlake Gardens, SC
A 72   Nicholls Gardens, VA
A 82   Pleasure Iris Gardens, NM
A 91   Santa Barbara Water Gardens, CA
A 104   Tranquil Lake Nursery, MA
A 110   Wayside Gardens, SC

IRIS, LOUISIANA
A 1   Adamgrove, MO
A 8   Bay View Gardens, CA
A 21   Comanche Acres Iris Gardens, MO
A 22   Cooper's Garden, MN
A 22   Cordon Bleu Farms, CA
A 61   Lilypons Water Gardens, MD
(continued next page)

IRIS, LOUISIANA (continued)

A 63	Louisiana Nursery, LA
A 65	Magnolia Nursery & Display Garden, AL
A 66	Maryland Aquatic Nurseries, MD
A 67	Maxim's Greenwood Gardens, CA
A 72	Nicholls Gardens, VA
A 82	Pleasure Iris Gardens, NM
A 91	Santa Barbara Water Gardens, CA
A 95	Shepard Iris Garden, AZ

IRIS, MEDIAN BEARDED

A 1	Adamgrove, MO
A 2	Aitken's Salmon Creek Garden, WA
A 10	Borbeleta Gardens, MN
A 21	Comanche Acres Iris Gardens, MO
A 23	Country View Gardens, MI
A 24	C. Criscola Iris Garden, WA
A 37	Garden of the Enchanted Rainbow, AL
A 42	Hahn's Rainbow Iris Garden, MO
A 43	Hatfield Gardens, OH
A 49	Huggins Farm Irises, TX
A 51	Iris Acres, IN
A 51	Iris Gardens, MT
A 55	Keith Keppel, CA
A 56	Kirkland Iris Garden, WA
A 63	Long's Gardens, CO
A 64	McMillen's Iris Garden, ON
A 65	Maple Tree Gardens, NE
A 68	Mid-America Iris Gardens, OK
A 69	Miller's Manor Gardens, IN
A 70	Moonshine Gardens, CA
A 72	Nicholls Gardens, VA
A 73	North Pine Iris Gardens, NE
A 82	Pleasure Iris Gardens, NM
A 92	Schreiner's Gardens, OR
A 95	Shepard Iris Garden, AZ
A 99	Spruce Gardens, NE
A 106	21st Century Gardens, AZ
A 116	Worel's Iris Gardens, MN

IRIS, PACIFIC COAST NATIVES

A 2	Aitken's Salmon Creek Garden, WA
A 8	Bay View Gardens, CA
A 59	Larner Seeds, CA
A 59	Laurie's Garden, OR
A 67	Maxim's Greenwood Gardens, CA
A 82	Portable Acres, CA
A 96	Skyline Nursery, WA

IRIS, PUMILA

A 1	Adamgrove, MO
A 23	Country View Gardens, MI

IRIS, REBLOOMING

A 2	Aitken's Salmon Creek Garden, WA
A 6	Avonbank Iris Gardens, VA
A 21	Comanche Acres Iris Gardens, MO
A 37	Garden of the Enchanted Rainbow, AL
A 49	Huggins Farm Irises, TX
A 51	Iris Acres, IN
A 51	The Iris Pond, VA
A 68	Mid-America Iris Gardens, OK
A 70	Moonshine Gardens, CA
A 72	Nicholls Gardens, VA
A 78	Pacific Coast Hybridizers, CA
A 106	21st Century Gardens, AZ

IRIS, SIBERIAN

A 2	Aitken's Salmon Creek Garden, WA
A 3	Ambergate Gardens, MN

IRIS, SIBERIAN

A 10	Borbeleta Gardens, MN
A 14	Busse Gardens, MN
A 16	Caprice Farm, OR
A 19	Chehalem Gardens, OR
A 20	Clifford's Perennial & Vine, WI
A 22	Cooper's Garden, MN
A 23	Country View Gardens, MI
A 29	Englerth Gardens, MI
A 30	Ensata Gardens, MI
A 32	Fieldstone Gardens, Inc., ME
A 38	Gladside Gardens, MA
A 42	Dr. Joseph C. Halinar, OR
A 46	Hickory Hill Gardens, PA
A 48	Honeywood Lilies, SK
A 51	The Iris Pond, VA
A 56	Kimberly Garden on Oregon Hill, NY
A 56	Klehm Nursery, IL
A 59	Laurie's Garden, OR
A 61	Lilypons Water Gardens, MD
A 64	McMillen's Iris Garden, ON
A 65	Maple Tree Gardens, NE
A 67	Maxim's Greenwood Gardens, CA
A 69	Miller's Manor Gardens, IN
A 69	Monashee Gardens, BC
A 72	Nicholls Gardens, VA
A 82	Pleasure Iris Gardens, NM
A 91	Santa Barbara Water Gardens, CA
A 96	Anthony J. Skittone, CA
A 100	Stoecklein's Nursery, PA
A 104	Tranquil Lake Nursery, MA
A 109	Andre Viette Farm & Nursery, VA
A 116	Worel's Iris Gardens, MN
A 116	Wright Iris Nursery, CA

IRIS, SPECIES

A 1	Adamgrove, MO
A 2	Aitken's Salmon Creek Garden, WA
A 3	Alpenflora Gardens, BC
A 5	Appalachian Wildflower Nursery, PA
A 6	Avon Bulbs, En
A 12	Broadleigh Gardens, En
A 12	Joseph Brown, Native Seeds, VA
A 13	Bundles of Bulbs, MD
A 19	Paul Christian -- Rare Plants, Wa
A 20	Coastal Gardens & Nursery, SC
A 21	Colorado Alpines, Inc., CO
A 22	Cooper's Garden, MN
A 29	Eco-Gardens, GA
A 34	Forestfarm, OR
A 39	Russell Graham, Purveyor of Plants, OR
A 51	The Iris Pond, VA
A 52	Klaus R. Jelitto, We
A 57	P. Kohli & Co., In
A 59	Laurie's Garden, OR
A 63	Louisiana Nursery, LA
A 67	Messelaar Bulb Co., MA
A 72	Nicholls Gardens, VA
A 82	Pleasure Iris Gardens, NM
A 82	Portable Acres, CA
A 82	Potterton & Martin, En
A 88	Rocknoll Nursery, OH
A 90	Rust-En-Vrede Nursery, So
A 91	Santa Barbara Water Gardens, CA
A 93	Select Seeds, CT
A 96	Skyline Nursery, WA
A 108	Van Engelen, Inc., CT
A 111	We-Du Nurseries, NC

PAGE SOURCE

IRIS, SPURIA
A 8   Bay View Gardens, CA
A 19   Chehalem Gardens, OR
A 22   Cordon Bleu Farms, CA
A 67   Maxim's Greenwood Gardens, CA
A 82   Pleasure Iris Gardens, NM
A 95   Shepard Iris Garden, AZ

IRIS, TALL BEARDED
A 2   Aitken's Salmon Creek Garden, WA
A 4   American Daylily & Perennials, MO
A 4   Anderson Iris Gardens, MN
A 8   Bay View Gardens, CA
A 11   Brand Peony Farm, MN
A 21   Comanche Acres Iris Gardens, MO
A 22   Cooley's Gardens, OR
A 22   Cottage Gardens, CA
A 23   Country View Gardens, MI
A 24   C. Criscola Iris Garden, WA
A 24   Cruickshank's, Inc., ON
A 37   Garden of the Enchanted Rainbow, AL
A 39   Grandview Iris Gardens, NE
A 42   Hahn's Rainbow Iris Garden, MO
A 43   Hatfield Gardens, OH
A 46   Hickory Hill Gardens, PA
A 46   Hildenbrandt's Iris Gardens, NE
A 49   Huggins Farm Irises, TX
A 50   Inter-State Nurseries, IA
A 51   Iris Acres, IN
A 51   Iris Gardens, MT
A 51   The Iris Pond, VA
A 51   Iris Test Gardens, WA
A 52   Jasperson's Hersey Nursery, WI
A 52   Jernigan Gardens, NC
A 55   Keith Keppel, CA
A 56   Klehm Nursery, IL
A 63   Long's Gardens, CO
A 64   McMillen's Iris Garden, ON
A 65   Maple Tree Gardens, NE
A 66   Maryott's Gardens, CA
A 68   Mid-America Iris Gardens, OK
A 69   Miller's Manor Gardens, IN
A 70   Moonshine Gardens, CA
A 72   Nicholls Gardens, VA
A 73   North Pine Iris Gardens, NE
A 78   Pacific Coast Hybridizers, CA
A 84   Quality Dutch Bulbs, NJ
A 85   Randy's Iris Garden, UT
A 88   Roris Gardens, CA
A 92   Schreiner's Gardens, OR
A 94   Shannon Gardens of Oak Brook Farm, MN
A 95   Shepard Iris Garden, AZ
A 99   Spruce Gardens, NE
A 103 Territorial Seed Company, OR
A 106 21st Century Gardens, AZ
A 109 Andre Viette Farm & Nursery, VA
A 116 Worel's Iris Gardens, MN
A 116 Wright Iris Nursery, CA

IVY
A 26   Davidson-Wilson Greenhouses, IN
A 28   Donnelly's Nursery, NC
A 38   Gilson Gardens, OH
A 48   Homestead Division of Sunnybrook Farms, OH
A 51   Ivies of the World, FL
A 58   Lake Odessa Greenhouse, MI
A 67   Merry Gardens, ME
A 83   Prentiss Court Ground Covers, SC
A 91   Sandy Mush Herb Nursery, NC
A 101 Sunnybrook Farms Nursery, OH

PAGE SOURCE

IVY
A 103 Ter-El Nursery, PA

JASMINES
A 83   Prentiss Court Ground Covers, SC
A 92   Sedona Gardens, BC
A 99   Stallings Exotic Nursery, CA
A 101 Sunrise Oriental Seed Co., CT

JOJOBA
A 54   KSA Jojoba, CA

JOSTABERRY
A 73   North Star Gardens, MN

JOVIBARBA
A 3   Alpine Gardens & Calico Shop, WI
A 23   Country Cottage, KS
A 88   Grace Rollerson, BC
A 90   Jim & Irene Russ Quality Plants, CA
A 99   Squaw Mountain Gardens, OR

JUJUBE
A 68   Roger & Shirley Meyer, CA

KALMIAS
A 6   B & B Laboratories, WA
A 8   Beaver Creek Nursery, TN
A 12   Broken Arrow Nursery, CT
A 12   Brown's Kalmia & Azalea Nursery, WA
A 17   Carlson's Gardens, NY
A 20   Coenosium Gardens, OR
A 24   The Cummins Garden, NJ
A 27   DeGrandchamp's Blueberry Farm, MI
A 29   Eastern Plant Specialties, ME
A 35   Foxborough Nursery, Inc., MD
A 39   Gossler Farms Nursery, OR
A 42   Hall Rhododendrons, OR
A 54   Kelly Nurseries, NY
A 72   E. B. Nauman, Nurseryman, NY
A 89   Roslyn Nursery, NY
A 94   Sevenoaks Nursery, OR
A 105 Transplant Nursery, GA
A 110 Washington Evergreen Nursery, NC
A 112 Westgate Garden Nursery, CA
A 112 Whitney Gardens, WA

KIWI
A 16   California Nursery Co., CA
A 68   Roger & Shirley Meyer, CA
A 74   Northwoods Nursery, OR
A 76   Oregon Exotica Nursery, OR
A 98   South Seas Nursery, CA

KIWI, HARDY
A 1   Ahrens Nursery & Plant Labs, IN
A 8   Bear Creek Nursery, WA
A 14   Burnt Ridge Nursery, WA
A 20   Cloud Mountain Nursery, WA
A 29   Edible Landscaping, VA
A 43   Hartmann's Plantation, Inc., MI
A 46   Hidden Springs Nursery -- Edible Landscaping, TN
A 68   Roger & Shirley Meyer, CA
A 73   Northern Kiwi Nursery, ON
A 74   Northwoods Nursery, OR
A 95   Sherwood's Greenhouses, LA
A 104 Tolowa Nursery, OR
A 106 Tripple Brook Farm, MA

PAGE SOURCE

LAVENDERS
A 26   T. DeBaggio Herbs by Mail, VA
A 39   Good Hollow Greenhouse & Herbarium, TN
A 65   Maple Leaf Nursery, CA
A 72   Nichols Garden Nursery, Inc., OR
A 96   Sleepy Hollow Herb Farm, KY
A 109   Village Arbors, AL

LEPTOSPERMUMS
A 50   International Seed Supplies, Au
A 73   Nindethana Seed Service, Au
A 77   D. Orriell -- Seed Exporters, Au

LEUCODENDRONS
A 50   International Seed Supplies, Au
A 78   Parsley's Cape Seeds, So
A 84   Protea Seed & Nursery Suppliers, So

LEUCOSPERMUMS
A 78   Parsley's Cape Seeds, So
A 84   Protea Seed & Nursery Suppliers, So

LEWISIAS
A 6   Ashwood Nurseries, En
A 21   Colorado Alpines, Inc., CO
A 70   Mt. Tahoma Nursery, WA

LEYLAND CYPRESS
A 18   Catalpa Nursery, MD

LILACS
A 4   Ameri-Hort Research, OH
A 13   Buckley Nursery, WA
A 44   Heard Gardens, Ltd., IA
A 48   Hortico, Inc., ON
A 70   Morden Nurseries, Ltd., MB
A 97   Smith Nursery Co., IA
A 111   Wedge Nursery, MN

LILIES, HYBRID
A 3   Ambergate Gardens, MN
A 6   B & D Lilies, WA
A 7   Bakker of Holland, MO
A 10   Borbeleta Gardens, MN
A 13   The Bulb Crate, IL
A 13   Bundles of Bulbs, MD
A 20   Clifford's Perennial & Vine, WI
A 22   Cooper's Garden, MN
A 24   Cruickshank's, Inc., ON
A 26   Peter De Jager Bulb Co., MA
A 28   Dutch Gardens, Inc., NJ
A 31   Fairyland Begonia & Lily Garden, CA
A 38   Gladside Gardens, MA
A 42   Dr. Joseph C. Halinar, OR
A 46   Hildenbrandt's Iris Gardens, NE
A 48   Honeywood Lilies, SK
A 50   Inter-State Nurseries, IA
A 60   Orol Ledden & Sons, NJ
A 61   Lindel Lilies, BC
A 64   Mad River Imports, VT
A 67   Messelaar Bulb Co., MA
A 69   Monashee Gardens, BC
A 86   Rex Bulb Farms, WA
A 91   Saxton Gardens, NY
A 91   John Scheepers, Inc., NY
A 96   Skolaski's Glads & Field Flowers, WI
A 103   Territorial Seed Company, OR
A 107   TyTy Plantation, GA
A 108   Van Engelen, Inc., CT
A 108   Vandenberg, NY

LILIES, HYBRID
A 110   The Waushara Gardens, WI

LILIES, SPECIES
A 3   Jacques Amand, Ltd., En
A 6   Avon Bulbs, En
A 6   B & B Laboratories, WA
A 6   B & D Lilies, WA
A 8   Beersheba Wildflower Garden, TN
A 22   Cooper's Garden, MN
A 37   Gardens of the Blue Ridge, NC
A 39   Russell Graham, Purveyor of Plants, OR
A 42   Dr. Joseph C. Halinar, OR
A 56   Kline Nursery Co., OR
A 57   P. Kohli & Co., In
A 61   Lindel Lilies, BC
A 86   Rex Bulb Farms, WA
A 88   Robinett Bulb Farm, CA
A 91   Saxton Gardens, NY
A 98   Southwestern Native Seeds, AZ

LIMA BEANS
A 32   Fern Hill Farm, NJ

LIRIOPE
A 26   Daylily Discounters, FL
A 83   Prentiss Court Ground Covers, SC
A 103   Thomasville Nurseries, GA
A 106   Turnipseed Nursery Farms, GA
A 116   Woody's Liriope Farm, GA

LITHOPS
A 1   Abbey Gardens, CA
A 15   Cactus Gem Nursery, AR
A 46   Highland Succulents, OH
A 67   Mesa Garden, NM
A 86   Redlo Cacti, OR
A 88   Grace Rollerson, BC
A 98   Southwest Seeds, En
A 116   Roy Young, Seedsman, En

LOBELIA, PERENNIAL
A 113   The Wildwood Flower, NC

LOBIVIAS
A 15   Cactus by Dodie, CA
A 94   Shein's Cactus, CA

LOTUS
A 10   Bonsai of Georgia, GA
A 55   Kester's Wild Game Food Nurseries, WI
A 61   Lilypons Water Gardens, MD
A 70   Moore Water Gardens, ON
A 79   Perry's Water Gardens, NC
A 91   Santa Barbara Water Gardens, CA
A 96   Slocum Water Gardens, FL
A 103   Tilley's Nursery/The WaterWorks, PA
A 105   William Tricker, Inc., OH
A 110   Water Ways Nursery, VA
A 110   Waterford Gardens, NJ
A 112   Wicklein's Aquatic Farm & Nursery, Inc., MD

LUPINES
A 43   Hauser's Superior View Farm, WI
A 79   Theodore Payne Foundation, CA

LYCHEE
A 68   Roger & Shirley Meyer, CA

PAGE SOURCE

MACADAMIA NUTS
A 36   Fruit Spirit Botanical Gardens, Au
A 85   Rancho Nuez Nursery, CA

MAGNOLIAS
A 8   Beaver Creek Nursery, TN
A 33   Flora Lan Nursery, OR
A 39   Gossler Farms Nursery, OR
A 41   Greer Gardens, OR
A 63   Louisiana Nursery, LA
A 65   Magnolia Nursery & Display Garden, AL
A 94   Sheffield's Seed Co., NY
A 117 Yucca Do Nursery, TX

MAMMILLARIAS
A 5   Apacha Cactus, CA
A 6   Aztekakti/Desertland Nursery, TX
A 15   Cactus by Dodie, CA
A 15   Cactus by Mueller, CA
A 19   Christa's Cactus, AZ
A 27   Desert Nursery, NM
A 27   Desert Theatre, CA
A 41   Grigsby Cactus Gardens, CA
A 44   Henrietta's Nursery, CA
A 56   Gerhard Koehres Cactus & Succulent Nursery, We
A 59   Lauray of Salisbury, CT
A 67   Mesa Garden, NM
A 72   New Mexico Cactus Research, NM
A 86   Redlo Cacti, OR
A 84   Sand Ridge Greenhouse, OK
A 92   Schulz Cactus Gardens, CA
A 92   Scotty's Desert Plants, CA
A 93   The Seed Shop, MT
A 94   Shein's Cactus, CA
A 98   Southwest Seeds, En

MANZANITAS
A 21   Colvos Creek Nursery & Landscaping, WA
A 59   Las Pilitas Nursery, CA

MAPLES, JAPANESE
A 20   Coenosium Gardens, OR
A 27   Del's Japanese Maples, OR
A 33   Flora Lan Nursery, OR
A 35   Foxborough Nursery, Inc., MD
A 41   Greer Gardens, OR
A 41   Gulf Coast Plantsmen, LA
A 49   Hughes Nursery, WA
A 57   Michael & Janet Kristick, PA
A 58   Lamtree Farm, NC
A 63   Loucks Nursery, OR
A 65   Maplewood Seed Company, OR
A 66   Matsu-Momiji Nursery, PA
A 69   Miniature Plant Kingdom, CA
A 94   Sheffield's Seed Co., NY
A 96   Siskiyou Rare Plant Nursery, OR
A 105 Trans Pacific Nursery, OR
A 110 Wavecrest Nursery & Landscaping Co., MI

MAPLES, SPECIES
A 8   Beaver Creek Nursery, TN
A 16   Camellia Forest Nursery, NC
A 21   Cold Stream Farm, MI
A 21   Colvos Creek Nursery & Landscaping, WA
A 38   Golden Bough Tree Farm, ON
A 39   Gossler Farms Nursery, OR
A 45   Heronswood Nursery, WA
A 49   Hughes Nursery, WA
A 57   Michael & Janet Kristick, PA
A 65   Maplewood Seed Company, OR

MAPLES, SPECIES
A 66   Marrs Tree Farm, WA
A 68   Meta Horticultural Labs, KY
A 86   Recor Tree Seed, CO
A 92   F. W. Schumacher Co., MA
A 94   Sheffield's Seed Co., NY
A 112 Whitman Farms, OR

MEADOW PLANTS
A 113 Wildginger Woodlands, NY

MEDLARS
A 106 Tsolum River Fruit Trees, BC

MELALEUCAS
A 14   Bushland Flora (Australian Seed Specialists), Au
A 50   International Seed Supplies, Au

MELONS
A 44   Herb Gathering, Inc., MO
A 53   Jordan Seeds, MN
A 61   Liberty Seed Company, OH
A 62   Lockhart Seeds, CA
A 90   SPB Sales, TX
A 102 Talavaya Seeds, NM
A 112 Westwind Seeds, AZ
A 114 Willhite Seed Co., TX

MESEMBS
A 1   Abbey Gardens, CA
A 56   Gerhard Koehres Cactus & Succulent Nursery, We
A 72   New Mexico Cactus Research, NM
A 88   Grace Rollerson, BC

MINTS
A 109 Village Arbors, AL

MORAEA
A 16   Cape Seed & Bulb, So

MOSSES
A 2   Allgrove Farm, Inc., MA
A 54   Kartuz Greenhouses, CA
A 75   Orchid Gardens, MN

MULBERRIES
A 14   Burnt Ridge Nursery, WA
A 32   The Fig Tree Nursery, FL
A 37   Louis Gerardi Nursery, IL
A 38   Girard Nurseries, OH
A 58   LBG Nursery, MN
A 68   Meta Horticultural Labs, KY
A 90   Saginaw Valley Nut Nursery, MI
A 95   Sherwood's Greenhouses, LA
A 106 Tripple Brook Farm, MA
A 107 TyTy South Orchards, GA

MUSHROOM SPAWN
A 4   American Forest Foods Corp., NC
A 19   Choice Edibles, CA
A 32   Field and Forest Products, Inc., WI
A 36   Fungi Perfecti, WA
A 42   Hardscrabble Enterprises, WV
A 71   Mushroompeople, CA
A 74   Northwest Mycological Consultants, OR
A 111 Western Biologicals, Ltd., BC

MUSHROOMS, MOREL
A 19   Choice Edibles, CA
A 74   Northwest Mycological Consultants, OR

PAGE SOURCE

MUSHROOMS, OYSTER
A 4   American Forest Foods Corp., NC
A 19   Choice Edibles, CA
A 32   Field and Forest Products, Inc., WI
A 36   Fungi Perfecti, WA
A 74   Northwest Mycological Consultants, OR

MUSHROOMS, SHIITAKE
A 4   American Forest Foods Corp., NC
A 19   Choice Edibles, CA
A 32   Field and Forest Products, Inc., WI
A 36   Fungi Perfecti, WA
A 42   Hardscrabble Enterprises, WV
A 71   Mushroompeople, CA
A 74   Northwest Mycological Consultants, OR

NATIVE PLANTS
See specific plants
See specific regions

NATIVE PLANTS, AUSTRALIAN
A 6   B & T Associates, En
A 14   Bushland Flora (Australian Seed Specialists), Au
A 16   Callahan Seeds, OR
A 17   Carolina Exotic Gardens, NC
A 17   Carter Seeds, CA
A 22   Copacabana Gardens, CA
A 24   Cycad Gardens, CA
A 30   Exotic Seeds, Lothar Seik, We
A 36   Fruit Spirit Botanical Gardens, Au
A 49   J. L. Hudson, Seedsman, CA
A 50   International Seed Supplies, Au
A 73   Nindethana Seed Service, Au
A 77   D. Orriell -- Seed Exporters, Au
A 78   Palms for Tropical Landscaping, FL
A 105 Trans Pacific Nursery, OR
A 114 Wildwood Nursery, CA

NATIVE PLANTS, CALIFORNIAN
A 16   Callahan Seeds, OR
A 30   Exotic Seeds, Lothar Seik, We
A 40   Greenlee Nursery, CA
A 49   Hummingbird Gardens, CA
A 59   Larner Seeds, CA
A 59   Las Pilitas Nursery, CA
A 79   Theodore Payne Foundation, CA
A 86   Redwood City Seed Co., CA
A 88   Robinett Bulb Farm, CA
A 110 Wapumne Native Plant Nursery, CA
A 114 Wildwood Nursery, CA

NATIVE PLANTS, HAWAIIAN
A 7   The Banana Tree, PA
A 30   Exotic Seeds, Lothar Seik, We
A 30   Exotica Rare Fruit Nursery, CA
A 78   Palms for Tropical Landscaping, FL

NATIVE PLANTS, HIMALAYAN
A 18   Chadwell Himalayan Seed, En
A 39   Gossler Farms Nursery, OR
A 49   J. L. Hudson, Seedsman, CA
A 57   P. Kohli & Co., In
A 61   Life-Form Replicators, MI

NATIVE PLANTS, INDIAN
A 7   The Banana Tree, PA
A 30   Exotic Seeds, Lothar Seik, We
A 57   P. Kohli & Co., In

NATIVE PLANTS, MEXICAN/CENTRAL AMERICAN
A 6   Aztekakti/Desertland Nursery, TX
A 9   Bird Rock Tropicals, CA
A 24   Cycad Gardens, CA
A 44   Heliconia Haus, FL
A 49   J. L. Hudson, Seedsman, CA
A 78   Palms for Tropical Landscaping, FL
A 98   Southwest Seeds, En
A 98   Southwestern Native Seeds, AZ
A 116 Guy Wrinkle Exotic Plants, CA

NATIVE PLANTS, MIDWESTERN U.S.
A 3   Alpine Gardens & Calico Shop, WI
A 10   Boehlke's Woodland Gardens, WI
A 23   Country Wetlands Nursery, WI
A 35   The Fragrant Path, NE
A 58   LaFayette Home Nursery, Inc., IL
A 59   Landscape Alternatives, Inc., MN
A 61   Life-Form Replicators, MI
A 62   Little Valley Farm, WI
A 68   Milaeger's Gardens, WI
A 75   Oikos Tree Crops, MI
A 75   Orchid Gardens, MN
A 83   Prairie Moon Nursery, MN
A 83   Prairie Nursery, WI
A 83   Prairie Ridge Nursery/CRM Ecosystems, Inc., WI
A 97   Smith Nursery Co., IA

NATIVE PLANTS, NEW ZEALAND
A 6   B & T Associates, En
A 7   The Banana Tree, PA
A 30   Exotic Seeds, Lothar Seik, We
A 98   Southern Seeds, Ne
A 105 Trans Pacific Nursery, OR

NATIVE PLANTS, NORTH AMERICAN
A 4   Amenity Plant Products, PA
A 7   Barber Nursery, OR
A 9   Blueberry Hill, ON
A 12   Brookside Wildflowers, NC
A 17   Carolina Exotic Gardens, NC
A 29   Eastern Plant Specialties, ME
A 30   Exotic Seeds, Lothar Seik, We
A 34   Forestfarm, OR
A 47   Holbrook Farm & Nursery, NC
A 58   Lamtree Farm, NC
A 60   Lee's Botanical Gardens, FL
A 61   Life-Form Replicators, MI
A 61   Linn Farm Perennials, VA
A 71   Musser Forests Inc., PA
A 71   Native Gardens, TN
A 71   Natural Gardens, TN
A 72   Niche Gardens, NC
A 79   Peace Seeds, OR
A 94   Shady Oaks Nursery, MN
A 97   Smith Nursery Co., IA
A 113 The Wildflower Source, IL
A 114 Wildwood Nursery, CA

NATIVE PLANTS, NORTHEASTERN U.S.
A 14   Butterbrooke Farm, CT
A 21   Companion Plants, OH
A 26   Daystar, ME
A 52   The Thomas Jefferson Center, VA
A 71   Natural Gardens, TN
A 75   Oakridge Nurseries, NH
A 83   The Primrose Path, PA
A 101 Sunlight Gardens, TN
A 113 The Wildflower Source, IL

PAGE SOURCE

NATIVE PLANTS, NORTHWESTERN U.S.
A 1   Abundant Life Seed Foundation, WA
A 7   Barber Nursery, OR
A 16   Callahan Seeds, OR
A 17   Carolina Exotic Gardens, NC
A 21   Colvos Creek Nursery & Landscaping, WA
A 36   Frosty Hollow Nursery, WA
A 39   Gossler Farms Nursery, OR
A 39   Russell Graham, Purveyor of Plants, OR
A 59   Larner Seeds, CA
A 59   Laurie's Garden, OR
A 70   Mt. Tahoma Nursery, WA
A 71   Native Seed Foundation, ID
A 72   Nature's Garden Nursery, OR
A 73   Northplan/Mountain Seed, ID
A 74   Northwest Biological Enterprises, OR
A 81   Plants of the Wild, WA
A 88   Robinett Bulb Farm, CA
A 94   Sevenoaks Nursery, OR
A 96   Silvaseed Company, Inc., WA
A 96   Silver Springs Nursery, ID
A 96   Siskiyou Rare Plant Nursery, OR
A 96   Skyline Nursery, WA
A 98   Southwestern Native Seeds, AZ
A 113   The Wildflower Source, IL

NATIVE PLANTS, ORIENT
A 2   Albiflora, Inc., Ja
A 18   Chadwell Himalayan Seed, En
A 111   We-Du Nurseries, NC

NATIVE PLANTS, ROCKY MOUNTAIN
A 59   Lawyer Nursery, Inc., MT
A 68   Midwest Cactus, MO
A 73   Northplan/Mountain Seed, ID
A 75   Old Farm Nursery, CO
A 86   Recor Tree Seed, CO
A 94   Sevenoaks Nursery, OR
A 97   Solar Green, Ltd., ID
A 98   Southwestern Native Seeds, AZ

NATIVE PLANTS, SOUTH AFRICAN
A 6   B & T Associates, En
A 9   Bio-Quest International, CA
A 16   Cape Seed & Bulb, So
A 17   Carolina Exotic Gardens, NC
A 22   Copacabana Gardens, CA
A 30   Exotic Seeds, Lothar Seik, We
A 78   Parsley's Cape Seeds, So
A 84   Protea Seed & Nursery Suppliers, So
A 90   Rust-En-Vrede Nursery, So
A 98   Southwest Seeds, En
A 100   Succulent Plants, MN
A 105   Trans Pacific Nursery, OR
A 116   Guy Wrinkle Exotic Plants, CA

NATIVE PLANTS, SOUTH AMERICAN
A 6   Aztekakti/Desertland Nursery, TX
A 16   Callahan Seeds, OR
A 22   Copacabana Gardens, CA
A 30   Exotic Seeds, Lothar Seik, We
A 78   Palms for Tropical Landscaping, FL
A 98   Southwest Seeds, En
A 102   Talavaya Seeds, NM

NATIVE PLANTS, SOUTHEASTERN U.S.
A 12   Joseph Brown, Native Seeds, VA
A 17   Carolina Exotic Gardens, NC
A 29   Eco-Gardens, GA
A 37   Gardens of the Blue Ridge, NC

NATIVE PLANTS, SOUTHEASTERN U.S.
A 39   Gossler Farms Nursery, OR
A 41   Gulf Coast Plantsmen, LA
A 47   Holland Wildflower Farm, AR
A 52   The Thomas Jefferson Center, VA
A 69   Montrose Nursery, NC
A 71   Native Gardens, TN
A 71   Natural Gardens, TN
A 72   Niche Gardens, NC
A 80   Piccadilly Farm, GA
A 90   Salter Tree Farm, FL
A 97   South Florida Seed Supply, FL
A 101   Sunlight Gardens, TN
A 105   Transplant Nursery, GA
A 111   We-Du Nurseries, NC
A 113   Wildflower Nursery, NC
A 113   The Wildflower Source, IL
A 113   The Wildwood Flower, NC
A 115   Woodlanders, Inc., SC

NATIVE PLANTS, SOUTHWESTERN U.S.
A 6   Artistic Plants, TX
A 6   Aztekakti/Desertland Nursery, TX
A 8   Bernardo Beach Native Plant Farm, NM
A 25   The Nursery at the Dallas Nature Center, TX
A 49   Hummingbird Gardens, CA
A 59   Larner Seeds, CA
A 63   The Lowrey Nursery, TX
A 69   Miller Grass Seed Company, TX
A 71   Native Seeds/SEARCH, AZ
A 75   Old Farm Nursery, CO
A 81   Plants of the Southwest, NM
A 98   Southwestern Native Seeds, AZ
A 102   Talavaya Seeds, NM
A 106   Turner Seed Company, TX
A 117   Yucca Do Nursery, TX

NECTARINES
A 1   Adams County Nursery, Inc., PA
A 24   Cumberland Valley Nurseries, Inc., TN
A 48   Hollydale Nursery, TN
A 97   Sonoma Antique Apple Nursery, CA
A 107   TyTy South Orchards, GA

NEOREGELIAS
A 26   Dane Company, TX
A 38   Golden Lake Greenhouses, CA
A 47   Holladay Jungle, CA
A 63   Paul P. Lowe, FL
A 84   Rainforest Flora, Inc., CA
A 94   Shelldance Nursery, CA

NEPENTHES
A 18   Cedar Ridge Nurseries, PA
A 60   Lee's Botanical Gardens, FL
A 66   Marston Exotics, En
A 77   Orgel's Orchids, FL

NOTOCACTUS
A 5   Apacha Cactus, CA
A 6   Aztekakti/Desertland Nursery, TX
A 15   Cactus by Dodie, CA
A 15   Cactus by Mueller, CA
A 27   Desert Theatre, CA
A 44   Henrietta's Nursery, CA
A 86   Redlo Cacti, OR
A 84   Sand Ridge Greenhouse, OK
A 92   Schulz Cactus Gardens, CA
A 93   The Seed Shop, MT

PAGE SOURCE

NUT TREES, HARDY
See also specific nuts
A 8   Vernon Barnes & Son Nursery, TN
A 8   Bear Creek Nursery, WA
A 14   Burnt Ridge Nursery, WA
A 17   Cascade Forestry Nursery, IA
A 21   Cold Stream Farm, MI
A 32   Fernald's Hickory Hill Nursery, IL
A 37   Louis Gerardi Nursery, IL
A 38   Golden Bough Tree Farm, ON
A 39   John H. Gordon, Jr., Grower, NY
A 41   Grimo Nut Nursery, ON
A 51   Ison's Nursery, GA
A 58   LBG Nursery, MN
A 69   J. E. Miller Nurseries, Inc., NY
A 70   Mt. Leo Nursery, TN
A 73   Nolin River Nut Tree Nursery, KY
A 74   Northwoods Nursery, OR
A 75   Oikos Tree Crops, MI
A 84   Raintree Nursery, WA
A 90   Saginaw Valley Nut Nursery, MI
A 90   St. Lawrence Nurseries, NY
A 97   Smith Nursery Co., IA
A 104   Tolowa Nursery, OR
A 114   Wiley's Nut Grove, OH

NUT TREES, LOW-CHILL
See also specific nuts
A 30   Exotica Rare Fruit Nursery, CA
A 36   Garden of Delights, FL
A 78   Pacific Tree Farms, CA
A 85   Rancho Nuez Nursery, CA
A 91   Savage Farms Nursery, TN
A 107   TyTy South Orchards, GA

OAKS
A 7   Barber Nursery, OR
A 14   Burnt Ridge Nursery, WA
A 16   Callahan Seeds, OR
A 17   Cascade Forestry Nursery, IA
A 21   Colvos Creek Nursery & Landscaping, WA
A 34   Forestfarm, OR
A 59   Las Pilitas Nursery, CA
A 71   Musser Forests Inc., PA
A 75   Oikos Tree Crops, MI
A 97   Smith Nursery Co., IA
A 112   Whitman Farms, OR
A 117   Yucca Do Nursery, TX

ONION PLANTS
A 6   Archias' Seed Store, MO
A 12   Brown's Omaha Plant Farms, Inc., TX
A 58   Lagomarsino Seeds, CA
A 80   Piedmont Plant Company, GA
A 82   Porter & Son, TX
A 90   SPB Sales, TX
A 99   Steele Plant Company, TN

ONIONS
A 14   D. V. Burrell Seed Growers Co., CO
A 25   Dacha Barinka, BC
A 30   Evergreen Y. H. Enterprises, CA
A 54   Kalmia Farm, VA
A 58   D. Landreth Seed Company, MD
A 62   Lockhart Seeds, CA
A 90   S & H Organic Acres, CA
A 98   Southern Exposure Seed Exchange, VA

ONIONS, SHORT DAY
A 98   Southern Seeds, FL

OPHIOPOGON
A 103   Thomasville Nurseries, GA

OPUNTIAS
A 5   Apacha Cactus, CA
A 15   The Cactus Patch, KS
A 27   Desert Nursery, NM
A 50   Intermountain Cactus, UT
A 68   Midwest Cactus, MO
A 72   New Mexico Cactus Research, NM
A 93   The Seed Shop, MT
A 101   Sunnyvale Cactus Nursery, MA

ORCHIDS, ANGRAECUM
A 4   The Angraecum House, CA
A 40   Green Valley Orchids, LA
A 40   Greenleaf Orchids, FL
A 76   Orchid Haven, ON
A 76   Orchid Thoroughbreds, PA
A 102   Sunswept Laboratories, CA

ORCHIDS, ASCOCENDAS
A 31   Farnsworth Orchids, HI
A 40   Green Valley Orchids, LA
A 53   Jones & Scully, FL
A 55   Kilworth Flowers, ON
A 56   Arnold J. Klehm Grower, Inc., IL
A 61   Limrick, Inc., FL
A 76   Orchid Thoroughbreds, PA
A 77   Orgel's Orchids, FL
A 91   Santa Barbara Orchid Estate, CA
A 92   Seagulls Landing Orchids, NY
A 114   Wilk Orchid Specialties, HI

ORCHIDS, BRASSAVOLAS
A 51   J. E. M. Orchids, FL
A 75   Orchibec, PQ
A 76   Orchid Species Specialties, CA
A 91   Santa Barbara Orchid Estate, CA

ORCHIDS, CATTLEYAS
A 1   Adagent Acres, CA
A 7   Baker & Chantry Orchids, WA
A 8   The Beall Orchid Company, WA
A 11   Breckinridge Orchids, NC
A 17   Carter & Holmes, Inc., SC
A 23   Creole Orchids, LA
A 31   Farnsworth Orchids, HI
A 31   Fennell's Orchid Jungle, FL
A 34   Fordyce Orchids, CA
A 35   Fox Orchids, Inc., AR
A 36   G & B Orchid Lab & Nursery, CA
A 40   Green Valley Orchids, LA
A 40   Greenleaf Orchids, FL
A 49   Spencer M. Howard Orchid Imports, CA
A 51   J. E. M. Orchids, FL
A 53   Jones & Scully, FL
A 53   Jungle Gems, Inc., MD
A 54   Kawamoto Orchid Nursery, HI
A 55   Kensington Orchids, MD
A 55   Kilworth Flowers, ON
A 56   Arnold J. Klehm Grower, Inc., IL
A 60   Lenette Greenhouses, NC
A 61   Limrick, Inc., FL
A 64   Rod McLellan Co., CA
A 67   Mauna Kea Orchids, HI
A 68   Miami Orchids, FL
A 74   Oak Hill Gardens, IL
A 75   Orchibec, PQ
A 76   Orchid Haven, ON
(continued next page)

PAGE SOURCE

ORCHIDS, CATTLEYAS (continued)
A 76   The Orchid House, CA
A 76   Orchid Species Specialties, CA
A 76   Orchid Thoroughbreds, PA
A 76   Orchids for Everyone, ON
A 77   Owens Orchids, NC
A 79   Penn Valley Orchids, PA
A 83   Prairie Orchid Company, MB
A 87   Riverbend Orchids, MS
A 92   Seagulls Landing Orchids, NY
A 100   Stewart Orchids, Inc., CA
A 102   Sunswept Laboratories, CA
A 111   Ken West Orchids, HI
A 114   Wilk Orchid Specialties, HI

ORCHIDS, CYMBIDIUMS
A 1   Adagent Acres, CA
A 4   Annabelle's Fuchsia Garden, CA
A 19   Charles Island Gardens, BC
A 23   Creole Orchids, LA
A 36   G & B Orchid Lab & Nursery, CA
A 55   Kensington Orchids, MD
A 55   Kilworth Flowers, ON
A 60   Lenette Greenhouses, NC
A 61   Limrick, Inc., FL
A 64   Rod McLellan Co., CA
A 74   Oak Hill Gardens, IL
A 76   The Orchid House, CA
A 76   Orchids for Everyone, ON
A 76   Orchids Royale, CA
A 91   Santa Barbara Orchid Estate, CA
A 92   Seagulls Landing Orchids, NY
A 102   Sunswept Laboratories, CA

ORCHIDS, DENDROBIUMS
A 11   Breckinridge Orchids, NC
A 23   Creole Orchids, LA
A 30   Exotics Hawaii, Ltd., HI
A 31   Fennell's Orchid Jungle, FL
A 36   G & B Orchid Lab & Nursery, CA
A 40   Green Valley Orchids, LA
A 49   Spencer M. Howard Orchid Imports, CA
A 51   J & L Orchids, CT
A 51   J. E. M. Orchids, FL
A 53   Jones & Scully, FL
A 54   Kawamoto Orchid Nursery, HI
A 61   Limrick, Inc., FL
A 68   Miami Orchids, FL
A 76   Orchid Haven, ON
A 76   Orchid Thoroughbreds, PA
A 76   Orchids for Everyone, ON
A 77   Orgel's Orchids, FL
A 79   Penn Valley Orchids, PA
A 92   Seagulls Landing Orchids, NY
A 114   Wilk Orchid Specialties, HI

ORCHIDS, DISA
A 16   Cape Seed & Bulb, So
A 73   Nooitgedag Disa Nursery, So
A 90   Rust-En-Vrede Nursery, So

ORCHIDS, DORITAENOPSIS
A 30   John Ewing Orchids, Inc., CA
A 40   Green Valley Orchids, LA
A 75   Orchibec, PQ

ORCHIDS, EPIDENDRUMS
A 35   Fox Orchids, Inc., AR
A 40   Green Valley Orchids, LA
A 49   Spencer M. Howard Orchid Imports, CA

PAGE SOURCE

ORCHIDS, EPIDENDRUMS
A 51   J & L Orchids, CT
A 51   J. E. M. Orchids, FL
A 61   Limrick, Inc., FL
A 75   Orchibec, PQ
A 76   Orchid Haven, ON
A 76   Orchid Species Specialties, CA
A 77   Orgel's Orchids, FL
A 79   Penn Valley Orchids, PA
A 91   Santa Barbara Orchid Estate, CA
A 102   Sunswept Laboratories, CA

ORCHIDS, HARDY
A 103   Terrorchids, We
A 113   Wildflower Nursery, NC
A 113   The Wildflower Source, IL

ORCHIDS, HYBRIDS
See also specific genera
A 1   A & P Orchids, MA
A 1   Adagent Acres, CA
A 2   Alberts & Merkel Bros., Inc., FL
A 4   Annabelle's Fuchsia Garden, CA
A 7   Baker & Chantry Orchids, WA
A 8   The Beall Orchid Company, WA
A 11   Breckinridge Orchids, NC
A 17   Carter & Holmes, Inc., SC
A 19   Charles Island Gardens, BC
A 20   City Gardens, MI
A 20   Clargreen Gardens, Ltd., ON
A 20   Cloud Forest Orchids, HI
A 23   Creole Orchids, LA
A 30   John Ewing Orchids, Inc., CA
A 31   Farnsworth Orchids, HI
A 31   Fennell's Orchid Jungle, FL
A 33   Floridel Gardens, ON
A 34   Fordyce Orchids, CA
A 34   Fort Caroline Orchids, FL
A 35   Fox Orchids, Inc., AR
A 36   G & B Orchid Lab & Nursery, CA
A 40   Green Valley Orchids, LA
A 40   Greenleaf Orchids, FL
A 48   Jerry Horne -- Rare Plants, FL
A 49   Huronview Nurseries & Garden Centre, ON
A 51   J & L Orchids, CT
A 51   J. E. M. Orchids, FL
A 53   Jones & Scully, FL
A 53   Jungle Gems, Inc., MD
A 54   Kawamoto Orchid Nursery, HI
A 55   Kensington Orchids, MD
A 56   Arnold J. Klehm Grower, Inc., IL
A 59   Lauray of Salisbury, CT
A 60   Lenette Greenhouses, NC
A 61   Limrick, Inc., FL
A 65   Ann Mann's Orchids, FL
A 67   Mauna Kea Orchids, HI
A 74   Oak Hill Gardens, IL
A 75   Orchibec, PQ
A 76   Orchid Haven, ON
A 76   The Orchid House, CA
A 76   Orchid Thoroughbreds, PA
A 76   Orchids by Hausermann, Inc., IL
A 76   Orchids for Everyone, ON
A 76   Orchids Royale, CA
A 77   Owens Orchids, NC
A 79   Penn Valley Orchids, PA
A 81   The Plant Shop's Botanical Gardens, CA
A 83   Prairie Orchid Company, MB
A 87   Riverbend Orchids, MS
A 91   Santa Barbara Orchid Estate, CA
(continued next page)

PAGE SOURCE

ORCHIDS, HYBRIDS (continued)
A 92   Seagulls Landing Orchids, NY
A 100 Stewart Orchids, Inc., CA
A 101 Sunshine Violets & Gesneriads, MA
A 102 Sunswept Laboratories, CA
A 111 Ken West Orchids, HI
A 117 Zuma Canyon Orchids, CA

ORCHIDS, LAELIAS
A 49   Spencer M. Howard Orchid Imports, CA
A 51   J & L Orchids, CT
A 51   J. E. M. Orchids, FL
A 75   Orchibec, PQ
A 76   Orchid Haven, ON
A 76   Orchid Species Specialties, CA
A 91   Santa Barbara Orchid Estate, CA
A 102 Sunswept Laboratories, CA
A 111 Ken West Orchids, HI

ORCHIDS, MASDEVALLIAS
A 7   Baker & Chantry Orchids, WA
A 8   The Beall Orchid Company, WA
A 51   J & L Orchids, CT
A 91   Santa Barbara Orchid Estate, CA

ORCHIDS, MERICLONES
A 7   Baker & Chantry Orchids, WA
A 17   Carter & Holmes, Inc., SC
A 20   Cloud Forest Orchids, HI
A 30   John Ewing Orchids, Inc., CA
A 30   Exotics Hawaii, Ltd., HI
A 35   Fox Orchids, Inc., AR
A 49   Huronview Nurseries & Garden Centre, ON
A 53   Jones & Scully, FL
A 54   Kawamoto Orchid Nursery, HI
A 56   Arnold J. Klehm Grower, Inc., IL
A 61   Limrick, Inc., FL
A 64   Rod McLellan Co., CA
A 75   Orchibec, PQ
A 76   Orchid Haven, ON
A 76   Orchid Thoroughbreds, PA
A 77   Owens Orchids, NC
A 83   Prairie Orchid Company, MB
A 87   Riverbend Orchids, MS
A 102 Sunswept Laboratories, CA
A 114 Wilk Orchid Specialties, HI

ORCHIDS, MILTONIAS
A 7   Baker & Chantry Orchids, WA
A 8   The Beall Orchid Company, WA
A 30   John Ewing Orchids, Inc., CA
A 31   Fennell's Orchid Jungle, FL
A 53   Jungle Gems, Inc., MD
A 55   Kensington Orchids, MD
A 64   Rod McLellan Co., CA
A 76   Orchid Haven, ON
A 76   Orchid Species Specialties, CA
A 76   Orchid Thoroughbreds, PA
A 76   Orchids Royale, CA
A 83   Prairie Orchid Company, MB
A 100 Stewart Orchids, Inc., CA

ORCHIDS, MINIATURE
A 7   Baker & Chantry Orchids, WA
A 11   Breckinridge Orchids, NC
A 19   Charles Island Gardens, BC
A 31   Farnsworth Orchids, HI
A 34   Fordyce Orchids, CA
A 40   Green Valley Orchids, LA
A 49   Spencer M. Howard Orchid Imports, CA

ORCHIDS, MINIATURE
A 51   J & L Orchids, CT
A 51   J. E. M. Orchids, FL
A 55   Kilworth Flowers, ON
A 60   Lenette Greenhouses, NC
A 68   Miami Orchids, FL
A 75   Orchibec, PQ
A 76   Orchid Species Specialties, CA
A 76   Orchid Thoroughbreds, PA
A 76   Orchids Royale, CA
A 77   Owens Orchids, NC
A 83   Prairie Orchid Company, MB
A 87   Riverbend Orchids, MS
A 91   Santa Barbara Orchid Estate, CA
A 92   Seagulls Landing Orchids, NY
A 102 Sunswept Laboratories, CA

ORCHIDS, NATIVE SPECIES (U.S.)
A 21   Conley's Garden Center, ME
A 37   Gardens of the Blue Ridge, NC
A 75   Orchid Gardens, MN

ORCHIDS, ODONTOGLOSSUMS
A 7   Baker & Chantry Orchids, WA
A 8   The Beall Orchid Company, WA
A 19   Charles Island Gardens, BC
A 64   Rod McLellan Co., CA
A 76   The Orchid House, CA
A 76   Orchids Royale, CA
A 91   Santa Barbara Orchid Estate, CA
A 92   Seagulls Landing Orchids, NY

ORCHIDS, ONCIDIUMS
A 7   Baker & Chantry Orchids, WA
A 8   The Beall Orchid Company, WA
A 23   Creole Orchids, LA
A 31   Fennell's Orchid Jungle, FL
A 35   Fox Orchids, Inc., AR
A 40   Green Valley Orchids, LA
A 49   Spencer M. Howard Orchid Imports, CA
A 51   J & L Orchids, CT
A 51   J. E. M. Orchids, FL
A 54   Kawamoto Orchid Nursery, HI
A 60   Lenette Greenhouses, NC
A 61   Limrick, Inc., FL
A 64   Rod McLellan Co., CA
A 68   Miami Orchids, FL
A 76   Orchid Haven, ON
A 76   The Orchid House, CA
A 76   Orchid Species Specialties, CA
A 79   Penn Valley Orchids, PA
A 83   Prairie Orchid Company, MB
A 91   Santa Barbara Orchid Estate, CA
A 102 Sunswept Laboratories, CA
A 114 Wilk Orchid Specialties, HI

ORCHIDS, PAPHIOPEDILUMS
A 1   A & P Orchids, MA
A 1   Adagent Acres, CA
A 4   Annabelle's Fuchsia Garden, CA
A 7   Baker & Chantry Orchids, WA
A 8   The Beall Orchid Company, WA
A 11   Breckinridge Orchids, NC
A 23   Creole Orchids, LA
A 35   Fox Orchids, Inc., AR
A 40   Green Valley Orchids, LA
A 49   Spencer M. Howard Orchid Imports, CA
A 55   Kensington Orchids, MD
A 56   Arnold J. Klehm Grower, Inc., IL
A 60   Lenette Greenhouses, NC
(continued next page)

PAGE SOURCE

ORCHIDS, PAPHIOPEDILUMS (continued)
A 61   Limrick, Inc., FL
A 75   Orchibec, PQ
A 76   Orchid Haven, ON
A 76   The Orchid House, CA
A 76   Orchid Thoroughbreds, PA
A 76   Orchids for Everyone, ON
A 76   Orchids Royale, CA
A 77   Orgel's Orchids, FL
A 79   Penn Valley Orchids, PA
A 83   Prairie Orchid Company, MB
A 87   Riverbend Orchids, MS
A 92   Seagulls Landing Orchids, NY
A 100   Stewart Orchids, Inc., CA
A 102   Sunswept Laboratories, CA

ORCHIDS, PHALAENOPSIS
A 1   A & P Orchids, MA
A 8   The Beall Orchid Company, WA
A 11   Breckinridge Orchids, NC
A 17   Carter & Holmes, Inc., SC
A 30   John Ewing Orchids, Inc., CA
A 30   Exotics Hawaii, Ltd., HI
A 31   Farnsworth Orchids, HI
A 33   Floridel Gardens, ON
A 35   Fox Orchids, Inc., AR
A 36   G & B Orchid Lab & Nursery, CA
A 40   Green Valley Orchids, LA
A 40   Greenleaf Orchids, FL
A 53   Jones & Scully, FL
A 53   Jungle Gems, Inc., MD
A 54   Kawamoto Orchid Nursery, HI
A 55   Kensington Orchids, MD
A 55   Kilworth Flowers, ON
A 56   Arnold J. Klehm Grower, Inc., IL
A 60   Lenette Greenhouses, NC
A 61   Limrick, Inc., FL
A 62   Logee's Greenhouses, CT
A 64   Rod McLellan Co., CA
A 67   Mauna Kea Orchids, HI
A 68   Miami Orchids, FL
A 75   Orchibec, PQ
A 76   Orchid Haven, ON
A 76   The Orchid House, CA
A 76   Orchid Thoroughbreds, PA
A 76   Orchids for Everyone, ON
A 77   Owens Orchids, NC
A 83   Prairie Orchid Company, MB
A 87   Riverbend Orchids, MS
A 92   Seagulls Landing Orchids, NY
A 100   Stewart Orchids, Inc., CA
A 102   Sunswept Laboratories, CA
A 109   Volkmann Gardens, TX
A 114   Wilk Orchid Specialties, HI
A 117   Zuma Canyon Orchids, CA

ORCHIDS, SPECIES
A 4   The Angraecum House, CA
A 7   Baker & Chantry Orchids, WA
A 8   Beersheba Wildflower Garden, TN
A 11   Breckinridge Orchids, NC
A 17   Carter & Holmes, Inc., SC
A 20   City Gardens, MI
A 20   Clargreen Gardens, Ltd., ON
A 20   Cloud Forest Orchids, HI
A 31   Farnsworth Orchids, HI
A 34   Fort Caroline Orchids, FL
A 36   G & B Orchid Lab & Nursery, CA
A 40   Greenleaf Orchids, FL
A 49   Spencer M. Howard Orchid Imports, CA

ORCHIDS, SPECIES
A 49   Huronview Nurseries & Garden Centre, ON
A 51   J & L Orchids, CT
A 51   J. E. M. Orchids, FL
A 53   Jones & Scully, FL
A 53   Jungle Gems, Inc., MD
A 54   Kawamoto Orchid Nursery, HI
A 55   Kilworth Flowers, ON
A 56   Arnold J. Klehm Grower, Inc., IL
A 59   Lauray of Salisbury, CT
A 61   Limrick, Inc., FL
A 63   Paul P. Lowe, FL
A 65   Ann Mann's Orchids, FL
A 66   Marilynn's Garden, CA
A 68   Miami Orchids, FL
A 74   Oak Hill Gardens, IL
A 75   Orchibec, PQ
A 76   Orchid Haven, ON
A 76   The Orchid House, CA
A 76   Orchid Species Specialties, CA
A 76   Orchid Thoroughbreds, PA
A 76   Orchids by Hausermann, Inc., IL
A 76   Orchids for Everyone, ON
A 77   Orgel's Orchids, FL
A 79   Penn Valley Orchids, PA
A 81   The Plant Shop's Botanical Gardens, CA
A 83   Prairie Orchid Company, MB
A 87   Riverbend Orchids, MS
A 91   Santa Barbara Orchid Estate, CA
A 102   Sunswept Laboratories, CA
A 103   Terrorchids, We
A 101   W. K. Quality Bromeliads, CA
A 116   Guy Wrinkle Exotic Plants, CA

ORCHIDS, VANDAS
A 11   Breckinridge Orchids, NC
A 23   Creole Orchids, LA
A 31   Farnsworth Orchids, HI
A 31   Fennell's Orchid Jungle, FL
A 40   Green Valley Orchids, LA
A 40   Greenleaf Orchids, FL
A 53   Jones & Scully, FL
A 54   Kawamoto Orchid Nursery, HI
A 56   Arnold J. Klehm Grower, Inc., IL
A 60   Lenette Greenhouses, NC
A 61   Limrick, Inc., FL
A 68   Miami Orchids, FL
A 76   Orchid Thoroughbreds, PA
A 77   Orgel's Orchids, FL
A 92   Seagulls Landing Orchids, NY
A 114   Wilk Orchid Specialties, HI

PACHYPODIUMS
A 54   K & L Cactus Nursery, CA

PACHYSANDRA
A 38   Gilson Gardens, OH
A 79   Peekskill Nurseries, NY
A 83   Prentiss Court Ground Covers, SC
A 103   Ter-El Nursery, PA

PALMS
A 21   Colvos Creek Nursery & Landscaping, WA
A 22   Copacabana Gardens, CA
A 30   Exotic Seeds, Lothar Seik, We
A 30   Exotica Rare Fruit Nursery, CA
A 36   Fruit Spirit Botanical Gardens, Au
A 36   Garden of Delights, FL
A 40   The Green Escape, FL
A 50   International Seed Supplies, Au

(continued next page)

PAGE	SOURCE

PALMS (continued)
A 56 Gerhard Koehres Cactus & Succulent Nursery, We
A 72 Neon Palm Nursery, CA
A 77 D. Orriell -- Seed Exporters, Au
A 78 Pacific Tree Farms, CA
A 78 Palms for Tropical Landscaping, FL
A 97 South Florida Seed Supply, FL
A 112 Westside Exotics Palm Nursery, CA
A 115 Woodlanders, Inc., SC

PALMS, RHAPIS
A 36 Garden of Delights, FL
A 40 The Green Escape, FL
A 86 Rhapis Gardens, TX
A 87 Rhapis Palm Growers, CA

PALMS, TROPICAL
A 6 B & T Associates, En
A 7 The Banana Tree, PA
A 17 Carter Seeds, CA
A 29 Endangered Species, CA
A 30 Exotic Seeds, Lothar Seik, We
A 36 Garden of Delights, FL
A 40 The Green Escape, FL
A 48 Jerry Horne -- Rare Plants, FL
A 74 Oak Hill Gardens, IL
A 78 Palms for Tropical Landscaping, FL
A 112 Westside Exotics Palm Nursery, CA

PAPAYAS
A 37 Garden World, TX
A 98 South Seas Nursery, CA
A 98 Southern Seeds, FL

PARODIAS
A 27 Desert Nursery, NM
A 56 Gerhard Koehres Cactus & Succulent Nursery, We
A 92 Schulz Cactus Gardens, CA
A 94 Shein's Cactus, CA

PASSIONFLOWERS
A 50 International Seed Supplies, Au
A 54 Kartuz Greenhouses, CA

PAWPAWS
A 26 Corwin Davis Nursery, MI
A 29 Edible Landscaping, VA
A 39 John H. Gordon, Jr., Grower, NY
A 43 Hartmann's Plantation, Inc., MI
A 68 Meta Horticultural Labs, KY
A 75 Oikos Tree Crops, MI
A 90 Saginaw Valley Nut Nursery, MI
A 95 Sherwood's Greenhouses, LA
A 104 Tolowa Nursery, OR
A 114 Wiley's Nut Grove, OH

PEACHES
A 1 Adams County Nursery, Inc., PA
A 4 Ames' Orchard and Nursery, AR
A 24 Cumberland Valley Nurseries, Inc., TN
A 48 Hollydale Nursery, TN
A 52 Johnson Nursery, GA
A 72 New York State Fruit Testing Coop. Assn., NY
A 97 Sonoma Antique Apple Nursery, CA
A 98 Southmeadow Fruit Gardens, MI
A 99 Stark Bro's Nurseries & Orchards Co., MO
A 107 TyTy South Orchards, GA
A 108 VanWell Nursery, Inc., WA
A 115 Womack's Nursery Co., TX

PEARS
A 1 Adams County Nursery, Inc., PA
A 4 Ames' Orchard and Nursery, AR
A 20 Cloud Mountain Nursery, WA
A 24 Cumberland Valley Nurseries, Inc., TN
A 32 The Fig Tree Nursery, FL
A 40 Greenmantle Nursery, CA
A 52 Johnson Nursery, GA
A 58 LBG Nursery, MN
A 62 Living Tree Centre, CA
A 69 J. E. Miller Nurseries, Inc., NY
A 70 Moosebell Flower, Fruit & Tree Co., ME
A 72 New York State Fruit Testing Coop. Assn., NY
A 88 Rocky Meadow Orchard & Nursery, IN
A 90 St. Lawrence Nurseries, NY
A 95 Sherwood's Greenhouses, LA
A 99 Stark Bro's Nurseries & Orchards Co., MO
A 104 Tolowa Nursery, OR
A 107 TyTy South Orchards, GA
A 108 VanWell Nursery, Inc., WA

PEARS, ANTIQUE
A 5 Arbor & Espalier, CA
A 97 Sonoma Antique Apple Nursery, CA
A 98 Southmeadow Fruit Gardens, MI
A 106 Tsolum River Fruit Trees, BC

PEARS, ORIENTAL
A 1 Adams County Nursery, Inc., PA
A 13 Buckley Nursery, WA
A 14 Burnt Ridge Nursery, WA
A 20 Cloud Mountain Nursery, WA
A 35 Fowler Nurseries, Inc., CA
A 41 Gulf Coast Plantsmen, LA
A 46 Hidden Springs Nursery -- Edible Landscaping, TN
A 76 Oregon Exotica Nursery, OR
A 88 Rocky Meadow Orchard & Nursery, IN
A 95 Sherwood's Greenhouses, LA
A 97 Sonoma Antique Apple Nursery, CA
A 104 Tolowa Nursery, OR
A 106 Tsolum River Fruit Trees, BC

PECANS
A 24 Cumberland Valley Nurseries, Inc., TN
A 32 Fernald's Hickory Hill Nursery, IL
A 35 Fowler Nurseries, Inc., CA
A 37 Louis Gerardi Nursery, IL
A 39 John H. Gordon, Jr., Grower, NY
A 41 Grimo Nut Nursery, ON
A 73 Nolin River Nut Tree Nursery, KY
A 75 Oikos Tree Crops, MI
A 76 Oregon Exotica Nursery, OR
A 90 Saginaw Valley Nut Nursery, MI
A 114 Wiley's Nut Grove, OH

PELARGONIUMS
A 22 Cook's Geranium Nursery, KS
A 26 Davidson-Wilson Greenhouses, IN
A 62 Logee's Greenhouses, CT
A 94 Shady Hill Gardens, IL
A 116 Young's Mesa Nursery, CA

PELARGONIUMS, SPECIES
A 16 Cape Seed & Bulb, So
A 22 Cook's Geranium Nursery, KS
A 52 The Thomas Jefferson Center, VA
A 78 Parsley's Cape Seeds, So
A 90 Rust-En-Vrede Nursery, So
A 94 Shady Hill Gardens, IL
A 116 Young's Mesa Nursery, CA

PAGE SOURCE

PENSTEMONS
A 8   Bernardo Beach Native Plant Farm, NM
A 21   Colorado Alpines, Inc., CO
A 36   Frosty Hollow Nursery, WA
A 42   Robert B. Hamm, CA
A 52   Klaus R. Jelitto, We
A 53   Joyce's Garden, OR
A 57   L. Kreeger, En
A 59   Las Pilitas Nursery, CA
A 75   Old Farm Nursery, CO
A 79   Theodore Payne Foundation, CA
A 81   Plants of the Wild, WA
A 83   Prairie Moon Nursery, MN
A 83   The Primrose Path, PA
A 93   Select Seeds, CT
A 111   We-Du Nurseries, NC
A 117   Yucca Do Nursery, TX

PEONIES, HERBACEOUS
A 1   Adamgrove, MO
A 4   American Daylily & Perennials, MO
A 4   Anderson Iris Gardens, MN
A 11   Brand Peony Farm, MN
A 13   The Bulb Crate, IL
A 13   Bundles of Bulbs, MD
A 14   Busse Gardens, MN
A 16   Caprice Farm, OR
A 32   Fieldstone Gardens, Inc., ME
A 37   Gardenimport, Inc., ON
A 43   Hatfield Gardens, OH
A 46   Hickory Hill Gardens, PA
A 46   Hildenbrandt's Iris Gardens, NE
A 48   Honeywood Lilies, SK
A 50   Inter-State Nurseries, IA
A 56   Klehm Nursery, IL
A 72   The New Peony Farm, MN
A 86   Reath's Nursery, MI
A 91   John Scheepers, Inc., NY
A 104   Tischler Peony Garden, MN
A 109   Andre Viette Farm & Nursery, VA
A 112   White Flower Farm, CT
A 113   Gilbert H. Wild & Son, Inc., MO

PEONIES, TREE
A 16   Caprice Farm, OR
A 32   Fieldstone Gardens, Inc., ME
A 56   Klehm Nursery, IL
A 86   Reath's Nursery, MI
A 97   Smirnow's Son, NY
A 112   White Flower Farm, CT

PEPEROMIAS
A 42   Robert B. Hamm, CA
A 58   Lake Odessa Greenhouse, MI
A 101   Sunshine State Tropicals, FL

PEPPERS, HOT
A 2   Alfrey -- Peter Pepper Seeds, TN
A 14   D. V. Burrell Seed Growers Co., CO
A 18   Catnip Acres Herb Nursery, CT
A 21   Companion Plants, OH
A 30   Evergreen Y. H. Enterprises, CA
A 48   Horticultural Enterprises, TX
A 60   Le Champion Heritage Seeds, CA
A 62   Lockhart Seeds, CA
A 69   Miller-Bowie County Farmers Assn., TX
A 71   Native Seeds/SEARCH, AZ
A 79   The Pepper Gal, FL
A 80   Piedmont Plant Company, GA
A 82   Porter & Son, TX

PEPPERS, HOT
A 86   Redwood City Seed Co., CA
A 89   Roswell Seed Co., NM
A 98   Southern Seeds, FL
A 104   Tomato Growers Supply Company, FL
A 111   Chris Weeks Peppers, NC
A 112   Westwind Seeds, AZ
A 114   Willhite Seed Co., TX

PEPPERS, SWEET
A 2   Alfrey -- Peter Pepper Seeds, TN
A 14   D. V. Burrell Seed Growers Co., CO
A 22   The Cook's Garden, VT
A 48   Horticultural Enterprises, TX
A 61   Liberty Seed Company, OH
A 62   Lockhart Seeds, CA
A 69   Miller-Bowie County Farmers Assn., TX
A 79   The Pepper Gal, FL
A 82   Porter & Son, TX
A 89   Roswell Seed Co., NM
A 98   Southern Seeds, FL
A 100   Stokes Seed Company, NY
A 104   Tomato Growers Supply Company, FL
A 108   Vermont Bean Seed Co., VT

PERENNIALS
See also specific plants
See also Flowers, Heirloom
A 2   Allen, Sterling & Lothrop, ME
A 3   Alpenflora Gardens, BC
A 3   Ambergate Gardens, MN
A 5   Appalachian Wildflower Nursery, PA
A 6   B & B Laboratories, WA
A 8   Vernon Barnes & Son Nursery, TN
A 8   Beaverlodge Nursery, AB
A 8   Bernardo Beach Native Plant Farm, NM
A 9   Birch Farm Nursery, En
A 9   Kurt Bluemel, Inc., MD
A 10   Bluestone Perennials, OH
A 10   Borbeleta Gardens, MN
A 11   Botanicals, MA
A 12   Brookside Wildflowers, NC
A 12   Joseph Brown, Native Seeds, VA
A 14   W. Atlee Burpee Company, PA
A 14   Busse Gardens, MN
A 14   The Butchart Gardens, BC
A 16   Camelot North, MN
A 16   Canyon Creek Nursery, CA
A 16   Caprice Farm, OR
A 17   Carroll Gardens, MD
A 18   Catnip Acres Herb Nursery, CT
A 18   Chadwell Himalayan Seed, En
A 19   Chiltern Seeds, En
A 20   Clargreen Gardens, Ltd., ON
A 20   Clifford's Perennial & Vine, WI
A 20   Coastal Gardens & Nursery, SC
A 21   Comstock, Ferre & Co., CT
A 21   Conley's Garden Center, ME
A 22   Cooper's Garden, MN
A 23   The Country Garden, WI
A 24   Cricklewood Nursery, WA
A 24   Crosman Seed Corp., NY
A 24   Crownsville Nursery, MD
A 24   Cruickshank's, Inc., ON
A 25   Dabney Herbs, KY
A 25   The Nursery at the Dallas Nature Center, TX
A 25   William Dam Seeds, ON
A 26   Dan's Garden Shop, MD
A 26   Daystar, ME
A 27   DeGiorgi Seed Company, NE
(continued next page)

PAGE	SOURCE

PERENNIALS (continued)

PAGE	SOURCE
A 27	Dominion Seed House, ON
A 28	Donaroma's Nursery, MA
A 28	Dutch Mill Herb Farm, OR
A 28	E & H Products, CA
A 28	Early's Farm & Garden Centre, Inc., SK
A 29	Earthstar Herb Gardens, AZ
A 29	Eco-Gardens, GA
A 29	Englerth Gardens, MI
A 31	F W H Seed Exchange, CA
A 31	Far North Gardens, MI
A 31	Farmer Seed & Nursery, MN
A 31	Fedco Seeds, ME
A 32	Henry Field Seed & Nursery Co., IA
A 32	Fieldstone Gardens, Inc., ME
A 33	Flora Favours, WI
A 33	Flowerland, NE
A 34	Flowerplace Plant Farm, MS
A 34	Forestfarm, OR
A 35	The Fragrant Path, NE
A 36	Frosty Hollow Nursery, WA
A 37	Garden Perennials, NE
A 37	Garden Place, OH
A 37	Gardenimport, Inc., ON
A 38	Gilson Gardens, OH
A 38	Gladside Gardens, MA
A 38	Glasshouse Works, OH
A 39	Good Hollow Greenhouse & Herbarium, TN
A 39	Goodwin Creek Gardens, OR
A 39	Russell Graham, Purveyor of Plants, OR
A 40	Green Horizons, TX
A 41	Grianan Gardens, CA
A 41	Gurney Seed & Nursery Co., SD
A 43	Harris Seeds, NY
A 43	Hartman's Herb Farm, MA
A 43	Hauser's Superior View Farm, WI
A 43	Havasu Hills Herbs, CA
A 45	Heritage Gardens, IA
A 45	Heymaqua Seed Service, CA
A 46	Hickory Hill Gardens, PA
A 47	Holbrook Farm & Nursery, NC
A 48	Hortico, Inc., ON
A 49	J. L. Hudson, Seedsman, CA
A 49	Ed Hume Seeds, Inc., WA
A 49	Huronview Nurseries & Garden Centre, ON
A 50	Indigo Knoll Perennials, MD
A 50	Inter-State Nurseries, IA
A 51	Island Seed Mail Order, BC
A 52	Klaus R. Jelitto, We
A 52	Johnny's Selected Seeds, ME
A 53	Joyce's Garden, OR
A 53	J. W. Jung Seed Co., WI
A 54	Kelly Nurseries, NY
A 56	Kimberly Garden on Oregon Hill, NY
A 56	Kings Herb Seeds, Au
A 56	Klehm Nursery, IL
A 56	Kline Nursery Co., OR
A 57	P. Kohli & Co., In
A 58	Lakeshore Tree Farms, Ltd., SK
A 59	Landscape Alternatives, Inc., MN
A 60	Orol Ledden & Sons, NJ
A 60	Ledgecrest Greenhouses, CT
A 61	Liberty Seed Company, OH
A 61	Life-Form Replicators, MI
A 61	Linn Farm Perennials, VA
A 63	Lost Prairie Herb Farm, MT
A 63	Louisiana Nursery, LA
A 64	McConnell Nurseries, Inc., ON
A 64	McFayden Seeds, MB
A 65	Maple Leaf Nursery, CA

PERENNIALS

PAGE	SOURCE
A 66	Mary's Plant Farm, OH
A 67	Earl May Seed & Nursery Co., IA
A 61	Meadowbrook Herb Garden, RI
A 67	Mellinger's, Inc., OH
A 68	Milaeger's Gardens, WI
A 69	Montrose Nursery, NC
A 71	National Heirloom Flower Seed Exchange, MA
A 71	Native Gardens, TN
A 71	Natural Gardens, TN
A 72	Nature's Garden Nursery, OR
A 72	Niche Gardens, NC
A 74	Northwest Biological Enterprises, OR
A 75	Old Farm Nursery, CO
A 75	Ontario Seed Company, Ltd., ON
A 77	Owen Farms, TN
A 78	Park Seed Company, Inc., SC
A 79	Theodore Payne Foundation, CA
A 80	Piccadilly Farm, GA
A 80	Pinetree Garden Seeds, ME
A 83	Powell's Gardens, NC
A 83	Prairie Nursery, WI
A 83	The Primrose Path, PA
A 84	Putney Nursery, Inc., VT
A 85	Ravenswood Seeds, WI
A 87	Rice Creek Gardens, MN
A 88	Robyn's Nest Nursery, WA
A 88	Rocknoll Nursery, OH
A 89	Rose Hill Herbs and Perennials, VA
A 89	Roslyn Nursery, NY
A 91	Sandy Mush Herb Nursery, NC
A 91	John Scheepers, Inc., NY
A 92	Seed Centre, Ltd., AB
A 93	The Seed Source, NC
A 93	Seeds Blum, ID
A 93	Select Seeds, CT
A 94	Shady Oaks Nursery, MN
A 96	Skyline Nursery, WA
A 96	Sleepy Hollow Herb Farm, KY
A 98	Specialty Seeds, Au
A 99	Spring Hill Nurseries Co., IL
A 99	Springvale Farm Nursery, IL
A 100	Stoecklein's Nursery, PA
A 100	Stokes Seed Company, NY
A 101	Sunlight Gardens, TN
A 101	Sunnybrook Farms Nursery, OH
A 102	Surry Gardens, ME
A 102	T & T Seeds, Ltd., MB
A 103	Ter-El Nursery, PA
A 103	Thompson & Morgan, NJ
A 104	Torbay's Plant World, En
A 105	Tregunno Seeds, ON
A 106	Triple Oaks Nursery, NJ
A 106	Tripple Brook Farm, MA
A 106	Otis Twilley Seed Co., PA
A 107	Twombly Nursery, CT
A 108	Vandenberg, NY
A 108	Vermont Bean Seed Co., VT
A 109	Vesey's Seeds, Ltd., PE
A 109	Andre Viette Farm & Nursery, VA
A 109	Village Arbors, AL
A 110	Mary Walker Bulb Company, GA
A 110	Wayside Gardens, SC
A 111	We-Du Nurseries, NC
A 111	Weiss Brothers Nursery, CA
A 111	Well-Sweep Herb Farm, NJ
A 112	Whayes End Nursery, VA
A 112	White Flower Farm, CT
A 113	Wild Seeds, Wa
A 113	Wildflower Nursery, NC

(continued next page)

PAGE SOURCE

PERENNIALS (continued)
A 113   The Wildwood Flower, NC
A 114   Wildwood Nursery, CA
A 115   Winter Greenhouse, WI
A 115   Woodlanders, Inc., SC
A 116   Wrenwood of Berkeley Springs, WV
A 116   Wyatt-Quarles Seed Co., NC

PERSIMMONS
A 7   Barber Nursery, OR
A 14   Burnt Ridge Nursery, WA
A 16   California Nursery Co., CA
A 19   Chestnut Hill Nursery, Inc., FL
A 29   Edible Landscaping, VA
A 36   Fruit Spirit Botanical Gardens, Au
A 37   Louis Gerardi Nursery, IL
A 39   John H. Gordon, Jr., Grower, NY
A 68   Meta Horticultural Labs, KY
A 73   Nolin River Nut Tree Nursery, KY
A 74   Northwoods Nursery, OR
A 95   Sherwood's Greenhouses, LA
A 104   Tolowa Nursery, OR
A 107   TyTy South Orchards, GA
A 114   Wiley's Nut Grove, OH

PHILODENDRONS
A 98   Southern Exposure, TX

PHLOX
A 5   Appalachian Wildflower Nursery, PA
A 10   Bluestone Perennials, OH
A 14   Busse Gardens, MN
A 21   Colorado Alpines, Inc., CO
A 32   Fieldstone Gardens, Inc., ME
A 33   Flora Favours, WI
A 37   Garden Place, OH
A 45   Heritage Gardens, IA
A 47   Holbrook Farm & Nursery, NC
A 53   Joyce's Garden, OR
A 57   L. Kreeger, En
A 58   Lamb Nurseries, WA
A 68   Milaeger's Gardens, WI
A 69   Montrose Nursery, NC
A 83   Powell's Gardens, NC
A 83   The Primrose Path, PA
A 88   Rocknoll Nursery, OH
A 109   Andre Viette Farm & Nursery, VA
A 111   We-Du Nurseries, NC
A 115   Winter Greenhouse, WI

PIERIS
A 12   Broken Arrow Nursery, CT
A 27   DeGrandchamp's Blueberry Farm, MI
A 29   Eastern Plant Specialties, ME
A 33   Flora Lan Nursery, OR
A 35   Foxborough Nursery, Inc., MD
A 42   Hall Rhododendrons, OR
A 43   Hass Nursery, OR
A 89   Roslyn Nursery, NY
A 97   Sorum's Nursery, OR

PISTACHIOS
A 16   California Nursery Co., CA
A 32   Fiddyment Farms, CA

PLATYCERIUMS
A 35   Fox Orchids, Inc., AR
A 44   Heliconia Haus, FL
A 47   Holladay Jungle, CA
A 48   Jerry Horne -- Rare Plants, FL

PAGE SOURCE

PLATYCERIUMS
A 81   The Plant Shop's Botanical Gardens, CA
A 84   Rainforest Flora, Inc., CA

PLEIONES
A 6   Avon Bulbs, En
A 82   Potterton & Martin, En
A 103   Terrorchids, We

PLUMERIAS
A 19   Christa's Cactus, AZ
A 66   Marilynn's Garden, CA
A 81   The Plant Shop's Botanical Gardens, CA
A 82   The Plumeria People, TX

PLUMS
A 1   Adams County Nursery, Inc., PA
A 20   Cloud Mountain Nursery, WA
A 24   Cumberland Valley Nurseries, Inc., TN
A 48   Hollydale Nursery, TN
A 51   Ison's Nursery, GA
A 52   Johnson Nursery, GA
A 58   LBG Nursery, MN
A 72   New York State Fruit Testing Coop. Assn., NY
A 74   Northwoods Nursery, OR
A 88   Rocky Meadow Orchard & Nursery, IN
A 90   St. Lawrence Nurseries, NY
A 97   Sonoma Antique Apple Nursery, CA
A 98   Southmeadow Fruit Gardens, MI
A 104   Tolowa Nursery, OR
A 106   Tsolum River Fruit Trees, BC
A 107   TyTy South Orchards, GA
A 108   VanWell Nursery, Inc., WA

POPCORN
A 22   Corns, OK
A 24   Cross Seed Company, KS
A 31   Farmer Seed & Nursery, MN
A 90   SPB Sales, TX
A 93   Seedway, Inc., NY
A 95   Shissler Seed Company, IL
A 108   Vermont Bean Seed Co., VT

POPLARS, HYBRID
A 21   Cold Stream Farm, MI

POPPIES, ORIENTAL
A 20   Clifford's Perennial & Vine, WI
A 37   Garden Place, OH
A 46   Hildenbrandt's Iris Gardens, NE
A 52   Klaus R. Jelitto, We
A 56   Kimberly Garden on Oregon Hill, NY
A 58   Lamb Nurseries, WA
A 69   Mohns, Inc., CA
A 102   Surry Gardens, ME
A 109   Andre Viette Farm & Nursery, VA

POTATOES, SEED
A 8   Becker's Seed Potatoes, ON
A 27   Dominion Seed House, ON
A 28   Early's Farm & Garden Centre, Inc., SK
A 36   Garden City Seeds, MT
A 39   Good Seed Co., WA
A 68   MicroCulture, Inc., OR
A 79   Peace Seeds, OR
A 80   Pinetree Garden Seeds, ME
A 88   Ronniger's Seed Potatoes, ID
A 114   Wilton's Organic Seed Potatoes, CO

PAGE SOURCE

PRAIRIE PLANTS
See also Grasses, Prairie
See also Wildflowers, Prairie
A 8   Bernardo Beach Native Plant Farm, NM
A 10   Boehlke's Woodland Gardens, WI
A 12   Joseph Brown, Native Seeds, VA
A 25   The Nursery at the Dallas Nature Center, TX
A 36   Frosty Hollow Nursery, WA
A 40   Greenlee Nursery, CA
A 58   LaFayette Home Nursery, Inc., IL
A 59   Landscape Alternatives, Inc., MN
A 62   Little Valley Farm, WI
A 68   Milaeger's Gardens, WI
A 75   Old Farm Nursery, CO
A 83   Prairie Moon Nursery, MN
A 83   Prairie Nursery, WI
A 83   Prairie Ridge Nursery/CRM Ecosystems, Inc., WI
A 83   Prairie Seed Source, WI
A 100 Stock Seed Farms, Inc., NE
A 101 Sunlight Gardens, TN

PRIMULAS
A 2   Albiflora, Inc., Ja
A 5   Appalachian Wildflower Nursery, PA
A 7   Bailey's, WA
A 9   Blackmore & Langdon, En
A 18   Chadwell Himalayan Seed, En
A 19   Chehalis Rare Plant Nursery, WA
A 21   Colorado Alpines, Inc., CO
A 24   Cricklewood Nursery, WA
A 26   Daystar, ME
A 31   Far North Gardens, MI
A 39   Russell Graham, Purveyor of Plants, OR
A 50   Brenda Hyatt, En
A 52   Klaus R. Jelitto, We
A 69   Montrose Nursery, NC
A 72   Nature's Garden Nursery, OR
A 83   The Primrose Path, PA
A 90   Saltspring Primroses, BC
A 93   Seedalp, Sw
A 102 Surry Gardens, ME
A 104 Torbay's Plant World, En

PROTEACEAE
A 6   B & T Associates, En
A 84   Protea Seed & Nursery Suppliers, So
A 96   Anthony J. Skittone, CA

PROTEAS
A 7   The Banana Tree, PA
A 22   Copacabana Gardens, CA
A 50   International Seed Supplies, Au
A 78   Parsley's Cape Seeds, So
A 105 Trans Pacific Nursery, OR

PUMPKINS, GIANT
A 27   Howard W. Dill, NS
A 70   Mountain Valley Seeds & Nursery, UT
A 78   Paul's Premium Seeds, CA
A 109 Vesey's Seeds, Ltd., PE
A 114 Willhite Seed Co., TX

PYRETHRUMS
A 43   Hauser's Superior View Farm, WI

PYRRHOCACTUS
A 72   New Mexico Cactus Research, NM

QUINCES (FRUIT)
A 7   Barber Nursery, OR

QUINCES (FRUIT)
A 46   Hidden Springs Nursery -- Edible Landscaping, TN
A 62   Living Tree Centre, CA
A 106 Tsolum River Fruit Trees, BC

RASPBERRIES
A 1   Ahrens Nursery & Plant Labs, IN
A 2   Allen Company, MD
A 4   Ames' Orchard and Nursery, AR
A 9   Blue Star Lab, NY
A 10   Boston Mountain Nurseries, AR
A 12   Brittingham Plant Farms, MD
A 18   Champlain Isle Agro Associates, VT
A 20   Cloud Mountain Nursery, WA
A 29   Emlong Nurseries, MI
A 43   Hartmann's Plantation, Inc., MI
A 51   Ison's Nursery, GA
A 58   LBG Nursery, MN
A 65   Makielski Berry Farm & Nursery, MI
A 72   New York State Fruit Testing Coop. Assn., NY
A 73   North Star Gardens, MN
A 74   Nourse Farms, Inc., MA
A 77   Pacific Berry Works, WA
A 79   Pense Nursery, AR
A 87   Rider Nurseries, IA
A 99   Stanek's Garden Center, WA
A 115 Windy Ridge Nursery, AB

REBUTIAS
A 94   Shein's Cactus, CA

RHIPSALIS
A 5   Apacha Cactus, CA
A 38   Golden Lake Greenhouses, CA
A 40   Greenlife Gardens Greenhouses, GA
A 42   Robert B. Hamm, CA
A 84   Rainbow Gardens Nursery & Bookshop, CA

RHODODENDRONS, HYBRIDS
A 6   B & B Laboratories, WA
A 11   The Bovees Nursery, OR
A 11   Briarwood Gardens, MA
A 12   Broken Arrow Nursery, CT
A 13   Bull Valley Rhododendron Nursery, PA
A 16   Cardinal Nursery, NC
A 17   Carlson's Gardens, NY
A 18   Chambers Nursery, OR
A 24   The Cummins Garden, NJ
A 27   DeGrandchamp's Blueberry Farm, MI
A 29   Eastern Plant Specialties, ME
A 33   Flora Lan Nursery, OR
A 40   The Greenery, WA
A 41   Greer Gardens, OR
A 42   Hall Rhododendrons, OR
A 42   Hammond's Acres of Rhodys, WA
A 47   Holly Hills, Inc., IN
A 53   Justice Gardens, GA
A 70   Mowbray Gardens, OH
A 71   Musser Forests Inc., PA
A 72   E. B. Nauman, Nurseryman, NY
A 73   North Coast Rhododendron Nursery, CA
A 89   Roslyn Nursery, NY
A 97   Sorum's Nursery, OR
A 105 Transplant Nursery, GA
A 106 Trillium Lane Nursery, CA
A 110 Washington Evergreen Nursery, NC
A 112 Westgate Garden Nursery, CA
A 112 Whitney Gardens, WA

PAGE SOURCE

RHODODENDRONS, SPECIES
A 11   The Bovees Nursery, OR
A 12   Broken Arrow Nursery, CT
A 17   Carlson's Gardens, NY
A 24   The Cummins Garden, NJ
A 39   Gossler Farms Nursery, OR
A 40   The Greenery, WA
A 41   Greer Gardens, OR
A 42   Hall Rhododendrons, OR
A 42   Hammond's Acres of Rhodys, WA
A 53   Justice Gardens, GA
A 58   Lamtree Farm, NC
A 70   Mowbray Gardens, OH
A 73   North Coast Rhododendron Nursery, CA
A 89   Roslyn Nursery, NY
A 90   Salter Tree Farm, FL
A 92   F. W. Schumacher Co., MA
A 93   The Seed Source, NC
A 105   Transplant Nursery, GA
A 106   Trillium Lane Nursery, CA
A 112   Westgate Garden Nursery, CA
A 112   Whitney Gardens, WA
A 115   Woodlanders, Inc., SC

RHODODENDRONS, VIREYA
A 11   The Bovees Nursery, OR
A 41   Greer Gardens, OR
A 86   Red's Rhodies, OR
A 109   Vireya Specialties Nursery, CA

RHUBARB
A 1   Ahrens Nursery & Plant Labs, IN
A 52   Jackson & Perkins Co., OR
A 58   D. Landreth Seed Company, MD
A 74   Nourse Farms, Inc., MA
A 87   Rider Nurseries, IA

RIBES
A 59   Las Pilitas Nursery, CA
A 81   Plants of the Wild, WA
A 94   Sevenoaks Nursery, OR
A 112   Whitman Farms, OR

ROCK GARDEN PLANTS
See also specific plants
A 2   Albiflora, Inc., Ja
A 3   Alpenflora Gardens, BC
A 5   Appalachian Wildflower Nursery, PA
A 9   Birch Farm Nursery, En
A 10   Bluestone Perennials, OH
A 11   The Bovees Nursery, OR
A 12   Brookside Wildflowers, NC
A 14   Bushland Flora (Australian Seed Specialists), Au
A 14   The Butchart Gardens, BC
A 19   Chehalis Rare Plant Nursery, WA
A 19   Chiltern Seeds, En
A 20   Coenosium Gardens, OR
A 21   Colorado Alpines, Inc., CO
A 24   Cricklewood Nursery, WA
A 24   The Cummins Garden, NJ
A 25   The Nursery at the Dallas Nature Center, TX
A 26   Daystar, ME
A 29   Eco-Gardens, GA
A 31   Fancy Fronds, WA
A 31   Far North Gardens, MI
A 32   Fieldstone Gardens, Inc., ME
A 33   Flora Favours, WI
A 36   Frosty Hollow Nursery, WA
A 37   Garden Perennials, NE
A 37   Gardens of the Blue Ridge, NC

ROCK GARDEN PLANTS
A 41   Grianan Gardens, CA
A 43   Havasu Hills Herbs, CA
A 47   Holbrook Farm & Nursery, NC
A 50   Indigo Knoll Perennials, MD
A 52   Klaus R. Jelitto, We
A 53   Joyce's Garden, OR
A 56   Kimberly Garden on Oregon Hill, NY
A 56   Kline Nursery Co., OR
A 57   P. Kohli & Co., In
A 57   L. Kreeger, En
A 57   Michael & Janet Kristick, PA
A 58   Lamb Nurseries, WA
A 59   Landscape Alternatives, Inc., MN
A 61   Life-Form Replicators, MI
A 63   Lost Prairie Herb Farm, MT
A 63   McClure & Zimmerman, WI
A 66   Mary's Plant Farm, OH
A 69   Montrose Nursery, NC
A 70   Mt. Tahoma Nursery, WA
A 71   Native Gardens, TN
A 72   Nature's Garden Nursery, OR
A 72   Niche Gardens, NC
A 74   Northwest Biological Enterprises, OR
A 75   Old Farm Nursery, CO
A 79   Theodore Payne Foundation, CA
A 81   Plants of the Wild, WA
A 83   Prairie Nursery, WI
A 83   The Primrose Path, PA
A 87   Rice Creek Gardens, MN
A 88   Robyn's Nest Nursery, WA
A 88   Rock Spray Nursery, MA
A 88   Rocknoll Nursery, OH
A 90   Jim & Irene Russ Quality Plants, CA
A 90   Rust-En-Vrede Nursery, So
A 91   Sandy Mush Herb Nursery, NC
A 93   The Seed Source, NC
A 93   Seedalp, Sw
A 96   Siskiyou Rare Plant Nursery, OR
A 96   Skyline Nursery, WA
A 97   Solar Green, Ltd., ID
A 98   Southern Seeds, Ne
A 98   Southwestern Native Seeds, AZ
A 99   Springvale Farm Nursery, IL
A 99   Squaw Mountain Gardens, OR
A 101   Sunlight Gardens, TN
A 102   Surry Gardens, ME
A 103   Thompson & Morgan, NJ
A 104   Torbay's Plant World, En
A 107   Twombly Nursery, CT
A 111   We-Du Nurseries, NC
A 111   Well-Sweep Herb Farm, NJ
A 113   Wildginger Woodlands, NY
A 113   The Wildwood Flower, NC
A 114   Wildwood Gardens, OH
A 114   Wildwood Nursery, CA
A 115   Winter Greenhouse, WI
A 116   Wrenwood of Berkeley Springs, WV

ROOTSTOCKS, FRUIT TREES
A 8   Bear Creek Nursery, WA
A 41   Grootendorst Nurseries, MI
A 84   Raintree Nursery, WA
A 88   Rocky Meadow Orchard & Nursery, IN
A 97   Sonoma Antique Apple Nursery, CA

ROOTSTOCKS, GRAPES
A 97   Sonoma Grapevines, CA

PAGE SOURCE

ROSEMARY
A 26   T. DeBaggio Herbs by Mail, VA
A 47   Hilltop Herb Farm, TX
A 65   Maple Leaf Nursery, CA
A 96   Sleepy Hollow Herb Farm, KY
A 109 Village Arbors, AL

ROSES
A 7   BDK Nursery, FL
A 20   Clargreen Gardens, Ltd., ON
A 23   Country Bloomers Nursery, CA
A 29   Emlong Nurseries, MI
A 31   Farmer Seed & Nursery, MN
A 40   Greenmantle Nursery, CA
A 41   Gurney Seed & Nursery Co., SD
A 43   Hastings, GA
A 45   Heritage Gardens, IA
A 45   Heritage Rosarium, MD
A 45   Heritage Rose Gardens, CA
A 47   Historical Roses, OH
A 48   Hortico, Inc., ON
A 49   Huronview Nurseries & Garden Centre, ON
A 50   Inter-State Nurseries, IA
A 52   Jackson & Perkins Co., OR
A 54   Kelly Nurseries, NY
A 57   V. Kraus Nurseries, Ltd., ON
A 57   Krider Nurseries, IN
A 63   Lowe's own-root Roses, NH
A 64   McConnell Nurseries, Inc., ON
A 67   Earl May Seed & Nursery Co., IA
A 68   Milaeger's Gardens, WI
A 70   Morden Nurseries, Ltd., MB
A 78   Carl Pallek & Son Nursery, ON
A 80   Pickering Nurseries, Inc., ON
A 87   Rice Creek Gardens, MN
A 87   Rider Nurseries, IA
A 88   Rose Acres, CA
A 89   Roses by Fred Edmunds, OR
A 89   Roses of Yesterday & Today, CA
A 93   Sequoia Nursery -- Moore Miniature Roses, CA
A 95   R. H. Shumway Seedsman, SC
A 99   Spring Hill Nurseries Co., IL
A 99   Stanek's Garden Center, WA
A 99   Stark Bro's Nurseries & Orchards Co., MO
A 100 Stocking Rose Nursery, CA
A 102 T & T Seeds, Ltd., MB
A 103 Thomasville Nurseries, GA
A 110 Wayside Gardens, SC
A 112 White Flower Farm, CT
A 115 Windy Ridge Nursery, AB
A 115 Womack's Nursery Co., TX
A 116 Yesterday's Rose, CA

ROSES, MINIATURE
A 3   Alpenflora Gardens, BC
A 7   BDK Nursery, FL
A 23   Country Bloomers Nursery, CA
A 38   Gloria Dei, NY
A 46   Hidden Garden Nursery, Inc., OR
A 53   Justice Miniature Roses, OR
A 57   Krider Nurseries, IN
A 64   McDaniel's Miniature Roses, CA
A 69   Miniature Plant Kingdom, CA
A 73   Nor'East Miniature Roses, MA
A 77   Oregon Miniature Roses, OR
A 80   Pixie Treasures Miniature Rose Nursery, CA
A 88   Rose Acres, CA
A 89   The Rose Garden & Mini Rose Nursery, SC
A 89   Rosehill Farm, MD
A 93   Sequoia Nursery -- Moore Miniature Roses, CA

PAGE SOURCE

ROSES, MINIATURE
A 100 Stocking Rose Nursery, CA
A 103 Thomasville Nurseries, GA
A 104 Tiny Petals Nursery, CA
A 111 Wee Gems Minature Roses, MN

ROSES, MODERN SHRUB
A 34   Forevergreen Farm, ME
A 40   Greenmantle Nursery, CA
A 45   Heritage Rosarium, MD
A 45   Heritage Rose Gardens, CA
A 46   High Country Rosarium, CO
A 47   Historical Roses, OH
A 57   Krider Nurseries, IN
A 63   Lowe's own-root Roses, NH
A 78   Carl Pallek & Son Nursery, ON
A 80   Pickering Nurseries, Inc., ON
A 88   Rose Acres, CA
A 89   Roses of Yesterday & Today, CA
A 103 Thomasville Nurseries, GA
A 116 Yesterday's Rose, CA

ROSES, OLD GARDEN
A 4   Antique Rose Emporium, TX
A 7   BDK Nursery, FL
A 23   Country Bloomers Nursery, CA
A 34   Forevergreen Farm, ME
A 40   Greenmantle Nursery, CA
A 45   Heritage Rosarium, MD
A 45   Heritage Rose Gardens, CA
A 46   High Country Rosarium, CO
A 47   Historical Roses, OH
A 52   The Thomas Jefferson Center, VA
A 57   Krider Nurseries, IN
A 63   Lowe's own-root Roses, NH
A 66   Mary's Plant Farm, OH
A 78   Carl Pallek & Son Nursery, ON
A 80   Pickering Nurseries, Inc., ON
A 88   Rose Acres, CA
A 89   Roses of Yesterday & Today, CA
A 116 Yesterday's Rose, CA

ROSES, SPECIES
A 7   BDK Nursery, FL
A 7   Barber Nursery, OR
A 12   Joseph Brown, Native Seeds, VA
A 18   Chadwell Himalayan Seed, En
A 23   Country Bloomers Nursery, CA
A 34   Forestfarm, OR
A 34   Forevergreen Farm, ME
A 40   Greenmantle Nursery, CA
A 45   Heritage Rosarium, MD
A 45   Heritage Rose Gardens, CA
A 46   High Country Rosarium, CO
A 47   Historical Roses, OH
A 63   Lowe's own-root Roses, NH
A 80   Pickering Nurseries, Inc., ON
A 89   Roses of Yesterday & Today, CA
A 92   F. W. Schumacher Co., MA

RUDBECKIAS
A 23   The Country Garden, WI
A 43   Hauser's Superior View Farm, WI

SALVIAS
A 16   Canyon Creek Nursery, CA
A 18   Catnip Acres Herb Nursery, CT
A 21   Companion Plants, OH
A 28   Dutch Mill Herb Farm, OR
A 29   Earthstar Herb Gardens, AZ
(continued next page)

PAGE SOURCE

SALVIAS (continued)
A 47 Hilltop Herb Farm, TX
A 59 Las Pilitas Nursery, CA
A 69 Montrose Nursery, NC
A 75 Old Farm Nursery, CO
A 96 Sleepy Hollow Herb Farm, KY
A 99 Stallings Exotic Nursery, CA
A 102 Surry Gardens, ME
A 117 Yucca Do Nursery, TX

SANSEVIERIAS
A 29 Endangered Species, CA
A 38 Glasshouse Works, OH
A 41 Grigsby Cactus Gardens, CA
A 96 Singers' Growing Things, CA
A 100 Succulent Plants, MN
A 100 Succulenta, CA

SARRACENIAS
A 66 Marston Exotics, En
A 77 Orgel's Orchids, FL

SASKATOONS
A 28 Early's Farm & Garden Centre, Inc., SK
A 46 Hidden Springs Nursery -- Edible Landscaping, TN
A 58 Lakeshore Tree Farms, Ltd., SK
A 115 Windy Ridge Nursery, AB

SCIONWOOD, FRUIT TREES
A 37 Louis Gerardi Nursery, IL

SEDUMS
A 3 Alpine Gardens & Calico Shop, WI
A 5 Apacha Cactus, CA
A 10 Bluestone Perennials, OH
A 15 Cactus Gem Nursery, AR
A 23 Country Cottage, KS
A 33 Flora Favours, WI
A 34 Flowerplace Plant Farm, MS
A 36 Frosty Hollow Nursery, WA
A 37 Garden Place, OH
A 38 Gilson Gardens, OH
A 44 The Herbfarm, WA
A 50 Indigo Knoll Perennials, MD
A 53 Joyce's Garden, OR
A 56 Kimberly Garden on Oregon Hill, NY
A 58 Lamb Nurseries, WA
A 69 Montrose Nursery, NC
A 72 Nature's Garden Nursery, OR
A 83 Powell's Gardens, NC
A 87 Rice Creek Gardens, MN
A 90 Jim & Irene Russ Quality Plants, CA
A 93 The Seed Source, NC
A 99 Squaw Mountain Gardens, OR
A 103 Ter-El Nursery, PA
A 104 Tranquil Lake Nursery, MA
A 116 Wrenwood of Berkeley Springs, WV

SEED EXCHANGES
A 22 Corns, OK
A 31 F W H Seed Exchange, CA
A 33 The Flower & Herb Exchange, IA
A 38 Global Seed Exchange, WA
A 39 The Grain Exchange, KS
A 71 National Heirloom Flower Seed Exchange, MA
A 85 Rare Seed Locator Network, CA
A 93 Seed Saving Project, CA

SEMPERVIVUMS
A 3 Alpine Gardens & Calico Shop, WI

PAGE SOURCE

SEMPERVIVUMS
A 5 Apacha Cactus, CA
A 15 Cactus Gem Nursery, AR
A 21 Colorado Alpines, Inc., CO
A 23 Country Cottage, KS
A 44 The Herbfarm, WA
A 53 Joyce's Garden, OR
A 58 Lamb Nurseries, WA
A 86 Redlo Cacti, OR
A 88 Rocknoll Nursery, OH
A 88 Grace Rollerson, BC
A 90 Jim & Irene Russ Quality Plants, CA
A 99 Squaw Mountain Gardens, OR
A 103 Ter-El Nursery, PA
A 116 Wrenwood of Berkeley Springs, WV

SHADE PLANTS
See also specific plants
See also Woodland Plants
A 3 Ambergate Gardens, MN
A 12 Brookside Wildflowers, NC
A 14 Busse Gardens, MN
A 20 Coastal Gardens & Nursery, SC
A 21 Color Farm Growers, FL
A 22 Cooper's Garden, MN
A 25 Dabney Herbs, KY
A 29 Eastern Plant Specialties, ME
A 29 Eco-Gardens, GA
A 29 Englerth Gardens, MI
A 31 Fancy Fronds, WA
A 34 Foliage Gardens, WA
A 39 Good Hollow Greenhouse & Herbarium, TN
A 40 Greenlee Nursery, CA
A 41 Gurney Seed & Nursery Co., SD
A 43 Havasu Hills Herbs, CA
A 56 Kimberly Garden on Oregon Hill, NY
A 56 Klehm Nursery, IL
A 57 V. Kraus Nurseries, Ltd., ON
A 59 Landscape Alternatives, Inc., MN
A 63 The Lowrey Nursery, TX
A 66 Mary's Plant Farm, OH
A 71 Native Gardens, TN
A 72 Niche Gardens, NC
A 79 Theodore Payne Foundation, CA
A 79 Peekskill Nurseries, NY
A 84 Putney Nursery, Inc., VT
A 88 Robyn's Nest Nursery, WA
A 91 Savory's Gardens, Inc., MN
A 94 Shady Oaks Nursery, MN
A 100 Stoecklein's Nursery, PA
A 101 Sunlight Gardens, TN
A 103 Thompson & Morgan, NJ
A 106 Tripple Brook Farm, MA
A 109 Andre Viette Farm & Nursery, VA
A 110 Wayside Gardens, SC
A 111 We-Du Nurseries, NC
A 113 The Wildflower Source, IL
A 114 Wildwood Nursery, CA

SHALLOTS
A 17 Casa Yerba Gardens, OR
A 35 Fox Hollow Herbs, PA
A 44 Herb Gathering, Inc., MO
A 54 Kalmia Farm, VA
A 90 S & H Organic Acres, CA
A 98 Southern Exposure Seed Exchange, VA

SHASTA DAISIES
A 10 Bluestone Perennials, OH
A 37 Garden Place, OH
(continued next page)

PAGE SOURCE

SHASTA DAISIES (continued)
A 43   Hauser's Superior View Farm, WI
A 50   Indigo Knoll Perennials, MD
A 112   Whayes End Nursery, VA

SHRUBS, DWARF
See also Bonsai, Plants for
A 3   Alpenflora Gardens, BC
A 24   The Cummins Garden, NJ
A 26   Daystar, ME
A 29   Eastern Plant Specialties, ME
A 47   Holbrook Farm & Nursery, NC
A 58   Lakeshore Tree Farms, Ltd., SK
A 69   Miniature Plant Kingdom, CA
A 77   Owen Farms, TN
A 88   Rocknoll Nursery, OH
A 99   Springvale Farm Nursery, IL
A 114   Wildwood Gardens, OH

SHRUBS, FLOWERING
See also specific plants
A 5   Appalachian Gardens, PA
A 6   B & B Laboratories, WA
A 8   Beaver Creek Nursery, TN
A 8   Beaverlodge Nursery, AB
A 11   Botanicals, MA
A 11   The Bovees Nursery, OR
A 13   Buckley Nursery, WA
A 14   W. Atlee Burpee Company, PA
A 16   Callahan Seeds, OR
A 16   Camellia Forest Nursery, NC
A 17   Carroll Gardens, MD
A 18   Chadwell Himalayan Seed, En
A 19   Chiltern Seeds, En
A 20   Coenosium Gardens, OR
A 21   Cold Stream Farm, MI
A 26   Daystar, ME
A 29   Emlong Nurseries, MI
A 31   Farmer Seed & Nursery, MN
A 34   Forestfarm, OR
A 35   The Fragrant Path, NE
A 37   Gardens of the Blue Ridge, NC
A 38   Girard Nurseries, OH
A 45   Heritage Gardens, IA
A 45   Heronswood Nursery, WA
A 47   Holbrook Farm & Nursery, NC
A 48   Hortico, Inc., ON
A 57   P. Kohli & Co., In
A 57   V. Kraus Nurseries, Ltd., ON
A 58   Lakeshore Tree Farms, Ltd., SK
A 58   Lamtree Farm, NC
A 59   Lawyer Nursery, Inc., MT
A 62   Little Valley Farm, WI
A 63   Louisiana Nursery, LA
A 64   McConnell Nurseries, Inc., ON
A 67   Mellinger's, Inc., OH
A 69   J. E. Miller Nurseries, Inc., NY
A 70   Morden Nurseries, Ltd., MB
A 70   Mt. Leo Nursery, TN
A 74   Northwoods Nursery, OR
A 75   Old Farm Nursery, CO
A 81   Plant World, TN
A 82   The Plumeria People, TX
A 82   Pony Creek Nursery, WI
A 83   Powell's Gardens, NC
A 90   Salter Tree Farm, FL
A 91   Savage Farms Nursery, TN
A 92   F. W. Schumacher Co., MA
A 93   The Seed Source, NC
A 94   Sheffield's Seed Co., NY

SHRUBS, FLOWERING
A 97   Smith Nursery Co., IA
A 99   Spring Hill Nurseries Co., IL
A 99   Stallings Exotic Nursery, CA
A 99   Stark Bro's Nurseries & Orchards Co., MO
A 106   Tripple Brook Farm, MA
A 107   Twombly Nursery, CT
A 107   TyTy Plantation, GA
A 107   Valley Nursery, MT
A 110   Wayside Gardens, SC
A 112   White Flower Farm, CT
A 113   Wildflower Nursery, NC
A 113   The Wildwood Flower, NC
B 43   Winterthur Museum & Gardens, DE
A 115   Woodlanders, Inc., SC
A 117   Yucca Do Nursery, TX

SHRUBS, FOLIAGE
See also specific plants
A 8   Beaver Creek Nursery, TN
A 45   Heritage Gardens, IA
A 45   Heronswood Nursery, WA
A 62   Little Valley Farm, WI
A 74   Northwest Biological Enterprises, OR
A 75   Old Farm Nursery, CO
A 77   Owen Farms, TN
A 92   F. W. Schumacher Co., MA
A 94   Sheffield's Seed Co., NY
A 107   Valley Nursery, MT
A 117   Yucca Do Nursery, TX

SHRUBS, SMALL GARDEN
A 17   Carroll Gardens, MD
A 24   The Cummins Garden, NJ
A 29   Eco-Gardens, GA
A 39   Gossler Farms Nursery, OR
A 41   Greer Gardens, OR
A 58   Lakeshore Tree Farms, Ltd., SK
A 65   Maple Leaf Nursery, CA
A 74   Northwoods Nursery, OR
A 75   Old Farm Nursery, CO
A 81   Plant World, TN
A 87   Rice Creek Gardens, MN
A 89   Roslyn Nursery, NY
A 99   Springvale Farm Nursery, IL
A 107   Valley Nursery, MT
A 110   Washington Evergreen Nursery, NC
A 110   Wavecrest Nursery & Landscaping Co., MI
A 115   Woodlanders, Inc., SC

SINNINGIAS
A 13   Buell's Greenhouse, Inc., CT
A 36   Lorine Friedrich, TX
A 54   Karleens Achimenes, GA
A 54   Kartuz Greenhouses, CA
A 60   Les Violettes Natalia, PQ
A 64   McKinney's Glasshouse, KS
A 81   Pleasant Hill African Violets, TX
A 103   Tiki Nursery, NC

SPIREAS
A 66   Mary's Plant Farm, OH

STAPELIADS
A 19   Christa's Cactus, AZ
A 42   Robert B. Hamm, CA

STEWARTIAS
A 8   Beaver Creek Nursery, TN
A 39   Gossler Farms Nursery, OR
(continued next page)

PAGE SOURCE

STEWARTIAS (continued)
A 41 Greer Gardens, OR
A 112 Westgate Garden Nursery, CA
A 112 Whitman Farms, OR

STRAWBERRIES
A 1 Ahrens Nursery & Plant Labs, IN
A 2 Allen Company, MD
A 6 Archias' Seed Store, MO
A 10 Boston Mountain Nurseries, AR
A 13 Buckley Nursery, WA
A 22 Cooley's Strawberry Nursery, AR
A 29 Emlong Nurseries, MI
A 36 Garden City Seeds, MT
A 57 Krohne Plant Farms, MI
A 61 Lewis Strawberry Nursery, NC
A 65 Makielski Berry Farm & Nursery, MI
A 72 New York State Fruit Testing Coop. Assn., NY
A 74 Nourse Farms, Inc., MA
A 77 Pacific Berry Works, WA
A 86 Rayner Bros., MD
A 87 Rider Nurseries, IA

STRAWBERRIES, HARDY
A 1 Ahrens Nursery & Plant Labs, IN
A 2 Allen Company, MD
A 12 Brittingham Plant Farms, MD
A 22 Cooley's Strawberry Nursery, AR
A 57 Krohne Plant Farms, MI
A 61 Lewis Strawberry Nursery, NC
A 86 Rayner Bros., MD
A 115 Windy Ridge Nursery, AB

STRAWBERRY, MUSK
A 82 Plumtree Nursery, NY

STREPTOCARPUS
A 13 Buell's Greenhouse, Inc., CT
A 16 Cape Cod Violetry, MA
A 31 Fairyland Begonia & Lily Garden, CA
A 32 Fischer Greenhouses, NJ
A 60 Les Violettes Natalia, PQ
A 63 Lyndon Lyon Greenhouses, Inc., NY
A 103 Tiki Nursery, NC

SUCCULENTS
See also specific plants
A 1 Abbey Gardens, CA
A 5 Apacha Cactus, CA
A 6 Artistic Plants, TX
A 6 Aztekakti/Desertland Nursery, TX
A 6 B & T Associates, En
A 9 Betsy's Brierpatch, NY
A 15 Cactus by Dodie, CA
A 15 Cactus by Mueller, CA
A 15 Cactus Gem Nursery, AR
A 19 Christa's Cactus, AZ
A 27 Desert Nursery, NM
A 27 Desert Theatre, CA
A 40 Greenlife Gardens Greenhouses, GA
A 41 Grigsby Cactus Gardens, CA
A 42 Robert B. Hamm, CA
A 44 Henrietta's Nursery, CA
A 46 Highland Succulents, OH
A 53 Joyce's Garden, OR
A 54 K & L Cactus Nursery, CA
A 56 Gerhard Koehres Cactus & Succulent Nursery, We
A 59 Lauray of Salisbury, CT
A 62 Logee's Greenhouses, CT
A 66 Marilynn's Garden, CA

PAGE SOURCE

SUCCULENTS
A 67 Mesa Garden, NM
A 72 Neon Palm Nursery, CA
A 78 The PanTree, CA
A 81 The Plant Shop's Botanical Gardens, CA
A 81 Plants of the Southwest, NM
A 84 Rainbow Gardens Nursery & Bookshop, CA
A 86 Redlo Cacti, OR
A 88 Grace Rollerson, BC
A 92 Scotty's Desert Plants, CA
A 93 The Seed Shop, MT
A 94 Shein's Cactus, CA
A 96 Singers' Growing Things, CA
A 98 Southwest Seeds, En
A 100 Succulent Plants, MN
A 101 Sunshine Violets & Gesneriads, MA
A 116 Guy Wrinkle Exotic Plants, CA
A 116 Roy Young, Seedsman, En

SUNFLOWERS
A 23 The Country Garden, WI
A 24 Crosman Seed Corp., NY
A 24 Cross Seed Company, KS
A 41 Grianan Gardens, CA
A 55 Kester's Wild Game Food Nurseries, WI
A 98 Southern Exposure Seed Exchange, VA

SWEET PEAS
A 11 S & N Brackley, En
A 19 Chiltern Seeds, En
A 23 The Country Garden, WI
A 41 Grianan Gardens, CA
A 70 Mountain Valley Seeds & Nursery, UT
A 85 Ravenswood Seeds, WI
A 93 Select Seeds, CT
A 98 Specialty Seeds, Au

SWEET POTATO PLANTS
A 6 Archias' Seed Store, MO
A 36 Fred's Plant Farm, TN
A 58 Lagomarsino Seeds, CA
A 80 Piedmont Plant Company, GA
A 99 Steele Plant Company, TN
A 108 Vermont Bean Seed Co., VT

TERRARIUM PLANTS
See also specific plants
A 2 Allgrove Farm, Inc., MA
A 6 Artistic Plants, TX
A 18 Cedar Ridge Nurseries, PA
A 54 Kartuz Greenhouses, CA
A 60 Lee's Botanical Gardens, FL
A 64 McKinney's Glasshouse, KS
A 74 Oak Hill Gardens, IL
A 79 Peter Pauls Nurseries, NY

THYMES
A 47 Hilltop Herb Farm, TX
A 102 Surry Gardens, ME

TILLANDSIAS
A 9 Bird Rock Tropicals, CA
A 10 Arthur Boe Distributor, LA
A 26 Dane Company, TX
A 29 Enchanted Garden, WA
A 37 Garden World, TX
A 38 Golden Lake Greenhouses, CA
A 47 Holladay Jungle, CA
A 53 Jungle Gems, Inc., MD
A 56 Gerhard Koehres Cactus & Succulent Nursery, We

(continued next page)

PAGE SOURCE

TILLANDSIAS (continued)
A 66   Marilynn's Garden, CA
A 84   Rainforest Flora, Inc., CA
A 94   Shelldance Nursery, CA
A 97   Tropical Imports, CA
A 101 W. K. Quality Bromeliads, CA
A 116 Guy Wrinkle Exotic Plants, CA

TOBACCO
A 36   Fred's Plant Farm, TN

TOMATOES
A 2   Alfrey -- Peter Pepper Seeds, TN
A 14   D. V. Burrell Seed Growers Co., CO
A 44   Herb Gathering, Inc., MO
A 104 Tomato Growers Supply Company, FL
A 104 The Tomato Seed Company, Inc., NJ

TOMATOES, HEIRLOOM
A 3   Alston Seed Growers, NC
A 33   Floating Mountain Seeds, WA
A 44   Heirloom Seeds, PA
A 53   J. W. Jung Seed Co., WI
A 60   Le Champion Heritage Seeds, CA
A 78   Paul's Premium Seeds, CA
A 79   Peace Seeds, OR
A 98   Southern Exposure Seed Exchange, VA
A 104 The Tomato Seed Company, Inc., NJ

TOMATOES, HYBRID
A 43   Harris Seeds, NY
A 53   Jordan Seeds, MN
A 53   J. W. Jung Seed Co., WI
A 55   Kilgore Seed Company, FL
A 69   Miller-Bowie County Farmers Assn., TX
A 80   Piedmont Plant Company, GA
A 82   Porter & Son, TX
A 87   Ripley's Believe It or Not Seed Catalog, CT
A 90   SPB Sales, TX
A 93   Seedway, Inc., NY
A 100 Stokes Seed Company, NY
A 104 Tomato Growers Supply Company, FL
A 104 The Tomato Seed Company, Inc., NJ
A 114 Willhite Seed Co., TX

TOPIARY, PLANTED
A 91   Sandy Mush Herb Nursery, NC

TREES, FLOWERING
See also specific plants
A 5   Appalachian Gardens, PA
A 6   B & B Laboratories, WA
A 6   B & T Associates, En
A 8   Beaver Creek Nursery, TN
A 8   Beaverlodge Nursery, AB
A 11   The Bovees Nursery, OR
A 12   Joseph Brown, Native Seeds, VA
A 16   Camellia Forest Nursery, NC
A 17   Carroll Gardens, MD
A 17   Carter Seeds, CA
A 18   Chadwell Himalayan Seed, En
A 19   Chiltern Seeds, En
A 22   Copacabana Gardens, CA
A 29   Emlong Nurseries, MI
A 30   Exotica Rare Fruit Nursery, CA
A 32   Henry Field Seed & Nursery Co., IA
A 33   Flickingers' Nursery, PA
A 38   Golden Bough Tree Farm, ON
A 39   Gossler Farms Nursery, OR
A 45   Heritage Gardens, IA

TREES, FLOWERING
A 48   Hortico, Inc., ON
A 52   Jackson & Perkins Co., OR
A 54   Kelly Nurseries, NY
A 57   P. Kohli & Co., In
A 57   V. Kraus Nurseries, Ltd., ON
A 59   Lawson's Nursery, GA
A 59   Lawyer Nursery, Inc., MT
A 63   Louisiana Nursery, LA
A 67   Mellinger's, Inc., OH
A 70   Mt. Leo Nursery, TN
A 73   Nindethana Seed Service, Au
A 77   Owen Farms, TN
A 78   Pacific Tree Farms, CA
A 81   Plant World, TN
A 89   Roslyn Nursery, NY
A 92   F. W. Schumacher Co., MA
A 94   Sheffield's Seed Co., NY
A 99   Spring Hill Nurseries Co., IL
A 99   Stark Bro's Nurseries & Orchards Co., MO
A 107 Twombly Nursery, CT
A 107 Valley Nursery, MT
A 110 Wayside Gardens, SC
A 112 Westgate Garden Nursery, CA
B 43   Winterthur Museum & Gardens, DE
A 115 Womack's Nursery Co., TX
A 115 Woodlanders, Inc., SC
A 117 Yucca Do Nursery, TX

TREES, FOLIAGE
See also specific plants
A 5   Appalachian Gardens, PA
A 7   The Banana Tree, PA
A 8   Vernon Barnes & Son Nursery, TN
A 16   Callahan Seeds, OR
A 16   Camellia Forest Nursery, NC
A 17   Carter Seeds, CA
A 17   Cascade Forestry Nursery, IA
A 20   Clargreen Gardens, Ltd., ON
A 20   Coenosium Gardens, OR
A 29   Emlong Nurseries, MI
A 31   Farmer Seed & Nursery, MN
A 57   V. Kraus Nurseries, Ltd., ON
A 64   McConnell Nurseries, Inc., ON
A 69   J. E. Miller Nurseries, Inc., NY
A 70   Morden Nurseries, Ltd., MB
A 70   Mt. Leo Nursery, TN
A 71   Musser Forests Inc., PA
A 77   Owen Farms, TN
A 84   Raintree Nursery, WA
A 90   Salter Tree Farm, FL
A 92   F. W. Schumacher Co., MA
A 94   Sheffield's Seed Co., NY
A 112 Whitman Farms, OR
A 117 Yucca Do Nursery, TX

TREES, SEEDLING
See also specific plants
A 7   Barber Nursery, OR
A 17   Carino Nurseries, PA
A 17   Cascade Forestry Nursery, IA
A 21   Cold Stream Farm, MI
A 30   Ernst Crownvetch Farms, PA
A 33   Flickingers' Nursery, PA
A 38   Girard Nurseries, OH
A 45   Heronswood Nursery, WA
A 58   Lamtree Farm, NC
A 59   Lawyer Nursery, Inc., MT
A 71   Musser Forests Inc., PA
A 75   Oikos Tree Crops, MI
(continued next page)

PAGE SOURCE

TREES, SEEDLING (continued)
A 77   Owen Farms, TN
A 81   Plants of the Wild, WA
A 84   Qualitree Nursery, OR
A 96   Silvaseed Company, Inc., WA
A 112   Whitman Farms, OR

TREES, SMALL GARDEN
A 5   Appalachian Gardens, PA
A 8   Beaver Creek Nursery, TN
A 12   Broken Arrow Nursery, CT
A 17   Carroll Gardens, MD
A 41   Greer Gardens, OR
A 45   Heronswood Nursery, WA
A 58   Lakeshore Tree Farms, Ltd., SK
A 65   Maple Leaf Nursery, CA
A 67   Mellinger's, Inc., OH
A 74   Northwoods Nursery, OR
A 77   Owen Farms, TN
A 81   Plant World, TN
A 89   Roslyn Nursery, NY
A 90   Salter Tree Farm, FL
A 91   Savage Farms Nursery, TN
A 93   The Seed Source, NC
A 96   Skyline Nursery, WA
A 107   Valley Nursery, MT
A 110   Wavecrest Nursery & Landscaping Co., MI
A 113   Wildflower Nursery, NC
A 115   Woodlanders, Inc., SC

TRILLIUMS
A 6   Avon Bulbs, En
A 8   Beersheba Wildflower Garden, TN
A 19   Paul Christian -- Rare Plants, Wa
A 24   Cruickshank's, Inc., ON
A 37   Gardens of the Blue Ridge, NC
A 40   The Greenery, WA
A 56   Kline Nursery Co., OR
A 113   Wildflower Nursery, NC
A 113   The Wildflower Source, IL
A 113   Wildginger Woodlands, NY

TULIPS
A 3   Jacques Amand, Ltd., En
A 7   Bakker of Holland, MO
A 11   Breck's, IL
A 12   Broadleigh Gardens, En
A 12   Brooksfield Farm, WA
A 13   Bundles of Bulbs, MD
A 25   The Daffodil Mart, VA
A 26   Peter De Jager Bulb Co., MA
A 28   Dutch Gardens, Inc., NJ
A 28   Early's Farm & Garden Centre, Inc., SK
A 37   Gardenimport, Inc., ON
A 63   McClure & Zimmerman, WI
A 64   Mad River Imports, VT
A 67   Messelaar Bulb Co., MA
A 84   Quality Dutch Bulbs, NJ
A 91   John Scheepers, Inc., NY
A 107   Van Bourgondien Bros., Inc., NY
A 108   Van Engelen, Inc., CT
A 108   Mary Mattison van Schaik, VT
A 108   Vandenberg, NY
A 108   Veldheer Tulip Gardens, MI
A 110   Wayside Gardens, SC

VEGETABLE PLANTS
A 12   Brown's Omaha Plant Farms, Inc., TX
B 28   The Natural Gardening Company, CA
A 80   Piedmont Plant Company, GA

PAGE SOURCE

VEGETABLE PLANTS
A 99   Steele Plant Company, TN

VEGETABLES - WIDE ASSORTMENT
See also specific vegetables
A 1   Abundant Life Seed Foundation, WA
A 2   Allen, Sterling & Lothrop, ME
A 14   W. Atlee Burpee Company, PA
A 14   D. V. Burrell Seed Growers Co., CO
A 14   Butterbrooke Farm, CT
A 21   Comstock, Ferre & Co., CT
A 24   Crosman Seed Corp., NY
A 26   Dan's Garden Shop, MD
A 27   DeGiorgi Seed Company, NE
A 27   Dominion Seed House, ON
A 28   Early's Farm & Garden Centre, Inc., SK
A 31   Farmer Seed & Nursery, MN
A 31   Fedco Seeds, ME
A 32   Henry Field Seed & Nursery Co., IA
A 37   Gardenimport, Inc., ON
A 41   Gurney Seed & Nursery Co., SD
B 19   Harmony Farm Supply, CA
A 43   Harris Seeds, NY
A 43   Hastings, GA
A 49   Ed Hume Seeds, Inc., WA
A 51   Island Seed Mail Order, BC
A 52   Johnny's Selected Seeds, ME
A 53   Jordan Seeds, MN
A 53   J. W. Jung Seed Co., WI
A 56   Kings Herb Seeds, Au
A 58   Lagomarsino Seeds, CA
A 58   D. Landreth Seed Company, MD
A 60   Le Champion Heritage Seeds, CA
A 60   Orol Ledden & Sons, NJ
A 61   Liberty Seed Company, OH
A 62   Lockhart Seeds, CA
A 64   McFayden Seeds, MB
A 67   Earl May Seed & Nursery Co., IA
A 68   Meyer Seed Co., MD
A 69   Miller-Bowie County Farmers Assn., TX
A 70   Mountain Valley Seeds & Nursery, UT
A 72   Nichols Garden Nursery, Inc., OR
A 73   Northplan/Mountain Seed, ID
A 75   Ontario Seed Company, Ltd., ON
A 78   Park Seed Company, Inc., SC
A 79   Peace Seeds, OR
A 80   Piedmont Plant Company, GA
A 80   Pinetree Garden Seeds, ME
A 82   Pony Creek Nursery, WI
A 82   Porter & Son, TX
A 85   Rawlinson Garden Seed, NS
A 86   Redwood City Seed Co., CA
A 89   Roswell Seed Co., NM
A 90   SPB Sales, TX
A 91   Sanctuary Seeds/Folklore Herb Co., Ltd., BC
A 92   Seed Centre, Ltd., AB
A 93   Seeds Blum, ID
A 93   Seedway, Inc., NY
A 95   Shepherd's Garden Seeds, CA
A 95   R. H. Shumway Seedsman, SC
A 95   Siegers Seed Co., MI
A 100   Stokes Seed Company, NY
A 103   Thompson & Morgan, NJ
A 105   Tregunno Seeds, ON
A 106   Otis Twilley Seed Co., PA
A 108   Vermont Bean Seed Co., VT
A 114   Willhite Seed Co., TX
A 116   Wyatt-Quarles Seed Co., NC

PAGE SOURCE

VEGETABLES, EUROPEAN
See also specific vegetables
A 22   The Cook's Garden, VT
A 25   William Dam Seeds, ON
A 35   Fox Hollow Herbs, PA
A 44   Heirloom Seeds, PA
A 44   Herb Gathering, Inc., MO
A 46   High Altitude Gardens, ID
A 72   Nichols Garden Nursery, Inc., OR
A 80   Pinetree Garden Seeds, ME
A 86   Redwood City Seed Co., CA
A 95   Shepherd's Garden Seeds, CA

VEGETABLES, GIANT
A 27   Howard W. Dill, NS
A 31   Farmer Seed & Nursery, MN
A 87   Ripley's Believe It or Not Seed Catalog, CT

VEGETABLES, HEIRLOOM
See also specific vegetables
A 1   Abundant Life Seed Foundation, WA
A 3   Alta Seeds, CA
A 11   Bountiful Gardens, CA
A 14   Butterbrooke Farm, CT
A 22   The Cook's Garden, VT
A 31   F W H Seed Exchange, CA
A 33   Floating Mountain Seeds, WA
A 35   Fox Hollow Herbs, PA
A 39   Good Seed Co., WA
A 44   Heirloom Garden Project, NY
A 44   Heirloom Seeds, PA
A 45   Heymaqua Seed Service, CA
A 46   High Altitude Gardens, ID
A 52   The Thomas Jefferson Center, VA
A 58   D. Landreth Seed Company, MD
A 60   Le Champion Heritage Seeds, CA
A 71   Native Seeds/SEARCH, AZ
A 78   Paul's Premium Seeds, CA
A 79   Peace Seeds, OR
A 86   Redwood City Seed Co., CA
A 88   Ronniger's Seed Potatoes, ID
A 93   Seed Saving Project, CA
A 95   R. H. Shumway Seedsman, SC
A 98   Southern Exposure Seed Exchange, VA

VEGETABLES, HYBRID
See also specific vegetables
A 3   Alta Seeds, CA
A 6   Archias' Seed Store, MO
A 14   W. Atlee Burpee Company, PA
A 22   The Cook's Garden, VT
A 43   Harris Seeds, NY
A 50   Intermountain Seeds, ID
A 55   Kilgore Seed Company, FL
A 62   Lockhart Seeds, CA
A 80   Piedmont Plant Company, GA
A 95   Siegers Seed Co., MI
A 106 Otis Twilley Seed Co., PA

VEGETABLES, LATIN AMERICAN
A 48   Horticultural Enterprises, TX
A 98   Southern Seeds, FL

VEGETABLES, MINIATURE
A 2   Alberta Nurseries & Seed Company, AB
A 95   Shepherd's Garden Seeds, CA

VEGETABLES, NATIVE AMERICAN
A 39   Good Seed Co., WA
A 71   Native Seeds/SEARCH, AZ

VEGETABLES, NATIVE AMERICAN
A 81   Plants of the Southwest, NM
A 86   Redwood City Seed Co., CA
A 102 Talavaya Seeds, NM

VEGETABLES, OPEN-POLLINATED
See also specific vegetables
A 1   Abundant Life Seed Foundation, WA
A 3   Alta Seeds, CA
A 11   Bountiful Gardens, CA
A 14   Butterbrooke Farm, CT
A 33   Floating Mountain Seeds, WA
A 36   Garden City Seeds, MT
A 39   Good Seed Co., WA
A 43   Harris Seeds, NY
A 44   Heirloom Seeds, PA
A 45   Heymaqua Seed Service, CA
A 46   High Altitude Gardens, ID
A 49   J. L. Hudson, Seedsman, CA
A 55   Kilgore Seed Company, FL
A 58   D. Landreth Seed Company, MD
A 60   Le Champion Heritage Seeds, CA
A 61   Liberty Seed Company, OH
A 62   Lockhart Seeds, CA
A 70   Mountain Valley Seeds & Nursery, UT
A 71   Native Seeds/SEARCH, AZ
A 77   Ozark National Seed Order, NY
A 78   Paul's Premium Seeds, CA
A 79   Peace Seeds, OR
A 80   Piedmont Plant Company, GA
A 86   Redwood City Seed Co., CA
A 91   Sanctuary Seeds/Folklore Herb Co., Ltd., BC
A 93   Seed Saving Project, CA
A 93   Seeds Blum, ID
A 95   R. H. Shumway Seedsman, SC
A 95   Siegers Seed Co., MI
A 98   Southern Exposure Seed Exchange, VA
A 98   Southern Seeds, FL
A 102 Talavaya Seeds, NM
A 103 Territorial Seed Company, OR
A 112 Westwind Seeds, AZ

VEGETABLES, ORIENTAL
A 25   Dacha Barinka, BC
A 25   William Dam Seeds, ON
A 30   Evergreen Y. H. Enterprises, CA
A 39   Good Seed Co., WA
A 53   Jordan Seeds, MN
A 56   Kings Herb Seeds, Au
A 56   Kitazawa Seed Co., CA
A 62   Lockhart Seeds, CA
A 72   Nichols Garden Nursery, Inc., OR
A 80   Piedmont Plant Company, GA
A 80   Pinetree Garden Seeds, ME
A 98   Southern Seeds, FL
A 100 Stokes Seed Company, NY
A 101 Sunrise Oriental Seed Co., CT
A 106 Tsang & Ma, CA
A 108 Vermont Bean Seed Co., VT

VEGETABLES, ORNAMENTAL
A 2   Alfrey -- Peter Pepper Seeds, TN
A 22   The Cook's Garden, VT
A 95   Shepherd's Garden Seeds, CA
A 109 Vesey's Seeds, Ltd., PE

VEGETABLES, PATIO-SIZED PLANTS
A 25   William Dam Seeds, ON
A 78   Park Seed Company, Inc., SC
A 80   Piedmont Plant Company, GA

PAGE SOURCE

VEGETABLES, SALAD
A 22   The Cook's Garden, VT
A 31   Fedco Seeds, ME
A 39   Good Seed Co., WA
A 43   Harris Seeds, NY
A 44   Heirloom Seeds, PA
A 44   Herb Gathering, Inc., MO
A 45   Heymaqua Seed Service, CA
A 46   High Altitude Gardens, ID
A 58   D. Landreth Seed Company, MD
A 60   Le Champion Heritage Seeds, CA
A 80   Piedmont Plant Company, GA
A 95   Shepherd's Garden Seeds, CA
A 108   Vermont Bean Seed Co., VT
A 112   Westwind Seeds, AZ

VEGETABLES, SHORT-SEASON
See also specific vegetables
A 2   Alberta Nurseries & Seed Company, AB
A 2   Allen, Sterling & Lothrop, ME
A 3   Alta Seeds, CA
A 14   D. V. Burrell Seed Growers Co., CO
A 14   Butterbrooke Farm, CT
A 25   William Dam Seeds, ON
A 31   Fedco Seeds, ME
A 46   High Altitude Gardens, ID
A 49   Ed Hume Seeds, Inc., WA
A 50   Intermountain Seeds, ID
A 52   Johnny's Selected Seeds, ME
A 58   D. Landreth Seed Company, MD
A 70   Mountain Valley Seeds & Nursery, UT
A 73   Northplan/Mountain Seed, ID
A 78   Paul's Premium Seeds, CA
A 85   Rawlinson Garden Seed, NS
A 92   Seed Centre, Ltd., AB
A 93   Seeds Blum, ID
A 100   Stokes Seed Company, NY
A 102   T & T Seeds, Ltd., MB
A 103   Territorial Seed Company, OR
A 109   Vesey's Seeds, Ltd., PE
A 112   Westwind Seeds, AZ

VENUS FLY TRAP
A 9   Black Copper Kits, NJ
A 17   Carolina Exotic Gardens, NC
A 60   Lee's Botanical Gardens, FL
A 66   Marston Exotics, En
A 79   Peter Pauls Nurseries, NY

VERONICAS
A 33   Flora Favours, WI
A 53   Joyce's Garden, OR
A 102   Surry Gardens, ME

VIBURNUMS
A 5   Appalachian Gardens, PA
A 8   Beaver Creek Nursery, TN
A 11   The Bovees Nursery, OR
A 16   Camellia Forest Nursery, NC
A 17   Carroll Gardens, MD
A 21   Colvos Creek Nursery & Landscaping, WA
A 44   Heard Gardens, Ltd., IA
A 45   Heronswood Nursery, WA
A 66   Mary's Plant Farm, OH
A 92   F. W. Schumacher Co., MA
A 94   Shady Oaks Nursery, MN
A 94   Sheffield's Seed Co., NY
A 97   Smith Nursery Co., IA
A 107   Twombly Nursery, CT

PAGE SOURCE

VINCAS
A 33   Flickingers' Nursery, PA
A 38   Gilson Gardens, OH
A 79   Peekskill Nurseries, NY
A 83   Prentiss Court Ground Covers, SC
A 106   Turnipseed Nursery Farms, GA

VINES
See also specific plants
A 20   Clifford's Perennial & Vine, WI
A 21   Conley's Garden Center, ME
A 35   The Fragrant Path, NE
A 38   Gilson Gardens, OH
A 54   Kartuz Greenhouses, CA
A 57   P. Kohli & Co., In
A 62   Little Valley Farm, WI
A 62   Logee's Greenhouses, CT
A 63   Louisiana Nursery, LA
A 67   Merry Gardens, ME
A 82   The Plumeria People, TX
A 97   Smith Nursery Co., IA
A 99   Stallings Exotic Nursery, CA
A 99   Arthur H. Steffen, Inc., NY
A 106   Tripple Brook Farm, MA
A 115   Woodlanders, Inc., SC

VIOLAS
A 10   Bluestone Perennials, OH
A 16   Canyon Creek Nursery, CA
A 18   Richard G. M. Cawthorne, En
A 21   Conley's Garden Center, ME
A 31   Far North Gardens, MI
A 37   Gardens of the Blue Ridge, NC
A 43   Hauser's Superior View Farm, WI
A 52   Klaus R. Jelitto, We
A 57   L. Kreeger, En
A 58   Lamb Nurseries, WA
A 69   Montrose Nursery, NC
A 72   Nature's Garden Nursery, OR
A 75   Orchid Gardens, MN
A 105   Trans Pacific Nursery, OR
A 113   Wildginger Woodlands, NY
A 115   Winter Greenhouse, WI

VRIESEAS
A 47   Holladay Jungle, CA
A 94   Shelldance Nursery, CA

WALNUTS
A 7   Barber Nursery, OR
A 8   Bear Creek Nursery, WA
A 14   Burnt Ridge Nursery, WA
A 29   Emlong Nurseries, MI
A 32   Fernald's Hickory Hill Nursery, IL
A 35   Fowler Nurseries, Inc., CA
A 37   Louis Gerardi Nursery, IL
A 39   John H. Gordon, Jr., Grower, NY
A 41   Grimo Nut Nursery, ON
A 68   Meta Horticultural Labs, KY
A 73   Nolin River Nut Tree Nursery, KY
A 90   Saginaw Valley Nut Nursery, MI
A 90   St. Lawrence Nurseries, NY
A 97   Somers' Greenhaven Farm Nursery, MI
A 99   Stark Bro's Nurseries & Orchards Co., MO
A 114   Wiley's Nut Grove, OH
A 115   Windy Ridge Nursery, AB

WATER LILIES
A 10   Bonsai of Georgia, GA
A 20   City Gardens, MI
(continued next page)

PAGE SOURCE

WATER LILIES (continued)
A 55 Kester's Wild Game Food Nurseries, WI
A 61 Lilypons Water Gardens, MD
A 66 Maryland Aquatic Nurseries, MD
A 70 Moore Water Gardens, ON
A 78 Paradise Water Gardens, MA
A 79 Perry's Water Gardens, NC
A 91 Santa Barbara Water Gardens, CA
A 91 S. Scherer & Sons, NY
A 96 Slocum Water Gardens, FL
A 103 Tilley's Nursery/The WaterWorks, PA
A 105 William Tricker, Inc., OH
A 108 Van Ness Water Gardens, CA
A 110 Water Ways Nursery, VA
A 110 Waterford Gardens, NJ
A 112 Wicklein's Aquatic Farm & Nursery, Inc., MD

WATERMELONS
A 3 Alston Seed Growers, NC
A 14 D. V. Burrell Seed Growers Co., CO
A 53 Jordan Seeds, MN
A 55 Kilgore Seed Company, FL
A 60 Le Champion Heritage Seeds, CA
A 61 Liberty Seed Company, OH
A 69 Miller-Bowie County Farmers Assn., TX
A 82 Porter & Son, TX
A 89 Roswell Seed Co., NM
A 90 SPB Sales, TX
A 106 Otis Twilley Seed Co., PA
A 114 Willhite Seed Co., TX

WATERMELONS, GIANT
A 114 Willhite Seed Co., TX

WILD RICE
A 55 Kester's Wild Game Food Nurseries, WI

WILDFLOWERS
See specific plants
See specific regions

WILDFLOWERS, AUSTRALIAN
A 14 Bushland Flora (Australian Seed Specialists), Au
A 50 International Seed Supplies, Au
A 73 Nindethana Seed Service, Au
A 77 D. Orriell -- Seed Exporters, Au
A 96 Anthony J. Skittone, CA

WILDFLOWERS, BRITISH
A 18 John Chambers, En
A 113 Wild Seeds, Wa

WILDFLOWERS, CALIFORNIAN
A 45 Heymaqua Seed Service, CA
A 59 Larner Seeds, CA
A 59 Las Pilitas Nursery, CA
A 70 Moon Mountain Wildflowers, CA
A 79 Theodore Payne Foundation, CA
A 87 Clyde Robin Seed Co., CA
A 88 Robinett Bulb Farm, CA
A 107 Twin Peaks Seeds, CA
A 113 Wildflower Seed Company, CA
A 114 Wildwood Nursery, CA

WILDFLOWERS, HIMALAYAN
A 57 P. Kohli & Co., In

WILDFLOWERS, JAPAN
A 2 Albiflora, Inc., Ja

WILDFLOWERS, MANY REGIONS
A 11 Botanic Garden Company, NY
A 11 Botanicals, MA
A 16 Camelot North, MN
A 17 Carter Seeds, CA
A 18 John Chambers, En
A 28 Donaroma's Nursery, MA
A 28 E & H Products, CA
A 39 Goodwin Creek Gardens, OR
A 41 Grianan Gardens, CA
A 42 Halcyon Gardens, PA
A 50 Indigo Knoll Perennials, MD
A 53 Johnson Seed Company, CA
A 61 Life-Form Replicators, MI
A 62 Lofts Seed, Inc., NJ
A 70 Moon Mountain Wildflowers, CA
A 71 Native Seeds, Inc., MD
A 72 Nature's Garden Nursery, OR
A 72 Niche Gardens, NC
A 79 Peaceful Valley Farm Supply, CA
A 83 The Primrose Path, PA
A 87 Clyde Robin Seed Co., CA
A 93 Seeds Blum, ID
A 96 Siskiyou Rare Plant Nursery, OR
A 108 Vermont Wildflower Farm, VT
A 111 We-Du Nurseries, NC
A 113 Wildflower Seed Company, CA
A 113 Wildseed, Inc., TX

WILDFLOWERS, MIDWESTERN U.S.
A 10 Boehlke's Woodland Gardens, WI
A 21 Companion Plants, OH
A 29 Englerth Gardens, MI
A 33 Flowerland, NE
A 47 Holland Wildflower Farm, AR
A 50 Indigo Knoll Perennials, MD
A 58 LaFayette Home Nursery, Inc., IL
A 59 Landscape Alternatives, Inc., MN
A 70 Moon Mountain Wildflowers, CA
A 75 Orchid Gardens, MN
A 83 Prairie Moon Nursery, MN
A 83 Prairie Ridge Nursery/CRM Ecosystems, Inc., WI
A 88 Rocknoll Nursery, OH
A 100 Stock Seed Farms, Inc., NE
A 108 Vermont Wildflower Farm, VT
A 113 Wildflower Seed Company, CA
A 113 The Wildflower Source, IL
A 113 Wildseed, Inc., TX

WILDFLOWERS, NEW ZEALAND
A 98 Southern Seeds, Ne

WILDFLOWERS, NORTH AMERICAN
A 4 Amenity Plant Products, PA
A 11 Botanic Garden Company, NY
A 12 Brookside Wildflowers, NC
A 12 Joseph Brown, Native Seeds, VA
A 24 Crosman Seed Corp., NY
A 34 Forestfarm, OR
A 47 Holland Wildflower Farm, AR
A 49 J. L. Hudson, Seedsman, CA
A 49 Huronview Nurseries & Garden Centre, ON
A 50 Indigo Knoll Perennials, MD
A 55 Kester's Wild Game Food Nurseries, WI
A 61 Linn Farm Perennials, VA
A 66 Mary's Plant Farm, OH
A 70 Moon Mountain Wildflowers, CA
A 71 Native Gardens, TN
A 71 Native Seeds, Inc., MD
A 71 Natural Gardens, TN

(continued next page)

PAGE SOURCE

WILDFLOWERS, NORTH AMERICAN (continued)
A 94   Shady Oaks Nursery, MN
A 101   Sunlight Gardens, TN
A 107   Van Bourgondien Bros., Inc., NY
A 108   Vermont Wildflower Farm, VT

WILDFLOWERS, NORTHEASTERN U.S.
A 2   Allen, Sterling & Lothrop, ME
A 21   Conley's Garden Center, ME
A 22   Cooper's Garden, MN
A 43   Harris Seeds, NY
A 50   Indigo Knoll Perennials, MD
A 52   Johnny's Selected Seeds, ME
A 59   Landscape Alternatives, Inc., MN
A 70   Moon Mountain Wildflowers, CA
A 71   Native Seeds, Inc., MD
A 71   Natural Gardens, TN
A 75   Oakridge Nurseries, NH
A 84   Putney Nursery, Inc., VT
A 87   Clyde Robin Seed Co., CA
A 101   Sunlight Gardens, TN
A 108   Vermont Wildflower Farm, VT
A 109   Vesey's Seeds, Ltd., PE
A 110   Wyrttun Ward, MA
A 113   Wildflower Seed Company, CA
A 113   The Wildflower Source, IL
A 113   Wildginger Woodlands, NY
A 113   Wildseed, Inc., TX

WILDFLOWERS, NORTHWESTERN U.S.
A 1   Abundant Life Seed Foundation, WA
A 36   Frosty Hollow Nursery, WA
A 49   Ed Hume Seeds, Inc., WA
A 56   Kline Nursery Co., OR
A 57   L. Kreeger, En
A 59   Larner Seeds, CA
A 70   Moon Mountain Wildflowers, CA
A 73   Northplan/Mountain Seed, ID
A 87   Clyde Robin Seed Co., CA
A 88   Robinett Bulb Farm, CA
A 96   Skyline Nursery, WA
A 98   Southwestern Native Seeds, AZ
A 108   Vermont Wildflower Farm, VT
A 113   Wildflower Seed Company, CA
A 113   Wildseed, Inc., TX

WILDFLOWERS, PRAIRIE
A 40   Green Horizons, TX
A 47   Holland Wildflower Farm, AR
A 50   Indigo Knoll Perennials, MD
A 58   LaFayette Home Nursery, Inc., IL
A 62   Little Valley Farm, WI
A 70   Moon Mountain Wildflowers, CA
A 71   Native Seeds, Inc., MD
A 83   Prairie Moon Nursery, MN
A 83   Prairie Nursery, WI
A 83   Prairie Ridge Nursery/CRM Ecosystems, Inc., WI
A 83   Prairie Seed Source, WI
A 108   Vermont Wildflower Farm, VT
A 113   Wildflower Seed Company, CA
A 113   Wildseed, Inc., TX

WILDFLOWERS, ROCKY MOUNTAIN
A 46   High Altitude Gardens, ID
A 57   L. Kreeger, En
A 73   Northplan/Mountain Seed, ID
A 81   Plants of the Southwest, NM
A 97   Solar Green, Ltd., ID
A 98   Southwestern Native Seeds, AZ
A 108   Vermont Wildflower Farm, VT

PAGE SOURCE

WILDFLOWERS, ROCKY MOUNTAIN
A 113   Wildseed, Inc., TX

WILDFLOWERS, SOUTH AFRICAN
A 9   Bio-Quest International, CA
A 90   Rust-En-Vrede Nursery, So
A 96   Anthony J. Skittone, CA

WILDFLOWERS, SOUTHEASTERN U.S.
A 8   Vernon Barnes & Son Nursery, TN
A 8   Beersheba Wildflower Garden, TN
A 17   Carolina Exotic Gardens, NC
A 34   Flowerplace Plant Farm, MS
A 37   Gardens of the Blue Ridge, NC
A 43   Hastings, GA
A 47   Holland Wildflower Farm, AR
A 71   Native Gardens, TN
A 71   Natural Gardens, TN
A 72   Niche Gardens, NC
A 87   Clyde Robin Seed Co., CA
A 101   Sunlight Gardens, TN
A 108   Vermont Wildflower Farm, VT
A 109   Andre Viette Farm & Nursery, VA
A 111   We-Du Nurseries, NC
A 113   Wildflower Nursery, NC
A 113   Wildflower Seed Company, CA
A 113   Wildseed, Inc., TX
A 113   The Wildwood Flower, NC
A 115   Woodlanders, Inc., SC

WILDFLOWERS, SOUTHWESTERN U.S.
A 8   Bernardo Beach Native Plant Farm, NM
A 25   The Nursery at the Dallas Nature Center, TX
A 40   Green Horizons, TX
A 63   The Lowrey Nursery, TX
A 69   Miller Grass Seed Company, TX
A 81   Plants of the Southwest, NM
A 87   Clyde Robin Seed Co., CA
A 98   Southwestern Native Seeds, AZ
A 108   Vermont Wildflower Farm, VT

WILDLIFE FOOD PLANTS
A 4   Amenity Plant Products, PA
A 8   Bernardo Beach Native Plant Farm, NM
A 17   Carino Nurseries, PA
A 17   Cascade Forestry Nursery, IA
A 23   Country Wetlands Nursery, WI
A 24   Cross Seed Company, KS
A 34   Forestfarm, OR
A 36   Garden of Delights, FL
A 38   Glendale Enterprises, FL
A 55   Kester's Wild Game Food Nurseries, WI
A 59   Landscape Alternatives, Inc., MN
A 59   Larner Seeds, CA
A 59   Lawyer Nursery, Inc., MT
A 61   Life-Form Replicators, MI
A 62   Little Valley Farm, WI
A 63   The Lowrey Nursery, TX
A 71   Native Seed Foundation, ID
A 71   Natural Gardens, TN
A 72   Niche Gardens, NC
A 73   Northplan/Mountain Seed, ID
A 74   Northwoods Nursery, OR
A 79   Theodore Payne Foundation, CA
A 81   Plants of the Wild, WA
A 83   Prairie Ridge Nursery/CRM Ecosystems, Inc., WI
A 95   R. H. Shumway Seedsman, SC
A 98   Southmeadow Fruit Gardens, MI
A 106   Tripple Brook Farm, MA
A 106   Turner Seed Company, TX
(continued next page)

PAGE SOURCE

WILDLIFE FOOD PLANTS (continued)
A 113   Wildlife Nurseries, WI

WOODLAND PLANTS
See also Shade Plants
A 7   Bamboo Sourcery, CA
A 10   Boehlke's Woodland Gardens, WI
A 11   The Bovees Nursery, OR
A 12   Broken Arrow Nursery, CT
A 12   Brookside Wildflowers, NC
A 16   Canyon Creek Nursery, CA
A 18   Chadwell Himalayan Seed, En
A 29   Eastern Plant Specialties, ME
A 31   Fancy Fronds, WA
A 31   Far North Gardens, MI
A 33   Flora Favours, WI
A 34   Foliage Gardens, WA
A 36   Frosty Hollow Nursery, WA
A 37   Gardens of the Blue Ridge, NC
A 39   Russell Graham, Purveyor of Plants, OR
A 47   Holland Wildflower Farm, AR
A 56   Kimberly Garden on Oregon Hill, NY
A 56   Klehm Nursery, IL
A 56   Kline Nursery Co., OR
A 59   Landscape Alternatives, Inc., MN
A 59   Larner Seeds, CA
A 62   Little Valley Farm, WI
A 71   Natural Gardens, TN
A 72   Nature's Garden Nursery, OR
A 72   Niche Gardens, NC
A 75   Orchid Gardens, MN
A 79   Theodore Payne Foundation, CA
A 79   Peter Pauls Nurseries, NY
A 80   Piedmont Gardens, CT
A 81   Plants of the Wild, WA
A 83   Prairie Moon Nursery, MN
A 83   Prairie Ridge Nursery/CRM Ecosystems, Inc., WI
A 87   Rice Creek Gardens, MN
A 94   Sevenoaks Nursery, OR
A 94   Shady Oaks Nursery, MN
A 96   Siskiyou Rare Plant Nursery, OR
A 100   Stoecklein's Nursery, PA
A 101   Sunlight Gardens, TN
A 103   Thompson & Morgan, NJ
A 108   Vandenberg, NY
A 110   Wyrttun Ward, MA
A 111   We-Du Nurseries, NC
A 113   Wild Seeds, Wa
A 113   Wildflower Nursery, NC
A 113   The Wildflower Source, IL
A 113   Wildginger Woodlands, NY
A 113   The Wildwood Flower, NC
A 114   Wildwood Nursery, CA

YAM PLANTS
A 58   Lagomarsino Seeds, CA
A 99   Steele Plant Company, TN

YEWS
A 35   Foxborough Nursery, Inc., MD
A 71   Musser Forests Inc., PA

YUCCAS
A 5   Apacha Cactus, CA
A 6   Aztekakti/Desertland Nursery, TX
A 15   The Cactus Patch, KS
A 21   Colvos Creek Nursery & Landscaping, WA
A 50   International Seed Supplies, Au
A 59   Las Pilitas Nursery, CA
A 67   Mesa Garden, NM

PAGE SOURCE

YUCCAS
A 72   Neon Palm Nursery, CA
A 117   Yucca Do Nursery, TX

ZELKOVAS
A 35   Foxborough Nursery, Inc., MD

© Old Farm Nursery
Artist: Larry D. Schlichenmeyer

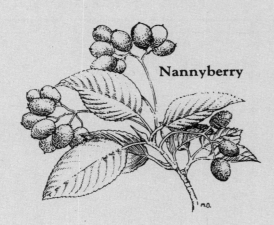

Nannyberry

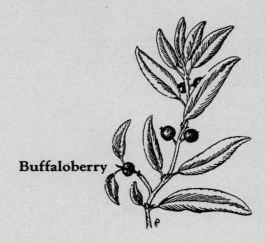

Buffaloberry

Bog Cranberry

Sand Cherry

Lingonberry

Edible Honeysuckle

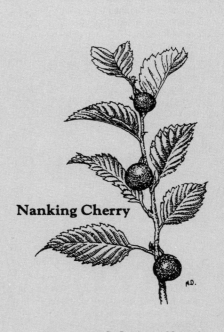

Nanking Cherry

Pixwell Gooseberry

© St. Lawrence Nurseries
Artist: Michael DiGiorgio

PAGE	CITY/ZIP	⌂ NURSERY ▼ GARDEN		SOURCE

ALABAMA

A 109	Auburn, 36830	⌂	▼	Village Arbors
A 86	Birmingham, 35206	⌂	▼	Steve Ray's Bamboo Gardens
A 65	Chunchula, 36521	⌂	▼	Magnolia Nursery & Display Garden
A 64	Dothan, 36303	⌂	▼	Ma-Dot-Cha Hobby Nursery
A 37	Killen, 35645	⌂		Garden of the Enchanted Rainbow

ALBERTA, CANADA

A 2	Bowden, T0M 0K0	⌂		Alberta Nurseries & Seed Company
A 50	Coaldale, T0K 0L0	⌂		Inland African Violets
A 92	Edmonton, T5L 4K1	⌂		Seed Centre, Ltd.
A 115	Hythe, T0H 2C0	⌂	▼	Windy Ridge Nursery

ARIZONA

A 29	Chino Valley, 86323	⌂	▼	Earthstar Herb Gardens
A 19	Coolidge, 85228	⌂	▼	Christa's Cactus
A 95	Phoenix, 85051	⌂	▼	Shepard Iris Garden
A 106	Prescott, 86303		▼	21st Century Gardens
A 71	Tucson, 85719	⌂	▼	Native Seeds/SEARCH
A 98	Tucson, 85703			Southwestern Native Seeds
A 112	Tucson, 85719			Westwind Seeds

ARKANSAS

A 22	Augusta, 72006			Cooley's Strawberry Nursery
A 15	Batesville, 72501	⌂		Cactus Gem Nursery
A 14	Benton, 72015	⌂	▼	Burk's Nursery
A 47	Elkins, 72727	⌂	▼	Holland Wildflower Farm
A 4	Fayetteville, 72703			Ames' Orchard and Nursery
A 30	Fouke, 71837	⌂		Enoch's Berry Farm
A 35	Little Rock, 72205	⌂	▼	Fox Orchids, Inc.
A 10	Mountainburg, 72946			Boston Mountain Nurseries
A 79	Mountainburg, 72946			Pense Nursery
A 46	Pettigrew, 72752	⌂	▼	Highlander Nursery

AUSTRALIA

A 36	Dorroughby, 2480			Fruit Spirit Botanical Gardens
A 80	Everton Hills, 4053			Pine Heights Nursery
A 56	Glenbrook, NSW, 2773			Kings Herb Seeds
A 14	Hillarys, 6025	⌂		Bushland Flora (Australian Seed Specialists)
A 98	Jolimont, Victoria, 3002	⌂		Specialty Seeds
A 77	Mt. Yokine, WA, 6060	⌂		D. Orriell -- Seed Exporters
A 50	Nowra, NSW, 2541			International Seed Supplies
A 73	Woogenilup, 6324	⌂		Nindethana Seed Service

BRITISH COLUMBIA, CANADA

A 111	Aldergrove, V0X 1A0	⌂		Western Biologicals, Ltd.
A 88	Burnaby, V5J 2L8	⌂	▼	Grace Rollerson
A 25	Chilliwack, V2P 3T2			Dacha Barinka
A 61	Langley, V3A 7N6	⌂	▼	Lindel Lilies
A 106	Merville, V0R 2M0	⌂	▼	Tsolum River Fruit Trees
A 92	Osoyoos, V0H 1V0			Sedona Gardens
A 3	Surrey, V3S 4N8	⌂		Alpenflora Gardens
A 90	Vancouver, V6M 2N2			Saltspring Primroses
A 91	Vancouver, V6K 1P1	⌂		Sanctuary Seeds/Folklore Herb Co., Ltd.
A 111	Vancouver, V5R 3C1	⌂	▼	West Coast Violets
A 69	Vernon, V1T 7Z3			Monashee Gardens
A 14	Victoria, V8X 3X4		▼	The Butchart Gardens
A 51	Victoria, V8X 3X8			Island Seed Mail Order
A 19	West Vancouver, V7V 3P2	⌂		Charles Island Gardens

PAGE	CITY/ZIP	⌂ NURSERY	▼ GARDEN	SOURCE
CALIFORNIA				
A 74	Altadena, 91003	⌂		Nuccio's Nurseries
A 30	Anaheim, 92817			Evergreen Y. H. Enterprises
A 116	Arroyo Grande, 93420	⌂	▼	Young's Mesa Nursery
A 69	Atascadero, 93423			Mohns, Inc.
A 15	Bakersfield, 93312	⌂	▼	Cactus by Mueller
A 85	Berkeley, 94704			Rare Seed Locator Network
A 114	Berkeley, 94708			Nancy Wilson Species & Miniature Narcissus
A 28	Bermuda Dunes, 92201			E & H Products
A 73	Bodega, 94922			North Coast Rhododendron Nursery
A 59	Bolinas, 94924	⌂	▼	Larner Seeds
A 62	Bolinas, 94924	⌂		Living Tree Centre
A 104	Calpella, 95418	⌂	▼	Tradewinds Nursery
A 78	Campbell, 95009	⌂	▼	Pacific Coast Hybridizers
A 19	Carlotta, 95528			Choice Edibles
A 9	Carlsbad, 92009	⌂	▼	Bird Rock Tropicals
A 1	Carpinteria, 90313	⌂	▼	Abbey Gardens
A 76	Carpinteria, 93013	⌂	▼	Orchids Royale
A 100	Carpinteria, 93013	⌂	▼	Stewart Orchids, Inc.
A 87	Castro Valley, 94546	⌂		Clyde Robin Seed Co.
A 50	Chula Vista, 92012	⌂		Hurov's Tropical Seeds
A 78	Chula Vista, 92010	⌂	▼	Pacific Tree Farms
A 104	Chula Vista, 92010	⌂	▼	Tiny Petals Nursery
A 114	Claremont, 91711	⌂	▼	Wildwood Nursery
A 56	Clements, 95227	⌂	▼	King's Mums
A 76	Coarsegold, 93614	⌂	▼	Orchid Species Specialties
A 43	Coulterville, 95311	⌂	▼	Havasu Hills Herbs
A 93	Davis, 95616			Seed Saving Project
A 88	Diamond Springs, 95619	⌂	▼	Rose Acres
A 99	Encinitas, 92024	⌂	▼	Stallings Exotic Nursery
A 107	Eureka, 95501			Twin Peaks Seeds
A 112	Eureka, 95501	⌂	▼	Westgate Garden Nursery
A 85	Fallbrook, 92028	⌂	▼	Rancho Nuez Nursery
A 95	Felton, 95018	⌂	▼	Shepherd's Garden Seeds
A 4	Fort Bragg, 95437	⌂	▼	Annabelle's Fuchsia Garden
A 68	Fountain Valley, 92708	⌂	▼	Roger & Shirley Meyer
A 60	Freedom, 95019			Le Champion Heritage Seeds
A 16	Fremont, 94536			California Nursery Co.
A 34	Fremont, 94539	⌂		Four Winds Growers
A 44	Fresno, 93722	⌂	▼	Henrietta's Nursery
A 47	Fresno, 93711	⌂	▼	Hill 'n dale
A 47	Fresno, 93755	⌂	▼	Holladay Jungle
A 45	Ft. Bragg, 95437		▼	Heritage Rose Gardens
A 106	Ft. Bragg, 95437			Trillium Lane Nursery
A 54	Galt, 95632	⌂		K & L Cactus Nursery
A 40	Garberville, 95440	⌂	▼	Greenmantle Nursery
A 45	Garberville, 95440			Heymaqua Seed Service
A 84	Gardena, 90249	⌂	▼	Rainforest Flora, Inc.
A 116	Gilroy, 95020	⌂	▼	Wright Iris Nursery
A 4	Grass Valley, 95945	⌂		The Angraecum House
A 79	Grass Valley, 95945	⌂		Peaceful Valley Farm Supply
A 111	Grass Valley, 95945	⌂		Weiss Brothers Nursery
A 44	Guerneville, 95446			Heirloom Garden Seeds
A 97	Healdsburg, 95448	⌂		Sonoma Antique Apple Nursery
A 90	Igo, 96047	⌂	▼	Jim & Irene Russ Quality Plants
A 71	Inverness, 94937		▼	Mushroompeople
A 87	La Conchita, 93001	⌂	▼	Richardson's Seaside Banana Garden
A 49	La Honda, 94020	⌂	▼	Hummingbird Gardens
A 64	Lemon Grove, 92045	⌂	▼	McDaniel's Miniature Roses
A 109	Lincoln, 95648	⌂	▼	Violets Collectible
A 110	Lincoln, 95648			Wapumne Native Plant Nursery
A 34	Livermore, 94550	⌂	▼	Fordyce Orchids
A 15	Lodi, 95242	⌂	▼	Cactus by Dodie
A 24	Los Angeles, 90041	⌂		Cycad Gardens
A 100	Los Angeles, 90048			Succulenta
A 109	Los Angeles, 90064			Vireya Specialties Nursery
A 76	Los Osos, 93402	⌂	▼	The Orchid House
A 117	Malibu, 90265	⌂		Zuma Canyon Orchids
A 94	Marina, 93933	⌂	▼	Shein's Cactus

(continued next page)

PAGE	CITY/ZIP	⌂ NURSERY ▼ GARDEN	SOURCE

CALIFORNIA (continued)

PAGE	CITY/ZIP	Nursery	Garden	SOURCE
A 31	McKinleyville, 95521	⌂		Fairyland Begonia & Lily Garden
A 38	Moorpark, 93021			Golden Lake Greenhouses
A 22	Moraga, 94556	⌂	▼	Copacabana Gardens
A 92	Morgan Hill, 95037	⌂	▼	Schulz Cactus Gardens
A 70	Morro Bay, 93442	⌂	▼	Moon Mountain Wildflowers
A 35	Newcastle, 95658	⌂	▼	Fowler Nurseries, Inc.
A 49	North Hollywood, 91607	⌂	▼	Spencer M. Howard Orchid Imports
A 116	North Hollywood, 91601	⌂	▼	Guy Wrinkle Exotic Plants
A 54	Northridge, 91324	⌂		KSA Jojoba
A 96	Northridge, 91325	⌂	▼	Singers' Growing Things
A 57	Ojai, 93023			Kusa Research Foundation
A 23	Orange, 92669	⌂	▼	Country Bloomers Nursery
A 16	Oroville, 95965	⌂		Canyon Creek Nursery
A 94	Pacifica, 94044	⌂		Shelldance Nursery
A 31	Pauma Valley, 92061			F W H Seed Exchange
A 82	Penngrove, 94951			Portable Acres
A 65	Placerville, 95667	⌂		Maple Leaf Nursery
A 40	Pomona, 91766	⌂		Greenlee Nursery
A 3	Potrero, 92063			Alta Seeds
A 70	Potter Valley, 95469	⌂	▼	Moonshine Gardens
A 84	Ramona, 92065	⌂	▼	Ramona Gardens
A 42	Rancho Cordova, 95670	⌂		Robert B. Hamm
A 67	Redding, 96001	⌂	▼	Maxim's Greenwood Gardens
A 87	Redlands, 92373	⌂	▼	Rhapis Palm Growers
A 49	Redwood City, 94064			J. L. Hudson, Seedsman
A 86	Redwood City, 94064			Redwood City Seed Co.
A 106	Redwood City, 94063			Tsang & Ma
A 5	Redwood Valley, 95470	⌂	▼	Apacha Cactus
A 81	Reseda, 91335	⌂		The Plant Shop's Botanical Gardens
A 32	Roseville, 95678	⌂	▼	Fiddyment Farms
A 58	Sacramento, 95824	⌂		Lagomarsino Seeds
A 68	Sacramento, 95828	⌂	▼	Mighty Minis
A 88	Sacramento, 95829	⌂	▼	Roris Gardens
A 36	Salinas, 93907			G & G Gardens and Growers
A 78	San Diego, 92137			Paul's Premium Seeds
A 5	San Francisco, 94117	⌂		Arbor & Espalier
A 41	San Francisco, 94114			Grianan Gardens
A 96	San Francisco, 94132	⌂		Anthony J. Skittone
A 101	San Gabriel, 91775			Sunnyslope Gardens
A 66	San Jose, 95125	⌂	▼	Maryott's Gardens
A 100	San Jose, 95133	⌂	▼	Stocking Rose Nursery
A 90	San Luis Obispo, 93401	⌂	▼	SLO Gardens
A 22	San Marcos, 92069	⌂	▼	Cordon Bleu Farms
A 116	San Rafael, 94903	⌂	▼	Yesterday's Rose
A 54	Sanger, 93657			Kelly's Plant World
A 66	Santa Ana, 92705	⌂		Marilynn's Garden
A 9	Santa Barbara, 93150	⌂		Bio-Quest International
A 91	Santa Barbara, 93111	⌂	▼	Santa Barbara Orchid Estate
A 91	Santa Barbara, 93140	⌂	▼	Santa Barbara Water Gardens
A 56	Santa Clara, 95051			Kitazawa Seed Co.
A 5	Santa Cruz, 95062	⌂	▼	Antonelli Brothers, Inc.
A 8	Santa Cruz, 95060			Bay View Gardens
A 59	Santa Margarita, 93453	⌂	▼	Las Pilitas Nursery
A 1	Santa Rosa, 95403			Adagent Acres
A 3	Santa Rosa, 95404	⌂	▼	Alpine Valley Gardens
A 72	Santa Rosa, 95407	⌂		Neon Palm Nursery
A 97	Santa Rosa, 95403			Sonoma Grapevines
A 7	Sebastopol, 95472	⌂	▼	A Bamboo Shoot
A 7	Sebastopol, 95472	⌂	▼	Bamboo Sourcery
A 69	Sebastopol, 95472	⌂	▼	Miniature Plant Kingdom
A 88	Sebastopol, 95473			Robinett Bulb Farm
A 92	Selma, 93662			Scotty's Desert Plants
A 117	Solvang, 93463	⌂	▼	Zaca Vista Nursery
A 30	Soquel, 95076	⌂	▼	John Ewing Orchids, Inc.
A 64	South San Francisco, 94080	⌂	▼	Rod McLellan Co.
A 113	St. Helena, 94574			Wildflower Seed Company
A 55	Stockton, 95208	⌂	▼	Keith Keppel
A 62	Stockton, 95201	⌂		Lockhart Seeds

(continued next page)

PAGE	CITY/ZIP	⌂ NURSERY ▼ GARDEN	SOURCE
CALIFORNIA (continued)			
A 102	Studio City, 91604	⌂ ▼	Sunswept Laboratories
A 79	Sun Valley, 91352	⌂ ▼	Theodore Payne Foundation
A 29	Tustin, 92681		Endangered Species
A 108	Upland, 91786	⌂ ▼	Van Ness Water Gardens
A 98	Ventura, 93004	⌂	South Seas Nursery
A 93	Visalia, 93277	⌂ ▼	Sequoia Nursery -- Moore Miniature Roses
A 17	Vista, 92083	⌂	Carter Seeds
A 30	Vista, 92083	⌂ ▼	Exotica Rare Fruit Nursery
A 36	Vista, 92084	⌂ ▼	G & B Orchid Lab & Nursery
A 41	Vista, 92084	⌂ ▼	Grigsby Cactus Gardens
A 54	Vista, 92083	⌂ ▼	Kartuz Greenhouses
A 78	Vista, 92084		The PanTree
A 84	Vista, 92084	⌂ ▼	Rainbow Gardens Nursery & Bookshop
A 102	Vista, 92084	⌂	Taylor's Herb Gardens
A 82	Walnut Creek, 94596	⌂	Pollen Bank
A 27	Watsonville, 95076	⌂ ▼	Desert Theatre
A 89	Watsonville, 95076	⌂ ▼	Roses of Yesterday & Today
A 90	Watsonville, 95077	⌂	S & H Organic Acres
A 112	Westley, 95387	⌂ ▼	Westside Exotics Palm Nursery
A 41	Whittier, 90601	⌂ ▼	Greenwood Daylily Gardens
A 11	Willits, 95490	⌂ ▼	Bountiful Gardens
A 22	Wilton, 95693	⌂ ▼	Cottage Gardens
A 53	Woodacre, 94973		Johnson Seed Company
A 80	Yorba Linda, 92686	⌂ ▼	Pixie Treasures Miniature Rose Nursery
A 27	Yountville, 94599		Delegeane Garlic Farms
COLORADO			
A 114	Aspen, 81612		Wilton's Organic Seed Potatoes
A 21	Avon, 81620	⌂	Colorado Alpines, Inc.
A 63	Boulder, 80306	⌂ ▼	Long's Gardens
A 46	Denver, 80209	⌂ ▼	High Country Rosarium
A 86	Denver, 80221		Recor Tree Seed
A 109	Englewood, 80110	⌂	The Violet Showcase
A 75	Golden, 80403	⌂ ▼	Old Farm Nursery
A 14	Rocky Ford, 81067		D. V. Burrell Seed Growers Co.
CONNECTICUT			
A 62	Danielson, 06239	⌂ ▼	Logee's Greenhouses
A 13	Eastford, 06242	⌂ ▼	Buell's Greenhouse, Inc.
A 51	Easton, 06612	⌂ ▼	J & L Orchids
A 101	Elmwood, 06110		Sunrise Oriental Seed Co.
A 12	Gaylordsville, 06755	⌂ ▼	Lee Bristol Nursery
A 12	Hamden, 06518	⌂ ▼	Broken Arrow Nursery
A 108	Litchfield, 06759		Van Engelen, Inc.
A 112	Litchfield, 06759	⌂ ▼	White Flower Farm
A 107	Monroe, 06468	⌂ ▼	Twombly Nursery
A 14	Oxford, 06483	⌂ ▼	Butterbrooke Farm
A 18	Oxford, 06483	⌂ ▼	Catnip Acres Herb Nursery
A 59	Salisbury, 06068	⌂ ▼	Lauray of Salisbury
A 94	Stamford, 06903	⌂	Shanti Bithi Nursery
A 60	Storrs, 06268	⌂	Ledgecrest Greenhouses
A 93	Union, 06076	⌂ ▼	Select Seeds
A 80	Waterbury, 06706	⌂ ▼	Piedmont Gardens
A 87	Westport, 06880		Ripley's Believe It or Not Seed Catalog
A 21	Wethersfield, 06109	⌂ ▼	Comstock, Ferre & Co.
ENGLAND			
A 57	Ashtead, Surrey, KT21 1NN		L. Kreeger
A 11	Aylesbury, Bucks., HP22 4QB	⌂ ▼	S & N Brackley
A 98	Bedford, MK42 8ND	⌂ ▼	Southwest Seeds
A 103	Benenden, Kent, TN17 4LB		Tile Barn Nursery
A 6	Bradford-on-Avon, BA15 2AT		Avon Bulbs
A 6	Bridgewater, Somerset, TA5 1JE		B & T Associates
A 9	Bristol, BS18 4JL	⌂	Blackmore & Langdon
A 82	Caistor, Lincs., LN7 6HX		Potterton & Martin
A 50	Chatham, Kent, ME5 9QT	⌂	Brenda Hyatt
A 9	East Grinstead, R19 4LE		Birch Farm Nursery
A 3	Hassocks, W. Sussex, BN6 9NB	⌂	Allwood Bros.

(continued next page)

PAGE	CITY/ZIP	⌂ NURSERY ▼ GARDEN	SOURCE
ENGLAND (continued)			
A 102	Isles of Scilly, TR21 0JY	⌂ ▼	A. P. & E. V. Tabraham
A 18	Kettering, Northants, NN15 5AJ	⌂	John Chambers
A 116	King's Lynn, Norfolk, PE33 0QH	⌂	Roy Young, Seedsman
A 6	Kingswinford, W.Mid., DY6 0AE		Ashwood Nurseries
A 66	Madley, Hereford, HR1 9LX	⌂ ▼	Marston Exotics
A 104	Newton Abbot, Devon,		Torbay's Plant World
A 18	Slough, Berks., SL3 8BE		Chadwell Himalayan Seed
A 3	Stanmore, Middlesex, HA7 3JS		Jacques Amand, Ltd.
A 18	Swanley, Kent, BR8 7NU		Richard G. M. Cawthorne
A 12	Taunton, Somerset, TA4 1AE		Broadleigh Gardens
A 19	Ulverston, Cumbria, LA12 7PB		Chiltern Seeds
FLORIDA			
A 19	Alachua, 32615	⌂ ▼	Chestnut Hill Nursery, Inc.
A 26	Alachua, 32615	⌂ ▼	Daylily Discounters
A 7	Apopka, 32712		BDK Nursery
A 115	Archer, 32618		Tom Wood, Nurseryman
A 21	Auburndale, 33823		Color Farm Growers
A 2	Boynton Beach, 33435	⌂ ▼	Alberts & Merkel Bros., Inc.
A 13	Brandon, 33511		John Brudy Exotics
A 40	Crystal River, 32629	⌂	Greenleaf Orchids
A 38	DeFuniak Springs, 32433	⌂	Glendale Enterprises
A 51	Delray Beach, 33446	⌂ ▼	J. E. M. Orchids
A 64	Eustis, 32726	⌂	McCrory's Sunny Hill Herb Farm
A 104	Fort Myers, 33902		Tomato Growers Supply Company
A 114	Gainesville, 32605	⌂	Wimberlyway Gardens
A 102	Green Cove Springs, 32043	⌂ ▼	Dave Talbott Nursery
A 32	Gulf Hammock, 32639	⌂	The Fig Tree Nursery
A 36	Hollywood, 33020	⌂ ▼	Garden of Delights
A 31	Homestead, 33031	⌂ ▼	Fennell's Orchid Jungle
A 33	Homestead, 33032	⌂ ▼	Florida Colors Nursery
A 60	Homestead, 33031	⌂	W. O. Lessard Nursery
A 34	Jacksonville, 32225	⌂ ▼	Fort Caroline Orchids
A 79	Largo, 34643		The Pepper Gal
A 97	Loxahatchee, 33470	⌂	South Florida Seed Supply
A 90	Madison, 32340	⌂ ▼	Salter Tree Farm
A 98	Melbourne, 32902		Southern Seeds
A 44	Miami, 33186	⌂ ▼	Heliconia Haus
A 48	Miami, 33173	⌂ ▼	Jerry Horne -- Rare Plants
A 53	Miami, 33187	⌂ ▼	Jones & Scully
A 60	Miami, 33184	⌂ ▼	Lee's Botanical Gardens
A 61	Miami, 33173	⌂ ▼	Limrick, Inc.
A 68	Miami, 33170	⌂ ▼	Miami Orchids
A 77	Miami, 33187	⌂ ▼	Orgel's Orchids
A 78	Miami, 33155	⌂ ▼	Palms for Tropical Landscaping
A 82	Miami, 33187	⌂ ▼	Possum Trot Tropical Fruit Nursery
A 86	Oneco, 34264	⌂	Reasoner's, Inc.
A 40	Palm Harbor, 34682		The Green Escape
A 101	Port Richey, 34673	⌂ ▼	Sunshine State Tropicals
A 26	Sanford, 32772	⌂ ▼	Daylily World
A 55	Sanford, 32771	⌂	Kilgore Seed Company
A 15	Sebring, 33871	⌂ ▼	Caladium World
A 101	Sebring, 33871		Sunshine Caladium Farms
A 33	Tavernier, 33070		Florida Keys Native Nursery, Inc.
A 51	Weirsdale, 32195	⌂	Ivies of the World
A 63	West Palm Beach, 33415		Paul P. Lowe
A 65	Windemere, 34786	⌂	Ann Mann's Orchids
A 96	Winter Haven, 33880	⌂ ▼	Slocum Water Gardens
GEORGIA			
A 80	Albany, 31703		Piedmont Plant Company
A 10	Atlanta, 30341	⌂ ▼	Bonsai of Georgia
A 43	Atlanta, 30310		Hastings
A 59	Ball Ground, 30107	⌂ ▼	Lawson's Nursery
A 80	Bishop, 30621	⌂ ▼	Piccadilly Farm
A 51	Brooks, 30205	⌂ ▼	Ison's Nursery
A 29	Decatur, 30031	⌂ ▼	Eco-Gardens
A 52	Ellijay, 30540	⌂ ▼	Johnson Nursery

(continued next page)

PAGE	CITY/ZIP	⌂ NURSERY	▼ GARDEN	SOURCE
GEORGIA (continued)				
A 106	Fayetteville, 30214			Turnipseed Nursery Farms
A 81	Gainesville, 30501	⌂	▼	Plant City Bonsai
A 77	Gay, 30218	⌂		Owen's Vineyard & Nursery
A 40	Griffin, 30223			Greenlife Gardens Greenhouses
A 105	Lavonia, 30553	⌂	▼	Transplant Nursery
A 43	Lawrenceville, 30245			James Harris Hybrid Azaleas
A 105	Ochlochnee, 31773	⌂		Travis' Violets
A 110	Omega, 31775			Mary Walker Bulb Company
A 116	Royston, 30662			Woody's Liriope Farm
A 103	Thomasville, 31799	⌂	▼	Thomasville Nurseries
A 107	TyTy, 31795	⌂	▼	TyTy Plantation
A 107	TyTy, 31795	⌂		TyTy South Orchards
A 54	Valdosta, 31601	⌂	▼	Karleens Achimenes
A 53	Watkinsville, 30677			Justice Gardens
HAWAII				
A 31	Haiku, Maui, 96708	⌂	▼	Farnsworth Orchids
A 67	Hilo, 96720			Mauna Kea Orchids
A 20	Honokaa, 96727	⌂	▼	Cloud Forest Orchids
A 30	Honolulu, 96816	⌂		Exotics Hawaii, Ltd.
A 54	Honolulu, 96816	⌂	▼	Kawamoto Orchid Nursery
A 84	Honolulu, 96814	⌂	▼	Rainforest Plantes et Fleurs, Inc.
A 40	Kaaawa, 96730	⌂	▼	Green Plant Research
A 106	Kailua, 96734			Tropicals Unlimited
A 114	Kaneohe, 96744	⌂	▼	Wilk Orchid Specialties
A 111	Pahoa, 96778	⌂	▼	Ken West Orchids
IDAHO				
A 93	Boise, 83706			Seeds Blum
A 46	Ketchum, 83340	⌂	▼	High Altitude Gardens
A 97	Moore, 83255			Solar Green, Ltd.
A 73	Moscow, 83843	⌂	▼	Northplan/Mountain Seed
A 71	Moyie Springs, 83845			Native Seed Foundation
A 88	Moyie Springs, 83845	⌂		Ronniger's Seed Potatoes
A 96	Moyie Springs, 83845			Silver Springs Nursery
A 50	Rexburg, 83440			Intermountain Seeds
ILLINOIS				
A 94	Batavia, 60510	⌂	▼	Shady Hill Gardens
A 81	Belleville, 62221	⌂	▼	Plant Villa
A 50	Champaign, 61820	⌂		Illinois Foundation Seeds, Inc.
A 5	Chapin, 62628			Applesource
A 74	Dundee, 60118	⌂	▼	Oak Hill Gardens
A 7	Elmhurst, 60126			Fred Bach Epiphyllums
A 95	Elmwood, 61529	⌂		Shissler Seed Company
A 113	Fox Lake, 60020			The Wildflower Source
A 99	Hamburg, 62045			Springvale Farm Nursery
A 56	Hampshire, 60193	⌂		Arnold J. Klehm Grower, Inc.
A 58	Lafayette, 61449			LaFayette Home Nursery, Inc.
A 32	Monmouth, 61462	⌂	▼	Fernald's Hickory Hill Nursery
A 37	O'Fallon, 62269	⌂		Louis Gerardi Nursery
A 11	Peoria, 61656			Breck's
A 99	Peoria, 61656			Spring Hill Nurseries Co.
A 13	Riverwoods, 60015			The Bulb Crate
A 9	San Jose, 62682			Blue Dahlia Gardens
A 56	South Barrington, 60010		▼	Klehm Nursery
A 60	Tremont, 61568			Lee's Gardens
A 83	Trilla, 62469	⌂		Prairie State Commodities
A 76	Villa Park, 60181	⌂	▼	Orchids by Hausermann, Inc.
INDIA				
A 57	Srinagar, Kashmir, 190009			P. Kohli & Co.
INDIANA				
A 26	Crawfordsville, 47933	⌂	▼	Davidson-Wilson Greenhouses
A 47	Evansville, 47711	⌂	▼	Holly Hills, Inc.
A 80	Floyds Knob, 47119	⌂	▼	Pinecliffe Daylily Gardens
A 1	Huntingburg, 47542	⌂	▼	Ahrens Nursery & Plant Labs

(continued next page)

PAGE	CITY/ZIP	♤ NURSERY ▼ GARDEN	SOURCE

INDIANA (continued)

A 57	Middlebury, 46540	♤ ▼	Krider Nurseries
A 88	New Salisbury, 47161	♤ ▼	Rocky Meadow Orchard & Nursery
A 69	Ossian, 46777	♤ ▼	Miller's Manor Gardens
A 20	Valparaiso, 46383	♤ ▼	Coburg Planting Fields
A 51	Winamac, 46996	♤ ▼	Iris Acres

IOWA

A 17	Cascade, 52033		Cascade Forestry Nursery
A 97	Charles City, 50616	♤	Smith Nursery Co.
A 33	Decorah, 52101		The Flower & Herb Exchange
A 87	Farmington, 52626	♤	Rider Nurseries
A 50	Hamburg, 51640		Inter-State Nurseries
A 44	Johnston, 50131	♤ ▼	Heard Gardens, Ltd.
A 45	Marshalltown, 50158	♤ ▼	Herbs-Liscious
A 32	Shenandoah, 51602		Henry Field Seed & Nursery Co.
A 45	Shenandoah, 51602		Heritage Gardens
A 67	Shenandoah, 51603	♤ ▼	Earl May Seed & Nursery Co.

JAPAN

| A 2 | Ichikawa, Chiba, 272-0 | | Albiflora, Inc. |

KANSAS

A 24	Bunker Hill, 67626	♤ ▼	Cross Seed Company
A 49	Burlington, 66839	♤ ▼	Huff's Garden Mums
A 22	Lyons, 67554	♤	Cook's Geranium Nursery
A 15	Radium, 67550	♤ ▼	The Cactus Patch
A 39	Salina, 67401		The Grain Exchange
A 23	Sedgwick, 67135	♤ ▼	Country Cottage
A 64	Wichita, 67207	♤	McKinney's Glasshouse

KENTUCKY

A 96	Danville, 40422		Sleepy Hollow Herb Farm
A 25	Louisville, 40222		Dabney Herbs
A 68	Meta, 41501	♤	Meta Horticultural Labs
A 80	Tomkinsville, 42167	♤ ▼	Pick's Ginseng
A 73	Upton, 42784	♤ ▼	Nolin River Nut Tree Nursery

LOUISIANA

A 3	Baton Rouge, 70821	♤	Amaryllis, Inc.
A 41	Baton Rouge, 70810	♤	Gulf Coast Plantsmen
A 40	Folsom, 70437	♤ ▼	Green Valley Orchids
A 19	Livingston, 70754		David Chopin Nursery
A 23	New Orleans, 70184	♤ ▼	Creole Orchids
A 63	Opelousas, 70570	♤	Louisiana Nursery
A 95	Sibley, 71073	♤	Sherwood's Greenhouses
A 52	Terrytown/Gretna, 70056	♤ ▼	Jeannette's Jesneriads

MAINE

A 52	Albion, 04910	♤ ▼	Johnny's Selected Seeds
A 21	Boothbay Harbor, 04538	♤ ▼	Conley's Garden Center
A 67	Camden, 04843	♤ ▼	Merry Gardens
A 107	East Lebanon, 04027	♤ ▼	Valente Gardens
A 2	Falmouth, 04105	♤	Allen, Sterling & Lothrop
A 29	Georgetown, 04548	♤ ▼	Eastern Plant Specialties
A 26	Litchfield, 04350	♤ ▼	Daystar
A 80	New Gloucester, 04260	♤	Pinetree Garden Seeds
A 34	North Yarmouth, 04021	♤ ▼	Forevergreen Farm
A 70	St. Francis, 04774		Moosebell Flower, Fruit & Tree Co.
A 102	Surry, 04684	♤ ▼	Surry Gardens
A 32	Vassalboro, 04989	♤ ▼	Fieldstone Gardens, Inc.
A 31	Waterville, 04901		Fedco Seeds

MANITOBA, CANADA

A 64	Brandon, R7A 6A6		McFayden Seeds
A 70	Morden, R0G 1J0	♤	Morden Nurseries, Ltd.
A 102	Winnepeg, R3C 3P6	♤	T & T Seeds, Ltd.
A 83	Winnipeg, R3R 0V2	♤ ▼	Prairie Orchid Company

PAGE	CITY/ZIP	⌂ NURSERY	▼ GARDEN	SOURCE
MARYLAND				
A 9	Baldwin, 21013	⌂	▼	Kurt Bluemel, Inc.
A 58	Baltimore, 21230	⌂		D. Landreth Seed Company
A 68	Baltimore, 21231			Meyer Seed Co.
A 112	Baltimore, 21234	⌂		Wicklein's Aquatic Farm & Nursery, Inc.
A 45	Brookville, 20833	⌂		Heritage Rosarium
A 24	Crownsville, 21032			Crownsville Nursery
A 71	Dayton, 21036			Native Seeds, Inc.
A 18	Easton, 21601	⌂		Catalpa Nursery
A 53	Edgewood, 21040	⌂	▼	Jungle Gems, Inc.
A 26	Frederick, 21701			Dan's Garden Shop
A 89	Galena, 21635	⌂	▼	Rosehill Farm
A 66	Jarrettsville, 21084	⌂	▼	Maryland Aquatic Nurseries
A 55	Kensington, 20895	⌂	▼	Kensington Orchids
A 112	Lanham, 20706			Frank B. White, Jr.
A 61	Lilypons, 21717	⌂	▼	Lilypons Water Gardens
A 50	Mt. Airy, 21771			Indigo Knoll Perennials
A 13	Owings Mills, 21117	⌂	▼	Bundles of Bulbs
A 10	Riderwood, 21139			Boordy Nursery
A 2	Salisbury, 21801	⌂		Allen Company
A 12	Salisbury, 21801	⌂		Brittingham Plant Farms
A 86	Salisbury, 21801			Rayner Bros.
A 35	Street, 21154	⌂	▼	Foxborough Nursery, Inc.
A 17	Westminster, 21157	⌂		Carroll Gardens
MASSACHUSETTS				
A 81	Agawam, 01001	⌂		Pleasant Valley Glads
A 43	Barre, 01005	⌂	▼	Hartman's Herb Farm
A 101	Barre, 01005	⌂		Sunshine Violets & Gesneriads
A 71	Cambridge, 02138			National Heirloom Flower Seed Exchange
A 92	Carlisle, 01741	⌂	▼	Seawright Gardens
A 11	East Sandwich, 02537	⌂	▼	Briarwood Gardens
A 28	Edgartown, 02539	⌂	▼	Donaroma's Nursery
A 16	Falmouth, 02540	⌂		Cape Cod Violetry
A 67	Ipswich, 01938	⌂		Messelaar Bulb Co.
A 110	Middleboro, 02346	⌂		Wyrttun Ward
A 38	Northfield, 01360	⌂	▼	Gladside Gardens
A 101	Reading, 01867			Sunnyvale Cactus Nursery
A 104	Rehoboth, 02769	⌂	▼	Tranquil Lake Nursery
A 23	Rowley, 01969	⌂	▼	Cricket Hill Herb Farm, Ltd.
A 73	Rowley, 01969	⌂	▼	Nor'East Miniature Roses
A 92	Sandwich, 02563	⌂		F. W. Schumacher Co.
A 74	South Deerfield, 01373	⌂	▼	Nourse Farms, Inc.
A 26	South Hamilton, 01982	⌂		Peter De Jager Bulb Co.
A 106	Southampton, 01073	⌂	▼	Tripple Brook Farm
A 1	Swansea, 02777	⌂	▼	A & P Orchids
A 88	Truro, 02666	⌂		Rock Spray Nursery
A 11	Wayland, 01778			Botanicals
A 78	Whitman, 02382			Paradise Water Gardens
A 2	Wilmington, 01887	⌂		Allgrove Farm, Inc.
MICHIGAN				
A 26	Bellevue, 49021	⌂		Corwin Davis Nursery
A 90	Birch Run, 48415			Saginaw Valley Nut Nursery
A 23	Chesaning, 48616	⌂	▼	Country View Gardens
A 13	Clifford, 48727	⌂		Elizabeth Buck African Violets
A 20	Detroit, 48234	⌂	▼	City Gardens
A 57	Dowagiac, 49047	⌂	▼	Krohne Plant Farms
A 110	Fennville, 49408	⌂		Wavecrest Nursery & Landscaping Co.
A 61	Fowlerville, 48836	⌂	▼	Life-Form Replicators
A 21	Free Soil, 49411	⌂		Cold Stream Farm
A 30	Galesburg, 49053	⌂	▼	Ensata Gardens
A 43	Grand Junction, 49056	⌂		Hartmann's Plantation, Inc.
A 108	Holland, 49424	⌂	▼	Veldheer Tulip Gardens
A 29	Hopkins, 49328	⌂	▼	Englerth Gardens
A 75	Kalamazoo, 49007	⌂	▼	Oikos Tree Crops
A 58	Lake Odessa, 48849	⌂	▼	Lake Odessa Greenhouse
A 41	Lakeside, 49116	⌂	▼	Grootendorst Nurseries
A 98	Lakeside, 49116	⌂		Southmeadow Fruit Gardens

(continued next page)

PAGE	CITY/ZIP	⌂ NURSERY ▼ GARDEN	SOURCE

MICHIGAN (continued)

PAGE	CITY/ZIP	⌂	▼	SOURCE
A 31	Livonia, 48154			Far North Gardens
A 66	Livonia, 48154	⌂	▼	Marvelous Minis
A 35	Parma, 49269	⌂	▼	Fox Hill Farm
A 97	Perrinton, 48871			Somers' Greenhaven Farm Nursery
A 27	South Haven, 49090	⌂		DeGrandchamp's Blueberry Farm
A 29	Stevensville, 49127	⌂	▼	Emlong Nurseries
A 86	Vulcan, 49892			Reath's Nursery
A 65	Ypsilanti, 48197	⌂		Makielski Berry Farm & Nursery
A 95	Zeeland, 49464	⌂		Siegers Seed Co.

MINNESOTA

PAGE	CITY/ZIP	⌂	▼	SOURCE
A 31	Albert Lea, 56007	⌂		Fairway Enterprises
A 111	Albert Lea, 56000			Wedge Nursery
A 75	Andover, 55304	⌂	▼	Orchid Gardens
A 14	Cokato, 55321	⌂	▼	Busse Gardens
A 91	Edina, 55435	⌂	▼	Savory's Gardens, Inc.
A 10	Faribault, 55021	⌂	▼	Borbeleta Gardens
A 31	Faribault, 55021	⌂		Farmer Seed & Nursery
A 104	Faribault, 55021			Tischler Peony Garden
A 4	Forest Lake, 55025	⌂	▼	Anderson Iris Gardens
A 66	Hastings, 55033	⌂	▼	Maroushek Gardens
A 28	Hutchinson, 55350	⌂		Dooley Gardens
A 73	Marine, 55047	⌂	▼	North Star Gardens
A 87	Minneapolis, 55432	⌂	▼	Rice Creek Gardens
A 100	Minneapolis, 55418	⌂		Succulent Plants
A 94	Northfield, 55057		▼	Shannon Gardens of Oak Brook Farm
A 116	Osseo, 55369			Worel's Iris Gardens
A 16	Pequot Lakes, 56472	⌂	▼	Camelot North
A 58	Princeton, 55371	⌂	▼	LBG Nursery
A 22	Roseville, 55113	⌂	▼	Cooper's Garden
A 11	St. Cloud, 56302			Brand Peony Farm
A 59	St. Paul, 55108	⌂	▼	Landscape Alternatives, Inc.
A 72	St. Paul, 55118		▼	The New Peony Farm
A 111	St. Paul, 55116			Wee Gems Minature Roses
A 3	Waconia, 55387	⌂	▼	Ambergate Gardens
A 94	Waseca, 56093			Shady Oaks Nursery
A 18	West St. Paul, 55118	⌂	▼	Cascade Daffodils
A 83	Winona, 55987	⌂	▼	Prairie Moon Nursery
A 53	Woodbury, 55125			Jordan Seeds

MISSISSIPPI

PAGE	CITY/ZIP	⌂	▼	SOURCE
A 87	Biloxi, 39532	⌂	▼	Riverbend Orchids
A 34	Meridian, 39304	⌂		Flowerplace Plant Farm
A 13	Olive Branch, 38654	⌂	▼	Brussel's Bonsai Nursery

MISSOURI

PAGE	CITY/ZIP	⌂	▼	SOURCE
A 1	California, 65018			Adamgrove
A 42	Deslet, 63601	⌂	▼	Hahn's Rainbow Iris Garden
A 21	Gower, 64454	⌂	▼	Comanche Acres Iris Gardens
A 4	Grain Valley, 64029			American Daylily & Perennials
A 27	Kansas City, 64161	⌂	▼	Don's Daylily Garden
A 44	Kansas City, 64110			Herb Gathering, Inc.
A 7	Louisiana, 63353			Bakker of Holland
A 99	Louisiana, 63353	⌂		Stark Bro's Nurseries & Orchards Co.
A 68	New Melle, 63365			Midwest Cactus
A 113	Sarcoxie, 64862	⌂	▼	Gilbert H. Wild & Son, Inc.
A 6	Sedalia, 65301			Archias' Seed Store
A 2	Waynesville, 65583	⌂		Alice's Violet Room

MONTANA

PAGE	CITY/ZIP	⌂	▼	SOURCE
A 51	Bozeman, 59715	⌂	▼	Iris Gardens
A 107	Helena, 59601	⌂	▼	Valley Nursery
A 3	Kalispell, 59901	⌂	▼	Alpen Gardens
A 63	Kalispell, 59901	⌂	▼	Lost Prairie Herb Farm
A 93	Mile City, 59301			The Seed Shop
A 59	Plains, 59859			Lawyer Nursery, Inc.
A 36	Victor, 59875			Garden City Seeds

PAGE	CITY/ZIP	△ NURSERY	▼ GARDEN	SOURCE
NEBRASKA				
A 55	Arlington, 68002	△	▼	Kent's Flowers
A 39	Bayard, 69334		▼	Grandview Iris Gardens
A 35	Ft. Calhoun, 68023			The Fragrant Path
A 46	Lexington, 68850	△	▼	Hildenbrandt's Iris Gardens
A 100	Murdock, 68407			Stock Seed Farms, Inc.
A 73	Norfolk, 68701	△		North Pine Iris Gardens
A 27	Omaha, 68104	△		DeGiorgi Seed Company
A 65	Ponca, 68770		▼	Maple Tree Gardens
A 37	Wayne, 68787	△	▼	Garden Perennials
A 99	Wisner, 68791	△	▼	Spruce Gardens
A 33	Wynot, 68792			Flowerland
NEW HAMPSHIRE				
A 75	East Kingston, 03872			Oakridge Nurseries
A 63	Nashua, 03062		▼	Lowe's own-root Roses
NEW JERSEY				
A 28	Adelphia, 07710			Dutch Gardens, Inc.
A 32	Bargaintown, 08221	△	▼	Fischer Greenhouses
A 62	Bound Brook, 08805			Lofts Seed, Inc.
A 81	Cinnaminson, 08077	△	▼	Plant Factory
A 32	Clarksboro, 08020			Fern Hill Farm
A 106	Franklinville, 08322	△	▼	Triple Oaks Nursery
A 101	Glassboro, 08028			Alex Summerville
A 84	Hillsdale, 07642			Quality Dutch Bulbs
A 103	Jackson, 08527	△		Thompson & Morgan
A 24	Marlboro, 07746	△	▼	The Cummins Garden
A 104	Metuchen, 08840			The Tomato Seed Company, Inc.
A 9	Pompton Lakes, 07442			Black Copper Kits
A 111	Port Murray, 07865	△	▼	Well-Sweep Herb Farm
A 110	Saddle River, 07458	△	▼	Waterford Gardens
A 60	Sewell, 08080	△	▼	Orol Ledden & Sons
A 47	Voorhees, 08043	△	▼	Hillhouse Nursery
NEW MEXICO				
A 67	Belen, 87002	△	▼	Mesa Garden
A 72	Belen, 87002	△	▼	New Mexico Cactus Research
A 82	Chaparral, 88021		▼	Pleasure Iris Gardens
A 27	Deming, 88030	△	▼	Desert Nursery
A 102	Espanola, 87532	△	▼	Talavaya Seeds
A 89	Roswell, 88202	△		Roswell Seed Co.
A 81	Santa Fe, 87501	△	▼	Plants of the Southwest
A 8	Veguita, 87062	△	▼	Bernardo Beach Native Plant Farm
NEW YORK				
A 23	Albany, 12210	△		The Cottage Herb Farm Shop
A 107	Babylon, 11702	△		Van Bourgondien Bros., Inc.
A 11	Brooklyn, 11201			Botanic Garden Company
A 100	Buffalo, 14240		▼	Stokes Seed Company
A 69	Canandaigua, 14424	△	▼	J. E. Miller Nurseries, Inc.
A 79	Canandaigua, 14424			Peter Pauls Nurseries
A 62	Cato, 13033	△	▼	Lloyd's African Violets
A 108	Chester, 10918	△		Vandenberg
A 54	Dansville, 14437	△	▼	Kelly Nurseries
A 89	Dix Hills, 11746	△	▼	Roslyn Nursery
A 63	Dolgeville, 13329	△	▼	Lyndon Lyon Greenhouses, Inc.
A 60	East Moriches, 11940	△		Henry Leuthardt Nurseries, Inc.
A 24	East Rochester, 14445	△		Crosman Seed Corp.
A 99	Fairport, 14450			Arthur H. Steffen, Inc.
A 34	Fredonia, 14063			Foster Nurseries
A 72	Geneva, 14456			New York State Fruit Testing Coop. Assn.
A 92	Glen Head, 11545	△	▼	Seagulls Landing Orchids
A 30	Greenlawn, 11740	△	▼	Evergreen Acres Dahlia Gardens
A 93	Hall, 14463	△		Seedway, Inc.
A 38	High Falls, 12440	△		Gloria Dei
A 97	Huntington, 11743			Smirnow's Son
A 9	Ithaca, 14850			Betsy's Brierpatch
A 44	Ithaca, 14853			Heirloom Garden Project

(continued next page)

PAGE	CITY/ZIP	⌂ NURSERY ▼ GARDEN	SOURCE
NEW YORK (continued)			
A 56	Lisle, 13797		Kimberly Garden on Oregon Hill
A 94	Locke, 13092	⌂	Sheffield's Seed Co.
A 91	Middletown, 10940		John Scheepers, Inc.
A 82	New Paltz, 12561		Plumtree Nursery
A 39	North Tonawanda, 14120	⌂ ▼	John H. Gordon, Jr., Grower
A 91	Northport, 11768	⌂ ▼	S. Scherer & Sons
A 90	Potsdam, 13676	⌂ ▼	St. Lawrence Nurseries
A 43	Rochester, 14606		Harris Seeds
A 91	Saratoga Springs, 12866	⌂ ▼	Saxton Gardens
A 72	Schenectady, 12309		E. B. Nauman, Nurseryman
A 34	Setauket, 11733	⌂ ▼	Floyd Cove Nursery
A 79	Shrub Oak, 10588		Peekskill Nurseries
A 10	Smithtown, 11787	⌂	The Bonsai Shop
A 17	South Salem, 10590	⌂	Carlson's Gardens
A 113	Webster, 14580		Wildginger Woodlands
A 9	Williamstown, 13493	⌂ ▼	Blue Star Lab
A 77	Woodstock, 12498		Ozark National Seed Order
NEW ZEALAND			
A 98	Canterbury, 8173	⌂ ▼	Southern Seeds
NEWFOUNDLAND, CANADA			
A 37	St. John's, A1C 5K8		Gaze Seed Company, Inc.
NO. IRELAND			
A 17	Ballymena, Co.Antrim, BT43 7HF		Carncairn Daffodils, Ltd.
NORTH CAROLINA			
A 32	Bailey, 27807		Finch Blueberry Nursery
A 12	Boone, 28607	⌂ ▼	Brookside Wildflowers
A 11	Brown Summit, 27214	⌂ ▼	Breckinridge Orchids
A 16	Chapel Hill, 27516	⌂ ▼	Camellia Forest Nursery
A 72	Chapel Hill, 27516	⌂ ▼	Niche Gardens
A 52	Dunn, 28334	⌂ ▼	Jernigan Gardens
A 28	Fairview, 28730	⌂ ▼	Donnelly's Nursery
A 103	Fairview, 28730	⌂ ▼	Tiki Nursery
A 47	Fletcher, 28732	⌂ ▼	Holbrook Farm & Nursery
A 79	Franklin, 28734	⌂ ▼	Perry's Water Gardens
A 116	Garner, 27529	⌂	Wyatt-Quarles Seed Co.
A 85	Godwin, 28344	⌂ ▼	Rasland Farm
A 17	Greenville, 27834		Carolina Exotic Gardens
A 4	Henderson, 27536	⌂	American Forest Foods Corp.
A 69	Hillsborough, 27278	⌂ ▼	Montrose Nursery
A 60	Kannapolis, 28081	⌂ ▼	Lenette Greenhouses
A 111	Kill Devil Hills, 27948		Chris Weeks Peppers
A 91	Leicester, 28748	⌂ ▼	Sandy Mush Herb Nursery
A 110	Leicester, 28748	⌂ ▼	Washington Evergreen Nursery
A 3	Littleton, 27850		Alston Seed Growers
A 111	Marion, 28752	⌂ ▼	We-Du Nurseries
A 113	Marshall, 28753	⌂ ▼	Wildflower Nursery
A 37	Pineola, 28662	⌂ ▼	Gardens of the Blue Ridge
A 77	Pisgah Forest, 28768	⌂ ▼	Owens Orchids
A 113	Pittsboro, 27312	⌂	The Wildwood Flower
A 83	Princeton, 27569	⌂ ▼	Powell's Gardens
A 61	Rocky Point, 28457	⌂	Lewis Strawberry Nursery
A 16	State Road, 28676	⌂	Cardinal Nursery
A 93	Tuckasegee, 28783		The Seed Source
A 58	Warrensville, 28693	⌂ ▼	Lamtree Farm
NOVA SCOTIA, CANADA			
A 85	Truro, B2N 2P6	⌂	Rawlinson Garden Seed
A 27	Windsor, B0N 2T0		Howard W. Dill
OHIO			
A 21	Athens, 45701	⌂ ▼	Companion Plants
A 8	Bedford, 44146		Bedford Dahlias
A 114	Chardon, 44024	⌂ ▼	Wildwood Gardens
A 48	Chesterland, 44026	⌂ ▼	Homestead Division of Sunnybrook Farms

(continued next page)

PAGE	CITY/ZIP	⌂ NURSERY ▼ GARDEN	SOURCE

OHIO (continued)

A 101	Chesterland, 44026	⌂ ▼	Sunnybrook Farms Nursery
A 70	Cincinnati, 45226		Mowbray Gardens
A 4	Dayton, 45402		American Bamboo Company
A 46	Gallipolis, 45631	⌂	Highland Succulents
A 38	Geneva, 44041	⌂ ▼	Girard Nurseries
A 66	Hamilton, 45013	⌂ ▼	Mary's Plant Farm
A 88	Hillsboro, 45133	⌂	Rocknoll Nursery
A 105	Independence, 44131	⌂ ▼	William Tricker, Inc.
A 10	Madison, 44057	⌂ ▼	Bluestone Perennials
A 114	Mansfield, 44907	⌂ ▼	Wiley's Nut Grove
A 4	Medina, 44258		Ameri-Hort Research
A 37	Mentor, 44061		Garden Place
A 61	New Philadelphia, 44663	⌂	Liberty Seed Company
A 67	North Lima, 44452	⌂ ▼	Mellinger's, Inc.
A 74	Novelty, 44072		Novelty Nurseries
A 47	Painesville, 44077	⌂	Historical Roses
A 38	Perry, 44081	⌂	Gilson Gardens
A 38	Stewart, 45778	⌂ ▼	Glasshouse Works
A 43	Stoutsville, 43154	⌂ ▼	Hatfield Gardens
A 28	Vincent, 45785	⌂ ▼	Dyke Bros. Nursery
A 89	Wauseon, 43567		Rupp Seeds, Inc.

OKLAHOMA

A 56	Lawton, 73506		Kinder Canna Farm
A 68	Oklahoma City, 73112	⌂ ▼	Mid-America Iris Gardens
A 22	Turpin, 73950	⌂	Corns

ONTARIO, CANADA

A 49	Bright's Grove, N0N 1C0	⌂ ▼	Huronview Nurseries & Garden Centre
A 57	Carlisle, L0R 1H0	⌂ ▼	V. Kraus Nurseries, Ltd.
A 25	Dundas, L9H 6M1	⌂ ▼	William Dam Seeds
A 27	Georgetown, L7G 4A2	⌂	Dominion Seed House
A 76	Glenburnie, K0H 1S0	⌂ ▼	Orchids for Everyone
A 87	Goodwood, L0C 1A0	⌂ ▼	Richters
A 105	Hamilton, L8R 1J4	⌂	Tregunno Seeds
A 55	Komoka, N0L 1R0	⌂ ▼	Kilworth Flowers
A 38	Marlbank, K0K 2L0		Golden Bough Tree Farm
A 9	Maynooth, K0L 2S0		Blueberry Hill
A 20	Mississauga, L5J 2Y4	⌂ ▼	Clargreen Gardens, Ltd.
A 41	Niagara on the Lake, L0S 1J0	⌂ ▼	Grimo Nut Nursery
A 73	Niagara-on-the-Lake, L0S 1J0	⌂ ▼	Northern Kiwi Nursery
A 64	Norwich, N0J 1P0	⌂ ▼	McMillen's Iris Garden
A 80	Pickering, L1V 1A6	⌂	Pickering Nurseries, Inc.
A 64	Port Burwell, N0J 1T0	⌂	McConnell Nurseries, Inc.
A 33	Port Stanley, N0L 2A0	⌂	Floridel Gardens
A 70	Port Stanley, N0L 2A0	⌂ ▼	Moore Water Gardens
A 100	St. Catharines, L2R 6R6		Stokes Seed Company
A 37	Thornhill, L3T 4A5	⌂	Gardenimport, Inc.
A 24	Toronto, M4P 2M1	⌂	Cruickshank's, Inc.
A 8	Trout Creek, P0H 2L0		Becker's Seed Potatoes
A 78	Virgil, L0S 1T0	⌂ ▼	Carl Pallek & Son Nursery
A 48	Waterdown, L0R 2H0		Hortico, Inc.
A 75	Waterloo, N2J 3Z9		Ontario Seed Company, Ltd.
A 76	Whitby, L1N 5R5	⌂ ▼	Orchid Haven

OREGON

A 72	Albany, 97321	⌂ ▼	Nichols Garden Nursery, Inc.
A 20	Aurora, 97002	⌂ ▼	Coenosium Gardens
A 72	Beaverton, 97007		Nature's Garden Nursery
A 77	Beaverton, 97007	⌂	Oregon Miniature Roses
A 53	Bend, 97701	⌂ ▼	Joyce's Garden
A 102	Canby, 97013	⌂ ▼	Swan Island Dahlias
A 16	Central Point, 97502	⌂	Callahan Seeds
A 63	Cloverdale, 97112	⌂ ▼	Loucks Nursery
A 10	Corbett, 97019	⌂ ▼	Bonnie Brae Gardens
A 77	Corbett, 97019	▼	Oregon Trail Daffodils
A 68	Corvallis, 97339		MicroCulture, Inc.
A 74	Corvallis, 97330		Northwest Mycological Consultants

(continued next page)

PAGE	CITY/ZIP	⌂ NURSERY	▼ GARDEN	SOURCE
OREGON (continued)				
A 79	Corvallis, 97333	⌂	▼	Peace Seeds
A 86	Corvallis, 97330	⌂		Redlo Cacti
A 94	Corvallis, 97330			Sevenoaks Nursery
A 17	Days Creek, 97429			Casa Yerba Gardens
A 42	Drain, 97435	⌂		Hall Rhododendrons
A 84	Eddyville, 97343	⌂	▼	Qualitree Nursery
A 99	Estacada, 97023	⌂	▼	Squaw Mountain Gardens
A 27	Eugene, 97404	⌂	▼	Del's Japanese Maples
A 41	Eugene, 97401	⌂	▼	Greer Gardens
A 48	Eugene, 97404	⌂		Hookland's Dahlias
A 28	Forest Grove, 97116	⌂	▼	Dutch Mill Herb Farm
A 33	Forest Grove, 97116	⌂	▼	Flora Lan Nursery
A 76	Grants Pass, 97527	⌂		Oregon Exotica Nursery
A 69	Hubbard, 97032		▼	Grant Mitsch Novelty Daffodils
A 18	Junction City, 97448			Chambers Nursery
A 56	Lake Oswego, 97035	⌂	▼	Kline Nursery Co.
A 65	Lake Oswego, 97470	⌂	▼	Maplewood Seed Company
A 103	Lorane, 97451	⌂	▼	Territorial Seed Company
A 105	McMinnville, 97128	⌂	▼	Trans Pacific Nursery
A 52	Medford, 97501		▼	Jackson & Perkins Co.
A 96	Medford, 97501	⌂	▼	Siskiyou Rare Plant Nursery
A 46	Milwaukie, 97222	⌂	▼	Hidden Garden Nursery, Inc.
A 74	Molalla, 97038	⌂	▼	Northwoods Nursery
A 19	Newberg, 97132		▼	Chehalem Gardens
A 43	Philomath, 97370	⌂		Hass Nursery
A 11	Portland, 97219	⌂	▼	The Bovees Nursery
A 59	Portland, 97201	⌂		Lazarus Enterprises
A 37	Roseburg, 97470	⌂		Garden Valley Dahlias
A 39	Salem, 97304	⌂	▼	Russell Graham, Purveyor of Plants
A 62	Salem, 97303	⌂		Lon's Oregon Grapes
A 92	Salem, 97303			Schreiner's Gardens
A 112	Salem, 97304			Whitman Farms
A 42	Scotts Mills, 97375	⌂	▼	Dr. Joseph C. Halinar
A 109	Scotts Mills, 97375	⌂	▼	Walden -- West
A 16	Sherwood, 97140	⌂	▼	Caprice Farm
A 86	Sherwood, 97140	⌂	▼	Red's Rhodies
A 97	Sherwood, 97140			Sorum's Nursery
A 22	Silverton, 97381	⌂	▼	Cooley's Gardens
A 39	Springfield, 97478	⌂	▼	Gossler Farms Nursery
A 59	Springfield, 97478	⌂	▼	Laurie's Garden
A 104	Talent, 97540	⌂		Tolowa Nursery
A 94	Troutdale, 97060	⌂	▼	Shackleton's Dahlias
A 7	Veneta, 97487	⌂	▼	Barber Nursery
A 74	West Linn, 97068	⌂	▼	Northwest Biological Enterprises
A 100	West Linn, 97068	⌂	▼	Stubbs Shrubs
A 34	Williams, 97544	⌂	▼	Forestfarm
A 39	Williams, 97544	⌂	▼	Goodwin Creek Gardens
A 53	Wilsonville, 97070	⌂		Justice Miniature Roses
A 89	Wilsonville, 97070	⌂	▼	Roses by Fred Edmunds
PENNSYLVANIA				
A 18	Allison Park, 15101			Cedar Ridge Nurseries
A 1	Aspers, 17304	⌂	▼	Adams County Nursery, Inc.
A 13	Aspers, 17304	⌂	▼	Bull Valley Rhododendron Nursery
A 44	Bodines, 17722	⌂		The Herb Barn
A 103	Coopersburg, 18036	⌂	▼	Tilley's Nursery/The WaterWorks
A 76	Dillsburg, 17019	⌂	▼	Orchid Thoroughbreds
A 7	Easton, 18042	⌂		The Banana Tree
A 37	Georgetown, 15043			Georgetown Greenhouse & Nursery
A 103	Huntingdon Valley, 19006	⌂	▼	Tinari Greenhouses
A 17	Indiana, 15701			Carino Nurseries
A 71	Indiana, 15701	⌂	▼	Musser Forests Inc.
A 46	Loretto, 15940	⌂	▼	Hickory Hill Gardens
A 35	McGrann, 16236			Fox Hollow Herbs
A 30	Meadville, 16335	⌂		Ernst Crownvetch Farms
A 89	Mechanicsburg, 17055	⌂	▼	The Rosemary House
A 107	Media, 19063	⌂	▼	Upper Bank Nurseries
A 4	Mt. Pleasant, 15666			Amenity Plant Products

(continued next page)

PAGE	CITY/ZIP	⌂ NURSERY ▼ GARDEN	SOURCE

PENNSYLVANIA (continued)

A 71	North East, 16428	⌂	Mums by Paschke
A 103	Orefield, 18069		Ter-El Nursery
A 66	Philadelphia, 19111	⌂ ▼	Matsu-Momiji Nursery
A 61	Port Matilda, 16870	⌂ ▼	Limerock Ornamental Grasses
A 5	Reedsville, 17084	⌂	Appalachian Wildflower Nursery
A 100	Renfrew, 16053	⌂ ▼	Stoecklein's Nursery
A 33	Sagamore, 16250	⌂	Flickingers' Nursery
A 83	Scottdale, 15683	⌂ ▼	The Primrose Path
A 106	Trevose, 19047		Otis Twilley Seed Co.
A 14	Warminster, 18974	⌂ ▼	W. Atlee Burpee Company
A 108	Warrington, 18976	⌂ ▼	Varga's Nursery
A 5	Waynesboro, 17268	⌂ ▼	Appalachian Gardens
A 57	Wellsville, 17365	⌂ ▼	Michael & Janet Kristick
A 44	West Elizabeth, 15088		Heirloom Seeds
A 42	Wexford, 15090		Halcyon Gardens
A 79	Wynnewood, 19096	⌂	Penn Valley Orchids

PRINCE EDWARD ISLAND, CANADA

A 109	Charlottetown, C0A 1P0	⌂ ▼	Vesey's Seeds, Ltd.

QUEBEC, CANADA

A 60	Sawyerville, J0B 3A0		Les Violettes Natalia
A 75	Ste. Foy, G2E 3L9	⌂ ▼	Orchibec

SASKATCHEWAN, CANADA

A 48	Parkside, S0J 2A0	⌂ ▼	Honeywood Lilies
A 28	Saskatoon, S7K 3S9	⌂	Early's Farm & Garden Centre, Inc.
A 58	Saskatoon, S7K 3J6	⌂ ▼	Lakeshore Tree Farms, Ltd.

SOUTH AFRICA

A 90	Constantia, 7848		Rust-En-Vrede Nursery
A 73	Rondebosch, Cape, 7700		Nooitgedag Disa Nursery
A 84	Sloanpark, 2152		Protea Seed & Nursery Suppliers
A 78	Somerset West, Cape, 7130		Parsley's Cape Seeds
A 16	Stellenbosch, Cape, 7609		Cape Seed & Bulb

SOUTH CAROLINA

A 115	Aiken, 29801	⌂ ▼	Woodlanders, Inc.
A 74	Clover, 29710	⌂ ▼	Oak Hill Farm
A 89	Cross Hill, 29332	⌂ ▼	The Rose Garden & Mini Rose Nursery
A 95	Graniteville, 29829	⌂	R. H. Shumway Seedsman
A 83	Greenville, 29604		Prentiss Court Ground Covers
A 78	Greenwood, 29648	⌂ ▼	Park Seed Company, Inc.
A 110	Hodges, 29695		Wayside Gardens
A 20	Myrtle Beach, 29575	⌂ ▼	Coastal Gardens & Nursery
A 17	Newberry, 29108	⌂ ▼	Carter & Holmes, Inc.
A 67	Walterboro, 29488	▼	Meadowlake Gardens

SOUTH DAKOTA

A 41	Yankton, 57078	⌂	Gurney Seed & Nursery Co.

SWITZERLAND

A 93	Meyrin, Geneve, CH 1217	⌂	Seedalp

TENNESSEE

A 101	Andersonville, 37705	⌂	Sunlight Gardens
A 8	Beersheba Springs, 37305	⌂	Beersheba Wildflower Garden
A 46	Cookeville, 38501	⌂ ▼	Hidden Springs Herb and Fuchsia Farm
A 46	Cookeville, 38501	⌂ ▼	Hidden Springs Nursery -- Edible Landscaping
A 74	Corryton, 37721	⌂ ▼	Oakes Daylilies
A 36	Dresden, 38225	⌂	Fred's Plant Farm
A 99	Gleason, 38229	⌂	Steele Plant Company
A 71	Greenback, 37742	⌂ ▼	Native Gardens
A 2	Knoxville, 37901		Alfrey -- Peter Pepper Seeds
A 8	Knoxville, 37938	⌂	Beaver Creek Nursery
A 64	Knoxville, 37920		Boris McCubbin
A 8	McMinnville, 37110		Vernon Barnes & Son Nursery
A 24	McMinnville, 37110		Cumberland Valley Nurseries, Inc.

(continued next page)

PAGE	CITY/ZIP	♠ NURSERY ▼ GARDEN	SOURCE

TENNESSEE (continued)

A 70	McMinnville, 37110	♠	Mt. Leo Nursery
A 81	McMinnville, 37110		Plant World
A 91	McMinnville, 37110	♠ ▼	Savage Farms Nursery
A 71	Oak Ridge, 37830		Natural Gardens
A 48	Pelham, 37366		Hollydale Nursery
A 62	Red Boiling Springs, 37150	♠ ▼	Long Hungry Creek Nursery
A 77	Ripley, 38063	♠ ▼	Owen Farms
A 42	Smithville, 37116		Haley Nursery Company, Inc.
A 39	Taft, 38488	♠ ▼	Good Hollow Greenhouse & Herbarium

TEXAS

A 98	Beaumont, 77702	♠	Southern Exposure
A 106	Breckenridge, 76024		Turner Seed Company
A 4	Brenham, 77833	♠ ▼	Antique Rose Emporium
A 81	Brenham, 77833		Pleasant Hill African Violets
A 114	Bryan, 77802	♠ ▼	Wilson's Violet Haven
A 6	Burleson, 76028	♠ ▼	Artistic Plants
A 63	Conroe, 77385	♠ ▼	The Lowrey Nursery
A 26	Corpus Christi, 78411	♠	Dane Company
A 25	Dallas, 75249	♠ ▼	The Nursery at the Dallas Nature Center
A 48	Dallas, 75381		Horticultural Enterprises
A 109	Dallas, 75219	♠ ▼	Volkmann Bros. Greenhouses
A 115	De Leon, 76444	♠	Womack's Nursery Co.
A 113	Eagle Lake, 77434	♠ ▼	Wildseed, Inc.
A 6	El Paso, 79927	♠ ▼	Aztekakti/Desertland Nursery
A 109	Flower Mound, 75028	♠ ▼	Volkmann Gardens
A 86	Gregory, 78359	♠ ▼	Rhapis Gardens
A 69	Hereford, 79045		Miller Grass Seed Company
A 49	Hico, 76457	♠ ▼	Huggins Farm Irises
A 1	Houston, 77026	♠	Air Expose
A 36	Houston, 77037		Lorine Friedrich
A 82	Houston, 77282	♠ ▼	The Plumeria People
A 40	Kerrville, 78028	♠	Green Horizons
A 37	Laredo, 78043	♠ ▼	Garden World
A 10	Lavernia, 78121		Bonsai Farm
A 8	Nacogdoches, 75961	♠ ▼	Barnee's Garden
A 90	Nash, 75569		SPB Sales
A 12	Omaha, 75571		Brown's Omaha Plant Farms, Inc.
A 114	Poolville, 76076		Willhite Seed Co.
A 47	Romayor, 77368	♠	Hilltop Herb Farm
A 48	San Antonio, 78233		Hortense's African Violets
A 54	San Antonio, 78221	♠ ▼	Kay's Greenhouses
A 82	Stephenville, 76401	♠ ▼	Porter & Son
A 69	Texarkana, 75502	♠	Miller-Bowie County Farmers Assn.
A 53	Victoria, 77904	♠ ▼	JoS Violets
A 117	Waller, 77484	▼	Yucca Do Nursery

UTAH

A 70	Logan, 84321	♠	Mountain Valley Seeds & Nursery
A 50	Salt Lake City, 84119	♠ ▼	Intermountain Cactus
A 85	Sunset, 84015	▼	Randy's Iris Garden

VERMONT

A 108	Cavendish, 05142		Mary Mattison van Schaik
A 108	Charlotte, 05445	♠ ▼	Vermont Wildflower Farm
A 108	Fair Haven, 05743	♠ ▼	Vermont Bean Seed Co.
A 18	Isle La Motte, 05463		Champlain Isle Agro Associates
A 22	Londonderry, 05148	▼	The Cook's Garden
A 64	Moretown, 05660		Mad River Imports
A 84	Putney, 05346	♠ ▼	Putney Nursery, Inc.
A 104	Tinmouth, 05773	♠	Tinmouth Channel Farm

VIRGINIA

A 29	Afton, 22920	♠	Edible Landscaping
A 89	Amherst, 24521		Rose Hill Herbs and Perénnials
A 26	Arlington, 22201	♠ ▼	T. DeBaggio Herbs by Mail
A 112	Burgess, 22432	♠ ▼	Whayes End Nursery
A 52	Charlottesville, 22902	♠ ▼	The Thomas Jefferson Center

(continued next page)

PAGE	CITY/ZIP	⌂ NURSERY ▼ GARDEN	SOURCE

VIRGINIA (continued)

A 54	Charlottesville, 22903		Kalmia Farm
A 61	Charlottesville, 22901		Linn Farm Perennials
A 12	Christiansburg, 24068		Brookfield Nursery & Tree Plantation
A 109	Fisherville, 22939	⌂ ▼	Andre Viette Farm & Nursery
A 72	Gainesville, 22065	⌂ ▼	Nicholls Gardens
A 25	Gloucester, 23061	⌂ ▼	The Daffodil Mart
A 12	Gloucester Point, 23062		Joseph Brown, Native Seeds
A 110	Lovettsville, 22080	⌂ ▼	Water Ways Nursery
A 51	McLean, 22101	▼	The Iris Pond
A 13	Monroe, 24574	⌂ ▼	Burford Brothers
A 97	Newport News, 23606	⌂ ▼	Solomon Daylilies
A 98	North Garden, 22959		Southern Exposure Seed Exchange
A 6	Radford, 24142	▼	Avonbank Iris Gardens

WALES

A 113	Llandderfel, Gwynedd, LL23 7RF		Wild Seeds
A 19	Wrexham, Clwyd, LL11 3DP		Paul Christian -- Rare Plants

WASHINGTON

A 42	Arlington, 98223	⌂ ▼	Hammond's Acres of Rhodys
A 8	Auburn, 98002	⌂ ▼	The Beall Orchid Company
A 34	Bellevue, 98005	⌂ ▼	Foliage Gardens
A 40	Bellevue, 98007	⌂	The Greenery
A 12	Blaine, 98230	⌂ ▼	Brown's Kalmia & Azalea Nursery
A 77	Bow, 98232	⌂ ▼	Pacific Berry Works
A 112	Brinnon, 98320	⌂ ▼	Whitney Gardens
A 13	Buckley, 98321	⌂ ▼	Buckley Nursery
A 12	Centralia, 98531		Brooksfield Farm
A 19	Chehalis, 98532	⌂	Chehalis Rare Plant Nursery
A 51	College Place, 99324	⌂ ▼	Iris Test Gardens
A 7	Edmonds, 98020		Bailey's
A 44	Elma, 98541	⌂ ▼	Heaths and Heathers
A 20	Everson, 98247	⌂	Cloud Mountain Nursery
A 44	Fall City, 98024	⌂ ▼	The Herbfarm
A 70	Graham, 98338	⌂ ▼	Mt. Tahoma Nursery
A 48	Humptulips, 98552		Hollyvale Farm
A 57	Kalama, 98625	⌂ ▼	Kordonowy's Dahlias
A 49	Kent, 98035		Ed Hume Seeds, Inc.
A 45	Kingston, 98346	⌂ ▼	Heronswood Nursery
A 56	Kirkland, 98033	⌂ ▼	Kirkland Iris Garden
A 36	Langley, 98260		Frosty Hollow Nursery
A 38	Longview, 98632		Global Seed Exchange
A 49	Montesano, 98563	⌂ ▼	Hughes Nursery
A 84	Morton, 98356	⌂ ▼	Raintree Nursery
A 6	Mt. Vernon, 98273	⌂	B & B Laboratories
A 8	Northport, 99157	⌂	Bear Creek Nursery
A 36	Olympia, 98507		Fungi Perfecti
A 14	Onalaska, 98570	⌂	Burnt Ridge Nursery
A 39	Oroville, 98844		Good Seed Co.
A 66	Payallup, 98373		Marrs Tree Farm
A 33	Port Angeles, 98362	⌂	Floating Mountain Seeds
A 1	Port Townsend, 98368	⌂ ▼	Abundant Life Seed Foundation
A 6	Port Townsend, 98368	⌂ ▼	B & D Lilies
A 86	Port Townsend, 98368	⌂	Rex Bulb Farms
A 25	Puyallup, 98373	⌂ ▼	Dahlias by Phil Traff
A 96	Roy, 98580	⌂	Silvaseed Company, Inc.
A 21	Seattle, 98101	⌂	Colvos Creek Nursery & Landscaping
A 29	Seattle, 98101	⌂	Enchanted Garden
A 31	Seattle, 98119	⌂ ▼	Fancy Fronds
A 92	Seattle, 98198	⌂ ▼	Sea-Tac Gardens
A 96	Sequim, 98382	⌂ ▼	Skyline Nursery
A 24	Snohomish, 98290	⌂ ▼	Cricklewood Nursery
A 58	Spokane, 99202	⌂	Lamb Nurseries
A 99	Spokane, 99223	⌂	Stanek's Garden Center
A 28	Sumner, 98390		Dunford Farms
A 21	Tacoma, 98446	⌂ ▼	Connell's Dahlias
A 81	Tekoa, 99033	⌂ ▼	Plants of the Wild
A 2	Vancouver, 98685	⌂ ▼	Aitken's Salmon Creek Garden

(continued next page)

PAGE	CITY/ZIP	⌂ NURSERY ▼ GARDEN	SOURCE
WASHINGTON (continued)			
A 88	Vancouver, 98662	⌂	Robyn's Nest Nursery
A 24	Walla Walla, 99362		C. Criscola Iris Garden
A 108	Wenatchee, 98801	⌂ ▼	VanWell Nursery, Inc.
A 7	Woodinville, 98072	⌂ ▼	Baker & Chantry Orchids
WEST GERMANY			
A 52	D 2000 Hamburg 56,	⌂	Klaus R. Jelitto
A 56	Erzhausen/Darmstadt, D-610		Gerhard Koehres Cactus & Succulent Nursery
A 30	Tubingen 1, D 7400		Exotic Seeds, Lothar Seik
A 103	Wolfenbuttel, 3340		Terrorchids
WEST VIRGINIA			
A 116	Berkeley Springs, 25411	⌂ ▼	Wrenwood of Berkeley Springs
A 42	Cherry Grove, 26804		Hardscrabble Enterprises
WISCONSIN			
A 43	Bayfield, 54814	⌂ ▼	Hauser's Superior View Farm
A 23	Crivitz, 54114	⌂ ▼	The Country Garden
A 20	East Troy, 53120		Clifford's Perennial & Vine
A 33	Elkhorn, 53121	⌂ ▼	Flora Favours
A 63	Friesland, 53935		McClure & Zimmerman
A 10	Germantown, 53022		Boehlke's Woodland Gardens
A 83	Mt. Horeb, 53572		Prairie Ridge Nursery/CRM Ecosystems, Inc.
A 23	Muskego, 53150	⌂ ▼	Country Wetlands Nursery
A 83	North Lake, 53064		Prairie Seed Source
A 55	Omro, 54963	⌂	Kester's Wild Game Food Nurseries
A 113	Oshkosh, 54903		Wildlife Nurseries
A 32	Peshtigo, 54157	⌂ ▼	Field and Forest Products, Inc.
A 110	Plainfield, 54966	⌂ ▼	The Waushara Gardens
A 68	Racine, 53402	⌂ ▼	Milaeger's Gardens
A 53	Randolph, 53957	⌂	J. W. Jung Seed Co.
A 62	Spring Green, 53588	⌂ ▼	Little Valley Farm
A 3	Stitzer, 53825	⌂ ▼	Alpine Gardens & Calico Shop
A 82	Tilleda, 54978	⌂ ▼	Pony Creek Nursery
A 96	Waunakee, 53597	⌂ ▼	Skolaski's Glads & Field Flowers
A 85	Wauwatosa, 53213		Ravenswood Seeds
A 83	Westfield, 53964	▼	Prairie Nursery
A 52	Wilson, 54027	⌂ ▼	Jasperson's Hersey Nursery
A 115	Winter, 54896	⌂ ▼	Winter Greenhouse

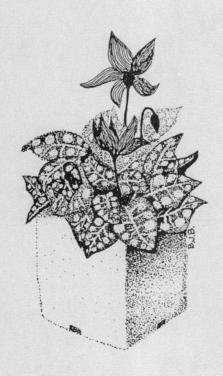

© Edible Landscaping
Artist: Sher Bell

PAGE	STATE	CITY	⌂ SHOP	SOURCE
ADD-IT FERTILIZER INJECTOR (TM)				
B 39	CA	Santee	⌂	TFS Systems
AFRICAN VIOLET SUPPLIES				
A 50	AB	Coaldale	⌂	Inland African Violets
A 111	BC	Vancouver	⌂	West Coast Violets
B 32	CA	El Cajon		Patches and Pots
A 68	CA	Sacramento	⌂	Mighty Minis
A 117	CA	Solvang	⌂	Zaca Vista Nursery
B 32	CA	Ventura	⌂	Phologistics
A 109	CO	Englewood	⌂	The Violet Showcase
B 42	FL	Gainesville	⌂	The Violet House
B 12	FL	Merritt Island	⌂	DoDe's Gardens, Inc.
A 105	GA	Ochlochnee	⌂	Travis' Violets
B 12	IN	Jeffersonville		Earlee, Inc.
A 16	MA	Falmouth	⌂	Cape Cod Violetry
B 22	MA	Lynnfield	⌂	Innis Violets
B 21	MI	Detroit		Indoor Gardening Supplies
A 32	NJ	Bargaintown	⌂	Fischer Greenhouses
A 81	NJ	Cinnaminson	⌂	Plant Factory
A 103	PA	Huntingdon Valley	⌂	Tinari Greenhouses
A 60	PQ	Sawyerville		Les Violettes Natalia
A 81	TX	Brenham		Pleasant Hill African Violets
A 114	TX	Bryan	⌂	Wilson's Violet Haven
A 109	TX	Dallas	⌂	Volkmann Bros. Greenhouses
A 109	TX	Flower Mound	⌂	Volkmann Gardens
A 53	TX	Victoria	⌂	JoS Violets
AGROSOKE (TM)				
B 18	TX	Ft. Worth		Grosoke, Inc.
ALPINE TROUGHS				
B 30	IN	Carmel		Old-World Garden Troughs
ANIMAL REPELLENTS				
See also Live Traps				
B 32	BC	Delta		Phero Tech, Inc.
B 28	IN	Sunman		Natural Gardening Research Center
B 29	MN	Park Rapids	⌂	North Star Evergreens
ARBORS				
B 7	MA	Bolton	⌂	Bow House, Inc.
B 22	PA	Fairview Village		Ivywood Gazebo
B 14	PA	Philadelphia		Exotic Blossoms
B 24	PA	Point Pleasant	⌂	Kinsman Company, Inc.
B 16	TN	Memphis	⌂	The Garden Concepts Collection
B 38	WI	Delafield	⌂	Sun Designs
AUTOMATIC VENT OPENERS				
See also Greenhouse Ventilators				
B 31	CA	Cotati	⌂	Pacific Coast Greenhouse Manufacturing Co.
B 38	CA	Huntington Beach	⌂	Superior Autovents
B 7	MA	Salem		Bramen Company, Inc.
B 40	NC	Goldsboro	⌂	Turner Greenhouses
B 33	NH	Exeter	⌂	Progressive Building Products
B 39	TX	Ft. Worth	⌂	Texas Greenhouse Co.
B 41	VA	Charlottesville	⌂	Victory Garden Supply Co.
B 9	WA	Mt. Vernon	⌂	Charley's Greenhouse Supply

PAGE	STATE	CITY	⌂ SHOP	SOURCE
BAMBOO TIMBERS				
B 31	CA	Albany		Orion Trading Company
BEES AND BEEKEEPING SUPPLIES				
B 23	KY	Clarkson		Walter T. Kelley Co.
A 6	MO	Sedalia		Archias' Seed Store
B 8	NC	Moravian Falls	⌂	Brushy Mountain Bee Farm, Inc.
A 89	NM	Roswell	⌂	Roswell Seed Co.
B 35	OH	Medina	⌂	A. I. Root Company
B 39	OR	Albany		Tec Laboratories, Inc.
B 38	PA	Eighty Four	⌂	Sunstream Bee Supply
BIO-FORCE (TM)				
A 37	TX	Laredo	⌂	Garden World
BIO-GRO (TM)				
A 37	TX	Laredo	⌂	Garden World
BIRD FEEDERS AND FOOD				
B 9	CA	Redondo Beach		J Collard
B 34	CA	Sebastopol	⌂	Reed Bros.
A 43	GA	Atlanta		Hastings
B 6	GA	Waynesboro		Birdsong
A 67	IA	Shenandoah	⌂	Earl May Seed & Nursery Co.
B 11	IL	Moline		John Deere Catalog
B 6	MA	Framingham		Bird 'n Hand
B 21	MA	Waltham		Hyde Bird Feeder Co.
A 2	ME	Falmouth	⌂	Allen, Sterling & Lothrop
A 110	MI	Fennville	⌂	Wavecrest Nursery & Landscaping Co.
B 25	NC	Colerain		Lazy Hill Farm Designs
B 12	NH	Penacook		Duncraft, Inc.
B 8	OH	Toledo	⌂	Carruth Studio
B 26	OK	Oklahoma City		MAC Industries
A 75	ON	Waterloo		Ontario Seed Company, Ltd.
B 22	PA	Fairview Village		Ivywood Gazebo
A 28	SK	Saskatoon	⌂	Early's Farm & Garden Centre, Inc.
B 16	TN	Memphis	⌂	The Garden Concepts Collection
B 33	VA	Orange	⌂	The Plow & Hearth
B 12	WI	Manitowoc		The Dramm Company
A 55	WI	Omro	⌂	Kester's Wild Game Food Nurseries
BIRD NETTING				
A 11	CA	Willits	⌂	Bountiful Gardens
B 28	IN	Sunman		Natural Gardening Research Center
B 22	MN	Minneapolis	⌂	InterNet, Inc.
B 21	WA	Wenatchee	⌂	I. F. M.
BIRD REPELLENTS				
B 36	CA	Emeryville	⌂	Seabright Enterprises
A 14	CO	Rocky Ford		D. V. Burrell Seed Growers Co.
B 12	IN	Jeffersonville		Earlee, Inc.
A 43	MI	Grand Junction	⌂	Hartmann's Plantation, Inc.
A 73	MN	Marine	⌂	North Star Gardens
B 30	WA	Seattle	⌂	Organic Pest Management
BIRDBATHS				
B 2	CA	Pt. Arena		American Sundials, Inc.
B 16	CA	San Francisco		Gardener's Eden
B 12	NH	Penacook		Duncraft, Inc.
B 15	NY	Long Island City	⌂	Florentine Craftsmen, Inc.
B 8	OH	Toledo	⌂	Carruth Studio
B 13	RI	Newport	⌂	Erkins Studios, Inc.
BIRDHOUSES				
B 9	CA	Redondo Beach		J Collard
B 16	CA	San Francisco		Gardener's Eden
B 34	CA	Sebastopol	⌂	Reed Bros.
B 13	CT	Stamford	⌂	The English Garden from Machin
B 43	DE	Dover	⌂	Winterthur Museum & Gardens

(continued next page)

PAGE	STATE	CITY	⌂ SHOP	SOURCE

BIRDHOUSES (continued)

PAGE	STATE	CITY	⌂ SHOP	SOURCE
B 6	GA	Waynesboro		Birdsong
A 67	IA	Shenandoah	⌂	Earl May Seed & Nursery Co.
B 2	IL	Galesburg		Alsto's Handy Helpers
B 20	KS	Overland Park		Holland's Organic Garden
B 29	MA	Topsfield	⌂	The Walt Nicke Company
B 21	MA	Waltham		Hyde Bird Feeder Co.
A 110	MI	Fennville	⌂	Wavecrest Nursery & Landscaping Co.
B 28	MN	Grand Rapids	⌂	Mr. Birdhouse
A 12	NC	Boone	⌂	Brookside Wildflowers
B 25	NC	Colerain		Lazy Hill Farm Designs
B 8	NC	Moravian Falls	⌂	Brushy Mountain Bee Farm, Inc.
B 16	NC	Raleigh	⌂	Garden Magic
B 12	NH	Penacook		Duncraft, Inc.
B 26	OK	Oklahoma City		MAC Industries
B 37	PA	Honey Brook		Simple's Creative Quality Trellises
B 14	PA	Philadelphia		Exotic Blossoms
B 24	PA	Point Pleasant	⌂	Kinsman Company, Inc.
B 16	TN	Memphis	⌂	The Garden Concepts Collection
B 33	VA	Orange	⌂	The Plow & Hearth
B 12	WI	Manitowoc		The Dramm Company
A 113	WI	Oshkosh		Wildlife Nurseries

BLOOMSAVER (TM)

PAGE	STATE	CITY	⌂ SHOP	SOURCE
B 6	CA	La Jolla		Bloomsaver, Ltd.

BONSAI POTS AND SUPPLIES

PAGE	STATE	CITY	⌂ SHOP	SOURCE
A 92	CA	Selma		Scotty's Desert Plants
A 94	CT	Stamford	⌂	Shanti Bithi Nursery
B 6	FL	Ft. Lauderdale		Bonsai Creations
A 10	GA	Atlanta	⌂	Bonsai of Georgia
A 81	GA	Gainesville	⌂	Plant City Bonsai
B 11	IA	Kelley	⌂	Dave's Aquariums & Greenhouse
A 99	IL	Hamburg		Springvale Farm Nursery
B 33	IL	Rock Island		Pot Lock
B 30	IN	Carmel		Old-World Garden Troughs
B 10	MA	Andover		Country House Floral Supply
B 31	MA	Sudbury	⌂	John Palmer Bonsai
B 6	MD	Baltimore	⌂	Bonsai Associates, Inc.
A 20	MI	Detroit	⌂	City Gardens
A 13	MS	Olive Branch	⌂	Brussel's Bonsai Nursery
A 20	ON	Mississauga	⌂	Clargreen Gardens, Ltd.
A 66	PA	Philadelphia	⌂	Matsu-Momiji Nursery
A 6	TX	Burleson	⌂	Artistic Plants
A 86	TX	Gregory	⌂	Rhapis Gardens
A 10	TX	Lavernia		Bonsai Farm
B 32	WA	Arlington	⌂	Pine Garden Pottery
B 19	WA	Kent	⌂	Heritage Arts

BONSAI TOOLS

PAGE	STATE	CITY	⌂ SHOP	SOURCE
A 94	CT	Stamford	⌂	Shanti Bithi Nursery
B 6	FL	Ft. Lauderdale		Bonsai Creations
A 10	GA	Atlanta	⌂	Bonsai of Georgia
A 81	GA	Gainesville	⌂	Plant City Bonsai
B 11	IA	Kelley	⌂	Dave's Aquariums & Greenhouse
A 99	IL	Hamburg		Springvale Farm Nursery
B 31	MA	Sudbury	⌂	John Palmer Bonsai
B 6	MD	Baltimore	⌂	Bonsai Associates, Inc.
A 13	MS	Olive Branch	⌂	Brussel's Bonsai Nursery
A 66	PA	Philadelphia	⌂	Matsu-Momiji Nursery
A 6	TX	Burleson	⌂	Artistic Plants
A 10	TX	Lavernia		Bonsai Farm
B 19	WA	Kent	⌂	Heritage Arts

BOOK CLUBS

PAGE	STATE	CITY	⌂ SHOP	SOURCE
B 16	NY	New York		The Garden Book Club

BOOK SEARCH SERVICE

PAGE	STATE	CITY	⌂ SHOP	SOURCE
B 7	CA	Concord	⌂	Brooks Books

(continued next page)

PAGE	STATE	CITY	⌂ SHOP	SOURCE
BOOK SEARCH SERVICE (continued)				
B 17	CA	Rancho Palos Verdes	⌂	V. L. T. Gardner
B 34	CA	Stanford	⌂	Quest Rare Books
B 16	DC	Washington		Garden Variety, Limited
B 26	En	Kew, Surrey	⌂	Lloyds' of Kew
B 2	IL	Chillicothe	⌂	The American Botanist
B 43	MA	Lincoln	⌂	Wilkerson Books
B 37	NH	Bedford		Edward F. Smiley, Bookseller
B 6	NJ	Englishtown	⌂	The Book Tree
B 6	NY	New York		Bookfinders General, Inc.
B 40	Ne	Hastings		Touchwood Books
B 33	ON	Rockton	⌂	Pomona Book Exchange
B 4	OR	Portland		Carol Barnett -- Books
B 20	So	Newlands, Cape Town	⌂	Honingklip Nurseries & Book Sales
B 44	WI	Madison	⌂	Wood Violet Books
BOOKS, AFRICAN VIOLETS				
A 117	CA	Solvang	⌂	Zaca Vista Nursery
A 109	CO	Englewood	⌂	The Violet Showcase
A 103	PA	Huntingdon Valley	⌂	Tinari Greenhouses
BOOKS, AGRICULTURAL				
B 1	CA	Davis	⌂	agAccess
B 2	IL	Chillicothe	⌂	The American Botanist
B 20	IN	Jamestown		Heritage Center for the Preservation
BOOKS, ALPINE & ROCK GARDENS				
A 2	Ja	Ichikawa, Chiba		Albiflora, Inc.
A 87	MN	Minneapolis	⌂	Rice Creek Gardens
A 96	OR	Medford	⌂	Siskiyou Rare Plant Nursery
BOOKS, AUSTRALIAN PLANTS				
B 23	Au	Cremorne, NSW		Johima Books
B 12	Au	Rose Bay, NSW		Direct Book Service
B 17	CA	Rancho Palos Verdes	⌂	V. L. T. Gardner
BOOKS, BEEKEEPING				
B 35	OH	Medina	⌂	A. I. Root Company
B 38	PA	Eighty Four	⌂	Sunstream Bee Supply
BOOKS, BONSAI				
B 17	CA	Rancho Palos Verdes	⌂	V. L. T. Gardner
A 94	CT	Stamford	⌂	Shanti Bithi Nursery
B 6	FL	Ft. Lauderdale		Bonsai Creations
A 10	GA	Atlanta	⌂	Bonsai of Georgia
B 11	IA	Kelley	⌂	Dave's Aquariums & Greenhouse
B 31	MA	Sudbury	⌂	John Palmer Bonsai
B 6	MD	Baltimore	⌂	Bonsai Associates, Inc.
A 13	MS	Olive Branch	⌂	Brussel's Bonsai Nursery
B 44	NJ	Hopewell	⌂	Elisabeth Woodburn
B 40	NY	Hauppauge		Tiny Trees Book Sales
B 40	Ne	Hastings		Touchwood Books
A 6	TX	Burleson	⌂	Artistic Plants
A 10	TX	Lavernia		Bonsai Farm
B 19	WA	Kent	⌂	Heritage Arts
BOOKS, BROMELIADS				
B 23	CA	Azusa		Myron Kimnach
B 7	CA	Concord	⌂	Brooks Books
B 17	CA	Rancho Palos Verdes	⌂	V. L. T. Gardner
A 84	CA	Vista	⌂	Rainbow Gardens Nursery & Bookshop
B 44	NJ	Hopewell	⌂	Elisabeth Woodburn
B 40	Ne	Hastings		Touchwood Books
BOOKS, BULBS				
A 64	VT	Moretown		Mad River Imports
A 63	WI	Friesland		McClure & Zimmerman

PAGE	STATE	CITY	⌂ SHOP	SOURCE

BOOKS, CACTI & SUCCULENTS

A 15	AR	Batesville	⌂	Cactus Gem Nursery
B 23	CA	Azusa		Myron Kimnach
A 1	CA	Carpinteria	⌂	Abbey Gardens
B 7	CA	Concord	⌂	Brooks Books
A 44	CA	Fresno	⌂	Henrietta's Nursery
A 54	CA	Galt	⌂	K & L Cactus Nursery
A 15	CA	Lodi	⌂	Cactus by Dodie
A 96	CA	Northridge	⌂	Singers' Growing Things
A 92	CA	Selma		Scotty's Desert Plants
A 84	CA	Vista	⌂	Rainbow Gardens Nursery & Bookshop
B 23	OR	Newburg	⌂	The Ken-L-Questor

BOOKS, CALIFORNIA NATIVE PLANTS

A 59	CA	Bolinas	⌂	Larner Seeds
B 7	CA	Concord	⌂	Brooks Books
A 79	CA	Sun Valley	⌂	Theodore Payne Foundation

BOOKS, CARNIVOROUS PLANTS

| A 66 | En | Madley, Hereford | ⌂ | Marston Exotics |

BOOKS, CONIFERS

| A 20 | OR | Aurora | ⌂ | Coenosium Gardens |

BOOKS, FERNS

| B 23 | CA | Azusa | | Myron Kimnach |
| B 23 | OR | Newburg | ⌂ | The Ken-L-Questor |

BOOKS, FLOWER ARRANGING

| B 23 | CA | Corona del Mar | | The Keth Company |
| B 5 | PA | Greeley | ⌂ | Dorothy Biddle Service |

BOOKS, GESNERIADS

| A 13 | CT | Eastford | ⌂ | Buell's Greenhouse, Inc. |

BOOKS, GREENHOUSE GROWING

| B 9 | WA | Mt. Vernon | ⌂ | Charley's Greenhouse Supply |

BOOKS, HEIRLOOM PLANTS

B 2	IL	Chillicothe	⌂	The American Botanist
B 20	IN	Jamestown		Heritage Center for the Preservation
A 52	VA	Charlottesville	⌂	The Thomas Jefferson Center

BOOKS, HERBS

A 43	CA	Coulterville	⌂	Havasu Hills Herbs
A 18	CT	Oxford	⌂	Catnip Acres Herb Nursery
B 2	IL	Chillicothe	⌂	The American Botanist
A 25	KY	Louisville		Dabney Herbs
B 43	MA	Lincoln	⌂	Wilkerson Books
A 23	MA	Rowley	⌂	Cricket Hill Herb Farm, Ltd.
A 35	MI	Parma	⌂	Fox Hill Farm
A 44	MO	Kansas City		Herb Gathering, Inc.
A 63	MT	Kalispell	⌂	Lost Prairie Herb Farm
A 111	NJ	Port Murray	⌂	Well-Sweep Herb Farm
A 101	OH	Chesterland	⌂	Sunnybrook Farms Nursery
A 87	ON	Goodwood	⌂	Richters
A 89	PA	Mechanicsburg	⌂	The Rosemary House
A 44	WA	Fall City	⌂	The Herbfarm
B 44	WI	Oregon	⌂	Wood Violet Books

BOOKS, HYDROPONICS

| B 20 | CA | Irvine | | Hollister's Hydroponics |
| B 22 | OR | Portland | ⌂ | JC's Garden Center |

BOOKS, LANDSCAPE ARCHITECTURE

B 17	CA	Rancho Palos Verdes	⌂	V. L. T. Gardner
B 43	MA	Lincoln	⌂	Wilkerson Books
B 24	NH	Exeter		Landscape Books
B 6	NJ	Englishtown	⌂	The Book Tree

(continued next page)

PAGE	STATE	CITY	⌂ SHOP	SOURCE
BOOKS, LANDSCAPE ARCHITECTURE (continued)				
B 44	NJ	Hopewell	⌂	Elisabeth Woodburn
B 7	NY	Lansingburgh	⌂	Warren F. Broderick -- Books
BOOKS, LILIES				
B 23	OR	Newburg	⌂	The Ken-L-Questor
BOOKS, MUSHROOMS				
A 111	BC	Aldergrove	⌂	Western Biologicals, Ltd.
A 71	CA	Inverness		Mushroompeople
A 74	OR	Corvallis		Northwest Mycological Consultants
B 23	OR	Newburg	⌂	The Ken-L-Questor
A 42	WV	Cherry Grove		Hardscrabble Enterprises
BOOKS, NEW				
See also specific subjects				
B 29	AR	Fayetteville	⌂	Nitron Industries, Inc.
B 12	Au	Rose Bay, NSW		Direct Book Service
A 91	BC	Vancouver	⌂	Sanctuary Seeds/Folklore Herb Co., Ltd.
B 8	CA	Berkeley	⌂	Builders Booksource
A 78	CA	Chula Vista	⌂	Pacific Tree Farms
B 7	CA	Concord	⌂	Brooks Books
B 1	CA	Davis	⌂	agAccess
B 37	CA	Mill Valley	⌂	Smith & Hawken
B 29	CA	Nevada City		Nelson-Miller
B 4	CA	Palo Alto	⌂	Bell's Book Store
B 17	CA	Rancho Palos Verdes	⌂	V. L. T. Gardner
A 96	CA	San Francisco	⌂	Anthony J. Skittone
A 84	CA	Vista	⌂	Rainbow Gardens Nursery & Bookshop
A 101	CT	Elmwood		Sunrise Oriental Seed Co.
B 16	DC	Washington		Garden Variety, Limited
B 43	En	Hitchin, Herts.	⌂	Wheldon & Wesley
B 26	En	Kew, Surrey	⌂	Lloyds' of Kew
B 19	En	London	⌂	Hatchard's
B 26	FL	Jacksonville	⌂	McQuerry Orchid Books
A 29	GA	Decatur	⌂	Eco-Gardens
A 93	ID	Boise		Seeds Blum
A 46	ID	Ketchum	⌂	High Altitude Gardens
B 20	IN	Jamestown		Heritage Center for the Preservation
B 29	MA	Topsfield	⌂	The Walt Nicke Company
B 9	MA	West Newton		The Clapper Co.
A 80	ME	New Gloucester	⌂	Pinetree Garden Seeds
A 31	ME	Waterville		Fedco Seeds
A 36	MT	Victor		Garden City Seeds
B 40	NC	Goldsboro	⌂	Turner Greenhouses
B 4	NC	Troutman		Bark Service Company
B 24	NH	Exeter		Landscape Books
B 6	NJ	Englishtown	⌂	The Book Tree
B 44	NJ	Hopewell	⌂	Elisabeth Woodburn
B 15	NY	Hamilton		Floribunda Books
B 16	NY	New York		The Garden Book Club
B 40	Ne	Hastings		Touchwood Books
A 67	OH	North Lima	⌂	Mellinger's, Inc.
B 12	OK	Mounds	⌂	Earthly Goods Farm & Garden Supply
B 9	OK	Tulsa		Cedar Hill Books
A 25	ON	Dundas	⌂	William Dam Seeds
A 27	ON	Georgetown	⌂	Dominion Seed House
B 5	ON	St. Thomas	⌂	Berry-Hill, Limited
B 25	ON	Toronto		Laurelbrook Book Services
A 72	OR	Albany	⌂	Nichols Garden Nursery, Inc.
A 41	OR	Eugene	⌂	Greer Gardens
A 103	OR	Lorane	⌂	Territorial Seed Company
A 35	PA	McGrann		Fox Hollow Herbs
B 2	PA	West Chester		American Arborist Supplies
A 115	SC	Aiken	⌂	Woodlanders, Inc.
B 20	So	Newlands, Cape Town	⌂	Honingklip Nurseries & Book Sales
A 82	TX	Houston	⌂	The Plumeria People
B 29	VA	New Castle	⌂	Necessary Trading Co.
A 84	WA	Morton	⌂	Raintree Nursery

(continued next page)

PAGE	STATE	CITY	⌂ SHOP	SOURCE

BOOKS, NEW (continued)

A 1	WA	Port Townsend	⌂	Abundant Life Seed Foundation
B 14	WA	Seattle	⌂	Flora & Fauna Books
B 8	WI	Deer Park	⌂	Capability's Books
B 44	WI	Oregon	⌂	Wood Violet Books

BOOKS, ORCHIDS

A 35	AR	Little Rock	⌂	Fox Orchids, Inc.
A 100	CA	Carpinteria	⌂	Stewart Orchids, Inc.
B 7	CA	Concord	⌂	Brooks Books
B 17	CA	Rancho Palos Verdes	⌂	V. L. T. Gardner
A 91	CA	Santa Barbara	⌂	Santa Barbara Orchid Estate
A 64	CA	South San Francisco	⌂	Rod McLellan Co.
A 84	CA	Vista	⌂	Rainbow Gardens Nursery & Bookshop
A 31	FL	Homestead	⌂	Fennell's Orchid Jungle
B 26	FL	Jacksonville	⌂	McQuerry Orchid Books
A 74	IL	Dundee	⌂	Oak Hill Gardens
A 76	IL	Villa Park	⌂	Orchids by Hausermann, Inc.
A 83	MB	Winnipeg	⌂	Prairie Orchid Company
A 55	MD	Kensington	⌂	Kensington Orchids
B 44	NJ	Hopewell	⌂	Elisabeth Woodburn
B 40	Ne	Hastings		Touchwood Books
A 49	ON	Bright's Grove	⌂	Huronview Nurseries & Garden Centre
A 55	ON	Komoka	⌂	Kilworth Flowers
B 40	WI	Greenfield		Twin Oaks Books

BOOKS, PRAIRIE PLANTING

A 62	WI	Spring Green	⌂	Little Valley Farm

BOOKS, RARE & ANTIQUARIAN

B 7	CA	Concord	⌂	Brooks Books
B 34	CA	Stanford	⌂	Quest Rare Books
B 43	En	Brighton, Sussex		Wheelbarrow Books
B 36	En	Great Malvern, Worcs	⌂	St. Ann's Books
B 43	En	Hitchin, Herts.	⌂	Wheldon & Wesley
B 22	En	Redhill, Surrey	⌂	Ivelet Books
B 26	FL	Jacksonville	⌂	McQuerry Orchid Books
B 2	IL	Chillicothe	⌂	The American Botanist
B 36	MA	Lanesboro	⌂	Savoy Books
B 37	NH	Bedford		Edward F. Smiley, Bookseller
B 24	NH	Exeter		Landscape Books
B 21	NH	Westmoreland	⌂	Hurley Books
B 44	NJ	Hopewell	⌂	Elisabeth Woodburn
B 40	Ne	Hastings		Touchwood Books
B 8	ON	Picton		Calendula
B 33	ON	Rockton	⌂	Pomona Book Exchange
B 21	ON	Toronto		Hortulus
B 23	OR	Newburg	⌂	The Ken-L-Questor
B 4	OR	Portland		Carol Barnett -- Books
B 27	OR	Salem		Max Marbles
B 3	RI	Newport	⌂	Anchor & Dolphin Books
B 14	WA	Seattle	⌂	Flora & Fauna Books
B 44	WI	Madison	⌂	Wood Violet Books

BOOKS, ROSES

B 7	CA	Concord	⌂	Brooks Books
B 4	CA	Palo Alto	⌂	Bell's Book Store
A 46	CO	Denver	⌂	High Country Rosarium
B 27	OR	Salem		Max Marbles

BOOKS, SOUTH AFRICAN PLANTS

B 8	CA	Camarillo	⌂	C 'n' C Protea
B 20	So	Newlands, Cape Town	⌂	Honingklip Nurseries & Book Sales

BOOKS, USED AND OUT-OF-PRINT
See also specific subjects

B 42	AL	Fort Payne		Gary Wayner -- Bookseller
B 23	CA	Azusa		Myron Kimnach
B 17	CA	Berkeley		Ian Jackson

(continued next page)

PAGE	STATE	CITY	⌂ SHOP	SOURCE
BOOKS, USED AND OUT-OF-PRINT (continued)				
B 7	CA	Concord	⌂	Brooks Books
B 4	CA	Palo Alto	⌂	Bell's Book Store
B 17	CA	Rancho Palos Verdes	⌂	V. L. T. Gardner
B 34	CA	Stanford	⌂	Quest Rare Books
A 84	CA	Vista	⌂	Rainbow Gardens Nursery & Bookshop
B 36	CT	Morris		Robert Shuhi -- Books
B 27	CT	New Preston		Timothy Mawson
B 43	En	Brighton, Sussex		Wheelbarrow Books
B 36	En	Great Malvern, Worcs	⌂	St. Ann's Books
B 43	En	Hitchin, Herts.	⌂	Wheldon & Wesley
B 26	En	Kew, Surrey	⌂	Lloyds' of Kew
B 22	En	Redhill, Surrey	⌂	Ivelet Books
B 26	FL	Jacksonville	⌂	McQuerry Orchid Books
B 2	IL	Chillicothe	⌂	The American Botanist
B 20	IN	Jamestown		Heritage Center for the Preservation
B 36	MA	Lanesboro	⌂	Savoy Books
B 43	MA	Lincoln	⌂	Wilkerson Books
B 44	ME	Hampden	⌂	Gary W. Woolson, Bookseller
B 37	NH	Bedford		Edward F. Smiley, Bookseller
B 24	NH	Exeter		Landscape Books
B 21	NH	Westmoreland	⌂	Hurley Books
B 44	NJ	Hopewell	⌂	Elisabeth Woodburn
B 13	NY	Boiceville		Editions
B 15	NY	Hamilton		Floribunda Books
B 7	NY	Lansingburgh	⌂	Warren F. Broderick -- Books
B 6	NY	New York		Bookfinders General, Inc.
B 40	Ne	Hastings		Touchwood Books
B 8	ON	Picton		Calendula
B 33	ON	Rockton	⌂	Pomona Book Exchange
B 21	ON	Toronto		Hortulus
B 5	OR	Gold Hill		Beth L. Bibby Books
B 23	OR	Newburg	⌂	The Ken-L-Questor
B 4	OR	Portland		Carol Barnett -- Books
B 27	OR	Salem		Max Marbles
B 3	RI	Newport	⌂	Anchor & Dolphin Books
B 20	So	Newlands, Cape Town	⌂	Honingklip Nurseries & Book Sales
B 14	WA	Seattle	⌂	Flora & Fauna Books
B 44	WI	Oregon	⌂	Wood Violet Books
B 6	Wa	Nr. Presteign		Mary Bland
BOOKS, VEGETABLE & FRUIT GROWING				
A 97	CA	Healdsburg	⌂	Sonoma Antique Apple Nursery
A 86	CA	Redwood City		Redwood City Seed Co.
A 11	CA	Willits	⌂	Bountiful Gardens
A 59	GA	Ball Ground	⌂	Lawson's Nursery
B 20	KS	Overland Park		Holland's Organic Garden
A 102	NM	Espanola	⌂	Talavaya Seeds
A 90	NY	Potsdam	⌂	St. Lawrence Nurseries
B 33	ON	Rockton	⌂	Pomona Book Exchange
A 39	WA	Oroville		Good Seed Co.
BOOKS, WATER GARDENING				
A 91	CA	Santa Barbara	⌂	Santa Barbara Water Gardens
A 108	CA	Upland	⌂	Van Ness Water Gardens
A 96	FL	Winter Haven	⌂	Slocum Water Gardens
A 78	MA	Whitman		Paradise Water Gardens
A 61	MD	Lilypons	⌂	Lilypons Water Gardens
A 79	NC	Franklin	⌂	Perry's Water Gardens
A 110	NJ	Saddle River	⌂	Waterford Gardens
A 105	OH	Independence	⌂	William Tricker, Inc.
A 70	ON	Port Stanley	⌂	Moore Water Gardens
A 103	PA	Coopersburg	⌂	Tilley's Nursery/The WaterWorks
BOOKS, WEATHER				
B 43	CA	Mendocino	⌂	Wind & Weather
BOOKS, WILDFLOWERS				
A 59	CA	Bolinas	⌂	Larner Seeds

(continued next page)

PAGE	STATE	CITY	⌂ SHOP	SOURCE
BOOKS, WILDFLOWERS (continued)				
A 87	CA	Castro Valley	⌂	Clyde Robin Seed Co.
B 7	CA	Concord	⌂	Brooks Books
A 79	CA	Sun Valley	⌂	Theodore Payne Foundation
A 12	NC	Boone	⌂	Brookside Wildflowers
A 40	TX	Kerrville	⌂	Green Horizons
BOOT SCRAPERS				
B 32	MA	Hingham		Pigeon Hill
B 12	NV	Silver City	⌂	Dressler & Co.
B 24	PA	Point Pleasant	⌂	Kinsman Company, Inc.
BOTANICAL PRINTS				
B 9	CA	Redondo Beach		J Collard
B 26	FL	Jacksonville	⌂	McQuerry Orchid Books
B 36	MA	Lanesboro	⌂	Savoy Books
B 15	NY	Palisades	⌂	Florilegium
B 17	Wa	Hawarden, Clwyd	⌂	Gladstone & Campbell
BRIDGES				
B 28	CA	Bayside		Nampara Gardens
B 7	MA	Bolton	⌂	Bow House, Inc.
B 20	NY	Canastota	⌂	Hermitage Gardens
B 16	TN	Memphis	⌂	The Garden Concepts Collection
B 38	WI	Delafield	⌂	Sun Designs
BRUSH CUTTERS				
B 24	MN	St. Paul	⌂	Kinco Manufacturing
B 4	NC	Matthews		BCS Mosa, Inc.
B 16	NY	Troy		Garden Way Manufacturing Co.
B 26	OH	London	⌂	Mainline of North America
B 22	OR	Eugene	⌂	International Reforestation Suppliers
B 10	VT	Charlotte	⌂	Country Home Products, Inc.
CACTUS JUICE (R)				
B 9	IL	Deerfield		Clarel Laboratories, Inc.
CALCIUM-25 (TM)				
B 5	VA	Falls Church		Bio-Gard Agronomics
CANNING SUPPLIES				
B 19	CA	Graton	⌂	Harmony Farm Supply
B 17	CT	Farmington		Gardener's Kitchen
B 17	IL	Arlington Heights		Glashaus/Weck Home Canning
A 64	MB	Brandon		McFayden Seeds
A 52	ME	Albion	⌂	Johnny's Selected Seeds
A 100	NY	Buffalo		Stokes Seed Company
A 27	ON	Georgetown	⌂	Dominion Seed House
B 5	ON	St. Thomas	⌂	Berry-Hill, Limited
A 41	SD	Yankton	⌂	Gurney Seed & Nursery Co.
CARRY-IT CART (R)				
B 40	NY	Saratoga Springs	⌂	Trimit Sales Company
CARTS				
B 34	CA	Point Arena		Peter Reimuller's Cart Warehouse
B 28	CA	San Anselmo	⌂	The Natural Gardening Company
B 11	FL	Miami	⌂	Day-Dex Co.
B 2	IL	Galesburg		Alsto's Handy Helpers
B 11	IL	Moline		John Deere Catalog
B 34	IL	Rockford		RAM Log Splitters
B 20	KS	Overland Park		Holland's Organic Garden
B 14	MA	Woburn	⌂	FXG Corporation
B 37	MO	Kansas City		The Stanley Forge Co., Inc.
B 4	NC	Matthews		BCS Mosa, Inc.
B 40	NY	Saratoga Springs	⌂	Trimit Sales Company
B 16	NY	Troy		Garden Way Manufacturing Co.
B 25	OH	Piqua	⌂	A. M. Leonard, Inc.
B 20	OR	Salem		Homestead Carts

(continued next page)

PAGE	STATE	CITY	⌂ SHOP	SOURCE
CARTS (continued)				
B 11	TN	Knoxville		Cross T Products, Inc.
B 18	TX	Littlefield		The Greener Thumb
B 17	VT	Burlington	⌂	Gardener's Supply Company
B 18	WA	Puyallup	⌂	Green Earth Organics
B 30	WI	Stoughton	⌂	Norway Industries
CHRISTMAS WREATHS & GREENERY				
B 38	CA	Santa Rosa		Starcross Community
B 33	OR	Estacada	⌂	Pleasant Hill Farm
B 18	OR	Grants Pass		Greenleaf Industries
CIDER AND WINE PRESSES				
B 19	KS	Paola	⌂	Happy Valley Ranch
A 10	MD	Riderwood		Boordy Nursery
B 5	ON	St. Thomas	⌂	Berry-Hill, Limited
A 41	SD	Yankton	⌂	Gurney Seed & Nursery Co.
COLD FRAMES				
B 7	MA	Salem		Bramen Company, Inc.
B 29	MA	Topsfield	⌂	The Walt Nicke Company
A 43	NY	Rochester		Harris Seeds
B 18	PA	Pineville	⌂	Growing Naturally
B 24	PA	Point Pleasant	⌂	Kinsman Company, Inc.
B 39	TX	Ft. Worth	⌂	Texas Greenhouse Co.
COMPOSTING EQUIPMENT				
B 29	AR	Fayetteville	⌂	Nitron Industries, Inc.
B 28	CA	San Anselmo	⌂	The Natural Gardening Company
B 28	IN	Sunman		Natural Gardening Research Center
B 29	MA	Topsfield	⌂	The Walt Nicke Company
B 34	MN	Eden Prairie	⌂	Ringer Corporation
B 23	PA	Lititz	⌂	Kemp Company
B 18	PA	Pineville	⌂	Growing Naturally
B 24	PA	Point Pleasant	⌂	Kinsman Company, Inc.
B 18	TX	Littlefield		The Greener Thumb
B 29	VA	New Castle	⌂	Necessary Trading Co.
B 17	VT	Burlington	⌂	Gardener's Supply Company
COMPOSTOST (R)				
B 7	GA	Augusta	⌂	Bricker's Organic Farm
COMPOSTUMBLER (R)				
B 23	PA	Lititz	⌂	Kemp Company
COMPUTEMP (R)				
B 35	NE	Columbus	⌂	Rodco Products Co., Inc.
COMPUTER PROGRAMS				
B 1	CA	Davis	⌂	agAccess
B 31	CA	Redlands	⌂	P.L.A.N.T.S.
B 13	FL	Daytona Beach		Economy Label Sales Co., Inc.
B 39	MA	Cambridge		Terrace Software
B 10	MD	Arnold		Computer/Management Services
A 35	MI	Parma	⌂	Fox Hill Farm
B 22	MO	Arcola		Infopoint Software
B 2	PA	Media	⌂	American Weather Enterprises
B 8	WI	Deer Park	⌂	Capability's Books
COMPUTERIZED GARDEN DESIGN				
B 39	MA	Cambridge		Terrace Software
B 9	MD	Silver Spring	⌂	CompuGarden, Inc.
B 27	NJ	Andover	⌂	Mindsun
B 1	OR	Eugene		Abracadata, Ltd.
COMPUTERIZED PLANT SELECTION				
B 31	CA	Redlands	⌂	P.L.A.N.T.S.
B 39	MA	Cambridge		Terrace Software
B 22	MO	Arcola		Infopoint Software

(continued next page)

PAGE	STATE	CITY	⌂ SHOP	SOURCE
COMPUTERIZED PLANT SELECTION (continued)				
B 39	NC	Raleigh		Taxonomic Computer
B 31	NY	East Hampton		Paradise Information, Inc.
B 39	OR	Astoria		Terisan
B 4	WA	Arlington		BCP/Custom Software Applications
CONSERVATORIES				
B 2	MA	Boston		Amdega Conservatories
B 14	MD	Columbia	⌂	Everlite Greenhouses, Inc.
COOKBOOKS (GARDEN PRODUCE)				
A 30	CA	Anaheim		Evergreen Y. H. Enterprises
A 43	CA	Coulterville	⌂	Havasu Hills Herbs
A 95	CA	Felton	⌂	Shepherd's Garden Seeds
A 97	CA	Healdsburg	⌂	Sonoma Antique Apple Nursery
A 71	CA	Inverness		Mushroompeople
A 106	CA	Redwood City		Tsang & Ma
A 90	CA	Watsonville	⌂	S & H Organic Acres
A 101	CT	Elmwood		Sunrise Oriental Seed Co.
A 59	GA	Ball Ground	⌂	Lawson's Nursery
A 1	IN	Huntingburg	⌂	Ahrens Nursery & Plant Labs
B 19	KS	Paola	⌂	Happy Valley Ranch
A 44	MO	Kansas City		Herb Gathering, Inc.
B 9	OK	Tulsa		Cedar Hill Books
A 77	WA	Bow	⌂	Pacific Berry Works
B 44	WI	Madison	⌂	Wood Violet Books
CUT FLOWER CONTAINERS				
B 6	CA	La Jolla		Bloomsaver, Ltd.
CYROFLEX (R)				
B 33	NH	Exeter	⌂	Progressive Building Products
DAFFODRILL (TM)				
B 11	NY	Salt Point		Daffodrill, Inc.
DE-BUG (TM)				
B 14	CO	Broomfield		Evans BioControl, Inc.
DEHYDRATORS				
B 17	VT	Burlington	⌂	Gardener's Supply Company
A 42	WV	Cherry Grove		Hardscrabble Enterprises
DIATOMACEOUS EARTH				
B 26	AR	Lowell	⌂	Maestro-Gro
B 7	GA	Augusta	⌂	Bricker's Organic Farm
B 39	ID	Boise	⌂	Thurston Distributing, Inc.
B 20	KS	Overland Park		Holland's Organic Garden
B 44	PA	Gap	⌂	Zook & Ranck, Inc.
DOG AND CAT PEST CONTROLS				
B 29	AR	Fayetteville	⌂	Nitron Industries, Inc.
B 30	FA	Odessa		Odessa Natural Enterprises
B 28	IN	Sunman		Natural Gardening Research Center
A 25	KY	Louisville		Dabney Herbs
A 44	MO	Kansas City		Herb Gathering, Inc.
A 63	MT	Kalispell	⌂	Lost Prairie Herb Farm
A 36	MT	Victor		Garden City Seeds
B 6	NY	Yorkville	⌂	Bonide Chemical Co., Inc.
B 30	OH	Hartville	⌂	Ohio Earth Food, Inc.
B 12	OK	Mounds	⌂	Earthly Goods Farm & Garden Supply
B 29	VA	New Castle	⌂	Necessary Trading Co.
A 44	WA	Fall City	⌂	The Herbfarm
B 30	WA	Seattle	⌂	Organic Pest Management
B 21	WA	Wenatchee	⌂	I. F. M.
DOOM (R)				
B 14	NY	Clinton Corners		Fairfax Biological Lab, Inc.

PAGE	STATE	CITY	⌂ SHOP	SOURCE
DOOM LARVO BT (R)				
B 14	NY	Clinton Corners		Fairfax Biological Lab, Inc.
DRIP IRRIGATION SUPPLIES				
B 29	AR	Fayetteville	⌂	Nitron Industries, Inc.
B 41	AZ	Bouse	⌂	UPCO Irrigation
B 34	CA	Chatsworth		Raindrip, Inc.
B 28	CA	Fremont		Misti Maid, Inc.
A 111	CA	Grass Valley	⌂	Weiss Brothers Nursery
B 37	CA	Huntington Beach	⌂	Spot Systems
B 16	CA	Redway	⌂	Full Circle Garden Products
B 28	CA	San Anselmo	⌂	The Natural Gardening Company
B 41	CA	San Francisco	⌂	The Urban Farmer Store
B 39	CA	Santee	⌂	TFS Systems
B 11	CA	Sun Valley	⌂	D.I.G. Corporation
B 21	CO	Colorado Springs	⌂	Hydro-Gardens, Inc.
B 28	FL	Palmetto		Moss Products, Inc.
A 43	MI	Grand Junction	⌂	Hartmann's Plantation, Inc.
B 32	MO	Grover	⌂	Plastic Plumbing Products, Inc.
B 38	MO	North Kansas City		Stuppy Greenhouse Manufacturing, Inc.
B 13	NY	Staten Island		East Coast Hydroponics
B 29	NY	Valley Stream		Netafim Irrigation
B 22	ON	St. Catharines	⌂	International Irrigation Systems
B 22	OR	Portland	⌂	JC's Garden Center
B 31	OR	Portland	⌂	Pacific Garden Supply
B 38	TX	Lubbock	⌂	Submatic Irrigation Systems
A 82	TX	Stephenville	⌂	Porter & Son
B 12	WI	Manitowoc		The Dramm Company
DRIP IRRIGATION SYSTEMS				
A 115	AB	Hythe	⌂	Windy Ridge Nursery
B 41	AZ	Bouse	⌂	UPCO Irrigation
B 34	CA	Chatsworth		Raindrip, Inc.
A 78	CA	Chula Vista	⌂	Pacific Tree Farms
B 31	CA	Cotati	⌂	Pacific Coast Greenhouse Manufacturing Co.
B 28	CA	Fremont		Misti Maid, Inc.
A 111	CA	Grass Valley	⌂	Weiss Brothers Nursery
B 37	CA	Huntington Beach	⌂	Spot Systems
B 41	CA	San Francisco	⌂	The Urban Farmer Store
B 39	CA	Santee	⌂	TFS Systems
B 11	CA	Sun Valley	⌂	D.I.G. Corporation
B 28	FL	Palmetto		Moss Products, Inc.
B 28	IN	Sunman		Natural Gardening Research Center
B 32	MO	Grover	⌂	Plastic Plumbing Products, Inc.
B 13	NY	Staten Island		East Coast Hydroponics
B 29	NY	Valley Stream		Netafim Irrigation
B 22	ON	St. Catharines	⌂	International Irrigation Systems
B 16	OR	Corvallis	⌂	Full Moon Farm Products
B 17	PA	Harleysville	⌂	E. C. Geiger, Inc.
A 14	PA	Warminster	⌂	W. Atlee Burpee Company
B 9	WA	Mt. Vernon	⌂	Charley's Greenhouse Supply
B 12	WI	Manitowoc		The Dramm Company
EARTH AUGER				
B 11	NY	Salt Point		Daffodrill, Inc.
EARTHWORMS				
B 41	CA	Citrus Heights		Unique Insect Control
B 12	CA	Corte Madera	⌂	Dirt Cheap Organics
B 30	CA	Los Angeles	⌂	Organic Control, Inc.
B 7	GA	Bronwood		Bronwood Worm Gardens
B 4	GA	Dawson		Beatrice Farms
B 8	GA	Plains		Carter Fishworm Farm
B 8	MA	Buzzards Bay		Cape Cod Worm Farm
EASY WEEDER (TM)				
B 42	NY	Rochester	⌂	Warnico/USA, Inc.

PAGE	STATE	CITY	⌂ SHOP	SOURCE
EMPLOYMENT SERVICES				
B 15	FL	Deland		Florapersonnel
ERTH-RITE (R)				
B 12	CA	Corte Madera	⌂	Dirt Cheap Organics
B 12	IN	Jeffersonville		Earlee, Inc.
B 20	KS	Overland Park		Holland's Organic Garden
B 44	PA	Gap	⌂	Zook & Ranck, Inc.
EZ-DIGGER (R)				
B 35	TX	Ft. Worth		Rudon International Trading Company
FERTIL-MATIC (R)				
B 22	ON	St. Catharines	⌂	International Irrigation Systems
FERTILIZERS				
See also specific type				
B 3	CA	San Rafael	⌂	Applied Hydroponics
B 39	CA	Santee	⌂	TFS Systems
B 21	CO	Colorado Springs	⌂	Hydro-Gardens, Inc.
A 109	CO	Englewood	⌂	The Violet Showcase
B 42	FL	Gainesville	⌂	The Violet House
B 30	FL	Miami	⌂	OFE International, Inc.
B 40	FL	Orlando	⌂	Tropical Plant Products, Inc.
A 55	FL	Sanford	⌂	Kilgore Seed Company
B 4	FL	West Palm Beach		Avant Horticultural Products
A 65	FL	Windemere	⌂	Ann Mann's Orchids
A 67	IA	Shenandoah	⌂	Earl May Seed & Nursery Co.
B 9	IL	Deerfield		Clarel Laboratories, Inc.
B 15	IL	Schaumburg	⌂	Florist Products, Inc.
B 2	IL	Streamwood	⌂	Alternative Garden Supply, Inc.
A 2	ME	Falmouth	⌂	Allen, Sterling & Lothrop
A 43	MI	Grand Junction	⌂	Hartmann's Plantation, Inc.
A 11	NC	Brown Summit	⌂	Breckinridge Orchids
A 60	NJ	Sewell	⌂	Orol Ledden & Sons
A 89	NM	Roswell	⌂	Roswell Seed Co.
B 32	NY	Buffalo		Plant Collectibles
B 26	OH	Perry		MacKenzie Nursery Supply
A 105	ON	Hamilton	⌂	Tregunno Seeds
B 1	OR	Junction City	⌂	Agrilite
B 31	OR	Portland	⌂	Pacific Garden Supply
B 17	PA	Harleysville	⌂	E. C. Geiger, Inc.
B 3	PQ	Montreal	⌂	Applied Hydroponics of Canada
A 60	PQ	Sawyerville		Les Violettes Natalia
B 27	TX	Hondo		Medina Agricultural Products Co.
A 82	TX	Houston	⌂	The Plumeria People
A 10	TX	Lavernia		Bonsai Farm
A 82	TX	Stephenville	⌂	Porter & Son
B 31	UT	North Logan		Pan Agro, Inc.
A 112	WA	Brinnon	⌂	Whitney Gardens
FERTILIZERS, ORGANIC				
B 29	AR	Fayetteville	⌂	Nitron Industries, Inc.
B 26	AR	Lowell	⌂	Maestro-Gro
B 12	CA	Corte Madera	⌂	Dirt Cheap Organics
B 20	CA	Fresno	⌂	Hortopaper Growing Systems
A 79	CA	Grass Valley	⌂	Peaceful Valley Farm Supply
B 19	CA	Graton	⌂	Harmony Farm Supply
B 30	CA	Los Angeles	⌂	Organic Control, Inc.
B 16	CA	Redway	⌂	Full Circle Garden Products
B 28	CA	San Anselmo	⌂	The Natural Gardening Company
B 34	CA	San Diego	⌂	Bargyla Rateaver
B 31	CA	Watsonville		Pat's "Mini-Pack" Labels
A 11	CA	Willits	⌂	Bountiful Gardens
B 1	CO	Boulder		Age-Old Garden Supply
B 28	CT	Avon		Mother Nature's Worm Castings
A 43	GA	Atlanta		Hastings
B 7	GA	Augusta	⌂	Bricker's Organic Farm
B 13	IL	Mendota	⌂	EnP Inc.

(continued next page)

PAGE	STATE	CITY	⌂ SHOP	SOURCE
FERTILIZERS, ORGANIC (continued)				
B 12	IN	Jeffersonville		Earlee, Inc.
B 28	IN	Sunman		Natural Gardening Research Center
B 20	KS	Overland Park		Holland's Organic Garden
B 7	MA	Salem		Bramen Company, Inc.
B 29	ME	Waldoboro		North American Kelp
B 34	MN	Eden Prairie	⌂	Ringer Corporation
A 36	MT	Victor		Garden City Seeds
B 18	OH	Cleveland		The Guano Company
B 30	OH	Hartville	⌂	Ohio Earth Food, Inc.
B 12	OK	Mounds	⌂	Earthly Goods Farm & Garden Supply
A 87	ON	Goodwood	⌂	Richters
B 16	OR	Corvallis	⌂	Full Moon Farm Products
B 44	PA	Gap	⌂	Zook & Ranck, Inc.
B 18	PA	Pineville	⌂	Growing Naturally
A 37	TX	Laredo	⌂	Garden World
B 18	TX	Littlefield		The Greener Thumb
B 5	VA	Falls Church		Bio-Gard Agronomics
B 29	VA	New Castle	⌂	Necessary Trading Co.
B 18	WA	Puyallup	⌂	Green Earth Organics
B 30	WA	Seattle	⌂	Organic Pest Management
B 21	WA	Wenatchee	⌂	I. F. M.
B 12	WI	Manitowoc		The Dramm Company
FERTILIZERS, SEAWEED				
B 1	CO	Boulder		Age-Old Garden Supply
B 13	IL	Mendota	⌂	EnP Inc.
B 7	MA	Salem		Bramen Company, Inc.
B 29	ME	Waldoboro		North American Kelp
FISH FOR GARDEN PONDS				
A 108	CA	Upland	⌂	Van Ness Water Gardens
A 112	MD	Baltimore	⌂	Wicklein's Aquatic Farm & Nursery, Inc.
A 61	MD	Lilypons	⌂	Lilypons Water Gardens
A 79	NC	Franklin	⌂	Perry's Water Gardens
A 110	NJ	Saddle River	⌂	Waterford Gardens
A 105	OH	Independence	⌂	William Tricker, Inc.
A 103	PA	Coopersburg	⌂	Tilley's Nursery/The WaterWorks
FLORALIGHT (TM)				
B 14	ON	Willowdale		Floralight Gardens Canada, Inc.
FLOWER ARRANGING SUPPLIES				
B 23	CA	Corona del Mar		The Keth Company
B 6	CA	La Jolla		Bloomsaver, Ltd.
B 9	IL	Deerfield		Clarel Laboratories, Inc.
B 14	IL	Lombard		The Floral Mailbox
B 10	MA	Andover		Country House Floral Supply
A 2	MA	Wilmington	⌂	Allgrove Farm, Inc.
A 13	MD	Owings Mills	⌂	Bundles of Bulbs
A 20	ON	Mississauga	⌂	Clargreen Gardens, Ltd.
B 5	PA	Greeley	⌂	Dorothy Biddle Service
B 14	VA	Rustburg		Floral Accents
FLOWER DRYING SUPPLIES				
B 14	IL	Lombard		The Floral Mailbox
B 10	MA	Andover		Country House Floral Supply
B 5	PA	Greeley	⌂	Dorothy Biddle Service
FORESTRY EQUIPMENT/SUPPLIES				
B 3	FL	Fort Lauderdale	⌂	Arborist Supply House, Inc.
B 29	MN	Park Rapids	⌂	North Star Evergreens
B 25	OH	Piqua	⌂	A. M. Leonard, Inc.
B 22	OR	Eugene	⌂	International Reforestation Suppliers
B 17	PA	Harleysville	⌂	E. C. Geiger, Inc.
B 2	PA	West Chester		American Arborist Supplies
B 30	PQ	Sherbrooke	⌂	Nova Sylva, Inc.

PAGE	STATE	CITY	⌂ SHOP	SOURCE

FOUNTAINS

B 35	AL	Alexander City		Robinson Iron
B 42	BC	Vancouver	⌂	The Well-Furnished Garden
B 24	CA	San Diego		La Jolla Sales
A 91	CA	Santa Barbara	⌂	Santa Barbara Water Gardens
B 26	CT	Wilton		Kenneth Lynch & Sons, Inc.
B 29	MA	North Brookfield	⌂	New England Garden Ornaments
A 61	MD	Lilypons	⌂	Lilypons Water Gardens
B 32	MO	Grover	⌂	Plastic Plumbing Products, Inc.
B 7	NC	Connelly Springs	⌂	Andy Brinkley Studios
B 16	NC	Raleigh	⌂	Garden Magic
B 33	NY	Bronxville		Pompeian Studios
B 20	NY	Canastota	⌂	Hermitage Gardens
B 15	NY	Long Island City	⌂	Florentine Craftsmen, Inc.
A 70	ON	Port Stanley	⌂	Moore Water Gardens
A 103	PA	Coopersburg	⌂	Tilley's Nursery/The WaterWorks
B 7	PA	Malvern		Brandywine Garden Furniture
B 14	PA	Philadelphia		Exotic Blossoms
B 13	RI	Newport	⌂	Erkins Studios, Inc.
B 35	VA	Hillsboro	⌂	Royal Tidewater Collection, Inc.
B 9	VT	Bristol	⌂	Robert Compton, Ltd.

FRUIT BOXES

B 21	MN	Osseo		Hubbard Folding Box Co.

GARDEN BANNERS

B 24	OR	Portland		Landscapes & Accents

GARDEN BENCHES, METAL

B 35	AL	Alexander City		Robinson Iron
B 42	BC	Vancouver	⌂	The Well-Furnished Garden
B 22	CT	Colebrook		Irving & Jones
B 31	DC	Washington	⌂	Park Place
B 29	MA	North Brookfield	⌂	New England Garden Ornaments
B 16	NC	Raleigh	⌂	Garden Magic
B 43	NE	Broken Bow		Wikco Industries, Inc.
B 7	PA	Malvern		Brandywine Garden Furniture
B 13	RI	Newport	⌂	Erkins Studios, Inc.
B 9	SC	Charleston	⌂	Charleston Battery Bench, Inc.
B 26	VA	Arlington	⌂	Mrs. McGregor's Garden Shop

GARDEN BENCHES, STONE

B 29	MA	North Brookfield	⌂	New England Garden Ornaments
B 33	NY	Bronxville		Pompeian Studios
B 14	PA	Philadelphia		Exotic Blossoms
B 13	RI	Newport	⌂	Erkins Studios, Inc.

GARDEN BENCHES, WOOD

B 28	CA	Bayside		Nampara Gardens
B 1	CA	Fort Bragg		Adirondack Designs
B 37	CA	Mill Valley	⌂	Smith & Hawken
B 9	CA	Redondo Beach		J Collard
B 34	CA	Sebastopol	⌂	Reed Bros.
B 2	CO	Lakewood	⌂	Alpine Millworks Company
B 31	DC	Washington	⌂	Park Place
B 11	IL	Moline		John Deere Catalog
B 29	MA	North Brookfield	⌂	New England Garden Ornaments
B 9	MA	West Newton		The Clapper Co.
B 10	MD	Germantown	⌂	Country Casual
B 44	NY	High Falls	⌂	Wood Classics, Inc.
B 43	NY	Keesville	⌂	Willsboro Wood Products
B 1	NY	Woodbourne	⌂	AMH Furniture
B 11	PA	Carlisle	⌂	Cumberland Woodcraft
B 7	PA	Malvern		Brandywine Garden Furniture
B 13	RI	Newport	⌂	Erkins Studios, Inc.
B 41	TN	Knoxville		Van Klassens Fine Garden Furniture
B 16	TN	Memphis	⌂	The Garden Concepts Collection
B 24	VA	Arlington		Kingsley-Bate, Ltd.
B 26	VA	Arlington	⌂	Mrs. McGregor's Garden Shop

(continued next page)

PAGE	STATE	CITY	⌂ SHOP	SOURCE
GARDEN BENCHES, WOOD (continued)				
B 33	VA	Orange	⌂	The Plow & Hearth
GARDEN CLOTHING				
See also Gloves				
B 12	CA	Brea	⌂	Denman & Co.
B 27	CA	Guerneville	⌂	Emi Meade, Importer
B 37	CA	Mill Valley	⌂	Smith & Hawken
B 16	CA	San Francisco		Gardener's Eden
B 39	CA	Santa Barbara		There's Always the Garden
B 6	GA	Cleveland	⌂	Blue Creek Valley Ventures
B 44	ME	Kennebunkport		Womanswork
B 33	NH	Wilton	⌂	Putnam's
B 26	WA	Freeland	⌂	MAN Productions
B 9	WI	Elkhart Lake	⌂	Clothcrafters, Inc.
GARDEN FURNITURE				
See also specific type				
B 35	AL	Alexander City		Robinson Iron
B 37	AL	Birmingham		Southern Statuary and Stone
B 42	BC	Vancouver	⌂	The Well-Furnished Garden
B 28	CA	Bayside		Nampara Gardens
B 1	CA	Fort Bragg		Adirondack Designs
B 36	CA	Laguna Hills		Ryans by Mail
B 37	CA	Mill Valley	⌂	Smith & Hawken
B 9	CA	Redondo Beach		J Collard
B 24	CA	San Diego		La Jolla Sales
B 16	CA	San Francisco		Gardener's Eden
B 34	CA	Sebastopol	⌂	Reed Bros.
B 2	CO	Lakewood	⌂	Alpine Millworks Company
B 22	CT	Colebrook		Irving & Jones
B 13	CT	Stamford	⌂	The English Garden from Machin
B 26	CT	Wilton		Kenneth Lynch & Sons, Inc.
B 31	DC	Washington	⌂	Park Place
B 43	DE	Dover	⌂	Winterthur Museum & Gardens
B 2	IL	Galesburg		Alsto's Hand Helpers
B 29	MA	North Brookfield	⌂	New England Garden Ornaments
B 9	MA	West Newton		The Clapper Co.
B 10	MD	Germantown	⌂	Country Casual
B 16	NC	Raleigh	⌂	Garden Magic
B 33	NY	Bronxville		Pompeian Studios
B 44	NY	High Falls	⌂	Wood Classics, Inc.
B 43	NY	Keesville	⌂	Willsboro Wood Products
B 15	NY	Long Island City	⌂	Florentine Craftsmen, Inc.
B 1	NY	Woodbourne	⌂	AMH Furniture
B 23	OH	Cleveland	⌂	David Kay Garden & Gift Catalogue, Inc.
B 7	PA	Malvern		Brandywine Garden Furniture
B 11	PA	Philadelphia		Dalton Pavilions, Inc.
B 9	SC	Charleston	⌂	Charleston Battery Bench, Inc.
B 41	TN	Knoxville		Van Klassens Fine Garden Furniture
B 16	TN	Memphis	⌂	The Garden Concepts Collection
B 24	VA	Arlington		Kingsley-Bate, Ltd.
B 33	VA	Orange	⌂	The Plow & Hearth
GARDEN MARKERS				
See also Plant Labels				
B 14	CA	Cloverdale		Evergreen Garden Plant Labels
B 31	CA	Watsonville		Pat's "Mini-Pack" Labels
B 41	DE	Wilmington		F. R. Unruh
B 13	FL	Daytona Beach		Economy Label Sales Co., Inc.
B 32	MA	Hingham		Pigeon Hill
A 23	MA	Rowley	⌂	Cricket Hill Herb Farm, Ltd.
B 32	MI	Paw Paw		Paw Paw Everlast Label Co.
A 44	MO	Kansas City		Herb Gathering, Inc.
B 19	NJ	Old Tappan		Harlane Company, Inc.
B 13	OH	Swanton		Eon Industries
B 2	ON	Sydenham		Amaranth Stoneware

PAGE	STATE	CITY	⌂ SHOP	SOURCE
GARDEN ORNAMENTS				
See also specific type				
B 35	AL	Alexander City		Robinson Iron
B 37	AL	Birmingham		Southern Statuary and Stone
B 42	BC	Vancouver	⌂	The Well-Furnished Garden
B 31	CA	Albany		Orion Trading Company
B 28	CA	Bayside		Nampara Gardens
B 43	CA	Mendocino	⌂	Wind & Weather
B 13	CA	Menlo Park		east/west Gardens
B 37	CA	Mill Valley	⌂	Smith & Hawken
B 9	CA	Redondo Beach		J Collard
B 16	CA	San Francisco		Gardener's Eden
B 34	CA	Sebastopol	⌂	Reed Bros.
B 26	CT	Wilton		Kenneth Lynch & Sons, Inc.
B 13	Ca	Gormley, ON		The Empire Gnome Manufacturing Co.
B 31	DC	Washington	⌂	Park Place
B 43	DE	Dover	⌂	Winterthur Museum & Gardens
B 4	FL	Orlando		Autumn Forge
B 2	IL	Galesburg		Alsto's Handy Helpers
B 11	IL	Moline		John Deere Catalog
B 43	IN	Indianapolis	⌂	Windleaves
B 32	MA	Hingham		Pigeon Hill
B 29	MA	North Brookfield	⌂	New England Garden Ornaments
B 9	MA	West Newton		The Clapper Co.
A 61	MD	Lilypons	⌂	Lilypons Water Gardens
B 20	ME	Yarmouth	⌂	Heritage Lanterns
B 25	NC	Colerain		Lazy Hill Farm Designs
B 16	NC	Raleigh	⌂	Garden Magic
B 36	NJ	Roosevelt	⌂	Sculpture Cast Editions
B 33	NY	Bronxville		Pompeian Studios
B 15	NY	Long Island City	⌂	Florentine Craftsmen, Inc.
B 23	OH	Cleveland	⌂	David Kay Garden & Gift Catalogue, Inc.
B 8	OH	Toledo	⌂	Carruth Studio
B 2	ON	Sydenham		Amaranth Stoneware
B 24	OR	Portland		Landscapes & Accents
B 11	PA	Carlisle	⌂	Cumberland Woodcraft
B 19	PA	Gulph Mills		Hen-Feathers & Company
B 37	PA	Honey Brook		Simple's Creative Quality Trellises
B 14	PA	Philadelphia		Exotic Blossoms
B 33	PA	Pittsburgh		Popovitch Associates, Inc.
B 19	PA	Pleasant Gap	⌂	Philip Hawk & Company
B 13	RI	Newport	⌂	Erkins Studios, Inc.
B 16	TN	Memphis	⌂	The Garden Concepts Collection
B 42	TX	Fredericksburg	⌂	Vintage Wood Works
B 26	VA	Arlington	⌂	Mrs. McGregor's Garden Shop
B 35	VA	Hillsboro	⌂	Royal Tidewater Collection, Inc.
B 33	VA	Orange	⌂	The Plow & Hearth
B 9	VT	Bristol	⌂	Robert Compton, Ltd.
GARDEN PLANS				
B 9	MD	Silver Spring	⌂	CompuGarden, Inc.
B 36	MI	Edwardsburg		SeedScapes
B 3	MN	Minnetonka		Anderson Horticultural Design Service
A 89	PA	Mechanicsburg	⌂	The Rosemary House
GARDEN STRUCTURES				
B 7	MA	Bolton	⌂	Bow House, Inc.
B 14	PA	Philadelphia		Exotic Blossoms
GARDEN STRUCTURES, PLANS FOR				
B 38	WI	Delafield	⌂	Sun Designs
GAZEBOS				
B 13	CT	Stamford	⌂	The English Garden from Machin
B 7	MA	Bolton	⌂	Bow House, Inc.
B 29	MA	North Brookfield	⌂	New England Garden Ornaments
B 44	NJ	Green Brook		The Wood Garden
B 11	PA	Carlisle	⌂	Cumberland Woodcraft
B 42	PA	Elverson		Vixen Hill Gazebos

(continued next page)

PAGE	STATE	CITY	⌂ SHOP	SOURCE
GAZEBOS (continued)				
B 22	PA	Fairview Village		Ivywood Gazebo
B 11	PA	Philadelphia		Dalton Pavilions, Inc.
B 16	TN	Memphis	⌂	The Garden Concepts Collection
B 42	TX	Fredericksburg	⌂	Vintage Wood Works
B 38	WI	Delafield	⌂	Sun Designs
GIFTS FOR GARDENERS				
See also all other categories				
A 47	AR	Elkins	⌂	Holland Wildflower Farm
B 37	CA	Mill Valley	⌂	Smith & Hawken
B 9	CA	Redondo Beach		J Collard
B 16	CA	San Francisco		Gardener's Eden
B 39	CA	Santa Barbara		There's Always the Garden
A 112	CT	Litchfield	⌂	White Flower Farm
B 43	DE	Dover	⌂	Winterthur Museum & Gardens
B 6	GA	Cleveland	⌂	Blue Creek Valley Ventures
A 5	IL	Chapin		Applesource
A 99	IL	Hamburg		Springvale Farm Nursery
B 11	IL	Moline		John Deere Catalog
B 15	IL	Schaumburg	⌂	Florist Products, Inc.
B 43	IN	Indianapolis	⌂	Windleaves
A 16	MA	Falmouth	⌂	Cape Cod Violetry
B 29	MA	Topsfield	⌂	The Walt Nicke Company
B 21	MN	Osseo		Hubbard Folding Box Co.
B 16	NC	Raleigh	⌂	Garden Magic
A 11	NY	Brooklyn		Botanic Garden Company
B 23	OH	Cleveland	⌂	David Kay Garden & Gift Catalogue, Inc.
B 8	OH	Toledo	⌂	Carruth Studio
B 33	OR	Estacada	⌂	Pleasant Hill Farm
B 18	OR	Grants Pass		Greenleaf Industries
B 24	OR	Portland		Landscapes & Accents
A 89	PA	Mechanicsburg	⌂	The Rosemary House
A 42	PA	Wexford		Halcyon Gardens
A 110	SC	Hodges		Wayside Gardens
A 47	TX	Romayor	⌂	Hilltop Herb Farm
A 26	VA	Arlington	⌂	T. DeBaggio Herbs by Mail
B 26	VA	Arlington	⌂	Mrs. McGregor's Garden Shop
B 33	VA	Orange	⌂	The Plow & Hearth
A 44	WA	Fall City	⌂	The Herbfarm
B 9	WA	Mt. Vernon	⌂	Charley's Greenhouse Supply
GLOVES				
B 37	CA	Mill Valley	⌂	Smith & Hawken
B 9	CA	Redondo Beach		J Collard
B 11	IL	Moline		John Deere Catalog
B 7	MA	Salem		Bramen Company, Inc.
B 44	ME	Kennebunkport		Womanswork
B 29	MN	Park Rapids	⌂	North Star Evergreens
B 33	NH	Wilton	⌂	Putnam's
B 19	NJ	Old Tappan		Harlane Company, Inc.
B 5	PA	Greeley	⌂	Dorothy Biddle Service
B 23	PA	Lititz	⌂	Kemp Company
B 18	PA	Pineville	⌂	Growing Naturally
B 9	WI	Elkhart Lake	⌂	Clothcrafters, Inc.
GNOMES				
B 13	Ca	Gormley, ON		The Empire Gnome Manufacturing Co.
GOPHER BASKETS				
B 12	CA	Soquel		Digger's Product Development Co.
GOPHERIT II (R)				
B 36	CA	Laguna Hills		Ryans by Mail
GOVERNMENT PUBLICATIONS				
B 41	MD	Lanham		Unipub

PAGE	STATE	CITY	⌂ SHOP	SOURCE

GRAFTING SUPPLIES

A 78	CA	Chula Vista	⌂	Pacific Tree Farms
B 8	FL	Naples		Brushking
A 88	IN	New Salisbury	⌂	Rocky Meadow Orchard & Nursery
B 25	OH	Piqua	⌂	A. M. Leonard, Inc.
B 12	WI	Manitowoc		The Dramm Company

GRANNY'S BLOOMERS (R)

B 9	IL	Deerfield		Clarel Laboratories, Inc.

GREENHOUSE BUILDING MATERIALS

B 21	CO	Colorado Springs	⌂	Hydro-Gardens, Inc.
B 38	IL	Elmhurst		Suncraft, Inc.
B 40	NC	Goldsboro	⌂	Turner Greenhouses
B 29	ND	Neche	⌂	Northern Greenhouse Sales
B 33	NH	Exeter	⌂	Progressive Building Products
B 37	NH	Manchester	⌂	Solar Components Corporation
B 41	NY	New York		Vegetable Factory, Inc.
B 25	OH	Piqua	⌂	A. M. Leonard, Inc.
B 9	WA	Mt. Vernon	⌂	Charley's Greenhouse Supply
B 3	WI	Hammond	⌂	Arctic Glass & Window Outlet

GREENHOUSE CONTROLS

B 36	CA	Camarillo	⌂	Santa Barbara Greenhouses
B 31	CA	Cotati	⌂	Pacific Coast Greenhouse Manufacturing Co.
B 14	MD	Columbia	⌂	Everlite Greenhouses, Inc.
B 23	MD	Laurel		Janco Greenhouses
B 38	MO	North Kansas City		Stuppy Greenhouse Manufacturing, Inc.
B 40	NC	Goldsboro	⌂	Turner Greenhouses
B 33	NH	Exeter	⌂	Progressive Building Products
B 37	NH	Manchester	⌂	Solar Components Corporation
B 33	NJ	Princeton	⌂	Qualimetrics, Inc.
B 13	NY	Staten Island		East Coast Hydroponics
B 10	OH	Medina	⌂	Cropking, Inc.
B 38	OR	Portland	⌂	Sturdi-Built Mfg. Co.
B 39	TX	Ft. Worth	⌂	Texas Greenhouse Co.
B 38	WA	Seattle	⌂	Sunglo Solar Greenhouses

GREENHOUSE EQUIPMENT & ACCESSORIES

B 17	AL	Mobile	⌂	Gothic Arch Greenhouses
B 31	CA	Cotati	⌂	Pacific Coast Greenhouse Manufacturing Co.
B 11	CA	Sun Valley	⌂	D.I.G. Corporation
B 31	CA	Watsonville		Pat's "Mini-Pack" Labels
B 21	CO	Colorado Springs	⌂	Hydro-Gardens, Inc.
B 30	FL	Miami	⌂	OFE International, Inc.
B 38	IL	Elmhurst		Suncraft, Inc.
B 14	MD	Columbia	⌂	Everlite Greenhouses, Inc.
B 23	MD	Laurel		Janco Greenhouses
B 29	MN	Park Rapids	⌂	North Star Evergreens
B 32	MO	Grover	⌂	Plastic Plumbing Products, Inc.
B 38	MO	North Kansas City		Stuppy Greenhouse Manufacturing, Inc.
B 40	NC	Goldsboro	⌂	Turner Greenhouses
B 35	NE	Columbus	⌂	Rodco Products Co., Inc.
B 41	NY	New York		Vegetable Factory, Inc.
B 10	OH	Medina	⌂	Cropking, Inc.
B 1	OR	Junction City	⌂	Agrilite
B 31	OR	Portland	⌂	Pacific Garden Supply
B 38	OR	Portland	⌂	Sturdi-Built Mfg. Co.
A 17	SC	Newberry	⌂	Carter & Holmes, Inc.
B 39	TX	Ft. Worth	⌂	Texas Greenhouse Co.
B 18	TX	Littlefield		The Greener Thumb
B 41	VA	Charlottesville	⌂	Victory Garden Supply Co.
B 9	WA	Mt. Vernon	⌂	Charley's Greenhouse Supply
B 30	WA	Redmond		Northwest Eden Sales, Inc.
B 38	WA	Seattle	⌂	Sunglo Solar Greenhouses

GREENHOUSE HEATERS

B 17	AL	Mobile	⌂	Gothic Arch Greenhouses
B 36	CA	Camarillo	⌂	Santa Barbara Greenhouses

(continued next page)

PAGE	STATE	CITY	⌂ SHOP	SOURCE
GREENHOUSE HEATERS (continued)				
B 31	CA	Cotati	⌂	Pacific Coast Greenhouse Manufacturing Co.
B 38	IL	Elmhurst		Suncraft, Inc.
B 14	MD	Columbia	⌂	Everlite Greenhouses, Inc.
B 38	MO	North Kansas City		Stuppy Greenhouse Manufacturing, Inc.
B 40	NC	Goldsboro	⌂	Turner Greenhouses
B 33	NH	Exeter	⌂	Progressive Building Products
B 41	NY	New York		Vegetable Factory, Inc.
B 10	OH	Medina	⌂	Cropking, Inc.
B 38	OR	Portland	⌂	Sturdi-Built Mfg. Co.
B 39	TX	Ft. Worth	⌂	Texas Greenhouse Co.
B 38	WA	Seattle	⌂	Sunglo Solar Greenhouses
GREENHOUSE SUPPLIES				
B 17	AL	Mobile	⌂	Gothic Arch Greenhouses
B 31	CA	Cotati	⌂	Pacific Coast Greenhouse Manufacturing Co.
B 13	FL	Ft. Lauderdale	⌂	Environmental Concepts
B 15	IL	Schaumburg	⌂	Florist Products, Inc.
B 38	MO	North Kansas City		Stuppy Greenhouse Manufacturing, Inc.
B 1	OR	Junction City	⌂	Agrilite
A 37	PA	Georgetown		Georgetown Greenhouse & Nursery
B 7	PA	New Brighton		Brighton By-Products Co., Inc.
GREENHOUSE VENTILATORS				
B 17	AL	Mobile	⌂	Gothic Arch Greenhouses
B 36	CA	Camarillo	⌂	Santa Barbara Greenhouses
B 31	CA	Cotati	⌂	Pacific Coast Greenhouse Manufacturing Co.
B 38	CA	Huntington Beach	⌂	Superior Autovents
B 38	IL	Elmhurst		Suncraft, Inc.
B 14	MD	Columbia	⌂	Everlite Greenhouses, Inc.
B 23	MD	Laurel		Janco Greenhouses
B 38	MO	North Kansas City		Stuppy Greenhouse Manufacturing, Inc.
B 40	NC	Goldsboro	⌂	Turner Greenhouses
B 33	NH	Exeter	⌂	Progressive Building Products
B 37	NH	Manchester	⌂	Solar Components Corporation
B 41	NY	New York		Vegetable Factory, Inc.
B 10	OH	Medina	⌂	Cropking, Inc.
B 38	OR	Portland	⌂	Sturdi-Built Mfg. Co.
B 39	TX	Ft. Worth	⌂	Texas Greenhouse Co.
B 41	VA	Charlottesville	⌂	Victory Garden Supply Co.
B 38	WA	Seattle	⌂	Sunglo Solar Greenhouses
GREENHOUSE WINDOWS				
B 14	MD	Columbia	⌂	Everlite Greenhouses, Inc.
B 32	MO	Shawnee Mission		Peerless Products, Inc.
B 41	NY	New York		Vegetable Factory, Inc.
B 26	NY	Niagara Falls		Lord & Burnham
B 3	WI	Hammond	⌂	Arctic Glass & Window Outlet
GREENHOUSES				
B 17	AL	Mobile	⌂	Gothic Arch Greenhouses
B 36	CA	Camarillo	⌂	Santa Barbara Greenhouses
B 31	CA	Cotati	⌂	Pacific Coast Greenhouse Manufacturing Co.
B 21	CO	Colorado Springs	⌂	Hydro-Gardens, Inc.
B 38	IL	Elmhurst		Suncraft, Inc.
B 15	IL	Schaumburg	⌂	Florist Products, Inc.
B 14	MD	Columbia	⌂	Everlite Greenhouses, Inc.
B 23	MD	Laurel		Janco Greenhouses
A 52	ME	Albion	⌂	Johnny's Selected Seeds
B 38	MO	North Kansas City		Stuppy Greenhouse Manufacturing, Inc.
B 40	NC	Goldsboro	⌂	Turner Greenhouses
B 33	NH	Exeter	⌂	Progressive Building Products
B 37	NH	Manchester	⌂	Solar Components Corporation
B 16	NY	Holbrook		Four Seasons Greenhouses
B 41	NY	New York		Vegetable Factory, Inc.
B 26	NY	Niagara Falls		Lord & Burnham
B 10	OH	Medina	⌂	Cropking, Inc.
B 5	ON	St. Thomas	⌂	Berry-Hill, Limited
B 38	OR	Portland	⌂	Sturdi-Built Mfg. Co.

(continued next page)

PAGE	STATE	CITY	⌂ SHOP	SOURCE

GREENHOUSES (continued)

PAGE	STATE	CITY	⌂ SHOP	SOURCE
B 17	PA	Harleysville	⌂	E. C. Geiger, Inc.
A 17	SC	Newberry	⌂	Carter & Holmes, Inc.
B 39	TX	Ft. Worth	⌂	Texas Greenhouse Co.
B 41	VA	Charlottesville	⌂	Victory Garden Supply Co.
B 17	VT	Burlington	⌂	Gardener's Supply Company
B 9	WA	Mt. Vernon	⌂	Charley's Greenhouse Supply
B 30	WA	Redmond		Northwest Eden Sales, Inc.
B 38	WA	Seattle	⌂	Sunglo Solar Greenhouses

GROWING SUPPLIES, GENERAL
See also Growing Supplies, Indoor
See also Propagation Supplies

PAGE	STATE	CITY	⌂ SHOP	SOURCE
A 2	AB	Bowden	⌂	Alberta Nurseries & Seed Company
A 92	AB	Edmonton	⌂	Seed Centre, Ltd.
B 16	CA	Redway	⌂	Full Circle Garden Products
A 14	CO	Rocky Ford		D. V. Burrell Seed Growers Co.
B 30	FA	Odessa		Odessa Natural Enterprises
A 104	FL	Fort Myers		Tomato Growers Supply Company
B 42	FL	Gainesville	⌂	The Violet House
B 30	FL	Miami	⌂	OFE International, Inc.
B 7	GA	Augusta	⌂	Bricker's Organic Farm
A 52	GA	Ellijay	⌂	Johnson Nursery
A 67	IA	Shenandoah	⌂	Earl May Seed & Nursery Co.
B 2	IL	Galesburg		Alsto's Handy Helpers
A 25	KY	Louisville		Dabney Herbs
A 64	MB	Brandon		McFayden Seeds
A 68	MD	Baltimore		Meyer Seed Co.
A 26	MD	Frederick		Dan's Garden Shop
A 2	ME	Falmouth	⌂	Allen, Sterling & Lothrop
B 34	MN	Eden Prairie	⌂	Ringer Corporation
A 31	MN	Faribault	⌂	Farmer Seed & Nursery
B 29	MN	Park Rapids	⌂	North Star Evergreens
A 99	MO	Louisiana	⌂	Stark Bro's Nurseries & Orchards Co.
A 6	MO	Sedalia		Archias' Seed Store
A 60	NJ	Sewell	⌂	Orol Ledden & Sons
A 89	NM	Roswell	⌂	Roswell Seed Co.
B 32	NY	Buffalo		Plant Collectibles
A 100	NY	Buffalo		Stokes Seed Company
A 43	NY	Rochester		Harris Seeds
B 6	NY	Yorkville	⌂	Bonide Chemical Co., Inc.
B 10	OH	Medina	⌂	Cropking, Inc.
A 61	OH	New Philadelphia	⌂	Liberty Seed Company
A 67	OH	North Lima	⌂	Mellinger's, Inc.
B 25	OH	Piqua	⌂	A. M. Leonard, Inc.
A 27	ON	Georgetown	⌂	Dominion Seed House
A 105	ON	Hamilton	⌂	Tregunno Seeds
A 24	ON	Toronto	⌂	Cruickshank's, Inc.
A 75	ON	Waterloo		Ontario Seed Company, Ltd.
A 72	OR	Albany	⌂	Nichols Garden Nursery, Inc.
B 16	OR	Corvallis	⌂	Full Moon Farm Products
A 103	OR	Lorane	⌂	Territorial Seed Company
A 35	PA	McGrann		Fox Hollow Herbs
B 7	PA	New Brighton		Brighton By-Products Co., Inc.
B 24	PA	Point Pleasant	⌂	Kinsman Company, Inc.
A 106	PA	Trevose		Otis Twilley Seed Co.
A 14	PA	Warminster	⌂	W. Atlee Burpee Company
A 109	PE	Charlottetown	⌂	Vesey's Seeds, Ltd.
A 78	SC	Greenwood	⌂	Park Seed Company, Inc.
A 28	SK	Saskatoon	⌂	Early's Farm & Garden Centre, Inc.
A 90	TX	Nash		SPB Sales
A 82	TX	Stephenville		Porter & Son
B 17	VT	Burlington	⌂	Gardener's Supply Company
A 108	VT	Fair Haven	⌂	Vermont Bean Seed Co.
B 18	WA	Puyallup	⌂	Green Earth Organics
A 53	WI	Randolph	⌂	J. W. Jung Seed Co.
A 82	WI	Tilleda	⌂	Pony Creek Nursery

PAGE	STATE	CITY	⌂ SHOP	SOURCE

GROWING SUPPLIES, INDOOR
See also Growing Supplies, General
See also Propagation Supplies

PAGE	STATE	CITY	⌂ SHOP	SOURCE
A 111	BC	Vancouver	⌂	West Coast Violets
B 16	CA	Redway	⌂	Full Circle Garden Products
B 3	CA	San Rafael	⌂	Applied Hydroponics
A 64	CA	South San Francisco	⌂	Rod McLellan Co.
A 109	CO	Englewood	⌂	The Violet Showcase
B 13	FL	Ft. Lauderdale	⌂	Environmental Concepts
B 42	FL	Gainesville	⌂	The Violet House
B 12	FL	Merritt Island	⌂	DoDe's Gardens, Inc.
B 40	FL	Orlando	⌂	Tropical Plant Products, Inc.
A 101	FL	Port Richey	⌂	Sunshine State Tropicals
A 74	IL	Dundee	⌂	Oak Hill Gardens
B 15	IL	Schaumburg	⌂	Florist Products, Inc.
B 2	IL	Streamwood	⌂	Alternative Garden Supply, Inc.
A 26	IN	Crawfordsville	⌂	Davidson-Wilson Greenhouses
A 64	KS	Wichita	⌂	McKinney's Glasshouse
A 26	MD	Frederick		Dan's Garden Shop
B 18	MI	Ann Arbor	⌂	Grower's Supply Co.
B 21	MI	Detroit		Indoor Gardening Supplies
B 32	NY	Buffalo		Plant Collectibles
A 43	NY	Rochester		Harris Seeds
B 6	NY	Yorkville	⌂	Bonide Chemical Co., Inc.
B 16	OR	Corvallis	⌂	Full Moon Farm Products
B 1	OR	Junction City	⌂	Agrilite
B 28	OR	Medford	⌂	Nature's Control
B 22	OR	Portland	⌂	JC's Garden Center
B 31	OR	Portland	⌂	Pacific Garden Supply
A 42	PA	Wexford		Halcyon Gardens
B 3	PQ	Montreal	⌂	Applied Hydroponics of Canada
A 60	PQ	Sawyerville		Les Violettes Natalia

GROWTH STIMULANTS

PAGE	STATE	CITY	⌂ SHOP	SOURCE
B 34	CA	San Diego	⌂	Bargyla Rateaver
B 40	FL	Bradenton	⌂	Tropexotic Growers, Inc.
B 12	FL	Merritt Island	⌂	DoDe's Gardens, Inc.
B 7	GA	Augusta	⌂	Bricker's Organic Farm
B 22	OR	Portland	⌂	JC's Garden Center
B 27	TX	Hondo		Medina Agricultural Products Co.
B 37	TX	Houston	⌂	Spray-N-Grow, Inc.
A 37	TX	Laredo	⌂	Garden World
B 5	VA	Falls Church		Bio-Gard Agronomics

GUANO, BAT

PAGE	STATE	CITY	⌂ SHOP	SOURCE
B 29	AR	Fayetteville	⌂	Nitron Industries, Inc.
B 12	CA	Corte Madera	⌂	Dirt Cheap Organics
B 16	CA	Redway	⌂	Full Circle Garden Products
B 1	CO	Boulder		Age-Old Garden Supply
B 12	IN	Jeffersonville		Earlee, Inc.
B 13	NY	Staten Island		East Coast Hydroponics
B 18	OH	Cleveland		The Guano Company
B 16	OR	Corvallis	⌂	Full Moon Farm Products
B 22	OR	Portland	⌂	JC's Garden Center
B 31	OR	Portland	⌂	Pacific Garden Supply
B 21	WA	Wenatchee	⌂	I. F. M.

GUANO, SEABIRD

PAGE	STATE	CITY	⌂ SHOP	SOURCE
B 13	NY	Staten Island		East Coast Hydroponics
B 18	OH	Cleveland		The Guano Company
B 22	OR	Portland	⌂	JC's Garden Center

HADDONSTONE (R)

PAGE	STATE	CITY	⌂ SHOP	SOURCE
B 14	PA	Philadelphia		Exotic Blossoms

HAMMOCKS

PAGE	STATE	CITY	⌂ SHOP	SOURCE
B 16	CA	San Francisco		Gardener's Eden
B 19	CO	Boulder	⌂	Hangouts
B 31	DC	Washington	⌂	Park Place

(continued next page)

PAGE	STATE	CITY	⌂ SHOP	SOURCE

HAMMOCKS (continued)

| B 11 | IL | Moline | | John Deere Catalog |

HANGING BASKETS

B 43	DE	Dover	⌂	Winterthur Museum & Gardens
B 30	FL	Miami	⌂	OFE International, Inc.
B 40	FL	Orlando	⌂	Tropical Plant Products, Inc.
B 32	NY	Buffalo		Plant Collectibles

HANGOUTS (R)

| B 19 | CO | Boulder | ⌂ | Hangouts |

HISTORICAL REPRODUCTIONS, ORNAMENTAL
See also specific type

B 35	AL	Alexander City		Robinson Iron
B 3	CA	Duarte		Arroyo Craftsman Lighting, Inc.
B 13	CA	Menlo Park		east/west Gardens
B 13	CT	Stamford	⌂	The English Garden from Machin
B 30	IN	Carmel		Old-World Garden Troughs
B 29	MA	North Brookfield	⌂	New England Garden Ornaments
B 16	NC	Raleigh	⌂	Garden Magic
B 20	NH	North Hampton	⌂	Historic Hardware, Ltd.
B 17	NJ	Vincentown	⌂	Genie House
B 12	NV	Silver City	⌂	Dressler & Co.
B 33	NY	Bronxville		Pompeian Studios
B 15	NY	Long Island City	⌂	Florentine Craftsmen, Inc.
B 11	PA	Carlisle	⌂	Cumberland Woodcraft
B 19	PA	Gulph Mills		Hen-Feathers & Company
B 14	PA	Philadelphia		Exotic Blossoms
B 9	SC	Charleston	⌂	Charleston Battery Bench, Inc.
B 16	TN	Memphis	⌂	The Garden Concepts Collection
B 42	TX	Fredericksburg	⌂	Vintage Wood Works

HONEYDEW (TM)

| B 5 | CA | Berry Creek | ⌂ | Bio-Control Co. |

HORTICULTURAL CLIP ART

| B 43 | IL | Champaign | | Wheeler Arts |

HORTICULTURAL TOURS

B 10	CA	Oakland		Coopersmith's England
B 17	CA	Rohnert Park	⌂	Geostar Travel
B 36	CA	Santa Barbara		Santa Barbara Orchid Garden & Library
B 10	En	London		Cox & Kings Travel
B 28	En	London		Raoul Moxley Travel
B 42	En	London		Voyages Jules Verne
A 31	FL	Homestead	⌂	Fennell's Orchid Jungle
B 4	FL	Miami		Leona Bee Tours & Travel
B 25	VT	Burlington		Limewalk Tours

HORTOPAPER (R)

| B 20 | CA | Fresno | ⌂ | Hortopaper Growing Systems |

HUMIDIFIERS

B 36	CA	Camarillo	⌂	Santa Barbara Greenhouses
B 31	CA	Cotati	⌂	Pacific Coast Greenhouse Manufacturing Co.
B 27	CA	San Francisco		Don Mattern
B 40	NC	Goldsboro	⌂	Turner Greenhouses
B 38	OR	Portland	⌂	Sturdi-Built Mfg. Co.
B 37	RI	Pawtucket	⌂	Standard Humidifier
B 9	WA	Mt. Vernon	⌂	Charley's Greenhouse Supply

HUSKY-FIBER (R)

| A 65 | FL | Windemere | ⌂ | Ann Mann's Orchids |

HYDRION (R) PAPERS

| B 27 | NY | Brooklyn | | Micro Essential Laboratory, Inc. |

PAGE	STATE	CITY	⌂ SHOP	SOURCE
HYDROFARM (R) SYSTEMS				
B 3	CA	San Rafael	⌂	Applied Hydroponics
HYDROGELS				
B 23	CA	Davis		Janziker
B 34	MN	Eden Prairie	⌂	Ringer Corporation
B 29	MN	Park Rapids	⌂	North Star Evergreens
B 23	OH	Cleveland	⌂	JRM Chemical, Inc.
A 46	OR	Milwaukie	⌂	Hidden Garden Nursery, Inc.
B 31	OR	Portland	⌂	Pacific Garden Supply
B 28	TN	Chattanooga		Multiple Concepts
B 18	TX	Ft. Worth		Grosoke, Inc.
B 31	UT	North Logan		Pan Agro, Inc.
HYDROPONIC SUPPLIES				
B 20	CA	Irvine		Hollister's Hydroponics
B 3	CA	San Rafael	⌂	Applied Hydroponics
B 17	CA	San Rafael		General Hydroponics
B 21	CO	Colorado Springs	⌂	Hydro-Gardens, Inc.
B 2	IL	Streamwood	⌂	Alternative Garden Supply, Inc.
B 13	NY	Staten Island		East Coast Hydroponics
B 10	OH	Medina	⌂	Cropking, Inc.
A 20	ON	Mississauga	⌂	Clargreen Gardens, Ltd.
B 16	OR	Corvallis	⌂	Full Moon Farm Products
B 22	OR	Portland	⌂	JC's Garden Center
B 31	OR	Portland	⌂	Pacific Garden Supply
B 3	PQ	Montreal	⌂	Applied Hydroponics of Canada
HYDROPONIC SYSTEMS				
B 20	CA	Irvine		Hollister's Hydroponics
B 16	CA	Redway	⌂	Full Circle Garden Products
B 3	CA	San Rafael	⌂	Applied Hydroponics
B 17	CA	San Rafael		General Hydroponics
B 25	CA	Sebastopol		Living Green, Inc.
B 21	CO	Colorado Springs	⌂	Hydro-Gardens, Inc.
B 2	IL	Streamwood	⌂	Alternative Garden Supply, Inc.
B 10	OH	Medina	⌂	Cropking, Inc.
B 16	OR	Corvallis	⌂	Full Moon Farm Products
B 22	OR	Portland	⌂	JC's Garden Center
B 3	PQ	Montreal	⌂	Applied Hydroponics of Canada
B 18	WI	Sheboygan	⌂	Green Thumb Hygro-Gardens
INFORMATION HOTLINES				
B 1				ATTRA
INSECT CONTROLS, INFORMATION				
B 1				ATTRA
B 21	CA	Davis		IPM Computer System
INSECT CONTROLS, ORGANIC				
See also Pest Controls, Organic				
B 29	AR	Fayetteville	⌂	Nitron Industries, Inc.
B 32	BC	Delta		Phero Tech, Inc.
B 37	CA	Arroyo Grande		Spalding Laboratories
B 5	CA	Berry Creek	⌂	Bio-Control Co.
B 41	CA	Citrus Heights		Unique Insect Control
B 15	CA	Corona	⌂	Foothill Agricultural Research, Inc.
B 43	CA	Gridley	⌂	West Coast Ladybug Sales
B 30	CA	Los Angeles	⌂	Organic Control, Inc.
B 4	CA	Oak Run		Beneficial Insectary
B 16	CA	Redway	⌂	Full Circle Garden Products
B 15	CA	Rough & Ready		Fountain Sierra Bug Company
B 28	CA	San Anselmo	⌂	The Natural Gardening Company
B 34	CA	San Diego	⌂	Bargyla Rateaver
B 5	CA	Santa Paula		Bio-Resources
A 11	CA	Willits	⌂	Bountiful Gardens
B 14	CO	Broomfield		Evans BioControl, Inc.
B 35	CO	Palisade		Rocky Mountain Insectary
B 42	FL	Gainesville	⌂	The Violet House

(continued next page)

PAGE	STATE	CITY	⌂ SHOP	SOURCE
INSECT CONTROLS, ORGANIC (continued)				
B 30	FL	Miami	⌂	OFE International, Inc.
A 55	FL	Sanford	⌂	Kilgore Seed Company
B 12	IN	Jeffersonville		Earlee, Inc.
B 28	IN	Sunman		Natural Gardening Research Center
B 20	KS	Overland Park		Holland's Organic Garden
A 52	ME	Albion	⌂	Johnny's Selected Seeds
B 34	MN	Eden Prairie	⌂	Ringer Corporation
B 29	MN	Park Rapids	⌂	North Star Evergreens
A 60	NJ	Sewell	⌂	Orol Ledden & Sons
B 14	NY	Clinton Corners		Fairfax Biological Lab, Inc.
B 6	NY	Yorkville	⌂	Bonide Chemical Co., Inc.
B 30	OH	Hartville	⌂	Ohio Earth Food, Inc.
B 26	OH	Perry		MacKenzie Nursery Supply
B 5	ON	Windsor	⌂	Better Yield Insects & Garden Houses
B 28	OR	Medford	⌂	Nature's Control
B 31	OR	Portland	⌂	Pacific Garden Supply
B 44	PA	Gap	⌂	Zook & Ranck, Inc.
B 6	PA	Willow Hill	⌂	BioLogic
B 24	TX	Quemado	⌂	Kunafin
B 8	VA	Lexington		Bug-Off, The Natural Alternative
B 29	VA	New Castle	⌂	Necessary Trading Co.
A 84	WA	Morton	⌂	Raintree Nursery
B 9	WA	Mt. Vernon	⌂	Charley's Greenhouse Supply
B 18	WA	Puyallup	⌂	Green Earth Organics
B 30	WA	Seattle	⌂	Organic Pest Management
B 21	WA	Wenatchee	⌂	I. F. M.
INSECT REPELLENTS				
B 3	MN	White Bear Lake		Aquacide Company
B 39	OR	Albany		Tec Laboratories, Inc.
INSECT TRAPS				
B 32	BC	Delta		Phero Tech, Inc.
A 111	BC	Vancouver	⌂	West Coast Violets
B 37	CA	Arroyo Grande		Spalding Laboratories
B 36	CA	Emeryville	⌂	Seabright Enterprises
B 4	CA	Oak Run		Beneficial Insectary
B 30	FA	Odessa		Odessa Natural Enterprises
B 28	IN	Sunman		Natural Gardening Research Center
B 18	MI	Vestaburg	⌂	Great Lakes IPM
B 30	OH	Hartville	⌂	Ohio Earth Food, Inc.
B 5	ON	Windsor	⌂	Better Yield Insects & Garden Houses
B 28	OR	Medford	⌂	Nature's Control
B 18	PA	Pineville	⌂	Growing Naturally
B 29	VA	New Castle	⌂	Necessary Trading Co.
B 24	VT	Burlington		Ladd Research Industries
B 30	WA	Seattle	⌂	Organic Pest Management
B 21	WA	Wenatchee	⌂	I. F. M.
INSECTS, BENEFICIAL				
B 37	CA	Arroyo Grande		Spalding Laboratories
B 5	CA	Berry Creek	⌂	Bio-Control Co.
B 41	CA	Citrus Heights		Unique Insect Control
B 15	CA	Corona	⌂	Foothill Agricultural Research, Inc.
B 12	CA	Corte Madera	⌂	Dirt Cheap Organics
A 79	CA	Grass Valley	⌂	Peaceful Valley Farm Supply
B 19	CA	Graton	⌂	Harmony Farm Supply
B 43	CA	Gridley	⌂	West Coast Ladybug Sales
B 29	CA	Lafayette		Nematec -- Biological Control Agents
B 30	CA	Los Angeles	⌂	Organic Control, Inc.
B 4	CA	Oak Run		Beneficial Insectary
B 16	CA	Redway	⌂	Full Circle Garden Products
B 15	CA	Rough & Ready		Fountain Sierra Bug Company
B 28	CA	San Anselmo	⌂	The Natural Gardening Company
B 5	CA	Santa Paula		Bio-Resources
B 21	CO	Colorado Springs	⌂	Hydro-Gardens, Inc.
B 35	CO	Palisade		Rocky Mountain Insectary
B 2	IL	Streamwood	⌂	Alternative Garden Supply, Inc.

(continued next page)

PAGE	STATE	CITY	⌂ SHOP	SOURCE
INSECTS, BENEFICIAL (continued)				
B 28	IN	Sunman		Natural Gardening Research Center
A 81	NM	Santa Fe	⌂	Plants of the Southwest
B 13	NY	Staten Island		East Coast Hydroponics
A 87	ON	Goodwood	⌂	Richters
B 5	ON	Windsor	⌂	Better Yield Insects & Garden Houses
B 16	OR	Corvallis	⌂	Full Moon Farm Products
B 28	OR	Medford	⌂	Nature's Control
B 18	PA	Pineville	⌂	Growing Naturally
B 6	PA	Willow Hill	⌂	BioLogic
B 24	TX	Quemado	⌂	Kunafin
B 29	VA	New Castle	⌂	Necessary Trading Co.
B 30	WA	Seattle	⌂	Organic Pest Management
B 21	WA	Wenatchee	⌂	I. F. M.
A 82	WI	Tilleda	⌂	Pony Creek Nursery
IRRIGATION SUPPLIES				
See also Drip Irrigation				
See also Mist Irrigation				
B 29	AR	Fayetteville	⌂	Nitron Industries, Inc.
B 41	AZ	Bouse	⌂	UPCO Irrigation
B 34	CA	Chatsworth		Raindrip, Inc.
B 19	CA	Graton	⌂	Harmony Farm Supply
B 41	CA	San Francisco	⌂	The Urban Farmer Store
B 2	IL	Galesburg		Alsto's Handy Helpers
B 15	IL	Schaumburg	⌂	Florist Products, Inc.
B 20	KS	Overland Park		Holland's Organic Garden
B 32	MO	Grover	⌂	Plastic Plumbing Products, Inc.
B 7	PA	New Brighton		Brighton By-Products Co., Inc.
B 38	TX	Lubbock	⌂	Submatic Irrigation Systems
B 34	VA	Lowesville	⌂	The Ram Company
B 17	VT	Burlington	⌂	Gardener's Supply Company
IRRIGRO (R)				
B 22	ON	St. Catharines	⌂	International Irrigation Systems
JAPIDEMIC (R)				
B 14	NY	Clinton Corners		Fairfax Biological Lab, Inc.
JUNGLE JUICE (R)				
B 9	IL	Deerfield		Clarel Laboratories, Inc.
KEEP 'EM BLOOMIN' (R)				
B 9	IL	Deerfield		Clarel Laboratories, Inc.
KRICKET KRAP (R)				
B 7	GA	Augusta	⌂	Bricker's Organic Farm
LANTERNS, STONE				
A 94	CT	Stamford	⌂	Shanti Bithi Nursery
B 19	PA	Pleasant Gap	⌂	Philip Hawk & Company
LASCOLITE (R)				
B 33	NH	Exeter	⌂	Progressive Building Products
LAWN VACUUMS				
B 32	NC	Arden		PeCo, Inc.
LIGHT FIXTURES, OUTDOOR				
B 35	AL	Alexander City		Robinson Iron
B 37	AL	Birmingham		Southern Statuary and Stone
B 28	CA	Bayside		Nampara Gardens
B 42	CA	Burbank	⌂	Wendelighting
B 3	CA	Duarte		Arroyo Craftsman Lighting, Inc.
B 9	CA	Redondo Beach		J Collard
B 16	CA	San Francisco		Gardener's Eden
B 31	DC	Washington	⌂	Park Place
B 21	ID	Sandpoint	⌂	Idaho Wood Industries, Inc.
B 20	ME	Yarmouth	⌂	Heritage Lanterns

(continued next page)

PAGE	STATE	CITY	⌂ SHOP	SOURCE

LIGHT FIXTURES, OUTDOOR (continued)

B 7	NC	Connelly Springs	⌂	Andy Brinkley Studios
B 16	NC	Raleigh	⌂	Garden Magic
B 20	NH	North Hampton	⌂	Historic Hardware, Ltd.
B 17	NJ	Vincentown	⌂	Genie House
B 1	OR	Junction City	⌂	Agrilite
B 25	OR	Portland		Liteform Designs
B 37	PA	Honey Brook		Simple's Creative Quality Trellises
B 7	PA	Malvern		Brandywine Garden Furniture
B 33	PA	Pittsburgh		Popovitch Associates, Inc.

LIGHTING SYSTEMS, OUTDOOR

B 31	DC	Washington	⌂	Park Place
B 9	MA	West Newton	⌂	The Clapper Co.
B 1	OR	Junction City	⌂	Agrilite

LIL SUCKER (TM)

B 39	OR	Albany		Tec Laboratories, Inc.

LIVE TRAPS, ANIMALS

See also Animal Repellents

B 36	CA	Emeryville	⌂	Seabright Enterprises
B 26	OK	Oklahoma City		MAC Industries
B 5	ON	St. Thomas	⌂	Berry-Hill, Limited
B 29	VA	New Castle	⌂	Necessary Trading Co.
B 30	WA	Seattle	⌂	Organic Pest Management

LOG SPLITTERS

B 34	IL	Rockford		RAM Log Splitters
B 14	MA	Woburn	⌂	FXG Corporation
B 43	NE	Broken Bow		Wikco Industries, Inc.
B 26	OH	London	⌂	Mainline of North America

LUWASA HYDROCULTURE (R)

B 3	PQ	Montreal	⌂	Applied Hydroponics of Canada

MAXICROP (R)

B 12	CA	Corte Madera	⌂	Dirt Cheap Organics
B 34	CA	San Diego	⌂	Bargyla Rateaver
B 12	IN	Jeffersonville		Earlee, Inc.
B 20	KS	Overland Park		Holland's Organic Garden
B 44	PA	Gap	⌂	Zook & Ranck, Inc.

METERS AND INSTRUMENTS

B 31	AR	Eureka Springs	⌂	Ozark Handle & Hardware
B 28	CA	San Anselmo	⌂	The Natural Gardening Company
B 3	CA	San Rafael	⌂	Applied Hydroponics
B 21	CO	Colorado Springs	⌂	Hydro-Gardens, Inc.
B 13	FL	Ft. Lauderdale	⌂	Environmental Concepts
B 42	FL	Gainesville	⌂	The Violet House
B 27	MA	New Bedford		Maximum, Inc.
B 21	MI	Detroit		Indoor Gardening Supplies
B 35	NE	Columbus	⌂	Rodco Products Co., Inc.
B 19	NJ	Old Tappan		Harlane Company, Inc.
B 33	NJ	Princeton	⌂	Qualimetrics, Inc.
B 13	NY	Staten Island		East Coast Hydroponics
B 30	OH	Hartville	⌂	Ohio Earth Food, Inc.
B 10	OH	Medina	⌂	Cropking, Inc.
B 22	OR	Portland	⌂	JC's Garden Center
B 31	OR	Portland	⌂	Pacific Garden Supply
B 5	PA	Greeley	⌂	Dorothy Biddle Service
B 17	PA	Harleysville	⌂	E. C. Geiger, Inc.
B 40	WA	Enumclaw	⌂	Trade-Wind Instruments
B 21	WA	Wenatchee	⌂	I. F. M.

MIST IRRIGATION SUPPLIES

B 41	AZ	Bouse	⌂	UPCO Irrigation
B 28	CA	Fremont		Misti Maid, Inc.
B 37	CA	Huntington Beach	⌂	Spot Systems

(continued next page)

PAGE	STATE	CITY	⌂ SHOP	SOURCE
MIST IRRIGATION SUPPLIES (continued)				
B 11	CA	Sun Valley	⌂	D.I.G. Corporation
B 21	CO	Colorado Springs	⌂	Hydro-Gardens, Inc.
B 30	FL	Miami	⌂	OFE International, Inc.
B 28	FL	Palmetto		Moss Products, Inc.
B 32	MO	Grover	⌂	Plastic Plumbing Products, Inc.
B 38	MO	North Kansas City		Stuppy Greenhouse Manufacturing, Inc.
B 40	NC	Goldsboro	⌂	Turner Greenhouses
B 3	NY	Huntington		Aquamonitor
B 38	OR	Portland	⌂	Sturdi-Built Mfg. Co.
B 17	PA	Harleysville	⌂	E. C. Geiger, Inc.
B 39	TX	Ft. Worth	⌂	Texas Greenhouse Co.
B 38	TX	Lubbock	⌂	Submatic Irrigation Systems
B 12	WI	Manitowoc		The Dramm Company
MIST IRRIGATION SYSTEMS				
B 41	AZ	Bouse	⌂	UPCO Irrigation
B 36	CA	Camarillo	⌂	Santa Barbara Greenhouses
B 31	CA	Cotati	⌂	Pacific Coast Greenhouse Manufacturing Co.
B 28	CA	Fremont		Misti Maid, Inc.
B 37	CA	Huntington Beach	⌂	Spot Systems
B 11	CA	Sun Valley	⌂	D.I.G. Corporation
B 28	FL	Palmetto		Moss Products, Inc.
B 32	MO	Grover	⌂	Plastic Plumbing Products, Inc.
B 3	NY	Huntington		Aquamonitor
B 9	WA	Mt. Vernon	⌂	Charley's Greenhouse Supply
B 12	WI	Manitowoc		The Dramm Company
MOISTURE MIZER (R)				
B 28	TN	Chattanooga		Multiple Concepts
MOONSHINE (R)				
B 9	IL	Deerfield		Clarel Laboratories, Inc.
MULCHES, FABRIC/PAPER/PLASTIC				
B 20	CA	Fresno	⌂	Hortopaper Growing Systems
B 44	GA	Cornelia	⌂	Yonah Manufacturing Co.
B 15	IL	Schaumburg	⌂	Florist Products, Inc.
B 28	IN	Sunman		Natural Gardening Research Center
B 7	MA	Salem		Bramen Company, Inc.
A 80	ME	New Gloucester	⌂	Pinetree Garden Seeds
B 22	NC	Charlotte		Innovative Geotextiles Corp
B 7	PA	New Brighton		Brighton By-Products Co., Inc.
MUSHROOM GROWING SUPPLIES				
A 111	BC	Aldergrove	⌂	Western Biologicals, Ltd.
A 71	CA	Inverness		Mushroompeople
A 4	NC	Henderson	⌂	American Forest Foods Corp.
A 74	OR	Corvallis		Northwest Mycological Consultants
A 36	WA	Olympia		Fungi Perfecti
A 42	WV	Cherry Grove		Hardscrabble Enterprises
NATURE'S WAY (R)				
B 12	IN	Jeffersonville		Earlee, Inc.
NOLO BAIT (R)				
B 14	CO	Broomfield		Evans BioControl, Inc.
ORCHARD SUPPLIES				
A 13	VA	Monroe	⌂	Burford Brothers
ORCHID SUPPLIES				
A 35	AR	Little Rock	⌂	Fox Orchids, Inc.
A 100	CA	Carpinteria	⌂	Stewart Orchids, Inc.
B 10	CA	Lincoln	⌂	Critter Creek Laboratory & Orchids
B 20	CA	Orange		Holz-Ems, Inc.
A 30	CA	Soquel	⌂	John Ewing Orchids, Inc.
A 64	CA	South San Francisco	⌂	Rod McLellan Co.
A 36	CA	Vista	⌂	G & B Orchid Lab & Nursery

(continued next page)

PAGE	STATE	CITY	⌂ SHOP	SOURCE

ORCHID SUPPLIES (continued)

PAGE	STATE	CITY	SHOP	SOURCE
B 42	FL	Gainesville	⌂	The Violet House
A 31	FL	Homestead	⌂	Fennell's Orchid Jungle
A 53	FL	Miami	⌂	Jones & Scully
A 68	FL	Miami	⌂	Miami Orchids
B 30	FL	Miami	⌂	OFE International, Inc.
B 40	FL	Orlando	⌂	Tropical Plant Products, Inc.
A 65	FL	Windemere	⌂	Ann Mann's Orchids
A 76	IL	Villa Park	⌂	Orchids by Hausermann, Inc.
A 83	MB	Winnipeg	⌂	Prairie Orchid Company
B 10	MD	Arnold		Computer/Management Services
A 55	MD	Kensington	⌂	Kensington Orchids
A 20	MI	Detroit	⌂	City Gardens
A 87	MS	Biloxi	⌂	Riverbend Orchids
A 11	NC	Brown Summit	⌂	Breckinridge Orchids
A 92	NY	Glen Head	⌂	Seagulls Landing Orchids
A 49	ON	Bright's Grove	⌂	Huronview Nurseries & Garden Centre
A 55	ON	Komoka	⌂	Kilworth Flowers
A 20	ON	Mississauga	⌂	Clargreen Gardens, Ltd.
A 33	ON	Port Stanley	⌂	Floridel Gardens
A 17	SC	Newberry	⌂	Carter & Holmes, Inc.
B 9	WA	Mt. Vernon	⌂	Charley's Greenhouse Supply

ORCHIDS EXOTICA (R)

PAGE	STATE	CITY	SHOP	SOURCE
B 9	IL	Deerfield		Clarel Laboratories, Inc.

ORGANIC GARDEN PRODUCTS

PAGE	STATE	CITY	SHOP	SOURCE
A 4	AR	Fayetteville		Ames' Orchard and Nursery
B 29	AR	Fayetteville	⌂	Nitron Industries, Inc.
B 20	CA	Fresno	⌂	Hortopaper Growing Systems
A 79	CA	Grass Valley	⌂	Peaceful Valley Farm Supply
B 19	CA	Graton	⌂	Harmony Farm Supply
B 16	CA	Redway	⌂	Full Circle Garden Products
B 28	CA	San Anselmo	⌂	The Natural Gardening Company
B 34	CA	San Diego	⌂	Bargyla Rateaver
B 1	CO	Boulder		Age-Old Garden Supply
B 14	CO	Broomfield		Evans BioControl, Inc.
B 30	FA	Odessa		Odessa Natural Enterprises
B 7	GA	Augusta	⌂	Bricker's Organic Farm
A 46	ID	Ketchum	⌂	High Altitude Gardens
B 13	IL	Mendota	⌂	EnP Inc.
B 12	IN	Jeffersonville		Earlee, Inc.
B 28	IN	Sunman		Natural Gardening Research Center
B 20	KS	Overland Park		Holland's Organic Garden
A 52	ME	Albion	⌂	Johnny's Selected Seeds
A 80	ME	New Gloucester	⌂	Pinetree Garden Seeds
A 31	ME	Waterville		Fedco Seeds
B 34	MN	Eden Prairie	⌂	Ringer Corporation
A 60	NJ	Sewell	⌂	Orol Ledden & Sons
A 81	NM	Santa Fe	⌂	Plants of the Southwest
B 13	NY	Staten Island		East Coast Hydroponics
B 6	NY	Yorkville	⌂	Bonide Chemical Co., Inc.
B 30	OH	Hartville	⌂	Ohio Earth Food, Inc.
B 12	OK	Mounds	⌂	Earthly Goods Farm & Garden Supply
A 25	ON	Dundas	⌂	William Dam Seeds
B 18	PA	Pineville	⌂	Growing Naturally
B 17	VT	Burlington	⌂	Gardener's Supply Company
B 18	WA	Puyallup	⌂	Green Earth Organics
B 30	WA	Seattle	⌂	Organic Pest Management

PATIO CARTS

PAGE	STATE	CITY	SHOP	SOURCE
B 34	CA	Sebastopol	⌂	Reed Bros.
B 1	MA	Bolton		Acorn Services Corporation
B 44	NY	High Falls	⌂	Wood Classics, Inc.
B 7	PA	Malvern		Brandywine Garden Furniture
B 44	WI	Janesville	⌂	Wisconsin Wagon Co.

PERMA-NEST PLANT TRAYS (R)

PAGE	STATE	CITY	SHOP	SOURCE
B 18	MI	Ann Arbor	⌂	Grower's Supply Co.

PAGE	STATE	CITY	⌂ SHOP	SOURCE
PEST CONTROLS, ORGANIC				
See also Insect Controls, Organic				
B 32	BC	Delta		Phero Tech, Inc.
B 41	CA	Citrus Heights		Unique Insect Control
B 15	CA	Corona	⌂	Foothill Agricultural Research, Inc.
B 12	CA	Corte Madera	⌂	Dirt Cheap Organics
B 36	CA	Emeryville	⌂	Seabright Enterprises
A 79	CA	Grass Valley	⌂	Peaceful Valley Farm Supply
B 19	CA	Graton	⌂	Harmony Farm Supply
B 29	CA	Lafayette		Nematec -- Biological Control Agents
B 36	CA	Laguna Hills		Ryans by Mail
B 4	CA	Oak Run		Beneficial Insectary
B 16	CA	Redway	⌂	Full Circle Garden Products
B 28	CA	San Anselmo	⌂	The Natural Gardening Company
B 34	CA	San Diego	⌂	Bargyla Rateaver
B 12	CA	Soquel		Digger's Product Development Co.
B 14	CO	Broomfield		Evans BioControl, Inc.
B 30	FA	Odessa		Odessa Natural Enterprises
B 42	FL	Gainesville	⌂	The Violet House
B 39	ID	Boise	⌂	Thurston Distributing, Inc.
B 12	IN	Jeffersonville		Earlee, Inc.
B 28	IN	Sunman		Natural Gardening Research Center
B 20	KS	Overland Park		Holland's Organic Garden
B 18	MI	Vestaburg	⌂	Great Lakes IPM
B 34	MN	Eden Prairie	⌂	Ringer Corporation
B 29	MN	Park Rapids	⌂	North Star Evergreens
A 63	MT	Kalispell	⌂	Lost Prairie Herb Farm
A 36	MT	Victor		Garden City Seeds
B 14	NY	Clinton Corners		Fairfax Biological Lab, Inc.
B 6	NY	Yorkville	⌂	Bonide Chemical Co., Inc.
B 30	OH	Hartville	⌂	Ohio Earth Food, Inc.
B 12	OK	Mounds	⌂	Earthly Goods Farm & Garden Supply
A 87	ON	Goodwood	⌂	Richters
B 16	OR	Corvallis	⌂	Full Moon Farm Products
B 1	OR	Junction City	⌂	Agrilite
B 28	OR	Medford	⌂	Nature's Control
B 18	PA	Pineville	⌂	Growing Naturally
B 18	TX	Littlefield		The Greener Thumb
B 8	VA	Lexington		Bug-Off, The Natural Alternative
B 29	VA	New Castle	⌂	Necessary Trading Co.
B 17	VT	Burlington	⌂	Gardener's Supply Company
B 18	WA	Puyallup	⌂	Green Earth Organics
B 21	WA	Wenatchee	⌂	I. F. M.
A 110	WI	Plainfield	⌂	The Waushara Gardens
PET DOORS				
B 32	CA	Torrance	⌂	Patio Pacific, Inc.
PHOTOGRAPHS, HORTICULTURAL				
B 41	CA	Soquel		VT Productions
B 14	En	Uxbridge, Middlesex	⌂	Floracolour
A 18	PA	Allison Park		Cedar Ridge Nurseries
B 19	VA	Seaford		Harper Horticultural Slide Library
B 41	WA	Seattle		Videodiscovery, Inc.
PLANT FINDING SERVICES				
B 11	En	Basildon, Essex		Dataplant
A 45	IA	Marshalltown	⌂	Herbs-Liscious
B 20	IN	Jamestown		Heritage Center for the Preservation
B 21	NE	Omaha		Hosta Resources
PLANT HANGERS				
B 20	CA	Orange		Holz-Ems, Inc.
B 4	FL	Orlando		Autumn Forge
B 32	MA	Hingham		Pigeon Hill
B 29	MA	Topsfield	⌂	The Walt Nicke Company
B 20	NH	North Hampton	⌂	Historic Hardware, Ltd.
B 24	OR	Portland		Landscapes & Accents
B 12	WI	Manitowoc		The Dramm Company

PAGE	STATE	CITY	⌂ SHOP	SOURCE
PLANT LABELS				
See also Garden Markers				
A 15	AR	Batesville	⌂	Cactus Gem Nursery
A 111	BC	Vancouver	⌂	West Coast Violets
B 27	CA	Buena Park		Malley Supply
A 15	CA	Lodi	⌂	Cactus by Dodie
B 31	CA	Watsonville		Pat's "Mini-Pack" Labels
B 13	FL	Daytona Beach		Economy Label Sales Co., Inc.
B 42	FL	Gainesville	⌂	The Violet House
B 12	FL	Merritt Island	⌂	DoDe's Gardens, Inc.
B 30	FL	Miami	⌂	OFE International, Inc.
A 26	MD	Frederick		Dan's Garden Shop
A 2	ME	Falmouth	⌂	Allen, Sterling & Lothrop
B 32	MI	Paw Paw		Paw Paw Everlast Label Co.
A 3	MN	Waconia	⌂	Ambergate Gardens
B 32	NY	Buffalo		Plant Collectibles
A 48	OH	Chesterland	⌂	Homestead Division of Sunnybrook Farms
B 37	OH	Cleveland		Signum Sign Systems
B 13	OH	Swanton		Eon Industries
B 19	OR	Junction City		Hall Enterprises
B 18	PA	Pineville	⌂	Growing Naturally
A 10	TX	Lavernia		Bonsai Farm
A 86	WA	Port Townsend	⌂	Rex Bulb Farms
PLANT LIGHTS				
B 16	CA	Redway	⌂	Full Circle Garden Products
B 3	CA	San Rafael	⌂	Applied Hydroponics
A 109	CO	Englewood	⌂	The Violet Showcase
B 41	CT	Greenwich		Verilux, Inc.
B 2	IL	Streamwood	⌂	Alternative Garden Supply, Inc.
B 18	MI	Ann Arbor	⌂	Grower's Supply Co.
B 21	MI	Detroit		Indoor Gardening Supplies
B 18	MI	Livonia		H. P. Supplies, Inc.
B 32	NY	Buffalo		Plant Collectibles
B 33	NY	New York		Public Service Lamp Corp.
B 13	NY	Staten Island		East Coast Hydroponics
B 16	OR	Corvallis	⌂	Full Moon Farm Products
B 1	OR	Junction City	⌂	Agrilite
B 22	OR	Portland	⌂	JC's Garden Center
B 31	OR	Portland	⌂	Pacific Garden Supply
B 3	PQ	Montreal	⌂	Applied Hydroponics of Canada
PLANT STANDS				
B 24	CA	San Diego		La Jolla Sales
B 16	CA	San Francisco		Gardener's Eden
A 109	CO	Englewood	⌂	The Violet Showcase
B 12	FL	Merritt Island	⌂	DoDe's Gardens, Inc.
B 11	FL	Miami	⌂	Day-Dex Co.
B 30	FL	Miami	⌂	OFE International, Inc.
A 105	GA	Ochlochnee	⌂	Travis' Violets
B 2	IL	Galesburg		Alsto's Handy Helpers
B 15	IL	Schaumburg	⌂	Florist Products, Inc.
B 1	MA	Bolton		Acorn Services Corporation
B 18	MI	Ann Arbor	⌂	Grower's Supply Co.
B 21	MI	Detroit		Indoor Gardening Supplies
B 18	MI	Livonia		H. P. Supplies, Inc.
B 20	NH	North Hampton	⌂	Historic Hardware, Ltd.
A 32	NJ	Bargaintown	⌂	Fischer Greenhouses
B 32	NY	Buffalo		Plant Collectibles
B 14	ON	Willowdale		Floralight Gardens Canada, Inc.
A 103	PA	Huntingdon Valley	⌂	Tinari Greenhouses
B 3	PQ	Montreal	⌂	Applied Hydroponics of Canada
B 16	TN	Memphis	⌂	The Garden Concepts Collection
A 109	TX	Dallas	⌂	Volkmann Bros. Greenhouses
PLANT SUPPORTS				
B 14	CA	Cloverdale		Evergreen Garden Plant Labels
B 32	CA	El Cajon		Patches and Pots
B 20	CA	Orange		Holz-Ems, Inc.

(continued next page)

PAGE	STATE	CITY	⌂ SHOP	SOURCE

PLANT SUPPORTS (continued)

A 3	En	Hassocks, W. Sussex	⌂	Allwood Bros.
B 7	MA	Salem		Bramen Company, Inc.
B 29	MA	Topsfield	⌂	The Walt Nicke Company
B 24	PA	Point Pleasant	⌂	Kinsman Company, Inc.

PLANTERS

See also Terra Cotta Pots/Planters

B 35	AL	Alexander City		Robinson Iron
B 13	CA	Menlo Park		east/west Gardens
B 24	CA	San Diego		La Jolla Sales
B 16	CA	San Francisco		Gardener's Eden
B 34	CA	Sebastopol	⌂	Reed Bros.
B 13	CT	Stamford	⌂	The English Garden from Machin
B 26	CT	Wilton		Kenneth Lynch & Sons, Inc.
B 31	DC	Washington	⌂	Park Place
B 43	DE	Dover	⌂	Winterthur Museum & Gardens
B 30	IN	Carmel		Old-World Garden Troughs
B 29	MA	North Brookfield	⌂	New England Garden Ornaments
B 10	MD	Germantown	⌂	Country Casual
B 34	ME	Georgetown		Joe Reed, Woodsmith
B 16	NC	Raleigh	⌂	Garden Magic
B 7	ND	Luverne		Broadview Station
B 44	NJ	Green Brook		The Wood Garden
B 44	NY	High Falls	⌂	Wood Classics, Inc.
B 20	NY	Lake Peekskill	⌂	Hollowbrook Pottery and Tile
B 15	NY	Long Island City	⌂	Florentine Craftsmen, Inc.
B 25	NY	Rochester	⌂	Living Wall Gardening Co.
B 1	NY	Woodbourne	⌂	AMH Furniture
B 23	OH	Cleveland	⌂	David Kay Garden & Gift Catalogue, Inc.
B 8	OH	Toledo	⌂	Carruth Studio
B 19	PA	Gulph Mills		Hen-Feathers & Company
B 7	PA	Malvern		Brandywine Garden Furniture
B 14	PA	Philadelphia		Exotic Blossoms
B 3	PQ	Montreal	⌂	Applied Hydroponics of Canada
B 13	RI	Newport	⌂	Erkins Studios, Inc.
B 16	TN	Memphis	⌂	The Garden Concepts Collection
B 24	VA	Arlington		Kingsley-Bate, Ltd.
B 26	VA	Arlington	⌂	Mrs. McGregor's Garden Shop
B 28	WA	Seattle		Mitchells & Son

PLANTERS, HYDROPONIC

B 3	CA	San Rafael	⌂	Applied Hydroponics
B 25	CA	Sebastopol		Living Green, Inc.
B 21	CO	Colorado Springs	⌂	Hydro-Gardens, Inc.
B 13	NY	Staten Island		East Coast Hydroponics
B 22	OR	Portland	⌂	JC's Garden Center
B 3	PQ	Montreal	⌂	Applied Hydroponics of Canada

PLANTERS, SELF-WATERING

B 42	FL	Gainesville	⌂	The Violet House

PLASTIC TIES/STRAPPING

B 40	NY	Glen Head		Tyz-All Plastics, Inc.

PLAY STRUCTURES

B 10	WI	McFarland		Creative Playgrounds, Ltd.

POISON OAK/IVY CLEANSER

B 39	OR	Albany		Tec Laboratories, Inc.

POLYETHYLENE GROWING BAGS

B 19	OR	Junction City		Hall Enterprises

POLYETHYLENE, WOVEN

B 31	AR	Eureka Springs	⌂	Ozark Handle & Hardware
B 29	ND	Neche	⌂	Northern Greenhouse Sales

PAGE	STATE	CITY	⌂ SHOP	SOURCE
PONDS AND POOLS				
A 108	CA	Upland	⌂	Van Ness Water Gardens
B 26	CT	Wilton		Kenneth Lynch & Sons, Inc.
A 112	MD	Baltimore	⌂	Wicklein's Aquatic Farm & Nursery, Inc.
A 66	MD	Jarrettsville	⌂	Maryland Aquatic Nurseries
A 61	MD	Lilypons	⌂	Lilypons Water Gardens
A 110	NJ	Saddle River	⌂	Waterford Gardens
B 43	NJ	Wickatunk		Wickatunk Marine, Inc.
B 20	NY	Canastota	⌂	Hermitage Gardens
A 91	NY	Northport	⌂	S. Scherer & Sons
A 105	OH	Independence	⌂	William Tricker, Inc.
A 70	ON	Port Stanley	⌂	Moore Water Gardens
A 103	PA	Coopersburg	⌂	Tilley's Nursery/The WaterWorks
POTPOURRI SUPPLIES				
A 91	BC	Vancouver	⌂	Sanctuary Seeds/Folklore Herb Co., Ltd.
A 43	CA	Coulterville	⌂	Havasu Hills Herbs
A 45	IA	Marshalltown	⌂	Herbs-Liscious
A 43	MA	Barre	⌂	Hartman's Herb Farm
A 23	MA	Rowley	⌂	Cricket Hill Herb Farm, Ltd.
A 85	NC	Godwin	⌂	Rasland Farm
A 111	NJ	Port Murray	⌂	Well-Sweep Herb Farm
A 101	OH	Chesterland	⌂	Sunnybrook Farms Nursery
A 87	ON	Goodwood	⌂	Richters
A 72	OR	Albany	⌂	Nichols Garden Nursery, Inc.
A 89	PA	Mechanicsburg	⌂	The Rosemary House
A 39	TN	Taft	⌂	Good Hollow Greenhouse & Herbarium
A 44	WA	Fall City	⌂	The Herbfarm
POTS				
A 111	BC	Vancouver	⌂	West Coast Violets
B 27	CA	Buena Park		Malley Supply
A 54	CA	Galt	⌂	K & L Cactus Nursery
A 15	CA	Lodi	⌂	Cactus by Dodie
A 109	CO	Englewood	⌂	The Violet Showcase
B 42	FL	Gainesville	⌂	The Violet House
B 30	FL	Miami	⌂	OFE International, Inc.
B 40	FL	Orlando	⌂	Tropical Plant Products, Inc.
B 15	IL	Schaumburg	⌂	Florist Products, Inc.
B 22	MA	Lynnfield	⌂	Innis Violets
A 26	MD	Frederick		Dan's Garden Shop
A 11	NC	Brown Summit	⌂	Breckinridge Orchids
B 16	NC	Raleigh	⌂	Garden Magic
B 32	NY	Buffalo		Plant Collectibles
B 13	NY	Staten Island		East Coast Hydroponics
B 17	PA	Harleysville	⌂	E. C. Geiger, Inc.
B 14	PA	Philadelphia		Exotic Blossoms
B 3	PQ	Montreal	⌂	Applied Hydroponics of Canada
A 53	TX	Victoria	⌂	JoS Violets
POTTING BENCHES				
B 36	CA	Camarillo	⌂	Santa Barbara Greenhouses
B 31	CA	Cotati	⌂	Pacific Coast Greenhouse Manufacturing Co.
B 31	CA	Watsonville		Pat's "Mini-Pack" Labels
B 1	MA	Bolton		Acorn Services Corporation
B 14	MD	Columbia	⌂	Everlite Greenhouses, Inc.
B 38	MO	North Kansas City		Stuppy Greenhouse Manufacturing, Inc.
B 7	ND	Luverne		Broadview Station
B 39	TX	Ft. Worth	⌂	Texas Greenhouse Co.
B 41	VA	Charlottesville	⌂	Victory Garden Supply Co.
PROPAGATION SUPPLIES				
See also Growing Supplies, General				
See also Growing Supplies, Indoor				
B 27	CA	Buena Park		Malley Supply
B 16	CA	Redway	⌂	Full Circle Garden Products
B 15	IL	Schaumburg	⌂	Florist Products, Inc.
B 1	MA	Bolton		Acorn Services Corporation
B 7	MA	Salem		Bramen Company, Inc.

(continued next page)

PAGE	STATE	CITY	⌂ SHOP	SOURCE
PROPAGATION SUPPLIES (continued)				
B 29	MA	Topsfield	⌂	The Walt Nicke Company
A 26	MD	Frederick		Dan's Garden Shop
B 11	ME	Manset		Deer Meadow
B 21	MI	Detroit		Indoor Gardening Supplies
B 38	MO	North Kansas City		Stuppy Greenhouse Manufacturing, Inc.
B 40	NC	Goldsboro	⌂	Turner Greenhouses
B 32	NY	Buffalo		Plant Collectibles
B 3	NY	Huntington		Aquamonitor
A 61	OH	New Philadelphia	⌂	Liberty Seed Company
A 67	OH	North Lima	⌂	Mellinger's, Inc.
B 16	OR	Corvallis	⌂	Full Moon Farm Products
B 31	OR	Portland	⌂	Pacific Garden Supply
B 38	OR	Portland	⌂	Sturdi-Built Mfg. Co.
B 17	PA	Harleysville	⌂	E. C. Geiger, Inc.
B 7	PA	New Brighton		Brighton By-Products Co., Inc.
A 103	PA	Orefield		Ter-El Nursery
A 78	SC	Greenwood	⌂	Park Seed Company, Inc.
A 115	TX	De Leon	⌂	Womack's Nursery Co.
B 39	TX	Ft. Worth	⌂	Texas Greenhouse Co.
A 10	TX	Lavernia		Bonsai Farm
B 31	UT	North Logan		Pan Agro, Inc.
B 17	VT	Burlington	⌂	Gardener's Supply Company
A 96	WA	Roy	⌂	Silvaseed Company, Inc.
B 38	WA	Seattle	⌂	Sunglo Solar Greenhouses
PUMPS, WATER POWERED				
B 34	VA	Lowesville	⌂	The Ram Company
QUICK ART (TM)				
B 43	IL	Champaign		Wheeler Arts
RACHET-CUT (R)				
B 2	CT	Plantsville	⌂	American Standard Co.
RAIN-O-MATIC (R)				
B 35	NE	Columbus	⌂	Rodco Products Co., Inc.
ROLCUT (R)				
B 7	MA	Salem		Bramen Company, Inc.
ROOT GUARD GOPHER WIRE BASKETS (TM)				
B 12	CA	Soquel		Digger's Product Development Co.
ROOTS 'N' ALL (TM)				
B 42	NY	Rochester	⌂	Warnico/USA, Inc.
ROSE GROWING SUPPLIES				
B 14	CA	Cloverdale		Evergreen Garden Plant Labels
A 100	CA	San Jose	⌂	Stocking Rose Nursery
A 46	CO	Denver	⌂	High Country Rosarium
B 19	NJ	Old Tappan		Harlane Company, Inc.
B 6	NY	Yorkville	⌂	Bonide Chemical Co., Inc.
B 35	OH	Van Wert		Rose Tender
A 89	OR	Wilsonville	⌂	Roses by Fred Edmunds
ROW COVERS				
A 115	AB	Hythe	⌂	Windy Ridge Nursery
A 98	FL	Melbourne		Southern Seeds
A 52	ME	Albion	⌂	Johnny's Selected Seeds
A 31	ME	Waterville		Fedco Seeds
B 34	MN	Eden Prairie	⌂	Ringer Corporation
A 61	OH	New Philadelphia	⌂	Liberty Seed Company
A 75	ON	Waterloo		Ontario Seed Company, Ltd.
A 44	PA	West Elizabeth		Heirloom Seeds
A 109	PE	Charlottetown	⌂	Vesey's Seeds, Ltd.
B 30	PQ	Sherbrooke	⌂	Nova Sylva, Inc.
B 17	VT	Burlington	⌂	Gardener's Supply Company
B 18	WA	Puyallup	⌂	Green Earth Organics

(continued next page)

PAGE	STATE	CITY	⌂ SHOP	SOURCE
ROW COVERS (continued)				
B 21	WA	Wenatchee	⌂	I. F. M.
B 9	WI	Elkhart Lake	⌂	Clothcrafters, Inc.
SCANMASK (R)				
B 20	KS	Overland Park		Holland's Organic Garden
B 6	PA	Willow Hill	⌂	BioLogic
SEED FLATS, WOODEN				
B 11	ME	Manset		Deer Meadow
SEED SAVING SUPPLIES				
B 20	IN	Jamestown		Heritage Center for the Preservation
A 98	VA	North Garden		Southern Exposure Seed Exchange
SHADE CLOTH				
A 115	AB	Hythe	⌂	Windy Ridge Nursery
B 17	AL	Mobile	⌂	Gothic Arch Greenhouses
B 36	CA	Camarillo	⌂	Santa Barbara Greenhouses
B 31	CA	Cotati	⌂	Pacific Coast Greenhouse Manufacturing Co.
A 11	CA	Willits	⌂	Bountiful Gardens
B 21	CO	Colorado Springs	⌂	Hydro-Gardens, Inc.
B 11	FL	Miami	⌂	Day-Dex Co.
B 44	GA	Cornelia	⌂	Yonah Manufacturing Co.
B 38	MO	North Kansas City		Stuppy Greenhouse Manufacturing, Inc.
B 40	NC	Goldsboro	⌂	Turner Greenhouses
B 37	NH	Manchester	⌂	Solar Components Corporation
B 10	OH	Medina	⌂	Cropking, Inc.
B 17	PA	Harleysville	⌂	E. C. Geiger, Inc.
B 39	TX	Ft. Worth	⌂	Texas Greenhouse Co.
B 9	WA	Mt. Vernon	⌂	Charley's Greenhouse Supply
SHREDDERS				
B 37	CA	Mill Valley	⌂	Smith & Hawken
B 34	MN	Eden Prairie	⌂	Ringer Corporation
B 4	NC	Matthews		BCS Mosa, Inc.
B 43	NE	Broken Bow		Wikco Industries, Inc.
B 16	NY	Troy		Garden Way Manufacturing Co.
B 25	OH	Piqua	⌂	A. M. Leonard, Inc.
B 27	PA	Huntingdon Valley	⌂	Mantis Manufacturing Co.
B 23	PA	Lititz	⌂	Kemp Company
B 24	PA	Point Pleasant	⌂	Kinsman Company, Inc.
B 17	VT	Burlington	⌂	Gardener's Supply Company
SICKLE-BAR MOWERS				
B 24	MN	St. Paul	⌂	Kinco Manufacturing
B 4	NC	Matthews		BCS Mosa, Inc.
B 16	NY	Troy		Garden Way Manufacturing Co.
B 26	OH	London	⌂	Mainline of North America
SNAIL BARRIERS				
B 28	CA	San Anselmo	⌂	The Natural Gardening Company
B 30	FL	Miami	⌂	OFE International, Inc.
B 18	PA	Pineville	⌂	Growing Naturally
SOIL AMENDMENTS				
B 29	AR	Fayetteville	⌂	Nitron Industries, Inc.
B 26	AR	Lowell	⌂	Maestro-Gro
B 12	CA	Corte Madera	⌂	Dirt Cheap Organics
B 19	CA	Graton	⌂	Harmony Farm Supply
B 34	CA	San Diego	⌂	Bargyla Rateaver
A 64	CA	South San Francisco	⌂	Rod McLellan Co.
B 13	IL	Mendota	⌂	EnP Inc.
B 12	IN	Jeffersonville		Earlee, Inc.
B 29	ME	Waldoboro		North American Kelp
B 34	MN	Eden Prairie	⌂	Ringer Corporation
A 89	NM	Roswell	⌂	Roswell Seed Co.
B 6	NY	Yorkville	⌂	Bonide Chemical Co., Inc.
B 31	OR	Portland	⌂	Pacific Garden Supply

(continued next page)

PAGE	STATE	CITY	⌂ SHOP	SOURCE

SOIL AMENDMENTS (continued)

PAGE	STATE	CITY	⌂ SHOP	SOURCE
B 44	PA	Gap	⌂	Zook & Ranck, Inc.
B 18	PA	Pineville	⌂	Growing Naturally
B 18	TX	Ft. Worth		Grosoke, Inc.
B 27	TX	Hondo		Medina Agricultural Products Co.
B 18	WA	Puyallup	⌂	Green Earth Organics

SOIL MOIST (TM)

PAGE	STATE	CITY	⌂ SHOP	SOURCE
B 23	OH	Cleveland	⌂	JRM Chemical, Inc.

SOIL TESTING BY MAIL

PAGE	STATE	CITY	⌂ SHOP	SOURCE
B 16	CA	Freedom	⌂	Freedom Soil Lab
A 79	CA	Grass Valley	⌂	Peaceful Valley Farm Supply
B 30	OH	Hartville	⌂	Ohio Earth Food, Inc.
B 12	OK	Mounds	⌂	Earthly Goods Farm & Garden Supply
B 44	PA	Gap	⌂	Zook & Ranck, Inc.
B 29	VA	New Castle	⌂	Necessary Trading Co.
B 21	WA	Wenatchee	⌂	I. F. M.
A 110	WI	Plainfield	⌂	The Waushara Gardens
B 24	WY	Laramie		LaRamie Soils Service

SOIL TESTING PRODUCTS

PAGE	STATE	CITY	⌂ SHOP	SOURCE
B 32	CA	Ventura	⌂	Phologistics
A 55	FL	Sanford	⌂	Kilgore Seed Company
B 38	MO	North Kansas City		Stuppy Greenhouse Manufacturing, Inc.
B 27	NY	Brooklyn		Micro Essential Laboratory, Inc.
B 30	OH	Hartville	⌂	Ohio Earth Food, Inc.
A 37	ON	Thornhill	⌂	Gardenimport, Inc.
B 22	OR	Portland	⌂	JC's Garden Center
A 90	TX	Nash		SPB Sales
B 29	VA	New Castle	⌂	Necessary Trading Co.

SPRAY-N-GROW (TM)

PAGE	STATE	CITY	⌂ SHOP	SOURCE
B 37	TX	Houston	⌂	Spray-N-Grow, Inc.

SPRAYERS

PAGE	STATE	CITY	⌂ SHOP	SOURCE
B 41	AZ	Bouse	⌂	UPCO Irrigation
B 11	CA	Sun Valley	⌂	D.I.G. Corporation
B 30	FL	Miami	⌂	OFE International, Inc.
B 8	FL	Naples		Brushking
B 21	IL	Chicago		H. D. Hudson Mfg. Co.
B 29	MN	Park Rapids	⌂	North Star Evergreens
B 32	NC	Arden		PeCo, Inc.
B 4	NC	Matthews		BCS Mosa, Inc.
B 24	NJ	Blairstown		Langenbach Fine Tool Co.
B 26	OH	Perry		MacKenzie Nursery Supply
B 25	OH	Piqua	⌂	A. M. Leonard, Inc.
B 12	OK	Mounds	⌂	Earthly Goods Farm & Garden Supply
A 105	ON	Hamilton	⌂	Tregunno Seeds
B 22	OR	Eugene	⌂	International Reforestation Suppliers
B 17	PA	Harleysville	⌂	E. C. Geiger, Inc.
B 27	PA	Huntingdon Valley	⌂	Mantis Manufacturing Co.
B 2	PA	West Chester		American Arborist Supplies
B 30	PQ	Sherbrooke	⌂	Nova Sylva, Inc.
A 115	TX	De Leon	⌂	Womack's Nursery Co.
B 18	TX	Littlefield		The Greener Thumb
B 12	WI	Manitowoc		The Dramm Company

SPRINKLERS

See also Irrigation Supplies

PAGE	STATE	CITY	⌂ SHOP	SOURCE
B 41	AZ	Bouse	⌂	UPCO Irrigation
B 19	CA	Graton	⌂	Harmony Farm Supply
B 37	CA	Huntington Beach	⌂	Spot Systems
B 11	CA	Sun Valley	⌂	D.I.G. Corporation
B 28	FL	Palmetto		Moss Products, Inc.
B 34	MN	Eden Prairie	⌂	Ringer Corporation
B 32	MO	Grover	⌂	Plastic Plumbing Products, Inc.
B 24	NJ	Blairstown		Langenbach Fine Tool Co.
B 25	OH	Piqua	⌂	A. M. Leonard, Inc.

(continued next page)

PAGE	STATE	CITY	⌂ SHOP	SOURCE
SPRINKLERS (continued)				
B 35	OH	Van Wert		Rose Tender
B 39	TX	Ft. Worth	⌂	Texas Greenhouse Co.
B 8	TX	Hereford	⌂	C & C Products
B 18	TX	Littlefield		The Greener Thumb
B 38	TX	Lubbock	⌂	Submatic Irrigation Systems
B 12	WI	Manitowoc		The Dramm Company
STATUES				
B 35	AL	Alexander City		Robinson Iron
B 37	AL	Birmingham		Southern Statuary and Stone
B 42	BC	Vancouver	⌂	The Well-Furnished Garden
B 13	CA	Menlo Park		east/west Gardens
B 26	CT	Wilton		Kenneth Lynch & Sons, Inc.
B 31	DC	Washington	⌂	Park Place
B 43	DE	Dover	⌂	Winterthur Museum & Gardens
B 29	MA	North Brookfield	⌂	New England Garden Ornaments
B 16	NC	Raleigh	⌂	Garden Magic
B 36	NJ	Roosevelt	⌂	Sculpture Cast Editions
B 33	NY	Bronxville		Pompeian Studios
B 15	NY	Long Island City	⌂	Florentine Craftsmen, Inc.
B 8	OH	Toledo	⌂	Carruth Studio
B 1	ON	Pakenham		Abbey Garden Sundials
B 19	PA	Gulph Mills		Hen-Feathers & Company
B 14	PA	Philadelphia		Exotic Blossoms
B 13	RI	Newport	⌂	Erkins Studios, Inc.
B 35	VA	Hillsboro	⌂	Royal Tidewater Collection, Inc.
SUN-PORCH (R)				
B 41	NY	New York		Vegetable Factory, Inc.
SUNBIRD TILLERS (TM)				
B 38	OH	Mt. Vernon	⌂	Sunbird Products, Inc.
SUNDIALS				
B 42	BC	Vancouver	⌂	The Well-Furnished Garden
B 43	CA	Mendocino	⌂	Wind & Weather
B 2	CA	Pt. Arena		American Sundials, Inc.
B 9	CA	Redondo Beach		J Collard
B 16	CA	San Francisco		Gardener's Eden
B 26	CT	Wilton		Kenneth Lynch & Sons, Inc.
B 31	DC	Washington	⌂	Park Place
B 32	MA	Hingham		Pigeon Hill
B 29	MA	North Brookfield	⌂	New England Garden Ornaments
B 15	NY	Long Island City	⌂	Florentine Craftsmen, Inc.
B 1	ON	Pakenham		Abbey Garden Sundials
B 19	PA	Gulph Mills		Hen-Feathers & Company
B 2	PA	Media	⌂	American Weather Enterprises
B 14	PA	Philadelphia		Exotic Blossoms
B 13	RI	Newport	⌂	Erkins Studios, Inc.
B 26	VA	Arlington	⌂	Mrs. McGregor's Garden Shop
B 35	VA	Hillsboro	⌂	Royal Tidewater Collection, Inc.
B 33	VA	Orange	⌂	The Plow & Hearth
SUPERSORB-C (R)				
B 23	CA	Davis		Janziker
SUPERTHRIVE (TM)				
B 40	FL	Bradenton	⌂	Tropexotic Growers, Inc.
SWINGS AND GLIDERS				
B 1	CA	Fort Bragg		Adirondack Designs
B 31	DC	Washington	⌂	Park Place
B 11	IL	Moline		John Deere Catalog
B 9	MA	West Newton		The Clapper Co.
B 10	MD	Germantown	⌂	Country Casual
B 44	NY	High Falls	⌂	Wood Classics, Inc.
B 7	PA	Malvern		Brandywine Garden Furniture
B 41	TN	Knoxville		Van Klassens Fine Garden Furniture

(continued next page)

PAGE	STATE	CITY	⌂ SHOP	SOURCE
SWINGS AND GLIDERS (continued)				
B 16	TN	Memphis	⌂	The Garden Concepts Collection
B 33	VA	Orange	⌂	The Plow & Hearth
TECNU (R)				
B 39	OR	Albany		Tec Laboratories, Inc.
TERRA COTTA POTS/PLANTERS				
See also Planters				
B 42	BC	Vancouver	⌂	The Well-Furnished Garden
B 13	CA	Menlo Park		east/west Gardens
B 23	OH	Cleveland	⌂	David Kay Garden & Gift Catalogue, Inc.
B 8	OH	Toledo	⌂	Carruth Studio
B 13	RI	Newport	⌂	Erkins Studios, Inc.
TERRARIUMS				
A 42	CA	Rancho Cordova	⌂	Robert B. Hamm
A 68	CA	Sacramento	⌂	Mighty Minis
A 64	KS	Wichita	⌂	McKinney's Glasshouse
B 22	MA	Lynnfield	⌂	Innis Violets
A 9	NJ	Pompton Lakes		Black Copper Kits
THERMOFOR (R)				
B 7	MA	Salem		Bramen Company, Inc.
TIER BENCHES				
B 11	FL	Miami	⌂	Day-Dex Co.
B 11	IL	Moline		John Deere Catalog
B 41	NY	New York		Vegetable Factory, Inc.
TILLERS				
B 4	NC	Matthews		BCS Mosa, Inc.
B 43	NE	Broken Bow		Wikco Industries, Inc.
B 16	NY	Troy		Garden Way Manufacturing Co.
B 26	OH	London	⌂	Mainline of North America
B 38	OH	Mt. Vernon	⌂	Sunbird Products, Inc.
B 27	PA	Huntingdon Valley	⌂	Mantis Manufacturing Co.
B 3	WI	Cumberland		Ardisam, Inc.
TISSUE CULTURE, CUSTOM				
A 111	BC	Aldergrove	⌂	Western Biologicals, Ltd.
A 19	CA	Carlotta		Choice Edibles
A 1	IN	Huntingburg	⌂	Ahrens Nursery & Plant Labs
A 18	VT	Isle La Motte		Champlain Isle Agro Associates
A 6	WA	Mt. Vernon		B & B Laboratories
TISSUE CULTURE, ORCHIDS				
B 30	NY	Burdett		Orchis Laboratories
TOMAHAWK (R)				
B 16	NY	Troy		Garden Way Manufacturing Co.
TOOL HANDLES, REPLACEMENT				
B 31	AR	Eureka Springs	⌂	Ozark Handle & Hardware
B 30	PQ	Sherbrooke	⌂	Nova Sylva, Inc.
TOOLS				
A 92	AB	Edmonton	⌂	Seed Centre, Ltd.
A 79	CA	Grass Valley	⌂	Peaceful Valley Farm Supply
B 19	CA	Graton	⌂	Harmony Farm Supply
B 37	CA	Mill Valley	⌂	Smith & Hawken
B 9	CA	Redondo Beach		J Collard
B 28	CA	San Anselmo	⌂	The Natural Gardening Company
A 32	IA	Shenandoah		Henry Field Seed & Nursery Co.
A 67	IA	Shenandoah	⌂	Earl May Seed & Nursery Co.
B 2	IL	Galesburg		Alsto's Handy Helpers
B 11	IL	Moline		John Deere Catalog
B 34	IL	Rockford		RAM Log Splitters
B 29	MA	Topsfield	⌂	The Walt Nicke Company

(continued next page)

PAGE	STATE	CITY	⌂ SHOP	SOURCE
TOOLS (continued)				
B 34	MN	Eden Prairie	⌂	Ringer Corporation
B 24	NJ	Blairstown		Langenbach Fine Tool Co.
B 11	NY	Salt Point		Daffodrill, Inc.
A 67	OH	North Lima	⌂	Mellinger's, Inc.
B 26	OH	Perry		MacKenzie Nursery Supply
A 27	ON	Georgetown	⌂	Dominion Seed House
B 5	ON	St. Thomas	⌂	Berry-Hill, Limited
A 37	ON	Thornhill	⌂	Gardenimport, Inc.
B 24	PA	Point Pleasant	⌂	Kinsman Company, Inc.
A 14	PA	Warminster	⌂	W. Atlee Burpee Company
A 28	SK	Saskatoon	⌂	Early's Farm & Garden Centre, Inc.
A 82	TX	Stephenville	⌂	Porter & Son
B 17	VT	Burlington	⌂	Gardener's Supply Company
B 18	WA	Puyallup	⌂	Green Earth Organics
TOOLS, HAND				
B 12	CA	Brea	⌂	Denman & Co.
B 23	CA	Corona del Mar		The Keth Company
B 37	CA	Mill Valley	⌂	Smith & Hawken
B 9	CA	Redondo Beach		J Collard
B 16	CA	San Francisco		Gardener's Eden
A 112	CT	Litchfield	⌂	White Flower Farm
B 2	CT	Plantsville	⌂	American Standard Co.
B 2	IL	Galesburg		Alsto's Handy Helpers
B 14	IL	Lombard		The Floral Mailbox
B 11	IL	Moline		John Deere Catalog
B 29	MA	Topsfield	⌂	The Walt Nicke Company
B 9	MA	West Newton		The Clapper Co.
A 68	MD	Baltimore		Meyer Seed Co.
A 80	ME	New Gloucester	⌂	Pinetree Garden Seeds
B 29	MN	Park Rapids	⌂	North Star Evergreens
B 24	NJ	Blairstown		Langenbach Fine Tool Co.
A 11	NY	Brooklyn		Botanic Garden Company
B 42	NY	Rochester	⌂	Warnico/USA, Inc.
A 48	OH	Chesterland	⌂	Homestead Division of Sunnybrook Farms
B 23	OH	Cleveland	⌂	David Kay Garden & Gift Catalogue, Inc.
B 25	OH	Piqua	⌂	A. M. Leonard, Inc.
B 12	OK	Mounds	⌂	Earthly Goods Farm & Garden Supply
B 17	PA	Harleysville	⌂	E. C. Geiger, Inc.
B 24	PA	Point Pleasant	⌂	Kinsman Company, Inc.
B 35	TX	Ft. Worth		Rudon International Trading Company
B 18	TX	Littlefield		The Greener Thumb
B 26	VA	Arlington	⌂	Mrs. McGregor's Garden Shop
B 33	VA	Orange	⌂	The Plow & Hearth
A 86	WA	Port Townsend	⌂	Rex Bulb Farms
B 18	WA	Puyallup	⌂	Green Earth Organics
TOOLS, PRUNING				
B 12	CA	Brea	⌂	Denman & Co.
B 2	CT	Plantsville	⌂	American Standard Co.
B 3	FL	Fort Lauderdale	⌂	Arborist Supply House, Inc.
B 8	FL	Naples		Brushking
A 52	GA	Ellijay	⌂	Johnson Nursery
B 15	IL	Schaumburg	⌂	Florist Products, Inc.
B 19	KS	Paola	⌂	Happy Valley Ranch
B 10	MA	Andover		Country House Floral Supply
B 7	MA	Salem		Bramen Company, Inc.
B 29	MA	Topsfield	⌂	The Walt Nicke Company
B 9	MA	West Newton		The Clapper Co.
B 29	MN	Park Rapids	⌂	North Star Evergreens
B 24	NJ	Blairstown		Langenbach Fine Tool Co.
B 19	NJ	Old Tappan		Harlane Company, Inc.
B 26	OH	Perry		MacKenzie Nursery Supply
B 25	OH	Piqua	⌂	A. M. Leonard, Inc.
B 22	OR	Eugene	⌂	International Reforestation Suppliers
A 89	OR	Wilsonville	⌂	Roses by Fred Edmunds
A 1	PA	Aspers	⌂	Adams County Nursery, Inc.
B 5	PA	Greeley	⌂	Dorothy Biddle Service

(continued next page)

PAGE	STATE	CITY	⌂ SHOP	SOURCE
TOOLS, PRUNING (continued)				
B 18	PA	Pineville	⌂	Growing Naturally
B 2	PA	West Chester		American Arborist Supplies
B 30	PQ	Sherbrooke	⌂	Nova Sylva, Inc.
A 115	TX	De Leon	⌂	Womack's Nursery Co.
B 18	TX	Littlefield		The Greener Thumb
A 90	TX	Nash		SPB Sales
A 8	WA	Northport	⌂	Bear Creek Nursery
A 24	WA	Snohomish	⌂	Cricklewood Nursery
TOPIARY FRAMES				
B 26	CT	Wilton		Kenneth Lynch & Sons, Inc.
B 40	FL	Tampa		Topiary, Inc.
B 16	NC	Raleigh	⌂	Garden Magic
B 42	OR	Portland		Vine Arts
TRAKE (TM)				
A 5	PA	Waynesboro	⌂	Appalachian Gardens
TRELLISES				
B 11	GA	Atlanta		Cross VINYLattice
B 1	MA	Bolton		Acorn Services Corporation
B 29	MA	North Brookfield	⌂	New England Garden Ornaments
B 44	NJ	Green Brook		The Wood Garden
B 37	PA	Honey Brook		Simple's Creative Quality Trellises
TROY-BILT (R)				
B 16	NY	Troy		Garden Way Manufacturing Co.
TRUBLOOM (R)				
B 41	CT	Greenwich		Verilux, Inc.
VIDEO CASSETTES				
B 34	CA	Chatsworth		Raindrip, Inc.
B 10	CA	El Cajon		Cottage Garden Collection
B 28	CA	Fremont		Misti Maid, Inc.
A 71	CA	Inverness		Mushroompeople
B 30	CA	San Francisco		One Up Productions
A 14	CT	Oxford	⌂	Butterbrooke Farm
B 27	CT	Southport		The Matrix Group
B 36	IN	Battle Ground		Seeker Press
A 35	MI	Parma	⌂	Fox Hill Farm
B 8	NC	Moravian Falls	⌂	Brushy Mountain Bee Farm, Inc.
A 34	WA	Bellevue	⌂	Foliage Gardens
A 49	WA	Kent		Ed Hume Seeds, Inc.
B 8	WI	Deer Park	⌂	Capability's Books
VIDEODISCS				
B 41	CA	Soquel		VT Productions
B 27	CT	Southport		The Matrix Group
B 39	OR	Astoria		Terisan
B 41	WA	Seattle		Videodiscovery, Inc.
VIRUS TESTING				
B 10	CA	Lincoln	⌂	Critter Creek Laboratory & Orchids
B 30	NY	Burdett		Orchis Laboratories
WATER GARDEN SUPPLIES				
See also Fish for Garden Ponds				
See also Ponds and Pools				
A 91	CA	Santa Barbara	⌂	Santa Barbara Water Gardens
A 108	CA	Upland	⌂	Van Ness Water Gardens
A 96	FL	Winter Haven	⌂	Slocum Water Gardens
A 78	MA	Whitman		Paradise Water Gardens
A 112	MD	Baltimore	⌂	Wicklein's Aquatic Farm & Nursery, Inc.
A 66	MD	Jarrettsville	⌂	Maryland Aquatic Nurseries
A 20	MI	Detroit	⌂	City Gardens
B 3	MN	White Bear Lake		Aquacide Company
A 79	NC	Franklin	⌂	Perry's Water Gardens

(continued next page)

PAGE	STATE	CITY	⌂ SHOP	SOURCE

WATER GARDEN SUPPLIES (continued)

PAGE	STATE	CITY	⌂ SHOP	SOURCE
A 110	NJ	Saddle River	⌂	Waterford Gardens
B 20	NY	Canastota	⌂	Hermitage Gardens
A 91	NY	Northport	⌂	S. Scherer & Sons
A 105	OH	Independence	⌂	William Tricker, Inc.
A 70	ON	Port Stanley	⌂	Moore Water Gardens
A 103	PA	Coopersburg	⌂	Tilley's Nursery/The WaterWorks
A 113	WI	Oshkosh		Wildlife Nurseries

WATER PURIFIERS

PAGE	STATE	CITY	⌂ SHOP	SOURCE
B 29	AR	Fayetteville	⌂	Nitron Industries, Inc.
B 12	CA	Corte Madera	⌂	Dirt Cheap Organics
B 20	CA	Irvine		Hollister's Hydroponics
B 32	CA	Ventura	⌂	Phologistics

WATERING CANS

PAGE	STATE	CITY	⌂ SHOP	SOURCE
B 26	OH	Perry		MacKenzie Nursery Supply
B 24	PA	Point Pleasant	⌂	Kinsman Company, Inc.

WEATHER INSTRUMENTS

PAGE	STATE	CITY	⌂ SHOP	SOURCE
B 43	CA	Mendocino	⌂	Wind & Weather
B 15	IL	Schaumburg	⌂	Florist Products, Inc.
B 27	MA	New Bedford		Maximum, Inc.
B 35	NE	Columbus	⌂	Rodco Products Co., Inc.
B 33	NJ	Princeton	⌂	Qualimetrics, Inc.
B 22	OR	Eugene	⌂	International Reforestation Suppliers
B 17	PA	Harleysville	⌂	E. C. Geiger, Inc.
B 2	PA	Media	⌂	American Weather Enterprises
B 40	WA	Enumclaw	⌂	Trade-Wind Instruments

WEATHERVANES

PAGE	STATE	CITY	⌂ SHOP	SOURCE
B 43	CA	Mendocino	⌂	Wind & Weather
B 26	CT	Wilton		Kenneth Lynch & Sons, Inc.
B 11	IL	Moline		John Deere Catalog
B 43	IN	Indianapolis	⌂	Windleaves
B 27	MA	New Bedford		Maximum, Inc.
B 33	NJ	Princeton	⌂	Qualimetrics, Inc.
B 15	NY	Long Island City	⌂	Florentine Craftsmen, Inc.
B 5	ON	St. Thomas	⌂	Berry-Hill, Limited
B 24	OR	Portland		Landscapes & Accents
B 2	PA	Media	⌂	American Weather Enterprises
B 24	PA	Point Pleasant	⌂	Kinsman Company, Inc.

WECK (R) HOME CANNING

PAGE	STATE	CITY	⌂ SHOP	SOURCE
B 17	IL	Arlington Heights		Glashaus/Weck Home Canning

WEED CUTTERS, GAS/ELECTRIC

PAGE	STATE	CITY	⌂ SHOP	SOURCE
B 8	FL	Naples		Brushking
B 25	OH	Piqua	⌂	A. M. Leonard, Inc.
B 2	PA	West Chester		American Arborist Supplies
B 10	VT	Charlotte	⌂	Country Home Products, Inc.

WEED CUTTERS, SUPPLIES

PAGE	STATE	CITY	⌂ SHOP	SOURCE
B 42	GA	Dahlonega		Weed Wizard, Inc.

WEEDERS, HAND

PAGE	STATE	CITY	⌂ SHOP	SOURCE
B 29	MA	Topsfield	⌂	The Walt Nicke Company
A 73	MN	Marine	⌂	North Star Gardens
B 34	OR	Jacksonville		RNM Sales
B 35	TX	Ft. Worth		Rudon International Trading Company

WHEELBARROWS

PAGE	STATE	CITY	⌂ SHOP	SOURCE
B 11	FL	Miami	⌂	Day-Dex Co.
B 7	ND	Luverne		Broadview Station
B 24	NJ	Blairstown		Langenbach Fine Tool Co.
B 44	NJ	Green Brook		The Wood Garden
B 25	OH	Piqua	⌂	A. M. Leonard, Inc.
B 44	WI	Janesville	⌂	Wisconsin Wagon Co.

PAGE	STATE	CITY	⌂ SHOP	SOURCE
WINDOW BOXES				
B 24	VA	Arlington		Kingsley-Bate, Ltd.
B 26	VA	Arlington	⌂	Mrs. McGregor's Garden Shop
WINEMAKING EQUIPMENT				
B 19	KS	Paola	⌂	Happy Valley Ranch
A 10	MD	Riderwood	⌂	Boordy Nursery
B 5	ON	St. Thomas	⌂	Berry-Hill, Limited
WONDERLITE (R)				
B 33	NY	New York		Public Service Lamp Corp.
B 3	PQ	Montreal	⌂	Applied Hydroponics of Canada
WORM CASTINGS				
B 29	AR	Fayetteville	⌂	Nitron Industries, Inc.
B 30	CA	Los Angeles	⌂	Organic Control, Inc.
A 11	CA	Willits	⌂	Bountiful Gardens
B 28	CT	Avon		Mother Nature's Worm Castings
B 4	GA	Dawson		Beatrice Farms
B 8	GA	Plains		Carter Fishworm Farm
B 8	MA	Buzzards Bay		Cape Cod Worm Farm
B 18	OH	Cleveland		The Guano Company
B 18	WA	Puyallup	⌂	Green Earth Organics

HEUCHERA SANGUINEA

© Life-Form Replicators
Artist: Layne Stewart

PAGE SOCIETY

AFRICAN VIOLETS
D 1   African Violet Society of America, Inc.
D 1   African Violet Society of Canada
D 20   The Saintpaulia and Houseplant Society
D 20   Saintpaulia International

AGRICULTURAL HISTORY
C 2   Association for Living History Farms

ALOES
D 1   Aloe, Cactus & Succulent Society of Zimbabwe

ALPINE PLANTS
D 1   Alpine Garden Club of British Columbia
D 1   Alpine Garden Society
D 4   American Rock Garden Society
D 17   The New Zealand Alpine Garden Society
D 17   Newfoundland Alpine & Rock Garden Club
D 20   Scottish Rock Garden Club

AMARYLLIDS
D 4   American Plant Life Society

AQUATIC PLANTS
D 14   Water Lily Society

AROIDS
D 12   International Aroid Society

ASCLEPIADS
D 13   International Asclepiad Society

AUSTRALIAN PLANTS
D 5   The Australian Plant Society of California
D 21   The Society for Growing Australian Plants

AZALEAS
D 4   American Rhododendron Society
D 6   Azalea Society of America, Inc.

BAMBOO
D 1   American Bamboo Society

BEGONIAS
D 1   American Begonia Society
D 6   British Columbia Fuchsia & Begonia Society

BONSAI
D 2   American Bonsai Society
D 6   Bonsai Clubs International
D 22   The Toronto Bonsai Society

BOXWOOD
D 2   American Boxwood Society

BROMELIADS
D 7   Bromeliad Society, Inc.
D 7   Bromeliad Study Group of Northern California
D 9   The Cryptanthus Society

BULBOUS PLANTS
D 12   Indigenous Bulb Growers Assn. of South Africa

CACTUS
D 1   Aloe, Cactus & Succulent Society of Zimbabwe
D 6   The British Cactus & Succulent Society
D 7   Cactus & Succulent Society of America
D 9   Desert Plant Society of Vancouver
D 22   The Toronto Cactus & Succulent Club

CALOCHORTUS
D 2   American Calochortus Society

CAMELLIAS
D 2   American Camellia Society
D 13   International Camellia Society
D 17   New Zealand Camellia Society

CARNIVOROUS PLANTS
D 13   International Carnivorous Plant Society

CEREAL GRAINS
D 14   The KUSA Society

CHRYSANTHEMUMS
D 8   Canadian Chrysanthemum & Dahlia Society
D 16   National Chrysanthemum Society (UK)
D 16   National Chrysanthemum Society, Inc. (USA)

CITRUS
D 12   Indoor Citrus & Rare Fruit Society

CLEMATIS
D 13   The International Clematis Society

PAGE SOCIETY

COMMUNITY GARDENING
C 1 American Community Gardening Association

CONIFERS
D 2 American Conifer Society

CRABAPPLES
D 13 International Ornamental Crabapple Society

CRYPTANTHUS
D 9 The Cryptanthus Society

CUT FLOWERS
C 2 Association of Specialty Cut Flower Growers

CYCADS
D 9 The Cycad Society

CYCLAMEN
D 9 Cyclamen Society

DAFFODILS
D 2 American Daffodil Society, Inc.
D 9 The Daffodil Society (UK)

DAHLIAS
D 2 American Dahlia Society
D 8 Canadian Chrysanthemum & Dahlia Society
D 19 Puget Sound Dahlia Association

DAYLILIES
D 3 American Hemerocallis Society

DELPHINIUMS
D 9 The Delphinium Society

DESERT PLANTS
D 9 Desert Plant Society of Vancouver

EPIPHYLLUMS
D 9 Epiphyllum Society of America

EUCALYPTUS
D 10 Eucalyptus Improvement Association

FERNS
D 2 American Fern Society, Inc.
D 14 International Tropical Fern Society
D 14 Los Angeles International Fern Society

FLOWERS, HEIRLOOM
D 9 Cottage Garden Society

FORESTS
D 2 American Forestry Association

PAGE SOCIETY

FRUIT
D 4 American Pomological Society
D 10 Friends of the Trees
D 12 Home Orchard Society
D 12 Indoor Citrus & Rare Fruit Society
D 13 International Dwarf Fruit Tree Association
D 17 North American Fruit Explorers
D 19 Permaculture Institute of North America
D 19 Rare Fruit Council International, Inc.
D 23 Vinifera Wine Growers Association

FRUIT, NEW VARIETIES
D 4 American Pomological Society
D 17 North American Fruit Explorers

FRUIT, SUBTROPICAL
D 8 California Rare Fruit Growers, Inc.
D 12 Indoor Citrus & Rare Fruit Society
D 19 Rare Fruit Council International, Inc.
D 19 Rare Fruit Council of Australia
D 19 Rare Pit & Plant Council
D 22 Southern Fruit Fellowship

FRUIT, TROPICAL
D 12 Indoor Citrus & Rare Fruit Society
D 19 Rare Fruit Council International, Inc.
D 19 Rare Fruit Council of Australia
D 19 Rare Pit & Plant Council
D 22 Southern Fruit Fellowship

FUCHSIAS
D 2 American Fuchsia Society
D 5 Australian Fuchsia Society
D 6 British Columbia Fuchsia & Begonia Society
D 7 British Fuchsia Society
D 16 National Fuchsia Society
D 17 New Zealand Fuchsia Society, Inc.
D 18 Northwest Fuchsia Society
D 21 South African Fuchsia Society

GARDEN CONSERVATION
C 3 The Garden Conservancy

GARDEN HISTORY
C 1 Alliance for Historic Landscape Preservation
D 5 Australian Garden History Society
C 3 The Garden Conservancy
D 10 Garden History Society
C 3 Historic Preservation Committee
D 16 New England Garden History Society
D 20 San Diego Historical Society
D 22 Southern Garden History Association

GARDENIAS
D 10 Gardenia Society of America

PAGE SOCIETY

GENERAL INTEREST
D 3   American Horticultural Society
D 7   California Horticultural Society
C 2   The Garden Club of America
C 3   Garden Clubs Canada
D 12   Horticultural Alliance of the Hamptons
D 12   Horticultural Society of New York
D 14   Long Island Horticultural Society
D 15   Massachusetts Horticultural Association
C 4   Men's Garden Clubs of America, Inc.
D 15   Minnesota State Horticultural Society
C 4   National Council of State Garden Clubs, Inc.
C 4   National Junior Horticulture Association
D 17   Northern Horticultural Society
D 18   Northwest Horticultural Society
D 18   The Pennsylvania Horticultural Society
D 20   The Royal Horticultural Society
D 21   Southern California Horticultural Institute
D 22   Texas State Horticultural Society
D 23   Western Horticultural Society
D 23   Worcester County Horticultural Society

GERANIUMS
D 5   Australian Geranium Society
D 6   British & European Geranium Society
D 7   British Pelargonium & Geranium Society
D 8   Canadian Geranium & Pelargonium Society
D 13   International Geranium Society

GERANIUMS, SPECIES
D 7   British Pelargonium & Geranium Society

GESNERIADS
D 3   American Gloxinia & Gesneriad Society, Inc.
D 10   Gesneriad Hybridizers Association
D 10   Gesneriad Society International
D 22   Toronto Gesneriad Society

GINGERS
D 3   American Ginger Society

GINKGOS
D 13   International Golden Fossil Tree Society

GLADIOLUS
D 8   Canadian Gladiolus Society
D 17   North American Gladiolus Council

GLOXINIAS
D 3   American Gloxinia & Gesneriad Society, Inc.

GOURDS
D 3   American Gourd Society

GRAINS
D 14   The KUSA Society

PAGE SOCIETY

GREENHOUSE GARDENING
D 11   Hobby Greenhouse Association

HARDY PLANTS
D 10   Hardy Plant Society - Mid-Atlantic Group
D 10   Hardy Plant Society (UK)
D 10   Hardy Plant Society of Oregon
D 17   Northern Horticultural Society
D 23   Woody Plant Society

HEATHERS
D 11   The Heather Society
D 17   North American Heather Society

HEBES
D 11   The Hebe Society

HELICONIA
D 11   Heliconia Society International

HERBS
D 3   American Herb Association
D 11   Herb Research Foundation
D 11   Herb Society of America, Inc.
C 3   International Herb Growers & Marketers Assn.

HIBISCUS
D 3   American Hibiscus Society
D 5   Australian Hibiscus Society

HOLLY
D 11   Holly Society of America, Inc.

HORTICULTURAL THERAPY
C 1   American Horticultural Therapy Association
C 2   Canadian Horticultural Therapy Association

HOSTAS
D 3   American Hosta Society

HOUSEPLANTS
D 11   Hobby Greenhouse Association
D 12   Indoor Gardening Society of America
D 19   Peperomia Society International
D 20   The Saintpaulia and Houseplant Society

HOYAS
D 12   The Hoya Society International

HYDROPONIC GROWING
D 12   Hydroponic Society of America
D 12   Hydroponic Society of Victoria

INDOOR GARDENING
D 12   Indoor Gardening Society of America

PAGE SOCIETY

IRIS
D 3   American Iris Society
D 5   Aril Society International
D 7   British Iris Society
D 8   Canadian Iris Society
D 19   The Reblooming Iris Society
D 21   The Society for Japanese Irises
D 21   Society for Louisiana Irises
D 21   Society for Pacific Coast Native Iris
D 22   Species Iris Group of North America

IRIS, HISTORICAL
D 11   Historical Iris Preservation Society

IVY
D 3   American Ivy Society
D 7   The British Ivy Society

LILACS
D 13   International Lilac Society

LILIES
D 7   British Columbia Lily Society
D 8   Canadian Prairie Lily Society
D 14   Manitoba Regional Lily Society
D 17   North American Lily Society, Inc.
D 18   Ontario Regional Lily Society
D 18   Pacific Northwest Lily Society

MAGNOLIAS
D 14   The Magnolia Society, Inc.

MARIGOLDS
D 14   Marigold Society of America, Inc.

MARKET GARDENING
D 9   The Croft Institute

MASTER GARDENERS
C 4   Master Gardeners, Cooperative Extension
D 15   Master Gardeners International Corp. (MaGIC)

NARCISSUS
D 2   American Daffodil Society, Inc.
D 9   The Daffodil Society (UK)

NATIVE PLANTS
D 1   Alaska Native Plant Society
D 5   Arizona Native Plant Society
D 5   Arkansas Native Plant Society
D 6   Botanical Club of Wisconsin
D 7   California Native Plant Society
C 2   Center for Plant Conservation
D 9   Colorado Native Plant Society
D 10   Georgia Botanical Society
D 11   Hawaiian Botanical Society

PAGE SOCIETY

NATIVE PLANTS
D 12   Idaho Native Plant Society
D 14   Louisiana Native Plant Society
D 15   Michigan Botanical Club
D 15   Minnesota Native Plant Society
D 15   Mississippi Native Plant Society
D 15   Missouri Native Plant Society
C 4   National Wildflower Research Center
D 16   Native Plant Society of New Mexico
D 16   Native Plant Society of Oregon
D 16   Native Plant Society of Texas
D 16   New England Botanical Club
D 17   New Jersey Native Plant Society
D 18   Northern Nevada Native Plant Society
D 18   Ohio Native Plant Society
D 19   Pennsylvania Native Plant Society
D 21   Southern California Botanists
D 22   Southern Illinois Native Plant Society
D 22   Tennessee Native Plant Society
D 23   Utah Native Plant Society
D 23   Virginia Native Plant Society
D 23   Washington Native Plant Society
D 24   Wyoming Native Plant Society

NUTS, HARDY
D 18   Northern Nut Growers Association

OAKS
D 13   International Oak Society

OLEANDERS
D 13   International Oleander Society

ORCHIDS
D 3   American Orchid Society
D 8   Canadian Orchid Society
D 9   Cymbidium Society of America
D 18   Pacific Orchid Society
D 20   Saskatchewan Orchid Society
D 23   Victoria Orchid Society

ORGANIC GARDENING
D 6   Bio-Dynamic Farming & Gardening Assn.
D 6   Bio-Integral Resource Center (BIRC)
D 6   Biological Urban Gardening Services
D 8   Canadian Organic Growers
D 8   Alan Chadwick Society
D 9   The Croft Institute
D 16   National Gardening Association
D 19   Permaculture Institute of North America
D 20   Seattle Tilth Association

PALMS
D 14   The International Palm Society

PAGE SOCIETY

PELARGONIUMS
D 7   British Pelargonium & Geranium Society
D 8   Canadian Geranium & Pelargonium Society

PENSTEMONS
D 4   American Penstemon Society

PEONIES
D 4   American Peony Society

PEPEROMIAS
D 19   Peperomia Society International

PERENNIALS
D 9   Cottage Garden Society
D 10   Hardy Plant Society - Mid-Atlantic Group
D 10   Hardy Plant Society (UK)
D 10   Hardy Plant Society of Oregon
D 18   Northwest Perennial Alliance
C 5   Perennial Plant Association
D 20   Sacramento Perennial Garden Club

PERMACULTURE
D 10   Friends of the Trees
D 19   Permaculture Institute of North America

PEST CONTROL, NON-TOXIC
D 6   Bio-Integral Resource Center (BIRC)
D 6   Biological Urban Gardening Services

PLANT CONSERVATION
C 2   Center for Plant Conservation

PLUMERIAS
D 19   The Plumeria Society of America, Inc.

POINSETTIAS
D 4   American Poinsettia Society

POTATOES
D 23   Tubers

PRIMROSES
D 4   American Primrose Society
D 15   National Auricula & Primula Society

PRUNING
D 19   Plant Amnesty

PUMPKINS, GIANT
D 23   World Pumpkin Confederation

RHODODENDRONS
D 4   American Rhododendron Society
D 6   Australian Rhododendron Society
D 19   Rhododendron Society of Canada

PAGE SOCIETY

RHODODENDRONS
D 19   Rhododendron Species Foundation

ROCK GARDENS
D 1   Alpine Garden Club of British Columbia
D 1   Alpine Garden Society
D 4   American Rock Garden Society
D 17   The New Zealand Alpine Garden Society
D 17   Newfoundland Alpine & Rock Garden Club
D 20   Scottish Rock Garden Club

ROSES
D 4   American Rose Society
D 8   Canadian Rose Society
D 10   Federation of International Rose Exhibitors
D 11   Heritage Rose Group
D 20   Rose Hybridizers Association
D 20   The Royal National Rose Society

SEDUMS
D 20   The Sedum Society

SEED SAVING
D 11   Heritage Seed Program
D 21   Seed Savers Exchange

SELF-SUFFICIENCY
D 10   Friends of the Trees
D 19   Permaculture Institute of North America

SEMPERVIVUMS
D 21   Sempervivum Fanciers Association
D 21   The Sempervivum Society

SOIL CONSERVATION
C 5   Soil & Water Conservation Society

SOLANACEAE
D 21   Solanaceae Enthusiasts

SOUTH AFRICAN PLANTS
D 6   Botanical Society of South Africa
D 12   Indigenous Bulb Growers Assn. of South Africa

SUCCULENTS
D 1   Aloe, Cactus & Succulent Society of Zimbabwe
D 6   The British Cactus & Succulent Society
D 7   Cactus & Succulent Society of America
D 22   The Toronto Cactus & Succulent Club

SWEET PEAS
D 16   National Sweet Pea Society

TERRARIUMS
D 22   The Terrarium Association

PAGE   SOCIETY

TREE PLANTING
C 4   National Arbor Day Foundation

TROPICAL FLOWERING TREES
D 22   Tropical Flowering Tree Society

VEGETABLE GARDENING
C 1   American Community Gardening Association
D 11   Heritage Seed Program
D 16   National Gardening Association
D 21   Seed Savers Exchange

WATER CONSERVATION
C 4   National Xeriscape Council, Inc.
C 5   Soil & Water Conservation Society

WATER LILIES
D 14   Water Lily Society

WILDFLOWERS
D 1   Alabama Wildflower Society
D 8   The Canadian Wildflower Society
C 2   Center for Plant Conservation
D 14   Kansas Wildflower Society
C 4   National Wildflower Research Center
D 16   New England Wild Flower Society
D 17   North Carolina Wild Flower

WILLOWS
D 4   American Willow Growers Network

WINE GRAPES
D 23   Vinifera Wine Growers Association

WOODY PLANTS
D 23   Woody Plant Society

© Vermont Bean Seed Co.
Artist: F. Allyn Massey

PAGE	MAGAZINE	* AVAILABLE TO MEMBERS ONLY	ISSUER
D 2	ABStracts (3)	*	American Bonsai Society
D 10	ARS Rosaceae (4)	*	Federation of International Rose Exhibitors
C 1	ASTA Newsletter (12)	*	American Seed Trade Association
D 1	African Violet Magazine (6)	*	African Violet Society of America, Inc.
E 1	Agricultural Review		North Carolina Dept. of Agriculture
E 1	Agriculture -- Kentucky's Pride		Kentucky Dept. of Agriculture
E 1	Alabama Farmers' Bulletin		Alabama Dept. of Agriculture & Industries
D 1	Alpine Gardening (4)	*	Alpine Garden Society
E 1	Amaranth Today		Rodale Press, Inc.
D 2	American Fern Journal (4)	*	American Fern Society
D 3	American Horticulturist (6)	*	American Horticultural Society
D 4	The American Rose Magazine (12)	*	American Rose Society
D 14	Amerigold Newsletter (4)	*	Marigold Society of America, Inc.
D 16	Annual	*	National Sweet Pea Society
D 18	Annual Report	*	Northern Nut Growers Association
D 9	Aquilegia (4-6)	*	Colorado Native Plant Society
C 4	Arbor Day (6)	*	National Arbor Day Foundation
C 1	Arboriculture Consultant (7)	*	American Society of Consulting Arborists
E 1	Arnoldia		Harvard Univ., The Arnold Arboretum
D 12	Aroideana (4)	*	International Aroid Society
E 1	Australian Garden Journal		Australian Garden Journal Pty., Ltd.
E 1	Australian Orchid Review		(See Magazines, Section E)
D 21	Australian Plants (4)	*	The Society for Growing Australian Plants
E 1	The Avant Gardener		Horticultural Data Processors
D 6	The Azalean (4)	*	Azalea Society of America
D 6	BUGS Flyer (4)	*	Biological Urban Gardening Services
E 1	Backyard Gardener Idea-Letter		James J. Martin
E 1	Baer's Garden Newsletter		John Baer's Sons
D 1	The Begonian (6)	*	American Begonia Society
E 2	Bev Dobson's Rose Letter		Beverly R. Dobson
D 6	Bio-Dynamics (4)	*	Bio-Dynamic Farming & Gardening Assn.
D 6	Bonsai Clubs International (6)	*	Bonsai Clubs International
D 2	Bonsai Journal (4)	*	American Bonsai Society
E 1	Bonsai Today		Stone Lantern Publishing Company
E 1	Botanical & Herb Reviews		Steven Foster
D 2	The Boxwood Bulletin (4)	*	American Boxwood Society
D 6	British Cactus and Succulent Journal (4)	*	The British Cactus & Succulent Society
D 7	The Bromeliad Hobbyist (12)	*	Bromeliad Study Group of Northern California
E 2	The Bu$iness of Herbs		Northwind Farm Publications
D 2	Bulletin (4)	*	American Conifer Society
D 10	Bulletin (2)	*	Hardy Plant Society (UK)
D 16	Bulletin/Panorama (2)	*	National Chrysanthemum Society (UK)
C 2	CHTA Newsletter (4)	*	Canadian Horticultural Therapy Association
D 8	COGnition (4)	*	Canadian Organic Growers
E 2	Cacti & Other Succulents		Marina J. Welham

PAGE	MAGAZINE	* AVAILABLE TO MEMBERS ONLY	ISSUER
E 2	Cactus & Succulent Journal		Allen Press
D 22	Cactus Factus (8)	*	The Toronto Cactus & Succulent Club
E 2	California Garden		San Diego Floral Association
D 2	The Camellia Journal (4)	*	American Camellia Society
D 8	Canadian Gladiolus Annual	*	Canadian Gladiolus Society
E 2	Canadian Horticultural History		Royal Botanical Gardens (CCHHS)
D 8	The Canadian Orchid Journal (4)	*	Canadian Orchid Society
D 8	Canadian Rose Annual	*	Canadian Rose Society
D 13	Carnivorous Plant Newsletter (4)	*	International Carnivorous Plant Society
E 2	Carolina Gardener		Tri-Star Communications Inc.
D 14	The Cerealist (2)	*	The KUSA Society
D 14	Chapter Bulletins	*	International Tropical Fern Society
D 1	Chatter (4)	*	African Violet Society of Canada
E 2	Chestnutworks		Chestnut Growers Exchange
D 16	The Chrysanthemum (5)	*	National Chrysanthemum Society, Inc. (USA)
D 6	Common Sense Pest Control (4)	*	Bio-Integral Resource Center (BIRC)
E 2	Connecticut Market Bulletin		Connecticut Dept. of Agriculture
E 2	Country Journal		Cowles Magazines
D 13	Crab Gab (4)	*	International Ornamental Crabapple Society
D 9	The Crofter (6)	*	The Croft Institute
D 21	Crossosoma (6)	*	Southern California Botanists
D 10	Crosswords (3)	*	Gesneriad Hybridizers Association
E 2	The Cultivar		UCSC Agroecology Program
C 2	Cut Flower Quarterly	*	Association of Specialty Cut Flower Growers
D 9	The Cycad Newsletter (4)	*	The Cycad Society
D 9	Cyclamen Journal (2)	*	Cyclamen Society
D 2	The Daffodil Journal (4)	*	American Daffodil Society, Inc.
D 3	Daylily Journal (4)	*	American Hemerocallis Society
D 9	Delphinium Year Book	*	The Delphinium Society
E 2	Desert Plants		Boyce Thompson Southwestern Arboretum
C 1	Discover the Pleasure of Gardening	*	American Association of Nurserymen
D 23	Douglasia (4)	*	Washington Native Plant Society
E 2	Dwarf Conifer Notes		Theophrastus
E 2	Elizabeth		Elizabeth Harris
D 9	Epiphyllum Society Bulletin (6)	*	Epiphyllum Society of America
D 1	Excelsa (biennial)	*	Aloe, Cactus & Succulent Society of Zimbabwe
D 2	Fiddlehead Forum (6)	*	American Fern Society
D 9	The Fig Leaflet (4)	*	Friends of the Fig
E 3	Fine Gardening		The Taunton Press
E 3	Flower & Garden		Modern Handcraft, Inc.
C 4	The Forum (12)	*	National Association of Women in Horticulture
E 3	The Four Seasons		Regional Parks Botanic Garden
D 7	Fremontia (4)	*	California Native Plant Society
D 8	The Fruit Gardener (4)	*	California Rare Fruit Growers, Inc.
D 4	Fruit Varieties Journal (4)	*	American Pomological Society
D 16	Fuchsia Fan (12)	*	National Fuchsia Society
D 18	The Fuchsia Flash (10)	*	Northwest Fuchsia Society
C 2	GCA Bulletin (2)	*	The Garden Club of America
C 2	GCA Newsletter (10)	*	Garden Centers of America
E 3	Garden		The Garden Society
D 12	Garden (6)	*	Horticultural Society of New York
E 3	The Garden		Home & Law Publishing, Ltd.
D 20	The Garden (12)	*	The Royal Horticultural Society

PAGE	MAGAZINE	* AVAILABLE TO MEMBERS ONLY	ISSUER
E 3	Garden Design		American Society of Landscape Architects
D 10	Garden History (2)	*	Garden History Society
E 3	Garden Network Monthly		Benedyk and Gabella
E 3	Garden Railways		Sidestreet Bannerworks, Inc.
C 4	The Gardener (6)	*	Men's Garden Clubs of America, Inc.
E 3	The Gardener's Eye		Harvey Childs, Hurricane Publishing Company
E 3	Gardener's Guide		Carol Honey, Wayne Newell
E 3	Gardener's Index		CompuDex Press
E 3	Gardeners Share		Peggy Byers
D 10	Gardenia Quarterly	*	Gardenia Society of America
E 4	Gardening Newsletter by Bob Flagg		Morningside Associates
E 3	Gardening from the Heartland		Karen Johnson
D 6	Gazette (3)	*	British & European Geranium Society
D 19	The Gazette (4)	*	Peperomia Society International
D 13	Geraniums around the World (4)	*	International Geranium Society
D 20	Gesneriad Saintpaulia News (6)	*	Saintpaulia International
E 4	Gil's Garden		Gil Whitton
D 3	The Gloxinian (6)	*	American Gloxinia & Gesneriad Society, Inc.
C 4	Going & Growing (3)	*	National Junior Horticulture Association
D 3	The Gourd (4)	*	American Gourd Society
D 18	The Green Scene (6)	*	The Pennsylvania Horticultural Society
E 4	The Green Thumb Companion		Robin Patten
E 4	Greener Gardening, Easier		E. Dexter Davis, Horticulturist
D 23	Grow With Us (6)	*	Worcester County Horticultural Society
E 4	The Growing Edge Magazine		Tom Alexander & Nancy Votrain
E 4	Growing from Seed		Thompson & Morgan
D 11	HSI Bulletin (4)	*	Heliconia Society International
D 12	HSNY Newsletter (6)	*	Horticultural Society of New York
E 4	Hardy Enough		Joe Hebert
D 10	The Hardy Plant (2)	*	Hardy Plant Society (UK)
E 4	Harrowsmith (Canada)		Camden House Publishing
E 4	Harrowsmith (US)		Camden House Publishing
C 3	Harvests Newsletter (4)	*	The Lawn Institute
D 17	Heather News (4)	*	North American Heather Society
D 11	Hebe News	*	The Hebe Society
E 4	The Herb Companion		Interweave Press, Inc.
E 4	The Herb Quarterly		Long Mountain Press, Inc.
E 4	The Herb, Spice and Medicinal Plant Digest		Univ. of Massachusetts
E 4	The Herbal Kitchen		Diane Lea Mathews
D 11	Herbalgram (4)	*	Herb Research Foundation
E 4	The Herbalist		(See Magazines, Section E)
E 5	Herban Lifestyles		Stone Acre Press
D 11	The Herbarist (1)	*	Herb Society of America
D 4	Herbertia (2)	*	American Plant Life Society
D 11	Heritage Rose Letter (4)	*	Heritage Roses Group
D 11	Heritage Seed Program (3)	*	Heritage Seed Program
D 5	The Hibiscus (6)	*	Australian Hibiscus Society
E 5	Himalayan Plant Journal		Primulaceae Books
D 11	Hobby Greenhouse (4)	*	Hobby Greenhouse Association
D 11	Holly Society Journal (4)	*	Holly Society of America
E 5	HortIdeas		HortIdeas Publishing
E 5	Horticulture		Horticulture Limited Partnership
E 5	Hortus		David Wheeler, Editor

PAGE	MAGAZINE	* AVAILABLE TO MEMBERS ONLY	ISSUER
D 3	Hosta Journal (2)	*	American Hosta Society
E 5	Houseplant Forum		HortiCom, Inc.
D 12	The Hoyan (4)	*	The Hoya Society International
D 12	Hydroponic/Soilless Grower (6)	*	Hydroponic Society of America
D 12	IBSA Bulletin (1)	*	Indigenous Bulb Growers Assn. of South Africa
D 12	IC&RF Society Newsletter (4)	*	Indoor Citrus & Rare Fruit Society
D 1	The INGENS Bulletin (2)	*	Aloe, Cactus & Succulent Society of Zimbabwe
E 5	The IPM Practitioner		Bio-Integral Resource Center
E 5	Indian Orchid Journal		Ganesh Mani Pradhan & Udai C. Pradhan
D 12	Indoor Garden (6)	*	Indoor Gardening Society of America
D 11	Inside Green (10)	*	The Indoor Gardening Society of Canada
E 5	International Bonsai		International Bonsai Arboretum
D 7	The Iris Year Book	*	British Iris Society
D13	Irregular Newsletter	*	International Golden Fossil Tree Society
C 3	Irrigation News (12)	*	The Irrigation Association
E 6	The Island Grower		Greenheart Publications
D 3	The Ivy Journal (2)	*	American Ivy Society
E 1	John E. Bryan Gardening Newsletter		John E. Bryan, Inc.
D 4	Journal (4)	*	American Rhododendron Society
D 7	Journal (6)	*	Bromeliad Society, Inc.
D 1	Journal (Irregular)	*	American Bamboo Society
E 6	Journal of Garden History		Taylor & Francis, Inc.
E 6	The Kew Magazine		Basil Blackwell, Ltd.
E 6	Kiwifruit Enthusiasts Journal		Friends of the Trees Society
D 14	LAIFS Journal	*	Los Angeles International Fern Society
C 1	Landscape Architecture (6)	*	American Society of Landscape Architects
C 3	Landscapes	*	Historic Preservation Committee
D 13	Lilacs (4)	*	International Lilac Society
D 17	Lily Yearbook (1)	*	North American Lily Society, Inc.
E 6	Lindleyana		American Orchid Society
E 6	Living Off the Land, Subtropic Newsletter		Geraventure
D 15	MaGIC Lantern (4)	*	Master Gardeners International Corp. (MaGIC)
D 14	Magnolia (2)	*	The Magnolia Society, Inc.
D 14	Magnolia, Jnl. of the AMS (2)	*	American Magnolia Society
E 6	The Maine Organic Farmer & Gardener		Maine Organic Farmers & Gardeners Association
D 2	Mariposa (quarterly newsletter)	*	American Calochortus Society
E 6	The Market Bulletin		West Virginia Dept. of Agriculture
D 18	Members Packet/Membership List (1)	*	Northwest Perennial Alliance
D 18	Menzelia (irregular)	*	Northern Nevada Native Plant Society
E 6	The Metropolitan Gardener		Karen Fausch
D 13	Mid-Year Newsletter (1)	*	International Camellia Society
D 15	Minnesota Horticulturist (9)	*	Minnesota State Horticultural Society
D 21	Monthly Bulletin	*	Southern California Horticultural Institute
D 14	Monthly Fern Lesson	*	Los Angeles International Fern Society
D 18	Na Okika O Hawaii/Hawaiian Orchid Journal (4)	*	Pacific Orchid Society
D 16	National Gardening (12)	*	National Gardening Association
D 13	Nerium News (4)	*	International Oleander Society
E 6	New England Farm Bulletin		Jacob' Meadow, Inc.
E 6	The New England Gardener		New England Horticultural Services, Inc.
C 5	The New Farm (7)	*	Regenerative Agriculture Association
D 17	New Zealand Camellia Bulletin (4)	*	New Zealand Camellia Society
D 22	News Bulletin (4)	*	Southern Garden History Society
D 10	News Letter (2)	*	Hardy Plant Society (UK)

PAGE	MAGAZINE	* AVAILABLE TO MEMBERS ONLY	ISSUER
D 1	Newsletter (8)	*	Alaska Native Plant Society
D 17	Northern Gardener (4)	*	Northern Horticultural Society
E 6	Northland Berry News		Minnesota Berry Growers Association
D 18	Nutshell (4)	*	Northern Nut Growers Association
D 23	Occasional Papers	*	Washington Native Plant Society
D 18	On the Fringe (6)	*	Ohio Native Plant Society
D 9	The Orchid Advocate (6)	*	Cymbidium Society of America
E 6	The Orchid Digest		Mrs. N. H. Atkinson, Memb. Secy.
E 7	The Orchid Hunter		Terry Ferraro, Editor
E 7	Orchid Information Exchange		Doreen Vander Tuin
E 7	The Orchid Review		The Orchid Review, Ltd.
E 7	Organic Gardening		Rodale Press, Inc.
D 18	PHS News (11)	*	The Pennsylvania Horticultural Society
E 7	Pacific Horticulture		Pacific Horticultural Foundation
E 7	The Palm Quarterly		Temperate Zone Chapter, IPS
D 7	Pelargonium News (3)	*	British Pelargonium & Geranium Society
C 5	Perennial Plant Symposium Proceedings (1)	*	Perennial Plant Association
C5	Perennial Plants (4)	*	Perennial Plant Association
E 7	Permaculture with Native Plants		Curtin Mitchell
E 7	Phalaenopsis Fancier		Doreen Vander Tuin
D 19	The Pits Newsletter	*	Rare Pit & Plant Council
C 2	Plant Conservation (4)	*	Center for Plant Conservation
D 5	Plant Press (4)	*	Arizona Native Plant Society
E 7	Plants & Gardens		Brooklyn Botanic Garden
E 7	The Plantsman		The Royal Horticultural Society
E 7	Play Dirt		Russell Webber
D 12	Pome News (4)	*	Home Orchard Society
D 17	Pomona (4)	*	North American Fruit Explorers
E 7	Potpourri Party-Line		Berry Hill Press
E 7	Potpourri from Herbal Acres		Pinerow Publications
D 4	Primroses (4)	*	American Primrose Society
D 14	Principes (4)	*	The International Palm Society
C 3	Proceedings (1)	*	International Plant Propagator's Society
C 1	The Public Garden (4)	*	American Assn. of Botanical Gardens
D 12	Quarterly Newsletter	*	Indoor Citrus & Rare Fruit Society
C 3	Quill & Trowel (6)	*	Garden Writers Association of America
D 19	RSF Newsletter (4)	*	Rhododendron Species Foundation
D 2	Resource Hotline (25)	*	American Forestry Association
D 21	The Review (2)	*	The Society for Japanese Irises
D 6	The Rhododendron (4)	*	Australian Rhododendron Society
D 20	The Rock Garden (2)	*	Scottish Rock Garden Club
D 8	The Rosarian (3)	*	Canadian Rose Society
D 20	The Rose (4)	*	Royal National Rose Society
E 7	Rosy Outlook Magazine		"Rosy" McKenney
D 22	SIGNA (2)	*	Species Iris Group of North America
D 21	SPCNI Almanac (2)	*	Society for Pacific Coast Native Iris
D 12	Sage Notes (6)	*	Idaho Native Plant Society
D 20	Saintpaulia International News (6)	*	Saintpaulia International
E 8	San Diego Garden Digest		Ralph Garcia
D 20	Sea-Tilth (12)	*	Seattle Tilth Association
D 3	The Seed Pod (4)	*	American Hibiscus Society
D 23	Sego Lily (12)	*	Utah Native Plant Society
E 8	Small Farm News		Small Farm Center, Cooperative Extension

PAGE	MAGAZINE	* AVAILABLE TO MEMBERS ONLY	ISSUER

PAGE	MAGAZINE	ISSUER
E 8	Solanaceae Quarterly	(See Magazines, Section E)
D 21	The South African Fuchsia Fanfare (3)	* South African Fuchsia Society
D 22	Southern Fruit Fellowship Newsletter (4)	* Southern Fruit Fellowship
E 8	Southern Living	H. B. Flora
E 8	Spice & Herb Arts	Kaye Cude
D 8	Storksbill	* Canadian Geranium & Pelargonium Society
E 8	Sunset Magazine	Lane Publishing Co.
E 8	TLC ... for plants	Gardenvale Publishing Company, Ltd.
D 19	Tallgrass Prairie News (4)	* Tallgrass Prairie Alliance
D 23	Tater Talk (2)	* Tubers
D 22	Texas Horticulturist (12)	* Texas State Horticultural Society
D 16	Texas Native Plant Society News (6)	* Native Plant Society of Texas
C 4	The Tree Book (6)	* National Arbor Day Foundation
D 20	Trellis	* San Diego Historical Society
D 19	Tropical Fruit News (12)	* Rare Fruit Council International, Inc.
E 8	The Twenty-First Century Gardener	Growers Press, Inc.
E 8	Urban Forest Forum	American Forestry Association
D 6	Veld & Flora (4)	* Botanical Society of South Africa
D 14	Water Garden Journal (4)	* International Water Lily Society
D 14	Water Lily Journal (4)	* Water Lily Society
E 8	The Weekend Garden Journal	Jim Bennett
E 8	Weekly Market Bulletin	New Hampshire Dept. of Agriculture
E 8	The Whole Chili Pepper	Out West Publishing Company
D 16	Wild Flower Notes (1-2)	* New England Wild Flower Society
D 8	Wildflower (4)	* The Canadian Wildflower Society
D 21	Winter Yearbook	* Seed Savers Exchange
D 6	Year Book	* British & European Geranium Society
D 5	Yearbook	* Aril Society International
D 3	Zingiber (2)	* American Ginger Society
C 2	Zoo Horticulture (4)	* Association for Zoological Horticulture

© Shepherd's Garden Seeds
Artist: Mimi Osborne

Practical Matters

This section contains some practical forms which I hope you will find useful. All can be removed or photocopied for your use. As a matter of "good formsmanship" and to be sure you get what you request, carefully print or type your name and address.

❀ **Catalog and Information Request:** use this form to request catalogs or ask for information from societies and magazines, or ask companies if they can supply specific items on your "want list."

The best use of this form is to photocopy it once, print or type in your name and address, and then photocopy it again as many times as you like. You can then check off the appropriate boxes for each specific request. If you don't use this form, please mention *Gardening by Mail.*

❀ **Record of Catalog and Information Requests:** leave this form in the book so that you can keep a record of the requests you have sent and the replies you have received.

❀ **Reader Feedback and Update Order Form:** I'm eager to hear your opinions of and suggestions for *Gardening by Mail.* Please let us know what you like and don't like, any improvements you'd like to see, and how you use the book — readers have suggested many improvements.

Please list sources and organizations that you think we should list on a separate sheet. Before you recommend a source, please check to see if it sells by mail order; Weston Nurseries and Western Hills Nursery do not!

You can subscribe to all the updates in advance. Changes to the listings in this edition are cumulative, so you only have to order the **latest** update to be current. New sources and books received will be mentioned in each update as space allows.

❀ **Listing Request and Update of Current Listing:** if you feel your company, society, publication or library should be listed in the next edition of *Gardening by Mail,* please let us know by filling in and sending us this form as soon as possible. The information requested on the form is the minimum we need to know about you. Companies and organizations already listed in this edition may use this form to update their listing; all information will be verified before the publication of the next edition. We include changes and new sources in our periodic updates.

❀ **Changes and Corrections:** room has been left at the back of the book for including changes and corrections in subsequent printings.

❀ **Mailing Labels:** Tusker Press will sell mailing labels for the various listings in this book. Inquire about prices.

❀ **Computer Disks:** we are currently investigating the possibility of making data disks available with software for data searching; these would be available for IBM or Macintosh computers. Please write to Tusker Press if you are interested, and tell us to what specific use you would put such data.

Readers are reminded that photocopying, scanning or storing the information in this book in a computer for any personal or business use is against copyright law.

Catalog and Information Request Form

Date: _____

Dear: _____

[ ] Please send me your free catalog.

[ ] I enclose a long self-addressed envelope with $ _____ postage.

[ ] Please send me your catalog, for which I enclose $ _____ .

[ ] You did not provide the price of your catalog; please send me one or advise me of the cost.

[ ] Please send me information on joining your society.

[ ] I'd like to subscribe to your periodical; please tell me your current rates.

[ ] Please let me know if you have _____

_____

[ ] Other information I need: _____

_____

My name and address are:

Name: _____

Address: _____

City and State: _____

Country:_____ Postal Code: _____

Phone Number: (Daytime): _____ (Evenings): _____

Gardening by Mail : A Source Book
Published by Houghton Mifflin, Boston, MA

Record of Catalog Orders and Requests

Company/Organization	Date of Request	Received

Company/Organization	Date of Request	Received

Request for Listing in Gardening By Mail or Update of Current Listing

If you would like to be listed in the next edition of **Gardening By Mail,** please return this form as soon as possible. **We also list new sources in our regular updates as space allows.**

Current listees: Please use this form to notify us of any changes. **Changes will be included in our updates.**

To be listed in **Gardening by Mail**:

Seed companies, nurseries, other plant suppliers, and garden suppliers must sell direct by mail order to buyers in the U.S. and/or Canada and **must enclose their most recent catalog with this request.**

Plant and horticultural societies must welcome members from the U.S. and/or Canada and **must include a current issue of their periodical with this request.**

Libraries must allow members of their sponsoring organizations and/or the public to use their facilities for reference.

Questionnaires will be sent when a new edition is planned. Those listed in the current edition will automatically receive one but must meet the same conditions AND return the completed questionnaire and their catalog or literature to be listed again.

Questionnaires vary by type of company or organization. Please specify your **primary** category:

Date:_____

    [ ]   Seed company

    [ ]   Nursery

    [ ]   Garden suppliers: Category _____

    [ ]   Trade, professional or umbrella organization

    [ ]   Plant or horticultural society

    [ ]   Horticultural library

    [ ]   Gardening/ horticultural magazine or newsletter

    [ ]   Other (be specific and indicate why you should be listed): _____

Final selection of those listed is at the discretion of the author.

Please type or print – if we can't read it, we can't use it.

    [ ]   Request for listing   [ ] Current listing update (provide current listing name, and new name, if changed).

Name of Business or Organization: _____

Proprietor/Manager: _____

Mailing Address: _____

City and State: _____

Country: _____ Postal Code: _____

Phone Number(s): _____

Please send this form to:

Tusker Press, Database Department
P.O. Box 1338, Sebastopol, CA 95473

Please continue on back. ⟶

[　] We have added Tusker Press to our mailing list.

[　] Name of the individual who will promptly complete and return your future questionnaires.

_____

The following information is the **minimum** Tusker Press needs to know now:

The price of our catalog is $ _____ [　] Long SASE　　[　] Free

[　] Minimum retail order is $_____

[　] Telephone orders accepted with credit cards – $_____ minimum.

[　] We sell wholesale AS WELL AS retail by mail order.

[　] We ship to (　) USA (　) Canada (　) overseas

[　] We ship live/perishable materials in the months _____

[　] We sell MAIL ORDER ONLY (no nursery or shop/sales location).

[　] We also sell at this sales address: _____

[　] We have a display garden or many plants/products on display at sales location.

The twelve most important plants/products that we sell are:

_____

_____

_____

_____

_____

_____

_____

_____

Comments/other information:

_____

_____

_____

_____

_____

Reader Feedback & Update Order Form

Date:_____

What I like about *Gardening by Mail*

_____

_____

_____

_____

_____

_____

What I don't like about *Gardening by Mail*

_____

_____

_____

_____

Suggestions for improvements in the next edition

_____

_____

_____

_____

_____

Please list your recommendations for new plant and product sources, societies, magazines, etc. on a separate sheet of paper.

Name: _____

Mailing Address: _____

City: _____ State/Province: _____

Country: _____ Postal Code: _____

Daytime Phone _____ Evening Phone _____

Send this form to:

Tusker Press
P.O. Box 1338, Sebastopol, CA 95473

Please continue on back. ⟶

By identifying your special interests, the following information will help us improve the contents of the book.

I am a [ ] home gardener   [ ] professional/commercial horticulturist   [ ] both
     [ ] new gardener   [ ] experienced gardener   [ ] very experienced gardener

I have a [ ] small garden   [ ] medium-sized garden   [ ] large garden (acre or more)

I grow [ ] lawn   [ ] flowers   [ ] vegetables
     [ ] fruit   [ ] ornamental shrubs   [ ] trees
     [ ] greenhouse plants   [ ] indoor plants   [ ] special interests (list below)

_____

_____

I Use Gardening by Mail for:

[ ] mail orders   [ ] finding societies
[ ] finding local sources   [ ] finding libraries
[ ] visiting display gardens   [ ] making professional contacts
[ ] reference when traveling   [ ] buying plants/products for resale
[ ] finding plants by climate zone   [ ] selling plants/products to retailers
[ ] finding products/services   [ ] compiling a mailing list for prospects
[ ] finding gardening books   [ ] finding unusual plants or products for customers
[ ] finding magazines

[ ] Other uses:_____

_____

Order for Updates to Gardening by Mail

Over the years that we have been collecting information about horticultural sources, we have learned one sobering lesson: things change — and rapidly. As fast as we gather information, our listees are changing their names, addresses and ownership, going out of business or ceasing to fill mail orders. We try to keep current and we're constantly on the lookout for changes, but it's like trying to catch sand in a hairnet.

In addition, we are continually finding new and exciting sources of plants and supplies, new societies, libraries, magazines and books which we'd like to share with our readers.

Tusker Press issues periodic updates to *Gardening by Mail* which include any name and address changes that **we know about** for the listings in the book and new sources as space allows.

To order updates, send **U.S.$1.00 for each update desired** to Tusker Press and check the updates you wish.

Please send me _____ update(s) to *Gardening by Mail as checked below* :

Updates are cumulative, so order **only** the most recent or future issues:

[ ] August 1990   [ ] August 1991

[ ] January 1991   [ ] January 1992

[ ] May 1991   [ ] May 1992

Total Enclosed: $ _____